P9-DNB-676

THE QUALITY OF LIFE IN AMERICA

Edited by
A. DAVID HILL
University of Colorado
ERNEST A. CHAPLES, Jr.
University of Maryland
MATTHEW T. DOWNEY
University of Colorado
LARRY D. SINGELL
University of Colorado
DAVID M. SOLZMAN
University of Illinois at Chicago Circle
GERALD M. SWATEZ
University of Illinois at Chicago Circle

THE QUALITY OF

LIFE IN AMERICA
POLLUTION
POVERTY
POWER
AND FEAR

HOLT, RINEHART AND WINSTON, INC.
New York Chicago San Francisco Atlanta
Dallas Montreal Toronto

Library of Congress Catalog Card Number: 72–90647
ISBN: 0–03–005981–x
Printed in the United States of America
3456 090 987654321

 This work was developed under a grant from the U.S. Office of Education, Department of Health, Education and Welfare. However, the opinions and other content do not necessarily reflect the position or policy of that Agency, and no official endorsement should be inferred.

PREFACE

This book is dedicated to the American college student who seeks to understand the problems of his society and strives to remedy them. As such the editors have addressed themselves to the student of the liberal arts and to those of his teachers who wish to respond to the need for a broad and integrating perspective, one that defines as significant subject-matter social problems rather than compartmentalized disciplinary knowledge. For example, if the student is preparing to be a social studies teacher, he may well ask how he can relate knowledge from the courses he has taken in economics, political science, sociology, geography, or history to help him be an effective teacher in tomorrow's world. If he is majoring in one of the social science disciplines, he may inquire how that discipline both helps and hinders his understanding of the world. If he is one of the expanding number of students in integrated or distributive studies programs, he may be seeking materials specifically designed to meet his interdisciplinary purpose. The editors have tried to focus this book to meet such an array of needs.

This volume is the child of a diverse and unusual parentage. In a trial form it was used by hundreds of students as a course of study in several colleges and universities. It is the offspring of a federally funded project that attempted to meet the multiple goals of several professional associations and of a multidisciplinary group of individuals.

The project developed in response to the urging of a group of social scientists representing a number of professional associations. This group met in Asheville, North Carolina, June 10–15, 1969, to consider "The Disciplines in the Continuum of Teacher Education," a conference sponsored by the Consortium of Professional Associations (CONPASS) under a grant from the U.S. Office of Education. A resolution of the interdisciplinary group

> ". . . agreed that, in view of the present extensive employment of social studies courses at the high school level, for the offering of which it is important that the training of social studies teachers should be strengthened, it clearly would be desirable for prospective teachers of these courses to be given an integrated course in social sciences at the junior or senior level in college. . . ."

The group further resolved that CONPASS seek financing for a pilot project in the development of such a course.

Representatives from four professional associations (Ernest A. Chaples, Jr., American Political Science Association; Warren Nystrom, Association of American Geographers; Henry A. Villard, American Economic Association; Paul L. Ward, American Historical Association) later agreed to carry out the intent of the resolution, and Warren Nystrom was asked by this group to secure a director for the project. A. David Hill, Professor of Geography, University of Colorado, and then (1969–1970) Acting Director of the Center for Education in the Social Sciences at the University of Colorado, agreed to serve as director, write the proposal to U.S.O.E., and assemble the project personnel. CONPASS held planning meetings in March 1970, at which several persons representing various disciplines reacted to early drafts of the proposal.

As envisaged in the subsequently funded proposal, the project was to gather together and try out a package of curriculum materials for a one-semester interdisciplinary course especially designed for the training of social studies teachers during their junior and senior years in college. The materials were to be chosen so as to: (1) illustrate a few central features of each of several disciplines and their interrelations, especially to include economics, geography, history, political science, and sociology; (2) use contemporary problems (e.g., environmental quality, racial conflict, etc.) as their substantive focus; and (3) incorporate innovative modes of multimedia presentation and inquiry-oriented teaching strategies that involve students using the materials in order to provide a positive teaching model.

The proposal called for these materials to be initially gathered in the spring of 1970 by scholars (Chaples, Downey, Singell, Solzman, and Swatez) from their own individual disciplinary perspectives, brought together in the summer of 1970, and interrelated into an available package capable of being used and evaluated by students and teachers in pilot courses throughout the country during the spring of 1971. A revision of the course was planned during the summer of 1971 to incorporate ideas stemming from these evaluations and from commissioned scholarly reviews. Matthew Edel of the Massachusetts Institute of Technology provided a very helpful review of the trial materials. It was not until this revision session that the developers decided to seek commercial publication, since the trials had brought favorable reactions to the materials.

The editors wish to gratefully acknowledge the help throughout the course of the project of numerous individuals; in the process, goals and approaches changed and evolved to those described in the Introduction. In the spring of 1970, the six developers conceived the course to focus on the theme, "The Quality of Life in America: Pollution, Poverty, Power, and Fear," and subsequently they received helpful criticism from the project's Advisory Committee, composed of Paul L. Ward, Executive Secretary of the American Historical Association and Committee Chairman; Earl Baker, Acting Executive Secretary of the American Political Science Association; Wayne Gordon, Graduate School of Education, University of California at Los Angeles, representing the American Sociological Association; Salvatore J. Natoli, Educational Affairs Director, Association of American Geographers; and Wyn F. Owen, Department of Economics, University of Colorado, representing the American Economics Association.

Also, the editors were fortunate to have during the course of the funded project the following consultants: Loyal L. Darr, teacher, Thomas Jefferson High School, Denver, Colorado; John D. Haas, Director, Center for Education in the Social Sciences, University of Colorado; Dana Kurfman, Social Studies Supervisor, Prince Georges County, Maryland; Irving Morrissett, Executive Director, Social Science Education Consortium, Inc., and Professor of Economics, University of Colorado; and Roberta Ann Raithel, Social Studies Supervisor, Texas Education Agency, Austin, Texas.

Thanks are also owing to Joseph P. Palaia, then Director of CONPASS, and to his Assistant, Polly Bartholomew, for their help in the early coordination of the project as well as to Charles R. Foster, Division of College Programs, U.S. Office of Education.

Evaluative comments on the trial version of the materials came from hundreds of college students and from their teachers. The pilot teachers were Lee F. Anderson, Director of the American Political Science Association's Political Science Education Project, who taught the course at Indiana University; George W. Sorensen, Department of Sociology, and John W. Soule, Department of Political Science, San Diego State College; Al Redsun, Social Science Department, Oregon College of Education; Mary A. Hepburn, Department of Social Science Education, University of Georgia; and Ford Cleere, Department of Sociology, University of Northern Colorado. The editors also used the trial materials in courses at the University of Colorado, University of Illinois at Chicago Circle, and the University of Maryland.

Theodore Lowi, as consultant to Holt, Rinehart and Winston, Inc., was receptive to the editors' vision and gave them critical guidance as they transformed the trial course materials into the book's manuscript. This list of indebtedness would be incomplete without mentioning Mary Axe, who did the extensive work of securing publication permissions. Finally, special thanks are due Nancy A. Davis, who served throughout as the Project Assistant. All of those named above, as well as the hundreds of unnamed students in the pilot courses, have helped the six editors who, ultimately, bear the responsibility for the faults of this volume.

The Editors

CONTENTS

PART THREE POWER 255

THE QUALITY OF LIFE IN AMERICA

Introduction

American society has entered the decade of the 1970s caught in a web of paradoxes. Although it is the wealthiest society in the history of the world, it still tolerates a condition of poverty for millions of Americans. A nation capable of producing enormous food surpluses permits malnutrition to cut short the lives of thousands of its citizens each year. A people whose technological achievements have placed men on the moon is as yet unable to keep streams and air free from pollution. Pledged to peace and international order, it is a nation whose principal public expenditure is for weapons of war. A society that officially recognizes no distinction on the bases of race, creed, or color still sustains racial segregation in its ghettos and suburbs. A country proud for having introduced to the world the idea of quality universal education now agonizes over the large numbers of its youth who drop out of its schools, and is beginning to recognize that quality education is by no means universal. In America, which has most of the world's greatest universities, students are rushing headlong to revive America's dormant antiintellectualism. A people whose various religious creeds affirm the sanctity of human life cannot enact even rudimentary gun control legislation to protect the lives of its citizens. It is a nation that espouses law and order but has not stemmed a rising tide of violent crimes. Where once the American Dream prevailed a nightmare intrudes and cynicism haunts the land. Such is the social legacy, and some of the major social problems that the generation coming of age in the 1970s will inherit. The future of American society, possibly its very existence, will depend upon how well that generation resolves these paradoxes of contemporary American life.

In inheriting both an imperfect world and a backlog of unresolved problems, the coming generation will not be unique. Each generation of Americans has had to cope with perplexing social problems. The struggle for existence in the wilderness of colonial America, the quest for social justice and a living wage in industrialized America, and the search for economic security in years of recurring depressions posed major challenges for past generations. Perhaps the principal difference is that the problems facing this generation concern, for the most part, the quality rather than the quantity of life in America. Polluted beaches and streams, the social malaise of the inner cities, the fear of walking the streets at night, or the inability of ordinary citizens to have a voice in public decision making affect the quality of our lives. Even in the instance of poverty, it is no longer a question of insufficient wealth in the society at large, but of the inequality of its distribution.

This change in the nature of social problems does not necessarily make their solution easier—if anything, the difficulty of solving them is compounded. Because our society structures reality by rational *quantitative* analysis, qualitative analysis proves especially difficult. In many instances the problems of today have their roots in the value system and institutional structures that were created or reinforced to solve the problems of past generations. Mind sets and social arrangements identified with past success are always highly resistant to change. Efforts to remove the racial injustice of segregated ghettos will, for example, threaten the social arrangements that are the success symbols of upwardly mobile suburban Americans. A lasting solution to the problems of environmental deterioration will require a reduction of the resource consumption that supported the economic achievements of an older generation. Certainly, the success of any effort to improve the quality of life in America will depend first upon how well we understand the dimensions and complexities of the problems involved.

We are all aware that problems exist in contemporary American society, but awareness is not necessarily the same thing as understanding. It has become almost commonplace to lament that modern America is a society in crisis. We are deluged with an enormous volume of such popular literature as nonfiction best sellers and articles in magazines and Sunday supplements that are devoted to one or another of the "critical problems of our time," to say nothing of scholarly articles and monographs, television specials, and the barrage of "concerned" movies from Hollywood's radical chic. It may well be that future historians will conclude from the sheer volume of such literature that ours was, if not the Age of Crises, at least an age obsessed with the idea of crisis. While it is wise for a society to recognize a crisis when it sees one, it is unhealthy to deal with a social crisis by substituting rhetoric for understanding. Because this is a temptation that we have not always been able to resist, we must continually reexamine not only the problems that face us, but the nature and depth of our own understanding of them.

Perhaps the central crisis of our times is the intellectual crisis that has its roots in how we organize and use knowledge. The heart of the problem lies in the images or mental constructs that we tend to use when we look at and think about our social environment. For example, the images of cities that we carry around with us may exist at the most commonplace level of travel posters, scenes from movies, or highly selected memories from personal experience. But we quickly recognize that posters and memories have limited value as analytical tools; for the purpose of understanding cities or urban social problems we need more encompassing and sophisticated abstractions. The various social science disciplines have provided us with productive mental constructs, with concepts such as social class and the market system, with racial categories, and with behavioral typologies. While these are only a few examples, they should be sufficient to illustrate that what we know about society and its problems is a product of the kind of images that we have selected to gain that understanding. The problem is that in this age of increasing specialization, impressions and information that we have of the world around us have also become highly specialized. Moreover, as what we know and how we know it have become organized along formal disciplinary lines, knowledge has become increasingly compartmentalized. In their research and teaching, economists, political scientists, and geographers use conceptual tools that produce quite different perceptions of reality. Thus our own perceptions of the social environment have become fractured and fragmented. Both as scholars and as students we have become very much like the blind men in the fable, whose perceptions of the elephant were equally compartmentalized and incomplete.

This book mounts a critical analysis of some of the major problems of contemporary American society. It attempts to challenge conventional wisdom about the quality of life in America and to sketch an alternative for radical social change. As a point of departure we have selected four problem areas—pollution, poverty, power, and fear—that relate to the quality of life in America. While the choice of any particular problem area is somewhat arbitrary, these four best filled our requirements: Each is broad enough to encompass a variety of contemporary issues, yet none is so abstract that it cannot do justice to problems as tangible as a polluted river and as elusive as the impulse that makes suburbanites convert their homes into miniature arsenals.

Although these four problem areas are arranged as four separate parts of the book, they are but aspects of a single social reality. For example, it is impossible to discuss poverty without knowing how power and influence are allocated in the United States. It is doubtful that anyone can know poverty without knowing fear. Pollution of the environment raises questions about the use and impact of technology in modern America. Questions about poverty evoke other questions about racism, and inquiries about the uses of power provide insights into the educational system and its problems. We consider the problem areas into which we have divided these materials only as portals of entry into the complex fabric of American society.

This volume is an attempt to deal with the intellectual as well as the social crises of our times, and thus we also use pollution, poverty, power, and fear as new ordering concepts to enlarge understanding. Traditionally, readings books about contemporary society have been edited from the perspective of a particular discipline. Although the present editors came together as representatives of five different social science disciplines, we quickly learned that no single discipline can effectively deal with questions about the quality of life in America. There is no sociology of pollution, and the histories of pollution and fear largely remain to be written. The geography of fear is a field yet to be developed, and economists have told us more about the quantity than the quality of life in America. We discovered when working as a group that in many ways the "disciplinary" approach itself was a barrier to the meaningful analysis of the very problems we were attempting to analyze. This is not to fault these disciplines, whose purpose it is to advance knowledge along their respective specialized fronts, but to recognize that individually they simply cannot cope with the issue of the quality of life. Economics, geography, history, sociology, and political science provide only narrow constructs that separately are inadequate when viewing any broad-based social problem. Furthermore, the sum of the parts never equals the whole. Seeing this, we began to pay less attention to formal disciplinary perspectives. The materials we brought together represent points of view about some aspects of problems by observers who use varied insights that quite often cannot easily be categorized by discipline. The principle of selection was simply whether a piece, when combined with or juxtaposed to others, helped in any way to illuminate the nature and complexity of the problem. Our readers may have difficulty separating the "geographical," "historical," and "economic." We did. But we have found this approach comes closer to capturing the essence of the problems we have explored together.

Although the editors are all social scientists, we recognize that the social sciences do not represent the only possible or desirable modes for understanding social problems. The book deals with issues that require attention from the natural and physical sciences, with practical problems awaiting public action, and with human problems that cry out for our empathy as fellow human beings. We have included pieces from popular literature, poems, and music because they add layers of understanding and feeling to the perspective of the social sciences. Pollution, poverty, powerlessness, and fear may be analyzed with clinical detachment by the writer at his desk, but they are tragically experienced by millions of Americans. Some of the data included are important for the feelings they evoke in us—after all, we are America, and the quality of life in America is not just how we think but also how we feel.

What is clear to us is that the new crisis—the deteriorating quality of life in America—combined with the inability of the traditional, fragmented disciplines to respond effectively to this crisis has led, probably inevitably, to an intellectual crisis: the phenomenon of diminished faith in organized knowledge. School dropouts, hippies, the youth cults of drugs, mysticism, and communes, the middle-class populism and reaction, and the pervasive frustration of most college students who seek, but do not find, easy solutions, are all various manifestations of this phenomenon.

When organized knowledge does not meet the needs of society, it will be rejected, and new adaptive forms must be created to replace it. This book, although a mere beginning, is an attempt to respond to this challenge. It does not, of course, provide easy answers, but it does combine and structure the useful, however limited statements of the social sciences with expressive essays, poems, music, and still other statements written by "laymen," all to the purpose of providing new materials leading toward the actual expansion of the horizons of the social sciences. It is our hope that we are in fact making a contribution to the next round of social science, that is, that ultimately social scientists will take these and other materials and convert them into new, better organized knowledge, a more useful analytical knowledge responsive to society's problems.

While the book sets contrary points of view against each other, the materials were not primarily selected to present all possible perspectives. Rather, they were chosen to offer a radical alternative to the present quality of life in America. That alternative is based upon an ecological rather than a materialistic–technological ethic. We think the roots of the crises that face us lie in the latter. Pollution, poverty, power, and fear are age-old problems, but they take on new and significant dimensions in our materially and technically affluent society. The uninhibited development of technology used to exploit nature and other human beings has become a threat to human survival itself. We have begun to realize in the area of nuclear technology, for example, that the technological threat to survival is so great that its use must be greatly restricted and its use in its original, destructive form absolutely prohibited. We have still to realize that technical developments in many other areas of life pose similar dangers. When men have the intent to exploit and destroy others and have the technological ability to accomplish the task, the necessity of moral and social commitment to action becomes absolute. But such action cannot be mindless: it must be grounded upon a social ethic as powerful and reasonable as the obsolete one that must now be replaced. In the economically underdeveloped America of the past, the amoral, materialistic ethic did make some sense; in the technological, sophisticated society of contemporary America it is a prescription for ecological suicide. Either the technology must be dismantled or the moral and social commitments and structures of society must be altered—or both—or survival is impossible. Hence, a major contention of this book is that an ecological ethic is essential to the continued existence of man as well as to the quality of our life.

The book also focuses on the ways in which the current social, political, economic, and spatial structures are inconsistent with the ecological ethic, and how those same structures effectively prohibit change. The reader may infer from this that "I am not part of the problem" or "I am powerless in bringing about change." We want to stress that we think neither of these conclusions is justified.

Moral and value change must start with the individual's willingness to encounter the fear associated with nonsubmissive behavior. The direction of this value change must also allow new collectivities to form that will provide reinforcement for new values and help to develop the power to act.

Unless this happens other aspects of solution will be irrelevant because the choice will be quite literally beyond us. What is involved is not just the quality of life, but life itself.

Finally, we would like to stress the critical importance of an acceptance, better, a cherishing, of cultural relativity in reaching for a solution. A very wide variety of lifestyles is consistent with and is required for concretizing the ecological ethic. In fact, to judge a person's value, his commitment, or his approach to solving problems solely according to the norms of any single group is fundamentally nonecological.

Truth, of course, has many shapes. Conclusions differing from those of the editors or authors of the selections may be equally consistent with the data that are used. Search for your own data and draw your own conclusions. You will not find extensive chapter introductions or article headnotes because we believe that only you, by reading and discussing this material, can find meanings in the whole and go beyond the individual perspective of the editors and authors. Our assumption in assembling these materials is that useful and important data for analyzing American society can be found lying about underfoot. It exists in popular music, the press, television, films, in the sensory experiences of everyday living as well as in scholarly journals and monographs. That should be your guiding assumption in approaching the questions raised in these materials. Be patient. Trust yourself. Help each other.

PART ONE
POLLUTION

If you visit American city
You will find it very pretty.
Just two things of which you must beware:
Don't drink the water and don't breathe the air!
Tom Lehrer

"When you're in MY tax bracket, son—you don't have to worry about the 'the quality of life'!"

Reprinted by permission of Newspaper Enterprise Association.

The problem of pollution is an obvious point of entry into a discussion of the quality of life in America. Smog that stings the eyes and hangs grey-brown in the air over the cities, the refuse in streets and fence rows, the unseen mercury in the water and the DDT in the evening meal affect the quality of the lives of all of us. Probably in no other area have Americans arrived at such an apparent consensus that a problem exists and that something must be done about it. But to deplore and to react to the recognizable signs of the deteriorating quality of the environment is not necessarily to understand or to be able to cope with the problem of pollution. Like the proverbial iceberg, its larger dimensions lie hidden from view. The fact that we can see and feel and sometimes taste pollution—the fact that it is so obvious—can also blind us to the real complexity of the problem. Several of the selections in Part One argue that the problem is that we have not defined the problem itself broadly enough. In effect, we have taken a social problem whose roots lie deep within the complex reality of modern American society and have given it a narrow technical definition. Thus we attack only the shadow of the problem rather than the problem itself.

The danger of that, as Ehrlich suggests in Chapter 1, is that ecological catastrophe may overtake us before we are even aware of the prospect. We do not, of course, have to take such pessimistic forecasts at face value. Who can really predict that life on earth will soon perish with the death of the sea or ultimately end in a giant smogbank? That is to go beyond what we know for certain and as such it is fantasy. But other fantasies of the past have found ways to become our present realities. The possibility of ecological disaster is itself the partial result of earlier fantasies of man's dominion over nature and other men. The question here is not whether fantasies come true, but whether the more pessimistic ecologists have defined the problem more accurately than most of us. Certainly they have called our attention to the breadth of the problem.

Pollution is already a global problem. As Gordon points out in Chapter 2, it threatens the quality of life in Durban, South Africa, and Kobe, Japan, as well as in New York and Los Angeles. We pollute each other. Air contaminated by smokestacks and automobile exhausts in Chicago is breathed in the towns of Wisconsin; radioactive dust from the atomic bomb tests of a decade ago circle the globe. While all nations are polluters, the essential difference lies in their level of technological and industrial development. The average American contributes far more than his share to the global problem of pollution. With his technologically endowed capacity to consume resources, he may have the same detrimental effect on the environment as twenty-five people in India. The technological variable is so obvious that we find it easy to define pollution as essentially a technological problem.

This definition of pollution as a technological problem prompts us also to look for technological solutions. The automobile manufacturers are confronted with federal directives to "clean up" the internal combustion engine; public utility companies are given deadlines for installing mechanical and chemical devices that will filter the smoke from their smokestacks. To solve the problems of technology, we ask for more technology. We have always done so. As Blake points out in Chapter 3, the earliest pollution problem in America, the contamination of public water supplies, was solved by developing a technically more advanced water and sanitation system. When the unanticipated results of technology, population increase, and mass consumption rose to the surface, we sought the addict's cure of another technological "fix." And because we are "hooked" on technology, the nonrenewable resources of half the world fill our junkyards, crowd our streets, slick our waters, and foul our air. One of the central questions posed in Part One, therefore, is whether environmental problems caused by technology can be solved by technology.

But what if this is not the solution? Some have pointed to population control, insisting that overpopulation is killing us. We are inundated with waste because there are too many people. Yet birth control programs are focused upon the poor, who are not the major source of pollution. The affluent consume many times more of the earth's resources than do the poor. Even if the world attained zero population growth, increasing individual wants would continue to deplete our finite resources. Others have insisted upon government action to control pollution and to make polluters legally responsible for their actions. Yet as Gordon clearly points out in *Sick Cities*, our metropolitan areas are so politically fragmented that effective regional control of pollution is extremely difficult. Can we create effective regional governments and still have the local control and autonomy that we so highly value? Still others have argued that our concept of free goods is outmoded and must be changed—the air is no longer "free" and those who use it for disposing of wastes must pay the price for cleansing it. But ultimately it is us, the consumers, who must pay for the added costs of production for the goods that we so greatly desire. Are we willing to pay the price? And will even that solve the problem? We deal with the problem as if it were something quite distant rather than within each of us and within the roots of our society.

It is time that we consider whether the social forces that lead us to exploit other human beings are not fundamentally the same as those which lead us to exploit nature. Our value system and the social, economic, and political institutions that perpetuate it sanction competitiveness, acquisitiveness, and the wasting of resources through conspicuous consumption. The plundered landscape and the wasted people of our ghettos have this much in common: Both are the victims of the same social syndrome of exploitation, and both are explained away in the name of progress. Perhaps it is in large part for this reason that we define pollution as a technical problem, for defining it in social terms would pose the threat of social change. As Slater says in Chapter 4, we have fashioned a technologically radical, but socially conservative, society that has traditionally dealt with problems by giving free reign to technological change while obstructing social change. To get at the basic causes of pollution will require, then, not just a remedial technology, but fundamental social change. We must radically revise our view of the purpose of life and the social activities and institutions that sustain that view. But this is more easily said than done.

Every society erects barriers to change and American society is no exception. Those barriers are the props of the existing social order that are kept there by interests concerned with perpetuating the existing structure of things. In Chapter 5, Harrington examines the most visible of these interests that obstruct ecologically beneficial change—the large corporations whose concern for profits anesthetize their sense of social responsibility. Yet we too often think of such barriers as those constructed by powerful people, the "others" who are not like us. Barriers are also erected by people like us. These include, as Langer notes, the barriers that urban living has imposed between city people and the rhythm of nature. They are also the barriers that we erect against each other, barriers of fear, mistrust, and hatred. Until we can break through our own separations to understand our common needs, we shall be incapable of planning for social change. Like Prometheus bound with the chains he had forged, we shall struggle within our own isolation. Our neurotic self-interest in the social pollution that we have created may prove to be the most resistant barrier to change.

In the face of such difficulties is there any hope for constructive change? Spot technological cures have been tried for generations—every day we *feel* the results. This suggests that we must break out of our conventional pattern of thinking if we are to deal effectively with the problem of pollution. In Chapter 6, Berube contends that we must take an ecological approach, one that recognizes that every living thing on earth bears an interdependent relationship to every other living thing and to the habitat. The implications of such an ecological approach are explored in Chapter 6, for we feel that, while ecology is a formula for a steady state and its goal is ecological stability for survival sake, it is a socially radical idea in a society in which technological change is commonplace. It means seeing oneself as symbiotic with nature and with other human beings, not independent of them or dominant over them. Stability means cooperation; it means that enough is enough. Yet our goals that are formed by the family and school and the larger society require competition, striving, and achievement. Can knowledge of this subtle symbiosis provide the basis for a new kind of society? Apocalypse in the form of ecological catastrophe assuredly provides the setting for invention, for innovation, for new social fantasies. It challenges us to orient ourselves and our society toward harmony with nature and each other. The chief irony of the ecology movement is that those who have the most pessimistic view of our environmental future have produced the most helpful blueprint for the future of American society.

1 Crisis

ECO-CATASTROPHE!

Paul Ehrlich

I

The end of the ocean came late in the summer of 1979, and it came even more rapidly than the biologists had expected. There had been signs for more than a decade, commencing with the discovery in 1968 that DDT slows down photosynthesis in marine plant life. It was announced in a short paper in the technical journal, *Science*, but to ecologists it smacked of doomsday. They knew that all life in the sea depends on photosynthesis, the chemical process by which green plants bind the sun's energy and make it available to living things. And they knew that DDT and similar chlorinated hydrocarbons had polluted the entire surface of the earth, including the sea.

But that was only the first of many signs. There had been the final gasp of the whaling industry in 1973, and the end of the Peruvian anchovy fishery in 1975. Indeed, a score of other fisheries had disappeared quietly from overexploitation and various eco-catastrophes by 1977. The term "eco-catastrophe" was coined by a California ecologist in 1969 to describe the most spectacular of man's attacks on the systems which sustain his life. He drew his inspiration from the Santa Barbara offshore oil disaster of that year, and from the news which spread among naturalists that virtually all of the Golden State's seashore bird life was doomed because of chlorinated hydrocarbon interference with its reproduction. Eco-catastrophes in the sea became increasingly common in the early 1970s. Mysterious "blooms" of previously rare microorganisms began to appear in offshore waters. Red tides—killer outbreaks of a minute single-celled plant—returned to the Florida Gulf coast and were sometimes accompanied by tides of other exotic hues.

It was clear by 1975 that the entire ecology of the ocean was changing. A few types of phytoplankton were becoming resistant to chlorinated hydrocarbons and were gaining the upper hand. Changes in the phytoplankton community led inevitably to changes in the community of zooplankton, the tiny animals which eat the phytoplankton. These changes were passed on

From *Ramparts*, vol. 8, no. 3 (September 1969), pp. 24–28.

up the chains of life in the ocean to the herring, plaice, cod and tuna. As the diversity of life in the ocean diminished, its stability also decreased.

Other changes had taken place by 1975. Most ocean fishes that returned to fresh water to breed, like the salmon, had become extinct, their breeding streams so dammed up and polluted that their powerful homing instinct only resulted in suicide. Many fishes and shellfishes that bred in restricted areas along the coasts followed them as onshore pollution escalated.

By 1977 the annual yield of fish from the sea was down to 30 million metric tons, less than one-half the per capita catch of a decade earlier. This helped malnutrition to escalate sharply in a world where an estimated 50 million people per year were already dying of starvation. The United Nations attempted to get all chlorinated hydrocarbon insecticides banned on a worldwide basis, but the move was defeated by the United States. This opposition was generated primarily by the American petrochemical industry, operating hand in glove with its subsidiary, the United States Department of Agriculture. Together they persuaded the government to oppose the U.N. move—which was not difficult since most Americans believed that Russia and China were more in need of fish products than was the United States. The United Nations also attempted to get fishing nations to adopt strict and enforced catch limits to preserve dwindling stocks. This move was blocked by Russia, who, with the most modern electronic equipment, was in the best position to glean what was left in the sea. It was, curiously, on the very day in 1977 when the Soviet Union announced its refusal that another ominous article appeared in *Science*. It announced that incident solar radiaton had been so reduced by worldwide air pollution that serious effects on the world's vegetation could be expected.

II

Apparently it was a combination of ecosystem destabilization, sunlight reduction, and a rapid escalation in chlorinated hydrocarbon pollution from massive Thanodrin applications which triggered the ultimate catastrophe. Seventeen huge Soviet-financed Thanodrin plants were operating in underdeveloped countries by 1978. They had been part of a massive Russian "aid offensive" designed to fill the gap caused by the collapse of America's ballyhooed "Green Revolution."

It became apparent in the early '70s that the "Green Revolution" was more talk than substance. Distribution of high yield "miracle" grain seeds had caused temporary local spurts in agricultural production. Simultaneously, excellent weather had produced record harvests. The combination permitted bureaucrats, especially in the United States Department of Agriculture and the Agency for International Development (AID), to reverse their previous pessimism and indulge in an outburst of optimistic propaganda about staving off famine. They raved about the approaching transformation of agriculture in the underdeveloped countries (UDCs). The reason for the propaganda reversal was never made clear. Most historians agree that a combination of utter ignorance of ecology, a desire to justify past errors, and pressure from agroindustry (which was eager to sell pesticides, fertilizers, and farm machinery to the UDCs and agencies helping the UDCs) was behind the campaign. Whatever the motivation, the results were clear. Many concerned people, lacking the expertise to see through the Green Revolution drivel, relaxed. The population–food crisis was "solved."

But reality was not long in showing itself. Local famine persisted in northern India even after good weather brought an end to the ghastly Bihar famine of the mid-'60s. East Pakistan was next, followed by a resurgence of general famine in northern India. Other foci of famine rapidly developed in Indonesia, the Philippines, Malawi, the Congo, Egypt, Colombia, Ecuador, Honduras, the Dominican Republic, and Mexico.

Everywhere hard realities destroyed the illusion of the Green Revolution. Yields dropped as the progressive farmers who had first accepted the new seeds found that their higher yields brought lower prices—effective demand (hunger plus cash) was not sufficient in poor countries to keep prices up. Less progressive farmers, observing this, refused to make the extra effort required to cultivate the "miracle" grains. Transport systems proved inadequate to bring the necessary fertilizer to the fields where the new and extremely fertilizer-sensitive grains were being grown. The same systems were also inadequate to move produce to markets. Fertilizer plants were not built fast enough, and most of the underdeveloped countries could not scrape together funds to purchase supplies, even on concessional terms. Finally, the inevitable happened, and pests began to reduce yields in even the most carefully cultivated fields. Among the first were the famous "miracle rats" which invaded Philippine "miracle rice" fields early in 1969. They were quickly followed by many insects and viruses, thriving on the relatively pest-susceptible new grains, encouraged by the vast and dense plantings, and rapidly acquiring resistance to the chemicals used against them. As chaos spread until even the most obtuse agriculturists and economists realized that the Green Revolution had turned brown, the Russians stepped in.

In retrospect it seems incredible that the Russians, with the American mistakes known to them, could launch an even more incompetent program of aid to the underdeveloped world. Indeed, in the early 1970s there were cynics in the United States who claimed that outdoing the stupidity of American foreign aid would be physically impossible. Those critics were, however, obviously unaware that the Russians had been busily destroying their own environment for many years. The virtual disappearance of sturgeon from Russian rivers caused a great shortage of caviar by 1970. A standard joke among Russian scientists at that time was that they had created an artificial caviar which was indistinguishable from the real thing—except by taste. At any rate the Soviet Union, observing with interest the progressive deterioration of relations between the UDCs and the United States, came up with a solution. It had recently developed what it claimed was the ideal insecticide, a highly lethal chlorinated hydrocarbon complexed with a special agent for penetrating the external skeletal armor of insects. Announcing that the new pesticide, called Thanodrin, would truly produce a Green Revolution, the Soviets entered into negotiations with various UDCs for the construction of massive Thanodrin factories. The USSR would bear all the costs; all it wanted in return were certain trade and military concessions.

It is interesting now, with the perspective of years, to examine in some detail the reasons why the UDCs welcomed the Thanodrin plan with such open arms. Government officials in these countries ignored the protests of their own scientists that Thanodrin would not solve the problems which plagued them. The governments now knew that the basic cause of their problems was overpopulation, and that these problems had been exacerbated by the dullness, daydreaming, and cupidity endemic to all governments. They knew that only population control and limited development aimed primarily at agriculture could have spared them the horrors they now faced. They knew it, but they were not about to admit it. How much easier it was simply to accuse the Americans of failing to give them proper aid; how much simpler to accept the Russian panacea.

And then there was the general worsening of relations between the United States and the UDCs. Many things had contributed to this. The situation in America in the first half of the 1970s deserves our close scrutiny. Being more dependent on imports for raw materials than the Soviet Union, the United States had, in the early 1970s, adopted more and more heavy-handed policies in order to insure continuing supplies. Military adventures in Asia and Latin America had further lessened the international credibility of the United States as a great defender of freedom—an image which had begun to deteriorate rapidly during the pointless and fruitless Viet-Nam conflict. At home, acceptance of the carefully manufactured image lessened dramatically, as even the more romantic and chauvinistic citizens began to understand the role of the military and the industrial system in what John Kenneth Galbraith had aptly named "The New Industrial State."

At home in the USA the early '70s were traumatic times. Racial violence grew and the habitability of the cities diminished, as nothing substantial was done to ameliorate either racial inequities or urban blight. Welfare rolls grew as automation and general technological progress forced more and more people into the category of "unemployable." Simultaneously a taxpayers' revolt occurred. Although there was not enough money to build the schools, roads, water systems, sewage systems, jails, hospitals, urban transit lines, and all the other amenities needed to support a burgeoning population, Americans refused to tax themselves more heavily. Starting in Youngstown, Ohio, in 1969 and followed closely by Richmond, California, community after community was forced to close its schools or curtail educational operations for lack of funds. Water supplies, already marginal in quality and quantity in many places by 1970, deteriorated quickly. Water rationing occurred in 1723 municipalities in the summer of 1974, and hepatitis and epidemic dysentery rates climbed about 500 percent between 1970–1974.

III

Air pollution continued to be the most obvious manifestation of environmental deterioration. It was, by 1972, quite literally in the eyes of all Americans. The year 1973 saw not only the New York and Los Angeles smog disasters, but also the publication of the Surgeon General's massive report on air pollution and health. The public had been partially prepared for the worst by the publicity given to the U.N. pollution conference held in 1972. Deaths in the late '60s caused by smog were well known to scientists, but the public had ignored them because they mostly involved the early demise of the old and sick rather than people dropping dead on the freeways. But suddenly our citizens were faced with nearly 200,000 corpses and massive documentation that they could be the next to die from respiratory disease. They were not ready for that scale of disaster. After all, the U.N. conference had not predicted that accumulated air pollution would make the planet uninhabitable until almost 1990. The population was terrorized as TV screens became filled with scenes of horror from the disaster areas. Especially vivid was NBC's coverage of hundreds of unattended people choking out their lives outside of New York's hospitals. Terms like nitrogen oxide, acute bronchitis and cardiac arrest began to have real meaning for most Americans.

The ultimate horror was the announcement that chlorinated hydrocarbons were now a major constituent of air pollution in all American cities. Autopsies of smog disaster victims revealed an average chlorinated hydrocarbon load in fatty tissue equivalent to 26 parts per million of DDT. In October, 1973, the Department of Health, Education and Welfare announced studies which showed unequivocally that increasing death rates from hypertension, cirrhosis of the liver, liver cancer and a series of other diseases had resulted from the chlorinated hydrocarbon load. They estimated that Americans born since 1946 (when DDT usage began) now had a life expectancy of only 49 years, and predicted that if current patterns continued, this expectancy would reach 42 years by 1980, when it might level out. Plunging insurance stocks triggered a stock market panic. The president of Velsicol, Inc., a major pesticide producer, went on television to "publicly eat a teaspoonful of DDT" (it was really powdered milk) and announce that HEW had been infiltrated by Communists. Other giants of the petrochemical industry, attempting to dispute the indisputable evidence, launched a massive pressure campaign on Congress to force HEW to "get out of agriculture's business." They were aided by the agro-chemical journals, which had decades of experience in misleading the public about the benefits and dangers of pesticides. But by now the public realized that it had been duped. The Nobel Prize for medicine and physiology was given to Drs. J. L. Radomski and W. B. Deichmann, who in the late 1960s had pioneered in the documentation of the long-term lethal effects of chlorinated hydrocarbons. A Presidential Commission with unimpeachable credentials directly accused the agro-chemical complex of "condemning many millions of Americans to an early death." The year 1973 was the year in which Americans finally came to understand the direct threat to their existence posed by environmental deterioration.

And 1973 was also the year in which most people finally comprehended the indirect threat. Even the president of Union Oil Company and several other industrialists publicly stated their concern over the reduction of bird populations which had resulted from pollution by DDT and other chlorinated hydrocarbons. Insect populations boomed because they were resistant to most pesticides and had been freed, by the incompetent use of those pesticides, from most of their natural enemies. Rodents swarmed over crops, multiplying rapidly in the absence of predatory birds. The effect of pests on the wheat crop was especially disastrous in the summer of 1973, since that was also the year of the great drought. Most of us can remember the shock which greeted the announcement by atmospheric physicists that the shift of the jet stream which had caused the drought was probably permanent. It signalled the birth of the Midwestern desert. Man's air-polluting activities had by then caused gross changes in climatic patterns. The news, of course, played hell with commodity and stock markets. Food prices skyrocketed, as savings were poured into hoarded canned goods. Official assurances that good supplies would remain ample fell on deaf ears, and even the government showed signs of nervousness when California migrant field workers went out on strike again in protest against the continued use of pesticides by growers. The strike burgeoned into farm burning and riots. The workers, calling themselves "The Walking Dead," demanded immediate compensation for their shortened lives, and crash research programs to attempt to lengthen them.

It was in the same speech in which President Edward Kennedy, after much delay, finally declared a national emergency and called out the National Guard to harvest California's crops, that the first mention of population control was made. Kennedy pointed out that the United States would no longer be able to offer any food aid to other nations and was likely to suffer food shortages herself. He suggested that, in view of the manifest failure of the Green Revolution, the only hope of the UDCs lay in population control. His statement, you will recall, created an uproar in the underdeveloped countries. Newspaper editorials accused the United States of wishing to prevent small countries from becoming large nations and thus threatening American hegemony. Politicians asserted that President Kennedy was a "creature of the giant drug combine" that wished to shove its pills down every woman's throat.

Among Americans, religious opposition to population control was very slight. Industry in general also backed the idea. Increasing poverty in the UDCs was both destroying markets and threatening supplies of raw materials. The seriousness of the raw material situation had been brought home during the Congressional Hard Resources hearings in 1971. The exposure of the ignorance of the cornucopian economists had been quite a spectacle—a spectacle brought into virtually every American's home in living color. Few would forget the distinguished geologist from the University of California who suggested that economists be legally required to learn at least the most elementary facts of geology. Fewer still would forget that an equally distinguished Harvard economist added that they might be required to learn some economics, too. The overall message was clear: America's resource situation was bad and bound to get worse. The hearings had led to a bill requiring the Departments of State, Interior, and Commerce to set up a joint resource procurement council with the express purpose of "insuring that proper consideration of American resource needs be an integral part of American foreign policy."

Suddenly the United States discovered that it had a national consensus: population control was the only possible salvation of the underdeveloped world. But that same consensus led to heated debate. How could the UDCs be persuaded to limit their populations, and should not the United States lead the way by limiting its own? Members of the intellectual community wanted America to set an example. They pointed out that the United States was in the midst of a new baby boom: her birth rate, well over 20 per thousand per year, and her growth rate of over 1 percent per annum were among the very highest of the developed countries. They detailed the deterioration of the American physical and psychic environments, the growing health threats, the impending food shortages, and the insufficiency of funds for desperately needed public works. They contended that the nation was clearly unable or unwilling to properly care for the people it already had. What possible reason could there be, they queried, for adding any more? Besides, who would listen to requests by the United States for population control when that nation did not control her own profligate reproduction?

Those who opposed population controls for the U.S. were equally vociferous. The military-industrial complex, with its all-too-human mixture of ignorance and avarice, still saw strength and prosperity in numbers. Baby food magnates, already worried by the growing nitrate pollution of their products, saw their market disappearing. Steel manufacturers saw a decrease in aggregate demand and slippage for that holy of holies, the Gross National Product. And military men saw, in the growing population–food–environment crisis, a serious threat to their carefully nurtured Cold War. In the end, of course, economic arguments held sway, and the "inalienable right of every American couple to determine the size of its family," a freedom invented for the occasion in the early '70s, was not compromised.

The population control bill, which was passed by Congress early in 1974, was quite a document, nevertheless. On the domestic front, it authorized an increase from 100 to 150 million dollars in funds for "family planning" activities. This was made possible by a general feeling in the country that the growing army on welfare needed family planning. But the gist of the bill was a series of measures designed to impress the need for population control on the UDCs. All American aid to countries with overpopulation problems was required by law to consist in part of population control assistance. In order to receive any assistance each nation was required not only to accept the population control aid, but also to match it according to a complex formula. "Overpopulation" itself was defined by a formula based on U.N. statistics, and the UDCs were required not only to accept aid, but also to show progress in reducing birth rates. Every five years the status of the aid program for each nation was to be re-evaluated.

The reaction to the announcement of this program dwarfed the response to President Kennedy's speech. A coalition of UDCs attempted to get the U.N. General Assembly to condemn the United States as a "genetic aggressor." Most damaging of all to the American cause was the famous "25 Indians and a dog" speech by Mr. Shankarnarayan, Indian Ambassador to the U.N. Shankarnarayan pointed out that for several decades the United States, with less than six percent of the people of the world had consumed roughly 50 percent of the raw materials used every year. He described vividly America's contribution to worldwide environmental deterioration, and he scathingly denounced the miserly record of United States foreign aid as "unworthy of a fourth-rate power, let alone the most powerful nation on earth."

It was the climax of his speech, however, which most historians claim once and for all destroyed the image of the United States. Shankarnarayan informed the assembly that the average American family dog was fed more animal protein per week than the average Indian got in a month. "How do you justify taking fish from protein-starved Peruvians and feeding them to your animals?" he asked. "I contend," he concluded, "that the birth of an American baby is a greater disaster for the world than that of 25 Indian babies." When the applause had died away, Mr. Sorensen, the American representative, made a speech which said essentially that "other countries look after their own self-interest, too." When the vote came, the United States was condemned.

IV

This condemnation set the tone of U.S.–UDC relations at the time the Russian Thanodrin proposal was made. The proposal seemed to offer the masses in the UDCs an opportunity to save themselves and humiliate the United States at the same time; and in human affairs, as we all know, biological realities could never interfere with such an opportunity. The scientists were silenced, the politicians said yes, the Thanodrin plants were built, and the results were what any beginning ecology student could have predicted. At first Thanodrin seemed to offer excellent control of many pests. True, there was a rash of human fatalities from improper use of the lethal chemical, but, as Russian technical advisors were prone to note, these were more than compensated for by increased yields. Thanodrin use skyrocketed throughout the underdeveloped world. The Mikoyan design group developed a dependable, cheap agricultural aircraft which the Soviets donated to the effort in large numbers. MIG sprayers became even more common in UDCs than MIG interceptors.

Then the troubles began. Insect strains with cuticles resistant to Thanodrin penetration began to appear. And as streams, rivers, fish culture ponds and onshore waters became rich in Thanodrin, more fisheries began to disappear. Bird populations were decimated. The sequence of events was standard for broadcast use of a synthetic pesticide: great success at first, followed by removal of natural enemies and development of resistance by the pest. Populations of crop-eating insects in areas treated with Thanodrin made steady comebacks and soon became more abundant than ever. Yields plunged, while farmers in their desperation increased the Thanodrin dose and shortened the time between treatments. Death from Thanodrin poisoning became common. The first violent incident occurred in the Canete Valley of Peru, where farmers had suffered a similar chlorinated hydrocarbon disaster in the mid-'50s. A Russian advisor serving as an agricultural pilot was assaulted and killed by a mob of enraged farmers in January, 1978. Trouble spread rapidly during 1978, especially after the word got out that two years earlier Russia herself had banned the use of Thanodrin at home because of its serious effects on ecological systems. Suddenly Russia, and not the United States, was the *bête noir* in the UDCs. "Thanodrin parties" became epidemic, with farmers, in their ignorance, dumping carloads of Thanodrin concentrate into the sea. Russian advisors fled, and four of the Thanodrin plants were leveled to the ground. Destruction of the plants in Rio and Calcutta led to hundreds of thousands of gallons of Thanodrin concentrate being dumped directly into the sea.

Mr. Shankarnarayan again rose to address the U.N., but this time it was Mr. Potemkin, representative of the Soviet Union, who was on the hot seat. Mr. Potemkin heard his nation described as the greatest mass killer of all time as Shankarnarayan predicted at least 30 million deaths from crop failures due to overdependence on Thanodrin. Russia was accused of "chemical aggression," and the General Assembly, after a weak reply by Potemkin, passed a vote of censure.

It was in January, 1979, that huge blooms of a previously unknown variety of diatom were reported off the coast of Peru. The blooms were accompanied by a massive die-off of sea life and of the pathetic remainder of the birds which had once feasted on the anchovies of the area. Almost immediately another huge bloom was reported in the Indian ocean, centering around the Seychelles, and then a third in the South Atlantic off the African coast. Both of these were accompanied by spectacular die-offs of marine animals. Even more ominous were growing reports of fish and bird kills at oceanic points where there were no spectacular blooms. Biologists were soon able to explain the phenomena: the diatom had evolved an enzyme which broke down Thanodrin; that enzyme also produced a breakdown product which interfered with the transmission of nerve impulses, and was therefore lethal to animals. Unfortunately, the biologists could suggest no way of repressing the poisonous diatom bloom in time. By September, 1979, all important animal life in the sea was extinct. Large areas of coastline had to be evacuated, as windrows of dead fish created a monumental stench.

But stench was the least of man's problems. Japan and China were faced with almost instant starvation from a total loss of the seafood on which they were so dependent. Both blamed Russia for their situation and demanded immediate mass shipments of food. Russia had none to send. On October 13, Chinese armies attacked Russia on a broad front. . . .

V

A pretty grim scenario. Unfortunately, we're a long way into it already. Everything mentioned as happening before 1970 has actually occurred; much of the rest is based on projections of trends already appearing. Evidence that pesticides have long-term lethal effects on human beings has started to accumulate, and recently Robert Finch, Secretary of the Department of Health, Education and Welfare, expressed his extreme apprehension about the pesticide situation. Simultaneously the petrochemical industry continues its unconscionable poison-peddling. For instance, Shell Chemical has been carrying on a high-pressure campaign to sell the insecticide Azodrin to farmers as a killer of cotton pests. They continue their program even though they know that Azodrin is not only ineffective, but often *increases* the pest density. They've covered themselves nicely in an advertisement which states, "Even if an overpowering migration [sic] develops, the flexibility of Azodrin lets you regain control fast. Just increase the dosage according to label recommendations." It's a great game—get people to apply the poison and kill the natural enemies of the pests. Then blame the increased pests on "migration" and sell even more pesticide!

Right now fisheries are being wiped out by over-exploitation, made easy by modern electronic equipment. The companies producing the equipment know this. They even boast in advertising that only their equipment will keep fishermen in business until the final kill. Profits must obviously be maximized in the short run. Indeed, Western society is in the process of completing the rape and murder of the planet for economic gain. And, sadly, most of the rest of the world is eager for the opportunity to emulate our behavior. But the underdeveloped peoples will be denied that opportunity—the days of plunder are drawing inexorably to a close.

Most of the people who are going to die in the greatest cataclysm in the history of man have already been born. More than three and a half billion people already populate our moribund globe, and about half of them are hungry. Some 10 to 20 million will starve to death *this year.* In spite of this, the population of the earth will increase by 70 million souls in 1969. For mankind has artifically lowered the death rate of the human population, while in general birth rates have remained high. With the input side of the population system in high gear and the output side slowed down, our fragile planet has filled with people at an incredible rate. It took several million years for the population to reach a total of two billion people in 1930, while a *second two billion will have been added by 1975!* By that time some experts feel that food shortages will have escalated the present level of world hunger and starvation into famines of unbelievable proportions. Other experts, more optimistic, think the ultimate food-population collision will not occur until the decade of the 1980s. Of course more massive famine may be avoided if other events cause a prior rise in the human death rate.

Both worldwide plague and thermonuclear war are made more probable as population growth continues. These, along with famine, make up the trio of potential "death rate solutions" to the population problem—solutions in which the birth rate–death rate imbalance is redressed by a rise in the death rate rather than by a lowering of the birth rate. Make no mistake about it, *the imbalance will be redressed.* The shape of the population growth curve is one familiar to the biologist. It is the outbreak part of an outbreak–crash sequence. A population grows rapidly in the presence of abundant resources, finally runs out of food or some other necessity, and crashes to a low level or extinction. Man is not only running out of food, he is also destroying the life support systems of the Spaceship Earth. The situation was recently summarized very succinctly: "It is the top of the ninth inning. Man, always a threat at the plate, has been hitting Nature hard. It is important to remember, however, that NATURE BATS LAST."*

* Show in class 3 minute color film "Pollution," music by Tom Lehrer. Available from National Medical Audiovisual Center, Atlanta, Ga., 30333. No charge.

The Nature of the Environmental Crisis

Concern with environmental deterioration is an old story for the human race. One can find distinct overtones of it in the Book of Jeremiah. Within the last hundred years of unprecedented economic development, Jevons was worrying about the exhaustion of British coal as long ago as 1865, and Sir William Crookes was lamenting the imminent exhaustion of Chilean nitrates in 1899. Teddy Roosevelt was associated with the big conservation movement in the 1900s, with the extension of national parks and national forests, and the establishment of the Bureau of Reclamation. In the 1930s came the dust bowl and the Soil Conservation Act. The present excitement about the environment, which tends to center on atmospheric and water pollution and the adverse effects of insecticides, poisons, and radiation, is at least the third wave of excitement of this kind in this century, but perhaps is the first one that has become really worldwide in its implications.

It is a little puzzling why so much excitement has been generated at this particular time. Some of the present awareness stems from frustration with the nagging war in Vietnam, the continuing plight of the poor, the slow action on civil rights, and the pervasive threat of nuclear destruction. Part of it comes from increasing scientific knowledge of deteriorating environmental quality. . . .

University of Colorado Commission on Environmental Studies, "The University's Response to the Environmental Crisis," (August 3, 1970).

2 "Don't drink the water and don't breathe the air!"

. . . we must not forget that air pollution is a global problem. Madisonians sometimes breathe Chicago's air, Hong Kong receives pollution from Canton, and the dust and smoke from the deserts and fires of Asia spread eastward across the Pacific. Radioactive fallout from American, British, Chinese, French and Russian nuclear bombs and tests, while concentrated along the stormtracks of the northern hemisphere, has encircled the globe.

Air Pollution: Commission on College Geography Resource Paper Number 2 (Washington, D.C.: Association of American Geographers, 1968), p. 35.

SICK CITIES

Mitchell Gordon

Beware of the Air

For four years, from 1952 to 1956, while he was Associate Professor of Pathology at the School of Medicine at the University of Southern California, Dr. Paul Kotin conducted an interesting series of experiments involving several hundred mice and some painstakingly collected particles of Los Angeles smog. His findings hold some frightening implications for urban humans.

Large blowers located next to Los Angeles County Hospital and on a portable rig parked near the city's four-level downtown freeway interchange drew in foul air. Tiny particles and gases in the air were caught in filter paper. Solutions were then made from the particles and painted on the skins of some 100 mice as often as 3 times a week over a period of 14 months.

By the end of that time, 75 percent of the mice had developed skin cancers.

Dr. Kotin admits his experiments do not prove smog causes cancer in humans. The cancers produced on the mice, he concedes, may have been due to an unusual concentration of regularly applied pollutants not necessarily dangerous to humans in the highly diluted, airy forms in which they make highly irregular appearances.

"Nevertheless," Dr. Kotin states, "the experiments do prove there are chemical carcinogens (agents capable of producing cancer) in Los Angeles smog. Solutions made from washed and filtered air produced no cancers on test mice painted just as frequently over the same period of time. Furthermore, we know that what is capable of producing cancer in one mammal is generally capable of producing it in another.

"We know also," he said, "that the state in which these agents exist makes them capable of being breathed by humans and deposited on the lining of the lung where they can survive long enough to do damage." . . .

In 1960 Dr. Geoffrey Dean, of the Union of South Africa's Eastern Cape Provincial Hospital, told a medical conference, "There seems to be very strong evidence that lung cancer results from environmental factors and that it has not been primarily genetically determined, that it results, in fact, from the air we breathe."

In Japan, where mortality rates from lung cancer quadrupled in the years from 1948 to 1960, belief is rising that some of the contributory causes, at least, may be found in polluted air, particularly from the rapid growth in vehicular traffic.

One of the most emphatic statements of all comes from former Surgeon General, Dr. LeRoy E. Burney. "There is a very definite association between community air pollution," says he, "and high mortality rates due to cancer of the respiratory tract, cancer of the stomach, esophagus and arteriosclerotic heart disease."

Consider some of the evidence.

Not long ago, Dr. David F. Eastcott, of New Zealand, found that lung cancer among Britons who emigrated to the down-under isles after they were thirty years old was 75 percent more common than among natives who had lived in New Zealand all their lives, though New Zealanders are known to be among the heaviest smokers in the world. New Zealand's air is nowhere near as badly polluted as Britain's, though it is getting fouler and fouler as additional autos and factories dot its scenic landscape. The theory, of course, is that polluted air breathed in Britain may have started a physiological sequence in the émigrés which the native-born, inhaling cleaner air, escaped.

Studies of cancer victims in England and Wales revealed a doubling of mortality from lung cancer in a ten-year period from 1944, but no increase at all in larynx cancer deaths. The lung, of course, is more exposed to air pollutants than the larynx. . . .

More than a score of studies in Britain and elsewhere have established the role of air pollution in chronic bronchitis. The ailment has taken more lives in Britain in some recent years than lung cancer and tuberculosis combined, and is one of the leading causes of death in that country.

In the decade when California's automotive population grew the fastest —from 1950 to 1960—mortality rate from emphysema, a chronic lung disease that many physicians contend is aggravated by foul air, quadrupled. The most notable increases, twice as many, in fact, were experienced by urban as compared with rural regions. . . .

Water: Filthier and Farther

"Every time you take a glass of water from a faucet in St. Louis," says Richard Amberg, publisher of that city's morning *Globe-Democrat*, "you are drinking from every flush toilet from here to Minnesota."

The rival afternoon paper, the *Post-Dispatch*, commented not long ago on a Public Health Service report concerning pollution of the Mississippi in this manner: "The world's cleanest people, using only the purest oils and spices in exorcising grime witches, are drinking the garbage dump trickles of whatever town lies up the line. We bathe with scented fats and drink a factory's slime."

St. Louis is not unique among the nation's cities. A good many municipalities these days are drinking water that contains the inadequately treated discharge of communities upriver from them. And a good many more, from the looks of things, will be doing so in the future as water use increases along the nation's streams.

The prospect is not a pretty one. It was painted in vivid strokes some years back by Congressman Brent Spence, Kentucky Democrat: "I was born in sight of the Ohio River and I lived most of my life in a home that overlooked the river. I have seen it turn from a beautiful river in which I swam as a boy to a polluted sewer." The open sewer got so bad that eight states finally banded together in 1948 to form the Ohio River Valley Sanitation Commission to clean up the stream. By mid-1962, over 1000 cities representing all but 13 percent of the area's population had poured over $1 billion into sanitation facilities, and the job still was not complete. The multi-state body hired a helicopter to film the dumping of oily wastes into the river by factories along its banks for showing to the general public, in the hope of pressuring industry into cleaning up its liquid waste before discarding it.

The tide, apparently, is finally being turned against the forces of pollution on the Ohio, but it is rising on a good many other waterways. The father of our country is fortunate he's not crossing the Potomac today. A joint House and Senate committee on the capital's urban problems recently found the river so foul as to have become entirely uninhabitable to a wide variety of marine life that once thrived there.

Tulsa no longer draws water from the Arkansas River, it is so fouled with briny discharge. Chicago, which has spent over $400 million on sewage-treatment facilities to remove some 90 percent of the solids from its sewage, still disturbs communities as far as fifty miles downstream with its discard. And in Utah, contamination of the Great Salt Lake has become a matter of increasing concern to recreation-minded municipalities on that vast inland sea.

Authorities estimate well over 50 million pounds of solid wastes are pouring into the nation's waterways daily. Municipal sewer systems were already dumping twice as much waste into streams in 1961 as the maximum that was considered allowable as recently as 1955. A fourth of all the wastes cities are sending into streams is raw sewage. Another third is sewage that has had only the most cursory treatment. According to Dr. Abel Wolman, former chairman of the National Water Resources Board and more recently a top official of the National Research Council in Washington, D.C., practically every major waterway in the United States is now polluted in one degree or another.

President John F. Kennedy told Congress: "Pollution of our country's rivers and streams has—as a result of our rapid population and industrial growth and change—reached alarming proportions."

Water authorities figure that unless pollution is more effectively arrested at the source, the chemical methods that most cities use for treating water, when they treat it at all, will be incapable of producing palatable water by 1980 in many metropolitan areas.

The United States Senate Select Committee on National Water Resources has predicted the nation's daily discharge of used water will nearly double between 1954 and 1980—from 17 billion to 29 billion gallons. By the year 2000, it forecasts, that volume will rise another 50 percent. The late Senator Robert S. Kerr, the Oklahoma Democrat who headed that committee, told the National Watershed Congress in Tucson in 1961: "Well before the end of the century most Americans will be drinking, cooking with, bathing and otherwise using secondhand or thirdhand water."

The problem, for the most part, is not a lack of water. The United States as a nation has been well endowed in this respect. Besides its vast lakes, rivers, and groundwater resources, its average replenishment from precipitation is a deluging 4.3 billion gallons daily—an average of 30 inches a year across the nation's entire surface. Nearly three-quarters of this precipitation, mostly rain and snow, is lost through evaporation, runoff to the sea, and seepage. Only about half of the approximately 1.2 billion gallons that remain is considered economically recoverable. Still, this quantity of new fresh water was double the nation's 1960 usage. Furthermore, only a small portion of the water that's used disappears from circulation altogether. Only about 10 percent of it, in fact, is lost through evaporation, manufacturing, and other processes. Most of the rest is used and then discarded.

Hence, even though the nation's water usage is expected to double between 1960 and 1980 to approximately 600 billion gallons a day—about equal to the volume considered economically recoverable from precipitation—there is little concern, except in the more arid regions of the country, over actual water shortages. The worry, rather, is over a shortage of clean water. More and more water that's needed for home, factory, and other uses will have to come from sources that have already served one, and in some cases, several purposes.

In reusing the fresh water available to them, municipalities face a dual problem: not only is the volume of pollutants rising but the pollutants themselves are growing increasingly complex and troublesome. Until relatively recently, man's watery wastes posed no special problems to the processes of nature: they were largely organic and therefore easily decomposed by bacteria. Technological progress, however, is releasing a swelling variety of substances extremely impervious to nature's ways. And more are being developed all the time. It is estimated that well over four hundred new chemical substances are created yearly in the nation's research laboratories. Many of them participate in industrial processes and end up in the discard.

Furthermore, a vast increase in factory waste is in prospect. Industrial activity is expected to treble between 1950 and 1980, and the use of water for manufacturing purposes to rise even faster—perhaps to six times the 1950 level. The headaches of tomorrow are thus likely to be many times greater than those of today. And not all of these have been particularly easy to handle.

Consider one liquid miracle wrought in the recent past: the household detergent. It came into common use shortly after the end of World War II and now does about three times the wash volume in this country that natural soaps do. Detergents are customarily made from petroleum derivates, which means they are practically impervious to breakdown by bacteria. They have been known to retain their chemical identity even in water that has been treated several times. And, to the great dismay of treatment-plant operators, their sudsing ability is similarly unimpaired. Whether their sudsing ability helps them wash better is highly questionable, but market surveys consistently show housewives think they do, so manufacturers make them sudsy.

The indestructible suds whip up all kinds of trouble at the sewage plant. Porter W. Homer, City Manager of Tucson, Arizona, recalls seeing "suds froth as high as 10 to 15 feet in our primary treatment beds. When the wind came along," says he, "it would take a big foamy gob full of partially treated sewage and spread it over the neighborhood, on lawns and backyards and even on some of the clean laundry hanging on the line that perhaps helped produce it in the first place."

Sewage plant operators are attempting to keep the foam down with overhead sprinklers. The installation runs as high as $200,000 per plant, and even then the suds are not destroyed. They may bubble up all over again on the journey downstream, perhaps to other users of the water.

Some twelve thousand residents of the town of Chanute, Kansas, were somewhat taken aback not very long ago when they found water issuing from their taps foaming like beer. A severe drought had turned the town's usual water source, the Neosho River, to a trickle. To make up for the loss, the city decided to recirculate its sewage plant effluent through its treatment plant and dilute it with fresh water stored behind a dam. Five months of the circular expediency resulted in the accumulation of enough detergent to put a head on water flowing under pressure from city faucets.

Canadian physicist C. E. Hollborn recently reported detergents were turning Lake Winnipeg into a "giant bucket of suds." In the United States, a Senate report in 1959 stated that "most surface waters" and "many ground waters" were showing traces of detergents in them. Britain, West Germany, and other countries where the use of washing machines has increased considerably in recent years, have also had to grapple with the problem. Bargemen on the Neckar River in Germany complain that banks of suds three feet high are menacing navigation. . . .

Pollution of surface water is serious enough, but when contaminants find their way into groundwater supplies, which meet almost a fifth of the nation's needs, the problem may be infinitely worse. A Senate Committee on National Water Resources put it this way: "When streams become polluted, the situation can usually be remedied by treatment or by removing the source of pollution. In any case, the polluted waters move rapidly downstream and pass out of the picture in a relatively short time. Underground waters, on the other hand, are out of reach and move perhaps only a few feet a day. Years or decades may pass before pollution is detected, but once it has occurred, recovery may require an equal number of years." The affected water, the committee warns, "may never again regain its original quality."

Crowding too many septic tanks or cesspools in an area is one way to contaminate groundwater. And altogether too many suburban housing subdivisions have been doing exactly that. Where they should have provided sewage systems or forgone development until such systems were practical, some subdividers have packed up to eight times as many septic tanks in a given area as soil conditions were deemed to allow. Water contaminated by septic-tank seepage has been drawn from wells in such places as Peoria, Illinois; Dania, Florida; Lac de Flambeau, Wisconsin, and elsewhere.

Sewer lines, however, are costly to lay in communities where residents are widely scattered and connections to other systems are remote. Thus, they may not be constructed until the consequences come home to roost in danger or disaster. The Minnesota Health Department recently tested wells in a suburban subdivision with septic tanks just outside Minneapolis–St. Paul. Some 24 percent of the wells it tested produced water too contaminated for use in baby formulas. In the nearby town of Bloomington, 80 percent of the wells "showed traces of contamination from sewage."

On New York's Long Island, Suffolk County Executive H. Lee Dennison calls the threat of contamination to groundwater in that area "the most desperately urgent problem in the history of the county's development." Glasses of water from the area's wells have been known to overflow with suds before they were half full. Residents call their well water the "detergent cocktail," but they don't think it's very funny. . . .

True, the consequences of water pollution were once vastly more tragic in terms of human life than they are today. Housewives in England up to a little over a century ago still emptied their chamber pots from their windows with little more concern for the folks below than a hardy "Gardy-loo!" The cholera epidemics in London and Paris in the early and middle 1800s have all been traced to watery wastes, and typhoid carried in polluted waters to this day remains a vicious killer of humans in many parts of Asia and other less-developed regions of the world.

While water pollution is not the menace to human life in most parts of the globe that it once was, thanks to advances in water-treatment technique, new threats to human health are beginning to appear. Scientists at the Robert A. Taft Engineering Center in Cincinnati, for example, recently reported an explosive outbreak of poliomyelitis in Edmonton, Canada, was "reasonably correlated" with sewage pollution in that area. Polluted water was a prime suspect in a spate of polio cases reported in Nebraska. Senator Kerr in his book *Land, Wood and Water* (Fleetwood, 1960) cited a report from Camden, New Jersey, which showed "an amazing statistical connection" between paralytic polio cases in the area and open sewers; all but one of the cases reported over a period of eight years came from areas with open sewers.

Polluted water of late has also brought an upsurge in another, less frequently fatal but highly debilitating disease known as infectious hepatitis. The federal government's Communicable Disease Center in Atlanta traced thirty-two cases of the disease in 1961 to oysters taken at the highly polluted mouth of the Pascagoula River in Mississippi. The state dispatched two patrol boats to stop all oyster gathering in the area until the pollution problem was cleared up.

Some forty cases of hepatitis in the northeastern United States in 1961 were traced to the eating of raw clams taken from highly polluted Raritan Bay between New York and New Jersey. Another seventeen cases were traced to clams collected off Greenwich Point, Connecticut. Cooking shellfish generally kills hepatitis germs, but steaming them may not be enough: two of thc Connecticut victims were found to have eaten steamed oysters.

Hepatitis, which is caused by a virus, can also be brought on directly by drinking polluted water. Contaminated well water reportedly caused hepatitis recently among 52 schoolchildren in West Virginia. Chlorination doesn't always prevent the disease, either: polluted drinking water treated with chlorine was suspected of causing several cases of hepatitis in one eastern community in 1961.

Hepatitis, like water pollution, is riding a sharp upward curve. The United States Public Health Service estimated the total number of reported hepatitis cases in 1961 at a record 60,000—50 percent over the 1960 figure and three times the 1959 total. Unreported and undiagnosed cases are probably ten times the reported totals, medical authorities estimate. The Public Health Service has begun describing hepatitis as "a major infectious disease." It says the disease, which can cause confinement for three months or longer and recurs with the slightest strain or overindulgence in food and drink, is generally spread by contact but that the "most explosive epidemics" appear to be waterborne.

The damage bad water does to human health is not always immediately

"We don't have a retirement plan. We don't think the country will last that long."

Reproduced by special permission of PLAYBOY Magazine; copyright © 1971 by Playboy.

obvious. The Baker Water and Sanitation District just outside Denver recently investigated complaints of dirty water in its territory. As it did so, it turned up the fact that the area had twice as much intestinal illness as a nearby water district where there were no pollution complaints.

Considerably less than half of the nation's municipalities and only about a fifth of its factories are bothering to treat their sewage before dumping it into streams, according to authorities. Representative John Blatnik, Minnesota Democrat, reciting the record to the United States Conference of Mayors in 1960, declared that only 6700 of the 11,600 municipal sewage systems then in operation, and only 2600 of 10,400 known factory waste outlets, had any treatment facilities whatsoever for their outflow.

Many treatment plants now being operated have long since been considered obsolete. The Public Health Service in 1959 estimated about one-third of the municipal treatment plants then in operation were in desperate need of modernization. Sewer lines may be in similarly poor shape: a recent survey of New York City revealed that not one of its five boroughs met sewer maintenance and repair standards set by the Water Pollution Control Federation, a Washington-based organization of sanitation specialists and municipal officials.

AND NOW, MERCURY

Daniel Zwerdling

People didn't think mercury pollution would be a problem. It costs so damn much that they couldn't envision companies throwing it out in their wastes.

Interior Department spokesman

Government officials are only beginning to grasp the magnitude of the mercury pollution crisis which exploded in March when the Canadians suddenly found lethal doses of the chemical in Lake St. Clair fish. One month later, Americans found the Detroit River and Lake Erie were full of the poison. Since then, four states (Michigan, Ohio, Vermont, Alabama) have shut down their lakes and rivers to fishing, and at least sixteen other states have found potentially dangerous contamination levels in their fish and drinking water. Some investigators talk about declaring the entire Mississippi off limits. There is even the specter of widespread contamination in food crops and animals.

Hardly anyone in America had bothered thinking about mercury pollution before a Swedish doctoral student happened to take a close look at the St. Clair fish. Chemical manufacturers, especially alkali and caustic soda plants, use more than six million pounds of the poisonous metal each year, spewing back 1.2 million pounds somewhere in the environment. Factories like the Dow Chemical Corp. on the shores of St. Clair have been dumping up to 200 pounds a day each for up to forty years, building huge sludge banks on river and lake bottoms, where bacteria transform the inert metal into lethal methyl mercury which then concentrates in fish. The public has been eating the contaminated fish and drinking the water for just as long, possibly undergoing mild mercury poisoning with symptoms such as muscle tremors, nausea, nervousness and depression.

Dow Chemical spokesmen say they didn't know that metallic mercury undergoes a poisonous transformation in water. Yet more than 100 people died between 1953 and 1960 in Minamata Bay in Japan after eating mercury poisoned fish. Sweden banned some fish as early as 1967, and the prestigious scientific journal, *Nature,* wrote about the problem two years ago.

Major fault lies with the federal government, which has failed to enforce strict water quality standards and has carved up responsibility for checking water pollution among a dozen different agencies.

The Army Corps of Engineers should have stopped the mercury from ever reaching the water in the first place. Under the Refuse Control Act of 1889, the Corps is charged with monitoring all discharge in navigable waterways; factories must apply for permits before they start dumping, and pledge that their waste contains no toxic substances. Until a year ago, Corps officials merely asked companies to itemize any substances which they felt "might have environmental effects," according to Corps general counsel Jacobus Lankhorst. He doesn't recall any company mentioning mercury. But Lankhorst also notes that "most, if not all, of the companies discharging mercury do not have permits"; the Corps never asked for them. "For many years we have been interested primarily in navigational aspects of pollution," reports Lankhorst. "It's only recently that we realized that the broader aspects of pollution include environmental effects as well."

Once the companies dump their mercury sludge, it's up to the Federal Water Quality Administration—the Interior Department's chief water inspector—to find it. FWQA investigators never thought of looking for mercury, although 1968 guidelines list it as a poisonous substance. "We only monitor for constituents that we expect to find in the water," explains William Sayers, chief of the FWQA Surveillance systems. "We never looked for mercury. It's not a cheap analysis to perform, especially on a mass production basis. There are more than 100,000 substances that could have harmful effects. When you don't have the money you must pick out the two or three things that can be analyzed at relatively modest cost." (That might explain why an exhaustive 1965 federal study of water pollution in Michigan, one of the worst contaminated states, failed to mention any mercury.)

"Our monitor system is very, very modest," Sayers notes. Only 140 investigators are hired to monitor all of the nation's waterways, take inventory of every industry dumping wastes, and compile and analyze the data for Washington officials. "We couldn't tell you what the state of this nation's water supply is."

If no one else spots it, mercury that trickles into your drinking water might conceivably come under scrutiny by the Public Health Service's Bureau of Water Hygiene, which monitors interstate water sources and establishes quality guidelines for states. But PHS toxic substances guidelines, written in 1925 and last updated in 1962, don't list mercury. "There was a time when there was a specification for certain minerals," says C. B. Kelly, a bureau research assistant. "But about a year ago they [PHS administrators] ruled we could act only against substances that cause infectious diseases."

Since the government first learned in March and April about mercury pollution, it has done little to stop the poison pouring from the 46 identified factories across the country. Only on July 14 did Interior Secretary Walter Hickel warn that the government will take "immediate" and "aggressive" action against any polluters, unless corrective measures are taken "swiftly" on local levels. Michigan quickly hit its major polluter, the Wynandotte Corp., with an injunction, but the rest of the states have done little but plead with the factories to reduce their mercury discharge. So far, the most aggressive federal action has been a six-month warning, under the 1965 Pollution Act, against the Analine Film Corp. in New Jersey. Fortunately, Analine has complied—but under this statute, a 200 pound per day polluter like Dow could dump 180 more tons of mercury before the government could take action. Then, it might take months of suits and appeals before the Justice Department ever could bring the pollution to a halt. The best enforcement possibility lies under the Refuse Control Act, which permits the Justice Department to seek immediate injunctions against polluters or fines of up to $2500 per day. Justice officials could have filed injunctive suits against polluters on their own long ago, as early as the April Erie and Detroit river reports, but they have doggedly insisted on waiting for the Interior Department. Last week Sec. Hickel finally requested action under the Refuse Act against 13 major companies. That's at least a start.

Some factories *have* cut down on their mercury discharge (Interior officials say the only acceptable level is no discharge at all). But any legal action taken against polluters won't do anything about the tons of mercury already lying on river and lake bottoms, continually poisoning the water and fish: mercury stays active for centuries. Science hasn't figured out a way to deactivate the metal, and costs of physically removing it by dredging run up to one million dollars for a trough 150 feet wide, three feet deep and one mile long. Anyway, dredging would upset mercury which so far has lain dormant, and it would cause untold damage to the aquatic environment. To date, no one in the government is making a concentrated effort to find a solution. "The staff [of FWQA] has recommended such a study, but no decisions have been made," says Interior spokesman Dick Hoffman.

While citizens across the country wait anxiously to see whether their own neighborhood stream has mercury pollution, some authorities have raised the possibility that mercury also poisons us via the air, our food and everyday products. The chemical is used widely in hospitals, laundries, paints and paper products; it evaporates easily and is absorbed through the skin. Three children in New Mexico suffered irreversible brain damage in February after eating a hog fed with mercury-treated seed. Seed manufacturers have used mercurial compounds for years to protect vegetable, grain and fruit seeds from fungi. Government officials could have learned a lesson several years ago when Sweden found dead birds and wildlife poisoned by mercurial seeds. After the New Mexico tragedy, the Agriculture Department did forbid further production and interstate shipment of mercury-treated seeds, but a federal district court in Chicago has issued an injunction against the ban. The poisonous seeds continue to be marketed. Even if the government should appeal and win the case, the seed will sit on the nation's shelves for years. No laws can force private citizens to cease using banned products, and the Department of Agriculture doesn't have the manpower to seize stock supplies.

Besides playing havoc with ecology by killing animals, the seed mercury finds its way into the human food chain in small amounts which may have toxic effects after continued exposure. The mercury compounds may even grow directly from the seeds into their plants, contaminating foodstuffs, from tomatoes and peaches to potatoes and wheat. No one knows the extent of the contamination or its effects; the government hasn't allocated much money for research, and existing analytical tools aren't sensitive enough to trace the mercury.

Sen. Philip Hart (D, Mich.) is delving into this crisis on July 29 and 30, in hearings before his Senate environmental subcommittee. Committee aides say they may ask the President to use his powers of executive order to get anti-pollution gears moving. "The mercury pollution cuts across agency lines," notes a staff counsel. "We need emergency action to fight it." One immediate problem concerns the thousands of fishermen wiped out by the fishing bans, and the seafood restaurants forced to close or fire employees. Federal disaster aid doesn't cover "man-made" or "unnatural" catastrophes, and unemployment compensation will account for only a fraction of fishermen's salaries.

There is almost no restriction on the propagation of sound waves in the public medium. The shopping public is assaulted with mindless music, without its consent. Our government is paying out billions of dollars to create supersonic transport which will disturb 50,000 people for every one person who is whisked from coast to coast 3 hours faster. Advertisers muddy the airwaves of radio and television and pollute the view of travelers.*

* Show in class the 23 minute film "The Tragedy of the Commons" based on Garrett Hardin's article of the same name. Available from King Screen Productions, 320 Aurora Avenue N., Seattle, Wash., 98109.

Garrett Hardin, "The Tragedy of the Commons," *Science,* vol. 162, no. 13 (December 1968), p. 1248.

Air Pollution: The Empire State Building rises above smog-shrouded Manhattan.

United Press International Photo

OVERPOPULATED AMERICA

Wayne H. Davis

I define as most seriously overpopulated that nation whose people by virtue of their numbers and activities are most rapidly decreasing the ability of the land to support human life. With our large population, our affluence and our technological monstrosities the United States wins first place by a substantial margin.

Let's compare the U.S. to India, for example. We have 203 million people, whereas she has 540 million on much less land. But look at the impact of people on the land.

The average Indian eats his daily few cups of rice (or perhaps wheat, whose production on American farms contributed to our one percent per year drain in quality of our active farmland), draws his bucket of water from the communal well and sleeps in a mud hut. In his daily rounds to gather cow dung to burn to cook his rice and warm his feet, his footsteps, along with those of millions of his countrymen, help bring about a slow deterioration of the ability of the land to support people. His contribution to the destruction of the land is minimal.

An American, on the other hand, can be expected to destroy a piece of land on which he builds a home, garage and driveway. He will contribute his share to the 142 million tons of smoke and fumes, seven million junked cars, 20 million tons of paper, 48 billion cans, and 26 billion bottles the overburdened environment must absorb each year. To run his air conditioner we will strip-mine a Kentucky hillside, push the dirt and slate down into the stream, and burn coal in a power generator, whose smokestack contributes to a plume of smoke massive enough to cause cloud seeding and premature precipitation from Gulf winds which should be irrigating the wheat farms of Minnesota.

In his lifetime he will personally pollute three million gallons of water, and industry and agriculture will use ten times this much water in his behalf. To provide these needs the US Army Corps of Engineers will build dams and flood farmland. He will also use 21,000 gallons of leaded gasoline containing boron, drink 28,000 pounds of milk and eat 10,000 pounds of meat. The latter is produced and squandered in a life pattern unknown to Asians. A steer on a Western range eats plants containing minerals necessary for plant life. Some of these are incorporated into the body of the steer which is later shipped for slaughter. After being eaten by man these nutrients are flushed down the toilet into the ocean or buried in the cemetery, the sur-

From *The New Republic*, vol. 162, no. 2, issue 2872 (January 10, 1970), pp. 13–15.

face of which is cluttered with boulders called tombstones and has been removed from productivity. The result is a continual drain on the productivity of range land. Add to this the erosion of overgrazed lands, and the effects of the falling water table as we mine Pleistocene deposits of groundwater to irrigate to produce food for more people, and we can see why our land is dying far more rapidly than did the great civilizations of the Middle East, which experienced the same cycle. The average Indian citizen, whose fecal material goes back to the land, has but a minute fraction of the destructive effect on the land that the affluent American does.

Thus I want to introduce a new term, which I suggest be used in future discussions of human population and ecology. We should speak of our numbers in "Indian equivalents." An Indian equivalent I define as the average number of Indian citizens required to have the same detrimental effect on the land's ability to support human life as would the average American. This value is difficult to determine, but let's take an extremely conservative working figure of 25. To see how conservative this is, imagine the addition of 1000 citizens to your town and 25,000 to an Indian village. Not only would the Americans destroy much more land for homes, highways and a shopping center, but they would contribute far more to environmental deterioration in hundreds of other ways as well. For example, their demand for steel for new autos might increase the daily pollution equivalent of 130,000 junk autos which *Life* tells us that US Steel Corp. dumps into Lake Michigan. Their demand for textiles would help the cotton industry destroy the life in the Black Warrior River in Alabama with endrin. And they would contribute to the massive industrial pollution of our oceans (we provide one third to one half the world's share) which has caused the precipitous downward trend in our commercial fisheries landings during the past seven years.

The per capita gross national product of the United States is 38 times that of India. Most of our goods and services contribute to the decline in the ability of the environment to support life. Thus it is clear that a figure of 25 for an Indian equivalent is conservative. It has been suggested to me that a more realistic figure would be 500.

In Indian equivalents, therefore, the population of the United States is at least four billion. And the rate of growth is even more alarming. We are growing at one percent per year, a rate which would double our numbers in 70 years. India is growing at 2.5 percent. Using the Indian equivalent of 25, our population growth becomes 10 times as serious as that of India. According to the Reinows in their recent book *Moment in the Sun*, just one year's crop of American babies can be expected to use up 25 billion pounds of beef, 200 million pounds of steel and 9.1 billion gallons of gasoline during their collective lifetime. And the demands on water and land for our growing population are expected to be far greater than the supply available in the year 2000. We are destroying our land at a rate of over a million acres a year. We now have only 2.6 agricultural acres per person. By 1975 this will be cut to 2.2, the critical point for the maintenance of what we consider a decent diet, and by the year 2000 we might expect to have 1.2.

You might object that I am playing with statistics in using the Indian equivalent on the rate of growth. I am making the assumption that today's Indian child will live 35 years (the average Indian life span) at today's level of affluence. If he lives an American 70 years, our rate of population growth would be 20 times as serious as India's.

But the assumption of continued affluence at today's level is unfounded. If our numbers continue to rise, our standard of living will fall so sharply that by the year 2000 any surviving Americans might consider today's average Asian to be well off. Our children's destructive effects on their environment will decline as they sink ever lower into poverty.

The United States is in serious economic trouble now. Nothing could be more misleading than today's affluence, which rests precariously on a crumbling foundation. Our productivity, which had been increasing steadily at about 3.2 percent a year since World War II, has been falling during 1969. Our export over import balance has been shrinking steadily from $7.1 billion in 1964 to $0.15 billion in the first half of 1969. Our balance of payments deficit for the second quarter was $3.7 billion, the largest in history. We are now importing iron ore, steel, oil, beef, textiles, cameras, radios and hundreds of other things.

Our economy is based upon the Keynesian concept of a continued growth in population and productivity. It worked in an underpopulated nation with excess resources. It could continue to work only if the earth and its resources were expanding at an annual rate of 4 to 5 percent. Yet neither the number of cars, the economy, the human population, nor anything else can expand indefinitely at an exponential rate in a finite world. We must face this fact *now*. The crisis is here. When Walter Heller says that our economy will expand by 4 percent annually through the latter 1970s he is dreaming. He is in a theoretical world totally unaware of the realities of human ecology. If the economists do not wake up and devise a new system for us now somebody else will have to do it for them.

A civilization is comparable to a living organism. Its longevity is a function of its metabolism. The higher the metabolism (affluence), the shorter the life. Keynesian economics has allowed us an affluent but shortened life span. We have now run our course.

The tragedy facing the United States is even greater and more imminent than that descending upon the hungry nations. The Paddock brothers in their book, *Famine 1975!*, say that India "cannot be saved" no matter how much food we ship her. But India will be here after the United States is gone. Many millions will die in the most colossal famines India has ever known, but the land will survive and she will come back as she always has before.

The United States, on the other hand, will be a desolate tangle of concrete and ticky-tacky, of strip-mined moonscape and silt-choked reservoirs. The land and water will be so contaminated with pesticides, herbicides, mercury fungicides, lead, boron, nickel, arsenic and hundreds of other toxic substances, which have been approaching critical levels of concentration in our environment as a result of our numbers and affluence, that it may be unable to sustain human life.

Thus as the curtain gets ready to fall on man's civilization let it come as no surprise that it shall first fall on the United States. And let no one make the mistake of thinking we can save ourselves by "cleaning up the environment." Banning DDT is the equivalent of the physician's treating syphilis by putting a bandaid over the first chancre to appear. In either case you can be sure that more serious and widespread trouble will soon appear unless the disease itself is treated. We cannot survive by planning to treat the symptoms such as air pollution, water pollution, soil erosion, etc.

What can we do to slow the rate of destruction of the United States as a land capable of supporting human life? There are two approaches. First, we must reverse the population growth. We have far more people now than we can continue to support at anything near today's level of affluence. American women average slightly over three children each. According to the *Population Bulletin* if we reduced this number to 2.5 there would still be 330 million people in the nation at the end of the century. And even if we reduced this to 1.5 we would have 57 million more people in the year 2000 than we have now. With our present longevity patterns it would take more than 30 years for the population to peak even when reproducing at this rate, which would eventually give us a net decrease in numbers.

Do not make the mistake of thinking that technology will solve our population problem by producing a better contraceptive. Our problem now is that people want too many children. Surveys show the average number of children wanted by the American family is 3.3. There is little difference between the poor and the wealthy, black and white, Catholic and Protestant. Production of children at this rate during the next 30 years would be so catastrophic in effect on our resources and the viability of the nation as to be beyond my ability to contemplate. To prevent this trend we must not only make contraceptives and abortion readily available to everyone, but we must establish a system to put severe economic pressure on those who produce children and reward those who do not. This can be done within our system of taxes and welfare.

The other thing we must do is to pare down our Indian equivalents. Individuals in American society vary tremendously in Indian equivalents. If we plot Indian equivalents versus their reciprocal, the percentage of land surviving a generation, we obtain a linear regression. We can then place individuals and occupation types on this graph. At one end would be the starving blacks of Mississippi; they would approach unity in Indian equivalents, and would have the least destructive effect on the land. At the other end of the graph would be the politicians slicing pork for the barrel, the highway contractors, strip-mine operators, real estate developers, and public enemy number one—the US Army Corps of Engineers.

We must halt land destruction. We must abandon the view of land and minerals as private property to be exploited in any way economically feasible for private financial gain. Land and minerals are resources upon which the very survival of the nation depends, and their use must be planned in the best interests of the people.

Rising expectations for the poor is a cruel joke foisted upon them by the Establishment. As our new economy of use it once-and-throw-it-away produces more and more products for the affluent, the share of our resources available for the poor declines. Blessed be the starving blacks of Mississippi with their outdoor privies, for they are ecologically sound, and they shall inherit a nation. Although I hope that we will help these unfortunate people attain a decent standard of living by diverting war efforts to fertility control and job training, our most urgent task to assure this nation's survival during the next decade is to stop the affluent destroyers.

THE BLACKS CRY GENOCIDE

Ralph Z. Hallow

Not long ago a family planning center in Cleveland was burned to the ground after militant Negroes had labeled its activities "black genocide." More recently, the anti-poverty board of Pittsburgh became the first in the nation to vote down OEO appropriations to continue Planned Parenthood clinics in six of the city's eight poverty neighborhoods. The move resulted from intense pressure and threats of violence by blacks—all males—who have kept the genocide issue boiling since one of the clinics was threatened with fire bombing last fall. Although a coalition of women, black and white, has succeeded in rescuing the program, national officers of Planned Parenthood-World Population fear the Pittsburgh example may encourage black opponents to lay siege to similar programs in other cities. Organized opposition can be found in cities from California to New York, and summer could bring the violence which militant critics of the clinics have threatened.

Although concerted opposition to the Planned Parenthood Association (PPA) programs in the ghettos has centered in Pittsburgh, the issue has been gaining national currency through articles published in *Muhammad Speaks,* the newspaper of the Black Muslims. The author of the articles is Dr. Charles

From *The Nation*, vol. 208, no. 17 (April 28, 1969), pp. 335–336. Reprinted with permission of the publisher.

Greenlee, a respected black physician in Pittsburgh who first raised the issue nearly two years ago. Dr. Greenlee contends that the birth control information and "propaganda" of federally financed family planning programs are carried into the homes of poor blacks by "home visitors" and public assistance workers, who allegedly coerce indigent black women into visiting the clinics. Greenlee says, and welfare officials deny, that the intimidation takes the form of implicit or explicit threats that welfare payments will be cut off if the recipient has more children. Thus it is argued, the free clinics constitute "genocide," a conscious conspiracy by whites to effect a kind of Hitlerian solution to the "black problem" in the United States.

Dr. Greenlee's formula for leading his people out of white America's cul-de-sac is: black babies equal black votes equal Black Power. Recognizing this logic, he said recently on a local television panel discussion, the white power structure is using the neighborhood clincs to "decimate the black population in America within a generation." The Planned Parenthood national office sent a black representative to sit on the panel. The two top white executives of PPA in Pittsburgh decided their presence on the panel would only lend credence to Dr. Greenlee's charges. But, they point out, the neighborhood community action committees have representatives, including blacks, on the local PPA board.

Also arguing PPA's side of the question was Mrs. Frankie Pace, a resident of the city's largest black ghetto, the Hill District, where most of the "action" occurred during the civil disorders last April. Mrs. Pace believes that most black women in poor neighborhoods not only want the clinics but also desperately need such help because they are often ignorant of scientific methods of birth control. (Health department and welfare workers in nearly every U.S. city report that they still occasionally encounter indigent women who believe that urinating after intercourse prevents conception.)

The television panel illustrated the new alliances that have grown up over the "black genocide" issue. Seated next to Dr. Greenlee was Msgr. Charles Owen Rice, who for more than thirty years has enjoyed the reputation of being the liberal's liberal. Always a champion of the cause of labor and more recently of peace and an end to the war in Vietnam, he has nevertheless enunciated a position on birth control that is closer to that of the Vatican than to the more liberal one held by a significant number of priests and lay Catholics in America. He said during the panel discussion that the term "black genocide" is not too strong; for, he observed, it is "passing strange" that no clinics exist in the city's two mostly white poverty neighborhoods. Local PPA officials point out, however, that the predominantly Catholic populations in those neighborhoods have rejected the establishment of clinics in their communities.

PPA supporters also suggest it was no accident that William "Bouie" Haden was the only black leader to whom the Catholic diocese of Pittsburgh recently gave a $10,000 annual grant—to help run the United Movement for

Progress, Haden's black self-help group. Haden, a fiery though not so young militant, was quick to pick up Dr. Greenlee's charges of "black genocide" and to force the temporary closing last summer of one of the clinics on his "turf," the city's Homewood-Brushton district. Although about seventy irate black women forced Haden to back off from the issue for a time, in early February he led the forces which, through skillful parliamentary maneuvering, got a divided and confused anti-poverty board to vote down an appropriation to continue the clinics. Although Haden's enemies flaunt his long criminal record, most observers recognize him as a sincere and effective leader who did much to keep Homewood-Brushton cool during the disorders last April.

In spite of his leadership abilities, Haden has only piecemeal support for his "black genocide" charges. Family planning supporters point out that it was the black women in the poverty neighborhoods who demanded that PPA set up a network of neighborhood clinics under the hegemony of the city's anti-poverty board. The women claimed that the PPA center in the downtown area was inaccessible to the indigent whose welfare allowances made no provision for babysitting fees and bus fares.

To complicate the issue still further, supporters of family planning programs in the ghettos include such eminent black men of the Left as Bayard Rustin and Dr. Nathan Wright, Jr., who was chairman of the Black Power conference. Writing on "Sexual Liberation" in the Newark *Star-Ledger*, Dr. Wright said the poor—both black and white—are discriminated against sexually and should seek the help of Planned Parenthood.

The term "family planning" is slightly euphemistic; except in the states where it is prohibited, birth control counseling is offered even to unmarried girls under 18, provided there is parental consent and usually if the girl has had one child. Women in the 15-to-19-year age group account for the highest percentage of illegitimate births (40.2 percent for whites and 41.9 for blacks), according to U.S. Public Health Service figures for 1964. Here again, defenders of birth control argue that the clinics help to alleviate one of the grossest hypocrisies practiced by our male-dominated legislatures. Lawmakers, they say, hand down so-called moral standards for American women in defiance of the sexual practices actually prevailing in the society. If young women from enlightened middle-class families are still undergoing unwanted pregnancies and are forced to seek expensive or dangerous abortions, how much worse must it be for the teen-age daughters of the indigent?

Everywhere the statistics are on the side of family planning—at least for those who view them in unideological terms. In New Orleans, for example, where the largest family planning program in the United States has been operating, an indigent female population of 26 percent accounted for 56 percent of all births, 88 percent of illegitimate births and 72 percent of stillbirths. Nationally, the infant mortality rate of blacks is twice that of whites. The United States ranks fifteenth in the world in infant mortality, and there is a surfeit of evidence relating the problem directly to poverty. A study by the U.S. Department of Health, Education and Welfare found that the most effective way to reduce infant mortality is to offer family planning. Finally, of the 5.3 million indigent women in the United States, only 850,000 receive family planning services, and only 30 percent of those who do are nonwhite.

All this, however, means nothing to the black militant and his white allies who believe that Black Power and "poor" power (and the consequent redistribution of wealth they would bring) are threatened by free family planning clinics whose representatives actively seek out black women. Caught in the middle is the indigent American woman who wishes to have the same freedom to choose sex without conception that her middle-class counterpart enjoys.

pp. 46-68

3 Looking backward

WATER FOR THE CITIES

Nelson Manfred Blake

Pure water . . . is the best drink for persons of all ages and temperaments. By its fluidity and mildness it promotes a free and equable circulation of the blood and humours through all the vessels of the body, upon which the due performance of every animal function depends; and hence water-drinkers are not only the most active and nimble, but also the most chearful and springtly of all people. . . . But to delicate or cold constitutions, and to persons unaccustomed to it, water without wine is a very improper drink.

Philadelphia Monthly Magazine (1798)

It was not enough that the cities should provide themselves with an abundant quantity of water. It was even more important that the water should be kept pure. Unless adequate safeguards were taken, the germs of disease might be carried into every house of the city. Water from a polluted source supplied to the entire population was obviously much more dangerous to public health than a contaminated well or spring serving a single neighborhood.

The need for protecting the purity of the water had been in some degree recognized from the beginning. When he wrote his famous will in 1789, Benjamin Franklin had stressed the danger that as the cities grew, the well water would "gradually grow worse" and in time be "unfit to drink." In each of the municipalities where Council committees and engineers had been appointed to study the water problem, the instructions had always been that provision should be made for an abundant supply of *pure* water. But just what made water pure or impure and just *how* contaminated water might cause disease were difficult questions. Not until the end of the nineteenth century did the science of bacteriology provide really satisfactory answers. But before this time, practical men dealing with the problem of municipal water supply had been moving—largely by intuition—in the right direction. . . .

By the 1830s chemistry had sufficiently advanced for scientists to venture quantitative analyses of water samples. In 1831, for example, George

Chilton reported that a pint of water from a New York well yielded 10 grains of solid matter, which he identified as follows:

Muriate of Magnesia	3.50
Muriate of Sodium	4.
Sulphate of Lime	.25
Carbonate of Lime and Magnesia	1.25
Carbonate of Potassium and Extractive	.75
Loss	.25
	10.

What did such an analysis mean in terms of health? The doctors of the day were not sure. Hard water like this was obviously bad for washing clothes. But was it also bad for the human system? The members of the New York Lyceum of Natural History struggled with this problem in their report to the New York City Council in 1831. Attributing the high mineral content of New York well water to contamination from graveyards and privies, these men of science added the not very comforting suggestion that it was only the absorption of large quantities of urine that prevented the water from being even worse.

> This liquid, when *stale or putrid,* has the remarkable property of precipitating the earthy salts from their solution, or in other words, it makes hard waters soft. Although the fastidious may revolt from the use of water thus sweetened to our palate, it is perhaps fortunate that this mixture is daily taking place, for otherwise the water of this city would become, in a much shorter space of time than it actually does, utterly unfit for domestic purposes.

The Lyceum committee observed that many New Yorkers had become so accustomed to the local water that they found pure spring water unappetizing. "The popular expression . . . is, 'This water is like wind—there is nothing substantial in it, nothing to bite upon.' " The committee attributed the prevalent dyspepsia and the often fatal bowel complaints of children to the daily use of excessively hard water. . . .

In Boston discussion of the purity of the well water followed a similar course. The water was obviously very hard, but doctors disagreed on whether it was injurious to health. In 1834, Mayor Lyman solicited the opinion of local physicians and received a variety of opinions. Dr. Warren blamed the local well water for disorders of the stomach and digestive organs, and added: "As many fevers are generated by derangements beginning in the digestive organs, I have been led to believe that this impure water is not an unfrequent cause of fever. . . ." Dr. Shurtleff thought that the well water predisposed Bostonians to "calculous" and "bilious" disorders. Dr. Hayward made the shrewd observation that none of the salts or minerals which had been detected by analysis were of themselves injurious to health, but that danger might arise out of certain "foreign bodies" that were mixed with the water. Dr. Randall agreed that the minerals in the local water were probably harmless to the regular inhabitants of the city, but that newcomers were likely to suffer digestive upsets. . . .

The great Boston water debate took an interesting turn when the disputants began to argue about the significance of minute organisms in the water. Some of these were visible to the naked eye; others could be detected only under the microscope. These "animalcules," as they were called, were alleged to abound in Long Pond. One of the Spot Pond faction undertook to warn his fellow-citizens against water "in which fishes are poisoned by the impurity—in whose current, as it flows to the sea, men's wounds fester when it touches them—and whose animalculi, now obvious to the naked eye, expanding, as they advance to the city, in a sluggish current, falling three inches to the mile, must be nearly ready, on their arrival, to swell into gallinippers or dragon flies."

John H. Wilkins used the animalcule argument to urge that Boston draw its water supply from the Charles River. *"Animalcules,"* he asserted, "are *much less likely to be found in running, or river water, than in pond water;* and when found, *are less numerous and less formidable* (if I may use the word) *in the former than in the latter."* He explained that he was speaking only of the creatures that were visible to the naked eye "for it is to such only that any one can attach much importance."

Nathan Hale protested that there were as many animalcules in the water of the Charles River as in that of Long Pond. He advised Bostonians to close their eyes to these organisms unless they became too conspicuous.

> It is . . . quite useless to expect to obtain water from a source which will be free from these repulsive living beings. The only remedy against them is, to avoid too curious a search by microscopic eyes, and in case they appear, as they will occasionally, of a size to be discernible by the naked eye, to adopt such methods as shall be found practicable, of removing them.

Some of the experts of the day expressed the opinion that the presence of animalcules in the water was evidence of the water's purity, since these delicate creatures could not be expected to live in water that contained poisonous substances. But this contention was subjected to heavy ridicule by the anti-Long Pond faction. In a cartoon broadside of the day, a drop of water magnified by microscope was depicted as teeming with ferocious animalcules. A spectator was represented as inquiring: "Why do you prefer Long Pond, doctor?" To which the physician replied: "Because with this water we can appease both thirst and hunger, whereas water from other sources is but little more than mere drink. It is obvious therefore that to the poor this water would prove a great blessing."

To appease public anxiety about animalcules, John B. Jervis and Walter Johnson, the Commissioners of 1845, sought the opinion of Professors Benjamin Silliman, Jr., of Yale and J. W. Bailey of West Point. These experts reported that "infusorial insects" were to be found in all waters, including those of the Charles River, the Schuylkill, and the Croton—indeed, "in this last mentioned celebrated excellent and beautiful river water more animalcules were found than in any other sample." . . .

The citizens of Philadelphia had particular reason to worry about the quality of their water. The city and the neighboring districts were entirely dependent upon the Schuylkill and Delaware Rivers, and the danger of pollution steadily increased with the growth of population and industry within these watersheds. In November, 1843, the Philadelphia College of Physicians passed a series of resolutions earnestly recommending to the City Council "the adoption of such measures as will perpetuate the purity of the water derived from the basin of the Fairmount Dam."

Among other measures suggested was that the city should purchase the Lemon Hill Estate on the east bank of the Schuylkill just above the Fairmount Water Works. This proposal was also urged upon the Councils in twenty-seven petitions bearing the signatures of 2,443 citizens. Behind this mobilization of public opinion certain motives other than disinterested benevolence were at work. The Lemon Hill Estate had been one of the assets of the bankrupt Bank of the United States, and the assignees were eager to find a customer for this famous property. Nevertheless, the argument that the purity of the Fairmount water would be endangered if houses, stores, and factories were built in the vicinity of the dam was a sound one, fully justifying the city's purchase of the tract for $75,000.

For some years the municipality did nothing with this acquisition, but in 1854 the Councils decided to develop it as a public park. A number of physicians and leading citizens presented a petition, commending this policy and urging that the city also purchase land to the north and south of Lemon Hill. At stake was not only the proper protection of the Fairmount Water Works, but also that of the Spring Garden Water Works, which had recently become a part of the Philadelphia system through the consolidation of the city. The project would be expensive, admitted the petitioners:

> But when we reflect that the measure we propose will not only be the means of protecting our drinking water from impurities, but furnish the citizens with a large, elegant central public Park, abounding in natural beauties, with extended lawns, groves, and water scenery, easy of access from all parts of our extended city, we are led to believe the purchase now recommended, and the dedication of the whole connected tract from Fairmount to the northern limits of the grounds of the Spring Garden Water Works, to the public use forever, will be hailed with heartfelt pleasure by all classes of our citizens.

In keeping with these suggestions, Fairmount Park was dedicated in 1855 and greatly extended and improved over the next several years.

Although these developments were steps in the right direction, the purity of the drinking water was still far from assured. The Kensington Water Works on the Delaware, which also became a part of the city system through the consolidation of 1854, were notoriously suspect. When a sample from this source was submitted to James C. Booth, a local chemist in 1856, his report was brief and caustic:

> The water from the Kensington Water Works, abounding with scum and sediment is so foul from putrifying organic matter, apparently of animal origin, that a chemical examination of it would be useless. I would not be willing personally to use the water from which the sample was drawn, nor even water which had a remote connection with it, believing it to be injurious to health.

The immediate cause of this pollution was found in a neighboring dock where fish were cleaned and the entrails thrown in the water. Even after this nuisance was eliminated, the Delaware water was not above suspicion, because sewers and drains continued to discharge into streams tributary to the river.

One reason why the municipal authorities were not more alarmed by such conditions was an over-optimistic reliance upon the ability of running water to purify itself and of water in storage to cleanse itself through sedimentation. In discussing measures necessary to protect the water supply in 1861, the Philadelphia Chief Engineer admitted that the city had more power under the law than it had attempted to exercise. "But how far it would be wise to interfere with the large manufacturing interests which add so greatly to our permanent prosperity" he left for the Councils to decide.

> Much can be done, however, without putting manufacturers to large expense or great inconvenience. They might be prohibited from making the river a common sewer to carry off all refuse, and especially the discharge of privies, as is the practice in most of the factories. Indeed, if nothing but what could not be otherwise disposed of, was drained into the river, it might be allowed, at least for the present. But from that part of the river south of Columbus Avenue, immediate steps should be taken to remove all accumulation of detritus, and prevent all encroachments, and the drainage into it of any objectionable matter; and the whole shore should be guarded with the most jealous care.

Apparently, it was only in the immediate vicinity of the water works that any really serious danger of pollution was felt to exist. . . .

The Philadelphia authorities continued to congratulate themselves on the signal purity of their water supply. A report on the situation in 1860 admitted that the upper Schuylkill was so polluted with mine water that it had destroyed all the fish in the river above Reading. But the creeks which emptied into the stream near that city were largely impregnated with lime. This, mixed with the mine water, formed a precipitate "and after flowing a few miles the water is pure and limpid. To this chemical action may be attributed in a great measure the remarkable purity of the water of this river."

Philadelphia was not alone in its belief that filtration would be an expensive and unnecessary nuisance. The Croton Aqueduct Board decided against constructing a trial filter in 1849, and most other American cities refused to consider the idea despite its wide acceptance in Europe. In 1832, Albert Stein, a German-American engineer, constructed the first American filter at Richmond, Virginia, but the device was too small to clarify the highly turbid water of the James River and had to be abandoned. In 1855, a small filter was installed at Elizabeth, New Jersey.

It was not until after the Civil War that American engineers began serious study of the techniques of filtration developed abroad. In 1869, James P. Kirkwood published a *Report on the Filtration of River Waters, for the Supply of Cities, as Practiced in Europe*. The city of St. Louis, which had commissioned this investigation, decided not to attempt the filtration of the muddy water of the Mississippi, but the city of Poughkeepsie, New York, had more courage. In 1872, Kirkwood was employed to construct a slow sand filter that would permit the highly suspect water of the Hudson River to be used as a municipal supply. Although the Poughkeepsie system was cumbersome, it was sufficiently successful to encourage similar ventures elsewhere.

Leadership in the serious study of the relationship between pure water supply and public health was now assumed by the state of Massachusetts. In 1869, the Massachusetts State Board of Health had been established, and in 1878 this agency sent Professor William Ripley Nichols to Europe to study techniques of water purification. In 1887, the State Board of Health established an experiment station at Lawrence, where investigations of great significance were carried out. Five years later a sand filter for the public water supply of Lawrence was built.

More than anything else, the growing fear of typhoid fever convinced municipal authorities that pure water was a matter of life and death. It would be interesting to know the extent to which this disease prevailed in the days when the larger American cities still depended on neighborhood wells for their water supply, but such statistics do not exist. Indeed, final proof that typhoid fever was a separate disease and not merely a variety of typhus was not forthcoming until about 1850. The Boston Board of Health began to list typhoid fever as a cause of death in 1856, but in most other cities reliable statistics were not compiled until the 1870s or 1880s. In 1880, one of the first years for which the comparison can be made, the death rate from typhoid fever was about 31.9 per 100,000 population for New York, 57.6 for Philadelphia, 42.4 for Boston, and 59.0 for Baltimore—all shockingly high by present-day standards.

One of the landmarks of the infant science of bacteriology was the discovery of the typhoid bacillus by the German investigator, Karl Eberth, in 1880. Even before this event, however, the close relationship between polluted drinking water and typhoid fever was strongly suspected. In a useful work on the practical aspects of water supply engineering, published in 1877, Colonel John T. Fanning listed diarrhea, dysentery, and typhoid as ailments which were carried by impure water. In a pamphlet, entitled *The Dangers from the Domestic Use of Polluted Water,* published in 1883, Dr. Morton Prince of Boston asserted:

> The diseases which may be conveyed by water are many. The most common are typhoid fever, cholera, diarrhoea, and numerous smaller ailments. The most typical of this class is typhoid fever. This is probably, and especially in small towns, conveyed more frequently by poisoned water than in any other way.

To support this contention, he cited numerous examples from English medical history of the 1870s. Typhoid fever, he concluded, was a filth disease. The "poison" which gave rise to it was bred in filth, especially in sewage from houses. "No water supply should be contaminated with the slightest amount of sewage or polluted with organic matter of any kind. The neglect of these precautions means disease."

Shocking proof that whole cities might be endangered from sources of pollution miles away was soon forthcoming. In the spring of 1885, for example, typhoid fever struck the town of Plymouth, Pennsylvania, in a ferocious assault. Out of a total population of some 8,000, over 1,100 persons contracted the disease and 114 died. In the words of a contemporary report:

> The origin of all this sorrow and desolation occurred miles away on the mountain side, far removed from the populus town, and in a solitary house situated upon the banks of a swift-running stream. The attending physician did not know that this stream supplied the reservoirs with drinking-water. Here, if at any place, it might seem excusable to take less than ordinary precautions. . . .

The lessons from such an episode were obvious. Doctors and nurses must exercise the most scrupulous care in disinfecting and disposing of the body wastes from every typhoid fever patient; sanitary authorities must vigilantly protect the entire watershed from which municipal supplies were drawn; if watersheds could not be adequately safeguarded, filtration and other forms of water treatment must be introduced.

Municipal authorities could no longer blandly assume that anything too small to be visible to the naked eye was too small to be injurious to the human body. Through ingenious techniques drinking water was now examined to determine how many bacteria and other microorganisms it contained. The chances of isolating the elusive typhoid fever bacillus in any particular water sample were small, but a high count of the colon bacillus was presumptive evidence that the water was polluted with sewage and potentially dangerous.

Between 1890 and 1910, American cities made remarkable progress in safeguarding their water supplies. The danger of using untreated water from the rivers which ran conveniently through so many great centers of population was at last realized. Newark, Jersey City, and Paterson had all been drawing their supply from the badly polluted Passaic River. In 1890, Newark had a typhoid death rate of over 100 per 100,000 population; Jersey City's rate was just under 100; and Paterson's was about 30. Within the next fifteen years all three cities took important steps of reform. After Newark abandoned the Passaic in favor of purer upland supplies in 1892, its annual typhoid death rate dropped to about 20. Jersey City took the same step with similar results in 1896. Paterson continued to use the Passaic, but introduced filtration in 1902, thereby reducing the typhoid death rate to about 15.

The Merrimac River, which ran through another famous industrial district, also played the part of villain in this drama of public health. From 1887 to 1893, Lawrence, Massachusetts, was unmercifully scourged by typhoid fever. For seven years the death rate from this cause never fell below 80 and in 1890 it soared to 134. After building filters in 1893, the annual rate fell to between 20 and 30. Lowell was equally plagued so long as it drew its supply from the Merrimac. In 1887, its typhoid death rate was over 120 and in 1890, over 160. After 1893, the city began to draw more and more of its water supply from driven wells, finally abandoning the river completely in 1896.

The cities along the Great Lakes had their own problems. To use those huge bodies of water both for the disposal of their sewage and the supply of their drinking water was temptingly easy—and shockingly dangerous. In 1891, Chicago had almost 2,000 deaths from typhoid fever, and the death rate from this cause was over 173. The city sought to protect itself by building the Chicago Drainage Canal to reverse the flow of the Chicago River and allow most of the wastes of the community to pass down the Des Plaines and Illinois Rivers into the Mississippi instead of into Lake Michigan. This was an act of doubtful neighborliness to cities along these other streams, but Chicago's own typhoid death rate fell to an annual average of about 20 after the Drainage Canal was opened in 1900. In Cleveland, where the situation was similar but not as serious, the typhoid menace was measurably reduced in 1904 by extending the intake tunnel four miles out into Lake Erie.

The city of Philadelphia, once so proud of her leadership in matters of water supply, procrastinated dangerously in adopting adequate safeguards. During the twenty years between 1881 and 1900 the annual typhoid death rate never fell below 35 per 100,000 population and was often above 70. At long last the authorities decided to build filtration plants, and the first of these was put in operation in 1902. But a large part of the city still used unfiltered water, and the incidence of typhoid fever continued to be shockingly high. In 1906, there were 1,063 deaths from this cause, representing a typhoid death rate of over 80. Not until 1911 was the project so far completed that filtered water could be supplied to the whole city.

Technical progress in the treatment of water supplies had now become rapid. In addition to the earlier methods of slow sand filtration, new rapid filters were developed, particularly useful in clarifying highly turbid waters like those of the Ohio and the Mississippi. Disinfection by the use of liquid chlorine was another protective technique developed about 1910, with Philadelphia one of the first large cities to use it. Many communities undertook to improve the odor and taste of their water by aeration. When bad taste and odor resulted from algae and other organisms in the reservoirs, it proved possible to attack the nuisance by treating the water with copper sulphate.

Water supply engineering became a highly specialized field, with each local situation calling for its own policies. Cities like New York and Boston which took their supply from relatively safe upland sources were fortunate. Filtration was not necessary, and other measures of treatment could be held to a minimum. But such cities found it all the more important to guard carefully the watersheds from which their supplies were drawn. Many water authorities agreed that despite all the wonderful progress that had been made in filtration and other methods of water purification, the greatest protection that a city could have was to keep its water supply free from contamination in the first place.

A HISTORY OF URBAN AMERICA

Charles N. Glaab and A. Theodore Brown

In the 1830s and 40s, New York was often considered the showcase city of America—the exemplar of growth, change, and progress in the new society. Local residents were proud of its role, but not until past mid-century did the community do much to make the city presentable. Philip Hone, the ex-mayor of the city, had written in 1832 that New York was "one huge pigsty" but that a prudent farmer would avoid putting his pigs into it for fear they might catch the plague. In 1844 the editor of the *New World* made the same point: "That our streets have been horrible enough in times past no one denies, but they are now . . . more abominably filthy than ever; they are too foul to serve as the styes for the hogs which perambulate them. . . . The offal and filth, of which there are loads thrown from the houses in defiance of an ordinance which is never enforced, is scraped up with the usual deposits of mud and manure into big heaps and left *for weeks together* on the sides of the street." Not until after the establishment of the New York Metropolitan Board of Health in 1866 was there reasonably systematic and permanent clean-up of the city. As part of this program, hogs were finally eliminated from the city's streets.

The absence of adequate sewage facilities also contributed to the unpleasantness and unhealthiness of urban life in the nineteenth century. Before 1850 methods of removing waste were still largely those of the country, even in larger cities. Privies or water closets emptied into vaults or cesspools, and the waste material soaked into the soil or was hauled away as receptacles became filled. Kitchen waste was run into the street and left to evaporate or was led off by open drains to watercourses. Ditches provided for this purpose often carried urine and fecal matter as well as house slop, since privy facilities were often hopelessly inadequate in the congested districts of cities. A Cincinnati board of health report of 1865 told of a two-story tenement which housed 102 people for whom only one privy had been provided. When a municipal department of sewers was created in New York in 1849, only 70 miles of sewers had been built. Eight years later the mileage had grown to 158 for 500 miles of city streets, still leaving three-fourths of the city, including most of the slum areas, without facilities.

Inadequate sanitation, a laissez-faire governmental tradition which made measures of public control difficult, and erroneous beliefs about the causes of disease contributed to one of the most serious problems facing the nineteenth century urban dweller—epidemic. Diseases, particularly those spread through water contamination, flourished in the congested districts of cities; outbreaks of typhoid, dysentery, and typhus were continual. . . .

In view of the enormous health problems that resulted from the increased density of population in cities, new methods of removing waste and new methods of ensuring a pure water supply represented one of the more significant areas of technological change. Although the general relationship between unsatisfactory sewage disposal, water contamination and many diseases, such as typhoid fever and cholera, which decimated urban dwellers, was understood by European scientists in the 1860s and supported by many American public-health leaders, these contamination theories and the subsequent germ theory were not accepted widely enough to lead to any public demand for significant changes in methods of waste disposal. People continually complained about dirty water, but the specific health dangers of dirty water were not fully appreciated until the 1890s. The few miles of sewer that had been built in New York, Boston, Chicago, and a few other places proved completely inadequate in the face of the rapid growth of the 1870s. And most cities in the 1870s still used the old methods of private vaults and cesspools. In 1877, for example, Philadelphia had 82,000 vaults and cesspools, Washington had 56,000, and Chicago, despite its sewer system,

30,000. Chicago in 1871 had engaged in a large engineering project, headed by Ellis S. Chesbrough who had studied the sewer systems of European cities, to reverse the direction of the Chicago River, into which the city's sewers emptied, so that it discharged into the Illinois River rather than Lake Michigan. But this project had little effect. "The river stinks," commented the Chicago *Times* in 1880. "The air stinks. People's clothing, permeated by the foul atmosphere stinks. . . . No other word expresses it so well as stink. A stench means something finite. Stink reaches the infinite and becomes sublime in the magnitude of odiousness." Eventually the whole water supply and sewerage system of Chicago had to be drastically re-engineered.

Ironically, much of the advance in establishing better sewage facilities resulted from the agitations of an individual who tenaciously clung to older theories of disease and denounced the scientifically correct germ theory. George E. Waring, Jr., a scientific farmer, writer, and engineer, who achieved national attention as New York's Commissioner of Street Cleaning from 1895 to 1898, launched a crusade in the 1870s against America's inadequate sewerage methods. A contemporary commented that Waring made people so aware of the dangers to health from "sewer gas" that they "feared it perhaps more than they did the Evil One."

Waring was a vigorous anti-contagionist who accepted the idea that disease was the result of filth. He substituted "sewer gas" for the miasma which environmentalists had utilized as a disease-causing mechanism in earlier periods. In an 1878 essay, Waring argued persuasively that not only typhoid fever but most communicable diseases were the result of filth and decay. Outbreaks of disease, he argued, could often be traced to a foul-smelling house drain or the nearness of a drainage ditch. The poison itself might be the result of "the exhalations of decomposing matters in dung-heaps, pigsties, privy vaults, cellars, cess-pools, drains, and sewers; or it may be due . . . to the development of the poison deep in the ground, and its escape in an active condition in ground exhalations." To prevent disease-causing bad air, household sanitary fixtures were necessary, and whole communities would have to be systematically cleansed.

When a severe yellow-fever epidemic struck Memphis in 1878 killing nearly 5,000 people, Waring asserted that the epidemic was the result of the incredibly filthy condition of the city. As a consequence of the attention his argument received, Waring was hired to build a sewer system for Memphis in 1880. His well-advertised efforts in no way prevented yellow fever, which in its etiology is unrelated to filth, but they set off a general campaign in American cities to build sewers. By the earlier years of the twentieth century, especially after the real cause of yellow fever, the last of the mysterious epidemic diseases, had been established by the experiments of Walter Reed and others in Cuba, the germ theory of disease won general acceptance. City leaders, recognizing that typhoid in particular could be prevented, moved to ensure good sewage disposal systems and a pure water supply through tapping distant new sources and through techniques of filtration and purification. By 1910, over ten million urban residents drank filtered water which helped to cut the death rate at least a fifth in New York, Philadelphia, Boston, and New Orleans. Although cities were never able to solve the problem of pollution, at least the danger was recognized, so that technological means could be devised to combat it.

Thus between 1860 and 1910 technology and migration, in a national context of rapid economic growth, had drastically altered the American urban environment.

4 We are the problem

THE PURSUIT OF LONELINESS

Philip E. Slater

Our ideas about institutionalizing the aged, psychotic, retarded, and infirm are based on a pattern of thought that we might call the Toilet Assumption—the notion that unwanted matter, unwanted difficulties, unwanted complexities and obstacles will disappear if they are removed from our immediate field of vision. We do not connect the trash we throw from the car window with the trash in our streets, and we assume that replacing old buildings with new expensive ones will alleviate poverty in the slums. We throw the aged and psychotic into institutional holes where they cannot be seen. Our approach to social problems is to decrease their visibility: out of sight, out of mind. This is the real foundation of racial segregation, especially its most extreme case, the Indian "reservation." The result of our social efforts has been to remove the underlying problems of our society farther and farther from daily experience and daily consciousness, and hence to decrease, in the mass of the population, the knowledge, skill, resources, and motivation necessary to deal with them.

When these discarded problems rise to the surface again—a riot, a protest, an exposé in the mass media—we react as if a sewer had backed up. We are shocked, disgusted, and angered, and immediately call for the emergency plumber (the special commission, the crash program) to ensure that the problem is once again removed from consciousness.

The Toilet Assumption is not merely a facetious metaphor. Prior to the widespread use of the flush toilet all of humanity was daily confronted with the immediate reality of human waste and its disposal. They knew where it was and how it got there. Nothing miraculously vanished. Excrement was conspicuously present in the outhouse or chamber pot, and the slops that went out the window went visibly and noticeably into the street. The most aristocratic Victorian ladies strolling in fashionable city parks thought nothing of retiring to the bushes to relieve themselves. Similarly, garbage did not disappear down a disposal unit—it remained nearby.

As with physical waste, so with social problems. The biblical adage, "the poor are always with us," had a more literal meaning before World War I. The poor were visible and all around. Psychosis was not a strange phenomenon in a textbook but a familiar neighbor or village character. The aged were in every house. Everyone had seen animals slaughtered and knew what they were eating when they ate them; illness and death were a part of everyone's immediate experience.

In contemporary life the book of experience is filled with blank and mysterious pages. Occupational specialization and plumbing have exerted a kind of censorship over our understanding of the world we live in and how it operates. And when we come into immediate contact with anything that does not seem to fit into the ordinary pattern of our somewhat bowdlerized existence our spontaneous reaction is to try somehow to flush it away, bomb it away, throw it down the jail.

TOWARD AN ECOLOGICAL SOLUTION

Murray Bookchin

Popular alarm over environmental decay and pollution did not emerge for the first time merely in the late '60s, nor for that matter is it the unique response of the present century. Air pollution, water pollution, food adulteration and other environmental problems were public issues as far back as ancient times, when notions of environmental diseases were far more prevalent than they are today. All of these issues came to the surface again with the Industrial Revolution—a period which was marked by burgeoning cities, the growth of the factory system, and an unprecedented befouling and polluting of air and waterways.

Today the situation is changing drastically and at a tempo that portends a catastrophe for the entire world of life. What is not clearly understood in many popular discussions of the present ecological crisis is that the very nature of the issues has changed, that the decay of the environment is directly tied to the decay of the existing social structure. It is not simply certain malpractices or a given spectrum of poisonous agents that is at stake, but rather the very structure of modern agriculture, industry and the city. Consequently, environmental decay and ecological catastrophe cannot be averted merely by increased programs like "pollution control" which deal with sources rather than systems. To be commensurable to the problem, the solution must entail far-reaching revolutionary changes in society and in man's relation to man.

I

To understand the enormity of the ecological crisis and the sweeping transformation it requires, let us briefly revisit the "pollution problem" as it existed a few decades ago. During the 1930s, pollution was primarily a muckraking issue, a problem of exposé journalism typified by Kallet and Schlink's "100 Million Guinea Pigs."

This kind of muckraking literature still exists in abundance and finds an eager market among "consumers," that is to say, a public that seeks personal and legislative solutions to pollution problems. Its supreme pontiff is Ralph Nader, an energetic young man who has shrewdly combined traditional muckraking with a safe form of "New Left" activism. In reality, Nader's emphasis belongs to another historical era, for the magnitude of the pollution problem has expanded beyond the most exaggerated accounts of the '30s. The new pollutants are no longer "poisons" in the popular sense of the term; rather they belong to the problems of ecology, not merely pharmacology, and these do not lend themselves to legislative redress.

What now confronts us is not the predominantly specific, rapidly degradable poisons that alarmed an earlier generation, but long-lived carcinogenic and mutagenic agents, such as radioactive isotopes and chlorinated hydrocarbons. These agents become part of the very anatomy of the individual by entering his bone structure, tissues and fat deposits. Their dispersion is so global that they become part of the anatomy of the environment itself. They will be within us and around us for years to come, in many cases for generations to come. Their toxic effects are usually chronic rather than acute; the deadly and mutational effects they produce in the individual will not be seen until many years have passed. They are harmful not only in large quantities, but in trace amounts; as such, they are not detectable by human senses or even, in many cases, by conventional methods of analysis. They damage not only specific individuals but the human species as a whole and virtually all other forms of life.

No less alarming is the fact that we must drastically revise our traditional notions of what constitutes an environmental "pollutant." A few decades ago it would have been absurd to describe carbon dioxide and heat as "pollutants" in the customary sense of the term. Yet in both cases they may well rank among the most serious sources of future ecological imbalance and pose major threats to the viability of the planet. As a result of industrial and domestic combustion activities, the quantity of carbon dioxide in the atmosphere has increased by roughly 25 percent in the past 100 years, a figure that may well double again by the end of the century. The famous "greenhouse effect," which increasing quantities of the gas is expected to produce, has already been widely discussed: eventually, it is supposed, the gas will inhibit the dissipation of the earth's heat into space, causing a rise in overall temperatures which will melt the polar ice caps and result in an inundation of vast coastal areas. Thermal pollution, the result mainly of warm water discharged by nuclear and conventional power plants, has disastrous effects on the ecology of lakes, rivers and estuaries. Increases in water temperature not only damage the physiological and reproductive activities of fish; they also promote the great blooms of algae that have become such formidable problems in waterways.

What is at stake in the ecological crisis we face today is the very capacity of the earth to sustain advanced forms of life. The crisis is being drawn together by massive increases in "typical" forms of air and water pollution; by a mounting accumulation of nondegradable wastes, lead residues, pesticide residues and toxic additives in food; by the expansion of cities into vast urban belts; by increasing stresses due to congestion, noise and mass living; by the wanton scarring of the earth as a result of mining operations, lumbering, and real estate speculation. The result of all this is that the earth within a few decades has been despoiled on a scale that is unprecedented in the entire history of human habitation on the planet.

Finally, the complexity and diversity of life which marked biological evolution over many millions of years is being replaced by a simpler, more synthetic and increasingly homogenized environment. Aside from any esthetic considerations, the elimination of this complexity and diversity may prove to be the most serious loss of all. Modern society is literally undoing the work of organic evolution. If this process continues unabated, the earth may be reduced to a level of biotic simplicity where humanity—whose welfare depends profoundly upon the complex food chains in the soil, on the land surface and in the oceans—will no longer be able to sustain itself as a viable animal species.

II

In recent years a type of biological "cold warrior" has emerged who tends to locate the ecological crisis in technology and population growth, thereby divesting it of its explosive social content. Out of this focus has emerged a new version of "original sin" in which tools and machines, reinforced by sexually irresponsible humans, ravage the earth in concert. Both technology and sexual irresponsibility, so the argument goes, must be curbed —if not voluntarily, then by the divine institution called the state.

The naivete of this approach would be risible were it not for its sinister implications. History has known of many different forms of tools and machines, some of which are patently harmful to human welfare and the natural world, others of which have clearly improved the condition of man and the ecology of an area. It would be absurd to place plows and mutagenic defoliants, weaving machines and automobiles, computers and moon rockets, under a common rubric. Worse, it would be grossly misleading to deal with these technologies in a social vacuum.

Technologies consist not only of the devices humans employ to mediate their relationship with the natural world, but also the attitudes associated with these devices. These attitudes are distinctly social products, the results of the social relationships humans establish with each other. What is clearly needed is not a mindless deprecation of technology as such, but rather a reordering and redevelopment of technologies according to ecologically sound principles. We need an ecotechnology that will help harmonize society with the natural world.

The same over-simplification is evident in the neo-Malthusian alarm over population growth. The reduction of population growth to a mere ratio between birth rates and death rates obscures the many complex social factors that enter into both statistics. A rising or declining birth rate is not a simple biological datum, any more than is a rising or declining death rate. Both are subject to the influences of the economic status of the individual, the nature of family structure, the values of society, the status of women, the attitude toward children, the culture of the community, and so forth. A change in any single factor interacts with the remainder to produce the statistical data called "birth rate" and "death rate." Culled from such abstract ratios, population growth rates can easily be used to foster authoritarian controls and finally a totalitarian society, especially if neo-Malthusian propaganda and the failure of voluntary birth control are used as an excuse. In arguing that forcible measures of birth control and a calculated policy of indifference to hunger may eventually be necessary to stabilize world populations, the neo-Malthusians are already creating a climate of opinion that will make genocidal policies and authoritarian institutions socially acceptable.

What then happened to the lands of the New World in the three colonial centuries? In the first place, the aboriginal populations in contact with Europeans nearly everywhere declined greatly or were extinguished. Especially in the tropical lowlands, with the most notable exception of Yucatan, the natives faded away, and in many cases the land was quickly repossessed by forest growth. . . . The total population, white and other, of the areas under European control was less at the end of the eighteenth century than at the time of discovery. . . .

It is hardly an exaggeration to say that the early Europeans supported themselves on Indian fields.

Carl O. Sauer, "The Agency of Man on Earth," *Man's Role in Changing the Face of the Earth*, ed. William L. Thomas (Chicago: University of Chicago Press, 1956), p. 62.

It is supremely ironic that coercion, so clearly implicit in the neo-Malthusian outlook, has acquired a respected place in the public debate on ecology—for the roots of the ecological crisis lie precisely in the coercive basis of modern society. The notion that man must dominate nature emerges directly from the domination of man by man. The patriarchal family may have planted the seed of domination in the nuclear relations of humanity; the classical split between spirit and reality—indeed, mind and labor—may have nourished it; the anti-naturalistic bias of Christianity may have tended to its growth; but it was not until organic community relations, be they tribal, feudal or peasant in form, dissolved into market relationships that the planet itself was reduced to a resource for exploitation.

This centuries-long tendency finds its most exacerbating development in modern capitalism: a social order that is orchestrated entirely by the maxim "Production for the sake of production." Owing to its inherently competitive nature, bourgeois society not only pits humans against each other, but the mass of humanity against the natural world. Just as men are converted into commodities, so every aspect of nature is converted into a commodity, a resource to be manufactured and merchandised wantonly. Entire continental areas in turn are converted into factories, and cities into marketplaces. The liberal euphemisms for these unadorned terms are "growth," "industrial society" and "urban blight." By whatever language they are described, the phenomena have their roots in the domination of man by man.

Both science and technology can clearly be seen to have their historical roots in natural theology and the Christian dogma of man's rightful mastery over nature. Therefore, as [Lynn] White claims, it may be in vain that so many look to science and technology to solve our present ecological crisis.

From *Population, Resources, Environment: Issues in Human Ecology* by Paul R. Ehrlich and Anne H. Ehrlich, p. 191. W. H. Freeman and Company.

As technology develops, the maxim "Production for the sake of production" finds its complement in "Consumption for the sake of consumption." The phrase "consumer society" completes the description of the present social order as an "industrial society." Needs are tailored by the mass media to create a public demand for utterly useless commodities, each carefully engineered to deteriorate after a predetermined period of time. The plundering of the human spirit by the marketplace is paralleled by the plundering of the earth by capital. The tendency of the liberal to identify the marketplace with human needs, and capital with technology, represents a calculated error that neutralizes the social thrust of the ecological crisis.

The strategic ratios in the ecological crisis are not the population rates of India but the production rates of the United States, a country that produces more than 50 percent of the world's goods. Here, too, liberal euphemisms like "affluence" conceal the critical thrust of a blunt word like "waste." With a vast section of its industrial capacity committed to war production, the U.S. is literally trampling upon the earth and shredding ecological links that are vital to human survival. If current industrial projections prove to be accurate, the remaining 30 years of the century will witness a five-fold increase in electric power production, based mostly on nuclear fuels and coal. The colossal burden in radioactive wastes and other effluents that this increase will place on the natural ecology of the earth hardly needs description.

In shorter perspective, the problem is no less disquieting. Within the next five years, lumber production may increase an overall 20 percent; the output of paper, five percent annually; folding boxes, three percent annually; metal cans, four to five percent annually; plastics (which currently form one to two percent of municipal wastes), seven percent annually. Collectively, these industries account for the most serious pollutants in the environment. The utterly senseless nature of modern industrial activity is perhaps best illustrated by the decline in returnable (and reusable) beer bottles from 54 billion bottles in 1960 to 26 billion today. Their place has been taken over by "one-way bottles" (a rise from 8 to 21 billion in the same period) and cans (an increase from 38 to 53 billion). The "one-way bottles" and cans, of course, pose tremendous problems in solid waste disposal, but they do sell better.

It may be that the planet, conceived as a lump of minerals, can support these mindless increases in the output of trash. The earth, conceived as a complex web of life, certainly cannot. The only question is, can the earth survive its looting long enough for man to replace the current destructive social system with a humanistic, ecologically oriented society.

Poem from a Marine

Once I tried to interview a Marine officer, just home from Vietnam. On two occasions he refused. Then the mail brought a short poem from him one morning. He wrote that I could interpret it as I pleased, but to bear in mind Matthew XXV.

I was hungry, you destroyed my paddies . . .
I was homeless, you bombed my cities and burned my villages.
Inasmuch as you have done these things to the least of my brethren,
You have done it to me.

Murray Polner, "Vietnam War Stories," *Transaction,* vol. 6 (November, 1968), p. 18.

The apocalyptic tone that marks so many ecological works over the past decade should not be taken lightly. We are witnessing the end of a world, although whether this world is a long-established social order or the earth as a living organism still remains in question. The ecological crisis, with its threat of human extinction, has developed appositely to the advance of technology, with its promise of abundance, leisure and material security. Both are converging toward a single focus: At a point where the very survival of man is being threatened, the possibility of removing him from the trammels of domination, material scarcity and toil has never been more promising. The very technology that has been used to plunder the planet can now be deployed, artfully and rationally, to make it flourish.

It is necessary to overcome not only bourgeois society but also the long legacy of propertied society: the patriarchal family, the city, the state—indeed, the historic splits that separated mind from sensuousness, individual from society, town from country, work from play, man from nature. The spirit of spontaneity and diversity that permeates the ecological outlook toward the natural world must now be directed toward revolutionary change and utopian reconstruction in the social world. Propertied society, domination, hierarchy and the state, in all their forms, are utterly incompatible with the survival of the biosphere. Either ecology action is revolutionary action or it is nothing at all. Any attempt to reform a social order that by its very nature pits humanity against all the forces of life is a gross deception and serves merely as a safety valve for established institutions.

The application of ecological principles to social reconstruction, on the other hand, opens entirely new opportunities for imagination and creativity. The cities must be decentralized to serve the interests of both natural and social ecology. Urban gigantism is devastating not only to the land, the air, the waterways and the local climate, but to the human spirit. Having reached its limits in the megalopolis—an urban sprawl that can best be described as the "non-city"—the city must be replaced by a multitude of diversified, well-rounded communities, each scaled to human dimensions and to the carrying capacity of its ecosystem. Technology, in turn, must be placed in the service of meaningful human needs, its output gauged to permit a careful recycling of wastes into the environment.

One occurrence in particular had upset him. A soldier had murdered a peasant in an especially brutal fashion. After speaking with the soldier, Dr. Rosenberger came away shaken. "The fellow was absolutely untouched by what he had done. He had no emotional reaction. It was this, more than anything else, that finally made me wonder what this war is doing to these men so that they cannot bring themselves to *feel.*"

Murray Polner, "Vietnam War Stories," *Transaction,* vol. 6 (November, 1968), p. 11.

With the community and its technology sculptured to human scale, it should be possible to establish new, diversified energy patterns: the combined use of solar power, wind power and a judicious use of fossil and nuclear fuels. In this decentralized society, a new sense of tribalism, of face-to-face relations, can be expected to replace the bureaucratic institutions of propertied society and the state. The earth would be shared communally, in a new spirit of harmony between man and man and between man and nature.

In the early years of the 19th century, this image of a new, free and stateless society was at best a distant vision, a humanistic ideal which revolutionaries described as communism or anarchism, and their opponents as utopia. As the one century passed into its successor, the advance of technology increasingly brought this vision into the realm of possibility. The ecological crisis of the late 20th century has now turned the possibility of its early decades into a dire necessity. Not only is humanity more prepared for the realization of this vision than at any time in history—a fact intuited by the tribalism of the youth culture—but upon its realization depends the very existence of humanity in the remaining years ahead.

Perhaps the most important message of Marx a century ago was the concept that humanity must develop the means of survival in order to live. Today, the development of a flexible, open-ended technology has reversed this concept completely. We stand on the brink of a post-scarcity society, a society that can finally remove material want and domination from the human condition. Perhaps the most important message of ecology is the concept that man must master the conditions of life in order to survive.

During the May–June uprising of 1968, the French students sensed the new equation in human affairs when they inscribed the demand: "Be realistic! Do the impossible!" To this demand, the young Americans who face the next century can add the more solemn injunction: "If we don't do the impossible, we shall be faced with the unthinkable."

Gradually, very very gradually, mankind has begun to recognize his provincialism: that disasters are not really God-made floods or plagues of locusts, but human-made radioactivity; that the great destroyer, the great polluter, is not a naturally occurring dust storm. Man is his own problem.

William Bunge, "Field Notes," *The Detroit Geographical Expedition* (Discussion Paper No. 1), p. 2.

THE HILLS OF IXOPO

Maxwell Anderson and Kurt Weill

There is a lovely road
that runs from Ixopo into the hills.
These hills are grass covered and rolling
and they are lovely beyond any singing of it.
About you there is grass and bracken and you may hear
the forlorn crying of the ti-ti-ho-ya bird.
The grass of the veld is rich and matted,
you cannot see the soil.
The grass holds the rain and mist.
They seep into the ground, feeding the streams in every clove.
The clove is cool and green, and lovely beyond any singing of it.

Where you stand the grass is rich and matted,
but the green hills break down.
They fall to the valley below and falling change.
For they grow red and bare;
They cannot hold the rain and mist;
the streams run dry in the cloves.
Too many cattle feed on the grass;
it is not kept or guarded or cared for.
It no longer keeps men, guards men, cares for men.
The ti-ti-ho-ya cries here no more.
The great red hills stand desolate.
And the earth has torn away like flesh.
These are valleys of old men and old women.
The men are away,
The young men and the girls are away.
The soil cannot keep them any more.

. . . [R]emoval of resource from place of origin to place of demand tended to set up growing disturbance of whatever ecologic equilibrium had been maintained by the older rural communities sustained directly within their metes. . . .

The rise of civilizations has been accomplished and sustained by the development of powerful and elaborately organized states with a drive to territorial expansion, by commerce in bulk and to distant parts, by monetary economy, and by the growth of cities. Capital cities, port cities by sea and river, and garrison towns drew to themselves population and products from near and far. The ways of the country became subordinated to the demands of the cities, the *citizen* distinct from the *miserabilis plebs.* The containment of community by locally available resources gave way to the introduction of goods, especially foodstuffs, regulated by purchasing, distributing, or taxing power.

. . . The economic history of antiquity shows repeated shifts in the areas of supply of raw materials that are not explained by political events but raise unanswered questions as to decline of fertility, destruction of plant cover, and incidence of soil erosion. . . .

Have the elder civilizations fallen because their lands deteriorated?

Carl O. Sauer, "The Agency of Man on Earth," *Man's Role in Changing the Face of the Earth,* ed. William L. Thomas (Chicago: University of Chicago Press, 1956), p. 61.

When they had come down from the mountain, Gilgamesh seized the axe in his hand: he felled the cedar. When Humbaba heard the noise far off, he was enraged; he cried out,"who is this that has violated my woods and cut down my cedar?"

"The Epic of Gilgamesh," 2nd millennium B.C.

It is now generally agreed that the prevalent scrub vegetation of the Levantine highlands is the degraded remnant of an original cover of forest. Evidence of the degree and extent of the transformation has been accumulated by botanists, geographers, and other scholars in many parts of this complex realm. But the contrast between ancient and modern conditions is perhaps most strikingly evident on the humid, western versant of Mount Lebanon. From the time of the earliest Egyptian and Mesopotamian documents (*ca.* 2600 B.C.) until the reign of Emperor Hadrian (A.D. 117–138) this area was known for its valuable timber. Today much of it is as barren as the mountains of the Sahara. Only scattered remnants survive of the once extensive stands of cedar, fir, and juniper, and most of the oak forests have been reduced to scrub. What did Mount Lebanon look like in prehistoric time, and how and why was its vegetation so greatly modified? To answer these questions, even tentatively, is to come to grips with processes that offer unrivaled evidence of man's ability to transform nature.

Marvin W. Mikesell, "The Deforestation of Mount Lebanon," *The Geographical Review,* vol. 59, no. 1 (January 1969), p. 1.

The Enemy Is Plant Life: Near the Cambodian border, Vietnam, spewing a stream of vegetation-killing poison, two Air Force C-123 planes fly a mission against vegetation. The methodological defoliation, according to military tacticians, reduces hiding places available to enemy soldiers. Scientists and conservationists are concerned about the effects of widespread destruction of Vietnam's plant life.

United Press International Photo by Dennis Cook

ECOLOGICAL EFFECTS OF THE WAR IN VIETNAM

Gordon H. Orians and E. W. Pfeiffer

In Vietnam the chemical weapons of a technologically advanced society are being used massively for the first time in a guerrilla war. In this conflict there are no battle lines, no secure territory, and no fixed, permanent military installations which can serve as targets for attack. Rather, the military efforts are aimed at increasing the toll of fatalities, denying food to the enemy, and depriving him of the cover and concealment afforded by natural growth. This type of warfare is, therefore, extremely destructive, both of human lives and environment. Our own observations showed the profound effects of denuding the country of growth. The military is emphatic about the effectiveness of defoliation in reducing American casualties significantly. The demand for the services of 12th Air Commando Squadron greatly exceeds their ability to supply them. Although the total number of requests for defoliation missions was not disclosed, we were told that even if no further requests

From *Science,* vol. 168, no. 3931 (May 1, 1970), pp. 553–554. Copyright 1970 by the American Association for the Advancement of Science.

were made, the defoliation crews would be kept busy for years by the present backlog. The current extent of the defoliation program is not determined by military demand nor by any considerations of saving the ecology and viability of the land and natural resources of Vietnam, but solely by competition for equipment and personnel.

With general agreement among military experts that defoliation is a potent weapon in guerrilla warfare, it is to be expected that in any future wars of this nature more extensive use will be made of it. At the end of their war against the Vietnamese, the French discovered the usefulness of helicopters as field combat aircraft, but they had only about a dozen at their disposal. There are now several thousand helicopters in Vietnam as a major component of our offensive air power. Making a realistic appraisal of defoliation and its ecological consequences, we must, therefore, consider not only the present extent of use but also anticipate greatly expanded defoliation actions in the future.

We consider that the ecological consequences of defoliation are severe. Enough is now known to reveal that a significant fraction of mature trees in most forests are killed by single applications of herbicides and that almost complete kill, including destruction of seedlings and saplings, is to be expected if repeated sprayings are made. Because of military demands for respraying, we must expect virtual elimination of woody vegetation of defoliated sites as a common result of the military use of herbicides.

It is evident that the most stringent regulations for the application of defoliants cannot prevent the widespread dispersal of herbicides to areas far beyond those that were intended to be defoliated. We found abundant evidence of repeated moderate to severe defoliation of trees and herbs in areas many miles removed from sites of direct application. Every responsible Vietnamese person we met confirmed this. Moreover, a pilot in a war zone will jettison his load of defoliant, rather than jeopardize the safety of his crew and plane, and a spray plane will not return to its base with a full tank because its crew found the temperature or the wind velocity higher in the target area than anticipated. Military use of defoliants will inevitably result in herbicide damage to areas that are far more extensive than those specified as targets.

It is evident that the defoliation program has had tremendous psychological impact upon the Vietnamese people and has profoundly affected their attitude toward Americans. A farmer whose entire crop has been destroyed by herbicides, whose fruit trees do not bear fruit for 3 years, will inevitably be resentful. We were told repeatedly, though politely, that a significant deterioration of attitudes toward Americans has resulted from the massive use of defoliants. The claim that defoliation is more humane than other weapons of war because it does not directly cause human casualties, may appeal to those whose land has not been defoliated, but hardly to those whose food supply or property has been destroyed. A realistic assessment of the effects of defoliation must take into account the psychological effects upon the people.

The politically sensitive nature of effects of defoliation is fully recognized by the military authorities. Although they claim that defoliants produce no long-term effects on the environment, they have instituted the most stringent regulations to govern their use. The Army claims that it is more difficult to get permission for the defoliation of trees in Vietnam than for killing persons, and permission to spray rubber trees has never been granted, according to military sources, even when enemy forces were "known" to use plantations for concealment. It seems that preferential treatment of the politically powerful rubber interests in Vietnam has added to the hostility of the poorer Vietnamese.

THE PURSUIT OF LONELINESS

Philip E. Slater

All societies, optimally, must allow for both change and stability, since: (a) effective adaptation to the environment requires both modification and consolidation of existing responses; (b) social integration depends both upon the preservation and upon the periodic dissolution of existing structural differentiation; and (c) personal happiness rests upon both familiarity and novelty in everyday life. Every society evolves patterns for attempting to realize these mutually incompatible needs.

Our society, as many have pointed out, has traditionally handled the problem by giving completely free rein to technological change and opposing the most formidable obstacles to social change. Since, however, technological change in fact forces social changes upon us, this has had the effect of abdicating all control over our social environment to a kind of whimsical deity. While we think of ourselves as a people of change and progress, masters of our environment and our fate, we are no more entitled to this designation than the most superstitious savage, for our relation to change is entirely passive. We poke our noses out the door each day and wonder breathlessly what new disruptions technology has in store for us. We talk of technology as the servant of man, but it is a servant that now dominates the household, too powerful to fire, upon whom everyone is helplessly dependent. We tiptoe about and speculate upon his mood. What will be the effects of such-and-such

From Philip E. Slater, *The Pursuit of Loneliness: American Culture at the Breaking Point,* pp. 44–45.

an invention? How will it change our daily lives? We never ask, do we *want* this, is it worth it? (We did not ask ourselves, for example, if the trivial conveniences offered by the automobile could really offset the calamitous disruption and depersonalization of our lives that it brought about.) We simply say "You can't stop progress" and shuffle back inside.

We pride ourselves on being a "democracy" but we are in fact slaves. We submit to an absolute ruler whose edicts and whims we never question. We watch him carefully, hang on his every word; for technology is a harsh and capricious king, demanding prompt and absolute obedience. We laugh at the Luddites (Nat Turners in the struggle for human parity with the machine), but they were the last human beings seriously to confront this issue. Since then we have passively surrendered to every degradation, every atrocity, every enslavement that our technological ingenuity has brought about. We laugh at the old lady who holds off the highway bulldozers with a shotgun, but we laugh because we are Uncle Toms. We try to outdo each other in singing the praises of the oppressor, although in fact the value of technology in terms of human satisfaction remains at best undemonstrated. For when evaluating its effects we always adopt the basic assumptions and perspective of technology itself, and never examine it in terms of the totality of human experience. We say this or that invention is valuable because it generates other inventions—because it is a means to some other means—not because it achieves an ultimate human end. We play down the "side effects" that so often become the main effects and completely negate any alleged benefits. The advantages of *all* technological "progress" will after all be totally outweighed the moment nuclear war breaks out (an event which, given the inadequacy of precautions and the number of fanatical fingers close to the trigger, is only a matter of time unless radical changes are made).

Let me make clear what I am *not* saying here. I do not believe in the noble savage and I am not advocating any brand of bucolic romanticism. I do not want to put an end to machines. I only want to remove them from their position of mastery, to restore human beings to a position of equality and initiative. As a human I must protest that being able to sing and eat watermelon all day is no compensation for being beaten, degraded, and slaughtered at random, and this is the nature of our current relationship to our technological order.

The unexpected consequences of our technology have often worked to damage our environment; now we must turn that same technology to the work of its restoration and preservation.

—*Richard M. Nixon*

Fortune editors, *The Environment* (New York: Harper & Row, 1969), p. 13.

TECHNOLOGY AND GROWTH: THE PRICE WE PAY

E. J. Mishan

The social significance of both the market and the engineering criteria involved . . . may be better understood if, for a while, we skirt direct controversy and approach these issues by a sort of parable. Thus, without straining his credulity perhaps, the reader may be able to picture to himself a region of some continent, say, on the other side of the Atlantic, in which the traditional right to carry firearms is never questioned. Indeed, on the initiative of the manufacturers, who spend colossal sums in advertising their new wares, more than one pistol is to be seen in a man's belt. The young men in particular are anxious to be seen with the latest de-luxe "extra hard-hitting" model. Obviously the manufacture of holsters and other accessories flourishes as also does the manufacture of bullet-proof vests, leggings and helmets. These are not the only growth industries, however, for notwithstanding the purchase of bullet-proof items, the members of the undertakers association do a flourishing trade. The windows of all but the poorer houses are fitted with shatter-proof glass, while the bullet-proofing of rooms and offices in the more dangerous districts is a matter of ordinary precaution. No family is foolish enough to neglect the training of their sons, and even their daughters, in the art of the quick draw. In any case, a number of hours each week is devoted to target practice and dodgery in all the best schools. Life insurance is, of course, big business despite the exorbitant premia, and expenditure on medical attention continues to soar. For in addition to such normal ailments, as bullets embedded in various parts of the anatomy, there is widespread suffering from a variety of chafed skin diseases, the result of wearing the unavoidably heavy bullet-proof apparel. Moreover, owing to nervous diseases and anxiety, about every other adult is addicted either to strong liquor or to tranquillizing drugs. Taxes are burdensome for obvious reasons: a swollen police force employed mainly in trying to keep down the number of victims of the perennial feuds, extensive prisons and prison hospitals, to say nothing of the public funds devoted to guarding offices, banks, schools, and to the construction of special vans for transporting the children to and from schools.

In such an environment the most peace-loving man would be foolish to venture abroad unarmed. And since it is observed by the *laisser-faire* economist that men freely choose to buy guns, it would be regarded as an infringement of liberty to attempt to curb their manufacture. Moreover, since the market is working smoothly, the supply of firearms being such that no

From E. J. Mishan, *Technology and Growth: The Price We Pay.* (New York: Praeger Publishers, Inc., 1970), pp. 66–69. Reprinted by permission of the publisher.

one need wait if he is able to pay the market price, no government intervention to match industrial supplies to rising demand is called for. Provided there is enough competition in the production of firearms so that over the long period prices just cover costs (and tend also to equal marginal costs of production) the allocation economist is well satisfied. Looking at the promising signs of growth in the chief industries, firearms and accessories, the business economist pronounces the economy "sound." If, however, for any reason the Government begins to have misgivings about some of the more blatant social repercussions, it consults with the pistol economist, a highly paid and highly regarded expert. The pistol economist constructs models and, with the help of high-powered statisticians, amasses pistological data of all kinds, from which he calculates the optimal set of taxes on the sale of pistols and ammunition in recognition of those external diseconomies, such as occasional corpse-congestion on the better streets whose monetary costs can, he believes, be estimated.

Notwithstanding all his scientific advice, matters eventually come to a head, and amid much government fanfare a committee of inquiry is set up under the chairmanship of a highly competent engineer, Mr B. If there ever was a realist, Mr B. is one, and he soon satisfies himself that the economy is heavily dependent upon pistol production and all the auxiliary industries and services connected therewith. Besides, the evidence is incontrovertible: the demand for guns continues to grow year by year. It must, therefore, be accepted as a datum. Undaunted, Mr B. faces "the challenge" by proposing a radical remodelling of the chief towns and cities, at an unmentionable cost, in the endeavour to create an environment in which people can have both their guns and a peaceful life as well. The chief features of his plan are based on what he aptly calls "pistol architecture," and includes provision for no-shooting precincts fenced high with steel, the construction of circular and wavy road design to increase the difficulties of gun-duelling, the erection of high shatter-proof glass screens running down the centres of roads to prevent effective cross-firing, and the setting up of heavily protected television cameras at all strategic positions in the towns in order to relay information twenty-four hours a day to a vast new centralized police force equipped with fleets of helicopters. Every progressive journalist pays tribute to the foresight and realism of the B-plan and makes much of the virtues of "pistol architecture," the architecture of the future. Alas, the Government begins to realize that any attempt to raise the taxes necessary to implement the B-plan would start a revolution. So the plan is quietly shelved, new committees of inquiry are formed, masses of agenda are produced, and things continue much as before. We need not continue save to press home a few parallels. Over the last fifty years we have witnessed a transposition of ends and means. Originally the motor vehicle was designed for the roads. Today roads are designed for vehicles. Originally the motor vehicle was to be fitted into the pace of life. Today the pace of life is adapted to the speed of the vehicle, the saddest casualty of all being an irretrievable loss of the sense of ease, space and leisure.

The dominance exerted over our lives by this one invention is without precedent in history. So pervasive is its influence and so inextricably is it bound up with our way of life and habits of thought that the extent of its intrusion in our civilization is barely noticed. To insist on seeing it as no more than one of several alternative schemes of travel, and to propose a careful assessment of its benefits and costs smacks almost of the quixotic. Imagine a modern sceptic returning on a Wellsian time-machine to the second half of the eighteenth century and presenting the following conundrum to Dr Johnson: What gift to mankind is of such worth as to warrant an annual sacrifice of two hundred thousand lives, an annual list of five million people crippled, the transformation of the world's towns and cities into a concrete wasteland made hideous with noise, filth and danger, the dissipation of the countryside, the slow poisoning of the air in town and suburb, the enfeeblement of the health and the corruption of the character of peoples, and the creation of conditions favourable to the generation and execution of crimes of robbery and violence? What reply could the sage give, but that it must be of a nature, sir, that is beyond the bounds of man's imagination.

PLASTIC FANTASTIC LOVER

Marty Balin

Her neon mouth with its blinking soft smile is nothing but an electrical sign
You could say she has an individual style, she's a part of her carnival time
Super steel lady chrome colored clothes you wear 'cause you have no other
But I suppose no one knows you're my Plastic Fantastic Lover.

Her rattling cough that never shuts off is nothing but her used machines
Her aluminum finish is slightly diminished, is the best I ever have seen
Cosmetic baby plugged into me, you never ever find another
I realize no one's wise to my Plastic Fantastic Lover

The electrical dust is starting to rust her trapizoid thermometer taste
All the red tape is mechanical rape of the TV program waste
Data control and I.B.M. science is mankind's brother
But all I see is draining me on my Plastic Fantastic Lover

5 Barriers

The ordinary city-dweller knows nothing of the earth's productivity; he does not know the sunrise and rarely notices when the sun sets; ask him what phase the moon is in, or when the tide in the harbor is high, or even how high the average tide runs, and likely as not he cannot answer you. Seed time and harvest time are nothing to him. If he has never witnessed an earthquake, a great flood, or a hurricane, he probably does not feel the power of nature as a reality surrounding his life at all. His realities are the motors that run elevators, subway trains, and cars, the steady feed of water and gas through the mains and of electricity over the wires, the crates of food-stuff that arrive by night and are spread for his inspection before his day begins, the concrete and brick, bright steel and dingy woodwork that take the place of earth and waterside and sheltering roof for him. . . . Nature, as man has always known it, he knows no more.

Suzanne Langer, *Philosophy in a New Key, A Study in the Symbolism of Reason, Rite and Art* (New York: New American Library, 1951).

And television feeds us poison by lying to us about what life is really like, what people are really like. Communication between people is increasingly out of sync. Television has lied to us about ourselves, and because it shovels information at us in such quantities so relentlessly and with such impact, we believe it instead of believing our own guts. We find it harder to understand each other. We find it harder to understand ourselves.

Of course it's pollution.

Loring Mandel, "Television Pollutes Us All," *The New York Times,* March 15, 1970.

. . . It is not so much the case that feeling is "drying up" within us. But with so much feeling being channelled into the aptly-called "rat-race"—into the pursuit of worldly success and into the pursuit of fashion and prestige pastimes—there is little left to flow directly between people. Yet the thinner runs this flow of feeling between people the more impatient a man becomes to seek satisfactions in the external world of status and glamour, a world buzzing with perpetual expectancy wherein other people play but an incidental role in his schemes of personal triumph.

E. J. Mishan, *Technology and Growth: The Price We Pay* (New York: Praeger Publishers, Inc., 1970), p. 130.

A HISTORY OF URBAN AMERICA

Charles N. Glaab and A. Theodore Brown

From the beginning of the growth of towns and cities in the United States, the possibility of combining the benefits of the country with the advantages of the city—the "happy union of urbanity and rusticity"—had been a part of the American conception of community. The village of Brooklyn early in the nineteenth century provided a place where New Yorkers could escape the city; a Brooklyn real estate man in 1823 advertising lots on Brooklyn Heights encouraged this possibility in very modern terms: "Situated directly opposite the s-w part of the city, and being the nearest country retreat, and easiest of access from the centre of business that now remains unoccupied; the distance not exceeding an average fifteen to twenty-five minutes walk, including the passage of the river; the ground elevated and perfectly healthy at all seasons; views of water and landscape both extensive and beautiful; as a place of residence all the advantages of the country with most of the conveniences of the city. . . . Gentlemen whose business or profession require their daily attendance in the city, cannot better, or with less expense, secure the health and comfort of their families, than by uniting in such an association." A Cincinnati handbook in 1851 utilized considerable space in describing the advantages of suburban life in areas "unsurpassed for healthfulness, removed from the smoke and dust of the city, enjoying pure air and wholesome water." By the 1870s, Chicago promoters could claim the existence of nearly one hundred suburbs, with an aggregate population of 50,000, located along the railroads running from the city and offering the charms of "pure air, peacefulness, quietude, and natural scenery."

WHY HAVE WE LET OUR ENVIRONMENT DETERIORATE?

Paul R. Ehrlich and Anne H. Ehrlich

Historian Lynn White, Jr. of the University of California has suggested that the basic cause of Western man's destructive attitude toward nature lies in Judeo-Christian traditions. He points out, for instance, that before the Christian era men believed trees, springs, hills, streams and other objects of nature had guardian spirits. These spirits had to be approached and placated before one could safely invade their territories. As White says, "By destroying pagan animism, Christianity made it possible to exploit nature in a mood of indifference to the feelings of natural objects." Christianity fostered the basic idea of "progress" and of time as something linear, nonseparating, and absolute, flowing from the future into the past. Such ideas were foreign to the Greeks and Romans, who had a cyclical concept of time and did not envision the world as having a beginning. Although a physicist's concept of time might be somewhat closer to the Greeks than to that of the Christians, the Christian view is nevertheless the prevalent one, in which God designed and started the whole business for our benefit. The world is our oyster, made for man to dominate and exploit. The European ancestors of Americans had held and developed these attitudes long before the opportunity to exploit the Western Hemisphere arrived. The "frontier" or "cowboy" economy which has characterized the United States seems to be a natural extension of the Christian world view.

Both science and technology can clearly be seen to have their historical roots in natural theology and the Christian dogma of man's rightful mastery over nature. Therefore, as White claims, it may be in vain that so many look to science and technology to solve our present ecological crisis.

Air pollution (and its fallout on soil and water) is a form of domestic chemical and biological warfare. The efflux from motor vehicles, plants, and incinerators of sulfur oxides, hydrocarbons, carbon monoxide, oxides of nitrogen, particulates, and many more contaminants amounts to compulsory consumption of violence by most Americans. There is no full escape from such violent ingestions, for breathing is required. This damage, perpetuated increasingly in direct violation of local, state, and federal law, shatters people's health and safety but still escapes inclusion in crime statistics. "Smogging" a city or town has taken on the proportions of a massive crime wave, yet federal and state statistical compilations of crime pay attention to muggers and ignore "smoggers." As a nation which purports to apply law for preserving health, safety, and property, there is a curious permissiveness toward passing and enforcing laws against the primary polluters who harm our society's most valued rights. In testament to the power of corporations and their retained attorneys, enforcement scarcely exists. Violators are openly flouting the laws and an Administration allegedly dedicated to law and order sits on its duties.

John C. Esposito and Larry J. Silverman, *Vanishing Air* (New York: Grossman Publishers, 1970), p. viii.

TOO MANY GOVERNMENTS

Mitchell Gordon

"One of the most inspiring sights one could witness is the panorama of light and color of the spreading cities and populated county area of the Los Angeles basin when observed from a point on the partially surrounding mountain formation, especially from Mount Wilson on a smogless night. To the uninformed in local government matters, this is Los Angeles; to those who have been interested in metropolitan problems there is only a checkerboard of governmental areas in the third largest metropolitan area in the United States."

The words appear in a volume entitled *Metropolitan Los Angeles: Its Governments*, one of a series of studies on the area sponsored by the city's philanthropic Haynes Foundation. The volume was published in 1949. Today, the lights are spread even more broadly across the plains and amid the mountains which punctuate that vista.

The governments, too, are more numerous. Los Angeles County contained fewer than fifty cities in 1949. Today it has well over seventy, and more are being formed all the time. Counting school, water, mosquito-abatement, and hundreds of other districts and agencies which infest this once halcyon scene, there are presently over 600 different taxing bodies within the confines of the county.

Los Angeles' patchquilt of local governments is particularly interesting for the bizarre variety of its origins, but the pattern of administrative and fiscal frustration is repeated in practically every metropolitan area in the land. And it is getting considerably worse as sprawling growth knits existing cities together, physically if not politically, and governments, if they do little else, proliferate. Dr. Luther Gulick, Chairman of the Institute of Public Administration and New York's first City Administrator, recently counted the number of local governments operating in various metropolitan areas around the United States. He found the Pittsburgh area had even more than Los Angeles and that Chicago's was higher still: over 950. New York's total was even higher: 1,100, some 550 of them cities, towns, and villages. . . .

The mosaic of local authorities in a single metropolitan area should be of more than statistical interest to those who live among it or who one day might. It results in increasingly wasteful duplications of local services, conflict and confusion in their execution, inequities in taxation, and, in many instances, complete paralysis in the solution of more and more urgent area-wide needs, from the provision of a single metropolitan transit system to effective policing, and from the control of air and water pollution to the execution of regional planning.

Probably no aspect of the modern metropolitan scene is more thoroughly criticized and lamented among students of local government and practical administrators than the multiplicity of local governmental units, many of them obsolete but almost all of them indestructible. As Dr. Gulick puts it: "Our system of local government in America was set up in the 1700s and 1800s to fit conditions existing then. And it was a marvelous and brilliant invention. But the conditions have changed. The living city is no longer within the old city limits. The problems we are asking local governments to wrestle with now sprawl all over the map.

"Take any problem, like water or traffic," says he; "not only does it reach beyond the lines of any one organized governmental body, but it falls in several independent and often competing jurisdictions. Thus, you have problems which cannot even be thought about except on a comprehensive and unitary basis, fractionated among a score of separate political action units."

Professor William A. Robson, of the London School of Economics and Political Science and past president of the International Political Science Association, in a volume entitled *Great Cities of the World*, declares: "It is obvious that a large municipality, surrounded by a multiplicity of small local authorities of various kinds, cannot hope to meet the social, political or administrative needs of a great metropolitan area. A medley of scattered and disintegrated local authorities cannot provide the unity required for a coherent scheme of development." . . .

Consider, for a moment, the confusion produced by this welter of government. The city of La Mirada, which straddles the Los Angeles and Orange County lines, provided a poignant example not long ago. Residents of the city with "LAwrence" telephone exchanges generally were getting their fire service from the Los Angeles County Fire Department, but they weren't all doing so. New and nervous telephone operators occasionally became confused between which did and which did not. One day, a fire was reported in the two-year-old home of the John Broadbents. The operator mistakenly put the call through to the Orange County Fire Department. The department decided the call was outside its jurisdiction and passed it along to the police department of nearby Buena Park for action. The Buena Park Police desk made some quick checks and turned the call back to the Orange County Fire Department. Eventually, the call got to where it was supposed to go in the first place: the Los Angeles Fire Department. The LAFD had a station only two blocks from the Broadbent residence, but the house was wholly engulfed in flames by the time its engines arrived. A Los Angeles fire official testified later that the home could have been saved if the engines were dispatched correctly the moment the call was turned in.

Shortly after the incident, the Los Angeles Fire Station—Engine Company Number 29—distributed cards among residents of the area suggesting that next time they have a fire to report they should dial FAirview 8–7366. It was subsequently pointed out that the number could not be dialed from LAwrence exchanges in La Mirada but would have to go through an operator first, which could easily set the train of confusion back into motion again. An official of the nearby Buena Park Fire Department noted at the time: "This is a bad situation, and everyone in the area is aware of it. We get reports every time La Mirada has a fire." . . .

For the most part, the price of governmental confusion is paid unknowingly by the average citizen. He suffers it in such forms as time lost in trying to find an address as the name of a street and even its numbers vary as it crosses imperceptibly from one jurisdiction to another, or through the receipt of a traffic ticket innocently incurred as the regulations of one city vary from another. In Orange County, California, motorists are subjected to five different speed limits on a single two-mile stretch of street. In nearby Los Angeles County, one major artery changes names three times as it moves through three different cities—Claremont, Pomona, and La Verne. . . .

As it thickens, the jurisdictional jungle produces further duplication of facilities and services—and other costly waste. "It wasn't so bad when the snow plow stopped at the city limits and there was nothing beyond, but it seems a needless waste for the vehicle to turn around and go back to the garage now when it is just as built up on one side of the city as on the other," exclaims Samuel Resnic, Mayor of Holyoke, Massachusetts. At least four municipalities in his area, Mr. Resnic maintains, could benefit by pooling their public works departments—Holyoke, Chicopee, South Hadley, and West Springfield—but years of talk have yet to produce results. . . .

One of the most ominous of all the effects of splintered government is the paralysis it brings to the provision of necessary metropolitan areawide services. A special commission investigating government problems in the

New York City area, recently found control of water pollution and the development of an adequate regional park system were suffering seriously from the failure of local governments in the area to take common action. It noted that vast sums had been spent by some municipalities on incinerators and sewage plants but that others were highly neglectful about where they dumped their refuse and raw sewage. Water conditions had become so bad in the region, it stated, that the city was faced with "having all its beaches closed by health authorities." It concluded: "Divided authority for planning and constructing sewers is a contributory cause preventing solution to the problem of pollution." . . .

A certain amount of conflict, waste, and confusion is probably inevitable in any system of decentralized government and, no doubt, in highly centralized systems as well. But there are ways to cope with and perhaps even reverse the trend toward shattered local government. The most effective method of all, perhaps, for cities which can still do so, is annexation of surrounding areas before they develop and incorporate themselves.

THE POLITICS OF POLLUTION

Michael Harrington

Why Are the Corporations Cooperating?

One of the main reasons that the issue of the environment has suddenly become so popular and ubiquitous is that people wrongly think that it is noncontroversial. Nobody, David Brinkley said on a February newscast, is in favor of pollution; everybody is against it.

That is a dangerous half-truth (and I credit Brinkley for being one of the more astute, and sympathetic, newsmen). It is quite right to note that filthy air, noise, congestion and dirty water afflict the middle and upper classes as well as the poor. And that fact certainly does create a huge constituency, for, quite literally, everyone has an interest in cleaning up the environment. It is also true, but less happy, that the pollution crusade may turn out to be a genteel rest home for affluent idealists exhausted by their failures to end either poverty or the war in Vietnam.

But the consensus theory of environmental politics is also profoundly false (and I shall shortly summon up the memory of that great exponent of "reasoning together," Lyndon B. Johnson, to document the point). For just as everyone was against poverty, but powerful institutional forces refused to do what its abolition required, there are corporations which have become

From *Commonweal* (April 17, 1970), pp. 111–114. Reprinted with permission of Commonweal Publishing Co., Inc.

conscience-stricken about pollution only because they fear punitive legislation. They have enlisted in the crusade to ensure that it does not become militant and effective.

And the corollary of this analysis is that the democratic Left must have its own, quite distinctive program to save the environment. It must educate and organize around the proposition that the issue is political and conflict-laden and demands an assertion of social priorities in air and water which will override an entrenched private interest in their abuse.

One must thus prepare for vigorous contention for a simple reason. Ending pollution raises the most explosive of political questions: Who pays?

For we have now recognized that the failure of the market system is basic to our current environmental crisis. Air and water were considered to be "free" resources. Therefore a corporation which would invest enormous amounts of time and money in figuring out how to economize the costs of labor and capital did not give a second thought to using and destroying rivers, lakes and the atmosphere. The social costs of this pricing system, with its positive incentives for pollution, have now become intolerable, so we are going to decide, in one way or another, to charge for the environment. As Richard Nixon said in his State of the Union message, "We can no longer afford to consider air and water common property, free to be abused by anyone without regard to the consequences."

But whenever society determines that it is going to put a price tag on resources that were, up to yesterday, "free," there is an enormous potential for conflict. Moreover, although Mr. Nixon accurately stated the generality, he ignored some of the outstanding specifics. For the corporations which most notably squandered our "common property" of air and water are the largest in the land: pollution tends to grow along with economies of scale. So the industries which must now be forced to change their conduct, or else pay for it, include auto, oil, airlines, utilities and other giant types of enterprise.

And the recent past provides ample proof that these corporations will not passively submit to a reduction in their profit margins or restrictions on their operations. In his message on the environment Mr. Nixon had to falsify history to evade this reality.

On January 30, 1967, Lyndon Johnson sent Congress his message on "Protecting Our National Heritage." "It is in private laboratories," the President said, "and in private board rooms that the crucial decisions on new fuels, new control of technology and new means of developing power and locomotion will be made. We should support private efforts now to expand the range of their alternatives and make wiser choices possible." But on the very day that Mr. Johnson was thus engaging in his consensus rhetoric, the *New York Times* reported that Mr. Arjay Miller, the President of the Ford Company, was warning of the "threat of over-regulation by government" with regard to pollution. And the *Wall Street Journal* Washington office commented on the Johnson plan, "Business concerns, which have favored state control of anti-pollution programs, will probably fight hard against the proposal."

When Lyndon Johnson finally did sign the Air Quality Act of 1967, he pretended that he had won a great victory: "new power to stop pollution before it chokes our children and strangles our elderly—before it drives us indoors or into the hospital." The *Wall Street Journal* was, once again, more realistic about the law: "This was a major victory for such industrial groups as the coal producers, who vigorously opposed toughening Federal standards."

In his environment message this year, Nixon confirmed that the *Wall Street Journal* was right and Johnson wrong. For, as he documented, the "new powers" granted in 1967 had not even slowed down the crisis. But it would not do for an optimistic, preachy Republican President to admit the cause of this failure—that the very corporations to which he was now appealing had subverted the 1967 legislation. So he rewrote history: "Quite inadvertently, by ignoring environmental costs we have given an economic advantage to the careless polluter over his more conscientious rival." That "inadvertence," in point of fact, had been carefully lobbied through the Congress by the big polluters and they had prevailed over the wishes of the President of the United States.

But why, then, are the corporations cooperating now? An analogy to auto safety is helpful in understanding this development. Before Ralph Nader had awakened a national constituency and created enormous political pressure for new safety legislation, the auto giants tried to ridicule his charges and, for that matter, to conduct a private investigation of him in order to smear him, blackmail him, or both. But once Nader's crusade had succeeded, Detroit tried to head off the reform movement at the pass by proposing *its* safety program and ultimately by proudly advertising the devices which they had been forced to install at political gunpoint.

Today, I am suggesting, the polluting corporations are making a similar, tactical retreat: the 1967 strategy of vetoing effective legislation will no longer work; so the new emphasis is to be on making sure that the public, rather than the guilty companies, will pay the bill for cleaning up the environment.

General Motors has already announced that anti-pollution features in its cars will raise prices by $100. And in the February issue of *Fortune*, Max Ways quotes Henry Ford as proposing that the government spend money to generate a private, market demand for innovations in protecting the environment. These attitudes account for an interesting phenomenon on the stock market which the *Wall Street Journal* reported on February 3rd: in the midst of a bear market, the "ecological" stocks are bullish. If the speculators are right, there is going to be a new, multi-billion dollar environmental industry and filthy air and water will yield a profit.

This approach solves the question of who pays. The consumer is indirectly taxed by the corporation which passes on to him the cost of any government regulations. But there is an even more audacious proposal for seeing to it that the public supports the polluters. When *Fortune* magazine queried some of the most important executives in the nation on how to deal with the environmental crisis, the strategy favored by most of them (57 percent) was for the government to give industry a tax-cut so that it could finance anti-pollution devices. This would mean that the biggest polluters, with the greatest problems, would get the largest subsidies. It would, in effect, reward those who have befouled the atmosphere. And it would, like all other tax expenditures for the private sector, take money away from social uses.

Need for a Program

Ecology, then, is a highly political issue. And that is why the democratic Left has to begin immediately to develop a distinctive program aimed at charging the polluters, rather than the people, for the cost of cleaning up the environment and at relating the solution of this new problem to our older concerns with social needs. Above all the environmental campaign must not become an escape from the domestic priorities which we have identified, but not observed, in recent years.

First of all, the attempt to reclaim our air and water emphasizes the need for comprehensive planning.

In his message on the environment, President Nixon evoked an imminent apocalypse: "Based on present trends, it is quite possible that by 1980 the increase in the sheer number of cars in densely populated areas will begin outrunning the technological limits of our capacity to reduce pollution from the internal combustion engine." That is a clear warning of impending social doom. But in his budget, the very same President Nixon, after the usual glittering generalities, assigned mass transit 6 percent of the money he is spending on highways. Yet it is obvious that by reducing the "sheer number" of cars by providing new, pollution-free public transit one could take a major step toward dealing with suffocation in 1980. But Mr. Nixon, for all his talk, is actually putting the power of the Federal Government behind increasing auto congestion with all its fumes.

Here again, if Mr. Nixon observed the logic of his own priorities he would have to challenge some of the wealthiest vested interests in the nation, i.e., the auto-oil-construction alliance for paving the country. Indeed the *Wall Street Journal* has already warned the President that an attempt to produce an alternative to the internal combustion engine might lead to the "severe disruption of the nation's largest industries." Here, as in the case of most of the other crucial areas of American life, only a political movement based on a non-corporate and radical majority can put forth the solutions we need.

Secondly, the cost of fighting pollution must be charged to the polluters. And that means some price and profit controls.

If the funds for cleaning up the environment are not to be reflected in higher prices, steps will have to be taken so that industry cannot simply send the bill to the consumer. But then this is only one more case in which the right of huge corporations to follow a pricing policy without any social considerations has to be challenged. And that is precisely what Richard Nixon, with his ideological commitment to the values of the Old Economics, will not do. Under Kennedy-Johnson there were at least attempts to "jawbone" over prices and wages and sometimes, as in John Kennedy's famous confrontation with the steel companies, the policy worked.

But Mr. Nixon—as a good Republican—is keeping his hands off. The *London Economist*—hardly a radical periodical—commented at the end of January on one consequence of this policy: "With its usual lack of political sense the American steel industry, presumably managed almost entirely by Republicans, is celebrating a new year with yet another price increase." In the ten (mainly Democratic) years between 1959 and 1969, the *Economist* noted, steel prices were up by 6 percent; in the first twelve months of Richard Nixon they soared by 7 percent. And yet, in February the United States Steel Corporation explained that it was too poor to afford anti-pollution devices at its Duluth, Minnesota, plant.

This clearly will not do. As part of a general policy which insists that all major pricing decisions of large corporations be subject to public debate and that all the necessary data be made a matter of public record, the democratic Left should demand a policing of the price and profit policies of the major polluters. Only in this way can we see to it that corporate wealth pays for the profitable damage it has already done and be given an expensive reason to behave differently in the future.

Thirdly, the details of the Nixon program must be read carefully by experts with a social conscience. For there is already evidence that the President, for all his bold slogans, announced a resolute march to the rear in his pollution message.

As E. W. Kenworthy pointed out in the *New York Times*, Mr. Nixon suggests a "fair allocation of the total capacity of the waterways to absorb the user's particular kind of waste without becoming polluted." This, Kenworthy continued, is a statement of the doctrine of "assimilative capacity," i.e., one pollutes the water up to a safe limit. It is in contradiction to the present principle of "beneficial use" which states that one actually takes a positive view toward the value of the water. Under the Nixon refinement it may even be possible for industries to pollute waters which are now clean. After all, they have not been fouled up to their "assimilative capacity."

This point has larger implications. The Nixon philosophy is that the government should play an essentially negative, limiting role vis-à-vis the private sector. But in the case of water and in the area of the other profound social consequences of private investment, that is not enough. A technological innovation—the supersonic transport, for instance—affects many crucial areas of social life: pollution by fumes and by noise, airport congestion, public monies for highways to carry traffic to and from the planes, and so on. Therefore the major programs of all corporations should be tested for social consequence by an independent public agency. If we do not allow drug manufacturers to market a new product without first checking on its effect on health, we can no longer allow other industries to unilaterally impose their priorities on the nation. And "beneficial use" should be the criterion, not just for water, but for technology in general.

Finally, we cannot allow the environment to become a substitute for the struggle against poverty and urban blight. It must be an aid to it.

Mr. Nixon has been very bold in attacking the unions with the Philadelphia Plan (by following fiscal and government policies which cut back on construction at the same time he imposes a racial quota on the building industry, he makes a black-white struggle for scarce jobs inevitable—but then maybe that's precisely what he wants, for it splits the two most effective components of the opposition). And he is willing to pay a premium to car-makers who come up with pollution-free autos. But the democratic Left must insist that this entire new effort require that the burgeoning anti-pollution industry hire the unemployed and underemployed poor with special emphasis on the minorities, and that the location of facilities take social, as well as economic considerations into account.

We have already discovered through the "new careers" program that poor people can make effective contributions to the economy without a great deal of expensive training so long as jobs are designed for them (rather, so to speak, than "designing" them for the job). If there is now going to be a vanguard industry which does not now have a vested interest in the old ways, that provides a marvelous opportunity to redeem some of our promises to the poor, the blacks, and the Spanish-speaking—and to do so by giving the entire society a better place to live. In other words, we must be as concerned about the social effect of fighting pollution and not just about technology.

But to carry out this program will require political conflict. For recent experience and the present attitudes of the corporate sector show that it wants to deal with the environment in a conservative way which will yield a profit to those who created the problem in the first place. It is therefore quite wrong to think that all of us men of good will are going to get together and clean up our common air and water. We are going to have to prepare for vigorous conflict if this new crusade is actually going to achieve its goals and, in the process, benefit the entire society and not just the polluters.

TWENTIETH CENTURY PITTSBURGH: GOVERNMENT, BUSINESS AND ENVIRONMENTAL CHANGE

Roy Lubove

Smoke control, like housing legislation, represented a compromise between the desirable and feasible; and was further limited by difficulties of enforcement. Once again, the quest for bureaucratic rationalization led to the assumption of new regulatory powers by government, but the same reluctance to compromise seriously the autonomy of private business interests determined the character of public intervention. Enforcement would be achieved, if at all, by persuasion rather than coercion.

An address by Andrew Carnegie in 1899 led the Chamber of Commerce to appoint a Committee on Smoke Abatement. Consisting of engineers and manufacturers, it drafted an ordinance in 1906 that prohibited the emission of dense smoke for more than 8 minutes an hour. . . .

Following passage of the smoke ordinance, a Division of Smoke Inspection was created in the Bureau of Health in 1907; at the request of the mayor, the Chamber helped select the chief smoke inspector. The courts declared the ordinance unconstitutional in 1911 on the grounds that the city council had exceeded its authority, and that the measure was unreasonable. The state legislature promptly passed enabling legislation, and a new ordinance was enacted (which exempted mill heating and puddling furnaces). In 1912 the Chamber organized a Smoke and Dust Abatement League to support the work of the Division of Smoke Inspection (which was elevated to a Bureau of Smoke Regulation in 1914). Another assault against smoke was launched in 1911 when Robert Duncan Kennedy, a Pittsburgh businessman, provided funds to the Mellon Institute of the University of Pittsburgh for research. Under its sponsorship, scientists explored the economic costs, health hazards, and psychological consequences of a smoky atmosphere.

Business and scientific interest in smoke control, and the creation of a municipal regulatory machinery, had no perceptible results. Businessmen had to use government to extend their influence in civic affairs, but did not really want government power to compromise their autonomy. In smoke control, as in housing, they could reconcile these incompatible goals by creating a public bureaucracy with a feeble regulatory mandate and no constructive powers of intervention. Even the staunchest advocate of smoke control conceded that it would have to be sacrificed in the event of a conflict with local economic interests. The Civic Club, for one, "would be the last to advocate the passage of any law which would tend to lessen our prosperity." Legislation for the "many" was, according to the Congress of Women's Clubs of Allegheny County, permissible so long as their interests "can be subserved without . . . affecting the material prosperity of which we are all so justly proud." Unfortunately, smoke control could not be both effective and absolutely painless for all economic interests involved. Recognizing its ambiguous status, the Division of Smoke Inspection, like its housing counterparts, adopted a strategy of education and persuasion.

The chief smoke inspector noted that the tendency in Pittsburgh to equate smoke with prosperity inspired criticism of any regulatory legislation. It was, however, surely not the "purpose of the City of Pittsburgh . . . to harass or drive away the resident mill or factory operator," or to discourage the "prospective investor and manufacturer." In compliance with this policy, the Division rarely prosecuted offenders. It drove no manufacturer from Pittsburgh; neither did it reduce the volume of smoke by a wisp. . . .

There is no doubt that Pittsburgh confronted disaster in the 1940's. Despite record wartime production and employment, the district could "boast of few important new industries, and the gain in population has been limited." Many persons "have been apprehensive—some of them definitely pessimistic—regarding the prospects for the Pittsburgh district." By 1945 "large corporations which had long made their headquarters in Pittsburgh had actually taken options on properties in other cities and were laying plans to build skyscrapers there and move their offices." These included Westinghouse, Alcoa, and U. S. Steel. Corporate managerial and technical personnel and their wives "didn't want to live and raise their families under . . . prevailing environmental conditions." A blanket of smoke choked "the city much of the time. There are floods almost every year. Hundreds of communities dump their raw sewage into Pittsburgh's rivers. . . . Housing is substandard. No major highway has been built and none is in design." Pittsburgh, in short, was "not a fit place in which to live and work and raise a family. That being the case, the responsible citizenry of the city faced a tough decision. No longer could they vacillate, rationalize, compromise. . . . Either they would stay and eventually rebuild the core of the central city, or they would get out and take their industries with them."

One crucial circumstance that influenced the future of Pittsburgh was the assumption by a "whole group of younger leaders" of "positions of executive responsibility and power." Their emergence and involvement in the creation of Pittsburgh's reverse welfare state was, in turn, associated with one man's decision to rebuild rather than abandon Pittsburgh. Richard King Mellon assumed control of the family enterprises in the late 1930s, following the death of his father, Richard Beaty, and uncle, Andrew. In 1946 the family interests were consolidated in T. Mellon and Sons, and new executives arrived in Pittsburgh to head the Mellon concerns: General Brehon Somervell at Koppers; George H. Love at Pittsburgh Consolidation

Coal; Frank Denton at Mellon Bank; and Sidney W. Swensrud at Gulf Oil. "The blunt fact about Pittsburgh's changing scene," *Fortune* reported, "is that a new generation is in power. . . . It begins in the Mellon empire, extends through Big Steel, and runs through the other power groupings." . . .

Civic organization in Pittsburgh was not new; Pittsburgh and other American cities were the graveyard of citizen organizations established to promote environmental or social change. What made the ACCD unique was its success, and this requires explanation. Richard Mellon's leadership and the recruitment of the corporate elite provided the ACCD with extraordinary potential power; but a policy decision adopted when the Conference was first established in 1943 insured that the power would be exercised. This was the requirement that members of the executive committee participate personally in its deliberations, and as individuals rather than representatives of any corporation. . . .

The effectiveness of the ACCD depended ultimately upon the cooperation of Mayor David Lawrence and the City–County Democratic political machine. "The future," as Lawrence explained, "was to establish the working relationships between the Democratic administration and Richard Mellon." Lawrence paid particular tribute to Richard and to Mellon adviser Arthur B. Van Buskirk as the men who most "sensed the necessity of uniting public and private action for Pittsburgh's advancement." Through their efforts, in large measure, Pittsburgh pioneered "in municipal techniques which have since become commonplace." These techniques included extensive use of the "authority" mechanism in the renewal process and dependence upon the resources of every level of government. Thus the Pittsburgh civic coalition linked Democrat and Republican, businessman and politician, federal, state, and local government; and it adopted any administrative expedient that would serve its purposes.

Finally, the ACCD was successful because it forged a consensus on community policy. The ACCD could mold a powerful civic coalition because no one seriously challenged its proposition that the goal of community policy was revitalization of the CBD and ultimately the regional economy. "The need for preserving and protecting the stability of the Golden Triangle," Park Martin emphasized, "was recognized and accepted, and the program deliberately placed great emphasis on this area." Public officials agreed with the "civic leaders" that "the values of the Downtown must be preserved and strengthened before all else."

The establishment of the reverse welfare state, and the prestige of the ACCD, hinged upon three projects in the early days of the Renaissance. All three—Point Park, smoke control, and flood control—had long been advocated in Pittsburgh, and they demonstrated the use of public power or investment to promote private economic ends. As Wallace Richards explained, "the enterprise system itself has sought and established in Pittsburgh a partnership between private business and all levels of government." The irony of the environmental change process in twentieth century Pittsburgh was not that it ultimately hinged upon constructive public intervention, but that use of public resources was so closely identified with the corporate welfare. . . .

Lawrence inherited a smoke control law passed in 1941. Although the city council had abolished the Bureau of Smoke Control in 1939, councilman Abraham L. Wolk began a crusade for new legislation. The St. Louis smoke control ordinance of 1940 became the inspiration and model for Pittsburgh, where a strong alliance formed by the winter of 1941. Dr. I. Hope Alexander, Pittsburgh's health director, journeyed to St. Louis at the request of Mayor Scully and the city council. "Photographs and the evidence of Dr. Alexander's own eyes left no doubt about it—St. Louis is now as spotless as pre-War Rotterdam. And the experts agree that Pittsburgh can do what St. Louis has done." . . .

Mayor Scully and the council visited St. Louis in February, 1941. The Mayor then appointed a Smoke Commission under the chairmanship of Wolk. The Commission advanced several arguments on behalf of smoke control. Atmospheric pollution produced a high incidence of pneumonia, sinus ailments, and fibrosis of lung tissue. It destroyed vegetation and resulted in abnormally expensive cleaning bills. Not least important, "practically everyone has heard of persons who have refused to accept positions here because of Pittsburgh's reputation as a 'dirty city.' " Smoke control might even be the key to economic diversification. "With proper promotion, a considerable growth of smaller, lighter industries might well follow the elimination of the smoke nuisance here." The Commission recommended, and the council enacted, an ordinance based on the simple, but effective St. Louis policy. Consumers had to use smokeless fuel, or else install "fuelburning equipment which has been found to prevent the production of smoke." In contrast to previous legislation, private homes and multiple-dwellings with less than six units would have to comply. War-induced fuel shortages and production demands, however, prevented enforcement for the duration of the war.

A United Smoke Council, organized in 1945, soon became an affiliate of the ACCD. Its objectives included enforcement of the 1941 legislation and extension of smoke control to the county. The Council supported Mayor Lawrence's decision to require industry, railroads, and commercial buildings to comply by October 1, 1946, followed by residential dwellings one year later. Lawrence depended upon the ACCD to prevent obstruction from the coal companies. "Richard King Mellon and his associates in the Allegheny Conference," Lawrence observed, "gave their strong support. Without them I would not have been successful. I had not much influence with the Consolidation Coal Company, while Mr. Mellon's prestige with them was great." Lawrence and the ACCD also overcame opposition from the soft-coal miners. John Busarello, president of District No. 5, United Mine Workers, complained of a conspiracy to "reduce the market for Pittsburgh district coal." Someone, he insisted, "is trying to get the people of Allegheny County to buy their coal outside of the county and someone else is trying to get the people to throw out their furnaces and burn gas. They are trying to take work from our miners." Although smoke control was not a conspiracy, the mine workers' fears were not groundless. Smoke control depended, in large degree, upon reducing use of the district's high-volatile bituminous coal for engines and domestic heating. It hastened the conversion to diesel locomotives, and to gas in homes and apartments.

The influence of the Pennsylvania RR in Harrisburg posed the chief obstacle to extension of smoke control to the county. Enabling legislation for county smoke control, passed in 1943, had exempted the railroads. The ACCD sponsored a bill in 1947 that brought them under control; an understanding, presumably, had been reached with the Pennsylvania RR. The Conference delegation in Harrisburg was surprised and infuriated to find that the Pennsylvania's lobbyist, Rufus Flynn, nonetheless opposed the legislation. Wallace Richards contacted Mellon who informed the president of the Pennsylvania that other railroads would be delighted to handle his business. Benjamin Fairless of United States Steel also demanded that the Pennsylvania cooperate. The enabling legislation passed.

The ACCD then exerted its influence on behalf of a countywide smoke control law. The United Smoke Council organized smoke-abatement committees in each municipality, sponsored educational programs on the harmful effects of smoke, and circulated petitions requesting the county commissioners to enact an ordinance. The commissioners appointed a 17-member Smoke Abatement Advisory Committee under Edward Weidlein to prepare the legislation, which was passed in 1949. In 1957 the county absorbed the Pittsburgh Health Department, whose Bureau of Smoke Regulation had enforced the City ordinance. A new comprehensive regulation, administered by the County Bureau of Air Pollution Control, was passed in 1960.

By that date the urgency and sense of crisis had passed. The smoke control legislation of the 1940s had achieved its purpose; it eliminated the blatant ash and soot pollution that required street lighting at high noon, and thus enabled the civic coalition to proceed with its reconstruction program. Subsequently, progress under county auspices has been uneven. Gaseous and microdust pollution is extensive, including high levels of nitrogen and sulfur dioxide. Certain sections of the city, like Squirrel Hill and especially Hazelwood, still suffer at times from a thick, malodorous smog and a quick settling layer of black dust. Generous provision for staggered enforcement in the county legislation has permitted the use of obsolete equipment in steel plants. Pockets of old-style, thick grey-black smoke still existed in the 1960s in the river valley milltowns.

THE ECO-ESTABLISHMENT

Katherine Barkley and Steve Weissman

I

Ask Vietnam protesters about the April 22 National Environmental Teach-In and they'll tell you it's a scheme to contain their spring offensive against the ecological disaster in Southeast Asia. Ask young blacks about this new movement to save the ecosystem and they'll tell you that it is a way of distracting attention from the old movement that was supposed to save their skins.

Then go and talk to an environmental activist, a Survival Walker. Ask him why the ecology movement has turned its back on Vietnam and civil rights and he'll explain, with a convincing freshness the old New Left has lost, that the sky is falling. He'll point out that we all have to breathe and that none of us—white or black, Vietnamese peasant or American marine—has much of a future on CO_2. We all must eat, and a diet of pesticides is deadly. We all need water, and the dwindling supplies are unfit for human (or even industrial) consumption. We all depend on the same limited forests, mines, oceans and soil, and we are all going to choke on the same waste and pollution.

To this new ecology activist, nothing could be more obvious: we've all got to unite behind the overriding goal of unfouling our common nest before it's too late, turning back the pages of the environmental doomsday book. If we succeed, then we can get back to these other questions. There is no stopping, he will add, an idea whose time has come.

He will be right, too—though a bit naive about where ideas come from and where movements go. Environment *will be* the issue of the '70s, but not simply because the air got thicker or the oceans less bubbly, or even because the war in Vietnam got too bloody to have to think about every day. It will be the issue of the '70s because such stewards of the nation's wealth as the Ford Foundation, with its Resources for the Future, Inc. (RFF), and Laurance Rockefeller's Conservation Foundation needed a grass-roots movement to help consolidate their control over national policy-making, bolster their hold over world resources, and escalate further cycles of useless economic growth.

II

The environment bandwagon is not as recent a phenomenon as it seems. It began to gather momentum back in the mid-'60s under the leadership of Resources for the Future. "The relationship of people to resources, which usually has been expressed in terms of quantity, needs to be restated for modern times to emphasize what is happening to the quality of resources," warned RFF President Joseph L. Fisher in his group's 1964 report. "The wide variety of threats to the quality of the environment may well embrace the gravest U.S. resources problem for the next generation." The following year, Resources for the Future established a special research and educational program in environmental quality, funded with a $1.1 million grant from its parent organization, the Ford Foundation.

Created by Ford in the early '50s during the scare over soaring materials costs, RFF had just made its name in conservation by organizing the Mid-Century Conference on Resources for the Future, the first major national conservation conference since Teddy Roosevelt and Gifford Pinchot staged the National Governors' Conference in 1908. Held in 1953, the Mid-Century Conference mustered broad support from both the country's resource users and conservers for the national conservation policy already spelled out by President Truman's Materials Policy Commission. It was this Commission, headed by William S. Paley (board chairman of CBS and a founding director of RFF), which had openly affirmed the nation's inalienable right to extract cheap supplies of raw materials from the underdeveloped countries, and which set the background for Eisenhower and Dulles' oft-quoted concern over the fate of the tin and tungsten of Southeast Asia. Insuring adequate supplies of resources for the future became a conservationist byword.

By the mid-'60s, Resources for the Future had begun to broaden its concern to include resource quality, thus setting the tone for a decade of conservationist rhetoric and behavior. The trustees of the Ford Foundation, an executive committee of such international resource users and polluters as Esso and Ford Motor, established a separate Resources and Environment Division which, since 1966, has nourished such groups as Open Space Action Committee, Save-the-Redwoods League, Massachusetts Audubon Society, Nature Conservancy, and the Environmental Defense Fund. A year later, the Rockefeller Foundation set up an Environmental Studies Division, channelling money to the National Academy of Science and RFF and to Laurance Rockefeller's own pet project, the Conservation Foundation.

The conservationist-planners' new concern over threats to the quality of resources, and to life itself, was actually an outgrowth of their earlier success in assuring cheap and plentiful raw materials. It had become clear that supplies of resources would be less a problem than the immense amount of waste generated as a by-product of those now being refined. The more industry consumed, the more it produced and sold, the larger and more widespread the garbage dumps. Rivers and lakes required costly treatment to make water suitable for use in homes and industry. Smoggy air corroded machines, ruined timberlands, reduced the productivity of crop lands and livestock—to say nothing of its effect on the work capacity of the average man. Pesticides were killing more than pests, and raising the spectre of cumulative disaster. Cities were getting noisier, dirtier, uglier and more tightly packed, forcing the middle class to the suburbs and the big urban landowners to the wall. "Ugliness," Lyndon Johnson exclaimed sententiously, "is costly."

This had long been obvious to the conservationists. Something had to be done, and the elite resource planners took as their model for action the vintage 1910 American conservation movement, especially its emphasis on big business cooperation with big government.

III

When the 1890 census officially validated the fact that the frontier was closed, a generation of business and government leaders realized with a start that the American Eden had its bounds. Land, timber and water were all limited, as was the potential for conflicts over their apportionment. What resources should timbermen, grazers or farmers exploit? What should be preserved as a memory of the American past? Who would decide these questions? The conservationists—Teddy Roosevelt, Chief Forester Gifford Pinchot and some of the bigger timber, grazing and agricultural interests—pushed heavily for a new policy to replace the crude and wanton pillage which had been part of the frontier spirit. While preservationists like John Muir were fighting bitterly against any and all use of wild areas by private interests, the conservationists wanted only to make sure that the environment would be exploited with taste and efficiency.

Roosevelt and his backers won out, of course. And the strategy they used is instructive: failing initially to muster congressional support for their plan, they mobilized a broadly based conservation movement, supposedly to regulate the private interests which they in fact represented. Backed by the widespread public support it had whipped up, the conservationist juggernaut then began to move the country toward a more regulated—but still private—exploitation of its riches.

Of course, the private interests which had helped draft this policy also moved—to staff the regulatory agencies, provide jobs for retiring regulators, and generally to put the right man in the right niche most of the time. Within short order, the regulatory agencies were captives of the interests they were supposed to regulate, and they were soon being used as a screen which kept the public from seeing the way that small interests were squeezed out of the competition for resources. Their monopoly position thus strengthened by regulatory agencies, these large interests found it easy to pass the actual costs of regulation on to the citizen consumer.

IV

The old American conservation movement had reacted out of fear over resource scarcities; the new movement of the mid-'60s feared, as well, the destruction of resource quality. And the corporation conservationists and their professional planners in organizations like Resources for the Future once again looked to government regulations as an answer to the difficulties they foresaw. Only this time the stakes were much higher than they had been at the early part of the century. Many of the resource planners want an all-encompassing environmental agency or Cabinet level Department of Resources, Environment and Population. Holding enormous power over a wide range of decisions, this coordinating apparatus would be far more convenient for the elite than the present array of agencies, each influenced by its own interest groups.

Who will benefit from this increased environmental consciousness and who will pay is already quite clear to business, if not to most young ecology activists. "The elite of business leadership," reports Fortune, "strongly desire the federal government to step in, set the standards, regulate all activities pertaining to the environment, and help finance the job with tax incentives." The congressional background paper for the 1968 hearings on National Policy of Environmental Quality, prepared with the help of Rockefeller's Conservation Foundation, spells out the logic in greater detail: "Lack of national policy for the environment has now become as expensive to the business community as to the Nation at large. In most enterprises, a social cost can be carried without undue burden if all competitors carry it alike. For example, industrial waste disposal costs can, like other costs of production, be reflected in prices to consumers. But this becomes feasible only when public law and administration put all comparable forms of waste-producing enterprises under the same requirements." Only the truly powerful could be so candid about their intention to pick the pocket of the consumer to pay for the additional costs they will be faced with.

The resource planners are also quite frank about the wave of subsidies they expect out of the big clean-up campaign. "There will have to be a will to provide funds," explains Joseph Fisher, "to train the specialists, do the research and experimentation, build the laws and institutions through which more rapid progress [in pollution control] can be made, and of course, build the facilities and equipment." The coming boondoggles—replete with tax incentives, direct government grants, and new products—will make the oil depletion allowance seem tame. And what's more, it will be packaged as a critical social service.

The big business conservationists will doubtless be equally vocal about the need for new bond issues for local water and sewage treatment facilities; lead crusades to overcome reluctance of the average citizen to vote "yes" on bond measures; and then, as bond-holders themselves, skim a nice tax-free six or seven percent off the top.

It isn't just the citizen and taxpayer who will bear the burden, however. Bedraggled Mother Nature, too, will pay. Like the original conservation movement it is emulating, today's big business conservation is not interested in preserving the earth; it is rationally reorganizing for a more efficient rape of resources (e.g., the export of chemical-intensive agribusiness) and the production of an even grosser national product.

The seeming contradictions are mind-boggling: industry is combating waste so it can afford to waste more; it is planning to produce more (smog-controlled) private autos to crowd more highways, which means even more advertising to create more "needs" to be met by planned obsolescence. Socially, the result is disastrous. Ecologically, it could be the end.

Why don't the businessmen simply stop their silly growthmanship? They can't. If one producer slowed down in the mad race, he'd be eaten up by his competitors. If all conspired together to restrain growth permanently, the unemployment and cutbacks would make today's recession look like full employment, and the resulting unrest would make today's dissent look like play time at Summerhill.

V

They began in the mid-'60s in low key, mobilizing the academicians, sprinkling grants and fellowships at the "better" schools, and coordinating research efforts of Resources for the Future, the Conservation Foundation, RAND, Brookings Institution, the National Academy of Science and the Smithsonian Institution. Major forums were held in 1965 and 1966 on "The Quality of the Environment" and "Future Environments of North America." Research findings were programmed directly into industrial trade associations and business firms.

Then the resource people put their men and programs in the official spotlight: Laurance Rockefeller (founder of and major donor to the Conservation Foundation and also a director of RFF) chaired both the White House Conference on Natural Beauty and the Citizens' Advisory Committee on Recreation and Natural Beauty (which Nixon has rechristened his Citizens' Advisory Committee on Environmental Quality). Conservation Foundation President Russell Train headed up Nixon's Task Force on Resources and Environment, with help from Fisher and several other directors of RFF and the Conservation Foundation, and then became Undersecretary of Interior.

Then the media were plugged in, an easy task for men who have in their hands the direction of CBS, National Educational Television, Time-Life-Fortune, Christian Science Monitor, New York Times and Cowles publications, as well as many of the trade journals and conservation magazines.

Independent media, seeing that environment was now news, picked up and broadcast the studies which the conservation elite had produced. Public opinion leaders told their public, in Business Week's words, "to prepare for the approval of heavy public and private spending to fight pollution."

Finally, the grass roots were given the word. RFF, Ford and Rockefeller had long worked with and financed the old-time conservation groups, from Massachusetts Audubon to the Sierra Club, and now the big money moved beyond an appreciation of wilderness to a greater activism. When, for example, David Brower broke with the Sierra Club, it was Robert O. Anderson of Atlantic-Richfield and RFF who gave him $200,000 to set up Friends of the Earth (prudently channeling the donation through the organization's tax-exempt affiliate, the John Muir Institute).

When Senator Gaylord Nelson and Congressman Pete McCloskey got around to pushing the National Teach-In, it was the Conservation Foundation, the Audubon Society and the American Conservation Association which doled out the money while Friends of the Earth was putting together *The Environmental Handbook*, meant to be the Bible of the new movement.

The big business conservationists and their professionals didn't buy off the movement; they built it.

WATER SHORTAGE IS A FRAME OF MIND

William Bowen

Cheap Water Encourages Waste

For most users in the U.S., water is so cheap that the economic rewards for conserving it and the economic penalties for wasting it are too faint to matter much. Metered households pay, on the average, something like 40 cents a thousand gallons. The average price to industrial users of municipal water is lower than that, because many cities charge big users less per unit than small users. Irrigation water is cheaper still. And for most apartment dwellers the cost of using or wasting additional water (the "marginal cost," as economists call it) is zero—they pay a charge that is concealed in the rent and is unrelated to how much water they use.

Water is cheap because it is naturally abundant, but also because for many users it is priced below cost as a result of cheap water policies followed by various levels of government in the U.S. In the West, electric power revenues or property taxes are widely used to subsidize water for irrigation. Many municipal water systems do not charge enough to recover their costs. Some of them, in theory, supply water at cost or even make a profit on it, but the bookkeeping tends to understate costs.

From *Fortune,* vol. 71, no. 4 (April, 1965), p. 145. Reprinted from the April 1965 issue of *Fortune* Magazine by special permission;

Water pricing is pervaded with irrationalities and contradictions. California is moving ahead with a multi-billion-dollar project to bring water from the northern part of the state to the semi-arid south, yet the Metropolitan Water District of Los Angeles prices water below cost and levies a special property tax to make up the deficit. The desert city of Tucson gets its municipal water from deepening wells, and its threatened water scarcity in years ahead is among the arguments advanced for a proposed U.S. Bureau of Reclamation project to bring water to central Arizona; . . . yet water users in Tucson pay considerably less per unit than their counterparts in Indianapolis, St. Petersburg, and some other communities in the well-watered East.

"It's a living."

pp. 100–124

6 "Ecology is inherently radical"

The next hundred years will certainly see increased attention to what may be called the "re-entry problem," following the analogy of the "takeoff" into development. The re-entry problem is that of discovering a high-level circular technology. In this, raw materials are eventually recycled, we rely mainly on solar energy rather than on burning up the earth, and yet man can still enjoy a high standard of life and a large net utilization of goods. This problem is certainly not intrinsically insoluble, but it still remains to be solved, and we do not know how difficult it will be. It is certainly going to demand a major intellectual effort for mankind in the next hundred years. The problems of social technology which accompany this are perhaps even greater than that of physical technology. It requires, indeed, the development of what is increasingly coming to be called a "spaceship earth" with a stable population, a conservationist ideology, a circular technology, and a non-violent political order which will eliminate war and revolution—the greatest potential pollution—and still satisfy human demands both for freedom and for justice. This looks like a very large order, but it had better be on the menu or the whole human enterprise may end in total disaster, possibly sinking back into an endless cycle of starvation, misery, and violence.

University of Colorado Commission on Environmental Studies, "The University's Response to the Environmental Crisis," (August 3, 1970).

POPULATION, RESOURCES, ENVIRONMENT: ISSUES IN HUMAN ECOLOGY

Paul R. Ehrlich and Anne H. Ehrlich

The only trouble with our time is that the future is not what it used to be.
Paul Valéry (1891–1945)

The future is a cruel hoax . . . I am terribly saddened by the fact that the most humane thing for me to do is to have no children at all.
Valedictorian Stephanie Mills, 1969 *Mills College*

Summary

To recapitulate, we would summarize the present world situation as follows:

1. Considering present technology and patterns of behavior our planet is grossly overpopulated now.
2. The large absolute number of people and the rate of population growth are major hindrances to solving human problems.
3. The limits of human capability to produce food by conventional means have very nearly been reached. Problems of supply and distribution already have resulted in roughly half of humanity being undernourished or malnourished. Some 10–20 million people are starving to death annually now.
4. Attempts to increase food production further will tend to accelerate the deterioration of our environment, which in turn will eventually *reduce* the capacity of the Earth to produce food. It is not clear whether environmental decay has now gone so far as to be essentially irreversible; it is possible that the capacity of the planet to support human life has been permanently impaired. Such technological "successes," as automobiles, pesticides, and inorganic nitrogen fertilizers are major causes of environmental deterioration.
5. There is reason to believe that population growth increases the probability of a lethal worldwide plague and of a thermonuclear war. Either could provide an undesirable "death rate solution" to the population problem; each is potentially capable of destroying civilization and even of driving *Homo sapiens* to extinction.
6. There is no technological panacea for the complex of problems composing the population–food–environment crisis, although technology, properly applied in such areas as pollution abatement, communications, and fertility control can provide massive assistance. The basic solutions involve dramatic and rapid changes in human *attitudes*, especially those relating to reproductive behavior, economic growth, technology, the environment, and conflict resolution.

Recommendations: A Positive Program

Although our conclusions must seem rather pessimistic, we wish to emphasize our belief that the problems can be solved. Whether they *will* be solved is another question. A general course of action that we feel will have some chance of ameliorating the results of the current crisis is outlined below. Many of the suggestions will seem "unrealistic," and indeed that is how we view them. But the system has been allowed to run downhill for so long that only relatively idealistic programs offer any hope of salvation.

1. Population control is absolutely essential if the problems now facing mankind are to be solved. *It is not, however, a panacea.* If population growth were halted immediately, virtually all other human problems—poverty, racial tensions, urban blight, environmental decay, warfare—would remain. The situation is best summarized in the statement, "Whatever your cause, it's a lost cause without population control."

2. Political pressure must be applied immediately to induce the United States government to assume its responsibility to halt the growth of the American population. Once growth is halted, the government should undertake to regulate the birth rate so that the population is reduced to an optimum size and maintained there. It is essential that a grass-roots political movement be generated to convince our legislators and the executive branch of the government that they must act rapidly. The program should be based on what politicians understand best—votes. Presidents, Congressmen, Senators, and other elected officials who do not deal effectively with the crisis must be defeated at the polls and more intelligent and responsible candidates elected.

3. A massive campaign must be launched to restore a quality environment in North America and to *de-develop the United States*. De-development means bringing our economic system (especially patterns of consumption) into line with the realities of ecology and the world resource situation. This campaign would be largely political, especially with regard to our overexploitation of world resources, but the campaign should be strongly supplemented by legal and boycott action against polluters and others whose activities damage the environment. The need for de-development presents our economists with a major challenge. They must design a low-consumption economy of stability, and an economy in which there is a much more equitable distribution of wealth than in the present one. Marxists claim that capitalism is intrinsically expansionist and wasteful, and that it automatically produces a monied ruling class. Can our economists prove them wrong?

4. Once the United States has clearly started on the path of cleaning up its own mess it can then turn its attention to the problems of the de-development of the other DCs, population control, and ecologically feasible semi-development of the UDCs. It must use every peaceful means at its disposal to bring the Soviet Union and other DCs into the effort, in line with the general proposals of Lord Snow and Academician

Sakharov. Such action can be combined with attempts to achieve a general detente with the Soviets and the Chinese. Citizens, through the ballot, letter writing, and continued peaceful protest, must make clear to American leaders that they wish to move toward disarmament in spite of its possible risks. They must demand detailed appraisal of the risks of continuing the "balance of terror" versus the risk that the other side might "cheat" in a controlled disarmament situation. Americans should inform themselves of what is known about the causes and the psychology of conflict and about deterrence theory, and attempt to elect officials who are similarly informed.

5. It is unfortunate that at the time of the greatest crisis the United States and the world has ever faced, many Americans, especially the young, have given up hope that the government can be modernized and changed in direction through the functioning of the elective process. Their despair may have some foundation, but a partial attempt to institute a "new politics" very nearly succeeded in 1968. In addition many members of Congress and other government leaders, both Democrats and Republicans, are very much aware of the problems outlined in this book and are determined to do something about them. Others are joining their ranks as the dangers before us daily become more apparent. These people need public support in order to be effective. The world cannot, in its present critical state, be saved by merely tearing down old institutions, even if rational plans existed for constructing better ones from the ruins. We simply do not have the time. Either we will succeed by bending old institutions or we will succumb to disaster. Considering the potential rewards and consequences we see no choice but to make an effort to modernize the system. It may be necessary to organize a new political party with an ecological outlook and national and international orientation to provide an alternative to the present parties with their local and parochial interests. The environmental issue may well provide the basis for this.

6. Perhaps the major necessary ingredient that has been missing from a solution to the problems of both the United States and the rest of the world is a goal, a vision of the kind of Spaceship Earth that ought to be and the kind of crew that should man her. Society has always had its visionaries who talked of love, beauty, peace, and plenty. But somehow the "practical" men have always been there to praise the smog as a sign of progress, to preach "just" wars, and to restrict love while giving hate free rein. It must be one of the greatest ironies of the history of *Homo sapiens* that the only salvation for the practical men now lies in what they think of as the dreams of idealists. The question now is: can the "realists" be persuaded to face reality in time?

The ecological constraints on population and technological growth will inevitably lead to social and economic systems different from the ones in which we live today. In order to survive, mankind will have to develop what might be called a steady state. The steady state formula is so different from the philosophy of endless quantitative growth, which has so far governed Western Civilization, that it may cause widespread public alarm.

René Dubos, "A Social Design for Science," *Science*, vol. 166, no. 3907 (November 14, 1969), p. 823.

We had better know what we are about and take each step with great care. There is not enough time to study our present predicament and then design a total solution, even if it were possible. The parameters of this crisis are changing so quickly that a proper definition cannot be made. Only through intensive universal education and individual actions at all levels of organization can we mount an adequate and flexible response. If we have to wait for an agency to determine policy and implement federal programs, we may be waiting on our own extinction.

John G. Mitchell and Constance L. Stallings, *Ecotactics: The Sierra Club Handbook for Environmental Activists* (New York: Pocket Books, 1970), pp. 70–71.

THE ECO-ESTABLISHMENT

Katherine Barkley and Steve Weissman

Ecology activists out picketing a polluter or cleaning up a creek will have total freedom to make up their own minds about the threats to our environment, and they will have every right to choose their own course of constructive action. Yet they will surely never get a dime from Robert Anderson, or even a farthing from Ford or Rockefeller. And so far, the grass-roots ecology movement has done nothing but echo the eco-elite.

Ecology, unlike most of the fractured scientific field, is holistic. It talks of life and its environment as a totality: how organisms relate to each other and to the system which provides their life-support system. As a discipline applied to human affairs, then, ecology should help us get a whole view of our natural and social environment—from oxygen cycles to business cycles, from the jeopardized natural environment to the powerful institutional envi-

From *Eco-Catastrophe*, published by Canfield Press, San Francisco, 1970, pp. 21–24.

ronment which creates that jeopardy. If it revealed these interconnections, ecology would become, as it has been called, a "subversive science," subverting the polluters and resource-snatchers who now control the conservation of the nation's wealth. It would point the finger not simply at profit-making polluters or greedy consumers, but at the great garbage-creation system itself—the corporate capitalist economy.

But this is a far cry from the ecology movement as we have inherited it. Ecology, the science of interconnections, becomes a matter of cleaning up beaches and trying to change individuals' habits and attitudes, while ignoring the institutions which created them and practically all environmental damage.

The grass-roots ecology groups do have politics—the politics of consumer boycotts, shareholder democracy and interest group pluralism, all of which show a wonderfully anachronistic faith in the fairness of the market, political and economic. "If Dow pollutes," say the boycotters, "then we just won't buy Saran Wrap." If Super Suds won't make biodegradable soap, we'll buy Ivory. If Ford and Chevy won't make steam cars, we'll buy Japanese imports. From the planned obsolescence in automobiles, to 20 brands of toothpaste, much of what industry produces is insulting to the intelligence while also serving no real need; it is waste, to say nothing of the enormous pollution entailed in overproduction.

Consumer sovereignty has gone the way of the dodo, its passing noted two decades back by that stalwart defender of the new corporate capitalism, John Kenneth Galbraith. Consumers just don't control what gets produced, or how. To educate or build support for some stronger action, boycotts, like the picket line, work well. But to change production habits, an ecology movement will really have to pull the big plug at the other end of the TV transmitter, or better, at the production line itself.

Failing in the economic arena, the ecology groups can of course try their hand directly in the political marketplace. Oil has its lobby, the auto manufacturers theirs. Why not a People's Lobby? Californians have already created one, which is now pushing in Sacramento for a referendum "to make the polluters pay." The Environmental Defense League, geared primarily to the court system, is also defending the environment in Congress. The Sierra Club has already lost its tax-exempt status for being too political, and a number of the older conservation groups are pushing new, streamlined legislation. The strategy seems to be paying off, winning victories here and there. Most of the victories, however, merely strengthen the regulatory agencies, which, after public vigilance peters out, will become tools of the big corporations.

Where boycotts and stockholder strategies simply fail, the interest group politics may lead the ecology movement off the edge of a very well-conserved cliff. Eco-catastrophe threatens to kill us all—and Mother Nature, too. But to engage in the give-and-take of interest group politics, the ecologists must grant serious consideration to and must compromise with the oil interests, auto manufacturers and other powerful business groups. Standard Oil gets Indonesia only if they will market that country's prized sulphur-free oil here; the auto makers can keep producing their one-man-one-car civilization in return for making additional profit (and apparent compromise) on smog control. The world is dying: write your congressman today.

From lobbying, the eco-groups will move into the nearest election, trying to put Paul Ehrlich or David Brower in office. But elections aren't won on single issues. Allies must be wooed, coalitions built. Already parochial and out of sympathy with the blacks and other out-groups, the environmentalists, anxious to infiltrate the electoral system, will become even more respectable and more careful to avoid contamination by "extreme" positions or people. They will become further compartmentalized and will be at dead center, sacrificing even those of their own who refuse to compromise.

Avoiding "politics," the ecologists have taken up the old liberal shuck. Give equal freedom to aristocrats and the people, to bosses and workers, to landlords and tenants, and let both sides win. The scheme, of course, overlooks the one-sided distribution of resources, money and media-power. Some "reformers" will have all they need, but their solution, which will become *the* solution, is itself a good part of the problem. Profit-seekers and growth-mongers can't co-exist with Mother Nature and her fragile children without doing them irreparable harm.

To save any semblance of democracy, a decent relationship to the environment and perhaps the environment itself—ecology, the "in" movement, must become a movement of the outs. It must be committed to a long-term militant fight on more clearly understood grounds—its *own* grounds. That too might be impossible. But, as Eugene V. Debs once observed, it's a lot better to fight for what you want and not get it, than to fight for—and get—what you don't want.

Washington—(UPI)—Warning of possible "ecological disaster," President Nixon sent Congress an unprecedented report Monday calling for sweeping changes in American life to protect mankind against its own assaults on the land, air and water.

"We must seek nothing less than a basic reform in the way our society looks at problems and makes decisions," Nixon said in his message forewarding the 326-page report by the White House Council of Environmental Quality. ". . . in dealing with the environment we must learn not how to master nature but how to master ourselves, our institutions and our technology."

"Nixon Warns U.S. Life Style Must Change," *The Denver Post* (May 10, 1970).

They are playing a game. They are playing at not
playing a game. If I show them I see they are, I
shall break the rules and they will punish me.
I must play their game, of not seeing I see the game.

STRANGERS IN PARADISE

Philip E. Slater

We need now to consider seriously what the role of those over thirty is to be during the transition to and emergence of the new culture. Many will of course simply oppose it, with varying degrees of violence. A few will greet it with a sense of liberation, finding in it an answer they have long sought, but will experience a sense of awkwardness in trying to relate themselves to what has been so noisily appropriated by the young. Many more will be tormented with ambivalence, repelled by the new culture but disillusioned by the old.

It is to this latter group that what follows is addressed, for I do not believe that a successful transition can be made without their participation. If the issue is left to generational confrontation, with new-culture adherents attempting simply to push their elders out of the way and into the grave, the results will probably be catastrophic. The old culture will not simply fall of its own weight. It is not rotten but wildly malfunctioning, not weak and failing but strong and demented, not a sick old horse but a healthy runaway. It no longer performs its fundamental task of satisfying the needs of its adherents, but it still performs the task of feeding and perpetuating itself. Nor do the young have the knowledge and skill successfully to dismantle it. If the matter is left to the collision of generational change it seems to me inevitable that a radical-right revolution will occur as a last-ditch effort to stave off change.

Only those who have participated fully in the old culture can prevent this. Only they can dismantle the old culture without calamity. Furthermore, no revolution produces total change—much of the old machinery is retained more or less intact. Those intimate with the machinery are in the best position to facilitate the retooling and redirection.

But why should they? Why should they tear down what they have built? What place is there for them in the new culture? The new culture is contemptuous of age and rejects most of the values by which moderates have ordered their lives. Yet it must be remembered that the contempt for age and tradition, the worship of modernity, is not intrinsically a new-culture trait but a foundationstone of a technology-dominated culture. It is the old culture that systematically invalidates learning and experience, that worships innovation and turns its back on the past, on familial and community ties. The new culture is preoccupied with tradition, with community, with relationships—with many things that would reinstate the validity of accumulated wisdom. Social change is replete with paradox, and one of the most striking is the fact that the old culture worships novelty, while the new would resuscitate a more tradition-oriented way of life. The rhetoric of short-run goals, in which the young shout down the present and shout up the future, masks the fact that in the long run there is more room for the aged in the new culture than in the old. This is something about which new-culture adherents, however, are also confused, and old-culture participants will have much to do to stake out a rightful place for age in the new culture. If they fail the new culture will be corrupted into a reactionary parody of itself.

My main argument for rejecting the old culture is that it has been unable to keep any of the promises that have sustained it for so long, and as it struggles more and more violently to maintain itself, it is less and less able to hide its fundamental antipathy to human life and human satisfaction. It spends hundreds of billions of dollars to find ways of killing more efficiently, but almost nothing to enhance the joys of living. Against those who sought to humanize their physical environment in Berkeley the forces of "law and order" used a poison gas outlawed by the Geneva Conventions. The old culture is unable to stop killing people—deliberately in the case of those who oppose it, with bureaucratic indifference in the case of those who obey its dictates or consume its products trustingly. However familiar and comfortable it may seem, the old culture is threatening to kill us, like a trusted relative gone berserk so gradually that we are able to pretend to ourselves he has not changed.

But what can we cling to—what stability is there in our chaotic environment if we abandon the premises on which the old culture is based? To this I would answer that it is precisely these premises that have generated our chaotic environment. I recognize the desperate longing in America for stability, for some fixed reference point when all else is swirling about in endless flux. But to cling to old-culture premises is the act of a hopeless addict, who, when his increasingly expensive habit has destroyed everything else in his life, embraces his destroyer more fervently than ever. The radical change I am suggesting here is only the reinstatement of stability itself. It may appear highly unappealing, like all cold-turkey cures, but nothing else will stop the spiraling disruption to which our old-culture premises have brought us.

"As the addict's tolerance for drugs increases, his demand for drugs rises, and the cost of his habit grows." Richard Nixon, 7–15–69.

Reprinted by permission from The Boston Globe.

I am arguing, in other words, for a reversal of our old pattern of technological radicalism and social conservatism. Like most old-culture premises this is built upon a self-deception: we pretend that through it we actually achieve social stability—that technological change can be confined within its own sphere. Yet obviously this is not so. Technological instability creates social instability as well, and we lose both ways. Radical social change *has* occurred within the old culture, but unplanned and unheralded. The changes advocated by the new culture are changes that at least some people desire. The changes that have occurred under the old culture were desired by no one. They were not even foreseen. They just happened, and people tried to build a social structure around them; but it has always been a little like building sand castles in heavy surf and we have become a dangerously irritable people in the attempt. We have given technology carte blanche, much in the way Congress has always, in the past, given automatic approval to defense budgets, resulting in the most gigantic graft in history.

How long is it since anyone has said: "this is a pernicious invention, which will bring more misery than happiness to mankind"? Such comments occur only in horror and science-fiction films, and even there, in the face of the most calamitous outcomes that jaded and overtaxed brains can devise, the audience often feels a twinge of discomfort over the burning laboratory or the lost secret. Yet who would dare to defend even a small fraction of the technological innovations of the past century in terms of human satisfaction? The problem is that technology, industrialism, and capitalism have always been evaluated in their own terms. But it is absurd to evaluate capitalism in terms of the wealth it produces, or technology in terms of the inventions it generates, just as it would be absurd for a subway system to evaluate its service in terms of the number of tokens it manufactured. We need to find ways of appraising these systems in terms of criteria that are truly independent of the systems themselves. We need to develop a human-value index—a criterion that assesses the ultimate worth of an invention or a system or a product in terms of its total impact on human life, in terms of ends rather than means. We would then evaluate the achievements of medicine not in terms of man-hours of prolonged (and often comatose) life, or the volume of drugs sold, but in terms of the overall increase (or decrease) in human beings feeling healthy. We would evaluate city planning and housing programs not in terms of the number of bodies incarcerated in a given location, or the number of millions given to contractors, but in terms of the extent to which people take joy in their surroundings. We would evaluate the worth of an industrial firm not in terms of the money made or the number of widgets manufactured or sold, or how distended the organization has become, but in terms of how much pleasure or satisfaction has been given to people. It is not without significance that we tend to appraise a nation today in terms of its gross national product—a phrase whose connotations speak for themselves.

The problem is particularly acute in the case of technology. Freud suggested forty years ago that the much-touted benefits of technology were "cheap pleasures," equivalent to the enjoyment obtained by "sticking one's bare leg outside the bedclothes on a cold winter's night and then drawing it in again." "If there were no railway to make light of distances," he pointed out, "my child would never have left home and I should not need the telephone to hear his voice." Each technological "advance" is heralded as one that will solve problems created by its predecessors. None of them have done so, however, but have merely created new ones. Heroin was first introduced into this country as a heaven-sent cure for morphine addicts, and this is the model followed by technological "progress." We have been continually misled into supporting a larger and larger technological habit.

Lest I be accused of exaggeration, let me quote from a recent newspaper article: "How would you like to have your very own flying saucer? One that you could park in the garage, take off and land in your own driveway or office parking lot. . . . Within the new few years you may own and fly such an unusual aircraft and consider it as common as driving the family automobile. . . ." The writer goes on to describe a newly invented vertical-takeoff aircraft which will cost no more to own and operate than a sports car and is just as easy to drive. After an enthusiastic description of the design of the craft he attributes its development to the inventor's "concern for the fate of the motorist," citing the inability of the highways and city streets to handle the increasing number of automobiles. The inventor claims that his saucer "will help solve some of the big city traffic problems"!

The inventor is so confident of the public's groveling submission to every technological command that he does not even bother to defend this outlandish statement. Indeed, it is clear that he does not believe it himself, since he brazenly predicts that every family in the future will own a car *and* a saucer. He even acknowledges rather flippantly that air traffic might become a difficulty, but suggests that "these are not his problems," since he is "only the inventor."[1] He goes on to note that his invention would be useful in military operations (such as machine-gunning oriental farmers and gassing students, functions now performed by the helicopter) and in spraying poisons on our crops.

How can we account for the lack of public resistance to this arrogance? Why does the consumer abjectly comply with every technological whim, to the point where the seller scarcely bothers to justify it, or does so with tongue in cheek? Is the man in the street so punchdrunk with technological propaganda that he can conceive of the saucer as a solution to *any* problem? How can he greet with anything but horror an invention that will blot out the sky, increase a noise level which is already intense to unbearable levels, pollute the air further, facilitate crime immeasurably, and cause hundreds of thousands of horrible accidents (translating our highway death toll to the saucer domain requires the addition of bystanders, walking about the city, sitting in their yards, sleeping in their beds, or strolling in the park) each year? Is the American public really so insane or obtuse as to relish the prospect of the sky being as filled with motorized vehicles as the ground is now?

One reason for this docility is that Americans are trained by advertising media to identify immediately with the person who actually uses the new product. When he thinks of a saucer the American imagines himself inside it, flying about and having fun. He does not think of himself trying to sleep and having other Americans roaring by his window. Nor does he think of himself

[1] One is reminded of Tom Lehrer's brilliant song about the rocket scientist:

> *"Once they* [*the rockets*] *are up who cares where they come down:*
> *That's not my department," says Werner Von Braun.*

The Nuremberg and Eichmann trials were attempts to reverse the general rule that those who kill or make wretched a single person are severely punished, while those (heads of state, inventors, weapons manufacturers) who are responsible for the death, mutilation, or general wretchedness of thousands or millions are generally rewarded with fame, riches, and prizes. The old culture's rules speak very clearly: if you are going to rob, rob big; if you are going to kill, kill big.

trying to enjoy peace and quiet in the country with other Americans flying above. Nor does he even think of other Americans accompanying him in his flight and colliding with him as they all crowd into the city. The American in fact never thinks of other Americans at all—it is his most characteristic trait that he imagines himself to be alone on the continent.

Furthermore, Americans are always hung over from some blow dealt them by their technological environment and are always looking for a fix—for some pleasurable escape from what technology has itself created. The automobile, for example, did more than anything else to destroy community life in America. It segmented the various parts of the community and scattered them about so that they became unfamiliar with one another. It isolated travelers and decoordinated the movement of people from one place to another. It isolated and shrank living units to the point where the skills involved in informal cooperation among large groups of people atrophied and were lost. As the community became a less and less satisfying and pleasurable place to be, people more and more took to their automobiles as an escape from it. This in turn crowded the roads more which generated more road-building which destroyed more communities, and so on.

The saucers will simply extend this process further. People will take to their saucers to escape the hell of a saucer-filled environment, and the more they do the more unbearable that hell will become. Each new invention is itself a refuge from the misery it creates—a new hero, a new heroin.

How far can it go? What new inventions will be offered the staggering American to help him blow up his life? Will he finally flee to outer space, leaving the nest he has so industriously fouled behind him forever? Can he really find some means to propel himself so fast that he will escape his own inventive destructiveness? Is the man in orbit—the true Nowhere Man, whirling about in his metal womb unable to encounter anyone or anything—the destiny of all Americans?

The old-culture American needs to reconsider his commitment to technological "progress." If he fails to kick the habit he may retain his culture and lose his life. One often hears old-culture adherents saying, "what will you put in its place?" ("if you don't want me to kill you, give me something else to do"). But what does a surgeon put in the place of a malignant tumor? What does a policeman put in the place of a traffic jam? What does the Food and Drug Administration put in the place of the poisoned food it confiscates? What does a society put in the place of war when peace is declared? The question assumes, first, that what exists is safe and tolerable, and second, that social systems are mere inert mechanisms with no life of their own.

Some of this resistance comes from the old culture's dependence upon the substitutes and palliatives that its own pathology necessitates. "Without all these props, wires, crutches, and pills," its adherents ask, "how can I function? Without the 'extensions of man' I am not even a person. If you take away my gas mask, how can I breathe this polluted air? How will I get to the hospital without the automobile that had made me unfit to walk?" These questions are serious, since one cannot in fact live comfortably in our society without these props until radical changes have been made—until the diseases that necessitate these palliatives have been cured. Transitions are always fraught with risk and discomfort and insecurity, but we do not enjoy the luxury of postponement. No matter how difficult it seems to engage in radical change when all is changing anyway, the risk must be taken.

Our servility toward technology, however, is no more dangerous than our exaggerated moral commitment to the "virtues" of striving and individual achievement. The mechanized disaster that surrounds us is in no small part a result of our having deluded ourselves that a motley scramble of people trying to get the better of one another is socially useful instead of something to be avoided at all costs. It has taken us a long time to realize that seeking to surpass others might be pathological, and trying to enjoy and cooperate with others healthy, rather than the other way around.

The need to triumph over each other and the tendency to prostrate ourselves before technology are in fact closely related. We turn continually to technology to save us from having to cooperate with each other. Technology, meanwhile, serves to preserve and maintain the competitive pattern and render it ever more frantic, thus making cooperation at once more urgent and more difficult.

The essentially ridiculous premises of a competitive society are masked not only by technology, but also by the complexity of our economic system and our ability to compartmentalize our thinking about it. Since we are achievement-oriented rather than satisfaction-oriented, we always think of ourselves first as producers and only second as consumers. We talk of the "beleaguered consumer" as if this referred to some specialized group of befuddled little old ladies.

To some extent this convention is a maneuver in the American war between the sexes. Since men dominate production and women consumption, the man who produces shoddy merchandise can blame his wife for being incompetent enough to purchase it for him. Men have insulated themselves to this extent from having to deal with the consequences of their behavior.

What all of our complex language about money, markets, and profits tends to mask is the fact that ultimately, when the whole circuitous process has run its course, we are producing for our own consumption. When I exploit and manipulate others, through mass media or marketing techniques, I am also exploiting and manipulating myself. The needs I generate create a treadmill that I myself will walk upon. It is true that if I manufacture shoddy goods, create artificial needs, and sell vegetables, fruit, and meat that look well but are contaminated, I will make money. But what can I do with this money? I can buy shoddy goods and poisoned food, and satisfy ersatz needs. Our refusal to recognize our common economic destiny leads to the myth that if we all overcharge each other we will be better off.

This self-delusion is even more extraordinary when we consider issues of health and safety. Why are executives living in cities indifferent to the air pollution caused by their own factories, since it is the air they and their families breathe? Or do they all live in exurbia? And what of oil company executives: have they given up ocean beaches as places of recreation? Do they all vacation at mountain lakes? Do automobile manufacturers share a secret gas mask for filtering carbon monoxide out of the air? Are the families of canning company executives immune to botulism? Those of farming tycoons immune to insecticides?

These questions are not entirely facetious. To some extent wealth does purchase immunity from the effects of the crimes perpetrated to obtain it. But in many of the examples above the effects cannot be escaped even by those who caused them. When a tanker flushes its tanks at sea or an offshore well springs a leak the oil and tar will wash up on the most exclusive beach as well as the public one. The food or drug executive cannot tell his wife not to purchase his own product, since he knows his competitors probably share the same inadequate controls. We cannot understand the irresponsibility of corporations without recognizing that it includes and *assumes* a willingness on the part of corporate leaders to endanger themselves and their families for the short-run profit of the corporation. Men have always been able to subordinate human values to the mechanisms they create. They have the capacity to invest their libido in organizations that are then viewed as having independent life and superordinate worth. Man-as-thing (producer) can then enslave man-as-person (consumer), since his narcissism is most fully bound up in his "success" as a producer. What is overlooked, of course, is that the old-culture adherent's success as a producer may bring about his death as a consumer. Furthermore, since the Nuremberg and Eichmann trials there has been a gradual but increasing reluctance to allow individuals to hide behind the fiction of corporate responsibility.

One might object at this point that the preceding discussion places so much emphasis on individual motivation that it leaves us helpless to act. We cannot expect, after all, that everyone will arise one morning resolved simultaneously to act on different premises, and thus miraculously change the society. Competitive environments are difficult to modify, since whoever takes the first step is extremely likely to go under. "The system" is certainly a reality, no matter how much it is composed of fictions.

An action program must thus consist of two parts: (1) a long-term thrust at altering motivation and (2) a short-term attempt to redirect existing institutions. As the motivational underpinnings of the society change (and they are already changing) new institutions will emerge. But so long as the old institutions maintain their present form and thrust they will tend to overpower and corrupt the new ones. During the transitional period, then, those who seek peaceful and gradual change should work toward liberal reforms that shift the incentive *structure* as motivations in fact change.

TECHNOLOGY AND GROWTH: THE PRICE WE PAY

E. J. Mishan

If the moving spirit behind economic growth could speak, its motto would be: "Enough does not suffice." The classical description of an economic system makes sense in today's advanced economy only when stood on its head. Certainly the American economy presents us with the bizarre spectacle of growing resources pressing against limited wants. The least one can say of this phenomenon is that since consumers' wants have continuously to grow and change in response largely to the techniques of industry, the basis necessary to infer a *per capita* rise in welfare over time simply does not exist; even, that is, if human welfare were assumed to depend wholly on manufactured goods. Indeed, the rising tide of consumer goods may create as much diswelfare as welfare. The vagaries of fashion can become burdensome and the making of choices among a proliferation of models and brands can be time-consuming and disconcerting.

Once we move away from the economist's frame of reference, other factors bearing on social welfare loom large. Expanding markets in conditions of material abundance must depend upon men's dissatisfaction with their lot being perpetually renewed. Whether individual campaigns are successful or not, the institution of commercial advertising accentuates the materialistic propensities of men and promotes the view that the things which matter are the things money can buy—a view to which the young, who have plenty of need of the wherewithal if they are to avail themselves of the widely advertised opportunities for fast living and cool extravagance, are peculiarly vulnerable; a fact that explains much of their vociferous impatience and increasing violence.

. . . Rapid technical innovation may offer to add to men's material opportunities. But it does so only by increasing the risks of their obsolescence and by therefore adding to their anxieties. Swifter means of communication have had the paradoxical effect of isolating the individual: the increased speed of transport has led to more hours commuting, a result of over-response in terms of communal spread; increased automobilization is accompanied by increased family separation; more television entails less communication between neighbours and within the family. In a word, affection and intimacy have been exchanged for travel and entertainment; the substance exchanged for the shadow.

The pursuit of efficiency in general is in fact directed towards reducing

From E. J. Mishan, *Technology and Growth: The Price We Pay*. (New York: Praeger Publishers, Inc., 1970), pp. 163–165. Reprinted with permission from the publisher.

the dependence of people on one another and increasing their dependence, instead, on the machine. Indeed, by a gradual displacement of human effort from every aspect of living, technology will enable us eventually to slip through our allotted years with scarce enough sense of physical friction to be certain we are still alive.

Considerations such as these that do not lend themselves to formal treatment are crucial to the issue of human welfare. And the apparent inevitability of technological change does not thereby render them irrelevant. Death too is inevitable. Yet no one feels compelled to hurry towards it on that account. Once we descry the sort of world that technology is shaping for us, it is well worth discussing whether men are likely to find it congenial or otherwise. If, on reflection, we view the prospects with misgivings we are, at least, freed from obligation to join in the ritual incantations of our patriotic growth-men. More positively, we have an additional incentive to support a policy of reducing investment in manufactures in favour of large-scale re-planning of our cities, and of preserving, restoring, and enhancing the beauty of many of our villages, towns and resorts.

WOODEN SHIPS

David Crosby and Stephen Stills

If you smile at me, I will understand
'Cause that is something everybody everywhere does
In the same language.

I can see by your coat, my friend,
You're from the other side.
There's just one thing I've got to know,
Can you tell me please, who won?

Say, can I have some of your purple berries?
Yes, I've been eating them for six or seven weeks now,
Haven't got sick once.
Prob'ly keep us both alive.

Wooden ships on the water, very free,
Easy you know the way it's supposed to be.
Silver people on the shore line let us be.
Talkin' 'bout very free and easy.

Horror grips us as we watch you die,
All we can do is echo your anguished cries,

Stare as all human feelings die,
We are leaving, you don't need us.

Go take a sister, then, by the hand,
Lead her away from this foreign land
Far away, where we might laugh again.
We are leaving, you don't need us.

And it's a fair wind,
Blowin' warm out of the south
Over my shoulder.
Guess I'll set a course and go.

PROTECTING OUR ENVIRONMENT: MAKING PEACE WITH MAN AND NATURE

Allan Berube

Spurred by the obvious need to improve the quality of our environment many "Ecology Action" groups have sprung up across the nation and on college campuses. Some observers have thought this interest may supplant the protest movement, especially among youth groups, against the war in Vietnam. The following paper prepared by Mr. Berube of the Boston Area Ecology Action group suggests, however, a close relationship between environmental issues and those of war, poverty, population, social change and life styles. From "Ecology: Making Peace With Nature and With Each Other" by Allan Berube, A Green Paper, Feb. 6, 1970:

With all the current talk about pollution, conservation, and the deterioration of our environment, it is not always clear how pollution is related to the issues of the war, poverty, population, social change, and life style. Many government officials see young peoples' growing interest in "cleaning up environment" as a happy sign that they will be sweeping the streets and picking up garbage instead of protesting the war in Vietnam. For most government officials and much of the media, "meeting the environmental crisis" amounts to no more than demanding smog-control devices, sewage treatment plants, sanitary land fill, and air filtration systems on smokestacks.

When, however, pollution, garbage, and threatened wilderness are seen as symptoms of a larger ecological crisis, it becomes clear that "cleaning up the environment" involves revolutionary changes that would make many politicians wish young people were back on the streets only protesting the

From *Current* (April 1970), pp. 3–10. Reprinted with permission.

war. . . . [But let us] explore the implications of seeing "non-environmental" problems from an ecological perspective. If we ever end war and poverty, it may be through the back door of ecology. . . .

A strictly anti-pollution, conservation approach to the environment [suggests that] 1) environmental problems are more or less independent of one another . . . 2) pollution is a by-product of imperfect technology, and can be eliminated with more advanced technology . . . and 3) the protection of the environment is a series of defensive battles against anyone who would attack the environment.

The conservationist and anti-pollutionist approach is one of sure failure. Each year more attacks are made on the environment, exploiters gain more initiative, new and threatening technology is developed, and the same areas must be defended against new destruction. An alternative approach must be developed which places its faith in social and moral decisions instead of technological decisions, understands the inter-relatedness of all aspects of environmental destruction, and initiates a unified attack on the real sources of environmental deterioration.

The Ecological Approach

An ecological approach to environmental destruction is radically different from conservationist and anti-pollutionist approaches. It begins with an understanding of the processes, cycles, dynamics, and interactions in the natural world, and measures the behavior and values of men against these natural dynamics.

Ecology is easy to understand. It is, simply, the way living things, including man, inter-relate to one another and to the earth, air and water to support life on our planet. The root meaning of the word "ecology" is "earth household" or "housekeeping on earth." Some basic principles of ecology are:

(1) *Living things have organized themselves into ecosystems*, communities of mutual dependence and support, in which many species of plants and animals work together to insure their survival. The human body, a pond, a forest, and the planet earth are all ecosystems.

(2) *Every living thing is part of an ecosystem*, and since all ecosystems are related to each other, every living thing is somehow related to every other living thing.

(3) *Each species within an ecosystem has its own niche*, its own household. The wider the niche spectrum—the more life opportunities each species has—the more stable the ecosystem. If people could eat only lobsters, we would have been extinct long ago.

(4) *An ecosystem is also more stable if it includes a large variety of species.* A stable ecosystem preserves its balanced web of relationships from most natural threats.

(5) Some of the relationships that make species dependent on one another are: *Food chains*—grain, chickens, people. Plankton, little fish, bigger fish, pelicans. *Breathing cycles*—we breathe in oxygen and breathe out carbon dioxide; plants breathe in carbon dioxide and breathe out oxygen. *Nitrogen cycles*—we eat animals and produce wastes that bacteria break down into food for the plants that feed the animals we eat.

(6) *Nothing can be thrown away, really.* Everything has to go somewhere. When resources are extracted, shuffled, or discarded, they have an effect on the ecosystem they are taken from and on the ecosystem in which they are dumped.

(7) *Nothing is free.* Every change in an ecosystem effects another part of the ecosystem. Since the earth's resources are finite, any "progress," "development," "profit," or "expanding economy" in one area robs the resources of another area.

(8) *Human beings are not the center of the global ecosystem.* Human beings depend on a wide variety of species for survival, while almost no species depend on human beings for survival.

Every activity of man is done within the context of ecology. The demands that nature makes on the behavior of man and other species are non-negotiable. Living in accord with these ecological principles begins to insure a life of quality and meaning. Ignoring these principles is surely courting extinction.

Yet our life styles, our cultural and religious values, our industries, our economic expansion and population growth are in blatant defiance of these ecological laws. We throw anything into our garbage and down our drains. We see our relationships with nature and with each other as a never ending battle—we feel we must compete with each other and conquer nature. Our industries pour tons of poisons into whatever body of water they can find nearby. Our demand for endless economic growth, for a larger gross national product each year, results in mountains of garbage, cavities in the earth, and the permanent exhaustion of much of the earth's irreplaceable resources. Our unprecedented population growth—the global population will double in the next thirty years—will make even major attempts at solutions seem insignificant.

Horror stories about our present abuse of the planet could be listed for pages. But what is most important is that we feel the urgency to develop an ecological awareness and strategy, and begin acting to reverse this destruction of the life support systems of the planet. . . .

Ecology and Automobiles

Here, for example, is an excerpt from a paper written by a radical ecology group called "SURVIVAL?". It begins with air pollution, and is a good illustration of the kind of wholistic thinking that comes from an ecological awareness. Compare this approach with the band-aid anti-pollutionist approach to air pollution.

"Conservation proposals view air pollution primarily as an imperfection in automotive technology and therefore argue for a rationalization of that technology. This approach however overlooks the total impact of the automobile upon the environment—upon our visual and audial environments, upon our physical fitness, our use of space, upon our social relations, etc. The phenomenon of nightmarish traffic jams so common today and the consumption by automotive technology of at least 50 percent of the total space of urban areas, when combined with the problems of air destruction, represent more than enough cause for abolishing the privately owned and operated automobile. Improvements of the efficiency of the internal combustion engine or development of a steam or electric propulsion unit for private automobiles can never be more than halfway measures. In fact, they may well forestall even longer the necessary transformation of our transportation system. . . .

"We have not chosen the automobile as an example of the comprehensive nature of these issues by accident. The automobile is in large measure responsible for the geographically-controlled class structure of our society—the dichotomy between center city and suburb. By the same token, it is the primary technological factor which makes possible enormous waste, imperialistic styles of consumption and the directionless programs for urban expansion and development which are rapidly devouring our best agricultural lands, huge quantities of open greenery, and destroying the cohesiveness of neighborhoods and towns. De-automobilization ultimately means altering the structure of our everyday lives, reconstructing our society on a qualitatively different scale, with decentralized urban communities instead of sprawling characterless urban massifications—communities integrated into the ecology of their regions, dependent upon harmony with nature, instead of totally disfiguring and dominating nature with glass, asphalt, concrete and steel. Thus we would in fact have to re-think our basic concepts of transportation, urban living, political liberty, geographical mobility, and even our philosophical notions of time and space and personal identity."

When one approaches seemingly independent problems, such as air pollution, electric power, packaging, the SST, underground nuclear testing in Alaska, from an ecological perspective, the relationships of the problems to each other and to our values, life styles, expanding economy and population growth become clearer. It is important that more people become aware of and explore these interrelationships as a first step toward understanding our total ecosystem and as a basis for ecology actions.

Ecology people are now working out what shape and style their actions will take. Ecology actions so far have had elements of festivity and celebration, guerrilla theater, direct action, sabotage, and disruption. Some are symbolic and educational, some are beginnings of a change in life style, others are direct actions and disruptions that deal with the polluters and the pollution "regulation" agencies themselves. . . .

Ecology Actions

Berkeley Ecology Action held a mock funeral procession for the internal combustion engine. The engine, which came from a working Rambler, was carried in a casket and buried at the end of the procession. "Bury the smog-makers before they bury us!" . . .

In Boston, during recent air pollution hearings, over one hundred people marched in a clean air parade, which included balloons, gas masks, and a drum and kazoo corps, and went from the State House to the downtown headquarters of Boston Edison. Signs said "Polluters must Pay!", "If you're not a part of the solution, you're part of the pollution!", etc. The purpose of the parade was to award the "First Blue Ribbon Polluter Award" to the electric utility. At their headquarters an elaborate ceremony was held, a citation read, and a vice-president came down to accept the award. He claimed the award was both unfair and unjust, and passed out copies of Boston Edison policy on air pollution in embossed folders. The folders were returned to him on the spot for recycling.

Guerrilla theater groups have begun in several areas. Traffic Jam Rescue Squads, clad in white coats and wearing gas masks, circulate through traffic jams, talking to drivers and passing out leaflets about the inadequacies of an automobile-oriented transportation system and the need for cheap and efficient mass transit. Air Pollution Rescue Squads give air pollution victims artificial respiration and oxygen on downtown sidewalks. A mock funeral was held for the Don River in Toronto.

Boston Ecology Action is beginning an Ecology Food Store in which biodegradable soap and organic food will be sold only in returnable containers and minimal packaging. The store will be non-profit and run cooperatively. A Household Ecology Counseling Service will operate out of the store, offering free advice on how to reduce personal garbage, decrease water consumption, recycle paper, etc.

Recycling Waste

In many areas people are beginning to return all bottles and cans, whether returnable or not, to supermarkets. Paper and plastic packaging is also returned, and the store managers are asked to return it all to the manufacturers to be recycled.

Groups in several cities are working to make legal the distribution of all birth control information and methods to anyone regardless of age, marital status, or sex; to legalize pregnancy termination upon demand and under safe conditions; to legitimize non-nuclear families to enable childless or unmarried adults to care for or adopt children; to legalize alternative marriage relationships which may produce fewer children; to end all repressive legislation concerning sexual behavior between and among consenting persons; and to create alternatives for women so they can have meaningful lives without being mothers or housewives.

This spring Ecology Walks will begin in several parts of the country. Each walk will last for several weeks. Some of the reasons for the walks are to gain a physical sense of one's regional ecology, and to experience one's self as a part of that ecology, to meet people, to hold ecology festivals and celebrations and programs, and to do direct actions at ecological disaster areas: sites of nuclear power plants, proposed highway routes, polluted rivers, auto junk yards, marsh fills, etc.

Getting the Message

Most of these actions are not single-issue actions. Ecology actions usually make clear the source and context of a problem, and suggest in the style of the action the changes that are necessary to solve the problem. People picketing the opening of the International Auto Show (renamed the International Pollution Show) arrived by subway, by bicycle, on foot, and other forms of non-polluting locomotion. People who would never protest the war in Vietnam are willing to return all their packaging to supermarkets and to give up driving their cars. Many of these people would never even join a group, but are willing to begin changes in their lives. When one begins changing one's life style, even in the smallest ways and with the simplest awareness of ecology, one soon realizes how few meaningful, ecological alternatives (organic food, non-polluting yet convenient transportation, etc.) can be offered by our present system. Hopefully the awareness which follows from small actions will be a key to rapid social, economic and cultural change.

As our economy expands and our population grows and our faith in technology becomes near absolute, the side-effects of our "normal, necessary activities" become disasters. War is one of our "normal, necessary activities." Our weapons are now so "technologically advanced" that any of a number of them could destroy the ecosystems of whole continents if not the whole planet. The ecological destruction following a nuclear or biological war, even if millions of people survive, would be total. . . . Even if these weapons are never used, their testing, such as the underground explosion of a 2 megaton ABM warhead now scheduled for the Aleutian Islands, risks earthquakes, tidal waves, and contamination of air, sea water, and groundwater as possible but apparently acceptable side-effects. A vast underground grid, covering and disrupting several counties in northern Wisconsin, will be installed as part of our missile communications system. Even non-nuclear war—the saturation bombing, forced urbanization, rapid industrialization, paving, and defoliation in Vietnam—is becoming a conscious effort to destroy the ecology of the "enemy country."

Carrying Pollution Abroad

The addiction to economic expansion and uncontrolled technology, an addiction shared by most "over-developed" countries, has led to the space race and the race to "develop underdeveloped countries," or, in other words, to make "underdeveloped countries" extensions of the social and economic systems of the more advanced countries. For instance, an American diplomat, speaking about Laos, was recently quoted as saying, "To make progress in this country, it is necessary to level everything. The inhabitants must go back to zero, lose their traditional culture, for it blocks everything." DDT has been exported to the "underdeveloped" countries by the major powers in such quantities that DDT residues can be found in almost every living creature, body of water, and area of topsoil on the planet. Little research has been done to develop less catastrophic ways of controlling malaria and other diseases. Such international ventures as the Aswan Dam and the Mekong River Project are threatening to or have already disrupted the ecology of whole regions. . . .

These "unforeseen international ecological boomerangs" are not a series of blunders or mistakes but are the necessary ends of political and economic systems that have their security totally dependent on endless growth and expansion. These systems are forever looking for new markets, new consumers, new resources. If overpopulation is measured in terms of the destructive impact of a given population on its environment, the United States, with about six percent of the world's population and using up more than 60 percent of the earth's nonreplaceable resources, is the most overpopulated nation in the world. If our economy continues to expand, world population growth could be stabilized and we would still find that we are on the verge of using up all the nonreplaceable living and non-living resources in order to maintain economic security. This squandering of world resources is a joy ride that cannot last for many more years. . . .

It is becoming clear that we must work towards zero population growth and then a reduction in population growth, zero GNP growth and then a reduction in GNP, an end to economic exploitation, economic and political decentralization, and a redistribution of wealth and resources. . . .

The need for rapid ecological change is also closely related to the struggle of oppressed people for their own liberation. The Vietnamese people must be allowed to restore their culture and their former relationship to their land which, before the saturation bombings, napalming, forced urbanization, and massive defoliation, were ecologically sound. The U.S. Government and American industries must return to the American Indians all the land, water, and hunting and fishing rights that were stolen from them. Black people must be supported in their struggle to create communities and environments which they can relate to and which they can have creative control over: communities that are free of rats and roaches and the dangerous poisons used to kill them, communities that are free of lead poisoning and garbage, communities that provide adequate and humane housing without overcrowding, plenty of parks, easy access to cheap mass transit, communities that are controlled by the residents, not by absentee landlords, absentee polluters or outside police forces. Women must continue and gain support for their struggle to free themselves from the restricting and degrading roles of baby-producer, sex-object, housekeeper, and mindless consumer. Precautions must be made against those who will present subtle forms of genocide as ways to stabilize world population, against those who would place the burden of a stabilizing economy on the poor instead of on the rich, and against those who would have the consumers, rather than the polluters themselves, pay for clean air and water.

Toward New Life Styles

Ecology is inherently radical (i.e., "having roots"), and, while it points to fundamental changes in our economic, social, and political systems, it also points to changes in the quality of our lives and our sense of community. What does it mean to be alive? Does it mean increasing our control over other people and nature itself, an endless ego-trip? Do we have to specialize our activities and concerns—whether in offices, families, or universities—to the point of losing our perspective, our sense of wholeness, our wonder? Can we renew our relationships with each other and nature with a feeling of mutual respect, equality, interdependence? Are we willing to drop out of or begin radically transforming a way of life and a system that is oriented towards death, specialization, alienation, greed, manipulation, exclusion, and competition? Can we accept changes in our society—smaller families, living arrangements different from the customary marriage and nuclear family, changed moral codes which would accommodate the sex needs of as yet unmarried young people, availability of birth control information and pregnancy termination by anyone upon requrest that would make zero population growth, or negative population growth, possible? Do we have enough courage to lead lives of simplicity (not asceticism), celebration, and sharing? Are we willing to "take time" to get our own heads together, even if it means neglecting important political or movement work? Are we able to free ourselves from habits of ownership, property, acquisition? Can we begin caring about what food we put into our bodies? Are we able to begin moving our bodies freely over the earth without the aid of engines (can we learn to walk long distances, noticing and touching what we pass)? Can we begin holding each other without being embarrassed? Ecology is the way all living things, including men and women and children, commune together with the air, earth and water to support life on earth.

PART TWO
POVERTY

I am hurting because
I am hungry
I am sweating & eyes
are pissing down
my hungry face &
I am feeling sad
I am so hungry
I am nervous &
angry with all
I am hungry &
what I need
is someone
to feed me
some love

Ted Joans

We have examined the conventional wisdom that pollution is a by-product of technical progress and can be solved by technical know-how, given adequate time, investment, and skill. Part One argued that this kind of analysis is superficial, for invariably the causes of pollution are the aspirations, values, and social arrangements that most Americans have come to regard as essential to their way of life and to social progress. Pollution is at base a social problem, and its solution will therefore require social change.

A parallel analysis can be extended to poverty, a problem few of us regard as merely technical. Both the man on the street and the statesman agree that poverty is a condition of human misery. While we may put a price tag on cleansing polluted air or saving a dying stream, our wisdom holds that a human life is of incomparable value. How can we explain our affluent society's collective inaction in the face of starvation, rat-bitten children, miseducated youth, and ghettoized colonies of wasted human beings? Thus we are caught up in an inhumane paradox.

Part Two offers a framework through which the reader can begin to answer why such paradoxes exist. The analysis, however, raises other questions that illustrate the complexities involved in social changes designed to improve the quality of life for all Americans. Chapter 7 illustrates that the paradox of American poverty is due in some important way to three interrelated conditions: (1) the existence of widespread affluence; (2) a social, economic, political, and spatial structure that makes the poor invisible; and (3) pervasive myths regarding the causes of poverty. These myths persist because such experience is foreign to most Americans, but, as Harrington reminds us in *The Other America*, it is common to 40 to 50 million Americans who are "fat with hunger (for that is what cheap foods do) . . . without adequate housing and education and medical care." These people make up what Harrington calls the "other America" because they are invisible to those living in the "familiar America."

But how can 50 million impoverished people be hidden and invisible? The purpose of the materials in Part Two is to show how the social, political, spatial, and economic structures of American society hide the poor. The reader is asked to analyze the processes that lead to structures that separate people into different regions (city versus suburb), neighborhoods (middle-class Negro versus poor Black ghetto), social groups (country club versus street-corner society). Indeed, it is these processes that make poverty invisible to all but the poor themselves; we don't see or touch people who suffer in poverty, so we can believe the myths that are perpetuated in society regarding its causes. Thus, because of our widespread affluence and our social structure, we must press our imagination to experience the feeling of poverty. If necessary, vicarious experience can be called upon, such as that evoked in the following personal account from Sexton:

> Living the way I live in this slum house is miserable. I don't wish nobody to live the way I live. Inside a house in this condition, no steam, no hot water, ceiling falling on you, running water from the ceiling, to go to the bathroom you have to use an umbrella, rats everywhere. . . .

Chapter 8 shows the difficulty in discovering the invisible poor as well as the causes of their poverty. Included are several attempts to analyze the problem so as to prescribe "solutions." Although these analyses arrive at somewhat divergent conclusions, they are, for the most part, technical. Thus, they suggest (1) poverty is caused or maintained by unemployment, low productivity, and discrimination (Singell); (2) some poverty is caused by behavior arising out of business interests that rape the land, natural resources, and impoverish the people because it is profitable (Caudill); (3) that the extent and severity of poverty has lessened in the last several decades (Thernstrom).

While there are many questions that must be confronted in these analyses, a fundamental one is how to examine the problem of poverty. Because the poor are hidden to society, they are also hidden to the social analyst. Study of the subjective conditions of poverty may be made difficult by feelings of guilt, hatred, misunderstanding, and fear on the part of the observer. Hence, "progress," "reform," and "improvement," on the one hand, and "worsening conditions," "crisis proportions," and "increased deprivation," on the other, can be used to describe the same data. This dilemma has resulted in efforts to "objectively" and quantitatively define poverty according to various criteria (annual family income of less than $3000, the number of unskilled in the work force, the lowest decile in the income distribution), and then to analyze its causes—even though it may be recognized as a largely nontechnical problem. The danger in this approach is, however, that it perpetuates a situation described by Drew in which "Decent men could sit and discuss statistical reliability and administrative neatness and the importance of good precedents while people went hungry."

In studying Part Two, consider the alternative approaches to discovering poverty and make a judgment regarding their reliability and usefulness in making decisions to improve the quality of life in America. In each case, ask yourself to what extent your judgment is tempered by your past thinking, education, social role, and self-interest.

Chapter 9 argues that poverty is primarily a social, not a technical nor an individual problem. Thus the solution requires social change that must begin with the rehumanization of society in general and our concept of the poor in particular. This is required because, as Baldwin says, "it is a terrible, an inexorable, law that one cannot deny the humanity of another without diminishing one's own. . . ." But to restructure society for humanization requires an understanding of how the social, political, and economic development of the society produced the current condition of separation and to be aware of the obstacles to change. A major barrier to change that should be considered before proceeding to Chapter 10 is highlighted in the following juxtaposition: (1) "All white Americans gain some privileges and advantages from the colonization of Black communities. . . ." (see Blauner), and (2) "The program simply did not meet the needs of these young men. In fact, it was not really meant to. The Great Society was trying to 'run a game' on black youth" (see Wellman). These statements relate in intricate and confusing ways to Friedman's assertion that if the programs "for the poor" were abolished and outright cash grants were given, the incomes of the poorest families would be $6000 per year.

This leads to the most difficult question of all: To what extent does poverty persist in the affluent society due to our need for the poor? Answering this question requires not only individual honesty, but an ability to look at the social structure from more than one point of view. Hence, Chapter 10 summarizes and organizes major items presented earlier as a basis for considering questions such as: (1) What is the size, nature, and "cause" of poverty in America, and how has each of us gained our information? (Review Sexton, Zeitlin, Singell, Baldwin, Wellman, and then read Coser) (2) What and who must change if poverty is to be eliminated? In thinking about this, consider this: How would the capitalist be affected if there were no workers, the social worker if there were no poor clients, the college professor if there were no poverty research grants, the middle-class college student if there were no less-educated individuals? (Review Caudill, Thernstrom, Lumer, and then read Walinsky) (3) What are the steps society must take to move in the direction of solving the problem of poverty, and what are the steps each of us must take?

We must also try to resolve how much of the real problem of poverty arises out of the fact that though 40 to 50 million people are poor, they still represent a minority in American society. The overwhelming majority of the society is not poor, and this condition is unique in human history. While numerous factors undoubtedly account for this remarkable fact, some important ones are the acceptance of an individualistic and competitive ethic and the cherishing of ever higher levels of consumption and technology. Clearly, these factors are also important elements in the poverty problem. How would your strategy for solving the problem of poverty be affected by these (and other) factors you consider so important to the high standard of living in the United States?

7 Somebody's gotta be on the bottom

SIXTEEN TONS

Merle Travis

Now some people say a man's made out of mud,
But a poor man's made out of muscle and blood,
Muscle and blood, skin and bones,
A mind that's weak and a back that's strong.

CHORUS:
You load sixteen tons and what do you get?
Another day older and deeper in debt.
Saint Peter, don't you call me 'cause I can't go,
I owe my soul to the company store.

I was born one mornin' when the sun didn't shine,
I picked up my shovel and I walked to the mine,
I loaded sixteen tons of number nine coal
And the strawboss hollered, "Well, damn my soul!" (CHO.)

Now when you see me comin', you better step aside,
Another man didn't and another man died;
I've got a fist of iron and a fist of steel
If the right one don't get you, the left one will. (CHO.)

RENT STRIKE

Patricia C. Sexton

My days are swifter than a weaver's shuttle, and are spent without hope.
Job

It was natural that the rent strike, one of the most potent (if controversial and short-lived) direct action devices New York's poor have found, should have begun inside East Harlem.

The Community Council on Housing, led by Jesse Gray, had its offices in East Harlem. One of the first buildings struck was 16 East 117 Street, in East Harlem, owned by a matron living in Teaneck, New Jersey. After the strike began in this building, the landlord tried to dispossess the tenants. The court, inspecting building violations, ordered the rent paid to the court rather than the landlord. Later the city started receivership proceedings, and the rent money was returned to the tenants.

Mrs. Inocencia Flores, Apartment 3W, was among the striking tenants. Born in Puerto Rico, where she attended high school and for a time the University of Puerto Rico, she came to New York in 1944 and began work in the garment district, trimming and making clothes. At the time of the strike, she had four children, was on relief, and separated from her husband.

Her diary, kept while her building was on strike, tells part of her story.[1]

> *Wednesday, Feb. 5:* I got up at 6:45. The first thing to do was light the oven. The boiler was broke so not getting the heat. All the tenants together bought the oil. We give $7.50 for each tenant. But the boiler old and many things we don't know about the pipes, so one of the men next door who used to be superintendent is trying to fix. I make the breakfast for the three children who go to school. I give them orange juice, oatmeal, scrambled eggs, and Ovaltine. They have lunch in school and sometimes they don't like the food and won't eat, so I say you have a good breakfast. Miss Christine Washington stick her head in at 7:30 and say she go to work. I used to live on ground floor and she was all the time trying to get me move to third floor next door to her because this place vacant and the junkies use it and she scared the junkies break the wall to get into her place and steal everything because she live alone and go to work.

[1] Francis Sugrue, "Diary of a Rent Striker," *New York Herald Tribune*, February 16, 1964, p. 28. © 1964, New York Herald Tribune Inc.

I'm glad I come up here to live because the rats so big downstairs. We all say the "rats is big as cats." I had a baseball bat for the rats. It's lucky me and the children never got bit. The children go to school and I clean the house and empty the pan in the bathroom that catches the water dripping from pipe in the big hole in the ceiling. You have to carry umbrella to the bathroom sometimes. I go to the laundry place this afternoon and I wash again on Saturday because I change my kids clothes every day because I don't want them dirty to attract the rats.

At 12:15 I am fixing lunch for myself and the little one, Tom. I make for him two soft-boiled eggs and fried potatoes. He likes catsup and he has one slice of spam and a cup of milk. I have some spam for myself and salad because I only drink a cup of coffee at breakfast because I'm getting too fat. I used to work in the shipping department of bathing suits and the boss used to tell me to model for the buyers. I was a model, but now I'm too fat.

After I go out to a rent strike meeting at night, I come home and the women tell me that five policemen came and broke down the door of the vacant apartment of the ground floor where we have meetings for the tenants in our building. They come looking for something—maybe junkies, but we got nothing in there only paper and some chairs and tables. They knocked them all over. The women heard the policemen laughing. When I come up to my place the children already in bed and I bathe myself and then I go to bed and read the newspaper until 11:30.

Thursday, Feb. 6: I wake up at six o'clock and I went to the kitchen to heat a bottle for my baby. When I put the light on the kitchen I yelled so loud that I don't know if I disturbed the neighbors. There was a big rat coming out from the garbage pail. He looks like a cat. I ran to my room, I called my daughter Carmen to go to the kitchen to see if the coast was clear. She's not scared of the rats. So I could go back to the kitchen to heat the bottle for my baby. Then I left the baby with a friend and went downtown.

Friday, Feb. 7: This morning I woke up a little early. The baby woke up at five o'clock. I went to the kitchen but this time I didn't see the rat.

After the girls left for school I started washing the dishes and cleaning the kitchen. I am thinking about their school. Today they ain't teaching enough. My oldest girl is 5.9 in reading. This is low level in reading. I go to school and English teacher tell me they ain't got enough books to read and that's why my daughter behind. I doesn't care about integration like that. It doesn't bother me. I agree with boycott for some reasons. To get better education and better teachers and better materials in school. I don't like putting them in buses and sending them away. I like to stay here and change the system. Some teachers has to be changed. My girl take Spanish in junior high school, and I said to her, "Tell your teacher I'm going to be in school one day to teach him Spanish because I don't know where he learns to teach Spanish but it ain't Spanish."

I'm pretty good woman. I don't bother anyone. But I got my rights. I fight for them. I don't care about jail. Jail don't scare me. If have to go to jail, I go. I didn't steal. I didn't kill nobody. There's no record for me. But if I have to go, I go.

Saturday, Feb. 8: A tenant called me and asked me what was new in the building because she works daytimes. She wanted to know about the junkies. Have they been on the top floor where the vacant apartments is? That's why I have leaking from the ceiling. The junkies on the top floor break the pipes and take the fixtures and the sink and sell them and that's where the water comes. . . . I'm not ascared of the junkies. I open the door and I see the junkies I tell them to go or I call the police. Many people scared of them, but they scared of my face. I got a baseball bat for the rats and for the junkies. I sometimes see a junkie in the hallway taking the junk and I give him a broom and say "Sweep the hall." And he does what I tell him and hand me back the broom after he sweep the hall. I'm not scared of no junkies. I know my rights and I know my self-respect. After supper I played cards (casino) for two hours with the girls and later I got dressed and I went to a party for the rent strike. This party was to get funds to the cause. I had a good time. Mr. Gray was there dancing. He was so happy.

Sunday, Feb. 9: I dressed up in a hurry to go to church. When I go to church I pray for to have better house and have a decent living. I hope He's hearing. But I don't get discouraged on Him. I have faith. I don't care how cold I am I never lose my faith. When I come out of church I was feeling so good.

Monday, Feb. 10: At 9:30 a man came to fix the rat holes. He charged me only $3. Then one of the tenants came to tell me that we only had oil for today and every tenant have to give $7.50 to send for more oil. I went to see some tenants to tell them there is no more oil. We all have to co-operate with money for the oil. It's very hard to collect because some are willing to give but others start fussing. I don't know why because is for the benefit of all, especially those with children. We have to be our own land-lord and supers. We had to be looking for the building and I tell you we doing better than if there is an owner. Later I went down in the basement with another tenant to see about the boiler, but we found it missing water in the inside and she didn't light it up and anyway there was not too much oil in it. I hope nothing bad happens, because we too had given $5 each tenant to buy some material to repair the boiler. If something happens is going to be pretty hard to make another collection.

Tuesday, Feb. 11: This morning was too cold in the house that I had to light the oven and heat hot water. We had no steam, the boiler is not running good. I feel miserable. You know when the house is cold you can't do nothing. When the girls left for school I went back to bed. I just got up at 11:30 and this house is so cold. Living in a cold apartment is terrible. I wish I could have one of those kerosene stoves to heat myself.

My living room and my room is Alaska. I'm going to heat some pea soup and make coffee. I sat down in the kitchen by the stove to read some papers and keep warm. This is terrible situation. Living the way I live in this slum house is miserable. I don't wish no body to live the way I live. Inside a house in this condition, no steam, no hot water, ceiling falling on you, running water from the ceiling, to go to the bathroom you have to use an umbrella, rats everywhere. I suggest that landlords having human being living this way instead of sending them to jail they must make them live at least a month in this same conditions, so they know the way they pile up money in a bank.

Wednesday, Feb. 12: I wake up around 5 o'clock and the first thing I did was light the oven and the heater so when the girls wake up is a little warm. I didn't call them to 11 because they didn't have to go to school. It still so cold they trembling. You feel like crying looking your children in this way.

I think if I stay a little longer in this kind of living I'm going to be dead duck. I know that to get a project you have to have somebody prominent to back you up. Many people got to the projects and they don't even need them. I had been feeling [filling] applications I don't know since when. This year I feel another one. My only weapon is my vote. This year I *don't vote* for nobody. May be my vote don't count, but don't forget if you have fourteen cent you need another penny so you take the bus or the subway. At least I clean my house and you could eat on the floor. The rest of the day I didn't do nothing. I was so mad all day long. I cooked a big pot of soup. I leave it to God to help me. I have faith in Him.

Thursday, Feb. 13: I couldn't get up this morning. The house was so cold that I came out of bed at 7:15. I heated some water I leave the oven light up all night because the heater gave up. I fixed some oatmeal, eggs and some Ovaltine for the girls. I had some coffee. I clean the house. The baby was sleeping. Later on, the inspector came. They were supposed to come to every apartment and look all violations. They knock at the door and asked if anything had been fixed. I think even the inspectors are afraid of this slum conditions thats why they didn't dare to come inside. I don't blame them. They don't want to take a rat or any bug to their houses, or get dirty in this filthy houses. My little girl come from school with Valentine she made for me. Very pretty. At 8:30 I went downstairs to a meeting we had. We discuss about why there is no heat. We agreed to give $10 to fix the boiler for the oil. A man is coming to fix it. I hope everybody give the $10 so we have some heat soon.

Friday, Feb. 14: I didn't write this about Friday in my book until this Saturday morning, because Friday night I sick and so cold I go to bed and could not write in the book. But this about Friday. I got up at five and light the oven and put some water to heat. At seven I called the two oldest girls for school. I didn't send the little one, because she was coughing too much and with a running nose. I gave some baby aspirin and I put some Vick in her nose and chest and I gave some hot tea. I leaved her in bed.

It was so cold in here that I didn't want to do nothing in the house. I fixed some soup for lunch and read for a while in the kitchen and after a while I went out and clean the hallway. I didn't mop because there was no hot water, but at least the hallway looked a little clean.

Later on I fixed dinner I was not feeling good. I had a headache and my throat hurt. I hope I do not catch a cold. I hope some day God help me and all this experience I had be restore with a very living and happiness. It is really hard to believe that this happens here in New York and richest city in the world. But such is Harlem and hope. Is this the way to live. I rather go to the Moon in the next trip.

The building at 16 East 117 Street is one of 43,000 old-law tenements in New York City, which house about 900,000 people, a population the size of Baltimore, the nation's sixth largest city. Most old-law tenements, particularly those used by generations of poor and transient tenants, are not fit to live in and not economic to renovate. On the other hand, many old buildings, brownstones, and others, are often suitable for tenants or rehabilitation. Welfare Commissioner James Dumpson has said it will take fifty years to meet the housing needs of the city's welfare population alone at present construction rates, and another 100 years to house all the poor. By then the buildings that are habitable now will be in decay.

In the building on 117 Street, decay set in after a fast shuffle of owners who didn't care and often could not be located: "The superintendent was replaced by a handy man. Then the handy man was made to be handy in so many places that he became handy in none. When the bell system failed, it was left unrepaired; when the lock was broken, the front door stood open. Tenants endured broken windows, falling plaster, peeling paint, leaking pipes, cracked sinks and toilets, clogged drains, rotten window frames, jammed doors, unlighted halls, unswept stairs, winter days and nights without heat. Then too, there were rats. Traps were set and poisons laid out, but, though some of the rats were caught and some wandered off to die in the walls, a population established itself and fattened and bred on the trash that wasn't collected and the garbage left out in the halls."

None of the many owners of the house applied to raise rents under the law that guarantees landlords a fair return of at least 6 percent on investment, plus 2 percent for depreciation. Apparently the landlords made profits in excess of this legal guarantee.

A group of enterprising women from the Women's City Club of New York, instead of folding bandages or sponsoring talks on poverty, set out to learn for themselves what the slums are like. They chose a block of relatively "good" housing in East Harlem where the "decay of completely neglected slum areas was absent." In 59 apartments they found 1,319 violations of the housing code and unattended decay everywhere.

"Impoverishment" connotes the *absolute need and necessity* of subverting *intolerable* conditions of existence, and such absolute need appears in the beginnings of all revolution against the basic social institutions.

Herbert Marcuse, *One Dimensional Man* (Boston: Beacon Press, 1964), p. 26.

THE DARK SIDE OF THE MARKETPLACE

Warren G. Magnuson and Jean Carper

. . . Persons in poverty, especially minority groups are so ignorant or leery of the law that they won't seek out legal aid, and sometimes won't even wholeheartedly cooperate when legal redress is offered to them. Neighborhood Legal Services, a nationwide network of offices, funded by the Office of Economic Opportunity, which handles cases for the indigent, reports that their lawyers have great difficulty persuading their clients, mainly members of minority groups to go to court even when their case is strong. The poor cannot conceive of getting justice from a law which has so viciously exploited them in the past.

In an eloquent statement before the National Conference on Law and Poverty held in Washington, D. C., in June 1965, Nicholas de B. Katzenbach, then Attorney General of the United States, summarized the feelings of the poor toward the law: "Too often the poor man sees the law only as something which garnishees his salary; which repossesses his refrigerator; which evicts him from his house; which cancels his welfare; which binds him to usury; or which deprives him of his liberty because he cannot afford bail. The adversary system on which our courts are based fails whenever one side goes unrepresented, and judgment is entered by default.

"Small wonder then that the poor man does not always respect law. He has little reason to believe it is his guardian; he has every reason to believe it is an instrument of the Other Society, of the well-off, of the well educated, the well dressed and the well connected. The poor man is cut off from this society and from the protection of its laws. We make him a functional outlaw. . . ." . . .

When business and government—in fact, our whole enlightened society—strain to give equal employment opportunities to the Negro, we should also be far-sighted enough to guarantee that his earnings are not stolen from him through unethical business practices and antiquated laws. If we are not, it should hardly surprise us that his resentment might provide one more bit of fuel for the riot fires. . . .

. . . [I]t seems undeniable that the scandalous gouging of minority groups by dishonest merchants and salesmen contributes to a potentially explosive situation in every ghetto in America and is one of many discontents leading to riots. This is a fact that has been too little recognized or explored.

As Caryl Warner, a Los Angeles attorney who handles cases for the poor victimized by shady selling, said right after the Watts riots: "If that committee [the Governor's Commission to investigate the riots] is interested in finding out some of the real causes of trouble, they can come to this office and read a few of my files. . . . When historians write the story of all this trouble, they're going to wonder how in hell such an incendiary element could have been so complacently accepted and overlooked."*

AMERICA

Leonard Bernstein and Stephen Sondheim

Puerto Rico, my heart's devotion,
Let it sink back in the ocean
Always the hurricanes blowing
Always the population growing
And the money owing
And the sunlight streaming
And the natives steaming
I like the island Manhattan
Smoke on your pipe and put that in.

I like to be in America
Okay by me in America
Everything free in America
For a small fee in America.

Buying a present is so nice
One look at us and they charge twice
I have my own washing machine
What will you have though to keep clean.

Skyscrapers bloom in America
Airplanes zoom in America
Industry boom in America
Twelve in a room in America.

Lots of new housing with more space
Lots of doors slamming in our face
I'll get a terrace apartment
Better get rid of your accent.

* Show in class the two-part film "The Poor Pay More."

Life can be bright in America
If you can fight in America
Life is all right in America
If you're all white in America.

Here you are free and you have pride
Long as you stay on your own side
Free to be anything you choose
Free to wait tables and shine shoes.

Everywhere grime in America
Organized crime in America
Terrible time in America
You forget I'm in America.

I think I go back to San Juan
I know a boat you can get on
Everyone there will give big cheer
Everyone there will have moved here.

A NOTE ON DEATH IN VIETNAM

Maurice Zeitlin

Men from poor families are overrepresented among troops killed in Vietnam, according to the findings [of a study] by myself and Kenneth Lutterman, with James W. Russell.

The alleged universalistic standards of the armed forces are affected by the class origins of the enlisted men and officers. Based on individual data on all 380 servicemen from Wisconsin who died in Vietnam through 1967, we found that 27.6 percent came from families classified as "poor" by official standards, in contrast to the comparable cohort figure of 12.4 percent in the population. That is, about twice as many sons of poor families die in Vietnam as would if their share of the dead were equitable or proportional. The disproportionate representation of the poor is even greater among non-officers.

Most striking is the finding that *within each economic class*—farmers, workers, and middle class—the poor are also overrepresented among the "nonpoor."

The poor are probably overrepresented among the dead in Vietnam because they are least likely to qualify for—or know of—specific types of

From *American Society, Inc., Studies of the Social Structure and Political Economy of the United States* (Chicago: Markham Publishing Co., 1970), pp. 174–175. Reprinted with permission of the author and publisher.

draft deferments, especially college deferments; the same may apply, although less so, to manual workers who are not poor compared to the nonpoor in nonmanual occupations.

Deaths in Vietnam also occur from accidents and personal illness. Separating deaths from hostile action and deaths from other causes, we found that there is a general tendency for servicemen from poor families—in all ranks combined and in all branches of the service—to be more likely to die in hostile action than their counterparts from families that are not poor. Among workers' and farmers' (though not middle-class) sons—again, with all branches and ranks combined—the servicemen from poor families are more likely than nonpoor to be killed in hostile action. When poverty level is taken into account, the differences between economic classes are not systematic. However, of all strata, poor workers have the highest proportion of deaths from hostile action. The differences in death from hostile action may occur because jobs in the armed forces carry different amounts of risk with them, and job allocation probably falls along stratification lines, the poor (and poor workers in particular) are least likely to be assigned to administrative, supply, or other less risky positions, and more likely to be exposed to hostile action and the risk of death.

THE INVISIBLE LAND

Michael Harrington

There is a familiar America. It is celebrated in speeches and advertised on television and in the magazines. It has the highest mass standard of living the world has ever known.

In the 1950s this America worried about itself, yet even its anxieties were products of abundance. The title of a brilliant book was widely misinterpreted, and the familiar America began to call itself "the affluent society." There was introspection about Madison Avenue and tail fins; there was discussion of the emotional suffering taking place in the suburbs. In all this, there was an implicit assumption that the basic grinding economic problems had been solved in the United States. In this theory the nation's problems were no longer a matter of basic human needs, of food, shelter, and clothing. Now they were seen as qualitative, a question of learning to live decently amid luxury.

While this discussion was carried on, there existed another America. In it dwelt somewhere between 40,000,000 and 50,000,000 citizens of this land. They were poor. They still are.

To be sure, the other America is not impoverished in the same sense as those poor nations where millions cling to hunger as a defense against starvation. This country has escaped such extremes. That does not change the fact that tens of millions of Americans are, at this very moment, maimed in body and spirit, existing at levels beneath those necessary for human decency. If these people are not starving, they are hungry, and sometimes fat with hunger, for that is what cheap foods do. They are without adequate housing and education and medical care.

The Government has documented what this means to the bodies of the poor. . . . But even more basic, this poverty twists and deforms the spirit. The American poor are pessimistic and defeated, and they are victimized by mental suffering to a degree unknown in Suburbia.

This book is a description of the world in which these people live; it is about the other America. Here are the unskilled workers, the migrant farm workers, the aged, the minorities, and all the others who live in the economic underworld of American life. In all this, there will be statistics, and that offers the opportunity for disagreement among honest and sincere men. I would ask the reader to respond critically to every assertion, but not to allow statistical quibbling to obscure the huge, enormous, and intolerable fact of poverty in America. For, when all is said and done, that fact is unmistakable, whatever its exact dimensions, and the truly human reaction can only be outrage. . . .

The millions who are poor in the United States tend to become increasingly invisible. Here is a great mass of people, yet it takes an effort of the intellect and will even to see them.

I discovered this personally in a curious way. After I wrote my first article on poverty in America, I had all the statistics down on paper. I had proved to my satisfaction that there were around 50,000,000 poor in this country. Yet, I realized I did not believe my own figures. The poor existed in the Government reports; they were percentages and numbers in long, close columns, but they were not part of my experience. I could prove that the other America existed, but I had never been there.

My response was not accidental. It was typical of what is happening to an entire society, and it reflects profound social changes in this nation. The other America, the America of poverty, is hidden today in a way that it never was before. Its millions are socially invisible to the rest of us. No wonder that so many misinterpreted Galbraith's title and assumed that "the affluent society" meant that everyone had a decent standard of life. This misinterpretation was true as far as the actual day-to-day lives of two-thirds of the nation were concerned. Thus, one must begin a description of the other America by understanding why we do not see it.

There are perennial reasons that make the other America an invisible land.

Poverty is often off the beaten track. It always has been. The ordinary tourist never left the main highway, and today he rides interstate turnpikes. He does not go into the valleys of Pennsylvania where the towns look like movie sets of Wales in the thirties. He does not see the company houses in rows, the rutted roads (the poor always have bad roads whether they live in the city, in towns, or on farms), and everything is black and dirty. And even if he were to pass through such a place by accident, the tourist would not meet the unemployed men in the bar or the women coming home from a runaway sweatshop.

Then, too, beauty and myths are perennial masks of poverty. The traveler comes to the Appalachians in the lovely season. He sees the hills, the streams, the foliage—but not the poor. Or perhaps he looks at a run-down mountain house and, remembering Rousseau rather than seeing with his eyes, decides that "those people" are truly fortunate to be living the way they are and that they are lucky to be exempt from the strains and tensions of the middle class. The only problem is that "those people," the quaint inhabitants of those hills, are undereducated, underprivileged, lack medical care, and are in the process of being forced from the land into a life in the cities, where they are misfits.

These are normal and obvious causes of the invisibility of the poor. They operated a generation ago; they will be functioning a generation hence. It is more important to understand that the very development of American society is creating a new kind of blindness about poverty. The poor are increasingly slipping out of the very experience and consciousness of the nation.

If the middle class never did like ugliness and poverty, it was at least aware of them. "Across the tracks" was not a very long way to go. There were forays into the slums at Christmas time; there were charitable organizations that brought contact with the poor. Occasionally, almost everyone passed through the Negro ghetto or the blocks of tenements, if only to get downtown to work or to entertainment.

Now the American city has been transformed. The poor still inhabit the miserable housing in the central area, but they are increasingly isolated from contact with, or sight of, anybody else. Middle-class women coming in from Suburbia on a rare trip may catch the merest glimpse of the other America on the way to an evening at the theater, but their children are segregated in suburban schools. The business or professional man may drive along the fringes of slums in a car or bus, but it is not an important experience to him. The failures, the unskilled, the disabled, the aged, and the minorities are right there, across the tracks, where they have always been. But hardly anyone else is.

In short, the very development of the American city has removed poverty from the living, emotional experience of millions upon millions of middle-class Americans. Living out in the suburbs, it is easy to assume that ours is, indeed, an affluent society.

This new segregation of poverty is compounded by a well-meaning ignorance. A good many concerned and sympathetic Americans are aware that there is much discussion of urban renewal. Suddenly, driving through the city, they notice that a familiar slum has been torn down and that there are towering, modern buildings where once there had been tenements or hovels. There is a warm feeling of satisfaction, of pride in the way things are working out: the poor, it is obvious, are being taken care of.

The irony in this . . . is that the truth is nearly the exact opposite to the impression. The total impact of the various housing programs in postwar America has been to squeeze more and more people into existing slums. More often than not, the modern apartment in a towering building rents at $40 a room or more. For, during the past decade and a half, there has been more subsidization of middle- and upper-income housing than there has been of housing for the poor.

Clothes make the poor invisible too: America has the best-dressed poverty the world has ever known. For a variety of reasons, the benefits of mass production have been spread much more evenly in this area than in many others. It is much easier in the United States to be decently dressed than it is to be decently housed, fed, or doctored. Even people with terribly depressed incomes can look prosperous.

This is an extremely important factor in defining our emotional and existential ignorance of poverty. In Detroit the existence of social classes became much more difficult to discern the day the companies put lockers in the plants. From that moment on, one did not see men in work clothes on the way to the factory, but citizens in slacks and white shirts. This process has been magnified with the poor throughout the country. There are tens of thousands of Americans in the big cities who are wearing shoes, perhaps even a stylishly cut suit or dress, and yet are hungry. It is not a matter of planning, though it almost seems as if the affluent society had given out costumes to the poor so that they would not offend the rest of society with the sight of rags.

Then, many of the poor are the wrong age to be seen. A good number of them (over 8,000,000) are sixty-five years of age or better; an even larger number are under eighteen. The aged members of the other America are often sick, and they cannot move. Another group of them live out their lives in loneliness and frustration: they sit in rented rooms, or else they stay close to a house in a neighborhood that has completely changed from the old days. Indeed, one of the worst aspects of poverty among the aged is that these people are out of sight and out of mind, and alone.

The young are somewhat more visible, yet they too stay close to their neighborhoods. Sometimes they advertise their poverty through a lurid tabloid story about a gang killing. But generally they do not disturb the quiet streets of the middle class.

And finally, the poor are politically invisible. It is one of the cruelest ironies of social life in advanced countries that the dispossessed at the bottom of society are unable to speak for themselves. The people of the other America do not, by far and large, belong to unions, to fraternal organizations, or to political parties. They are without lobbies of their own; they put forward no legislative program. As a group, they are atomized. They have no face; they have no voice.

Thus, there is not even a cynical political motive for caring about the poor, as in the old days. Because the slums are no longer centers of powerful political organizations, the politicians need not really care about their inhabitants. The slums are no longer visible to the middle class, so much of the idealistic urge to fight for those who need help is gone. Only the social agencies have a really direct involvement with the other America, and they are without any great political power.

To the extent that the poor have a spokesman in American life, that role is played by the labor movement. The unions have their own particular idealism, an ideology of concern. More than that, they realize that the existence of a reservoir of cheap, unorganized labor is a menace to wages and working conditions throughout the entire economy. Thus, many union legislative proposals—to extend the coverage of minimum wage and social security, to organize migrant farm laborers—articulate the needs of the poor.

That the poor are invisible is one of the most important things about them. They are not simply neglected and forgotten as in the old rhetoric of reform; what is much worse, they are not seen. . . .

Forty to 50,000,000 people are becoming increasingly invisible. That is a shocking fact. But there is a second basic irony of poverty that is equally important: if one is to make the mistake of being born poor, he should choose a time when the majority of the people are miserable too.

Poverty in the 1960s is invisible and it is new, and both these factors make it more tenacious. It is more isolated and politically powerless than ever before. It is laced with ironies, not the least of which is that many of the poor view progress upside-down, as a menace and a threat to their lives. And if the nation does not measure up to the challenge of automation, poverty in the 1960s might be on the increase. . . .

There are mighty historical and economic forces that keep the poor down; and there are human beings who help out in this grim business, many of them unwittingly. There are sociological and political reasons why poverty is not seen; and there are misconceptions and prejudices that literally blind the eyes. The latter must be understood if anyone is to make the necessary act of intellect and will so that the poor can be noticed.

Here is the most familiar version of social blindness: "The poor are that way because they are afraid of work. And anyway they all have big cars. If they were like me (or my father or my grandfather), they could pay their own way. But they prefer to live on the dole and cheat the taxpayers."

This theory, usually thought of as a virtuous and moral statement, is one of the means of making it impossible for the poor ever to pay their way. There are, one must assume, citizens of the other America who choose impoverishment out of fear of work (though, writing it down, I really do not believe it). But the real explanation of why the poor are where they are is that they made the mistake of being born to the wrong parents, in the wrong section of the country, in the wrong industry, or in the wrong racial or ethnic group. Once that mistake has been made, they could have been paragons of will and morality, but most of them would never even have had a chance to get out of the other America.

There are two important ways of saying this: The poor are caught in a vicious circle; or, The poor live in a culture of poverty.

In a sense, one might define the contemporary poor in the United States as those who, for reasons beyond their control, cannot help themselves. All the most decisive factors making for opportunity and advance are against them. They are born going downward, and most of them stay down. They are victims whose lives are endlessly blown round and round the other America.

Here is one of the most familiar forms of the vicious circle of poverty. The poor get sick more than anyone else in the society. That is because they live in slums, jammed together under unhygienic conditions; they have inadequate diets, and cannot get decent medical care. When they become sick, they are sick longer than any other group in the society. Because they are sick more often and longer than anyone else, they lose wages and work, and find it difficult to hold a steady job. And because of this, they cannot pay for good housing, for a nutritious diet, for doctors. At any given point in the circle, particularly when there is a major illness, their prospect is to move to an even lower level and to begin the cycle, round and round, toward even more suffering.

This is only one example of the vicious circle. Each group in the other America has its own particular version of the experience, and these will be detailed throughout this book. But the pattern, whatever its variations, is basic to the other America.

The individual cannot usually break out of this vicious circle. Neither can the group, for it lacks the social energy and political strength to turn its misery into a cause. Only the larger society, with its help and resources, can really make it possible for these people to help themselves. Yet those who could make the difference too often refuse to act because of their ignorant, smug moralisms. They view the effects of poverty—above all, the warping of the will and spirit that is a consequence of being poor—as choices. Understanding the vicious circle is an important step in breaking down this prejudice.

There is an even richer way of describing this same, general idea: Poverty in the United States is a culture, an institution, a way of life.

There is a famous anecdote about Ernest Hemingway and F. Scott Fitzgerald. Fitzgerald is reported to have remarked to Hemingway, "The rich are different." And Hemingway replied, "Yes, they have money." Fitzgerald had much the better of the exchange. He understood that being rich was not a simple fact, like a large bank account, but a way of looking at reality, a series of attitudes, a special type of life. If this is true of the rich, it is ten times truer of the poor. Everything about them, from the condition of their teeth to the way in which they love, is suffused and permeated by the fact of their poverty. And this is sometimes a hard idea for a Hemingway-like middle-class America to comprehend.

The family structure of the poor, for instance, is different from that of the rest of the society. There are more homes without a father, there are less marriages, more early pregnancy and, if Kinsey's statistical findings can be used, markedly different attitudes toward sex. As a result of this, to take but one consequence of the fact, hundreds of thousands, and perhaps millions, of children in the other America never know stability and "normal" affection.

Or perhaps the policeman is an even better example. For the middle class, the police protect property, give directions, and help old ladies. For the urban poor, the police are those who arrest you. In almost any slum there is a vast conspiracy against the forces of law and order. If someone approaches asking for a person, no one there will have heard of him, even if he lives next door. The outsider is "cop," bill collector, investigator (and, in the Negro ghetto, most dramatically, he is "the Man").

While writing this book, I was arrested for participaton in a civil-rights demonstration. A brief experience of a night in a cell made an abstraction personal and immediate: the city jail is one of the basic institutions of the other America. Almost everyone whom I encountered in the "tank" was poor: skid-row whites, Negroes, Puerto Ricans. Their poverty was an incitement to arrest in the first place. (A policeman will be much more careful with a well-dressed, obviously educated man who might have political connections than he will with someone who is poor.) They did not have money for bail or for lawyers. And, perhaps most important, they waited their arraignment with stolidity, in a mood of passive acceptance. They expected the worst, and they probably got it.

There is, in short, a language of the poor, a psychology of the poor, a world view of the poor. To be impoverished is to be an internal alien, to grow up in a culture that is radically different from the one that dominates the society. The poor can be described statistically; they can be analyzed as a group. But they need a novelist as well as a sociologist if we are to see them. They need an American Dickens to record the smell and texture and quality of their lives. The cycles and trends, the massive forces, must be seen as affecting persons who talk and think differently.

I am not that novelist. Yet . . . I have attempted to describe the faces behind the statistics, to tell a little of the "thickness" of personal life in the other America. Of necessity, I have begun with large groups: the dispossessed workers, the minorities, the farm poor, and the aged. Then, there are three cases of less massive types of poverty, including the only single humorous component in the other America. And finally, there are the slums, and the psychology of the poor.

Throughout, I work on an assumption that cannot be proved by government figures or even documented by impressions of the other America. It is an ethical proposition, and it can be simply stated: In a nation with a technology that could provide every citizen with a decent life, it is an outrage and a scandal that there should be such social misery. Only if one begins with this assumption is it possible to pierce through the invisibility of 40,000,000 to 50,000,000 human beings and to see the other America. We must perceive passionately, if this blindness is to be lifted from us. A fact can be rationalized and explained away; an indignity cannot.

What shall we tell the American poor, once we have seen them? Shall we say to them that they are better off than the Indian poor, the Italian poor, the Russian poor? That is one answer, but it is heartless. I should put it another way. I want to tell every well-fed and optimistic American that it is intolerable that so many millions should be maimed in body and in spirit when it is not necessary that they should be. My standard of comparison is not how much worse things used to be. It is how much better they could be if only we were stirred.

pp. 148-178

8 Here come the white knight!

"The economy is finally under control. That bum said, 'Please, Sir.' "

APPALACHIA: THE DISMAL LAND

Harry Caudill

In the fall of 1963 Homer Bigart came to Eastern Kentucky and wrote an article for *The New York Times* that described the ragged, undernourished people with whom he talked, and the flimsy shacks in which they lived. He told of children so hungry they ate dry mud gouged out between chimney stones. Stung into action, an image-conscious President issued an executive order creating PARC, the President's Appalachian Regional Commission. In due time the commission made its report to President Johnson and to Congress, and in 1964 its recommendations became law. Americans may comfortably assume the problems of Appalachia have been fairly faced and are well on the road to being solved. Nothing could be further from the truth.

A great deal of superficial writing has given the nation a one-sided and misleading picture of the Appalachian South. The television camera has emphasized time and again that the Appalachian mountaineers are poor, that their land is tilted on its edge and badly eroded, and that the chief industry of the region—coal mining—is in the doldrums. They have told us that the people are undereducated, suspicious, and poorly motivated.

All this is true, after a fashion. Appalachia is a rugged land. Its once great timber stands have been reduced to pathetic remnants. Most highlanders still entertain a tenacious suspicion of government and of strangers, and out of this ancient suspicion flow many of the ills that beset the region today.

Mountaineers have traditionally looked at government as a dangerous tyrant, albeit a tyrant of the people's own creation. They have feared that if government is made strong enough to be effective it will be strong enough to enslave them. As a result the Appalachian states and people have deliberately kept their governments weak—and weak, underfinanced governments have kept the people ignorant and, in their ignorance, poor. . . .

We and our forebears had an opportunity to build a vigorous society, but we have opted for a low-key society instead, a society that places little emphasis on human development—on skills, competence, and inquisitiveness—and the result has been the enlargement of incompetence and dependency. A quarter of the dwindling population is on public assistance. Like most of the Appalachian South, the region has been turned into a pale-face reservation.

Sadly, the experience of Kentucky's eastern counties is in no sense unique. Its failure may have been greater in some respects than those of its kindred regions—southwestern Virginia, West Virginia, eastern Tennessee, western Maryland, and southern Pennsylvania; but in the main its tragic tale has been repeated: a backwoods people has moved into a primordial forest. They began decimating their timber to obtain "new grounds" which they wore out without replenishing them with cover crops. Failing to educate their descendants, the generations perpetuated a lack of understanding of the land and its capacities. When the region was rediscovered after the Civil War the people practically gave away its great riches, effectually disinheriting their children and their children's children. Some of the mineral tracts sold for as little as 10¢ an acre. The vast natural wealth passed into the hands of land companies organized by speculators with offices in Philadelphia, Pittsburgh, New York, and Baltimore.

For more than 50 years mountaineers have sat supinely and quietly by and allowed their land, kinsmen, and institutions to be exploited by people who have neither affection nor respect for Appalachia—whose only concern is to plunder it.

The hidden face of Appalachia must be brought into view and seen in proper focus. It is wondrously prosperous, for the coal depression has long since passed into history. It is studded with the names of great corporations—United States Steel, Bethlehem Steel, Inland Steel, Republic Steel, International Harvester, Jones & Laughlin, Ford Motor Company, and scores of others. And there are less famous corporations, the obscure firms that own immense tracts of minerals and lease them to operating companies for royalties payable on coal, oil, gas, and limestone. There is, for example, Virginia Coal & Iron with its 206,000 acres, almost certainly the most profitable investor-owned corporation in the United States. A few years ago the president of that company told a reporter for *Dunn's Review and Modern Industry* that he managed to "carry practically all of Virginia Coal & Iron's income down to net." Of its receipts 76 percent are tax-free at the federal level. In that year the company realized a net profit after taxes of 61 percent of gross. It paid a dividend of 45 percent of gross, nine times as high as that paid by General Motors.

The Kentucky River Coal Corporation owns 200,000 acres in eastern Kentucky, and during that same year its dividend was a trifle under half of its huge income.

The Big Sandy Corporation, with 75,000 acres in the fabulously rich Big Sandy region, is dominated by the Delano family and has its headquarters at Campo Bello. It has supported its investors in fine style for more than half a century.

These companies and a score of others like them have shaped the destiny of Appalachia for seventy-five years. They have set the policies followed in its courthouses and state houses, and governors and legislators have cowered before them, enacting laws that exempted them almost entirely from any effective taxation.

Consequently, Appalachia's counties are hollow shells, resting lightly on an enormously rich natural-resource foundation. In these once—and sometimes still—lovely valleys, whose scenic beauty should be worth fortunes to their inhabitants, the poor little counties huddle—shabby, starved for funds, in debt, deep in perpetual fiscal crisis. The shoddy schools and other public facilities frighten away potential investors. From their dreary ineffectiveness the more able, intelligent, and ambitious flee.

Appalachia is saddled with a colonial system. The colonial system was strapped onto Appalachia during the same historic interval when it was imposed on much of the world.

The colonialist sway in the rest of the world has ended. Only in our Appalachia does it proceed unchecked. In Tennessee, in my own Kentucky, in West Virginia, western Virginia, western Maryland, and Pennsylvania the colonial bastions erected in the 1870s, and 1880s and 1890s, and early in this century still stand. Once those same companies and their associates and minions dominated Africa, South America, and Asia. Now their benighted policies rejected so firmly elsewhere, continue in effect and force only in the Appalachian South. And there too, at last, they are being challenged!

If a New Appalachia is to arise out of the present tangle the people must be educated to comprehend the truth about their land. In classrooms, in courthouses, in community action centers, in every place where people meet, the possibility of Appalachian reform must be taught. The first battle ground in the struggle may well be the college classroom, but eventually it will be waged in PTA meetings and in state and local meetings of educational associations.

Teachers and their charges pay a terrible price for our regional backwardness. They would profit immensely from meaningful reform. A severance tax of 10 cents per ton of coal, barrel of oil, and comparable measure of gas would provide $30 million annually for education—for higher salaries, better buildings, enriched curricula. We must educate people

(a) to be discontented with the present arrangement;
(b) to appreciate the immense wealth of their land;
(c) to resent its exploitation by absentee owners;
(d) to understand the availability of funds to finance the institutions the people need;
(e) to grasp the vast power they can exercise—but have long neglected to exercise—over their basic wealth;
(f) to inspire a political movement to accomplish the far-reaching changes I have advocated.

We in the Congress for Appalachian Development have proposed that the people of the Southern mountains, whose forebears pioneered the institutions of freedom at Mecklenburg, South Carolina, and proclaimed America's first Declaration of Independence, should now assert a new Declaration of Independence and of Self-sufficiency; that as Americans we are a free-born people and intend to order our communities and affairs as such.

We seek to accomplish here no more and no less than has been accomplished in rich resource regions elsewhere in the world. We think the great wealth that was pilfered from our ancestors should be returned to the people of the mountains. We ask that those people who now hold legal title should be given a better and fairer deal than was afforded our forebears. The predecessors of the present-day companies came to the mountains when our ancestors were unschooled and inexperienced, and, taking advantage of their credulity, persuaded them to sign "broad form" deeds whereby coal companies in state after state claim the right to wreck and plunder the land, often without compensation to the people who live on and hold title to the "surface estate."

Whereas ignorant people were cozened into virtually giving away their substance, we would compensate these owners fairly according to modern values, vesting many of the great tracts of minerals in public ownership. We would put the title into public corporations, chartered under state enabling laws and governed by representatives of the people. These public corporations would have the right of eminent domain and would be empowered to sell bonds to finance the developmental efforts of their districts. These Economic Development Districts, these public corporations, would go to Wall Street or other money markets and raise their investment funds by offering a sound deal to the investing public. With these funds and by due process of law they would buy much of the vast mineral holdings now controlled by the economic royalists in distant cities.

With these acquisitions the people, acting through their Economic Development Districts, would undertake a comprehensive development program. They would build lakes and dams and coal-burning steam plants. They would turn the abundant resources of fuel and water into electricity and sell it in the world's largest and fastest-growing power market. They would send it by the fast-forming power grid to the electricity-hungry cities—including those now suffocating in grime and grit from antiquated generators on their outskirts. After debt retirement, Appalachia would use the profits from the sale of its power to finance the institutions and services the region desperately needs.

It is certain that Appalachian fossil fuels will power much of the nation in the future, as they have done for so long and so consistently in the past. *The coal and water will be turned into electricity, and the electricity will be sold at a profit.* Whether these profits will go out as dividends to distant stockholders or stay behind to finance the institutions our people need so desperately and have been promised for so long, remains to be seen.

This proposal is neither radical nor new. It has been thoroughly tested in the state of Washington over the last thirty years. A single county—Chelan—with a population of 40,000 has sold more than $500 million worth of bonds for its development. It built the Rocky Reach dam at a cost of $273.1 million. The Chelan County Public Utility District paid $1.5 million in taxes and donated another million to the county and county seat. The cheap power and good schools are attracting industry, and the county is booming.

The people who designed and now operate that Public Utility District have assured me that if Appalachia's counties were similarly organized they could raise many billions of dollars by the same means and finance local, grass-roots TVAs under the auspices of the states.

The scheme the federal authorities have devised for our highlands is not a development program at all. It is a depopulation program. Some 80 percent of the money Congress has authorized will go into roads, and these roads will lead to a few strategically located "growth centers," many of them completely outside the hills. The highways will act as efficient conveyors to move the people out of the hinterlands into a few places like Lexington, Kentucky, and Kingsport, Tennessee. There, the theory runs, they will find jobs and happiness.

I have a deeply-rooted suspicion that this undertaking reflects a scheme fostered by the great absentee holding corporations to empty the countryside in order to facilitate their extractive industries. Nothing could suit them better than to empty the long valleys of the Appalachian hinterland, to leave the little houses without inhabitants to witness or protest the destruction of the land. Then our latter-day colonialists could drill and dig and gouge and cut and blast to their heart's content. Then, without interference from troublesome local people, they could get out the minerals by the cheapest, the most technologically efficient method. Their profits would swell accordingly and their dividend rates would soar to new levels. Then, in God's good time, the strip-minded landscape and its hideous streams would be sold to the federal government for rehabilitation at the cost of the taxpayers.

Was this kind of a future for Appalachia sold to an unwitting Regional Commission in 1963–1964, and to an equally unquestioning Congress? How much better it would be to seize the dream President Johnson and Senators Ribicoff and Kennedy have expressed in recent months when they spoke of new cities springing up across America! They and others have proposed that the United States solve the problems of its people out in the countryside in new cities and towns, rather than in sprawling, crumbling ghettos in gargantuan supercities. They hold that new cities must be built because existing cities cannot be expanded to hold all who are destined to crowd into them. And where can we find a more likely spot for new population centers than in our own southern and central Appalachia?

The government of the United States is thinking of spending $100 billion to bring a river down from Alaska to southern California. A trifling part of this money would build scores of dams and lakes across the Appalachian South. This spangle of man-made lakes would provide flood control, industrial water, recreational water, and cheap electricity—all important underpinnings in the creation of a viable economy.

Government and private planners are at work devising the essential understanding for the fostering of new communities. The government is going to encourage them. Industry is going to move into them. Millions of people are going to inhabit them. It has been calculated that $3 trillion worth of new housing will go up in the United States by the beginning of the twenty-first century. Unless we act on the side of progress and positive good we will continue an immense American subterritory in the hands of ruthless exploiters who live far beyond its borders and care little or nothing about its destiny.*

* See Slater's "toilet assumption"; also "The Hills of Ixopo," both in Part One, Chap. 4.

GOING HUNGRY IN AMERICA: GOVERNMENT'S FAILURE

Elizabeth B. Drew

From time to time during the past few years, there has come to public attention the jarring news that a great many Americans do not get enough to eat because they are too poor. The words "starvation," "hunger," and "malnutrition" have all been used to describe the phenomenon. Each of these conditions is difficult to isolate, or even describe, or to separate from related diseases, because there has been little scientific or official interest in the problem. Yet it is generally agreed, even among government circles, that, at a minimum, ten million Americans are malnourished, and some of these are chronically hungry, even starving, because they are poor.

In 1967, a group of doctors, including Robert Coles of Harvard University, Joseph Brenner of MIT, Alan Mermann and Milton J. E. Senn of Yale, and private practitioners from Yazoo City, Mississippi, and Charlotte, North Carolina, took a foundation-sponsored trip to Mississippi to investigate the problem and returned to tell the Senate Subcommittee on Poverty what they had seen:

> In Delta counties . . . we saw children whose nutritional and medical condition we can only describe as shocking—even to a group of physicians whose work involves daily confrontation with disease and suffering. In child after child we saw: evidence of vitamin and mineral deficiencies; serious untreated skin infestation and ulcerations; eye and ear diseases, also unattended bone diseases secondary to poor food intake; the prevalence of bacterial and parasitic disease, as well as severe anemia . . . in boys and girls in every county we visited, obvious evidence of severe malnutrition, with injury to the body's tissues—its muscles, bones, and skin as well as an associated psychological state of fatigue, listlessness, and exhaustion. . . . We saw children who don't get to drink milk, don't get to eat fruit, green vegetables, or meat. They live on starches—grits, bread, Kool Aid. . . . In sum, we saw children who are hungry and who are sick—children for whom hunger is a daily fact of life and sickness, in many forms, an inevitability. We do not want to quibble over words, but "malnutrition" is not quite what we found. . . . They are suffering from hunger and disease and directly or indirectly they are dying from them—which is exactly what "starvation" means.

From *The Atlantic Monthly,* vol. 222 (December 1968), pp. 53–61 (excerpts).

There is developing, moreover, a disturbing body of scientific information that indicates a connection between malnutrition in children, in particular insufficient protein, and brain damage. Seventy-five percent of the mental retardation in this country is estimated to occur in areas of urban and rural poverty.

The situation in the Mississippi Delta has been particularly acute because of unemployment as a result of mechanization, and among other things, other government programs: controlled planting, and a new one-dollar-an-hour minimum wage, which led many plantation owners to lay workers off rather than pay it. Mississippi's welfare program pays an average of $50 a month to a family with four children, but payments are made only if the wage earner is old or disabled or blind or has left his family. Thus there are thousands of families in the Delta with no jobs and no income.

There are two basic government programs which are intended to improve the diet of the poor—the sale of food stamps and the distribution of food. The local county chooses one or the other—or neither. Government officials point out that for some time every county in Mississippi has had one of the programs. In response to the reports that people still were not getting enough to eat, the Secretary of Agriculture said to the same Senate subcommittee: "They got some food because they were obviously walking around. I don't know where they got it."

For some time, in fact, it has been known within the government that the food programs had serious shortcomings, in the number of people being reached and in the form of the assistance. In addition, over the past year and a half or so, domestic hunger has been the subject of a great deal of publicity. A solution would not be all that expensive: government studies have indicated that adequate food distribution for everyone who needed it would cost between $1.5 billion and $2 billion more than the roughly half billion being spent on stamps and commodities now. (No one had calculated, in terms of illness and wasted and dependent lives, what it costs not to provide everyone with an adequate diet.) There were also short-range and less expensive actions that could have been taken to alleviate the most severe distress. While it would be inaccurate to say that nothing was done, the response was slow, piecemeal, and, it often seemed, reluctant. More thorough responses, including a national commitment to see that no one was denied an adequate diet because of low income, were considered, and at several points they were almost made. Because of the impact on the lives, every day, of several million people, the reasons why they were not are worth exploring.

The food programs are run by the Department of Agriculture because they were begun not so much to help the poor as to dispose of embarrassing agricultural surpluses. Food packages are distributed once a month to the poor who live in counties which happen to want the distribution and are willing to pay for it. (Only recently, the federal government began to pay for the packages in a few of the poorest counties.) "But," Orville Freeman, the Secretary of Agriculture, has testified to Congress, "that doesn't mean that every person gets it, because a poor person who lives miles away from the distributing point where 100 pounds of food is made available for a month may very well (a) not even know about the distribution; (b) not be able to get there; and (c) not be able to carry it away." (One congressman replied: "I know dead soldiers who didn't miss out because they lived 10 miles from a recruiting office.")

The commodity packages have only recently approximated what even the Agriculture Department considers a "minimum adequate" diet, but the cheerful assumption is made that they are a "supplement" to a family's food supply. The commodity package has been periodically expanded, to the point where last summer, under public pressure, the Department announced that it would now contain some twenty-two items. The list is theoretical, however; whether the various items actually end up in the package depends on whether they are in sufficient supply and whether the local community elects to include them. It takes tolerance for tedium and some culinary ingenuity to make edible meals of the surplus packages, which until last summer consisted mainly of such things as flour, cornmeal, rice, dried peas, dried beans, bulgur. Formerly they contained thirty ounces of meat for each person for an entire month; now the packages are supposed to contain more meat, dried eggs, evaporated milk, canned chicken, canned vegetables, and some others. The wrapping is to be prettier, and recipes are to be supplied, although many of the recipients can't read.

The food stamp program, in which participants buy stamps which are worth more than the purchase price and use them to buy groceries, is preferred by just about everyone, including the local grocers. Long part of the Democrats' agenda, food stamps were started on a pilot basis in 1961, and were finally authorized by Congress three years later. The stamps are actually a form of income supplement, but that is not the sort of thing that is said out loud, and thus a great emphasis is always placed on how this, too, is to supplement a family's "normal" expenditure for food. It is difficult to divine just what was in the minds of the federal officials who worked out the details of how the food stamp program should work. Each month, a family may purchase a given amount's worth of stamps, depending on their income, in exchange for a given amount of bonus. Somehow, although people in general pay about 18 percent of their income for food, the poor, under the food stamp plan, are sometimes required to pay as much as 35 to 50 percent in order to obtain any stamps at all. If they cannot afford that because of the other demands on their income, or if they do not happen to have enough cash on hand on the day that the stamps are sold, they get no help at all. For example, after eight counties in Mississippi switched from commodity distribution to food stamps, some 32,000 fewer people were receiving food aid one year later. In Arkansas, of the 54,531 households on welfare in counties with the food stamp program, only 9700 buy the stamps. This is not peculiar to these states; while some 6 million people are estimated to be receiving either commodities or food stamps now—roughly 3 million under each program—it is seldom mentioned that six years ago even more people were being helped, albeit the great part by the inferior commodities program.

Another quirk is that the bonuses go up as the income goes up, so that the higher-income poor end up with more food than those at the bottom of the scale. The Agriculture Department explains that this is because it would not be wise to give those who are accustomed to being worst off too much too soon. In order to be certified as eligible for the program, families must run the gauntlet of the welfare agencies, many of which are not known for their sympathy toward Negroes. The food programs are sometimes used as an instrument of control: people who participate in civil rights activities or who are needed when it is time for the crops to be picked find that the programs are suddenly unavailable. In many areas, food prices go up on the day the stamps are issued.

When the uproar over these failings developed in 1967, the Agriculture Department made a study of the situation in Washington County, Mississippi. It found, among other things, that more than half of those qualified to receive food stamps were not doing so. The investigators were not, however, greatly perturbed. "In general," they reported, "the study indicates that low-income households in this Mississippi Delta county accommodate themselves to a diet which low-income families elsewhere would reject. . . . It may be that low-income families place less value on food than we think."

The Department of Agriculture should not, in all fairness, be expected to demonstrate dazzling expertise in the needs and life-styles of the poor. Its essential mission is to nurture the agricultural economy; the poor are somebody else's department. The typical employee in Agriculture has been there a long, long time. He may have come in with Henry Wallace, or he may have been a dirt farmer who was down and out during the Depression, got a government job measuring acreage, moved up through the ranks, and was promoted to Washington when he was in his fifties. . . .

Jamie Whitten, a fifty-eight-year-old Congressman from Charleston, Mississippi, chairman of the subcommittee which provides funds for the Agriculture Department's programs and one of the most powerful members of the House of Representatives, does not believe that anybody in this country is unavoidably hungry, "except," he says, "when there has been parental neglect through drunkenness or mental illness. You're dealing with people who for some reason or other are in a condition of poverty. If they had the training and foresight of other people, they wouldn't be in poverty." . . .

The House Agriculture Committee, which sets the policies for which Whitten's group then provides the money, is, to state it gently, disinterested in the poor. The committee's concerns are sheep scrapie and hog cholera and agricultural subsidies. The members of most committees see to it that the benefits of programs they preside over reach their constituents in full measure, but it is no accident that the home districts of a number of the Agriculture Committee members do not have food stamp programs. "These programs are not desired by the power structures back home," says one close observer, "and that's what elects them. The recipients of these programs don't vote."

The situation is similar in the Senate. In all cases, the Agriculture committees are almost entirely populated by representatives of Southern and midwestern farm districts, with, in a Democratic Congress, the representatives of Southern landholders in charge. Senator James O. Eastland, for example, is the third-ranking member of the Senate Agriculture Committee and its most important determiner of cotton policy. Last year, the Eastland family plantations in Sunflower County, Mississippi, received $211,364 in subsidies. Despite the slipping popularity of the farm programs, and the increasing urban and suburban orientation of Congress, these men have enough seniority, and serve on enough other important committees, to make their influence felt. To the extent that the Agriculture Department budget is under attack, they try to keep the budget down by curbing the Department's noncrop programs. "Freeman decided as a matter of policy," says one of his former colleagues, "that he was not going to antagonize these men. He checked out appointments with them and went to enormous lengths to cultivate them socially. When the food issue came up and he got caught in his conspiracy with the Southerners on the Hill, his instinctive reaction was to deny that anything was wrong. After all, he was relying on memos from his staff, and they were defending themselves, too."

In April, 1967, the Senate Labor and Public Welfare Committee's Subcommittee on Employment, Manpower, and Poverty went to Mississippi. The subcommittee, headed by Senator Joseph S. Clark of Pennsylvania, was making a nationwide study of the poverty program, and since Senator Robert Kennedy was a member of the group, wherever it went, the press went too. At a hearing in Jackson, Mississippi, Marian Wright, an attractive, soft-spoken attorney for the NAACP's Legal Defense Fund, Incorporated, who had been working in Mississippi, talked about welfare, poverty, and the situation in the Delta. "They are starving," she concluded. "They are starving, and those who can get the bus fare to go north are trying to go north. But there is absolutely nothing for them to do. There is nowhere to go, and somebody must begin to respond to them."

Kennedy and Clark said they would take it to the Department of Agriculture when they returned to Washington. Senator George Murphy went them one better and said that the group should "notify the President of the United States that there is an emergency situation, and send investigators and help in immediately." On the following day, Clark and Kennedy toured the Delta. The cameras were not there when Robert Kennedy sat on the floor in one particularly fetid shack watching a listless child toy with a plate of rice, feeling the child's body, trying to get the child to respond, and trying to comprehend. Until then, the senators really had not known how bad it was.

After they returned to Washington, all nine members of the subcommittee signed a letter to the President describing the situation as "shocking" and constituting an "emergency," and calling for specific Administration action. The White House, after trying not to receive it at all, bucked the letter to the Office of Economic Opportunity, which runs the poverty program, and OEO responded with a press release, its outlines dictated by the White House. The release said there was poverty in each of the senators' home states, too; that the crisis of poverty had been greater before Lyndon Johnson took office; that the Administration had started a lot of programs in Mississippi; that the Congress had cut funds for the poverty program; that "every recommendation in the letter by the Senators has the hearty concurrence of the administration," but there were some legal problems; and "we already know what needs to be done." . . .

There were two basic issues between the subcommittee and the Administration: the price of the food stamps, and the Secretary's authority to declare an emergency in the Delta and send in extra food. After several months of subcommittee pressure and after prodding by the White House and harassment by Shriver, the Agriculture Department did lower the price of food stamps for those with an income of less than $20 a month to 50 cents per person a month, with a maximum of $3 per family. (This buys $72 worth of food for a family of six, about half what the Department estimates such a family needs.) It also decided to charge all families only half the price in the first month. Prices could not be lowered generally until there was substantially more money for the program, a decision the President would have to make.

The Department resisted the argument that there were people with no income at all who should be charged nothing for their food stamps. For one thing, the Department thought that this was a problem in a small number of cases, and therefore not worthy of great concern. For another, the Secretary believed, as he told congressional committees on several occasions, that the poor could not be trusted with free stamps. "If you proceed, then, to have free stamps," he said, "and you give free stamps to everybody who wants them, what will happen to those stamps? Those stamps, I am afraid, in many cases will be bootlegged. That is what happened back in the 1940s and the 1930s, with the food stamp program. That destroyed the program. The food stamp program was discredited because those stamps became common currency for all kinds of things, from a wild party, to a beer party, to legitimate uses, to buy shoes." Another view of what ended the earlier program was the almost full employment during World War II.

The senators and others argued that the Secretary should have invoked his emergency power to send extra food to the Delta, using money from a special multipurpose fund (known as Section 32 for its place in an agriculture law), as he had used it to begin the food stamp program and expand the commodity packages. The Department argued that it didn't really have the power (despite the precedents), that the money really hadn't been budgeted, and it would be bad precedent and administratively inefficient to distribute free food where there were already food stamps; and there was also that danger that if there were two programs the people might start bootlegging. There was also the problem that the Agriculture committees frown on such use of the money.

As the arguments tumbled forth at one private meeting, Kennedy looked at Freeman and shook his head. "I don't know, Orville," he said, "I'd just get the food down there. I can't believe that in this country we can't get some food down there." . . .

In September of 1967, in the only public statement on the issue he was to make for a long time, President Johnson said that "we want no American in this country to go hungry. We believe that we have the knowledge, the compassion, and the resources to banish hunger and to do away with malnutrition if we only apply those resources and those energies." He ordered the Department of Agriculture to see to it that, one way or the other, every one of the thousand poorest counties in the nation had a food program. The Department said that there were 331 of those counties that did not, and, to give it a little of the old pizzazz, it embarked on "Project 331." As it turned out, it was a full year before each of the 331 was said to have a program, for the Department remained highly reluctant to fly in the face of tradition by using federal money and federal personnel to establish a program if the counties resisted. It was also concerned about what it felt was a bad precedent of having the federal government pay the full costs. In May of the following year, with the Poor People's Campaign beating at his door, Freeman finally announced that this would be done.

Extending the programs to more counties had nothing to do with improving matters for recipients, as in Mississippi. Since greater amounts of money were not committed, it also meant that other less poor counties that were on the waiting list for the food stamp program would have to continue to wait. Finally, sometime after Project 331 was under way it was discovered that Agriculture defined a "poorest" county as one with the lowest average income, rather than one with the largest number of poor people. Therefore, poor people who had the misfortune of living near too many rich people were out of luck. This covered more counties at less expense, and fewer people were helped.

The President's encouraging statement may have been prompted by the fact that by the fall of 1967 the White House had set up another secret task force, which once more reflected their deep conviction, they said, that every American should have an adequate nutritional diet. The task force, now headed by representatives of the Budget Bureau, reported that for another $1.5 to $2 billion and in relatively short time the government could provide that adequate diet to every American. Now, however, and for months to come, the Administration was locked in its fight to secure a 10 percent income surtax from Congress, and Congress' demand that there be substantial cuts in government spending in return. "I don't think anyone realizes how paralyzed we became by that fight," says one Administration official. "I don't think even we realized it." With the White House feeling under particular pressure to do something about the cities (the Detroit riot had just taken place), and with their own expertise tending in that direction, Califano's staff that fall concerned itself with devising new programs for jobs and housing. Whatever the limitations of these programs in terms of delayed spending, they at least represented a commitment and an effort at new approaches, which were not made on giving the poor sufficient food. Through it all, Mr. Johnson remained unconvinced that the problem was as serious as the critics said, reluctant to take the fight to the Hill, where he had enough problems, and annoyed that no one could tell him exactly how many people were going hungry. (No one knows exactly how many unemployed or how much substandard housing there is either.)

Moreover, there was now no great public pressure on the White House to act on hunger, as there was on behalf of the cities. During all of 1967 and 1968, only a small coterie made the issue a continuing preoccupation: Miss Wright; Peter Edelman of Kennedy's staff; William Smith of Clark's staff; and Robert Choate, a young businessman of some means who took a sabbatical to become a freelance, largely behind the scenes, and highly effective crusader on the issue. Of the enormous Washington press corps, only Nick Kotz of the Des Moines *Register* saw the hunger issue as worthy of continuing coverage, whether or not it was "in the news." Of all the lobby organizations, only a few of the more liberal labor groups found the issue to be of even intermittent concern.

The Citizens' Crusade Against Poverty, an organization with United Auto Workers backing, was the closest there was to a group with a fulltime concern. Early in 1968, it had established a Citizens' Board of Inquiry, which published "Hunger, U.S.A." a stinging indictment of the food programs. Around the same time, a coalition of women's organizations published a study of the federal school lunch program which could help children of the poor secure a better meal at least while they were in school. The women's groups found that of the 18 million children receiving free or reduced-price lunches under the program, only 2 million were poor; another 4 million poor children were not being helped. The Johnson Administration had tried to get Congress to restructure this so that less would go to the middle class and more to the poor, and Congress had adamantly refused. On May 21, CBS broadcast a powerful documentary called *Hunger in America.*

Several members of Congress reacted to all of this with outrage at the idea that anyone would charge that people in their areas were going hungry. Representative W. R. Poage of Texas, chairman of the House Agriculture Committee, wrote to county health officials, the very ones who would be most culpable, and asked if they personally knew of anyone in their county who was starving or seriously hungry. No, replied most of the health officers, and if the people were hungry it was mostly because they were lazy or ignorant. A few said the food programs were inadequate, but Poage did not emphasize that in his report to his colleagues.

The response of the politicians was understandable. More puzzling, in light of his professed zeal to get more done, were Freeman's own persistent attacks on the reports. Finding factual errors in the small (they didn't mention that grandma had a pension of $82-a-month), he condemned them in the large. The CBS telecast, he said, was "a biased, one-sided dishonest presentation of a serious national problem."

As the Poor People's Campaign, under the direction of the Southern Christian Leadership Conference, prepared for its March on Washington in the spring of 1968, strategists for both the SCLC and the federal government knew that, as always in these situations, there would have to be a governmental response which would enable the Campaign's leaders to make an honorable withdrawal from the city. First Attorney General Ramsey Clark, then the President himself asked the various government agencies to draw up a list of administrative actions—which would not cost money—which could alleviate some of the difficulties of the poor. A March on Washington by a grand coalition of white, black, brown, and red poor, who would encamp in the federal city, bringing their plight to the attention of the country, had been the idea of Martin Luther King. After Dr. King was assassinated, the leadership of the SCLC under Dr. Ralph Abernathy was in disarray. Goals and tactics became difficult to resolve. Miss Wright, who had moved to Washington, was placed in charge of the Campaign's dealings with the government agencies, and worked exhaustingly for weeks for a semblance of order and progress in the demands and responses. On the advice of Miss Wright and others, the Campaign leaders decided upon hunger as the central, most dramatic issue.

Now the issue was at its highest point of public attention. Most of the government agencies did what they could to respond to the marchers' demands. Agriculture, however, remained defensive. In the end, the Agriculture response consisted of promising to get a food program into each of the thousand counties—which the President had already done nine months earlier; making more commodities available for surplus distribution; regulations to improve the school lunch program; and improved food packages for infants and expectant mothers. Some Administration officials think the poor were not grateful enough.

As it happened, the major reason this response was so paltry was that the White House was preparing one on a grander scale for the President himself to present, probably in the form of a special message to Congress. It would have revised the entire food stamp schedule and perhaps lowered the cost to the very poorest to either nothing or a token amount; it would have expanded the size of the food programs so that many more areas could receive them; and it would have carried a commitment to build the programs over time, to the point where every American had an adequate diet. The Budget Bureau squirreled away some money to go with the message. The thought was that it would be delivered around the time of "Solidarity Day," on June 19, when thousands of others were to come to Washington to join the poor in a climactic march.

A number of reasons have been offered for why the President's Solidarity Day Message was never delivered: the mail in the White House was overwhelmingly against the Poor People's Campaign, and Resurrection City was out of control; Abernathy's final speech was likely to carry a stinging denunciation of the war in Vietnam; and the House of Representatives was going to vote at last on the tax bill the following day, and any move at that point by the President to increase government spending might jeopardize the long-negotiated compromise. The most important reason, however, was that the President simply did not want to be in the position of appearing to "respond to pressure." More startling to many was that after the poor had left town and the tax bill had passed, he still declined to move. He was focusing on the budget cuts that had to be made, annoyed at Freeman for getting out in front of him on the issue, still concerned at appearing to respond to pressure, and convinced that now that some legislation was moving on the Hill, it would be unseemly for him, the President, to appear to be running to catch up.

By this time, things were most uncomfortable for Freeman, and he began to press hard at the White House for help—belatedly, in the opinion of many. His friend Vice President Humphrey tried to help. First Humphrey offered his services as a mediator with the Poor People's Campaign, but the offer was rejected by the White House. Then the Vice President of the United States tried indirect means of communicating with the President. Humphrey wrote to Mrs. Arthur Krim, wife of the President's chief money raiser: "It is just intolerable to me that there is such a problem of malnutrition and undernourishment in the United States. . . . Through it all, there are ways the President could have helped—in approving some of Orville Freeman's budget requests, in supporting legislation on the Hill, and suggesting administrative change—but he has not. The thought came that you might be the person who could say a word or two to encourage him."

On Capitol Hill, a bill to expand the food stamp program was moving forward. Originally an Administration request to make a minimal expansion of $20 million (over the $225 million already authorized), under pressure from urban liberals who threatened to retaliate against a farm bill that was also in the mill, the bill ultimately authorized the program to grow by $90 million in the first year and more after that. After endorsing a substantial increase in the program, Freeman was reprimanded by both Poage and the White House, but when an increase seemed probable, the White House joined in. More spending for the school lunch program was approved, and a special Senate committee was established to "study" the food problem, with a view to trying to maneuver the food programs away from Agriculture committees.

In the very last days of the congressional session, with the President about to make a routine request for additional funds for various agencies that had fallen short of funds, the machinery around the government—in the Agriculture Department, in the Budget Bureau, in his own staff—geared up once more for a presidential request for more funds for food stamps and a major statement on the issue. Instead, he simply requested the $90 million and in the closing rush Congress gave him $55 million. Wait, it was said, for his farewell messages in 1969.

The failure of the Johnson Administration to make substantial progress toward feeding the poor is viewed by many as its most serious domestic failure. It is the cause of disappointment and even anguish on the part of many people within the government. Orville Freeman, for one, professes himself satisfied: "Everything I suggested from the beginning that should be in Lyndon Johnson's program, or damn near it, I have gotten. If he had gone up to Congress with a big feeding program like a bull in a china shop he'd have been under fire, and what would he have gotten? Some newspaper accolades and plaudits in some liberal magazines, and trouble with Congress."

The food issue is an unhappy example of a great deal that can go wrong in Washington. It is also an example, however, of the dangers of the latest fad of "local control." The food programs are examples of programs that *are* subject to local control—the local governments request, pay for, and run them—with the result that those areas which are least responsive to the needs of the poor can also deny them federally proffered food.

The problem is not nearly so insoluble as the events of the past two years would suggest. First of all, given enough money and flexibility, it is generally agreed the food stamp program is not at all a bad device. Choate, for one, suggests that in addition the program be federalized and computerized, to work as automatically and without continual harrassment for the recipient as social security. He and a number of others believe that ultimately the food programs ought to be recognized as income supplements and become part of an income maintenance system. That, however, seems a long way off. When asked by the space agency, the food companies have found ingenious ways to pack meals for astronauts in Tootsie-Roll–sized bars or toothpaste-sized tubes. The Pentagon seems to have no trouble keeping the troops in the field well nourished. There are problems of tastes and habits to meet, but if the food industry were less apprehensive about change, or did less cohabiting with the farm bloc in that great combine they call "agribusiness," a lot more could be done to feed the poor efficiently and inexpensively. The food companies have lately shown more interest in exploring this field—with government subsidies, of course.

Yet so little was accomplished not because of mechanical or industrial failures, but because of what can happen to men in policy-making positions in Washington. When they stay in a difficult job too long, they can be overwhelmed by the complexity of it all, and they become overly defensive. Man's pride, particularly the pride of a man who can tell himself he has done some good, can overtake his intellectual honesty. Thus, not Southern politicians, not Orville Freeman, not Lyndon Johnson could face the fact when it was pointed out that many people were hungry, that they weren't wearing any clothes. In this they reflected a national trait: it has been easier to stir sustained national concern over hunger in Bihar or Biafra than places at home for which we are more directly responsible. The problems are looked at in terms of the workings of Washington, not in terms of the problems. Decent men could sit and discuss statistical reliability and administrative neatness and the importance of good precedents while people went hungry.

The niceties of consensus politics were more important than the needs of some 10 million people. A new Congress and a new Administration ought to be able to improve on that kind of government.

The following dialogue occurred in Buffalo, N. Y., in October of 1960:

Reporter: "Vice-President Nixon, it has recently been stated that 5 million people in the United States go to bed hungry every night. Do you believe this is true?"

Mr. Nixon: "Well, I'd say if 5 million people go to bed hungry every night, it must be because 5 million Americans are on diets."

They are playing a game. They are playing at not
playing a game. If I show them I see they are, I
shall break the rules and they will punish me.
I must play their game, of not seeing I see the game.

BARRIERS TO EARNING INCOME

Larry D. Singell

The correctness of the statement, "ye have the poor always with you," depends on how poverty is defined, what its fundamental causes are, and the extent to which society allocates resources toward eliminating it. Indeed, poverty in the United States could be defined away by simply designating as poor any family having an income less than the median family income of Asia, Africa, or Latin America. The fact that poverty is considered to be a critical problem in the United States, even though it could be eliminated in this way, makes it clear that a fundamental basis for concern is the inequality in the distribution of income (with a conventional minimum higher than elsewhere).

An equally weighty concern, however, is that of eliminating barriers that create unequal opportunities to compete for income. It is significant that the major enabling legislation in the war on poverty is the Economic Opportunity Act, which has as its goal ". . . an America in which every citizen shares all the opportunities of his society, in which every man has a chance to advance his welfare to the limits of his capacities." . . .

The Problem of Defining Poverty

Since both the number of poor and the structure of poverty are sensitive to the definition of poverty utilized, a great deal of discussion and disagreement exists as to the appropriate definition. The fact that any definition must be arbitrary has led one economist to argue that no precise definition is needed ". . . save as a tactic for countering the intellectual obstructionist. . . ." However, unless a definition of poverty is agreed upon, efficient allocation of antipoverty resources is impossible. This is true because these resources may be allocated to people who by criteria society may use are really not poor and because the success of the alternative programs in reducing poverty cannot be evaluated.

Any definition must, in some sense, be arbitrary, but a fundamental difficulty to be resolved is whether poverty should be defined in relative or absolute terms. The Council of Economic Advisers (CEA), for example, adopted an absolute standard based on the acceptance of three criteria: (1) one-third of family income being spent on food, (2) a family of four as a base (the average size in 1960 was 3.65), and (3) Department of Agriculture estimates of cost of minimally nutritional meals of 22.8 cents a meal per person. On the basis of these three criteria a family would be designated poor if it had less than $3,000 a year in income. Utilizing this definition, the

From *Quarterly Review of Economics and Business,* vol. 8, no. 2 (Summer 1968), pp. 35–44 (excerpts). Reprinted with permission.

percentage of total families in poverty fell from 28.9 percent of the population in 1947 to 14.3 percent in 1966 (in 1966 prices). The CEA further predicted that if the economy continues to grow at its 1947–1963 rate (with 4 to 6 percent of the labor force unemployed) the percentage of families in poverty will fall to a level between 6.4 percent and 8.7 percent of the population by 1980. . . .

Socioeconomic Characteristics of the Poor

One way of appreciating the relative magnitude of the effect of barriers to earning income is to examine the characteristics of the poor. In Table 1 the 9.7 million poor families in 1959 (utilizing the CEA measure of poverty) are divided into seven mutually exclusive groups classified according to the characteristics of the family head. This breakdown is very suggestive of the major barriers to earning income: age, sex, education, and race.

TABLE 1 Number and Distribution of Poor Families by Characteristics of Family Head, 1959

Characteristic of Family Head	*Number of Families (thousands)*	*Percentage of All Poor Families*
All	9,651	100[a]
65 or over	2,992	31
Female under 65	1,641	17
Male under 25	597	6
Male 25–64 with less than 9 years education	2,799	29
Male 25–64 who dropped out of high school	676	7
Nonwhite male 25–64 who graduated from high school	97	1
White male 25–64 who graduated from high school	483	5

[a] Numbers of poor in categories given do not sum to the total and percentages in categories included do not sum to 100 because family heads 25–64 with greater than a high school education are omitted and because of rounding.

Source: Derived from Table 10, *Economic Report of the President Together with the Annual Report of the Council of Economic Advisers* (Washington, D.C.: U.S. Government Printing Office, 1964).

More than three-quarters of the poor families have a head who is either over 65 years of age, a female under 65, or a male between the ages of 25 and 64 with less than nine years of education. These characteristics as such cannot be taken as the "causes" of poverty. The percentage of the people with a given characteristic who are poor does, however, give some indication of the probability of someone with the characteristic of being poor. Table 2 gives the percentage of people in poverty (CEA definition) in 1962 with selected characteristics. Note, for example, that families headed by individuals over age 65 have two and one-half times more chance than the total population of being poor. It is equally important to realize that more than half of the households headed by those over 65 years of age, or by females, and almost two-thirds of the households with heads having less than eight years of education, were not in poverty in 1962. Therefore, these characteristics are associated with poverty with some probability. The size of these probabilities can, perhaps, be better understood by examining the causes of poverty.

The Causes of Poverty

An understanding of the relative importance of the fundamental causes of poverty is basic to a rational and efficient antipoverty program. Yet precise quantification is hampered by the circularity of the problem. This very often leads to the conventional wisdom of development economics: the cause of poverty for any family is that it lives in poverty, or

> Low real income is a reflection of low productivity, which in turn is due largely to lack of capital. The lack of capital is a result of a small capacity to save, and so the circle is complete.[1]

Fundamentally, however, the economic causes of poverty may be divided into three general types: (1) a level of aggregate demand inadequate to provide full employment, (2) low productivity, and (3) discrimination. Of course, these three types are not mutually exclusive because, for example, high levels of aggregate demand can affect both productivity and discriminatory barriers. However, the distinction is helpful at the outset, and thus these three types will be dealt with in order.

Poverty and employment opportunities

Post-Keynesian developments in macro theory assert that business cycle fluctuations are fundamentally interrelated with the growth behavior of the economy, with the result that the growth rate in income in the economy is related to the level of unemployment. Growth in median family or per capita income is likely to reduce poverty because some people "spill over" into affluence as income grows. Unemployment results in poverty simply because unemployment compensation and other transfers are not adequate to raise out of poverty those people who cannot find jobs. Variations in the rate of growth and unemployment thus cause the incidence of poverty to vary. Burton Weisbrod has shown that in the years of strong expansion between 1948 and 1963, poverty fell on the average of 667,000 families a year, and in the years of weak expansion it fell on the average of 425,000 families a year, whereas it increased by 400,000 families a year on the average in the years of no expansion or contraction.

[1] Ragnar Nurkse, *Problems of Capital Formation in Underdeveloped Countries* (Oxford: Blackwell, 1953). See Ch. 1 for the development of the vicious circle of poverty.

TABLE 2 Selected Characteristics of Poor Families, 1962

Selected Characteristics	*Number of Families (millions)*		*Incidence of Poverty (percent)*
	All Families	*Poor Families*	
Total	47.0	9.3	19.8
Age of head 65 and over	6.8	3.2	47.1
Female head	4.7	2.3	48.9
Nonwhite head	4.6	2.0	43.5
Head with less than 8 years of education	16.3	6.0	36.8

Source: *Economic Report of the President Together with the Annual Report of the Council of Economic Advisers* (Washington: U.S. Government Printing Office, 1964).

Lowell Gallaway and Henry Aaron have attempted to estimate empirically the effect that changes in median family income and the level of unemployment have on the incidence of poverty (as measured by the CEA). . . . These estimates are obtained from Aaron's regression equations under the assumptions that economic growth will continue at the 1947–1956 rate (median family income increased at an average annual rate of 2.93 percent in this period), and that unemployment will continue at 4 percent. Several observations may be made with respect to these results. First, rapid economic expansion and near full employment will significantly reduce the incidence of poverty for all groups (with an absolute measure of poverty). Second, the incidence of poverty for both white and nonwhite households with female heads will fall only half as fast as the incidence of poverty for households with male heads. Third, the incidence of poverty among nonwhites in 1980 will still be two to three times the rate for whites.

Assuming very rapid economic expansion and a level of unemployment lower than that experienced during most of the present decade in the United States (the unemployment rate was at or below 4 percent in only 7 of the last 20 years), 24.7 percent of the nonfarm households headed by white females, and over 43 percent of the nonwhite, nonfarm households with female heads will still be in poverty in 1980. However, under these conditions, poverty among nonfarm households headed by white males will be virtually eliminated.

Poverty caused by insufficient productivity

In a mixed free enterprise economy such as the United States, there is a tendency for output to be distributed in proportion to productive contributions. Hence, poverty is inevitable if productivity is low, unless transfer payments are adequate to make up the difference between the poverty line and productivity. From a theoretical and policy point of view it is helpful to distinguish between low productivity that results from market imperfections and that which would exist under perfect market conditions.

Even if the market worked perfectly, some poverty would exist. Low productivity resulting from the misfortunes of accident, disease, and mental illness accounted for at least 2.1 million poor individuals in 1960. In a perfect market economy the "life cycle" in productivity—the normal pattern in which productivity and income are low in the young ages, rise gradually to a peak in middle ages, and then decline as the family head grows older—may also result in poverty. However, the productivity life cycle as a contributor to poverty is very complex for those old enough to be in the labor market. For example, the mean income in 1960 for those family heads between 14 and 24 was $4,317, and for those heads over 65 it was $4,396; thus if every family had an income equal to the average for the age of its head there would be no poor families. Still, the probability of being poor for these groups is significantly higher than it is for the population in general.

Market imperfections cause poverty so far as they represent barriers which restrict resources from earning their potential productivity. Misallocation or underallocation of educational resources which results in undereducated, or miseducated, individuals can clearly be a source of low productivity and poverty. Immobility of resources, either through unwillingness or inability to change, reduces productivity. Numerous studies have shown that both geographic and occupational mobility are limited by low education, age, and family obligations; and hence it is significant that in 1960, 61 percent of the poor families had a head with no more than an elementary education, 17 percent of the poor families had a female head under 65, and 31 percent of the poor families had a head over age 65. Minimum wage laws at their current levels do not directly cause poverty, but they may cause unemployment, which may produce a culture of poverty which is passed on to future generations.

Poverty caused by discrimination

Discrimination results in an inefficient allocation of resources in the labor market because it creates barriers to allocation on the basis of relative productivities and factor costs. Hence, output and incomes are lower at full employment than those which exist in the absence of discrimination. Although there are a large number of discriminatory barriers in our economy, the major ones include race, age, and sex.

The existence of racial discrimination has been widely documented. With respect to poverty it is reflected by the following: (1) nonwhites had an incidence of poverty in the 1947–1963 period of two and one-half times that of whites, which is explained, at least in part, by the fact that nonwhites have over twice the unemployment rate of whites, and the duration of unemployment for nonwhites tends to be longer; (2) median family income among nonwhites is half that of whites, and the disparity in income between white and Negro males has been widening; and (3) nonwhites experience differential difficulty in moving out of poverty. For example, of the families who moved out of poverty between 1962 and 1963, 33 percent were white and 24 percent were nonwhite; and between 1947 and 1963 the incidence of poverty declined 45 percent for whites and only 34 percent for nonwhites.

It is beyond the scope of this paper to discuss in depth the problem of discrimination among the aged, but several factors may be noted in passing:

(1) Families with a head over 65 had, in the 1960s, a poverty rate two and one-half times that of the total population and two-thirds of the unrelated individuals over age 65 had an income of less than $1,500.

(2) The percentage of the poor who are over 65 years of age has been increasing, and this is likely to continue not only because the over-65 group is growing faster than the total population (the number of people over 65 increased from 2.9 percent in 1870 to 9.6 percent in 1963), but also because the relative number of the aged in the labor market has fallen substantially (in 1890 68.3 percent of the males over 65 were in the labor market compared with 27.6 percent in 1963).

(3) Those aged with the smallest incomes are the least likely or able to continue working after age 65. Thus, a recent survey by the Social Security Administration has shown that 69 percent of the male professional and technical class continue working after 65, whereas 57 percent of the male managers, officials, and proprietors and less than 45 percent of the craftsmen and service workers do.

(4) Leaving the labor market is tantamount to entering poverty for most of those over 65. For example, a survey by the Bureau of the Census in 1963 indicated that couples over 65 who usually worked full time had a median family income of $6,060 in 1962, whereas couples who did not work that year had a median family income of $1,805.

Discrimination against females in United States society is also far too complex to be dealt with in detail here. Women are, however, at a disadvantage in the labor market because they are given fewer educational opportunities and, in the period when males are obtaining on-the-job training which substantially adds to their productivity, the majority of females are relegated to the home to care for young children. Hence, if they become the head of the household the probability of poverty is very high. (In 1963, 48.9 percent of households headed by females, using CEA standards, were poor. See Table 2.) In addition, of course, a large number of jobs have become "male work" and females are clearly restricted.

The Causes of Poverty Combined

Consideration of the general causes of poverty separately does not allow one to determine quantitatively the relative importance of the various factors which contribute to the incidence of poverty. Lester Thurow has developed an econometric model to explain the incidence of poverty. The major factors discussed previously are included as the independent variables and are interpreted as representing the general causes of poverty. Table 3 gives Thurow's

TABLE 3 Poverty Regressed with Various Socioeconomic Characteristics for States and 135 SMSAs, 1960

	State		SMSAs	
Variable	*Regression Coefficient (standard error)*	*Mean (national average)*	*Regression Coefficient (standard error)*	*Mean (average for SMSAs)*
Percentage of families living on farms	.2978 (.0978)	7.4	..[a]	..[a]
Percentage of families headed by non-whites	.1133 (.0544)	9.4	.0888 (.0355)	10.5
Percentage of families with no one in the labor force	.5410 (.1677)	10.7	..[a]	..[a]
Percentage of family heads with less than 8 years of education	.4345 (.0480)	21.9	.3996 (.0552)	14.9
Percentage of the population who worked 50 to 52 weeks a year	—.5368 (.1117)	34.8	—.3793 (.0567)	36.0
An index of industrial structure[b]	—.7600 (.1978)	98.9	—.5131 (.0624)	100.0
Dummy variable—adjusts for: states, Alaska and Hawaii; cities, north and south	10.3777 (4.8210)	.04	—2.9297 (.7574)	.7
Percentage of the population 65 years of age and older	..[a]	..[a]	.2667 (.1419)	8.7
R^2, multiple coefficient of determination	.98		.82	
Standard error of the estimate	2.3		2.7	
Constant term	96.5125		74.8947	

[a] Not included in regression equation.

[b] The index of industrial structure was defined as $I = \sum_{i=1}^{n} X_i W_i$, where X_i is the percentage of the state's or SMSA's labor force in industry i; and W_i is the ratio of the US median income in industry i to the general US median income. Hence, the index measures the prevalence of high-wage industries in the state or SMSA.

results obtained by utilizing 1960 cross-section data for states, together with results I obtained using a similar model applied to the 135 standard metropolitan areas with 40,000 or more manufacturing employees.

Although these results do not allow one to test, with precision, the differences, or similarities, between urban and general (state) poverty, several observations can be made. Quantitatively, an increase in the industry mix variable, which represents the existence of high-paying industries in the city or state, is the most significant way in which a state or city can reduce the incidence of poverty. Drawing high-paying industries within the boundaries of a city or state has as its corollary growth in median family income at the national level. The only other variable which is subject to any state or local control is education, and a 1 percentage point reduction in the proportion with less than eight years of education is associated with a reduction of four-tenths of 1 percent in the incidence of poverty. However, the facts that states and cities are open economies and that the possibility of spillovers exists suggest that local decisions may be non-optimal—and hence national minimum standards may be necessary.

These results also make it clear that tight labor market conditions are fundamental to the elimination of poverty. For example, a change of 1 percentage point in the population working 50 to 52 weeks will reduce poverty by approximately one-half of 1 percent. It is interesting to note that the variable "families headed by non-whites" still enters both of these equations as a significant variable and thus, after holding constant the effect of education and activity in the labor force, nonwhites still account for more poverty. It might be argued that this variable picks up other direct and indirect effects of discrimination. Thus, for example, the fact that the state of Mississippi allocated substantially fewer resources to educating Negroes (between 1940 and 1960 the expenditure for educating Negro students in the public schools was, on the average, about one-half that spent on white students) suggests that nine years of education may not always be the same thing for white and nonwhite.

Conclusions

The purpose of this paper was to survey generally the barriers to earning income which result in or worsen poverty. These barriers are, essentially, (1) inadequate levels of demand, which result in unemployment, (2) low productivity, which in the United States is largely due to immobility of labor both geographically and occupationally (a major portion of this immobility can be explained by low levels of education, old age, and family restrictions for females), and (3) discrimination, which is a significant barrier to earning income for nonwhites, females, and the elderly.

The empirical work which has been done suggests that the percentage of the total population living in poverty (if defined in absolute terms) will decline significantly by 1980 if rapid economic growth and full employment can be maintained. This is true not only because expanding income and employment opportunities will pull people over the poverty line, but because these conditions tend to increase mobility of resources and reduce discriminatory practices. Hence, from an economic point of view rapid growth and full employment undoubtedly have top priority.

There is, however, evidence to suggest that even with rapid growth some groups (nonwhite families, those with inferior education, the aged) may be left in a backwash because substantial barriers exist that prevent them from gaining from economic growth. For these groups some efforts must be made to expand opportunities by either eliminating or reducing barriers to earning income or simply by paying them cash grants.

IS THERE REALLY A NEW POOR?

Stephan Thernstrom

A specter is haunting the imaginations of commentators upon the contemporary scene, the specter of the "new poor." In days of old (precise time conveniently unspecified), the cliché goes, "the immigrant saw poverty as a *temporary state* and looked forward to the day when he or his children could gain greater access to opportunity and financial resources. The poor of today are more inclined to regard poverty as a *permanent way of life* with little hope for themselves or their children. This change in the outlook of the poor can be explained by changes in the opportunity structure." (From Louis Furman's *Poverty in America.*) You can fill in the rest for yourself easily enough: the poor of old had aspirations; the poor today do not. The poor of old had a culture; the poor today have only a culture of poverty. The poor once had political machines which protected them; now they have only social workers who spy upon them. And the crucial contrast, from which so much else follows: the poor were once on the lowest rungs of a ladder most of them could climb; the poor today are a fixed underclass, a permanent proletariat.

A compelling, dramatic image, this, but is there any evidence that it is *true*? This is not the place for an exhaustive analysis of the data, but I suggest that the answer is negative. Much depends, of course, upon just whom we have in mind when we refer to "the poor"—the semantic hazards here are even larger than in most issues of social policy. If, for instance, we insist that

From *Poverty: Views from the Left*, ed. Jeremy Larner and Irving Howe, pp. 83–85, 87–89, 93. Excerpt reprinted with omissions by permission of William Morrow and Company, Inc.

the authentically poor are the kinds of people Oscar Lewis describes in his studies of "the culture of poverty," it is difficult to say anything at all about whether there are more or fewer of them and whether their lot is better or worse than it used to be, because the historical record provides few clues by which to make a judgment. But such simple operational definitions as income, concentration in unskilled or semi-skilled jobs, etc., yield relatively straightforward conclusions. These conclusions will not be palatable to the kind of mindless radical who reasons "things are terrible. Q.e.d: they are getting worse," though they certainly do not, I will argue, dictate a complacent view of the fate of the other America.

First, a word on the poor considered as an income class. There has been a good deal of heated argument about precisely where to draw the poverty line, but little attention to what seem the two points of greatest significance. One is that wherever the line is drawn—$3000, $4000, or whatever—an ever-smaller fraction of the American population falls below that line. The long-term trend of per capita income in this country is dramatically upward, and the way in which that income is distributed has not shifted abruptly in a direction unfavorable to those on the lower end of the scale. The rich have been getting richer, all right, but the poor have been getting richer at much the same rate. There has been no major increase in the proportion of the national income going to those on the bottom in recent decades—a fact American liberals have been pathetically slow to recognize. But the unpleasant truth that there is no pronounced trend toward more equal distribution of income in this country should not obscure the elementary fact that the disadvantaged are now receiving the same fraction of a pie which has grown substantially larger. Admittedly they *expect* more; in some ways it can be said that they *need* more, but that it *is* more is of considerable consequence, however it might seem to those of us who do not have to worry about the grocery bills.

A second observation is that it is very important to know whether the poverty line currently in favor in Washington, or some other (presumably higher) figure preferred by those of us on the left, marks off an *entity* with more or less stable membership, or whether it is a mere category into which Americans fall and out of which they climb in rapid succession. If we can assume that some fixed figure represents a minimal decent income for a family of a certain size, and that all those below it are living in poverty, it is obviously important to know if it is pretty much the same families who fall below that line year after year, as is commonly assumed by proponents of the "new poverty" thesis, or if there is a great deal of annual turnover in the composition of the group. Some people with desperately low incomes, after all, are graduate students. Are many of the poor temporary victims? No one has any idea about the extent of continuity in the lowest income categories in the American past—say, in the nineteenth and early twentieth centuries—

though there is a common and highly questionable assumption that there was little continuity then. . . .

If we turn to another aspect of the new poverty thesis—the assumption that it is now far more difficult for a low-skilled manual laborer to work his way up the occupational ladder than it once was—there is again a startling lack of evidence to buttress the claim. . . .

It is doubtful indeed that a new poverty has recently been created in this country because of creeping arteriosclerosis of the occupational structure. Unskilled and semiskilled laborers still do rise to a higher occupation during their lifetimes, in at least a minority of cases; their sons still make the jump more frequently than their fathers.

Impressive though it is, the evidence on rates and patterns of occupational mobility does not entirely dispose of the arguments of the pessimists. They would emphasize that the demand for unskilled labor, the capacity of the economy to absorb raw newcomers and assure them steady wages, is not what it was when the Golden Door was open to all. That could be true without lowering the rates of occupational mobility, of course. This has become a received truth in discussions of contemporary poverty without the benefit of the slightest critical examination, it seems to me. It is indubitable that the demand for unskilled labor is not what it used to be, if we take as our measure the proportion of jobs that are classified as unskilled; and indeed, discussions of this point often allude to the shrinking of the unskilled category in this century and the mushrooming of the white-collar group, as if that proves something. But what about the demand relative to the supply? To say that this relationship has changed in a way unfavorable to the unskilled is to assert that the pool of unemployed laborers—the Marxian industrial reserve army—is characteristically larger now than it was in the past; and that wage differentials between unskilled and other types of work are now larger. Neither of these propositions can be substantiated.

As to the first, we have a decent times series on average annual unemployment only back to 1900, and one broken down for specific occupational groups—which is really what we want—only since 1940. But you needn't dig at all deeply into historical data to arrive at the conclusion that, however hard it may be for many people to find steady employment in our society today, it was often still harder in the past. Robert Hunter's 1904 study *Poverty* pulls together a few chilling fragments we might profitably recall. In the year 1900, 44.3 percent of the unskilled laborers in the United States were unemployed at some time; of a sample of Italian workers in Chicago, for example, 57 percent had been out of a job some time during the previous year, with the average time unemployed running over seven months! The fact that horror stories like this become increasingly difficult to duplicate as we approach the present, plus the mild but distinct downward trend in the overall unemployment time series since 1900 makes me feel very skeptical about the common assumption that things are getting worse for those on the bottom.

It is possible, of course, that the unskilled labor market now offers fewer employment opportunities to certain kinds of people, and greater opportunities to others. The most obvious case would be the aged, who once were free to die with their boots on and now suffer compulsory retirement. But few of them lived *past* what we now consider retirement age, so that isn't much of an argument for the good old days. The case of the Negro naturally leaps to mind here. It is perfectly clear that the labor market today is not color-blind: at comparable skill levels the Negro receives lower wages, is more often unemployed, etc. If we are assessing trends, however, there is a question as to just what we compare this grossly inequitable situation with. If we compare Negro–white differentials in the past, the only way of arguing a long-term deterioration in the Negro position would be to assume that the sharecropper was better off than the urban laborer. Perhaps, however, a more fruitful point of comparison would be with the most recent immigrant group at other points in the past. Was the gap in wages and employment security between Irish and Yankee laborers in the 1850s or Italian and Yankee laborers in the 1890s as large as the racial gap today? Probably not, though no one has proved it yet.

To the extent, then, that in talking about poverty we really have in mind the problem of the Negro, the historical trend is open to debate (depending on the point of comparison we think most reasonable). With that exception—admittedly not a small one—I see no basis for the common cliché about the sluggish unskilled labor market. . . .

I do not, in sum, see any grounds for believing that this country is now threatened by a mass of "new poor" whose objective situations, especially their opportunities to rise out of poverty, are much worse than those of earlier generations. The real changes I see are generally encouraging, or at least mixed. Some families are worse off today because they can't reap the benefits of child labor: but in the long run, presumably, their children are better off.

I think that one can be clear-headed about what is happening without being complacent about the status quo. I have never understood why so many Americans believe that to assert that things are bad you must insist that they are getting worse. I would argue that they could well be getting a little better—as the situation of the poor in America is, on the whole—and still be intolerably bad. A little less unemployment can still be too damned much unemployment, in a culture where people have become civilized enough to understand that recurrent unemployment is due not to the will of God but to the inaction of man. To conjure up a Golden Age from which to judge the present and find it wanting is quite unnecessary, and as de Tocqueville pointed out long ago, it is even slightly unAmerican, for the American way is to reject the achievements of the past as a standard for the present or future; Americans, he said, use the past only as a means of information, and existing facts only as a lesson used in doing otherwise and doing better.

The following statements are based on data from the 1970 Economic Report of the President, and are based on inadequate income as the measure of poverty. To what extent does income adequately measure the quality (or lack of quality) of life of the poor? When it does not, how would the aspects you consider important change the size and structure of poverty? How do these aspects relate to the quality of life of the poor and the larger society?

1 The number of families in poverty has been cut in half since 1950—from 10.4 million in 1950 to 5.2 million in 1968.
2 When all poor families are considered, over three-quarters of the poor families are white.
3 Almost half the poor families live in the South, and almost half live on farms.
4 Only 6 percent of the heads of poor households are counted as unemployed.
5 About 20 percent of the families are poor even when the head of the household has a high-school education or greater.
6 While total poverty declined 22 percent between 1947 and 1962, families that had three or more children under age eighteen increased by 2 percent in that same period.

179-206

9 "No man is an Iland"

FIFTH AVENUE, UPTOWN: A LETTER FROM HARLEM

James Baldwin

There is a housing project standing now where the house in which we grew up once stood, and one of those stunted city trees is snarling where our doorway used to be. This is on the rehabilitated side of the avenue. The other side of the avenue—for progress takes time—has not been rehabilitated yet and it looks exactly as it looked in the days when we sat with our noses pressed against the windowpane, longing to be allowed to go "across the street." The grocery store which gave us credit is still there, and there can be no doubt that it is still giving credit. The people in the project certainly need it—far more, indeed, than they ever needed the project. The last time I passed by, the Jewish proprietor was still standing among his shelves, looking sadder and heavier but scarcely any older. Farther down the block stands the shoe-repair store in which our shoes were repaired until reparation became impossible and in which, then, we bought all our "new" ones. The Negro proprietor is still in the window, head down, working at the leather.

These two, I imagine, could tell a long tale if they would (perhaps they would be glad to if they could), having watched so many, for so long, struggling in the fishhooks, the barbed wire, of this avenue.

The avenue is elsewhere the renowned and elegant Fifth. The area I am describing, which, in today's gang parlance, would be called "the turf," is bounded by Lenox Avenue on the west, the Harlem River on the east, 135th Street on the north, and 130th Street on the south. We never lived beyond these boundaries; this is where we grew up. Walking along 145th Street—for example—familiar as it is, and similar, does not have the same impact because I do not know any of the people on the block. But when I turn east on 131st Street and Lenox Avenue, there is first a soda-pop joint, then a shoeshine "parlor," then a grocery store, then a dry cleaners', then the houses. All along the street there are people who watched me grow up, people who grew up with me, people I watched grow up along with my brothers and sisters; and, sometimes in my arms, sometimes underfoot, sometimes at my shoulder—or on it—their children, a riot, a forest of children, who include my nieces and nephews.

When we reach the end of this long block, we find ourselves on wide, filthy, hostile Fifth Avenue, facing that project which hangs over the avenue like a monument to the folly, and the cowardice, of good intentions. All along the block, for anyone who knows it, are immense human gaps, like craters. These gaps are not created merely by those who have moved away, inevitably into some other ghetto; or by those who have risen, almost always into a greater capacity for self-loathing and self-delusion; or yet by those who, by whatever means—War II, the Korean war, a policeman's gun or billy, a gang war, a brawl, madness, an overdose of heroin, or, simply, unnatural exhaustion—are dead. I am talking about those who are left, and I am talking principally about the young. What are they doing? Well, some, a minority, are fanatical churchgoers, members of the more extreme of the Holy Roller sects. Many, many more are "moslems," by affiliation or sympathy, that is to say that they are united by nothing more—and nothing less—than a hatred of the white world and all its works. They are present, for example, at every Buy Black street-corner meeting—meetings in which the "speaker urges his hearers to cease trading with white men and establish a separate economy. Neither the speakers nor his hearers can possibly do this, of course, since Negroes do not own General Motors or RCA or the A & P, nor, indeed, do they own more than a wholly insufficient fraction of anything else in Harlem (those who *do* own anything are more interested in their profits than in their fellows). But these meetings nevertheless keep alive in the participators a certain pride of bitterness without which, however futile this bitterness may be, they could scarcely remain alive at all. Many have given up. They stay home and watch the TV screen, living on the earnings of their parents, cousins, brothers, or uncles, and only leave the house to go to the movies or to the nearest bar. "How're you making it?" one may ask, running into them along the block, or in the bar. "Oh, I'm TV-ing it"; with the saddest, sweetest, most shamefaced of smiles, and from a great distance. This distance one is compelled to respect; anyone who has traveled so far will not easily be dragged again into the world. There are further retreats, of course, than the TV screen or the bar. There are those who are simply sitting on their stoops, "stoned," animated for a moment only, and hideously, by the approach of someone who may lend them the money for a "fix." Or by the approach of someone from whom they can purchase it, one of the shrewd ones, on the way to prison or just coming out.

And the others, who have avoided all of these deaths, get up in the morning and go downtown to meet "the man." They work in the white man's world all day and come home in the evening to this fetid block. They struggle to instill in their children some private sense of honor or dignity which will help the child to survive. This means, of course, that they must struggle, stolidly, incessantly, to keep this sense alive in themselves, in spite of the insults, the indifference, and the cruelty they are certain to encounter in their working day. They patiently browbeat the landlord into fixing the heat, the plaster, the plumbing; this demands prodigious patience; nor is patience usually enough. In trying to make their hovels habitable, they are perpetually throwing good money after bad. Such frustration, so long endured, is driving many strong, admirable men and women whose only crime is color to the very gates of paranoia.

One remembers them from another time—playing handball in the playground, going to church, wondering if they were going to be promoted at school. One remembers them going off to war—gladly, to escape this block. One remembers their return. Perhaps one remembers their wedding day. And one sees where the girl is now—vainly looking for salvation from some other embittered, trussed, and struggling boy—and sees the all-but-abandoned children in the streets.

Now I am perfectly aware that there are other slums in which white men are fighting for their lives, and mainly losing. I know that blood is also flowing through those streets and that the human damage there is incalculable. People are continually pointing out to me the wretchedness of white people in order to console me for the wretchedness of blacks. But an itemized account of the American failure does not console me and it should not console anyone else. That hundreds of thousands of white people are living, in effect, no better than the "niggers" is not a fact to be regarded with complacency. The social and moral bankruptcy suggested by this fact is of the bitterest, most terrifying kind.

The people, however, who believe that this democratic anguish has some consoling value are always pointing out that So-and-So, white, and So-and-So, black, rose from the slums into the big time. The existence—the public existence—of, say, Frank Sinatra and Sammy Davis, Jr. proves to them that America is still the land of opportunity and that inequalities vanish before the determined will. It proves nothing of the sort. The determined will is rare—at the moment, in this country, it is unspeakably rare—and the inequalities suffered by the many are in no way justified by the rise of a few. A few have always risen—in every country, every era, and in the teeth of regimes which can by no stretch of the imagination be thought of as free. Not all of these people, it is worth remembering, left the world better than they found it. The determined will is rare, but it is not invariably benevolent. Furthermore, the American equation of success with the big times reveals an awful disrespect for human life and human achievement. This equation has placed our cities among the most dangerous in the world and has placed our youth among the most empty and most bewildered. The situation of our youth is not mysterious. Children have never been very good at listening to their elders, but they have never failed to imitate them. They must, they have no other models. That is exactly what our children are doing. They are imitating our immorality, our disrespect for the pain of others.

All other slum dwellers, when the bank account permits it, can move out of the slum and vanish altogether from the eye of persecution. No Negro in this country has ever made that much money and it will be a long time before any Negro does. The Negroes in Harlem, who have no money, spend what they have on such gimcracks as they are sold. These include "wider" TV screens, more "faithful" hi-fi sets, more "powerful" cars, all of which, of course, are obsolete long before they are paid for. Anyone who has ever struggled with poverty knows how extremely expensive it is to be poor; and if one is a member of a captive population, economically speaking, one's feet have simply been placed on the treadmill forever. One is victimized, economically, in a thousand ways—rent, for example, or car insurance. Go shopping one day in Harlem—for anything—and compare Harlem prices and quality with those downtown.

The people who have managed to get off this block have only got as far as a more respectable ghetto. This respectable ghetto does not even have the advantages of the disreputable one—friends, neighbors, a familiar church, and friendly tradesmen; and it is not, moreover, in the nature of any ghetto to remain respectable long. Every Sunday, people who have left the block take the lonely ride back, dragging their increasingly discontented children with them. They spend the day talking, not always with words, about the trouble they've seen and the trouble—one must watch their eyes as they watch their children—they are only too likely to see. For children do not like ghettos. It takes them nearly no time to discover exactly why they are there.

The projects in Harlem are hated. They are hated almost as much as policemen, and this is saying a great deal. And they are hated for the same reason: both reveal, unbearably, the real attitude of the white world, no matter how many liberal speeches are made, no matter how many lofty editorials are written, no matter how many civil-rights commissions are set up.

The projects are hideous, of course, there being a law, apparently respected throughout the world, that popular housing shall be as cheerless as a prison. They are lumped all over Harlem, colorless, bleak, high, and revolting. The wide windows look out on Harlem's invincible and indescribable squalor: the Park Avenue railroad tracks, around which, about forty years ago, the present dark community began; the unrehabilitated houses, bowed down, it would seem, under the great weight of frustration and bitterness they contain; the dark, the ominous schoolhouses from which the child may emerge maimed, blinded, hooked, or enraged for life: and the churches, churches, block upon block of churches, niched in the walls like cannon in the walls of fortresses. Even if the administration of the projects were not so insanely humilitating (for example: one must report raises in salary to the management, which will then eat up the profit by raising one's rent; the management has the right to know who is staying in your apartment; the management can ask you to leave, at their discretion), the projects would still be hated because they are an insult to the meanest intelligence.

Harlem got its first private project, Riverton[1]—which is now, naturally, a slum—about twelve years ago because at that time Negroes were not allowed to live in Stuyvesant Town. Harlem watched Riverton go up, therefore, in the most violent bitterness of spirit, and hated it long before the builders arrived. They began hating it at about the time people began moving out of their condemned houses to make room for this additional proof of how thoroughly the white world despised them. And they had scarcely moved in, naturally, before they began smashing windows, defacing walls, urinating in the elevators, and fornicating in the playgrounds. Liberals, both white and black, were appalled at the spectacle. I was appalled by the liberal innocence—or cynicism, which comes out in practice as much the same thing. Other people were delighted to be able to point to proof positive that nothing could be done to better the lot of the colored people. They were, and are, right in one respect: that nothing can be done as long as they are treated like colored people. The people in Harlem know they are living there because white people do not think they are good enough to live anywhere else. No amount of "improvement" can sweeten this fact. Whatever money is now being earmarked to improve this, or any other ghetto, might as well be burnt. A ghetto can be improved in one way only: out of existence.

Similarly, the only way to police a ghetto is to be oppressive. None of the Police Commissioner's men, even with the best will in the world, have any way of understanding the lives led by the people they swagger about in twos and threes controlling. Their very presence is an insult, and it would be, even if they spent their entire day feeding gumdrops to children. They represent the force of the white world, and that world's real intentions are, simply, for that world's criminal profit and ease, to keep the black man corraled up here, in his place. The badge, the gun in the holster, and the swinging club make vivid what will happen should his rebellion become overt. Rare, indeed, is the Harlem citizen, from the most circumspect church member to the most shiftless adolescent, who does not have a long tale to tell of police incompetence, injustice, or brutality. I myself have witnessed and endured it more than once. The businessmen and racketeers also have a story. And so do the prostitutes. (And this is not, perhaps, the place

[1] The inhabitants of Riverton were much embittered by this description; they have, apparently, forgotten how their project came into being; and have repeatedly informed me that I cannot possibly be referring to Riverton, but to another housing project which is directly across the street. It is quite clear, I think, that I have no interest in accusing any individuals or families of the depredations herein described: but neither can I deny the evidence of my own eyes. Nor do I blame anyone in Harlem for making the best of a dreadful bargain. But anyone who lives in Harlem and imagines that he has *not* struck this bargain, or that what he takes to be his status (in whose eyes?) protects him against the common pain, demoralization, and danger, is simply self deluded.

to discuss Harlem's very complex attitude toward black policemen, nor the reasons, according to Harlem, that they are nearly all downtown.)

It is hard, on the other hand, to blame the policeman, blank, good-natured, thoughtless, and insuperably innocent, for being such a perfect representative of the people he serves. He, too, believes in good intentions and is astounded and offended when they are not taken for the deed. He has never, himself, done anything for which to be hated—which of us has?—and yet he is facing, daily and nightly, people who would gladly see him dead, and he knows it. There is no way for him not to know it: there are few things under heaven more unnerving than the silent, accumulating contempt and hatred of a people. He moves through Harlem, therefore, like an occupying soldier in a bitterly hostile country; which is precisely what, and where, he is, and is the reason he walks in twos and threes. And he is not the only one who knows why he is always in company: the people who are watching him know why, too. Any street meeting, sacred or secular, which he and his colleagues uneasily cover has as its explicit or implicit burden the cruelty and injustice of the white domination. And these days, of course, in terms increasingly vivid and jubilant, it speaks of the end of that domination. The white policeman standing on a Harlem street corner finds himself at the very center of the revolution now occurring in the world. He is not prepared for it—naturally, nobody is—and, what is possibly much more to the point, he is exposed, as few white people are, to the anguish of the black people around him. Even if he is gifted with the merest mustard grain of imagination, something must seep in. He cannot avoid observing that some of the children, in spite of their color, remind him of children he has known and loved, perhaps even of his own children. He knows that he certainly does not want *his* children living this way. He can retreat from his uneasiness in only one direction: into a callousness which very shortly becomes second nature. He becomes more callous, the population becomes more hostile, the situation grows more tense, and the police force is increased. One day, to everyone's astonishment, someone drops a match in the powder keg and everything blows up. Before the dust has settled or the blood congealed, editorials, speeches, and civil-rights commissions are loud in the land, demanding to know what happened. What happened is that Negroes want to be treated like men.

Negroes want to be treated like men: a perfectly straightforward statement, containing only seven words. People who have mastered Kant, Hegel, Shakespeare, Marx, Freud, and the Bible find this statement utterly impenetrable. The idea seems to threaten profound, barely conscious assumptions. A kind of panic paralyzes their features, as though they found themselves trapped on the edge of a steep place. I once tried to describe to a very well-known American intellectual the conditons among Negroes in the South. My recital disturbed him and made him indignant; and he asked me in perfect innocence, "Why don't all the Negroes in the South move North?"

I tried to explain what *has* happened, unfailingly, whenever a significant body of Negroes move North. They do not escape Jim Crow: they merely encounter another, not-less-deadly variety. They do not move to Chicago, they move to the South Side; they do not move to New York, they move to Harlem. The pressure within the ghetto causes the ghetto walls to expand, and this expansion is always violent. White people hold the line as long as they can, and in as many ways as they can, from verbal intimidation to physical violence. But inevitably the border which has divided the ghetto from the rest of the world falls into the hands of the ghetto. The white people fall back bitterly before the black horde; the landlords make a tidy profit by raising the rent, chopping up the rooms, and all but dispensing with the upkeep; and what has once been a neighborhood turns into a "turf." This is precisely what happened when the Puerto Ricans arrived in their thousands—and the bitterness thus caused is, as I write, being fought out all up and down those streets.

Northerners indulge in an extremely dangerous luxury. They seem to feel that because they fought on the right side during the Civil War, and won, they have earned the right merely to deplore what is going on in the South, without taking any responsibility for it; and that they can ignore what is happening in Northern cities because what is happening in Little Rock or Birmingham is worse. Well, in the first place, it is not possible for anyone who has not endured both to know which is "worse." I know Negroes who prefer the South and white Southerners, because "At least there, you haven't got to play any guessing games!" The guessing games referred to have driven more than one Negro into the narcotics ward, the madhouse, or the river. I know another Negro, a man very dear to me, who says, with conviction and with truth, "The spirit of the South is the spirit of America." He was born in the North and did his military training in the South. He did not, as far as I can gather, find the South "worse"; he found it, if anything, all too familiar. In the second place, though, even if Birmingham *is* worse, no doubt Johannesburg, South Africa, beats it by several miles, and Buchenwald was one of the worst things that ever happened in the entire history of the world. The world has never lacked for horrifying examples; but I do not believe that these examples are meant to be used as justification for our own crimes. This perpetual justification empties the heart of all human feeling. The emptier our hearts become, the greater will be our crimes. Thirdly, the South is not merely an embarrassingly backward region, but a part of this country, and what happens there concerns every one of us.

Negro death rates [have worsened] in Chicago over the last ten years in contrast to striking improvements in other parts of the nation and world. To cite but one example, the infant death rate of Chicago Negroes has increased by one-fourth since 1958 and today stands higher than the death rates of all 50 states and of all industrial nations. Tragic as is this needless sacrifice of babies before the altar of private medicine, even more tragic are the worsening conditions of health and living reflected by rising Negro death rates. The bankruptcy of private medicine and private health care in Negro areas is but a part of the larger failure of the free market economy to accommodate the urban Negro. The gradual withering of medical resources in Negro communities is but a by-product of the more general disintegration of Negro community life fostered by the push-and-pull forces of white decentralization and black centralization that are tearing asunder the social fabric of Chicago and other large American metropolitan communities.

Pierre de Vise, *Chicago's Widening Color Gap: Alienation of Negroes from the White Community* (Chicago: De Paul University, 1967).

As far as the color problem is concerned, there is but one great difference between the Southern white and the Northerner: the Southerner remembers, historically and in his own psyche, a kind of Eden in which he loved black people and they loved him. Historically, the flaming sword laid across this Eden is the Civil War. Personally, it is the Southerner's sexual coming of age, when, without any warning, unbreakable taboos are set up between himself and his past. Everything, thereafter, is permitted him except the love he remembers and has never ceased to need. The resulting, indescribable torment affects every Southern mind and is the basis of the Southern hysteria.

None of this is true for the Northerner. Negroes represent nothing to him personally, except, perhaps, the dangers of carnality. He never sees Negroes. Southerners see them all the time. Northerners never think about them whereas Southerners are never really thinking of anything else. Negroes are, therefore, ignored in the North and are under surveillance in the South, and suffer hideously in both places. Neither the Southerner nor the Northerner is able to look on the Negro simply as a man. It seems to be indispensable to the national self-esteem that the Negro be considered either as a kind of ward (in which case we are told how many Negroes, comparatively, bought Cadillacs last year and how few, comparatively, were lynched), or as a victim (in which case we are promised that he will never vote in our assemblies or go to school with our kids). They are two sides of the same coin and the South will not change—*cannot* change—until the North changes. The country will not change until it re-examines itself and discovers what it really means by freedom. In the meantime, generations keep being born, bitterness is increased by incompetence, pride, and folly, and the world shrinks around us.

It is a terrible, an inexorable, law that one cannot deny the humanity of another without diminishing one's own: in the face of one's victim, one sees oneself. Walk through the streets of Harlem and see what we, this nation, have become.

. . . a society

—which compels the vast majority of the population to "earn" their living in stupid, inhuman, and unnecessary jobs,

—which conducts its booming business on the back of ghettoes, slums, and internal and external colonialism,

—which is infested with violence and repression while demanding obedience and compliance from the victims of violence and repression,

—which, in order to sustain the profitable productivity on which its hierarchy depends, utilizes its vast resources for waste, destruction, and an ever more methodical creation of conformist needs and satisfactions.

Herbert Marcuse, *An Essay on Liberation* (Boston: Beacon Press, 1969), p. 62.

BLAMING POVERTY ON ITS VICTIMS

Hyman Lumer

The notion has been widely propagated in this country that if anyone is poor or unemployed it is because there is something wrong with him. The great depression of the thirties did much to dispel this fallacy, but it persists nevertheless as the stock-in-trade of reaction.

In its crudest version it takes the form of the slanderous allegation that the poor and the jobless are the lazy and the shiftless. This version is today part of the arsenal of the ultra-Right and its standard-bearer Barry Goldwater. Typical of his views are such pronouncements as these:

"I'm tired of professional chiselers walking up and down the streets who don't work and have no intention of working." (*New York Times*, July 19, 1964.)

"The fact is that most people who have no skills have no education for the same reason—low intelligence or low ambition." (*New York Times*, January 16, 1964.)

From Hyman Lumer, *Poverty: Its Roots and Its Future,* pp. 13–16. Reprinted by permission of International Publishers Co., Inc.

Similar views are expressed editorially by the *Wall Street Journal* (March 11, 1964), which regards poverty as an individual problem and its relief as the responsibility of the poor themselves. The editorial asserts that "almost all of us are up from poverty and almost none of our forebears considered it anybody's responsibility but his own to get up." Johnson's anti-poverty policy is condemned on the grounds that its logic "demands that the shiftless as well as the deserving have equal right to the fruits of the productive. Since there are those only too willing to live at the expense of others, that approach may only swell the ranks of the shiftless and help perpetuate poverty." To be sure, there are those who are "only too willing to live at the expense of others," but the successful practitioners of this philosophy are far more likely to be found within the clientele of the *Wall Street Journal* than among the poor.

There are others who would reject any such openly slanderous characterization of the poor, but who nevertheless ascribe poverty to individual peculiarities or shortcomings. Among these is Galbraith, who maintains that the general poverty of the working class has been abolished, leaving only individually-produced forms. He reduces present-day poverty, therefore, to what he calls "case poverty" and "insular poverty."

The former he defines as poverty related to "some quality peculiar to the individual or family involved—mental deficiency, bad health, inability to adapt to the discipline of modern economic life, excessive procreation, alcohol, insufficient education, or perhaps a combination of several of these handicaps. . . ." The latter he defines as a geographical "island" of poverty most of whose inhabitants do not wish to leave it, thus rejecting the solution to their poverty offered by emigration. (*The Affluent Society*, pp. 252–253.)

Herman P. Miller similarly argues that modern poverty reflects the shortcomings of the poor. In his book *Rich Man, Poor Man* (1964) he states (p. 81): "If a distribution has a top and a middle, it must also have a bottom and somebody must be there. The important question is why they are there and how much they get. People are not all equally endowed with good health, intelligence, creativity, drive, etc. In any society a premium will be paid to those who are most productive."

"There are," he says, "millions of fine, respectable, honest men whose native intelligence is quite low and who lack training to do any but the most menial work. They are poor because their productivity is low" (p. 69). On the other hand, "by and large, the wealthy in the United States contain some of the best and most essential talents—doctors, lawyers, engineers, entertainers, artists, plant managers, etc. While the association between ability and income is far from perfect, ordinary observation shows that many of the most talented are among the highest paid" (p. 125).

In short, the lazy and incompetent are generally poor; the talented and industrious are generally well off. One may help the poor by means of social welfare measures or private charity, but the divergence in status is inherent in the nature of things. A statistical distribution must have a lower range as well as an upper—in ability as in income. Again, the poor are reduced to a "statistical segment," and as such the category is eternal.

Such an explanation will not stand up. The basic causes of poverty are not individual but social. Individual differences can at most determine who is most apt to be poor, given the existence of poverty. But they cannot explain either its existence or its extent. The reasons for these must be sought in economic and social factors beyond the individual's control, ultimately in the character of the processes of production and distribution. True, there are people who suffer poverty because of personal handicaps or just plain misfortune. Such people need special consideration and help. But to take such a social work approach to the overall problem of poverty in our society is only to cover up the real causes.

First of all, the bulk of those in the lowest-paying jobs are not there because of lack of intelligence or other personal deficiencies but for quite other reasons. A large part of them, for example, are Negroes, Puerto Ricans or Mexican-Americans who are victims of discrimination. Others may be workers—particularly older workers—displaced from jobs by automation or the closing down of plants and unable to find anything better.

Secondly, the unemployed Appalachian coal miner or Pittsburgh steelworker is not out of a job because of his "low productivity." On the contrary, it is the multiplication of his productivity by means of new machinery and its utilization by his former employer to reduce the number of workers on his payroll that are responsible. If workers are victims of technological change in our society, this has nothing to do with their personal characteristics. "It was no sloth on the part of the coal miner," writes Bagdikian (*In the Midst of Plenty*, p. 182), "that caused petroleum to emerge as the more versatile fuel. It was no weakness in the railroad engineer that made the car and truck dominate transportation. Nor was it because farmers worked less hard that expensive machinery became more profitable than the simple plow. . . . Yet, the politics and social values of the commercial community, which depend on this versatility and change, assume that poverty and unemployment are casual, self-imposed and self-liquidating."

No man is an Iland, intire of it selfe; every man is a peece of the Continent, a part of the maine; if a Clod bee washed away by the Sea, Europe is the lesse, as well as if a Promontorie were, as well as if a Mannor of thy friends or of thine owne were; any mans death diminishes me, because I am involved in Mankinde; And therefore never send to know for whom the bell tolls; It tolls for thee. . . .

John Donne, "For Whom the Bell Tolls," *John Donne: Selected Prose*, ed. Evelyn Simpson (Oxford: Clarendon Press, 1967), p. 101.

HARLEM: THE MAKING OF A GHETTO

Gilbert Osofsky

The creation of Negro Harlem was only one example of the general development of large, segregated Negro communities within many American cities in the years *preceding* and following World War I. Harlem was New York's equivalent of the urban ghettos of the nation. "The Negroes are being relegated to the land of Goshen in all our great cities," Kelly Miller commented. "Niggertowns," "Buzzard's Alleys," "Nigger Rows," "Black Bottoms," "Smoketowns," "Bronzevilles," and "Chinch Rows" developed elsewhere, North and South, by 1913—and they would continue to emerge in the future. The District of Columbia was noted for its supposedly decadent Negro alleys: "Tin Can Alley," "Coon Alley," "Hog Alley," "Moonshine Alley," and "Goat Alley." (Life in "Goat Alley," was the subject of a play by that name in the 1920s.) "So closely have the terms Alleys and Negroes been associated," a historian of Washington's Negro section wrote, "that in the minds of the older citizens they are inseparable." "There is growing up in the cities of America a distinct Negro world," George Edmund Haynes said in 1913. These were neighborhoods "isolated from many of the impulses of the common life and little understood by the white world," he concluded.

Among these urban ghettos Harlem was unique. Initially, its name was a symbol of elegance and distinction, not derogation; its streets and avenues were broad, well-paved, clean and tree-lined, not narrow and dirty; its homes were spacious, replete with the best modern facilities, "finished in high-style." Harlem was originally not a slum, but an ideal place in which to live. For the first and generally last time in the history of New York City, Negroes were able to live in decent homes in a respectable neighborhood, "the best houses that they have ever had to live in": "It is no longer necessary for our people to live in small, dingy, stuffy tenements," *The New York Age* said in an editorial in 1906. Harlem was "a community in which Negroes as a whole are . . . better housed than in any other part of the country," an Urban League report concluded in 1914. "Those of the race who desire to live in grand style, with elevator, telephone and hall boy service, can now realize their cherished ambition."

It was expensive to live in "grand style." The rents paid by Harlem's Negroes were higher than those charged in any other Negro section of New York City and they continued to rise rapidly after World War I. In 1914 the average Negro family paid $23.45 per month for apartments in Harlem, and rents in the most elegant houses were much higher. As Negroes moved into the neighborhood they complained of being overcharged by landlords and, as a rule, most were paying higher rents than their incomes would warrant. . . .

The creation of a Negro community within one large and solid geographic area was unique in city history. New York had never been what realtors call an "open city"—a city in which Negroes lived wherever they chose—but the former Negro sections were traditionally only a few blocks in length, often spread across the island and generally interspersed with residences of white working-class families. Harlem, however, was a Negro world unto itself. A scattered handful of "marooned white families . . . stubbornly remained" in the Negro section, a United States census-taker recorded, but the mid-belly of Harlem was predominantly Negro by 1920.

And the ghetto rapidly expanded. Between the First World War and the Great Depression, Harlem underwent radical changes. When the twenties came to an end Negroes lived as far south as One Hundred and Tenth Street —the northern boundary of Central Park; practically all the older white residents had moved away; the Russian-Jewish and Italian sections of Harlem, founded a short generation earlier, were rapidly being depopulated; and Negro Harlem, within the space of ten years, became the most "incredible slum" in the entire city. In 1920 James Weldon Johnson was able to predict a glowing future for this Negro community: "Have you ever stopped to think what the future Harlem will be?" he wrote. "It will be the greatest Negro city in the world. . . . And what a fine part of New York City [the Negro] has come into possession of!" By the late 1920s and early 1930s, however, Harlem's former "high-class" homes offered, in the words of a housing expert, "the best laboratory for slum clearance . . . in the entire city." "Harlem conditions," a *New York Times* reporter concluded, are "simply deplorable." . . .

The most profound change that Harlem experienced in the 1920s was its emergence as a slum. Largely within the space of a single decade Harlem was transformed from a potentially ideal community to a neighborhood with manifold social and economic problems called "deplorable," "unspeakable," "incredible." "The State would not allow cows to live in some of these apartments used by colored people . . . in Harlem," the chairman of a city housing reform committee said in 1927. The Harlem slum of today was created in the 1920s.

The most important factor which led to the rapid deterioration of Harlem housing was the high cost of living in the community. Rents, traditionally high in Harlem, reached astounding proportions in the 1920s—they skyrocketed in response to the unprecedented demand created by heavy Negro migration and settlement within a restricted geographical area. "Crowded in a black ghetto," a sociologist wrote, "the Negro tenant is forced to pay exorbitant rentals because he cannot escape." In 1919 the average Harlemite paid somewhat above $21 or $22 a month for rent; by 1927 rentals had *doubled* and the "mean average market rent for Negro tenants in a typical block" was $41.77. In 1927 Harlem Negroes paid $8 more than the typical New Yorker for three-room apartments; $10 more for four rooms; and $7 more for five rooms, an Urban League survey noted. Another report concluded that the typical white working-class family in New York City in the late twenties paid $6.67 per room, per month, while Harlem Negroes were charged $9.50.

Realty values which had declined significantly prior to World War I *appreciated* in Harlem in the twenties. Harlem experienced a slum boom. "The volume of business done in the section . . . during the last year is . . . unprecedented," *Harlem Magazine* announced in 1920. "Renting conditions have been very satisfactory to the owners and the demand for space . . . is getting keener every year [due] to the steady increase in the negro population," a *New York Times* reporter wrote in 1923. There was, in the language of a Harlem businessman, an "unprecedented demand for Harlem real estate." For landlords—Negro and white (Negro tenants continually complained that Negro landlords fleeced them with equal facility as whites) —Harlem became a profitable slum.

High rents and poor salaries necessarily led to congested and unsanitary conditions. The average Negro Harlemite in the 1920s, as in the 1890s, held some menial or unskilled position which paid low wages—work which was customarily "regarded as Negro jobs." There were generally two types of businesses in New York in terms of Negro hiring policy, E. Franklin Frazier wrote: "Those that employ Negroes in menial positions and those that employ no Negroes at all." Macy's, for example, hired Negroes as elevator operators, escalator attendants and cafeteria workers; Gimbels used none. "We have felt it inadvisable to [hire] colored people," a Metropolitan Life Insurance Company executive explained in 1930, "not because of any prejudice on the part of the company, but because . . . there would be very serious objection on the part of our white employees. . . ." Throughout the city the vast majority of Negro men worked as longshoremen, elevator operators, porters, janitors, teamsters, chauffeurs, waiters and general laborers of all kinds. Negro women continued to work as domestics ("scrub women"), although in the 1920s an increasing number were employed as factory operatives in the garment industry and in laundries. Less than 20 percent of Harlem's businesses were owned by Negroes. The average Harlem family, according to President Hoover's Conference on Home Building and Home Ownership, earned $1,300 a year in the twenties; the typical white family in the city, $1,570. A variety of social investigations noted that working-class whites expended approximately 20 percent of their income for rent, considered the proper amount by economists; Harlemites, 33 percent and more. An Urban League study of 2,160 Harlem families demonstrated that almost half (48 percent) spent 40 or more percent of their earnings on rent. A 1928 sample of tenement families found that Harlemites paid 45 percent of their wages for housing. Similar conclusions were reached in a variety of local community studies. Whatever the exact figure, few Negroes looked to the first of the month with expectancy.

Added to the combination of "high rents and low wages" was the fact that Harlem's apartment houses and brownstones were originally built for people with a radically different family structure from that of the new residents. Seventy-five percent of Harlem's tenements had been constructed before 1900. The Negro community of the twenties, like all working-class peoples in times of great migration, continued to be most heavily populated by young adults—men and women between the ages of 15 and 44. Family life had not yet begun for many Negro Harlemites—as it had for older Americans and earlier immigrants who lived in the community previously. In 1930, 66.5 percent of Harlem Negroes were between the ages of 15 and 44, contrasted with 56.5 percent for the general population of Manhattan and 54.4 percent for New York City at large. Harlemites who were married had few children. In 1930, 17.5 percent of Harlem's population was under 14; the corresponding figure for New York City was 24.5 percent. The number of Harlemites under the age of 15 declined 14 percent between 1920 and 1930, as whites left the neighborhood. There was a corresponding decrease of 19 percent for those over 45 years of age.

What all these statistics mean is simply that apartments of five, six, and seven rooms were suitable for older white residents with larger families and larger incomes—they obviously did not meet the needs of the Negro community in the 1920s. "The houses in the section of Harlem inhabited by the Negro were not only built for another race," E. Franklin Frazier noted, "but what is more important, for a group of different economic level, and consisting of families and households of an entirely different composition from those which now occupy these dwellings." "Unfortunately," Eugene Kinckle Jones of the Urban League stated, "the houses built before [the Negroes'] arrival were not designed to meet the needs . . . of Negroes." "The class of houses we are occupying today are not suited to our economic needs," John E. Nail said in 1921. Negro Harlemites desperately needed small apartments at low rentals: "One of the community's greatest needs [is] small apartments for small families with a reasonable rent limit. . . ." Few realtors were philanthropic enough to invest their capital in new construction; older homes, properly subdivided, produced sufficient income. Only a handful of new houses were built in Harlem in the 1920s.

A variety of makeshift solutions were found to make ends meet: "What you gonna do when the rent comes 'round," had been an old Negro song. The most common solution was to rent an apartment larger than one's needs and means and make up the difference by renting rooms to lodgers—"commercializing" one's home. In the twenties, approximately one white

Manhattan family in nine (11.2 percent) took in roomers, contrasted with one in four (26 percent) for Negroes. Most lodgers were strangers people let into their homes because of economic necessity. It was difficult to separate "the respectable" from "the fast." "The most depraved Negroes lived side by side with those who were striving to live respectable lives," a contemporary complained. Urban reformers blamed many of Harlem's social problems on this "lodger evil."

Every conceivable space within a home was utilized to maximum efficiency: "Sometimes even the bathtub is used to sleep on, two individuals taking turns!" Negro educator Roscoe Conkling Bruce wrote. Boardinghouses were established which rented beds by the week, day, night or hour. A large number of brownstones were converted to rooming houses: "Private residences at one time characteristic of this part of the city have been converted into tenements. . . ." One landlord transformed apartments in nine houses into one-room flats, a state commission investigating New York housing reported. Space which formerly grossed $40 a month now brought in $100 to $125. People were said to be living in "coal bins and cellars." In an extreme case, one social investigator discovered seven children sleeping on pallets on the floor of a two-room apartment. More common was the "Repeating" or "Hot Bed System"—as soon as one person awoke and left, his bed was taken over by another.

An additional Harlem method devised to meet the housing crisis of the twenties was the "Rent Party." Tickets of admission were usually printed and sold for a modest price (25¢). All who wanted to come were invited to a party. Here is an example:

> If you're looking for a good time,
>   don't look no more,
> Just ring my bell and I'll answer
>   the door.
> Southern Barbecue
> Given by Charley Johnson and Joe
>   Hotboy, and How hot!

Chitterlings, pigs' feet, coleslaw and potato salad were sold. Money was raised in this way to pay the rent: "The rent party," *The New York Age* editorialized in 1926, "has become a recognized means of meeting the demands of extortionate landlords. . . ." The white world saw rent parties as picturesque affairs—in reality they were a product of economic exploitation and they often degenerated into rowdy, bawdy and violent evenings.

A significant part of the deterioration of the neighborhood was caused by the migrants themselves. Some needed rudimentary training in the simplest processes of good health and sanitation (Booker T. Washington, it will be remembered, preached the "gospel of the toothbrush"). E. Franklin Frazier called many Negro Harlemites "ignorant and unsophisticated peasant people without experience [in] urban living. . . ." They often permitted homes and buildings to remain in a state of uncleanliness and disrepair. Landlords complained that apartments were looted and fixtures stolen, that courtyards and hallways were found laden with refuse. Clothes and bedding were hung out of windows; trash sometimes thrown down air shafts; dogs walked on rooftops; profanities shouted across streets; "ragtime" played throughout the night. "Ragtime is a sufficient infliction of itself," one wag complained, "but when it keeps up all night, it becomes unbearable." "Since the so-called 'Negro invasion,' " a colored woman noted, "the streets, the property and the character of everything have undergone a change, and if you are honest, you will frankly acknowledge it has not been for the . . . improvement of the locality. . . . Are we responsible for at least some of the race prejudice which has developed since the entry of Negroes in Harlem?" Negro journals criticized "boisterous" men who laughed "hysterically" and hung around street corners, and those who used "foul language on the streets." An editorial in the *Age*, one of many, attacked "Careless Harlem Tenants": "A great deal might be said about the necessity for training some of the tenants in the matter of common decency," it suggested. The absence of a sense of social and community responsibility, characteristic of urban life, obviously affected Negro Harlemites.

All these factors combined to lead to the rapid decline of Harlem. The higher the rents, sociologists said, the greater the congestion: "Crowding is more prevalent in high-rent cities than in cities in which rent per room is more reasonable." In 1925, Manhattan's population density was 223 people per acre—in the Negro districts it was 336. Philadelphia, the second most congested Negro city in the country, had 111 Negroes to an acre of land; Chicago ranked third with 67. There were two streets in Harlem that were perhaps the most congested blocks in the entire world.

People were packed together to the point of "indecency." Some landlords, after opening houses to Negro tenants, lost interest in caring for their property and permitted it to run down—halls were left dark and dirty, broken pipes were permitted to rot, steam heat was cut off as heating apparatus wore out, dumb-waiters broke down and were boarded up, homes became vermin-infested. Tenants in one rat-infested building started what they called "a crusade against rats." They argued that the rats in their house were "better fed" and "better housed" than the people. Some common tenant complaints in the 1920s read: "No improvement in ten years"; "Rats, rat holes, and roaches"; "Very very cold"; "Not fit to live in"; "Air shaft smells"; "Ceilings in two rooms have fallen"; "My apartment is overrun with rats"; and so on. There were more disputes between tenants and landlords in Harlem's local district court—the Seventh District Court—than in any municipal court in the five boroughs. Traditionally, municipal courts were known as "poor-men's courts"; Harlemites called the Seventh District Court the "rent court." Occasionally, socially conscious judges of this court made personal inspections of local tenements that were subjects of litigation. Without exception what they saw horrified them: "Conditions in negro tenements in Harlem are deplorable"; "Found few fit for human habitation"; "Negro tenants are being grossly imposed upon by their landlords"; "On the whole I found a need for great reformation"; were some of their comments. One municipal official accurately called the majority of Harlem's houses "diseased properties."

INTERNAL COLONIALISM AND GHETTO REVOLT

Robert Blauner

It is becoming almost fashionable to analyze American racial conflict today in terms of the colonial analogy. I shall argue in this paper that the utility of this perspective depends upon a distinction between colonization as a process and colonialism as a social, economic, and political system. It is the experience of colonization that Afro-Americans share with many of the non-white people of the world. But this subjugation has taken place in a societal context that differs in important respects from the situation of "classical colonialism." In the body of this essay I shall look at some major developments in Black protest—the urban riots, cultural nationalism, and the movement for ghetto control—as collective responses to colonized status. Viewing our domestic situation as a special form of colonization outside a context of a colonial system will help explain some of the dilemmas and ambiguities within these movements.

The present crisis in America life has brought about changes in social perspectives and the questioning of long accepted frameworks. Intellectuals and social scientists have been forced by the pressure of events to look at old definitions of the character of our society, the role of racism, and the workings of basic institutions. The depth and volatility of contemporary racial conflict challenge sociologists in particular to question the adequacy of theoretical models by which we have explained American race relations in the past.

For a long time the distinctiveness of the Negro situation among the ethnic minorities was placed in terms of color, and the systematic discrimination that follows from our deep-seated racial prejudices. This was sometimes called the caste theory, and while provocative, it missed essential and dynamic features of American race relations. In the past ten years there has been a tendency to view Afro-Americans as another ethnic group not

Reprinted from "Internal Colonialism and Ghetto Revolt" by Robert Blauner in *Social Problems*, vol. 16, no. 4 (Spring 1969), pp. 393–400, 406–408. With permission from The Society for the Study of Social Problems and the author.

basically different in experience from previous ethnics and whose "immigration" condition in the North would in time follow their upward course. The inadequacy of this model is now clear—even the Kerner Report devotes a chapter to criticizing this analogy. A more recent (though hardly new) approach views the essence of racial subordination in economic class terms: Black people as an underclass are to a degree specially exploited and to a degree economically dispensable in an automating society. Important as are economic factors, the power of race and racism in America cannot be sufficiently explained through class analysis. Into this theory vacuum steps the model of internal colonialism. Problematic and imprecise as it is, it gives hope of becoming a framework that can integrate the insights of caste and racism, ethnicity, culture, and economic exploitation into an overall conceptual scheme. At the same time, the danger of the colonial model is the imposition of an artificial analogy which might keep us from facing up to the fact (to quote Harold Cruse) that "the American black and white social phenomenon is a uniquely new world thing."[1]

During the late 1950s, identification with African nations and other colonial or formerly colonized peoples grew in importance among Black militants.[2] As a result the U. S. was increasingly seen as a colonial power and the concept of domestic colonialism was introduced into the political analysis and rhetoric of militant nationalists. During the same period Black social theorists began developing this frame of reference for explaining American realities. As early as 1962, Cruse characterized race realtions in this country as "domestic colonialism."[3] Three years later in *Dark Ghetto,* Kenneth Clark demonstrated how the political, economic, and social structure of Harlem was essentially that of a colony.[4] Finally in 1967, a full-blown elaboration of "internal colonialism" provided the theoretical framework for Carmichael and Hamilton's widely read *Black Power.*[5] The following year the colonial analogy gained currency and new "respectability" when Senator McCarthy habitually referred to Black Americans as a colonized people during his campaign. While the rhetoric of internal colonialism was catching on, other social scientists began to raise questions about its appropriateness as a scheme of analysis.

[1] Harold Cruse, *Rebellion or Revolution,* New York: 1968, p. 214.

[2] Nationalism, including an orientation toward Africa, is no new development. It has been a constant tendency within Afro-American politics. See Cruse, *ibid,* esp. chaps. 5–7.

[3] This was six years before the publication of *The Crisis of the Negro Intellectual,* New York: Morrow, 1968, which brought Cruse into prominence. Thus the 1962 article was not widely read until its reprinting in Cruse's essays, *Rebellion or Revolution, op. cit.*

[4] Kenneth Clark, *Dark Ghetto,* New York: Harper and Row, 1965. Clark's analysis first appeared a year earlier in *Youth in the Ghetto,* New York: Haryou Associates, 1964.

[5] Stokely Carmichael and Charles Hamilton, *Black Power,* New York: Random, 1967.

The colonial analysis has been rejected as obscurantist and misleading by scholars who point to the significant differences in history and social-political conditions between our domestic patterns and what took place in Africa and India. Colonialism traditionally refers to the establishment of domination over a geographically external political unit, most often inhabited by people of a different race and culture, where this domination is political and economic, and the colony exists subordinated to and dependent upon the mother country. Typically the colonizers exploit the land, the raw materials, the labor, and other resources of the colonized nation; in addition a formal recognition is given to the difference in power, autonomy, and political status, and various agencies are set up to maintain this subordination. Seemingly the analogy must be stretched beyond usefulness if the American version is to be forced into this model. For here we are talking about group relations within a society; the mother country—colony separation in geography is absent. Though whites certainly colonized the territory of the original Americans, internal colonization of Afro-Americans did not involve the settlement of whites in any land that was unequivocably Black. And unlike the colonial situation, there has been no formal recognition of differing power since slavery was abolished outside the South. Classic colonialism involved the control and exploitation of the majority of a nation by a minority of outsiders. Whereas in America the people who are oppressed were themselves originally outsiders and are a numerical minority.

This conventional critique of "internal colonialism" is useful in pointing to the differences between our domestic patterns and the overseas situation. But in its bold attack it tends to lose sight of common experiences that have been historically shared by the most subjugated racial minorities in America and non-white peoples in some other parts of the world. For understanding the most dramatic recent developments on the race scene, this common core element—which I shall call colonization—may be more important than the undeniable divergences between the two contexts.

The common features ultimately relate to the fact that the classical colonialism of the imperialist era and American racism developed out of the same historical situation and reflected a common world economic and power stratification. The slave trade for the most part preceded the imperialist partition and economic exploitation of Africa, and in fact may have been a necessary prerequisite for colonial conquest—since it helped deplete and pacify Africa, undermining the resistance to direct occupation. Slavery contributed one of the basic raw materials for the textile industry which provided much of the capital for the West's industrial development and need for economic expansionism. The essential condition for both American slavery and European colonialism was the power domination and the technological superiority of the Western world in its relation to peoples of non-Western and non-white origins. This objective supremacy in technology and military power buttressed the West's sense of cultural superiority, laying the basis for racist ideologies that were elaborated to justify control and exploitation of non-white people. Thus because classical colonialism and America's internal version developed out of a similar balance of technological, cultural, and power relations, a common *process* of social oppression characterized the racial patterns in the two contexts—despite the variation in political and social structure.

There appear to be four basic components of the colonization complex. The first refers to how the racial group enters into the dominant society (whether colonial power or not). Colonization begins with a forced, involuntary entry. Second, there is an impact on the culture and social organization of the colonized people which is more than just a result of such "natural" processes as contact and acculturation. The colonizing power carries out a policy which constrains, transforms, or destroys indigenous values, orientations, and ways of life. Third, colonization involves a relationship by which members of the colonized group tend to be administered by representatives of the dominant power. There is an experience of being managed and manipulated by outsiders in terms of ethnic status.

A final fundament of colonization is racism. Racism is a principle of social domination by which a group seen as inferior or different in terms of alleged biological characteristics is exploited, controlled, and oppressed socially and psychically by a superordinate group. Except for the marginal case of Japanese imperialism, the major examples of colonialism have involved the subjugation of non-white Asian, African, and Latin American peoples by white European powers. Thus racism has generally accompanied colonialism. Race prejudice can exist without colonization—the experience of Asian-American minorities is a case in point—but racism as a system of domination is part of the complex of colonization.

The concept of colonization stresses the enormous fatefulness of the historical factor, namely the manner in which a minority group becomes a part of the dominant society.[6] The crucial difference between colonized Americans and the ethnic immigrant minorities is that the latter have always been able to operate fairly competitively within that relatively open section of the social and economic order because these groups came voluntarily in search of a better life, because their movements in society were not administratively controlled, and because they transformed their culture at their own pace—giving up ethnic values and institutions when it was seen as a desirable exchange for improvements in social position.

In present-day America, a major device of Black colonization is the powerless ghetto. As Kenneth Clark describes the situation:

[6] As Eldridge Cleaver reminds us, "Black people are a stolen people held in a colonial status on stolen land, and any analysis which does not acknowledge the colonial status of black people cannot hope to deal with the real problem." "The Land Question," *Ramparts,* 6 (May, 1968), p. 51.

> Ghettoes are the consequence of the imposition of external power and the institutionalization of powerlessness. In this respect, they are in fact social, political, educational, and above all—economic colonies. Those confined within the ghetto walls are subject peoples. They are victims of the greed, cruelty, insensitivity, guilt and fear of their masters. . . .
>
> The community can best be described in terms of the analogy of a powerless colony. Its political leadership is divided, and all but one or two of its political leaders are shortsighted and dependent upon the larger political power structure. Its social agencies are financially precarious and dependent upon sources of support outside the community. Its churches are isolated or dependent. Its economy is dominated by small businesses which are largely owned by absentee owners, and its tenements and other real property are also owned by absentee landlords.
>
> Under a system of centralization, Harlem's schools are controlled by forces outside of the community. Programs and policies are supervised and determined by individuals who do not live in the community . . .[7]

Of course many ethnic groups in America have lived in ghettoes. What make the Black ghettoes an expression of colonized status are three special features. First, the ethnic ghettoes arose more from voluntary choice, both in the sense of the choice to immigrate to America and the decision to live among one's fellow ethnics. Second, the immigrant ghettoes tended to be a one and two generation phenomenon; they were actually way-stations in the process of acculturation and assimilation. When they continue to persist as in the case of San Francisco's Chinatown, it is because they are big business for the ethnics themselves and there is a new stream of immigrants. The Black ghetto on the other hand has been a more permanent phenomenon, although some individuals do escape it. But most relevant is the third point. European ethnic groups like the Poles, Italians, and Jews generally only experienced a brief period, often less than a generation, during which their residential buildings, commercial stores, and other enterprises were owned by outsiders. The Chinese and Japanese faced handicaps of color prejudice that were almost as strong as the Blacks faced, but very soon gained control of their internal communities, because their traditional ethnic culture and social organization had not been destroyed by slavery and internal colonization. But Afro-Americans are distinct in the extent to which their segregated communities have remained controlled economically, politically, and administratively from the outside. One indicator of this difference is the estimate that the "income of Chinese-Americans from Chinese-owned businesses is in proportion to their numbers 45 times as great as the income of Negroes from Negro owned businesses."[8] But what is true of business is also true for the other

[7] *Youth in the Ghetto, op. cit.*, pp. 10–11; 79–80.

[8] N. Glazer and D. P. Moynihan, *Beyond the Melting Pot,* Cambridge, Mass.: M.I.T., 1963, p. 37.

social institutions that operate within the ghetto. The educators, policemen, social workers, politicians, and others who administer the affairs of ghetto residents are typically whites who live outside the Black community. Thus the ghetto plays a strategic role as the focus for the administration by outsiders which is also essential to the structure of overseas colonialism.[9]

The colonial status of the Negro community goes beyond the issue of ownership and decision-making within Black neighborhoods. The Afro-American population in most cities has very little influence on the power structure and institutions of the larger metropolis, despite the fact that in numerical terms, Blacks tend to be the most sizeable of the various interest groups. A recent analysis of policy-making in Chicago estimates that "Negroes really hold less than 1 percent of the effective power in the Chicago metropolitan area. [Negroes are 20 percent of Cook County's population.] Realistically the power structure of Chicago is hardly less white than that of Mississippi."[10]

Colonization outside of a traditional colonial structure has its own special conditions. The group culture and social structure of the colonized in America is less developed; it is also less autonomous. In addition, the colonized are a numerical minority, and furthermore they are ghettoized more totally and are more dispersed than people under classic colonialism. Though these realities affect the magnitude and direction of response, it is my basic thesis that the most important expressions of protest in the Black community during the recent years reflect the colonized status of Afro-America. Riots, programs of separation, politics of community control, the Black revolutionary movements, and cultural nationalism each represent a different strategy of attack on domestic colonialism in America. . . .

[9] "When we speak of Negro social disabilities under capitalism, . . . we refer to the fact that he does not own anything—*even what is ownable in his own community*. Thus to fight for black liberation *is to fight for his right to own*. The Negro is politically compromised today because he owns nothing. He has little voice in the affairs of state because he owns nothing. The fundamental reason why the Negro bourgeois-democratic revolution has been aborted is because American capitalism has prevented the development of a black class of capitalist owners of institutions and economic tools. To take one crucial example, Negro radicals today are severely hampered in their tasks of educating the black masses on political issues because Negroes do not own any of the necessary means of propaganda and communication. The Negro owns no printing presses, he has no stake in the networks of the means of communication. Inside his own communities he does not own the house he lives in, the property he lives on, nor the wholesale and retail sources from which he buys his commodities. He does not own the edifices in which he enjoys culture and entertainment or in which he socializes. In capitalist society, an individual or group that does not own anything is powerless." H. Cruse, "Behind the Black Power Slogan," in Cruse, *Rebellion or Revolution, op. cit.*, pp. 238–239.

[10] Harold M. Baron, "Black Powerlessness in Chicago," *Trans-action*, 6 (Nov., 1968), pp. 27–33.

Riot or Revolt?

The so-called riots are being increasingly recognized as a preliminary if primitive form of mass rebellion against a colonial status. There is still a tendency to absorb their meaning within the conventional scope of assimilation–integration politics: some commentators stress the material motives involved in looting as a sign that the rioters want to join America's middle-class affluence just like everyone else. That motives are mixed and often unconscious, that Black people want good furniture and television sets like whites is beside the point. The guiding impulse in most major outbreaks has not been integration with American society, but an attempt to stake out a sphere of control by moving against that society and destroying the symbols of its oppression.

In my critique of the McCone report I observed that the rioters were asserting a claim to territoriality, an unorganized and rather inchoate attempt to gain control over their community or "turf."[11] In succeeding disorders also the thrust of the action has been the attempt to clear out an alien presence, white men and officials, rather than a drive to kill whites as in a conventional race riot. The main attacks have been directed at the property of white businessmen and at the police who operate in the Black community "like an army of occupation" protecting the interests of outside exploiters and maintaining the domination over the ghetto by the central metropolitan power structure.[12] The Kerner report misleads when it attempts to explain riots in terms of integration: "What the rioters appear to be seeking was fuller participation in the social order and the material benefits enjoyed by the majority of American citizens. Rather than rejecting the American system, they were anxious to obtain a place for themselves in it."[13] More accurately, the revolts pointed to alienation from this system on the part of many poor and also not-so-poor Blacks. The sacredness of private property, that unconsciously accepted bulwark of our social arrangements, was rejected; people who looted apparently without guilt generally remarked that they were taking things that "really belonged" to them anyway.[14] Obviously the society's

[11] R. Blauner, "Whitewash Over Watts: The Failure of the McCone Report," *Trans-action*, 3 (March–April, 1966).

[12] "The police function to support and enforce the interests of the dominant political, social, and economic interests of the town" is a statement made by a former police scholar and official, according to A. Neiderhoffer, *Behind the Shield,* New York: Doubleday, 1967 as cited by Gary T. Marx, "Civil Disorder and the Agents of Control," *Journal of Social Issues,* forthcoming.

[13] Report of the National Advisory Commission on Civil Disorders, N.Y.: Bantam, March, 1968, p. 7.

[14] This kind of attitude has a long history among American Negroes. During slavery, Blacks used the same rationalization to justify stealing from their masters. Appropriating things from the master was viewed as "*taking* part of his property for the benefit of another part; whereas *stealing* referred to appropriating something from another slave, an offense that was not condoned." Kenneth Stampp, *The Peculiar Institution,* Vintage, 1956, p. 127.

bases of legitimacy and authority have been attacked. Law and order has long been viewed as the white man's law and order by Afro-Americans; but now this perspective characteristic of a colonized people is out in the open. And the Kerner Report's own data question how well ghetto rebels are buying the system: In Newark only 33 percent of self-reported rioters said they thought this country was worth fighting for in the event of a major war; in the Detroit sample the figure was 55 percent.[15]

One of the most significant consequences of the process of colonization is a weakening of the colonized's individual and collective will to resist his oppression. It has been easier to contain and control Black ghettoes because communal bonds and group solidarity have been weakened through divisions among leadership, failures of organization, and a general disspiritment that accompanies social oppression. The riots are a signal that the will to resist has broken the mold of accommodation. In some cities as in Watts they also represented nascent movements toward community identity. In several riot-torn ghettoes the outbursts have stimulated new organizations and movements. If it is true that the riot phenomenon of 1964–1968 has passed its peak, its historical import may be more for the "internal" organizing momentum generated than for any profound "external" response of the larger society facing up to underlying causes.

Despite the appeal of Frantz Fanon to young Black revolutionaries, American is not Algeria. It is difficult to foresee how riots in our cities can play a role equivalent to rioting in the colonial situation as an integral phrase in a movement for national liberation. In 1968 some militant groups (for example, the Black Panther Party in Oakland) had concluded that ghetto riots were self-defeating of the lives and interests of Black people in the present balance of organization and gunpower, though they had served a role to stimulate both Black consciousness and white awareness of the depths of racial crisis. Such militants have been influential in "cooling" their communities during periods of high riot potential. Theoretically oriented Black radicals see riots as spontaneous mass behavior which must be replaced by a revolutionary organization and consciousness. But despite the differences in objective conditions, the violence of the 1960s seems to serve the same psychic function, assertions of dignity and manhood for young Blacks in urban ghettoes, as it did for the colonized of North Africa described by Fanon and Memmi.[16] . . .

The Role of Whites

What makes the Kerner Report a less-than-radical document is its superficial treatment of racism and its reluctance to confront the colonized relationship between Black people and the larger society. The Report em-

[15] Report of the National Advisory Commission on Civil Disorders, *op. cit.*, p. 178.

[16] Frantz Fanon, *Wretched of the Earth,* New York: Grove, 1963; Albert Memmi, *The Colonizer and the Colonized,* Boston: Beacon, 1967.

phasizes the attitudes and feelings that make up white racism, rather than the system of privilege and control which is the heart of the matter.[17] With all its discussion of the ghetto and its problems, it never faces the question of the stake that white Americans have in racism and ghettoization.

This is not a simple question, but this paper should not end with the impression that police are the major villains. All white Americans gain some privileges and advantage from the colonization of Black communities.[18] The majority of whites also lose something from this oppression and division in society. Serious research should be directed to the ways in which white individuals and institutions are tied into the ghetto. In closing let me suggest some possible parameters.

1. It is my guess that only a small minority of whites make a direct economic profit from ghetto colonization. This is hopeful in that the ouster of white businessmen may become politically feasible. Much more significant, however, are the private and corporate interests in the land and residential property of the Black community; their holdings and influence on urban decision-making must be exposed and combated.

2. A much larger minority have occupational and professional interests in the present arrangements. The Kerner Commission reports that 1.3 million non-white men would have to be up-graded occupationally in order to make the Black job distribution roughly similar to the white. They advocate this without mentioning that 1.3 million specially privileged white workers would lose in the bargain.[19] In addition there are those professionals who carry out what Lee Rainwater has called the "dirty work" of administering the lives of the ghetto poor: the social workers, the school teachers, the urban development people, and of course the police.[20] The social problems of the Black community will ultimately be solved only by people and organizations from that community; thus the emphasis within these professions must shift toward training such a cadre of minority personnel. Social scientists who teach and study problems of race and poverty likewise have an obligation to replace themselves by bringing into the graduate schools and college faculties men of color who will become the future experts in these areas. For cultural and intellectual imperialism is as real as welfare colonialism, though it is currently screened behind such unassailable shibboleths as universalism and the objectivity of scientific inquiry.

[17] For a discussion of this failure to deal with racism, see Gary T. Marx, "Report of the National Commission: The Analysis of Disorder or Disorderly Analysis," 1968, unpublished paper.

[18] Such a statement is easier to assert than to document but I am attempting the latter in a forthcoming book tentatively titled *White Racism, Black Culture,* to be published by Little Brown, 1970.

[19] Report of the National Advisory Commission on Civil Disorders, *op. cit.,* pp. 253–256.

[20] Lee Rainwater, "The Revolt of the Dirty-Workers," *Trans-action,* 5 (Nov., 1967), pp. 2, 64.

3. Without downgrading the vested interests of profit and profession, the real nitty-gritty elements of the white stake are political power and bureaucratic security. Whereas few whites have much understanding of the realities of race relations and ghetto life, I think most give tacit or at least subconscious support for the containment and control of the Black population. Whereas most whites have extremely distorted images of Black Power, many —if not most—would still be frightened by actual Black political power. Racial groups and identities are real in American life; white Americans sense they are on top, and they fear possible reprisals or disruptions were power to be more equalized. There seems to be a paranoid fear in the white psyche of Black dominance; the belief that Black autonomy would mean unbridled license is so ingrained that such reasonable outcome as Black political majorities and independent Black police forces will be bitterly resisted.

On this level the major mass bulwark of colonization is the administrative need for bureaucratic security so that the middle classes can go about their life and business in peace and quiet. The Black militant movement is a threat to the orderly procedures by which bureaucracies and suburbs manage their existence, and I think today there are more people who feel a stake in conventional procedures than there are those who gain directly from racism. For in their fight for institutional control, the colonized will not play by the white rules of the game. These administrative rules have kept them down and out of the system; therefore they have no necessary intention of running institutions in the image of the white middle class.

The liberal, humanist value that violence is the worst sin cannot be defended today if one is committed squarely against racism and for self-determination. For some violence is almost inevitable in the decolonization process; unfortunately racism in America has been so effective that the greatest power Afro-Americans (and perhaps also Mexican-Americans) wield today is the power to disrupt. If we are going to swing with these revolutionary times and at least respond positively to the anti-colonial movement, we will have to learn to live with conflict, confrontation, constant change, and what may be real or apparent chaos and disorder.

A positive response from the white majority needs to be in two major directions at the same time. First, community liberation movements should be supported in every way by pulling out white instruments of direct control and exploitation and substituting technical assistance to the community when this is asked for. But it is not enough to relate affirmatively to the nationalist movement for ghetto control without at the same time radically opening doors for full participation in the institutions of the mainstream. Otherwise the liberal and radical position is little different than the traditional segregationist. Freedom in the special conditions of American colonization means that the colonized must have the choice between participation in the larger society and in their own independent structures.

To separate labor from other activities of life and to subject it to the laws of the market was to annihilate all organic forms of existence and to replace them by a different type of organization, an atomistic and individualistic one.

Such a scheme of destruction was best served by the application of the principle of freedom of contract. In practice this meant that the noncontractual organizations of kinship, neighborhood, profession, and creed were to be liquidated since they claimed the allegiance of the individual and thus restrained his freedom. To represent this principle as one of noninterference, as economic liberals were wont to do, was merely the expression of an ingrained prejudice in favor of a definite kind of interference, namely, such as would destroy noncontractual relations between individuals and prevent their spontaneous re-formation.

This effect of the establishment of a labor market is conspicuously apparent in colonial regions today. The natives are to be forced to make a living by selling their labor. To this end their traditional institutions must be destroyed, and prevented from re-forming, since, as a rule, the individual in primitive society is not threatened by starvation unless the community as a whole is in a like predicament.

Karl Polanyi, *The Great Transformation* (Boston: The Beacon Press, 1957), p. 163.

It is necessary to change social institutions so that they are more effectively responsive to the needs of the poor. . . . Poverty cannot be studied and changed without studying and changing society.

S. M. Miller and Martin Rein, "Poverty and Social Change," *The American Child* (March 1964), pp. 493–494.

THE WRONG WAY TO FIND JOBS FOR NEGROES

David Wellman

In the summer of 1966 I studied a Federal government program designed to help lower-class youths find jobs. The program was known as TIDE. It was run by the California Department of Employment, and classes were held five days a week in the Youth Opportunities Center of West Oakland.

The TIDE program was anything but a success. "I guess these kids just don't want jobs," one of the teacher-counselors told me. "The clothes they wear are loud. They won't talk decent English. They're boisterous. And they constantly fool around. They refuse to take the program seriously."

"But isn't there a job shortage in Oakland?" I asked. "Does it really *matter* how the kids act?"

"There's plenty of jobs. They're just not interested."

The students were 25 young men and 25 young women selected by poverty-program workers in the Bay Area. Their ages ranged from 16 to 22, and most were Negroes. The government paid them $5 a day to participate. Men and women usually met separately. I sat in on the men's classes.

The young men who took part in TIDE had a distinctive style. They were "cool." Their hair was "processed." All sported sunglasses—very lightly tinted, with small frames. They called them "pimp's glasses." Their clothes, while usually inexpensive, were loud and ingeniously altered to express style and individuality. They spoke in a "hip" vernacular. Their vocabularies were small but very expressive. These young men, as part of the "cool world" of the ghetto, represent a distinctively black working-class culture.

To most liberals these young men are "culturally deprived" or "social dropouts." Most had flunked or been kicked out of school. Few had any intention of getting a high school degree. They seemed uninterested in "making it." They had long and serious arrest and prison records. They were skeptical and critical of both the TIDE program and white society in general.

The TIDE workers were liberals. They assumed that if the young men would only act a little less "cool" and learn to smooth over some of their encounters with white authorities, they too could become full-fledged, working members of society. The aim of TIDE was not to train them for jobs, but to train them how to *apply* for jobs—how to take tests, how to make a good impression during a job interview, how to speak well, how to fill out an application form properly. They would play games, like dominoes, to ease the pain associated with numbers and arithmetic; they would conduct mock interviews, take mock tests, meet with management representatives, and tour places where jobs might be available. They were told to consider the TIDE program itself as a job—to be at the Youth Opportunities Center office on time, dressed as if they were at work. If they were late or made trouble, they would be docked. But if they took the program seriously and did well, they were told, they stood a pretty good chance of getting a job at the end of four weeks. The unexpressed aim of TIDE, then, was to prepare Negro youngsters for white society. The government would serve as an employment agency for white, private enterprise.

The program aimed to change the youngsters by making them more acceptable to employers. Their grammar and pronunciation were constantly corrected. They were indirectly told that, in order to get a job, their appearance would have to be altered: For example, "Don't you think you could shine your shoes?" Promptness, a virtue few of the youngsters possessed, was lauded. The penalty for tardiness was being put on a clean-up committee, or being docked.

For the TIDE workers, the program was a four-week exercise in futility. They felt they weren't asking very much of youngsters—just that they learn to make a good impression on white society. And yet the young men were uncooperative. The only conclusion the TIDE workers could arrive at was: "They just don't want jobs."

Yet most of the youngsters took *actual* job possibilities very seriously. Every day they would pump the Youth Opportunities Center staff about job openings. When told there was a job at such-and-such a factory and that a particular test was required, the young men studied hard and applied for the job in earnest. The TIDE program *itself*, however, seemed to be viewed as only distantly related to getting a job. The youngsters wanted jobs, but to them their inability to take tests and fill out forms was not the problem. Instead they talked about the shortage of jobs available to people without skills.

Their desire for work was not the problem. The real problem was what the program demanded of the young men. It asked that they change their manner of speech and dress, that they ignore their lack of skills and society's lack of jobs, and that they act as if their arrest records were of no consequence in obtaining a job. It asked, most important, that they pretend *they,* and not society, bore the responsibility for their being unemployed. TIDE didn't demand much of the men: Only that they become white.

Putting on the Program

What took place during the four-week program was a daily struggle between white, middle-class ideals of conduct and behavior and the mores and folkways of the black community. The men handled TIDE the way the black community in America has always treated white threats to Negro self-respect. They used subtle forms of subversion and deception. Historians and sociologists have pointed to slave subversion, to the content and ritual of Negro spirituals, and to the blues as forms of covert black resistance to white mores.

Today, "putting someone on," "putting the hype on someone," or "running a game on a cat" seem to be important devices used by Negroes to maintain their integrity. "Putting someone on," which is used as much with black people as with whites, allows a person to maintain his integrity in a hostile or threatening situation. To put someone on is to publicly lead him to believe that you are going along with what he has to offer to say, while privately rejecting the offer and subtly subverting it. The tactic fails if the other person recognizes what is happening. For one aim of putting someone on is to take pride in feeling that you have put something over on him, often at his expense. (Putting someone on differs from "putting someone down," which means active defiance and public confrontation.)

TIDE was evidently interpreted by the men as a threat to their self-respect, and this was the way they responded to it. Sometimes TIDE was put on. Sometimes it was put down. It was taken seriously only when it met the men's own needs.

There was almost no open hostility toward those in charge of TIDE, but two things quickly led me to believe that if the men accepted the program, they did so only on their own terms.

First, all of them appeared to have a "tuning-out" mechanism. They just didn't hear certain things. One young man was a constant joker and talked incessantly, even if someone else was speaking or if the group was supposed to be working. When told to knock it off, he never heard the command. Yet when he was interested in a program, he could hear perfectly.

Tuning-out was often a collective phenomenon. For instance, there was a radio in the room where the youngsters worked, and they would play it during lunch and coffee breaks. When the instructor would enter and tell them to begin work, they would continue listening and dancing to the music as if there were no one else in the room. When *they* were finished listening, the radio went off and the session began. The youngsters were going along with the program—in a way. They weren't challenging it. But they were undermining its effectiveness.

A second way in which the young men undermined the program was by playing dumb. Much of the program consisted of teaching the youngsters how to fill out employment applications. They were given lengthy lectures on the importance of neatness and lettering. After having filled out such forms a number of times, however, some students suddenly didn't know their mother's name, the school they last attended, or their telephone number.

This "stupidity" was sometimes duplicated during the mock job interviews. Five or more of the students would interview their fellow trainees for an imaginary job. These interviewers usually took their job seriously. But after it became apparent that the interview was a game, many of the interviewees suddenly became incredibly incompetent. They didn't have social-security numbers, they couldn't remember their last job, they didn't know what school they went to, they didn't know if they really wanted the job—to the absolute frustration of interviewers and instructors alike. Interestingly enough, when an instructor told them one morning that *this* time those who did well on the interview would actually be sent out on a real job interview with a real firm, the stupid and incompetent were suddently transformed into model job applicants.

The same thing happened when the youngsters were given job-preference tests, intelligence tests, aptitude tests, and tests for driver's licenses. The first few times the youngsters took these tests, most worked hard to master them. But after they had gotten the knack, and still found themselves without jobs and taking the same tests, their response changed. Some of them no longer knew how to do the test. Others found it necessary to cheat by looking over someone's shoulder. Still others flunked tests they had passed the day before. Yet when they were informed of actual job possibilities at the naval ship yard or with the post office, they insisted on giving and taking the tests themselves. In one instance, some of them read up on which tests were relevant for a particular job, then practiced that test for a couple of hours by themselves.

Tuning-out and playing stupid were only two of the many ways the TIDE program was "put-on." Still another way: Insisting on work "breaks." The young men "employed" by TIDE were well-acquainted with this ritual, and demanded that it be included as part of their job. Since they had been given a voice in deciding the content of the program, they insisted that breaks become part of their daily routine. And no matter what the activity, or who was addressing them, the young men religiously adhered to the breaks.

The program started at 9:30 A.M. The youngsters decided that their first break would be for coffee at 10:30. This break was to last until 11. And while work was never allowed to proceed a minute past 10:30, it was usually 11:15 or so before the young men actually got back to work. Lunch began exactly at 12. Theoretically, work resumed at 1. This usually meant 1:15, since they had to listen to "one more song" on the radio. The next break was to last from 2:30 to 3. However, because they were finished at 3:30 and because it took another 10 minutes to get them back to work the fellows could often talk their way out of the remaining half hour. Considering they were being paid $5 a day for five hours' work, of which almost half were regularly devoted to breaks, they didn't have a bad hustle.

Trips and Games

Games were another part of the TIDE program subverted by the put-on. Early in the program an instructor told the students that it might be helpful if they mastered arithmetic and language by playing games—dominoes, Scrabble, and various card games. The students considered this a fine idea. But what their instructor had intended for a pastime during the breaks, involving at most an hour a day, they rapidly turned into a major part of the instruction. They set aside 45 minutes in the morning and 45 minutes in the afternoon for games. But they participated in these games during their breaks as well, so that the games soon became a stumbling block to getting sessions back in order after breaks. When the instructor would say, "Okay, let's get back to work," the men would sometimes reply, "But we're already working on our math—we're playing dominoes, and you said that would help us with our math."

To familiarize the students with the kinds of jobs potentially available, the TIDE instructors took them on excursions to various work situations. These excursions were another opportunity for a put-on. It hardly seemed to matter what kind of company they visited so long as the visit took all day. On a trip to the Oakland Supply Naval Station, the men spent most of their time putting the make on a cute young WAVE who was their guide. One thing this tour did produce, however, was a great deal of discussion about the war in Vietnam. Almost none of the men wanted to serve in the armed forces. Through the bus windows some of them would yell at passing sailors: "Vietnam, baby!" or "Have a good time in Vietnam, man!"

The men would agree to half-day trips only if there was no alternative, or if the company would give away samples. Although they knew that the Coca-Cola Company was not hiring, they wanted to go anyway, for the free Cokes. They also wanted to go to many candy and cookie factories. Yet they turned down a trip to a local steel mill that they knew was hiring. TIDE, after all, was not designed to get them an interview—its purpose was to show them what sorts of jobs might be available. Given the circumstances, they reasoned, why not see what was *enjoyable* as well?

When the men were not putting-on the TIDE program and staff, they might be putting them down. When someone is put-down, he knows it. The tactic's success *depends* on his knowing it, whereas a put-on is successful only when its victim is unaware of it.

The Interview Technique

Among the fiercest put-downs I witnessed were those aimed at jobs the students were learning to apply for. These jobs were usually for unskilled labor: post-office, assembly-line, warehouse, and longshore workers, truck drivers, chauffeurs, janitors, bus boys, and so on.

The reaction of most of the students was best expressed by a question I heard one young man ask an instructor: "How about some tests for I.B.M.?" The room broke into an uproar of hysterical laughter. The instructor's response was typically bureaucratic, yet disarming: "Say, that's a good suggestion. Why don't you put it in the suggestion box?" The students didn't seem able to cope with that retort, so things got back to normal.

Actual employers, usually those representing companies that hired people only for unskilled labor, came to TIDE to demonstrate to the men what a good interview would be like. They did *not* come to interview men for real jobs. It was sort of a helpful-hints-for-successful-interviews session. Usually one of the more socially mobile youths was chosen to play the role of job applicant. The entire interview situation was played through. Some employers even went so far as to have the "applicant" go outside and knock on the door to begin the interview. The students thought this was both odd and funny, and one said to the employer: "Man, you've already *seen* the cat. How come you making him walk out and then walk back in?"

With a look of incredulity, the employer replied: "But that's how you get a job. You have to sell yourself from the moment you walk in that door."

The employer put on a real act, beginning the interview with the usual small talk.

"I see from your application that you played football in high school."

"Yeah."

"Did you like it?"

"Yeah."

"Football really makes men and teaches you teamwork."

"Yeah."

At this point, the men got impatient: "Man, the cat's here to get a job, not talk about football!"

A wisecracker chimed in: "Maybe he's interviewing for a job with the Oakland Raiders."

Usually the employer got the point. He would then ask about the "applicant's" job experience, draft status, school record, interests, skills, and so on. The young man being interviewed usually took the questions seriously and answered frankly. But after a while the rest of the group would tire of the game and (unrecognized, from the floor) begin to ask about the specifics of a real job:

"Say man, how much does this job pay?"

"What kind of experience do you need?"

"What if you got a record?"

It didn't take long to completely rattle an interviewer. The instructor might intervene and tell the students that the gentleman was there to help them, but this would stifle revolt for only a short while. During one interview, several of the fellows began loudly playing dominoes. That got the response they were looking for.

"Look!" shouted the employer. "If you're not interested in learning how to sell yourself, why don't you just leave the room so that others who are interested can benefit from this?"

"Oh no!" responded the ringleaders, "We work here. If you don't dig us, then *you* leave!"

Not much later, he did.

Sometimes during these mock interviews, the very nature of the work being considered was put-down. During one mock interview for a truck-driving job, some of the men asked the employer about openings for salesmen. Others asked him about executive positions. At one point the employer himself was asked point-blank how much he was paid, and what his experience was. They had turned the tables and were enjoying the opportunity to interview the interviewer. Regardless of a potential employer's status, the young men treated him as they would their peers. On one tour of a factory, the students were escorted by the vice-president in charge of hiring. To the TIDE participants, he was just another guide. After he had informed the students of the large number of unskilled positions available, they asked him if he would hire some of them, on the spot. He replied that this was just a tour and that he was in no position to hire anyone immediately. One youth looked at him and said: "Then you're just wasting our time, aren't you?"

Although shaken, the executive persisted. Throughout his talk, however, he innocently referred to his audience as "boys," which obviously bothered the students. Finally one of the more articulate men spoke up firmly: "We are young *men*, not boys!"

The vice-president blushed and apologized. He made a brave attempt to avoid repeating the phrase. But habit was victorious, and the word slipped in again and again. Each time he said "you boys" he was corrected, loudly, and with increasing hostility.

The students treated State Assemblyman Byron Rumford, a Negro, the same way. The meeting with Rumford was an opportunity for them to speak with an elected official about a job situation in the state. The meeting was also meant to air differences and to propose solutions. At the time, in fact, the men were quite angry about their rate of pay at TIDE. An instructor had suggested that they take the matter up with Rumford.

The meeting was attended by both the young men and women in the TIDE program. The young women were very well-dressed and well-groomed. Their clothes were not expensive, but were well cared for and in "good taste." Their hair was done in high-fashion styles. They looked, in short, like aspiring career women. The young men wore their usual dungarees or tight trousers, brightly colored shirts and sweaters, pointed shoes, and sunglasses.

The women sat quietly and listened politely. The men spoke loudly whenever they felt like it, and constantly talked among themselves.

Rumford, instead of speaking about the job situation in the Bay Area, chose to talk about his own career. It was a Negro Horatio Alger story. The moral was that if you work hard, you too can put yourself through college, become a successful druggist, then run for public office.

The moment Rumford finished speaking and asked for questions, one of the men jumped up and asked, "Hey man, how do we get a raise?" A male chorus of "Yeah!" followed. Before Rumford could complete a garbled answer (something like, "Well, I don't really know much about the procedures of a federally sponsored program"), the battle of the sexes had been joined. The women scolded the men for their "disrespectful behavior" toward an elected official. One said: "Here he is trying to help us and you-all acting a fool. You talking and laughing and carrying on while he talking, and then when he finishes you want to know about a raise. Damn!"

"Shit," was a male response. "You don't know what you talking about. We got a *right* to ask the cat about a raise. We elected him."

"We supposed to be talking about jobs," said another. "And we're talking about *our* job. If y'all like the pay, that's your business. We want more!"

The debate was heated. Neither group paid any attention to Rumford, who wisely slipped out of the room.

Battle of Sexes—or Class Conflict?

During the exchange it became clear to me that the differences in clothing and style between the sexes reflected their different orientations toward the dominant society and its values. In the minds of the young women, respect and respectability seemed paramount. At one point, a young woman said to the men, "You acting just like a bunch of *niggers*." She seemed to identify herself as a Negro, not as a "nigger." For the men, on the other hand, becoming a Negro (as opposed to a "nigger") meant giving up much that they considered positive. As one young man said in answer to the above, "You just ain't got no soul, bitch."

The women's identification with the values of white society became even clearer when the debate moved from what constituted respect and respectability to a direct attack on a personal level: "Do you all expect to get a job looking the way you do?" "Shit, I wouldn't wear clothes like that if I was on welfare."

The direction of the female attack corresponded closely with the basic assumptions of the TIDE program: People are without jobs because of themselves. This barrage hit the young men pretty hard. Their response was typical of any outraged male whose manhood has been threatened. In fact, when one young woman gibed, "You ain't no kinda man," some of the fellows had to be physically restrained from hitting her.

One of the men explained that "maybe the reason cats dress the way they do is because they can't afford anything else. Did you ever think of that?"

The woman's response was one I had not heard since the third or fourth grade: "Well, it doesn't matter what you wear as long as it's clean, pressed, and tucked-in. But hell, you guys don't even shine your shoes."

The battle of the sexes in the black community seems to be almost a class conflict. Many observers have noted that the black woman succeeds more readily in school than the black man. Women are also favored by parents, especially mothers. Moreover, the black woman has been for some time the most stable force and the major breadwinner of the Negro family. All these things put Negro women in harmony with the major values attached to work and success in our society. Black men, however, have been estranged from society, and a culture has developed around this estrangement—a male Negro culture often antagonistic to the dominant white society. The black woman stands in much the same relation to black men as white society does.

Even including Rumford, no group of officials was put down quite so hard as the Oakland police. Police brutality was constantly on the youngsters' minds. A day didn't pass without at least one being absent because he was in jail, or one coming in with a story about mistreatment by the police. A meeting was arranged with a sergeant from the Community Relations Bureau of the Oakland police. The students seemed excited about meeting the officer on their own turf and with the protection provided by the program.

In anticipation of his arrival, the fellows rearranged the room, placing all the separate tables together. Then they sat down in a group at one end of the table, waiting for the officer.

Putting down the Police

Sergeant McCormack was an older man. And while obviously a cop, he could also pass for a middle-aged businessman or a young grandfather.

"Hi boys," he said as he sat down. His first mistake. He began with the five-minute speech he must give to every community group. The talk was factual, uninteresting, and noncontroversial: how the department is run, what the qualifications for policemen are, and how difficult it is for police to do their work and still please everyone. His talk was greeted with complete silence.

"I understand you have some questions," McCormack finally said.

"What about police brutality?" asked one man.

"What is your definition of police brutality?" the sergeant countered.

"How long you been a cop?" someone shouted.

"Over 20 years."

"And you got the nerve to come on sounding like you don't know what we talking about. Don't be jiving us. Shit, if you've been a cop *that* long, you *got* to know what we talking about."

"Righteous on that, brother!" someone chimed in.

"Well, I've been around a while, all right, but I've never seen any brutality. But what about it?"

"What *about* it?" There was a tone of disbelief mixed with anger in the young man's voice. "Shit man, we want to know why you cats always kicking other cats' asses."

The officer tried to draw a distinction between necessary and unnecessary police violence. The fellows weren't buying that. They claimed the police systematically beat the hell out of them for no reason. The officer asked for examples and the fellows obliged with long, involved, and detailed personal experiences with the Oakland Police Department. The sergeant listened patiently, periodically interrupting to check details and inconsistencies. He tried to offer a police interpretation of the incident. But the fellows were simply not in a mood to listen. In desperation the sergeant finally said, "Don't you want to hear *our* side of the story?"

"Hell no, motherfucker, we *see* your side of the story every night on 14th Street."

One young man stood up, his back to the officer, and addressed his contemporaries: "We *tired* of talking! We want some action! There's a new generation now. We ain't like the old folks who took all this shit off the cops." He turned to the sergeant and said, "You take that back to your goddamn Chief Preston and tell him."

McCormack had a silly smile on his face.

Another youngster jumped up and hollered, "You all ain't going to be smiling when we put dynamite in your police station!"

The officer said simply, "You guys don't want to talk."

"You see," someone yelled, "the cat's trying to be slick, trying to run a game on us. First he comes in here all nice-talking, all that shit about how they run the police and the police is to protect us. And then when we tell him how they treat us he wants to say we don't want to talk. Shit! We want to talk, he don't want to listen."

From this point on, they ran over him mercilessly. I, with all my biases against the police, could not help feeling compassion for the sergeant. If the police are an authority figure in the black community, then this episode must be viewed as a revolt against authority—*all* authority. There was nothing about the man's life, both private and public, that wasn't attacked.

"How much money you get paid?"

"About $12,000 a year."

"For being a cop? Wow!"

"What do you do?"

"I work in the Community Relations Department."

"Naw, stupid, what *kind* of work?"

"I answer the telephone, speak to groups, and try to see if the police treat the citizens wrong."

"Shit, we could do that and we don't even have a high-school education. Is that all you do? And get that much money for it?"

"Where do you live?"

"I'll bet he lives up in the hills."

"I live in the east side of Oakland. And I want you to know that my next-door neighbor is a colored man. I've got nothing against colored people."

"You got any kids?"

"Yeah, two boys and a girl."

"Shit, bet they all went to college and got good jobs. Any of your kids been in trouble?"

"No, not really."

"What do they do?"

"My oldest boy is a fighter pilot in Vietnam."

"What the hell is he doing over there? That's pretty stupid."

"Yeah man, what are we fighting in Vietnam for? Is that your way of getting rid of us?"

"Well, the government says we have to be there and it's the duty of every citizen to do what his country tells him to do."

"We don't want to hear all that old bullshit, man."

"Hey, how come you wear such funny clothes? You even look like a goddam cop."

"Yeah baby, and he smells like one too!"

The barrage continued for almost half an hour. The instructor finally called a halt: "Sergeant McCormack has to get back, fellows. Is there anything specific that you'd like to ask him?"

"Yeah. How come Chief Preston ain't here? He's always talking to other people all over the country about how good the Oakland cops are and how there ain't going to be no riot here. Why don't he come and tell us that? We want to talk with the chief."

The next day, Deputy Chief Gain came—accompanied by the Captain of the Youth Division, the lieutenant of that division, and a Negro sergeant. It was a formidable display of police authority. The youngsters were noticeably taken aback.

Chief Gain is a no-nonsense, businesslike cop. He takes no static from anyone, vigorously defends what he thinks is correct, and makes no apologies for what he considers incorrect. He is an honest man in the sense that he makes no attempt to cover up or smooth over unpleasant things. He immediately got down to business: "All right now, I understand you guys have some beefs with the department. What's the story?"

The fellows started right in talking about the ways they had been mistreated by the police. The chief began asking specific questions: where it happened, when it happened, what the officer looked like, and so on. He never denied the existence of brutality. That almost seemed to be assumed. He did want details, however. He always asked whether the youth had filed a complaint with the department. The response was always No. He then lectured them about the need to file such complaints if the situation was to be changed.

He explained the situation as he saw it: "Look fellows, we run a police force of 654 men. Most of them are good men, but there's bound to be a few rotten apples in the basket. I know that there's a couple of men who mistreat people, but it's only a few and we're trying our best to change that."

"Shit, I know of a case where a cop killed a cat and now he's back on the beat."

"Now wait a minute—"

"No more waiting a minute!" someone interrupted. "You had two cops got caught taking bribes. One was black and the other Caucasian. The black cat was kicked off the force and the white cat is back on."

"Yeah, and what about that cat who killed somebody off-duty, what about him?"

"Hold on," Gain said firmly. "Let's take these things one at a time." He didn't get very far before he was back to the "few rotten apples" argument.

"If it's only a few cops, how come it happens all the time?"

The deputy chief told them that he thought it was the same few cops who were causing all the problems. "Unless you file complaints each time you feel you've been mistreated, we can't do anything about it. So it's up to you as much as it is up to us."

For the first time in weeks, I intruded into the discussion. I pointed out to Gain that he was asking citizens to police their own police force. He had argued that in most situations the department had a good deal of control over its own men—the same argument the police had used against a civilian-review board. Now he was saying the opposite: that it was up to the citizens. This seemed to break the impasse, and the students howled with delight.

"What happens if a cop beats my ass and I file a complaint?" demanded one. "Whose word does the judge take?"

"The judge takes the evidence and evaluates it objectively and comes to a decision."

"Yeah, but it's usually two cops against one of us, and if both testify against me, what happens? Do you think the judge is going to listen to me?"

"Bring some witnesses."

"That ain't going to do anything."

"That's your problem. If you don't like the legal system in this country, work to change it."

"Okay man," one fellow said to Gain, "You pretty smart. If I smack my buddy here upside the head and he files a complaint, what you gonna do?"

"Arrest you."

"Cool. Now let's say one of your ugly cops smacks *me* upside the head and I file a complaint—what you gonna do?"

"Investigate the complaint, and if there's anything to it, why we'll take action—probably suspend him."

"Why do *we* get arrested and *you* investigated?"

The deputy chief's response was that most private companies with internal difficulties don't want to be investigated by outside agencies. The fellows retorted: "Police are *not* a private business. You're supposed to work for the people!"

"And shit, you cats get to carry guns. No businessman carries guns. It's a different scene, man."

"How come you got all kinds of squad cars in this neighborhood every night? And have two and three cops in each of them?"

"The crime rate is high in this area," replied Gain, "and we get a lot of calls and complaints about it."

"Yeah, and you smart enough to know that when you come around here, you better be wearing helmets and carrying shotguns. If you that clever, you got to be smart enough to handle your own goddamn cops."

At this point the fellows all jumped on the deputy chief the same way they had jumped on the sergeant the day before:

"Why don't you just let us run our own damn community?"

"Yeah. There should be people on the force who've been in jail because they the only people who know what it means to be busted. People in West Oakland should be police because they know their community; you don't."

"Why do we get all the speeding tickets?"

"How come we got to fight in Vietnam?"

"Why the judges so hard on us? They don't treat white cats—I mean dudes—the way they do us."

The chief began assembling his papers and stood up. "You guys aren't interested in talking. You want to yell. When you want to talk, come down to my office and if I'm free we'll talk."

But the fellows had the last word. While he was leaving they peppered him with gibes about how *they* were tired of talking; promised to dynamite his office; and called the police chief a coward for not coming down to speak with them.

When the deputy chief had gone, the instructor asked the fellows why they insisted on ganging up on people like the police. The answer provides a lot of insight into the young men's actions toward the police, businessmen, and public officials:

"These people just trying to run a game on us. If we give them time to think about answers, they gonna put us in a trick. We've *got* to gang up on them because they gang up on us. Did you dig the way that cat brought three other cats with him? Besides, how else could we put them down?"

A Subtle Form of Racism

In effect, the young men had inverted the meaning and aims of the TIDE program. It was supposed to be an opportunity for them to plan careers and prepare themselves for their life's work. The immediate goal was to help them get started by showing them how to get a job. The youngsters had a different view. The program was a way to play some games and take some outings—an interesting diversion from the boredom and frustration of ghetto life in the summer. In some respects it was also a means of confronting, on equal terms, high-status people normally unavailable to them—and of venting on them their anger and hostility. But primarily they saw it as a $5-a-day job.

The program simply did not meet the needs of these young men. In fact, it was not really meant to. The Great Society was trying to "run a game on" black youth. TIDE asked them to stop being what they are. It tried to lead them into white middle-class America by showing that America was interested in getting them jobs. But America does not provide many jobs—let alone attractive jobs—for those with police records, with few skills, with black skins. The youths knew that; TIDE workers knew that, too. They did not train youths for work, but tried to make them believe that if they knew *how* to get a job, they could. The young men saw through the sham.

Ironically, the view that Negro youths, rather than society, are responsible for the employment problem is very similar to the familiar line of white racism. Negroes will not work because they are lazy and shiftless, the old Southern bigot would say. The Northern liberal today would put it a little differently: Negroes cannot get jobs because of their psychological and cultural impediments; what they need is cultural improvement, a proper attitude, the ability to sell themselves. Both views suggest that inequities in the job and opportunity structure of America are minor compared to the deficiencies of Negroes themselves. In the end, Northern liberals and Southern racists agree: The problem is mainly with Negroes, not with our society. This fallacy underlies much of the war on poverty's approach and is indicative of the subtle forms racism is taking in America today.

He does not think there is anything the matter with him
because
    one of the things that is
    the matter with him
    is that he does not think that there is anything
    the matter with him
therefore
    we have to help him realize that,
    the fact that he does not think there is anything
    the matter with him
    is one of the things that is
    the matter with him

CAPITALISM AND FREEDOM

Milton Friedman

The humanitarian and egalitarian sentiment which helped produce the steeply graduated individual income tax has also produced a host of other measures directed at promoting the "welfare" of particular groups. The most important single set of measures is the bundle misleadingly labeled "social security." Others are public housing, minimum wage laws, farm price supports, medical care for particular groups, special aid programs, and so on.

I shall first discuss briefly a few of the latter, mostly to indicate how different their actual effects may be from those intended, and shall then discuss at somewhat greater length the largest single component of the social security program, old age and survivor's insurance.

Miscellaneous Welfare Measures

1. *Public Housing* One argument frequently made for public housing is based on an alleged neighborhood effect: slum districts in particular, and other low quality housing to a lesser degree, are said to impose higher costs on the community in the form of fire and police protection. This literal neighborhood effect may well exist. But insofar as it does, it alone argues, not for public housing, but for higher taxes on the kind of housing that adds to social costs since this would tend to equalize private and social cost.

It will be answered at once that the extra taxes would bear on low-income people and that this is undesirable. The answer means that public housing is proposed not on the ground of neighborhood effects but as a means of helping low-income people. If this be the case, why subsidize housing in particular? If funds are to be used to help the poor, would they not be used more effectively by being given in cash rather than in kind? Surely, the families being helped would rather have a given sum in cash than in the form of housing. They could themselves spend the money on housing if they so desired. Hence, they would never be worse off if given cash; if they regarded other needs as more important, they would be better off. The cash subsidy would solve the neighborhood effect as well as the subsidy in kind, since if it were not used to buy housing it would be available to pay extra taxes justified by the neighborhood effect.

Public housing cannot therefore be justified on the grounds either of neighborhood effects or of helping poor families. It can be justified, if at all, only on grounds of paternalism; that the families being helped "need" housing more than they "need" other things but would themselves either not agree or would spend the money unwisely. The liberal will be inclined to reject this argument for responsible adults. He cannot completely reject it in the more indirect form in which it affects children; namely, that parents will neglect the welfare of the children, who "need" the better housing. But he will surely demand evidence much more persuasive and to the point than the kind usually given before he can accept this final argument as adequate justification for large expenditures on public housing.

So much could have been said in the abstract, in advance of actual experience with public housing. Now that we have had experience, we can go much farther. In practice, public housing has turned out to have effects very different indeed from those intended.

Far from improving the housing of the poor, as its proponents expected, public housing has done just the reverse. The number of dwelling units destroyed in the course of erecting public housing projects has been far larger than the number of new dwelling units constructed. But public housing as such has done nothing to reduce the number of persons to be housed. The effect of public housing has therefore been to raise the number of persons per dwelling unit. Some families have probably been better housed than the would otherwise have been—those who were fortunate enough to get occupancy of the publicly built units. But this has only made the problem for the rest all the worse, since the average density of all together went up.

Of course, private enterprise offsets some of the deleterious effect of the public housing program by conversion of existing quarters and construction of new ones for either the persons directly displaced or, more generally, the persons displaced at one or two removes in the game of musical chairs set in motion by the public housing projects. However, these private resources would have been available in the absence of the public housing program.

Why did the public housing program have this effect? For the general reason we have stressed time and again. The general interest that motivated many to favor instituting the program is diffuse and transitory. Once the program was adopted, it was bound to be dominated by the special interests that it could serve. In this case, the special interests were those local groups that were anxious to have blighted areas cleared and refurbished, either because they owned property there or because the blight was threatening local or central business districts. Public housing served as a convenient means to accomplish their objective, which required more destruction than construction. Even so, "urban blight" is still with us in undiminished force, to judge by the growing pressure for federal funds to deal with it.

Another gain its proponents expected from public housing was the reduction of juvenile delinquency by improving housing conditions. Here again, the program in many instances had precisely the opposite effect, entirely aside from its failure to improve *average* housing conditions. The income limitations quite properly imposed for the occupancy of public housing at subsidized rentals have led to a very high density of "broken" families—in particular, divorced or widowed mothers with children. Children of broken families are especially likely to be "problem" children and a high concentration of such children is likely to increase juvenile delinquency. One manifestation has been the very adverse effect on schools in the neighborhood of a public housing project. Whereas a school can readily absorb a few "problem" children it is very difficult for it to absorb a large number. Yet in some cases, broken families are a third or more of the total in a public housing project and the project may account for a majority of the children in the school. Had these families been assisted through cash grants, they would have been spread much more thinly through the community.

2. Minimum Wage Laws Minimum wage laws are about as clear a case as one can find of a measure the effects of which are precisely the opposite of those intended by the men of good will who support it. Many proponents of minimum wage laws quite properly deplore extremely low rates; they regard them as a sign of poverty; and they hope, by outlawing wage rates below some specified level, to reduce poverty. In fact, insofar as minimum wage laws have any effect at all, their effect is clearly to increase poverty. The state can legislate a minimum wage rate. It can hardly require employers to hire at that minimum all who were formerly employed at wages below the minimum. It is clearly not in the interest of employers to do so. The effect of the minimum wage is therefore to make unemployment higher than it otherwise would be. Insofar as the low wage rates are in fact a sign of poverty, the people who are rendered unemployed are precisely those who can least afford to give up the income they had been receiving, small as it may appear to the people voting for the minimum wage.

This case is in one respect very much like public housing. In both, the people who are helped are visible—the people whose wages are raised; the people who occupy the publicly built units. The people who are hurt are anonymous and their problem is not clearly connected to its cause: the people who join the ranks of the unemployed or, more likely, are never employed in particular activities because of the existence of the minimum wage and are driven to even less remunerative activities or to the relief rolls; the people who are pressed ever closer together in the spreading slums that seem to be rather a sign of the need for more public housing than a consequence of the existing public housing.

A large part of the support for minimum wage laws comes not from disinterested men of good will but from interested parties. For example, northern trade unions and northern firms threatened by southern competition favor minimum wage laws to reduce the competition from the South.

3. Farm Price Supports Farm price supports are another example. Insofar as they can be justified at all on grounds other than the political fact that rural areas are over-represented in the electoral college and Congress, it must be on the belief that farmers on the average have low incomes. Even if this be accepted as a fact, farm price supports do not accomplish the intended purpose of helping the farmers who need help. In the first place, benefits are, if anything, inverse to need, since they are in proportion to the amount sold on the market. The impecunious farmer not only sells less on the market than the wealthier farmer; in addition, he gets a larger fraction of his income from products grown for his own use, and these do not qualify for the benefits. In the second place, the benefits, if any, to farmers from the price-support program are much smaller than the total amount spent. This is clearly true of the amount spent for storage and similar costs which does not go to the farmer at all—indeed the suppliers of storage capacity and facilities may well be the major beneficiaries. It is equally true of the amount spent to purchase agricultural products. The farmer is thereby induced to spend additional sums on fertilizer, seed, machinery, etc. At most, only the excess adds to his income. And finally, even this residual of a residual overstates the gain since the effect of the program has been to keep more people on the farm than would otherwise have stayed there. Only the excess, if any, of what they can earn on the farm with the price-support program over what they can earn off the farm, is a net benefit to them. The main effect of the purchase program has simply been to make farm output larger, not to raise the income per farmer.

Some of the costs of the farm purchase program are so obvious and well-known as to need little more than mention: the consumer has paid twice, once in taxes for farm benefit payments, again by paying a higher price for food; the farmer has been saddled with onerous restrictions and detailed centralized control; the nation has been saddled with a spreading bureaucracy. There is, however, one set of costs which is less well-known. The farm program has been a major hindrance in the pursuit of foreign policy. In order to maintain a higher domestic than world price, it has been necessary to impose quotas on imports for many items. Erratic changes in our policy have had serious adverse effects on other countries.

The extraordinary economic growth experienced by Western countries during the past two centuries and the wide distribution of the benefits of free enterprise have enormously reduced the extent of poverty in any absolute sense in the capitalistic countries of the West. But poverty is in part a relative matter, and even in these countries, there are clearly many people living under conditions that the rest of us label as poverty.

One recourse, and in many ways the most desirable, is private charity. It is noteworthy that the heyday of laissez-faire, the middle and late nineteenth century in Britain and the United States, saw an extraordinary proliferation of private eleemosynary organizations and institutions. One of the major costs of the extension of governmental welfare activities has been the corresponding decline in private charitable activities.

It can be argued that private charity is insufficient because the benefits from it accrue to people other than those who make the gifts—again, a neighborhood effect. I am distressed by the sight of poverty; I am benefited by its alleviation; but I am benefited equally whether I or someone else pays for its alleviation; the benefits of other people's charity therefore partly accrue to me. To put it differently, we might all of us be willing to contribute to the relief of poverty, *provided* everyone else did. We might not be willing to contribute the same amount without such assurance. In small communities, public pressure can suffice to realize the proviso even with private charity. In the large impersonal communities that are increasingly coming to dominate our society, it is much more difficult for it to do so.

Suppose one accepts, as I do, this line of reasoning as justifying governmental action to alleviate poverty; to set, as it were, a floor under the standard of life of every person in the community. There remain the questions, how much and how. I see no way of deciding "how much" except in terms of the amount of taxes we—by which I mean the great bulk of us—are willing to impose on ourselves for the purpose. The question, "how," affords more room for speculation.

Two things seem clear. First, if the objective is to alleviate poverty, we should have a program directed at helping the poor. There is every reason to help the poor man who happens to be a farmer, not because he is a farmer but because he is poor. The program, that is, should be designed to help people as people, not as members of particular occupational groups or age groups or wage-rate groups or labor organizations or industries. This is a defect of farm programs, general old-age benefits, minimum-wage laws, pro-union legislation, tariffs, licensing provisions of crafts or professions, and so on in seemingly endless profusion. Second, so far as possible the program should, while operating through the market, not distort the market or impede its functioning. This is a defect of price supports, minimum-wage laws, tariffs and the like.

The arrangement that recommends itself on purely mechanical grounds is a negative income tax. We now have an exemption of $600 per person under the federal income tax (plus a minimum 10 percent flat deduction). If an individual receives $100 taxable income, i.e., an income of $100 in excess of the exemption and deductions, he pays a tax. Under the proposal, if his taxable income were minus $100, i.e., $100 less than the exemption plus deductions, he would pay a negative tax, i.e., receive a subsidy. If the rate of subsidy were, say, 50 percent, he would receive $50. If he had no income at all, and, for simplicity, no deductions, and the rate were constant, he would receive $300. He might receive more than this if he had deductions, for example, for medical expenses, so that his income less deductions, was negative even before subtracting the exemption. The rates of subsidy could, of course, be graduated just as the rates of tax above the exemption are. In this way, it would be possible to set a floor below which no man's net income (defined now to include the subsidy) could fall—in the simple example $300 per person. The precise floor set would depend on what the community could afford.

The advantages of this arrangement are clear. It is directed specifically at the problem of poverty. It gives help in the form most useful to the individual, namely, cash. It is general and could be substituted for the host of special measures now in effect. It makes explicit the cost borne by society. It operates outside the market. Like any other measures to alleviate poverty, it reduces the incentives of those helped to help themselves, but it does not eliminate that incentive entirely, as a system of supplementing incomes up to some fixed minimum would. An extra dollar earned always means more money available for expenditure.

No doubt there would be problems of administration, but these seem to me a minor disadvantage, if they be a disadvantage at all. The system would fit directly into our current income tax system and could be administered along with it. The present tax system covers the bulk of income recipients and the necessity of covering all would have the by-product of improving the operation of the present income tax. More important, if enacted as a substitute for the present rag bag of measures directed at the same end, the total administrative burden would surely be reduced.

A few brief calculations suggest also that this proposal could be far less costly in money, let alone in the degree of governmental intervention involved, than our present collection of welfare measures. Alternatively, these calculations can be regarded as showing how wasteful our present measures are, judged as measures for helping the poor.

In 1961, government spent something like $33 billion (federal, state, and local) on direct welfare payments and programs of all kinds: old age assistance, social security benefit payments, aid to dependent children, general assistance, farm price support programs, public housing, etc. I have excluded veterans' benefits in making this calculation. I have also made no allowance for the direct and indirect costs of such measures as minimum-wage laws, tariffs, licensing provisions, and so on, or for the costs of public health activities, state and local expenditures on hospitals, mental institutions, and the like.

There are approximately 57 million consumer units (unattached individuals and families) in the United States. The 1961 expenditures of $33 billion would have financed outright cash grants of nearly $6,000 per consumer unit to the 10 percent with the lowest incomes. Such grants would have raised their incomes above the average for all units in the United States. Alternatively, these expenditures would have financed grants of nearly $3,000 per consumer unit to the 20 percent with the lowest incomes. Even if one went so far as that one-third whom New Dealers were fond of calling ill-fed, ill-housed, and ill-clothed, 1961 expenditures would have financed grants of nearly $2,000 per consumer unit, roughly the sum which, after allowing for the change in the level of prices, was the income which separated the lower one-third in the middle 1930s from the upper two-thirds. Today, fewer than one-eighth of consumer units have an income, adjusted for the change in the level of prices, as low as that of the lowest third in the middle 1930s.

Clearly, these are all far more extravagant programs than can be justified to "alleviate poverty" even by a rather generous interpretation of that term. A program which *supplemented* the incomes of the 20 percent of the consumer units with the lowest incomes so as to raise them to the lowest income of the rest would cost less than half of what we are now spending.

The major disadvantage of the proposed negative income tax is its political implications. It establishes a system under which taxes are imposed on some to pay subsidies to others. And presumably, these others have a vote.

There is always the danger that instead of being an arrangement under which the great majority tax themselves willingly to help an unfortunate minority, it will be converted into one under which a majority imposes taxes for its own benefit on an unwilling minority. Because this proposal makes the process so explicit, the danger is perhaps greater than with other measures. I see no solution to this problem except to rely on the self-restraint and good will of the electorate. . . .

Liberalism and Egalitarianism

The heart of the liberal philosophy is a belief in the dignity of the individual, in his freedom to make the most of his capacities and opportunities according to his own lights, subject only to the proviso that he not interfere with the freedom of other individuals to do the same. This implies a belief in the equality of men in one sense; in their inequality in another. Each man has an equal right to freedom. This is an important and fundamental right precisely because men are different, because one man will want to do different things with his freedom than another, and in the process can contribute more than another to the general culture of the society in which many men live.

The liberal will therefore distinguish sharply between equality of rights and equality of opportunity, on the one hand, and material equality or equality of outcome on the other. He may welcome the fact that a free society in fact tends toward greater material equality than any other yet tried. But he will regard this as a desirable by-product of a free society, not its major justification.

228-253

10 Do we need the poor?

In America, everything is owned. Everything is held as private property. Someone has a brand on everything. There is nothing left over. Until recently, the blacks themselves were counted as part of somebody's property, along with the chickens and goats. The blacks have not forgotten this, principally because they are still treated as if they are part of someone's inventory. . . .

Eldridge Cleaver, *Soul on Ice* (New York: Dell Publishing Company, 1968), p. 134.

AMERICA'S SCHIZOPHRENIC VIEW OF THE POOR

Paul Jacobs

I

An ideological schizophrenia with a complex history characterizes the American view of poverty. On the one hand, we believe achievement is related primarily to self-reliance and self-help; on the other, we have been forced to concede that failure cannot always be laid at the door of the individual. Both these views are embodied in the constellation of ideas on which President Johnson's War Against Poverty is based. As a result, that program is schizophrenic, too. It assumes that poverty will be eliminated if only society can alter the circumstances which have barred the poor from access to work, the "American way of life." But it does not question whether such a way of life is possible for all in the new technological order, nor does it seek to alter, in any profound sense, the economic and political system. Instead, the existence of poverty is viewed as an impersonal—and soluble—"paradox." The program's cheerful optimism reflects an almost mystical belief in the infinite potentials of American society. Poverty, like polio, will be defeated when the right vaccine is found.

The first American colonists brought with them from Puritan England the comparatively new doctrine which combined the view that man had a religious duty to achieve material success with the concept that giving direct financial aid to the poor destroyed their character. . . .

In colonial America, such Puritan doctrines were buttressed by the belief that every man, except the Negro slave, could break through the class barriers that had held them down in aristocratic England and Europe. In this view, the poor were poor only because of some flaw in their character; therefore, not society, but only their families, bore any responsibility towards them. Only the Negro slaves, for whom poverty was considered the natural state, were exempt from this judgment, and their care was given to their masters. The only explanation for any others who were poor was the one characteristically offered by the Humane Society in 1809, when it said that "by a just and inflexible law of Providence, misery is ordained to be the companion and punishment of vice." . . .

Such attitudes began to waver, however, in the first quarter of the nineteenth century, when the vision of an eternally expanding and ever-more-prosperous country became clouded over by recurring economic depressions. Grudgingly, it was conceded that "non-employment" resulting in poverty was not necessarily the fault of the workers. For those "whose cry was, not for bread and fuel of charity but for Work!" as Horace Greeley described them, destitution was often the ugly consequence of unemployment. The popular faith in the American ideals of self-sufficiency and self help was shaken by this kind of talk. Nevertheless, as late as 1854 President Franklin Pierce, vetoing a bill to grant public land for the use of states to help care for the indigent insane, argued that the government could not become "the great almoner of public charity throughout the United States."

The severe depression of 1857–1859 forced changes in methods of dealing with the poor. Private charity funds weren't adequate to tide over the unemployed, and public funds had to be appropriated by cities. Now, for the first time in the country's brief history, the unemployed organized in protest, demonstrating and marching to force local governments to take action. Shortly there followed the Civil War, which left the South as an entire region of poverty. In the wake of the war, private charity and philanthropy developed on a large scale, while there grew a reluctant acceptance of the fact that the federal government had to assume responsibility for some part of veterans' care and provide for the families of dead soldiers.

But no one, except nineteenth century radicals, questioned the basic assumption that the free enterprise system was created by God to bring about the Kingdom of Heaven, or something close to it, here on earth. Economic dislocations were believed to be only temporary disturbances from which the country could, and would, always quickly recover. The depression of 1873, like that of the late 1850s, brought about demonstrations of the unemployed which were crushed by the police. Private charity remained the main form of welfare during the latter half of the nineteenth century. Public work projects were adopted only reluctantly, because administration of welfare programs by corrupt officials often led to their abuse for political purposes. In the spring of 1894, thousands of unemployed marchers from all parts of the country gathered in Washington to petition Congress. This was "Coxey's Army." Coxey and a few other marchers were arrested and received short prison sentences for "walking on the grass" and carrying banners. The House Committee on Labor refused to hear Coxey's proposals, and before the end of the year, the first national movement of the poor and unemployed had collapsed.

Meanwhile, the reform and settlement house movements had started focusing attention on the social and economic conditions creating poverty. Even so, these social workers remained committed to the thesis that the dole destroyed the character of the recipients. In 1883, Josephine Shaw Lowell, the great welfare worker, wrote that using public funds to support the poor in their homes was evil because "the principle underlying [the practice] is not that the proceeds of all men's labor is to be fairly divided among all but that the idle, improvident and even vicious man has the right to live in idleness and vice upon the proceeds of the labor of his industrious and virtuous fellow citizen."

Characteristically, Jane Addams poignantly describes her mixed reactions to this policy in the case of a young man who came to Hull House to secure help for his family:

> I told him one day of the opportunity for work on the drainage canal and intimated that if any employment were obtainable, he ought to exhaust that possibility before asking for help. The man replied that he had always worked indoors and that he could not endure outside work in the winter. . . . He did not come again for relief but worked for two days digging on the canal where he contracted pneumonia and died a week later. I have never lost trace of the two little children he left behind him although I cannot see them without a bitter consciousness that it was at their expense I learned that life cannot be administered by definite rules and regulations; that wisdom to deal with a man's difficulties comes only through some knowledge of his life and habits as a whole; and that to treat an isolated episode is almost sure to invite blundering.

The first old-age assistance law was passed in 1915—not in a state, but in the Territory of Alaska. In 1923 Montana and Nevada became the first states to enact such legislation. Only 28 states had such laws in 1934, and even then the restrictions on eligibility were very severe and the amount of aid very limited. During the depression that followed the panic of 1907, and during the depression of 1914–1915, the fate of the able-bodied unemployed was left almost completely in the hands of private charity.

The traditional commitment of the country to laissez-faire capitalism was still very strong in the postwar depression of 1920–1922. The federal government took the position that only private industry could solve the problem of unemployment and that the responsibility for relief of the unemployed rested with the local communities.

In September, 1921, President Warren Harding told the Nationwide Conference on Unemployment that "I would have little enthusiasm for any proposed relief which seeks either palliation or tonic from the public treasury. The excess of stimulation from that source is to be reckoned a cause of trouble rather than a source of cure. . . ." Curiously, organized labor sided with the President and the employer class in opposing public relief for the unemployed. The American Federation of Labor had always opposed such relief and continued its opposition to any form of federal unemployment insurance even after the Great Depression of 1929. At its 1930 convention, William Green spoke in ringing 18th-century terms: "The American workman, proud of his freedom and his liberty, is not yet willing to make himself a ward of the state and a ward of the government. . . . We cannot deal with such a tragedy in a visionary way."

Even in the following year, with at least 7,000,000 people expected to be unemployed during the winter, the AFL termed federal unemployment insurance as "unsuited to our economic and political requirements here and unsatisfactory to American working men and women." It was not until July, 1932, when 11,000,000 workers were unemployed, that the AFL executive council reluctantly instructed President Green to draft a plan of unemployment insurance. . . .

II

The argument over whether or not federal funds should be used to aid the needy had actually ended in the summer of 1932, when President Hoover had reluctantly approved federal loans to finance 80 percent of all state and local aid to the unemployed (loans which obviously were not going to be repaid). The summer of 1932 was catastrophic for the Republicans: thousands of unemployed veterans had converged on Washington to exert pressure for the passage of a bonus bill, and were driven from the capital by force—an act which outraged the country. Roosevelt, as President, took immediate steps to meet the terrible crisis. In March, 1933, the Civilian Conservation Corps was established to provide work camps for youth; in May, the Federal Emergency Relief Administration was created; in June, public employment offices to be operated by the states were authorized; and in November, Roosevelt issued an executive order setting up the Civilian Works Agency to operate a federal work program. In January, 1935, Roosevelt proposed that Congress set up the Works Progress Administration. But his message to Congress reflected his commitment to the traditional attitude toward the dole: "The lessons of History," he said, "show conclusively that continued dependence upon relief induces a spiritual and moral disintegration fundamentally destructive to the national fiber. To dole out relief in this way is . . . a subtle destroyer of the human spirit." . . .

The New Deal welfare program changed an essential tenet of American life, but only in a limited way. Responsibility for the economic well-being of individuals was now vested in the government, but the responsibilities were carried out in ways that did no violence to traditional attitudes. Unemployment insurance and social security pensions were not given to all citizens as a matter of right; unemployment insurance was paid only to those who had been working for specified periods of time; payments to the aged were based on a system to which the workers contributed. The amounts paid out varied, too, in relation to the amounts paid in; nor did anyone question the right of the state to refuse unemployment insurance payments to the unemployed worker who refused to accept what was considered a suitable job. States' rights were also carefully preserved, and the emphasis of the program—accepted by the political leaders, the administrative staff and their social-worker allies—was on helping the depression victims adjust to their now somewhat better condition.

The fear shared by reformers and conservatives alike that unemployment relief and unemployment insurance would have the effect of pauperizing the recipient turned out to be groundless. Bakke, in *The Unemployed Worker*, a study of the depression victims, came to the general conclusion that "Unemployment Insurance has not made paupers." Nevertheless, over and over again, the "no handout" theme was emphasized by the administrative liberals running the programs. Together with the social workers, they adopted a kind of progressive paternalism towards the poor in which Roosevelt represented the kindly father figure. . . .

In 1939 and 1940, another and more rebellious voice was raised—that of the Back of the Yards movement in Chicago, which brought together a variety of community, religious, and labor organizations centered in the stockyards. The BYM was overtly a pressure group, committed to tying local actions into programs of larger social reconstruction. In words that have a clear resonance today, for they are echoed by important segments of the civil rights movement, one of their spokesmen defined the organization's aims:

> We are sick of the social-worker approach. The battle against slum conditions and slum areas is our prime objective, as it must be the prime objective of all organizations and individuals who seek to do significant work for social betterment.
>
> Many liberals are disturbed by the Back of the Yards Neighborhood Council because they feel it is a pressure group which fights in a tough vicious way in which no holds are barred. It does fight viciously.

> We in Back of the Yards are fighting for our bread and butter, our homes, our families, and for our very lives. . . . These liberals fail to realize that the achievement and constructive use of power can help people better themselves.
>
> The force we rely upon is the power that can only be generated by democratic organizations. The liberals cannot believe this because they are remote from the people and have never seen or felt the vitality of democracy in action.

World War II brought an end to the depression, at least for the white majority, and with it also came a temporary easing of the ideological schizophrenia that the country had suffered during the thirties. The society concentrated its attention on the war efforts, which seemed, as a concomitant, to have brought prosperity to all. In fact, nothing of the sort had happened: the aged, the dependent, and the disabled were only a little better off than they had been during the depression, while the Negroes, the largest minority group, were only in a relatively better position.

At the end of World War II, memories of the depression resulted in the passage of the Full Employment Act of 1946, which again reflected the dual commitment so characteristic of American society. The Act affirmed federal responsibility for providing "conditions under which there will be afforded useful employment opportunities, including self-employment, for those willing, able and seeking to work and to promote maximum employment, production and purchasing power"; but, simultaneously, it insisted that this responsibility had to be carried out "in a manner calculated to foster and promote free competitive enterprise." . . .

III

Beginning in 1956, the unemployment rate rose steadily, from 4.2 percent to 5.6 percent. Even worse, inside the overall rate was buried a differential rate for Negroes that was having a sharp effect in the Negro community: Negroes were actually slipping backwards and were relatively worse off than they had been in the immediate postwar period. But now a more aggressive mood prevailed among the Negroes and other minority groups, stimulated in part by the expansion of community and race relations agencies that were often supported by foundation funds.

These agencies were the post-World War II counterparts of the social welfare and reform groups of the late nineteenth and early twentieth centuries. But their focus had shifted to the improvement of inter-group and inter-religious relations, primarily through the establishment of community agencies with broad representation from all segments of the community. Generally, their operations were in the hands of professional staffs, backed by a board whose individual members either had personal or organizational prestige. And although the agencies recognized very quickly that the problems they confronted had to be dealt with in an integrated fashion, involving all aspects of community life, their actual operations involved very few members of the groups on whose behalf they spoke. In this approach they differed sharply from such organizations as the Back of the Yards movement, with its emphasis on participation in decision-making by as many members of the community as possible.

Inevitably, then, reform became professionalized, and the reformers learned to operate within the context of society, rather than attempting to make radical changes in it. Even more important, the new breed of reformers became the experts to whom society deferred for dealing with community problems—including the one of poverty, which was again being discovered.

The discovery wasn't a sudden one, nor was it complete. In 1958, John Galbraith's *The Affluent Society* divided the "new poverty" into two main components: case and insular poverty. Case poverty referred to those individuals who suffer from some personal disability that prevents them from joining in the national upward trend, while insular poverty referred to an entire area, such as the Appalachians, where everybody was adversely affected by the economic downgrading that had taken place.

But most people were more heartened by the title of Galbraith's book than dismayed by its contents. And the civil rights movement, which was not yet directly connected with, nor concerned about, poverty absorbed the attention of the government and the reformers. Robert Lampman's work on unequal income distribution failed to draw the notice it deserved, and when, in 1962, Michael Harrington's *The Other America* was published, it received equally little attention. But a year later, Dwight MacDonald wrote a long review-article about poverty in *The New Yorker* praising Harrington's book, and the rush was on. Poverty had been rediscovered. . . .

The Peace Corps had attracted people to the Kennedy administration who might not otherwise have been willing to join the government: liberal professionals with genuine commitment to limited change, and sincere volunteers, especially young ones, who were becoming involved in social problems but who, for one reason or another, were outside the civil rights movement.

The "war on poverty" attracted the same kinds of people—in some cases, the very same people. And Shriver, who was familiar with these types, liked them, and has proved willing to take some risks on their behalf. Under him, the "war on poverty" did not so much professionalize reform as bring professional reformers into the governmental orbit.

But despite manifestly good intentions, the program was handicapped from the start by the schizophrenia that has always marked the American view of the poor. For political reasons, it had to be defined immediately, in

Shriver's words, as "not a hand-out program—or an individual case-work program." Instead, the main emphasis has been put on projects which, again in Shriver's words, are "prudent, practical, focused and patriotic." The program is designed to give some of the poor opportunity to participate more fully in the American way of life, through better education and jobs. The basic assumptions were stated by the President's Council of Economic Advisers in their 1964 report: "Americans want to *earn* the American standard of living by their own efforts and contributions." . . .

So it is the "deserving" poor who are the main targets of the antipoverty effort. Its major emphases are on youth education and employment, on planned regional and community development, and on vocational training and retraining. But the programs are severely limited, almost all of them merely extensions of older programs. And the "war on poverty" was sold to the American public as a "cheap" war—one that would cost taxpayers very little.

I get what I deserve
I deserve what I get.

I have it,
therefore I deserve it

I deserve it
because I have it.

You have not got it
therefore you do not deserve it

You do not deserve it
because you have not got it

You have not got it
because you do not deserve it

You do not deserve it
therefore you have not got it.

KEEPING THE POOR IN THEIR PLACE: NOTES ON THE IMPORTANCE OF BEING ONE-UP

Adam Walinsky

No significant shade of political opinion, from I. F. Stone to *Time* magazine, can be found to oppose outright the War on Poverty; the Great Society has thus far been received as an election-year counterpart of the Big Rock Candy Mountain. And yet most of us assume that Congress will not establish the giant public works program for which Gunnar Myrdal calls. Nor will it lower the work week to thirty hours, as Herbert Gans has suggested, nor follow the suggestion of the Ad Hoc Committee on the Triple Revolution and guarantee incomes to all regardless of the work they do. The reasons for Congressional reluctance are familiar; the poor are, by definition, without economic power; except for the Negroes, they are without effective leaders; they are only one fifth of a nation, and the rest of the country is roughly satisfied with things as they are.

The liberals who argue that larger programs are necessary admit readily that the critical barrier is the apathetic or even hostile attitude of the middle-class majority—for present purposes, whites who are not poor—which has been victimized by "myths": that a balanced budget is desirable; that the government economy should be run like a household budget; that free enterprise is inherently superior to government activity; that big government is a bad thing; that tax cuts stimulate economic activity more than government spending; that expenditures result not in a bigger pie, but only a smaller slice for solid taxpayers. If the public is educated in the truth about economics, one hears, these "myths" will disappear.

But the interesting question about a myth is not whether people believe it, but why. Myths are not capricious inventions of storytellers, but ways of organizing and rationalizing group-behavior patterns. They serve real needs; they are less affected by argument than by changes in the conditions to which they are responsive. Viewing these myths as a screen behind which tangible aims are pursued would require a second hypothesis: that the middle-class majority *does not want* to improve significantly the lot of the poor, or—a further step—that the middle-class actively desires to keep the poor where they are.

In present-day America, the middle class is defined largely by the fact that the poor exist. Doctors are middle class, but so are bookkeepers; factory workers vacation with lawyers, drive bigger cars than teachers, live next door to store-owners, and send their children to school with the children of

Reprinted by Permission of *The New Republic*, vol. 151, no. 1 (July 4, 1964), pp. 15–18;

bank tellers. In a middle class so diffuse, with almost no characteristic common to all, middle-class income, education, and housing are what the poor do not have. If the present poor should become middle class, no meaning would remain to that phrase; either it would be a euphemism for the lower part of a bipartite division, or it would cease to apply to those who now boast of their "middle" status. The middle class knows that the economists are right when they say that poverty can be eliminated if we only will it; they simply do not will it.

Such an explanation, of course, seems in direct conflict with American ideals of equality of opportunity and social justice—ideals on which the middle classes themselves insist. But the creed of equal opportunity is a very complex thing. Opportunity to better oneself is usually regarded as self-explanatory, a recognition of the basic human right to fully utilize one's talents and labor. And in part it is recognized as a refusal to admit that others are better than oneself, or (a variant of the last) that others' children are better than one's own. But it has other facets. Virtually everyone who has reached his final life-station must and does believe and say that choice, or more commonly "the breaks," or "the system," prevented him from rising higher. But this same man must and does believe and say that his own abilities are primarily responsible for how far he has risen above others. People above oneself are regarded as no better than equal; people below oneself are regarded as inferior.

It is of course necessary to tinker with the system occasionally. Not only is reform commanded by the ethic; but as long as they pose no threat of basic change, improvements in the opportunity-structure at once reaffirm the existence of the depressed who need help, and serve as further "proof" that their inferior position is the result of inherent inferiority. But since people will not and cannot admit to themselves that the inferior position of others is entirely, or even primarily, caused by an inherently unequal system, they do not support measures that could possibly eliminate all or even most of the inequalities. The result is tokenism.

I suspect that the tension between adherence to democratic ideals and a natural desire to preserve one's relative gains by denying them to others has been heightened by a general loss of middle-class security. One possible reason for such a loss of security is enlargement in the size of the middle class itself; by the social and economic elevation of production and service workers; by the slackening of immigration, which has produced an America 95 percent native-born and thus eliminated much "native" prestige; by the spread of education, high school and now college; by the general availability of inexpensive goods (especially clothing) virtually identical to those used by the well-to-do. For the old middle class, this has meant a dilution of status, which they have attempted to recapture by shifting the criteria of middle-class membership from income ("mere money") to sophistication of various sorts—education, community service, culture. For the new middle class, the gain in status is precarious; they attempt to reinforce it by appropriating the symbols of the old middle class, especially suburban housing and education for the children. For both old and new middle classes, the problem of preserving status becomes more acute in direct proportion to the technical ease with which poverty can be eliminated from the country.

"Variety of Dingbats"

But the central factor in the loss of security is a general decline in the significance of work. Observers have noted this loss in many different places: among the unemployed and underemployed: among factory hands whose labor is ever more routinized and uncertain; among paper-work employees of great corporations whose only function is the creation of artificial differences between what Pegler called "an ingenious variety of dingbats for the immature"; among craftsmen whose only means of delaying obsolescence is in Luddite strikes, and who are reminded of their uselessness at every well-publicized contract negotiation. Indeed, the meaninglessness of work has become one of the dominant themes of popular culture. But any decline thus far observed in the importance of work is but the start of a potential toboggan run. The impact of automation on the assembly line is increasingly clear. But white-collar workers are also being replaced by machines; and Donald N. Michael predicts that middle management, whose relatively unsophisticated job is being brought within computer capabilities, is the next threatened class. If present trends in the automation of factory and office continue, there will be fewer jobs, and most of them will be routine.

Understanding the full import of that development requires recognition of the function work has performed in the past. Work everywhere serves the obvious function of enabling men to eat and survive. But work in America has also been the primary source of status in the society. Men have marked out their relation to others through work. The rewards of the society—income, women, power, respect—have gone to men roughly in proportion to their market utility. (Divergences—such as great inherited wealth—have been remarkable chiefly for their tendency to gravitate toward the norm—as in the upper classes' compulsion to enter and subsidize public affairs.) But work has been the organizing principle of American society in more than an economic sense; it has in large part displaced and substituted for ancestry, social class, tradition, and family as bench-marks for men's knowledge of self and their relation to others. Reliance on work as the primary social ethic has been intimately bound up with the growth of a democratic, egalitarian society. For work is alone among our status-givers in its diversity and attendant uniqueness. No man can master all occupations; indeed, few can master more than one. No matter how brilliant a professor may be, he must still call the plumber when his water-pipes freeze, or a mechanic when his car's transmission slips, a butcher when he wants meat, and a laborer when he wants a drain dug. In a diversified economy, so long as a man has a trade or skill, he has something for which people in the community must turn to him —some claim of importance which is recognized by others. It is not even necessary that the job be itself intrinsically difficult to learn or perform, so long as it is important to other people and would not be done except for the labor of those doing it; thus Michael Harrington reports a striking pride of *metier* among many migrant fruit-pickers in California. It is the status conferred by work that allows people to live in reasonable contentment with themselves and others.

The alienation of factory operatives from their work is a story as old as the assembly line. But technological development continues the spiral. Automation removes workers from direct contact with the line, and most from the factory itself; fewer workers remain to do more highly skilled jobs. "Service industries" are to take up the employment slack of automation, in theory, but repairmen, for instance, are little more than salesclerks for replacement parts; consumer goods are built to be sold cheaply and discarded, not repaired when they fail. Printed electrical circuits, for example, are not, like their more expensive wired predecessors, repairable by the normal electrician. Other "service" workers—domestics, waiters, salesclerks, hospital orderlies—are menials easily replaced by anyone from the growing refuse-heap of the society.

But if work loses its diversity, and hence its importance, for a significant proportion of the society, we lose our only means for apportioning status on a roughly equal basis. Other status-givers can confer meaningful prestige only on those who have *more* than others.

Significance of Housing

The consequences of a decline in the prime importance of work are easily deduced. One is a rise in the status-importance of consumption, and of all consumption expenditures, housing has the greatest personal and financial importance; the one-family house with a plot of ground has always been the ideal American home. Its possession and quality have always been marks of social status. By excluding groups of people, communities have appropriated for themselves a mark of class superiority. In Washington, D.C., as in many other cities, houses in communities which exclude Jews (or Negroes) bring higher prices than equivalent houses in otherwise equal areas; the monetary value of such small differences in neighborhood quality should alert us to the fact that housing status is essentially predicated on success in excluding social "inferiors." The use of housing as a symbol of superior status has been increasing. Income-segregation, abetted by public-housing projects in which no member of the middle class will live, is well underway. Trends reported by the New York Metropolitan Region Study are being duplicated elsewhere: luxury apartments will soon house most older people who can afford them;

the exodus of white couples with children from the large cities will continue, indeed will probably accelerate as fewer remain. Fair-housing ordinances will be passed in some cities, perhaps even some states; but the trend will, in general, be toward maintenance of racial segregation. (Surely it is significant that California will probably repeal this year, by popular referendum, its established fair-housing law, and that cities like Seattle and Berkeley have voted down fair-housing ordinances.) In the Philadelphia suburb of Folcroft, a few months ago, residents rioted for weeks to prevent a Negro family from moving in; there is no reason to think that community unique.

Education is a second major heir to the status-giving function once dominated by work. The late ebbing of the Sputnik mentality arises only in part from our missile successes. In larger part, it is a way of raising a new standard of status—"liberal" education pursued for its own sake, which is particularly appropriate as a means of preserving present status-boundaries. First, it is an overexpensive luxury for the lower classes. Thus, Dr. Conant suggests that education for the poor should be vocational training suited to the jobs they can "reasonably" expect to get; a liberal education cannot be cheapened by too-wide distribution. Moreover, stressing the importance of liberal education insures the future position of the present middle class; its children will, by definition, score better on the class-biased tests which are used to determine their eligibility for such education. Lastly, the poor sense the futility of education in an economy where work (especially the kind for which they are trained) is declining, and shun and depreciate it; this phenomenon in turn serves as proof that opportunity is there, but is not taken advantage of by the poor.

A third critical status factor is income, which is important both in itself and as it affects access to other status-givers. In itself, income has been closely connected with work, often measuring the social worth of the work done; when inherited, it also reflects social class. But as work loses significance, income becomes most important as a determinant of consumption and education. To preserve status in these areas, income differentials will probably be preserved—as by making the tax structure more regressive, and keeping doles well below minimum-wage levels. People whose work is meaningless except as it allows them, by earning money, to differentiate themselves from the poor will continue to oppose large-scale employment projects. Instead, they will support transfer payments at a level too low to allow the recipients to compete for status in housing or education.

Two recent proposals, usually thought of as diametric opposites—the President's Poverty program and the Report of the Ad Hoc Committee on the Triple Revolution—are examples of programs which lend themselves to reinforcement of the social hierarchy.

The Kennedy–Johnson program does some excellent things. It attempts to train workers for jobs; to establish community-service programs for unoccupied youth; and to subsidize employment by special loans to municipalities and private employers. It directly will affect about half a million people. Christopher Jencks has stated its essential premise. . . .[1] The problems of poverty, he noted, will be solved by remedying imperfections in the opportunity-structure—education and jobs (with a side glance at motivation); the measures so far advanced, at any rate, are directed at these imperfections. A rationale advanced for the program's present modest size is that the tax cut will provide more jobs for the economy as a whole; some suggest the program will reach its full growth only after arms expenditures are cut as a result of lowered world tensions. It appears from his recent statements that the President plans to expand the government's domestic activities considerably; a program of rebuilding all our cities and countryside would itself be a major step toward the poverty war's expressed goals.

But if my earlier speculations are correct, expansion of the poverty war, or any government activity which tends to lessen class distinctions, will encounter resistance which increases in direct proportion to its size and probable effectiveness. Indeed, I would argue that the program thus far advanced has been received quietly because its fundamentally middle-class principles can be used by the middle class to prevent more significant action. Thus its concentration on opening up the opportunity-structure could be used to justify inaction on government employment programs tailored to large numbers of the un- and underemployed. Similarly, the emphasis on job training could be used to justify class segregation in education à la Dr. Conant and reliance for job expansion on the tax cut could justify regressive taxation as an economic policy to aid the poor.

Guaranteed Incomes

But for all the long-range political dangers of the poverty program's initial direction, it is on far firmer ground than that of the Ad Hoc Committee on the Triple Revolution. Starting from the premise that further increases in worker productivity will make a scarcity-based economy irrelevant, the Ad Hoc Committee sees the vital function of the economy shifted from production to consumption. If machines can produce everything that is within our capacity to consume, and work is available to only a small fraction of the society, then consumption should be separated from labor; manifestly, it is as pointless to deny the products of the automatic machines to those without work as it would be to deny them air or sunlight. Income, therefore, should be guaranteed and paid by the government, regardless of work done in exchange.

In fact, this report is more a projection of the economy in fifty years' time than it is a blueprint for today; in this respect, it is an admirable effort

[1] Jencks, Christopher, "Johnson vs. Poverty," *The New Republic,* March 28, 1964, pp. 15–18.

at advanced social planning. But its advanced liberal tone should not blind us to its danger. Of all the devices that have been invented to keep the status-poor in their place, putting them on a dole is by far the most effective. The size of the dole can be controlled so as to keep them always in comparative poverty, and thus unable to compete for higher status in the society; indeed, the fact of being on the dole itself leads to lessened aspiration and pride. Most of the present unemployed continue to covet work because the society's ethic commands it; to make the dole legitimate is to lessen significantly the pressure for reform from below.

The dole, of course, would be extended gradually, in the form of increasing present welfare payments and extending their coverage. The gradual change would start with the present poor; and since the middle class would still have jobs when the dole was extended, a substantial differentiation would be maintained between dole-income and prevailing middle-class wage rates. This differential would then serve as a method for preserving housing and educational segregation and quality differentials. As more of the middle class lose traditional work, however, they would not slip onto the dole and into the ranks of the status-poor. Instead in all probability, they would become social-service workers of an advanced sort—tending, of course, to the needs of the poor. Or they might find large-scale employment overseas, as in a "Management Corps" to aid administration in the poor nations. Means will be found to preserve their status vis-à-vis the poor simply because the middle class is larger and has higher cards.

These developments are not inevitable; they can, and should, be arrested and reversed. But the programs so far suggested, even the most radical, treat symptoms—the poor—and not the illness, which is a loss of meaningful work for most of the society. So long as they treat symptoms which are directed primarily at poverty, they will be restricted by the majority to glorified pilot projects; the existence of these limited projects will salve the conscience and the egos of the middle class.

It cannot be said too often that we are faced with a problem of time, that the resistance of the middle class to change will increase as their own assurance decreases and the lower classes (particularly Negroes) assert themselves more strongly. But neither can it be stressed too much that to castigate the middle class for their resistance to change is both useless and irresponsible. That resistance is based on sound fears that an effective drive on poverty will narrow status-differentials between them and the present poor. Those who criticize middle-class ignorance usually do so from privileged sanctuaries: a Harvard education, a house in an all-white suburb, and a firm position in the academic-political-foundation hierarchy guarantee status which will not be jeopardized no matter what improvement is made in the lot of the poor. But the increasingly useless middle class is being asked to surrender its claims to any superiority of status; even where jobs are insecure and meaningless, simply having one gives status superior to those who cannot support their families without public assistance. The middle class sense this perfectly, and no amount of talk about side effects on consumption and employment will convince them otherwise. A serious program must offer the middle class a new life style in return for the raise in status it would give to the poor; it must deal not only (or even primarily) with pockets of economic poverty, but with the poverty of satisfaction, purpose, and dignity that afflicts us all.

A Black Student's Comment, April 30, 1971
(during tryout class with this book)

I don't feel a part of this class because a lot of these people are "hippie types," whatever that is. I don't feel like *I* belong here. I guess I'm prejudiced. Children of rich white folks, tired of being rich, think it might be fun to act hip—stereotyped phrases stolen from us. A lot of them are full of bull—they can always go back. The right clothes . . . say the right things . . . I feel *very* hostile. I'm not very "hip," I can't act like I am not—I don't understand. Why should I have to go back to nature? I haven't had anything to give up yet. They are trying to get somewhere I'm trying to get away from. I come here and I get very confused and I don't like it. Maybe it's just been a bad week.

THE FIRE NEXT TIME BLUES

Ted Joans

you put me down when I needed you most
you kicked me out you were a very rude host
you maltreated me
I'll give you the fire next time

you mistreated me/ rejected me/ threatened me/ &
economically enslaved poor me
but I've got MY bag
I'll give you the fire next time

you ignored/floored/ became bored/
you cheated/taunted/ became conceited/
you exploited me
I'll give you the fire next time

I hate you, Wow!! You taught me how/so I'll give you the fire
R ight N ow!!!

THE SOCIOLOGY OF POVERTY

Lewis A. Coser

Historically, the poor emerge when society elects to recognize poverty as a special status and assigns specific persons to that category. The fact that some people may privately consider themselves poor is sociologically irrelevant. What *is* sociologically relevant is poverty as a socially recognized condition, as a social status. We are concerned with poverty as a property of the social structure. . . .

In modern societies the deprived are assigned to the core category of the poor only when they receive assistance. It might be objected that the category of the economically deprived is presently much larger than that of the assisted poor. Whereas the latter englobes around 8 million persons in contemporary America, between 40 and 50 million fall into the former category. However, the point is precisely that the current widespread discussion of the problems of poverty can be seen in large part as an effort to broaden the core category of the poor by insisting that millions not heretofore included deserve societal assistance. If I understand Michael Harrington and his co-thinkers aright, they argue in effect that a redefinition of the problem of poverty is required so that the very large number of deprived who have so far not received assistance can be included among the poor receiving societal help of one kind or another.

It is not a person's lack of economic means that makes him belong to the core category of the poor. As long as a man continues to be defined primarily in terms of his occupational status, he is not so classified. Doctors, farmers, or plumbers who have suffered financial reverses or strains are still typically called doctors, farmers, or plumbers. "The acceptance of assistance," argues Georg Simmel, "removes the man who has received it from the precondition of the previous status; it symbolized his formal declassification."[1] From that point on his private trouble becomes a public issue. In individual psychological terms the sequence of events leads from the experience of deprivation to a quest for assistance; the matter is reversed however in sociological perspective: those who receive assistance are defined as being poor. Hence, poverty cannot be understood sociologically in terms of low

[1] Georg Simmel, *Soziologie* (Leipzig: Duncker und Humblot, 1908), p. 489. I have relied very heavily on Simmel's hitherto untranslated essay, "Der Arme," in the above volume. In fact, much of what I say in the first part of this paper is little more than a restatement of some of Simmel's seminal ideas.

Reprinted from "The Sociology of Poverty" by Lewis A. Coser in *Social Problems,* vol. 13, no. 2 (1965), pp. 140–148 (excerpts). With permission from The Society for the Study of Social Problems and the author.

income or deprivation but rather in terms of the social response to such deprivations.

The modern poor are a stratum that is recruited from heterogeneous origins, and individual members of this stratum have a great number of differing attributes. They come to belong to the common category of the poor by virtue of an essentially passive trait, namely that society reacts to them in a particular manner. The poor come to be viewed and classified not in terms of criteria ordinarily used in social categorization, that is, not by virtue of what they do, but by virtue of what is done to them. To quote Simmel again: "Poverty hence presents a unique sociological constellation: a number of individuals occupy a specific organic position within the social whole through purely personal fate; but it is not personal destiny or personal conditions which determine the position but rather the fact that others—individuals, associations, or social totalities—attempt to correct this state of affairs. Hence it is not personal need which makes for poverty; rather, the sociological category of poverty emerges only when those who suffer from want are receiving assistance."[2]

Though the poor are recognized as having a special status in modern societies, it is still a status that is marked only by negative attributes, that is, by what the status-holder does *not* have. This distinguishes him from any other status-holder in that it does not carry with it the expectation of a social contribution. This lack of expectation of a social contribution by the poor is symbolized by their lack of social visibility. Those who are assigned to the status of the poor offend the moral sensibilities of other members of the society who, unwittingly, or wittingly, keep them out of their sight. What is at issue here is not only physical segregation into special areas and districts that right-minded citizens would not normally care to visit and that are typically not shown to tourists, but also a kind of moral invisibility. . . .

Lest it be believed that we deal here only with the more remote past it may be well to remind us of a very similar trend in the recent history of the United States. John K. Galbraith remarked upon this a few years ago when he wrote: "In the United States, the survival of poverty is remarkable. We ignore it because we share with all societies at all times the capacity for not seeing what we do not wish to see. Anciently this has enabled the nobleman to enjoy his dinner while remaining oblivious to the beggars around his door. In our own day it enables us to travel in comfort throughout South Chicago and the South."[3] At the present moment, when poverty is suddenly receiving frontline attention among politicians, scholars and the mass media, it is difficult to remember that only recently it seemed hardly visible at all. Five years ago the editors of *Fortune* magazine published a volume, *America*

[2] *Ibid.*, p. 493.

[3] John K. Galbraith, *The Affluent Society* (Boston: Houghton Mifflin, 1959), p. 333.

in the Sixties,[4] in which they attempted to forecast the major social and economic trends of the next decade. They concluded that soon deprivation would no longer be with us at all. They announced with self-congratulatory flourish that "only" 3,600,000 families have incomes under $2,000 and that if a family makes over $2,000 it cannot be considered deprived at all. Two years later Michael Harrington's *The Other America*,[5] followed by a spate of other books and articles, suddenly helped to picture deprivation as the central domestic issue in the United States and led to the emergence of a new social definition of poverty. The deprived in America now were seen as constituting about 25 percent of the population all of whom deserved assistance. The number of objectively deprived is not likely to have changed appreciably between the complacent fifties and the self-critical sixties, but the extent of perceived deprivation changed drastically. As a consequence, what appeared as a peripheral problem only a few years ago suddenly assumes considerable national salience. . . .

One cannot help but be struck by the fact that, to give one example, the number of underprivileged will vary greatly depending on where you fix the income line. Thus the aforementioned *Fortune* study defined deprivation as a family income under $2,000 and concluded that there were only 3,600,000 poor families. Robert Lampman used the $2,500 cut-off for an urban family of four and on this basis came to the conclusion that 19 percent of the American population, 32,000,000 people, were underprivileged. In the same period, the AFL–CIO, using a slightly higher definition of what constituted low income, found that 41,500,000 Americans—24 percent of the total population—have substandard incomes. After all these studies were published, the Bureau of Labor Statistics issued a report containing newly calculated budgets for urban families of four which showed that previous calculations had underestimated minimal budgetary requirements. Harrington concludes on the basis of these new figures that the deprived number more nearly 50,000,000.[6]

Enough has been said to indicate the extent to which objective misery and perceived deprivation may diverge. We can now return to the initial statement that, in modern societies, persons are assigned a position in the status category of the poor when they receive assistance. Receipt of such assistance is predicated upon the society's willingness to assume a measure of responsibility for the poor and upon its recognition of the fact that they are effectively a part of the community. But what are the terms upon which

[4] The Editors of Fortune, *America in the Sixties* (New York: Harper Torchbooks, 1960), p. 102. Note the following additional comment: "Only about a million domestic servants, marginal farm operators, and farm laborers and their families still look truly poor." *Ibid.*, p. 102.

[5] Michael Harrington, *The Other America* (Baltimore: Penguin Books), 1963.

[6] *Ibid.*, pp. 192–194.

such assistance is granted and what are the consequences for the recipient?

Here I would like to contend that the very granting of relief, the very assignment of the person to the category of the poor, is forthcoming only at the price of a degradation of the person who is so assigned.

To receive assistance means to be stigmatized and to be removed from the ordinary run of men. It is a status degradation through which, in Harold Garfinkel's words, "the public identity of an actor is transformed into something looked on as lower in the local schemes of social types."[7] In this perspective, the societal view of a person becomes significant in so far as it alters his face. Once a person is assigned to the status of the poor his role is changed, just as the career of the mental patient is changed by the very fact that he is defined as a mental patient.[8] Let me give a few illustrative instances of what is at issue here.

Members of nearly all status groups in society can make use of a variety of legitimate mechanisms to shield their behavior from observability by others; society recognizes a right to privacy, that is, the right to conceal parts of his role behavior from public observation. But this right is denied to the poor. At least in principle, facets of his behavior which ordinarily are not public are in this case under public control and are open to scrutiny by social workers or other investigators. In order to be socially recognized as poor a person is obligated to make his private life open to public inspection.[9] The protective veil which is available to other members of society is explicitly denied to him.

Whereas other recipients of social services may upon occasion be visited at home by investigators, most of their contact with the agency is likely to be in the agency rather than in their private homes. Generally, in modern society, the exercise of authority—except within the family—is separated from the home. With regard to the poor on relief, however, this is not the case. Here their home is the place in which most contacts with the agency investigators are likely to take place. They are typically being investigated *in situ* and hence have much less of a chance to conceal their private affairs from the superordinate observers. Such an invasion of home territory, because it prevents the usual stage management for the visit of outsiders, is necessarily experienced as humiliating and degrading.

When money is allocated to members of any other status groups in society, they have the freedom to dispose of it in almost any way they see fit.

[7] Harold Garfinkel, "Conditions of Successful Degradation Ceremonies," *American Journal of Sociology*, 61(1956), p. 420.

[8] Cf. Erving Goffman, *Asylums* (New York: Doubleday Anchor Books, 1961), *passim*.

[9] On the notion of observability cf. Robert K. Merton, *Social Theory and Social Structure* (Glencoe, Ill.: The Free Press, 1957), pp. 374–375, and Rose Laub Coser, "Insulation from Observability and Types of Social Conformity," *American Sociological Review*, 26, pp. 28–39.

Here again, the treatment of the poor differs sharply. When monies are allocated to them, they do not have free disposition over their use. They must account to the donors for their expenses and the donors decide whether the money is spent "wisely" or "foolishly." That is, the poor are treated in this respect much like children who have to account to parents for the wise use of their pocket money; the poor are infantilized through such procedures.

As the above examples make clear, in the very process of being helped and assisted, the poor are assigned to a special career that impairs their previous identity and becomes a stigma which marks their intercourse with others. Social workers, welfare investigators, welfare administrators and local volunteer workers seek out the poor in order to help them, and yet, paradoxically, they are the very agents of their degradation. Subjective intentions and institutional consequences diverge here. The help rendered may be given from the purest and most benevolent of motives, yet the very fact of being helped degrades.

Assistance can be given either by voluntary workers or by professionals. The former pattern prevailed till roughly World War I, the latter has come to predominate in our days. Such professionalization of assistance has had two divergent sets of consequences for the recipient. To be cared for by a professional who is paid for his work means that the recipient need not be grateful to him, he doesn't have to say thank you. In fact he can hate the person giving assistance and even display some of his antagonism without losing the institutionally provided aid. Professionalization removes the personal element in the relationship and marks it as an impersonal transaction thereby freeing the recipient both from personal embarrassment and from personal obligation. When the poor is, so to speak, "promoted" to a case he may be spared certain personal humiliations. Yet this is not the whole story. The very manner of bureaucratic procedure used in dealing with a person on relief is different from that employed with respect to, say, an unemployed person. Receipt of unemployment insurance is seen as an unquestioned right which has been earned. Control by the donor agency over the recipient is minimal. Here it stands in contrast to control over the person on relief where control is a precondition for relief. Hence the professional in an agency dealing with the unemployed has little power over persons he serves, but the welfare investigator or the case worker has a great deal of power over the assisted poor. This power was considerably increased, it may be remarked in passing, when the giving of assistance shifted from so-called categorical assistance to granting case workers leeway to vary assistance according to the specific needs of the client. This change of policy was instituted for humanitarian and benevolent reasons, to be sure. But it stands to reason that it has greatly increased the discretionary power of the case worker over the client.

Prescribed impersonality has still other effects on the relationship between professionalized welfare workers and the recipients of aid. As long as volunteers or other non-professionals were the main dispensers of charity, condescension was likely to mark the relationship between donors and recipients of aid, but it was also likely to be characterized by a fairly high level of spontaneity. The relationship was so defined as to make a *reciprocal* flow of affect and emotion between the two actors possible, even if it did not always, or usually, occur. But professionalization by definition prevents the flow of affect. This is not due to happenstance but to the institutionalization of a structurally asymmetrical type of relationship. Those who render assistance have a job to do; the recipient is a case. As in every type of bureaucratic procedure, the impersonal aspects of the case must of need take precedence over distracting personal considerations. In fact, case workers or investigators would be incapacitated in the exercise of their tasks were they to indulge in "over-rapport," that is, in an undue consideration of the personal needs of the client. Excessive sympathy would impair role performance. The welfare worker, moreover, is not supposed to deserve esteem for his accomplishments from the recipient of aid but rather from professional peers and superiors. The client who is defined as "poor" has little if any possibility of controlling his behavior. Hence there exist built-in insulating mechanisms which insure that professional concern with the poor does not corrupt the professional into considering the poor as anything but an object of care and a recipient of aid. In this way the status discrepancy between them is continuously reaffirmed. This is accentuated, moreover, in those cases where welfare workers are of lower middle class origin and feel that close association with clients might endanger the respectable status they have but recently achieved.

The professionals and the poor do in fact belong to two basically different worlds. In Alexander Solzhenitsyn's fine novel about Russian concentration camps, *One Day in the Life of Ivan Denisovich*,[10] occurs an episode in which the hero attempts to get some medical relief from the man in charge of the infirmary but is turned away with indifference. He thereupon reflects, "How can you expect a man who's warm to understand a man who's cold." This beautifully captures the gist of what I have been trying to say. As long as social workers and the poor belong to the opposite worlds of those who are warm and those who are cold, their relationship is necessarily an asymmetrical one. As in other aspects of case work, those in need address those who can relieve some of their wants as supplicants, and the asymmetry is not only one of feelings and attitudes, it is also an asymmetry of power. This is an extreme case of unilateral dependence. Peter Blau's formulation is helpful here: "By supplying services in demand to others, a person establishes power over them. If he regularly renders needed services they cannot readily obtain elsewhere, others become dependent on and obligated to him for

[10] Alexander Solzhenitsyn, *One Day in the Life of Ivan Denisovich* (New York: E. P. Dutton, 1963).

these services, and unless they can furnish other benefits to him that produce interdependence by making him equally dependent on them, their unilateral dependence obligates them to comply with his requests lest he ceases to continue to meet their needs."[11]

Blau stresses here that unilateral dependence comes into being when the receiver of benefits is not in a position to reciprocate with benefits that he can in turn bestow upon the donor. This, I believe, touches upon the crux of the matter. The poor, when receiving assistance, are assigned a low and degraded status by virtue of a determination that they cannot themselves contribute to society. Their inability to contribute in turn degrades them to the condition of unilateral receivers. Built into the system of relief is not only the definition of their being noncontributors, but the expectation that they are not even potential contributors. In an instrumentally oriented society, those who cannot give but only receive and who are not expected to give at a future time are naturally assigned the lowest status. They cannot engage in activities that establish interdependence and this is why they cannot be given social recognition. Poverty, therefore, can never be eliminated unless the poor are enabled to give as well as to receive. They can be fully integrated into the social fabric only if they are offered the opportunity to give.

In order to be able to serve, they must first be able to function at optimum capacity. Devices such as a guaranteed minimum income for every citizen, assuring him freedom from pressing want, may very well be a precondition for the abolition of dependency. But it is a precondition only. It needs to be considered not as an end in itself but only as a means which permits the poor to be free from anxiety while they train themselves for the rendering of such services to the community as will make them interdependent with others.

I showed earlier how the core category of the poor arises only when they come to be defined as recipients of assistance. We now see that correlatively the poor will be with us as long as we provide assistance so that the problem of poverty can be solved only through the abolition of a unilateral relationship of dependence.

This is not the place to spell out in detail concrete measures which will "solve" the problem of poverty. I know of no such global solutions at the present moment. But I wish to indicate at least the direction in which, I believe, such solutions are to be looked for. I am impressed, for example, by the number of recent experiments, from Mobilization for Youth to Alcoholics Anonymous, in which "some people who do not seem to benefit from *receiving* help often profit indirectly when they are *giving* help."[12]

[11] Peter Blau, *Exchange and Power in Social Life* (New York: Wiley, 1964), p. 118.

[12] Robert Reiff and Frank Riessman, *The Indigenous Nonprofessional* (New York: National Institute of Labor Education, Mental Health Program), mimeo, p. 11.

A number of such projects have of late used a variety of nonprofessionals recruited largely among the poor. The New York State Division for Youth and several other agencies for example employ former youthful offenders in interviewing and related tasks. Howard University's Community Apprentice Program trains delinquent youth to be recreation, child welfare, and research aides. Mobilization for Youth employs indigenous leaders as case aides, homework helpers, and the like. These jobs offer employment opportunities for the underprivileged and hence serve directly to reduce poverty by transforming dependent welfare cases into homemakers, and former delinquents into researchers.[13] This indigenous nonprofessional, as Frank Riessman and Robert Reiff have written, "is a peer of the client and can more readily identify with him. He possesses no special body of knowledge which makes him an expert and can feel, therefore, that in reversed circumstances the client could do the same job just as easily. In the place of subtle patronage or *noblesse oblige* concepts, he is likely to feel that 'there but for the grace of God go I.' To the indigenous nonprofessional, 'helping others' is a reciprocal process. . . ."[14]

These are only a few and still very feeble beginnings, but I believe that they point in the right direction. The task is to create valued status positions for those who were formerly passive recipients of assistance. Such valuable status positions can only be those in which they are required and enabled to make a social contribution and become active partners in a joint undertaking of mutual aid. This can be done through helping others with whom but recently they shared similar problems or through working in large-scale projects similar to a domestic Peace Corps or a replica of the New Deal's Civilian Conservation Corps. Yet another case in which the poor may themselves contribute to the abolition of the status they occupy arises when they cease "acting poor," i.e., when they reject the role behavior which is required by the status. When the poor begin to react actively, when they refuse to continue to be passive recipients of aid, they undermine the very status that they occupy. This is why rent strikes, demonstrations, and other political activities by the poor should be seen as avenues of activization which tend to lead to a restructuring of their relationships in the community.

Simmel observes that though the notion of assistance necessarily implies taking from the rich and giving to the poor, it nevertheless was never aimed at an equalization of their positions in society. As distinct from socialist endeavors, it does not even have the tendency to reduce the differences between rich and poor but rather accepts and bolsters them.[15] Or, as T. H. Marshall once put it, "The common purpose of statutory and voluntary effort was to abate the nuisance of poverty without disturbing the pattern of in-

[13] *Ibid.*, p. 6.
[14] *Ibid.*, p. 12.
[15] Simmel, *op. cit.*, p. 459.

equality of which poverty was the most obvious unpleasant consequence."[16] This is why what I have suggested diverges sharply from most previous policies. It aims not at alleviating poverty but at abolishing it through the elimination of the despised status of the receiver of assistance. It is, to be sure, a Utopian proposal. But, as Max Weber, that supreme realist, has argued, "Certainly all political experience confirms the truth—that man would not have attained the possible unless time and again he had reached out for the impossible."[17]

[16] T. H. Marshall, *Class Citizenship and Social Development* (New York: Doubleday, Anchor Books, 1965), p. 105.

[17] Gerth and Mills, eds., *From Max Weber* (New York: Oxford University Press, 1948), p. 128.

ADVICE TO A RULER

Gerald M. Swatez

Keep 'em all equally deprived,
And you're asking for trouble.
But advantage some
Relatively over the others,
And the advantaged ones
Will fall all over themselves
Lording their infinitesimally lesser
Deprivation over their
More deprived brothers,
Thereby controlling the more deprived
In your interest,
As well as themselves, similarly;
While those not at all advantaged
Will both grovel
In the hope
Of catching a crumb
From you or the advantaged,
And will establish among themselves
Hierarchies of deprivation
In compulsive imitation–emulation–anticipation–elaboration
Of your tripartite
Scheme of Oppression.

PART THREE
POWER

Do the thing, and you shall have the power. But they who do not do the thing, have not the powers.

Ralph Waldo Emerson

Certain . . . [things] can be done only together, for a society of men provides a sinew no man has alone.

M. C. Richards

America defines pollution too narrowly; thus the problem continues to grow and threatens to strangle America in its own affluence. We may think more broadly about poverty; still the poverty programs are defined such that we hit the technical symptoms and ignore the societal implications of American poverty.

In raising the issue of power, we look at some of the phenomena which keep us from dealing with pollution and poverty. We explore why power—the ability to do—and its correlates, authority and manipulation, restrict our participation in the social, political, and economic systems. We see why man so often ends up "doing" the very things that hurt his neighbors and himself.

Students feel it. Our schools teach us from the very beginning to conform, to get in step, to do what we are told when we are told to do it. In Chapter 11, Gracey's article, which draws an analogy between kindergarten and military boot camp, asserts that it is not only Kozol's ghetto children who face the prospect of "death at an early age." The good teacher is defined as the one who best achieves control over his brood, that is, the one who best prepares his pupils to stifle their own creative and individual impulses. The maintenance of traditional power relationships does not encourage creativity and individuality.

The educational system is but one example of the maintanance of control. In the economic system, workers must learn their jobs and, in so doing, nothing is more important than learning how to recognize authority and how to obey orders. They must perform their tasks in a hierarchical and highly bureaucratic system of competition. The system needs people who do their jobs in the way they are designed, and innovators, those who resist the directions of authority—whether in business, government, or education—can only be seen as competitors for power, as radicals of the most basic type.

In Part Three we are primarily concerned with who exercises power over whom and how that power is wielded. Institutions in America today are complex beyond understanding and, perhaps, beyond efficacy. (Indeed, these institutions mirror the complexity of life itself.) Large technical bureaucracies are characteristic of both public and private institutions, and act to channel the wants and the expectations of the members of the society they are presumed to serve. But here is the dilemma: On the one hand, when an individual or group attains power in any one realm (e.g., economic power) it becomes easier for that person or group to gain power in other realms as well; this is an insidious phenomenon giving rise to the concentration of general power in the hands of a relative few. On the other hand, how can we avoid the large concentrations of power? How can we afford to doubt the wisdom of the bureaucracy? We are, after all, nonspecialists; what can we know? Just tell us what to do!

Thus, as Chapter 12 illustrates, manipulation is central to the technocratic bureaucracy, and something happens to citizens who find themselves powerless in that society. Even the members of the bureaucracy themselves strangle in their own inability to be free, to control their own destinies, even to get something done. What happens to a people when they begin to realize their own lack of power? We note that representatives of many schools of thought, from the most conservative to the most radical, believe that overcoming these feelings of inadequacy and of helplessness is a matter of the highest priority in developing new policies, new programs, and new institutions. And a new quality of life for us, a new sense of community.

But just how deep does this penetrate? How deep *can* it penetrate, given common observation that those who have power are seldom interested in giving it up? Power brokers don't merely exist: They control the system of rewards and benefits. They can and usually do use these rewards and benefits to cripple efforts that challenge existing distributions of power. As Chapter 13 suggests, power is exercised over the powerless in many forms growing in number and subtlety. The role of the anonymous corporation in wielding psychological control over us suggests the degree to which we have become pawns of our own success. Corporations create wants and desires as well as the goods and services to fulfill them. It is a circular and cumulative process. Hence, the successful corporation is the one that is forever convincing large numbers of people that they want something for which they have very little need. So we no longer know what we need. Power is also institutionalized. Private power holders learn to accommodate to public power holders. The ultimate is the "military-industrial-complex," which produces both the materials for world destruction and the conditions that may result in its use. Is not such power a form of pollution?

How have we faced the problem of concentration of power and wealth? We have become increasingly dependent on government to restrain the power accruing from wealth, but our experience—even if we ponder only the military-industrial complex—teaches us that government may become the greatest source of accumulated and oppressive power. Government, operating under the assumption of public legitimacy and popular representation, can fall to those who recognize its capability to coerce. No controls are ever as effective as those exercised in the name of the public good. How does the individual protect himself from the witch hunters, from those who pick his trash can and bug his telephone, in the name of national security?

In a complex society, power is complex, and its potential is great. We have become so obsessed with the effective use of power that we have come to worship it. The great president is thought to be the one who gets everyone else to do what he wants them to do (for the public good, he says). To break this pattern of submission, Alinsky, in Chapter 14, asserts there is a higher form of leadership than that which results in building power to fulfill the social and personal desires of an individual leader. He tells us that the organizer is one who creates power which allows others to break down existing forms of control and to use to control their own destinies.

Yet, even Alinsky's counsel is discouraging. Is there not reason to suspect any form of power? Those with whom we have now to contend represent past efforts to break down past forms of control. If in our day the powerless resort to new organization in order to produce power for themselves, do they not also produce yet another organizational environment that could, for their children, be a pollutant?

We are convinced that new forms of human interaction are sorely needed in America today. Our wealth and technology, coupled with our fear of the unknown and the unfamiliar, seem to be leading the world much closer to destruction than to paradise. We fear that the ultimate result of increasing concentrations of power may well be the destruction of the very human strength that is required to rebuild our ever more dehumanizing institutions. Should we be so fortunate as to prevail in the face of such odds and thereby develop new sets of institutions, we shall have created another civilizing overlay for which later there will need to be new forms of power and new strength.

11 Learning submission

LEARNING THE STUDENT ROLE: KINDERGARTEN AS ACADEMIC BOOT CAMP

Harry L. Gracey

Introduction

Education must be considered one of the major institutions of social life today. Along with the family and organized religion, however, it is a "secondary institution," one in which people are prepared for life in society as it is presently organized. The main dimension of modern life, that is, the nature of society as a whole, is determined principally by the "primary institutions," which today are the economy, the political system, and the military establishment. Education has been defined by sociologists, classical and contemporary, as an institution which serves society by socializing people into it through a formalized, standardized procedure. At the beginning of this century Emile Durkheim told student teachers at the University of Paris that education "consists of a methodical socialization of the younger generation." He went on to add:

> It is the influence exercised by adult generations on those that are not ready for social life. Its object is to arouse and to develop in the child a certain number of physical, intellectual, and moral states that are demanded of him by the political society as a whole and by the special milieu for which he is specifically destined. . . . To the egoistic and asocial being that has just been born, (society) must, as rapidly as possible, add another, capable of leading a moral and social life. Such is the work of education.[1]

[1] Emile Durkheim, *Sociology and Education* (New York: The Free Press, 1956), pp. 71–72.

Abridgment of a chapter from *The American Elementary School, A Case Study in Bureaucracy and Ideology*. The research for this study was conducted under Grant MH9135 from the National Institute for Mental Health to the Bank Street College of Education. The author wishes to thank Dr. Arthur Vidich of the New School for Social Research for his helpful criticism and suggestions.

The educational process, Durkheim said, "is above all the means by which society perpetually recreates the conditions of its very existence."[2] The contemporary educational sociologist, Wilbur Brookover, offers a similar formulation in his recent textbook definition of education:

> Actually, therefore, in the broadest sense education is synonymous with socialization. It includes any social behavior that assists in the induction of the child into membership in the society or any behavior by which the society perpetuates itself through the next generation.[3]

The educational institution is, then, one of the ways in which society is perpetuated through the systematic socialization of the young, while the nature of the society which is being perpetuated—its organization and operation, its values, beliefs and ways of living—are determined by the primary institutions. The educational system, like other secondary institutions, *serves* the society which is *created* by the operation of the economy, the political system, and the military establishment.

Schools, the social organizations of the educational institution, are today for the most part large bureaucracies run by specially trained and certified people. There are few places left in modern societies where formal teaching and learning is carried on in small, isolated groups, like the rural, one-room schoolhouses of the last century. Schools are large, formal organizations which tend to be parts of larger organizations, local community School Districts. These School Districts are bureaucratically organized and their operations are supervised by state and local governments. In this context, as Brookover says:

> the term education is used . . . to refer to a system of schools, in which specifically designated persons are expected to teach children and youth certain types of acceptable behavior. The school system becomes a . . . unit in the total social structure and is recognized by the members of the society as a separate social institution. Within this structure a portion of the total socialization process occurs.[4]

Education is the part of the socialization process which takes place in the schools; and these are, more and more today, bureaucracies within bureaucracies.

Kindergarten is generally conceived by educators as a year of preparation for school. It is thought of as a year in which small children, five or six years old, are prepared socially and emotionally for the academic learning which will take place over the next twelve years. It is expected that a foun-

[2] *Ibid.*, p. 123.

[3] Wilbur Brookover, *The Sociology of Education* (New York: American Book Company, 1957), p. 4.

[4] *Ibid.*, p. 6.

dation of behavior and attitudes will be laid in kindergarten on which the children can acquire the skills and knowledge they will be taught in the grades. A booklet prepared for parents by the staff of a suburban New York school system says that the kindergarten experience will stimulate the child's desire to learn and cultivate the skills he will need for learning in the rest of his school career. It claims that the child will find opportunities for physical growth, for satisfying his "need for self-expression," acquire some knowledge, and provide opportunities for creative activity. It concludes, "The most important benefit that your five-year-old will receive from kindergarten is the opportunity to live and grow happily and purposefully with others in a small society." The kindergarten teachers in one of the elementary schools in this community, one we shall call the Wilbur Wright School, said their goals were to see that the children "grew" in all ways: physically, of course, emotionally, socially, and academically. They said they wanted children to like school as a result of their kindergarten experiences and that they wanted them to learn to get along with others.

None of these goals, however, is unique to kindergarten; each of them is held to some extent by teachers in the other six grades at the Wright School. And growth would occur, but differently, even if the child did not attend school. The children already know how to get along with others, in their families and their play groups. The unique job of the kindergarten in the educational division of labor seems rather to be teaching children the student role. The student role is the repertoire of behavior and attitudes regarded by educators as appropriate to children in school. Observation in the kindergartens of the Wilbur Wright School revealed a great variety of activities through which children are shown and then drilled in the behavior and attitudes defined as appropriate for school and thereby induced to learn the role of student. Observations of the kindergartens and interviews with the teachers both pointed to the teaching and learning of classroom routines as the main element of the student role. The teachers expended most of their efforts, for the first half of the year at least, in training the children to follow the routines which teachers created. The children were, in a very real sense, *drilled* in tasks and activities created by the teachers for their own purposes and beginning and ending quite arbitrarily (from the child's point of view) at the command of the teacher. One teacher remarked that she hated September, because during the first month "everything has to be done rigidly, and repeatedly, until they know exactly what they're supposed to do." However, "by January," she said, "they know exactly what to do [during the day] and I don't have to be after them all the time." Classroom routines were introduced gradually from the beginning of the year in all the kindergartens, and the children were drilled in them as long as was necessary to achieve regular compliance. By the end of the school year, the successful kindergarten teacher has a well-organized group of children. They follow classroom routines automatically, having learned all the command signals and the expected responses to them. They have, in our terms, learned the student role. The following observation shows one such classroom operating at optimum organization on an afternoon late in May. It is the class of an experienced and respected kindergarten teacher.

An Afternoon in Kindergarten

At about 12:20 in the afternoon on a day in the last week of May, Edith Kerr leaves the teachers' room where she has been having lunch and walks to her classroom at the far end of the primary wing of Wright School. A group of five- and six-year-olds peers at her through the glass doors leading from the hall cloakroom to the play area outside. Entering her room, she straightens some material in the "book corner" of the room, arranges music on the piano, takes colored paper from her closet and places it on one of the shelves under the window. Her room is divided into a number of activity areas through the arrangement of furniture and play equipment. Two easels and a paint table near the door create a kind of passageway inside the room. A wedge-shaped area just inside the front door is made into a teacher's area by the placing of "her" things there: her desk, file, and piano. To the left is the book corner, marked off from the rest of the room by a puppet stage and a movable chalkboard. In it are a display rack of picture books, a record player, and a stack of children's records. To the right of the entrance are the sink and clean-up area. Four large round tables with six chairs at each for the children are placed near the walls about halfway down the length of the room, two on each side, leaving a large open area in the center for group games, block building, and toy truck driving. Windows stretch down the length of both walls, starting about three feet from the floor and extending almost to the high ceilings. Under the windows are long shelves on which are kept all the toys, games, blocks, paper, paints and other equipment of the kindergarten. The left rear corner of the room is a play store with shelves, merchandise, and cash register; the right rear corner is a play kitchen with stove, sink, ironing board, and bassinette with baby dolls in it. This area is partly shielded from the rest of the room by a large standing display rack for posters and children's art work. A sandbox is found against the back wall between these two areas. The room is light, brightly colored and filled with things adults feel five- and six-year-olds will find interesting and pleasing.

At 12:25 Edith opens the outside door and admits the waiting children. They hang their sweaters on hooks outside the door and then go to the center of the room and arrange themselves in a semi-circle on the floor, facing the teacher's chair which she has placed in the center of the floor. Edith follows them in and sits in her chair checking attendance while waiting for the bell to ring. When she has finished attendance, which she takes by sight, she asks the children what the date is, what day and month it is, how many children are enrolled in the class, how many are present, and how many are absent.

The bell rings at 12:30 and the teacher puts away her attendance book. She introduces a visitor, who is sitting against the right wall taking notes, as someone who wants to learn about schools and children. She then goes to the back of the room and takes down a large chart labeled "Helping Hands." Bringing it to the center of the room, she tells the children it is time to change jobs. Each child is assigned some task on the chart by placing his name, lettered on a paper "hand," next to a picture signifying the task—e.g., a broom, a blackboard, a milk bottle, a flag, and a Bible. She asks the children who wants each of the jobs and rearranges their "hands" accordingly. Returning to her chair, Edith announces, "One person should tell us what happened to Mark." A girl raises her hand, and when called on says, "Mark fell and hit his head and had to go to the hospital." The teacher adds that Mark's mother had written saying he was in the hospital.

During this time the children have been interacting among themselves, as well as with Edith. Children have whispered to their neighbors, poked one another, made general comments to the group, waved to friends on the other side of the circle. None of this has been disruptive, and the teacher has ignored it for the most part. The children seem to know just how much of each kind of interaction is permitted—they may greet in a soft voice someone who sits next to them, for example, but may not shout greetings to a friend who sits across the circle, so they confine themselves to waving and remain well within understood limits.

At 12:35 two children arrive. Edith asks them why they are late and then sends them to join the circle on the floor. The other children vie with each other to tell the newcomers what happened to Mark. When this leads to a general disorder Edith asks, "Who has serious time?" The children become quiet and a girl raises her hand. Edith nods and the child gets a Bible and hands it to Edith. She reads the Twenty-third Psalm while the children sit quietly. Edith helps the child in charge begin reciting the Lord's Prayer, the other children follow along for the first unit of sounds, and then trail off as Edith finishes for them. Everyone stands and faces the American flag hung to the right of the door. Edith leads the pledge to the flag, with the children again following the familiar sounds as far as they remember them. Edith then asks the girl in charge what song she wants and the child replies, "My Country." Edith goes to the piano and plays "America," singing as the children follow her words.

Edith returns to her chair in the center of the room and the children sit again in the semi-circle on the floor. It is 12:40 when she tells the children, "Let's have boys' sharing time first." She calls the name of the first boy sitting on the end of the circle, and he comes up to her with a toy helicopter. He turns and holds it up for the other children to see. He says, "It's a helicopter." Edith asks, "What is it used for?" and he replies, "For the army.

Carry men. For the war." Other children join in, "For shooting submarines." "To bring back men from space when they are in the ocean." Edith sends the boy back to the circle and asks the next boy if he has something. He replies "No" and she passes on to the next. He says "Yes" and brings a bird's nest to her. He holds it for the class to see, and the teacher asks, "What kind of bird made the nest?" The boy replies, "My friend says a rain bird made it." Edith asks what the nest is made of and different children reply, "mud," "leaves" and "sticks." There is also a bit of moss woven into the nest and Edith tries to describe it to the children. They, however, are more interested in seeing if anything is inside it, and Edith lets the boy carry it around the semi-circle showing the children its insides. Edith tells the children of some baby robins in a nest in her yard, and some of the children tell about baby birds they have seen. Some children are asking about a small object in the nest which they say looks like an egg, but all have seen the nest now and Edith calls on the next boy. A number of children say, "I know what Michael has, but I'm not telling." Michael brings a book to the teacher and then goes back to his place in the circle of children. Edith reads the last page of the book to the class. Some children tell of books which they have at home. Edith calls the next boy, and three children call out, "I know what David has." "He always has the same thing." "It's a bang-bang." David goes to his table and gets a box which he brings to Edith. He opens it and shows the teacher a scale-model of an oldfashioned dueling pistol. When David does not turn around to the class, Edith tells him, "Show it to the children," and he does. One child says, "Mr. Johnson [the principal] said no guns." Edith replies, "Yes, how many of you know that?" Most of the children in the circle raise their hands. She continues, "That you aren't supposed to bring guns to school?" She calls the next boy on the circle and he brings two large toy soldiers to her which the children enthusiastically identify as being from "Babes in Toyland." The next boy brings an American flag to Edith and shows it to the class. She asks him what the stars and stripes stand for and admonishes him to treat it carefully. "Why should you treat it carefully?" she asks the boy. "Because it's our flag," he replies. She congratulates him, sayling, "That's right."

"Show and Tell" lasted twenty minutes and during the last ten one girl in particular announced that she knew what each child called upon had to show. Edith asked her to be quiet each time she spoke out, but she was not content, continuing to offer her comment at each "show." Four children from other classes had come into the room to bring something from another teacher or to ask for something from Edith. Those with requests were asked to return later if the item wasn't readily available.

Edith now asks if any of the children told their mothers about their trip to the local zoo the previous day. Many children raise their hands. As Edith calls on them, they tell what they liked in the zoo. Some children cannot wait to be called on, and they call out things to the teacher, who asks them to be quiet. After a few of the animals are mentioned, one child says, "I liked the spooky house," and the others chime in to agree with him, some pantomiming fear and horror. Edith is puzzled, and asks what this was. When half the children try to tell her at once, she raises her hand for quiet, then calls on individual children. One says, "The house with nobody in it"; another, "The dark little house." Edith asks where it was in the zoo, but the children cannot describe its location in any way which she can understand. Edith makes some jokes but they involve adult abstractions which the children cannot grasp. The children have become quite noisy now, speaking out to make both relevant and irrelevant comments, and three little girls have become particularly assertive.

Edith gets up from her seat at 1:10 and goes to the book corner, where she puts a record on the player. As it begins a story about the trip to the zoo, she returns to the circle and asks the children to go sit at the tables. She divides them among the tables in such a way as to indicate that they don't have regular seats. When the children are all seated at the four tables, five or six to a table, the teacher asks, "Who wants to be the first one?" One of the noisy girls comes to the center of the room. The voice on the record is giving directions for imitating an ostrich and the girl follows them, walking around the center of the room holding her ankles with her hands. Edith replays the record, and all the children, table by table, imitate ostriches down the center of the room and back. Edith removes her shoes and shows that she can be an ostrich too. This is apparently a familiar game, for a number of children are calling out, "Can we have the crab?" Edith asks one of the children to do a crab "so we can all remember how," and then plays the part of the record with music for imitating crabs by. The children from the first table line up across the room, hands and feet on the floor and faces pointing toward the ceiling. After they have "walked" down the room and back in this posture they sit at their table and the children of the next table play "crab." The children love this; they run from their tables, dance about on the floor waiting for their turns and are generally exuberant. Children ask for the "inch worm" and the game is played again with the children squirming down the floor. As a conclusion Edith shows them a new animal imitation, the "lame dog." The children all hobble down the floor, table by table, to the accompaniment of the record.

At 1:30 Edith has the children line up in the center of the room; she says, "Table one, line up in front of me," and children ask, "What are we going to do?" Then she moves a few steps to the side and says, "Table two over here, line up next to table one," and more children ask, "What for?" She does this for table three and table four and each time the children ask, "Why, what are we going to do?" When the children are lined up in four lines of five each, spaced so that they are not touching one another, Edith puts on a new record and leads the class in calisthenics, to the accompaniment of the record. The children just jump around every which way in their places instead of doing the exercises, and by the time the record is finished, Edith, the only one following it, seems exhausted. She is apparently adopting the President's new "Physical Fitness" program in her classroom.

At 1:35 Edith pulls her chair to the easels and calls the children to sit on the floor in front of her, table by table. When they are all seated she asks, "What are you going to do for worktime today?" Different children raise their hands and tell Edith what they are going to draw. Most are going to make pictures of animals they saw in the zoo. Edith asks if they want to make pictures to send to Mark in the hospital, and the children agree to this. Edith gives drawing paper to the children, calling them to her one by one. After getting a piece of paper, the children go to the crayon box in the right-hand shelves, select a number of colors, and go to the tables, where they begin drawing. Edith is again trying to quiet the perpetually talking girls. She keeps two of them standing by her so they won't disrupt the others. She asks them, "Why do you feel you have to talk all the time," and then scolds them for not listening to her. Then she sends them to their tables to draw.

Most of the children are drawing at their tables, sitting or kneeling in their chairs. They are all working very industriously and, engrossed in their work, very quietly. Three girls have chosen to paint at the easels, and having donned their smocks, they are busily mixing colors and intently applying them to their pictures. If the children at the tables are primitives and neo-realists in their animal depictions, these girls at the easels are the class abstract-expressionists, with their broad-stroked, colorful paintings.

Edith asks of the children generally, "What color should I make the cover of Mark's book?" Brown and green are suggested by some children "because Mark likes them." The other children are puzzled as to just what is going on and ask, "What book?" or "What does she mean?" Edith explains what she thought was clear to them already, that they are all going to put their pictures together in a "book" to be sent to Mark. She goes to a small table in the play-kitchen corner and tells the children to bring her their pictures when they are finished and she will write their message for Mark on them.

By 1:50 most children have finished their pictures and given them to Edith. She talks with some of them as she ties the bundle of pictures together —answering questions, listening, carrying on conversations. The children are playing in various parts of the room with toys, games and blocks which they have taken off the shelves. They also move from table to table examining each other's pictures, offering compliments and suggestions. Three girls at a table are cutting up colored paper for a collage. Another girl is walking about the room in a pair of high heels with a woman's purse over her arm. Three boys are playing in the center of the room with the large block set, with which they are building walk-ways and walking on them. Edith is very much concerned about their safety and comes over a number of times to fuss over them. Two or three other boys are driving trucks around the center of the room, and mild altercations occur when they drive through the block constructions. Some boys and girls are playing at the toy store, two girls are serving "tea" in the play kitchen and one is washing a doll baby. Two boys have elected to clean the room, and with large sponges they wash the movable blackboard, the puppet stage, and then begin on the tables. They run into resistance from the children who are working with construction toys on the tables and do not want to dismantle their structures. The class is like a room full of bees, each intent on pursuing some activity, occasionally bumping into one another, but just veering off in another direction without serious altercation. At 2:05 the custodian arrives pushing a cart loaded with half-pint milk containers. He places a tray of cartons on the counter next to the sink, then leaves. His coming and going is unnoticed in the room (as, incidentally, is the presence of the observer, who is completely ignored by the children for the entire afternoon).

At 2:15 Edith walks to the entrance of the room, switches off the lights, and sits at the piano and plays. The children begin spontaneously singing the song, which is "Clean up, clean up. Everybody clean up." Edith walks around the room supervising the cleanup. Some children put their toys, the blocks, puzzles, games, and so on back on their shelves under the windows. The children making a collage keep right on working. A child from another class comes in to borrow the 45-rpm adaptor for the record player. At more urging from Edith the rest of the children shelve their toys and work. The children are sitting around their tables now and Edith asks, "What record would you like to hear while you have your milk?" There is some confusion and no general consensus, so Edith drops the subject and begins to call the children, table by table, to come get their milk. "Table one," she says, and the five children come to the sink, wash their hands and dry them, pick up a carton of milk and a straw, and take it back to their table. Two talking girls wander about the room interfering with the children getting their milk and Edith calls out to them to "settle down." As the children sit many of them call out to Edith the name of the record they want to hear. When all the children are seated at tables with milk, Edith plays one of these records called "Bozo and the Birds" and shows the children pictures in a book which go with the record. The record recites, and the book shows the adventures of a clown, Bozo, as he walks through a woods meeting many different kinds of birds who, of course, display the characteristics of many kinds of people or, more accurately, different stereotypes. As children finish their milk they take blankets or pads from the shelves under the windows and lie on them in the center of the room, where Edith sits on her chair showing the pictures. By 2:30 half the class is lying on the floor on their blankets, the record is still playing and the teacher is turning the pages of the book. The child who came in previously returns the 45-rpm adaptor, and one of the kindergarteners tells Edith what the boy's name is and where he lives.

The record ends at 2:40. Edith says, "Children, down on your blankets."

All the class is lying on blankets now. Edith refuses to answer the various questions individual children put to her because, she tells them, "it's rest time now." Instead she talks very softly about what they will do tomorrow. They are going to work with clay, she says. The children lie quietly and listen. One of the boys raises his hand and when called on tells Edith, "The animals in the zoo looked so hungry yesterday." Edith asks the children what they think about this and a number try to volunteer opinions, but Edith accepts only those offered in a "rest-time tone," that is, softly and quietly. After a brief discussion of animal feeding, Edith calls the names of the two children on milk detail and has them collect empty milk cartons from the tables and return them to the tray. She asks the two children on clean-up detail to clean up the room. Then she gets up from her chair and goes to the door to turn on the lights. At this signal the children all get up from the floor and return their blankets and pads to the shelf. It is raining (the reason for no outside play this afternoon) and cars driven by mothers clog the school drive and line up along the street. One of the talkative little girls comes over to Edith and pointing out the window says, "Mrs. Kerr, see my mother in the new Cadillac?"

At 2:50 Edith sits at the piano and plays. The children sit on the floor in the center of the room and sing. They have a repertoire of songs about animals, including one in which each child sings a refrain alone. They know these by heart and sing along through the ringing of the 2:55 bell. When the song is finished, Edith gets up and coming to the group says, "Okay, rhyming words to get your coats today." The children raise their hands and as Edith calls on them, they tell her two rhyming words, after which they are allowed to go into the hall to get their coats and sweaters. They return to the room with these and sit at their tables. At 2:59 Edith says, "When you have your coats on, you may line up at the door." Half of the children go to the door and stand in a long line. When the three o'clock bell rings, Edith returns to the piano and plays. The children sing a song called "Goodbye," after which Edith sends them out.

Training for Learning and for Life

The day in kindergarten at Wright School illustrates both the content of the student role as it has been learned by these children and the processes by which the teacher has brought about this learning, or, "taught" them the student role. The children have learned to go through routines and to follow orders with unquestioning obedience, even when these make no sense to them. They have been disciplined to do as they are told by an authoritative person without significant protest. Edith has developed this discipline in the children by creating and enforcing a rigid social structure in the classroom through which she effectively controls the behavior of most of the children for most of the school day. The "living with others in a small society" which the school pamphlet tells parents is the most important thing the children will learn in kindergarten can be seen now in its operational meaning, which is learning to live by the routines imposed by the school. This learning appears to be the principal content of the student role.

Children who submit to school-imposed discipline and come to identify with it, so that being a "good student" comes to be an important part of their developing identities, *become* the good students by the school's definitions. Those who submit to the routines of the school but do not come to identify with them will be adequate students who find the more important part of their identities elsewhere, such as in the play group outside school. Children who refuse to submit to the school routines are rebels, who become known as "bad students" and often "problem children" in the school, for they do not learn the academic curriculum and their behavior is often disruptive in the classroom. Today schools engage clinical psychologists in part to help teachers deal with such children.

In looking at Edith's kindergarten at Wright School, it is interesting to ask how the children learn this role of student—come to accept school-imposed routines—and what, exactly, it involves in terms of behavior and attitudes. The most prominent features of the classroom are its physical and social structures. The room is carefully furnished and arranged in ways adults feel will interest children. The play store and play kitchen in the back of the room, for example, imply that children are interested in mimicking these activities of the adult world. The only space left for the children to create something of their own is the empty center of the room, and the materials at their disposal are the blocks, whose use causes anxiety on the part of the teacher. The room, being carefully organized physically by the adults, leaves little room for the creation of physical organization on the part of the children.

The social structure created by Edith is a far more powerful and subtle force for fitting the children to the student role. This structure is established by the very rigid and tightly controlled set of rituals and routines through which the children are put during the day. There is first the rigid "locating procedure" in which the children are asked to find themselves in terms of the month, date, day of the week, and the number of the class who are present and absent. This puts them solidly in the real world as defined by adults. The day is then divided into six periods whose activities are for the most part determined by the teacher. In Edith's kindergarten the children went through Serious Time, which opens the school day, Sharing Time, Play Time (which in clear weather would be spent outside), Work Time, Clean-up Time, after which they have their milk, and Rest Time, after which they go home. The teacher has programmed activities for each of these Times.

Occasionally the class is allowed limited discretion to choose between proffered activities, such as stories or records, but original ideas for activities are never solicited from them. Opportunity for free individual action is open only once in the day, during the part of Work Time left after the general class assignment has been completed (on the day reported the class assignment was drawing animal pictures for the absent Mark). Spontaneous interests or observations from the children are never developed by the teacher. It seems that her schedule just does not allow room for developing such unplanned events. During Sharing Time, for example, the child who brought a bird's nest told Edith, in reply to her question of what kind of bird made it, "My friend says it's a rain bird." Edith does not think to ask about this bird, probably because the answer is "childish," that is, not given in accepted adult categories of birds. The children then express great interest in an object in the nest, but the teacher ignores this interest, probably because the object is uninteresting to her. The soldiers from "Babes in Toyland" strike a responsive note in the children, but this is not used for a discussion of any kind. The soldiers are treated in the same way as objects which bring little interest from the children. Finally, at the end of Sharing Time the child-world of perception literally erupts in the class with the recollection of "the spooky house" at the zoo. Apparently this made more of an impression on the children than did any of the animals, but Edith is unable to make any sense of it for herself. The tightly imposed order of the class begins to break down as the children discover a universe of discourse of their own and begin talking excitedly with one another. The teacher is effectively excluded from this child's world of perception and for a moment she fails to dominate the classroom situation. She reasserts control, however, by taking the children to the next activity she has planned for the day. It seems never to have occurred to Edith that there might be a meaningful learning experience for the children in re-creating the "spooky house" in the classroom. It seems fair to say that this would have offered an exercise in spontaneous self-expression and an opportunity for real creativity on the part of the children. Instead, they are taken through a canned animal imitation procedure, an activity which they apparently enjoy, but which is also imposed upon them rather than created by them.

While children's perceptions of the world and opportunities for genuine spontaneity and creativity are being systematically eliminated from the kindergarten, unquestioned obedience to authority and rote learning of meaningless material are being encouraged. When the children are called to line up in the center of the room they ask "Why?" and "What for?" as they are in the very process of complying. They have learned to go smoothly through a programmed day, regardless of whether parts of the program make any sense to them or not. Here the student role involves what might be called "doing what you're told and never mind why." Activities which might "make sense" to the children are effectively ruled out and they are forced or induced to participate in activities which may be "senseless," such as the calisthenics.

At the same time the children are being taught by rote meaningless sounds in the ritual oaths and songs, such as the Lord's Prayer, the Pledge to the Flag, and "America." As they go through the grades children learn more and more of the sounds of these ritual oaths, but the fact that they have often learned meaningless sounds rather than meaningful statements is shown when they are asked to write these out in the sixth grade; they write them as groups of sounds rather than as a series of words, according to the sixth grade teachers at Wright School. Probably much learning in the elementary grades is of this character, that is, having no intrinsic meaning to the children, but rather being tasks inexplicably required of them by authoritative adults. Listening to sixth grade children read social studies reports, for example, in which they have copied material from encyclopedias about a particular country, an observer often gets the feeling that he is watching an activity which has no intrinsic meaning for the child. The child who reads, "Switzerland grows wheat and cows and grass and makes a lot of cheese" knows the dictionary meaning of each of these words but may very well have no conception at all of this "thing" called Switzerland. He is simply carrying out a task assigned by the teacher *because* it is assigned, and this may be its only "meaning" for him.

Another type of learning which takes place in kindergarten is seen in children who take advantage of the "holes" in the adult social structure to create activities of their own, during Work Time or out-of-doors during Play Time. Here the children are learning to carve out a small world of their own within the world created by adults. They very quickly learn that if they keep within permissible limits of noise and action they can play much as they please. Small groups of children formed during the year in Edith's kindergarten who played together at these times, developing semi-independent little groups in which they created their own worlds in the interstices of the adult-imposed physical and social world. These groups remind the sociological observer very much of the socalled "informal groups" which adults develop in factories and offices of large bureaucracies.[5] Here too, within authoritatively imposed social organizations people find "holes" to create little sub-worlds which support informal, friendly, nonofficial behavior. Forming and participating in such groups seems to be as much part of the student role as it is of the role of bureaucrat.

The kindergarten has been conceived of here as the year in which children are prepared for their schooling by learning the role of student. In the classrooms of the rest of the school grades, the children will be asked to submit to systems and routines imposed by the teachers and the curriculum. The days will be much like those of kindergarten, except that academic subjects will be substituted for the activities of the kindergarten. Once out of the school system, young adults will more than likely find themselves working in large-scale bureaucratic organizations, perhaps on the assembly line in the factory, perhaps in the paper routines of the white collar occu-

[5] See, for example, Peter M. Blau, *Bureaucracy in Modern Society* (New York: Random House, 1956), Chapter 3.

pations, where they will be required to submit to rigid routines imposed by "the company" which may make little sense to them. Those who can operate well in this situation will be successful bureaucratic functionaries. Kindergarten, therefore, can be seen as preparing children not only for participation in the bureaucratic organization of large modern school systems, but also for the large-scale occupational bureaucracies of modern society.

Miss Peach by Mell Lazarus. Courtesy of Publishers-Hall Syndicate.

WORKING CLASS HERO

John Lennon

As soon as you're born they make you feel small
By giving you no time instead of it all
Till the pain is so big you feel nothing at all
A working class hero is something to be
A working class hero is something to be

They hurt you at home and they hit you at school
They hate you if you're clever and they despise a fool
Till you're so fucking crazy you can't follow their rules
A working class hero is something to be
A working class hero is something to be

When they've tortured and scared you for 20-odd years
Then they expect you to pick a career
When you can't really function you're so full of fear
A working class hero is something to be
A working class hero is something to be

Keep you doped with religion and sex and TV
And you think you're so clever and classless and free
But you're still fucking peasants as far as I can see
A working class hero is something to be
A working class hero is something to be

There's room at the top they are telling you still
But first you must learn how to smile as you kill
If you want to be like the folks on the hill
A working class hero is something to be

Yes, a working class hero is something to be
If you want to be a hero well just follow me
If you want to be a hero well just follow me

DEATH AT AN EARLY AGE

Jonathan Kozol

There is a booklet published by the Boston Public Schools and bearing the title "A Curriculum Guide in Character Education." This booklet was in the desk of my new classroom and so, as few things are explicitly stated to you and so much must be done by guessing within these poorly run schools, I made the guess that I was supposed to look at it and perhaps make use of it. I did look at it but I did not make use of it. I kept it, however, and studied it and I have it in front of me now.

The booklet, really, is little more than an anthology broken down according to the values which the Boston School Committee hopes to instill or inspire in a child. This is the list of character traits which the teacher is encouraged to develop in a child:

> CHARACTER TRAITS TO BE DEVELOPED: OBEDIENCE TO DULY CONSTITUTED AUTHORITY . . . SELF-CONTROL . . . RESPONSIBILITY . . . GRATITUDE . . . KINDNESS . . . GOOD WORKMANSHIP AND PERSEVERANCE . . . LOYALTY . . . TEAMWORK . . . HONESTY . . . FAIR PLAY.

Two of the things that seem most striking about this list are (1) the emphasis upon obedience characteristics and (2) the way in which the personality has been dissected and divided and the way in which consequently each "character trait" has been isolated and dwelt upon in the manner of a list of favorable characteristics in the eulogy at a funeral or in the citation of an honorary degree during a commencement ceremony. You look in vain through this list for anything that has to do with an original child or with an independent style. You also look in vain for any evaluation or assessment or conception of the human personality as a full or organic or continuously living and evolving firmament rather than as a filing cabinet of acceptable traits.

The section on obedience characteristics begins with the following verse: "We must do the thing we must Before the thing we may; We are unfit for any trust Till we can and do obey." It goes on to list the forms that obedience can take and it recommends a list of "selected memory gems" having to do with compliance to authority. Some of them are good and some are by famous people, but all of them, coming at you this way, out of context, have a killing, dull effect. They come one after another, some good, some dumb, and leave you feeling very obedient:

> Honor thy father and thy mother [is the first one]. He who knows how to obey will know how to command . . . Obedience to God is the best evidence of sincere love for Him . . . True obedience is true liberty . . . The good American obeys the laws . . . Help me to be faithful to my country, careful for its good, valiant for its defense, and obedient to its laws . . . He who would command others must first learn to obey . . . The first law that ever God gave to man was a law of obedience . . . My son Hannibal will be a great general, because of all my soldiers he best knows how to obey . . . Obedience sums up our entire duty . . . The first great law is to obey . . . Children, obey your parents in all things; for this is well pleasing to the Lord . . . Wicked men obey from fear; good men from love . . . We are born subjects and to obey God is perfect liberty. He that does this shall be free, safe, and happy . . . Obedience is not truly performed by the body if the heart is dissatisfied . . . Every day, in every way it is our duty to obey. "Every way" means prompt and willing. Cheerfully, each task fulfilling. It means, too, best work achieving Habits of obedience, weaving. To form a cable firm and strong With links unbreakable and long: To do a thing, at once, when told A blessing, doth the act enfold. Obedience, first to God, we owe; It should in all our actions show . . . If you're told to do a thing, And mean to do it really, Never let it be by halves, Do it fully, freely! Do not make a poor excuse Waiting, weak, unsteady; All obedience worth the name Must be prompt and ready.

Of all the quotations included in this list, I think there are only two which are deeply relevant to the case at hand: "Wicked men obey from fear; good men from love"—this comes from Aristotle. And: "Obedience is not truly performed by the body if the heart is dissatisfied," which comes from the Talmudic scholar Saadia. Both of these quotations are directly applicable to the exact problem exemplified by the kind of school system in which such a list could be seriously employed. If it is true, as Aristotle wrote, that wicked men obey from fear and good men from love, then where else is this more likely to become manifest than within these kinds of penitential schools? One thinks of the pathos of anxiety with which teachers and principals go about their duties, seldom out of respect for their superiors, which in so many cases is impossible, but out of an abject fear of being condemned or of being kicked out. I think of the Art Teacher confiding to me in an excited whisper: "Can you imagine that this principal honestly and truly can stand there and call herself an educator? It's the biggest laugh of the school year." The Reading Teacher, with equal vehemence, talking about my supervisor: "That man doesn't know as much about elementary education as the first-year substitutes do. You'll have to agree to whatever he says and then ignore it when he's gone." To these people, whom they held in deeply justified contempt, both women paid ample lip-service. If ever they were honest, I do not see how they could have avoided holding both themselves and each other in some portion of the same contempt.

Saadia's eloquent statement that "obedience is not truly performed by the body if the heart is dissatisfied" seems also appropriate to the Boston public schools. For the heart *is* dissatisfied here, and the obedience *is* perfunctory, and the whole concept of respect for unearned and undeserved authority is bitter and brittle and back-breaking to children, whether rich or poor, or black or white, within these kinds of schools. Only the authority of visible character demands respect. No other kind deserves it. No child in his heart, unless drugged by passivity, will pay obeisance to authority unless authority has earned it, and authority based upon political maneuvering and upon the ingestion and assimilation of platitudes is an authority which no person, white or Negro, adult or child, should respect. There is too much respect for authority in the Boston schools, and too little respect for the truth. If there were more of the latter, there would be less need of the former and the atmosphere of the Boston schools would not have to be so nearly what it is today: the atmosphere of a crumbling dictatorship in time of martial law. The emphasis both in this one booklet and in the words of the school administration in general upon the need for dumb obedience belies its deepest fear.

It is our duty to bring up our children to love,
honour and obey us.
If they don't, they must be punished,
otherwise we would not be doing our duty.

If they grow up to love, honour and obey us
we have been blessed for bringing them up properly.

If they grow up not to love, honour and obey us
    either we have brought them up properly
    or we have not:
if we have
    there must be something the matter with them;
if we have not
    there is something the matter with us.

SUFFER THE LITTLE CHILDREN

Buffy Sainte-Marie

School bell go ding dong ding; the children all line up.
They do what they are told, take a little drink from the liar's cup.
Momma don't really care if what they learn is true or if it's only lies.
Just get them thru the factories into production, ah get them into line.

Late in the afternoon, the children all come home.
They mind their manners well; their little lives are all laid out.
Momma don't seem to care that she may break their hearts.
She clips their wings off; they never learn to fly.
Poor woman needs a source of pride—a doctor son she'll have
No matter what the cost to manhood or soul.

Sun shine down brightly shine down on all the land.
Shine down on all the newborn lambs,
The butcher's knife is in his hand.
Oh momma keeps them unprepared to meet the enemy common unto all.
Teach them that evil dwells across the sea,
Lives in a mountain like they see on T.V.

Down in the heart of town the devil dresses up.
He keeps his nails clean;
Didja think he'd be a boogie man?
Poor momma's stuck with the sagging dreams she'll sell a son or two,
Into some slavery that's lucrative and fine.
Just teach them not to criticize; to yes the bosses;
Impress the clients.
Oh teachers of the world,
Teach them to fake it well.

School bell go ding dong ding; the children all line up.
They do what they are told, take a little drink from the liar's cup.

279-306

12 Divide and rule

BLACK POWER: ITS NEED AND SUBSTANCE*

Stokely Carmichael and Charles V. Hamilton

"To carve out a place for itself in the politico-social order," V. O. Key, Jr. wrote in *Politics, Parties and Pressure Groups*, "a new group may have to fight for reorientation of many of the values of the old order" (p. 57). This is especially true when that group is composed of black people in the American society—a society that has for centuries deliberately and systematically excluded them from political participation. Black people in the United States must raise hard questions, questions which challenge the very nature of the society itself: its long-standing values, beliefs and institutions.

To do this, we must first redefine ourselves. Our basic need is to reclaim our history and our identity from what must be called cultural terrorism, from the depredation of self-justifying white guilt. We shall have to struggle for the right to create our own terms through which to define ourselves and our relationship to the society, and to have these terms recognized. This is the first necessity of a free people, and the first right that any oppressor must suspend.

In *Politics Among Nations*, Hans Morgenthau defined political power as "the psychological control over the minds of men" (p. 29). This control includes the attempt by the oppressor to have *his* definitions, *his* historical descriptions, *accepted* by the oppressed. This was true in Africa no less than in the United States. To black Africans, the word "Uhuru" means "freedom," but they had to fight the white colonizers for the right to use the term. The recorded history of this country's dealings with red and black men offers other examples. In the wars between the white settlers and the "Indians," a battle won by the Cavalry was described as a "victory." The "Indians'" triumphs, however, were "massacres." (The American colonists were not

* Show in class 60 minute film "Conventions: The Land Around Us," by Kaye Miller and Gerald M. Swatez. Social Sciences Research Film Unit at the University of Illinois, Chicago Circle, 1970. Available from Anagram Pictures, 7328 South Euclid, Chicago, Ill., 60649.

From *Black Power*, by Stokely Carmichael and Charles V. Hamilton, pp. 34–56 (excerpts).

unaware of the need to define their acts in their own terms. They labeled their fight against England a "revolution"; the English attempted to demean it by calling it "insubordination" or "riotous.")

The historical period following Reconstruction in the South after the Civil War has been called by many historians the period of Redemption, implying that the bigoted southern slave societies were "redeemed" from the hands of "reckless and irresponsible" black rulers. Professor John Hope Franklin's *Reconstruction* or Dr. W. E. B. Dubois' *Black Reconstruction* should be sufficient to dispel inaccurate historical notions, but the larger society persists in its own self-serving accounts. Thus black people came to be depicted as "lazy," "apathetic," "dumb," "shiftless," "good-timers." Just as red men had to be recorded as "savages" to justify the white man's theft of their land, so black men had to be vilified in order to justify their continued oppression. Those who have the right to define are the masters of the situation. Lewis Carroll understood this:

> "When I use a word," Humpty Dumpty said in a rather scornful tone, "it means just what I choose it to mean—neither more nor less."
>
> "The question is," said Alice, "whether you *can* make words mean so many different things."
>
> "The question is," said Humpty Dumpty, "which is to be master—that's all."[1]

Today, the American educational system continues to reinforce the entrenched values of the society through the use of words. Few people in this country question that this is "the land of the free and the home of the brave." They have had these words drummed into them from childhood. Few people question that this is the "Great Society" or that this country is fighting "Communist aggression" around the world. We mouth these things over and over, and they become truisms not to be questioned. In a similar way, black people have been saddled with epithets.

"Integration" is another current example of a word which has been defined according to the way white Americans see it. To many of them, it means black men wanting to marry white daughters; it means "race mixing" —implying bed or dance partners. To black people, it has meant a way to improve their lives—economically and politically. But the predominant white definition has stuck in the minds of too many people.

Black people must redefine themselves, and only *they* can do that. Throughout this country, vast segments of the black communities are beginning to recognize the need to assert their own definitions, to reclaim their history, their culture; to create their own sense of community and togetherness. There is a growing resentment of the word "Negro," for exam-

[1] Lewis Carroll, *Through the Looking Glass.* New York: Doubleday Books, Inc., p. 196.

ple, because this term is the invention of our oppressor; it is *his* image of us that he describes. Many blacks are now calling themselves African-Americans, Afro-Americans or black people because that is *our* image of ourselves. When we begin to define our own image, the stereotypes—that is, lies—that our oppressor has developed will begin in the white community and end there. The black community will have a positive image of itself that *it* has created. This means we will no longer call ourselves lazy, apathetic, dumb, good-timers, shiftless, and so on. Those are words used by white America to define us. If we accept these adjectives, as some of us have in the past, then we see ourselves only in a negative way, precisely the way white America wants us to see ourselves. Our incentive is broken and our will to fight is surrendered. From now on we shall view ourselves as African-Americans and as black people who are in fact energetic, determined, intelligent, beautiful and peace-loving.

There is a terminology and ethos peculiar to the black community of which black people are beginning to be no longer ashamed. Black communities are the only large segments of this society where people refer to each other as brother—soul-brother, soul-sister. Some people may look upon this as *ersatz*, as make-believe, but it is not that. It is real. It is a growing sense of community. It is a growing realization that black Americans have a common bond not only among themselves, but with their African brothers. In *Black Man's Burden*, John O. Killens described his trip to ten African countries as follows:

> Everywhere I went people called me brother. . . . "Welcome, American brother." It was a good feeling for me, to be in Africa. To walk in a land for the first time in your entire life knowing within yourself that your color would not be held against you. No black man ever knows this in America [p. 160].

More and more black Americans are developing this feeling. They are becoming aware that they have a history which pre-dates their forced introduction to this country. African-American history means a long history beginning on the continent of Africa, a history not taught in the standard textbooks of this country. It is absolutely essential that black people know this history, that they know their roots, that they develop an awareness of their cultural heritage. Too long have they been kept in submission by being told that they had no culture, no manifest heritage, before they landed on the slave auction blocks in this country. If black people are to know themselves as a vibrant, valiant people they must know their roots. And they will soon learn that the Hollywood image of man-eating cannibals waiting for, and waiting on, the Great White Hunter is a lie.

With redefinition will come a clearer notion of the role black Americans can play in this world. This role will emerge clearly out of the unique, common experiences of Afro-Asians. Killens concludes:

> I believe furthermore that the American Negro can be the bridge between the West and Africa–Asia. We black Americans can serve as a bridge to mutual understanding. The one thing we black Americans have in common with the other colored peoples of the world is that we have all felt the cruel and ruthless heel of white supremacy. We have all been "niggerized" on one level or another. And all of us are determined to "deniggerize" the earth. To rid the world of "niggers" is the Black Man's Burden, human reconstruction is the grand objective [p. 176].

Only when black people fully develop this sense of community, of themselves, can they begin to deal effectively with the problems of racism in *this* country. This is what we mean by a new consciousness; this is the vital first step.

The next step is what we shall call the process of political modernization—a process which must take place if the society is to be rid of racism. "Political modernization" includes many things, but we mean by it three major concepts: (1) questioning old values and institutions of the society; (2) searching for new and different forms of political structure to solve political and economic problems; and (3) broadening the base of political participation to include more people in the decision-making process. These notions (we shall take up each in turn) are central to our thinking throughout this book and to contemporary American history as a whole. As David Apter wrote in *The Politics of Modernization*, ". . . the struggle to modernize is what has given meaning to our generation. It tests our cherished institutions and our beliefs. . . . So compelling a force has it become that we are forced to ask new questions of our own institutions. Each country, whether modernized or modernizing, stands in both judgment and fear of the results. Our own society is no exception" (p. 2).

The values of this society support a racist system; we find it incongruous to ask black people to adopt and support most of those values. We also reject the assumption that the basic institutions of this society must be preserved. The goal of black people must *not* be to assimilate into middle-class America, for that class—as a whole—is without a viable conscience as regards humanity. The values of the middle class permit the perpetuation of the ravages of the black community. The values of that class are based on material aggrandizement, not the expansion of humanity. The values of that class ultimately support cloistered little closed societies tucked away neatly in tree-lined suburbia. The values of that class do *not* lead to the creation of an open society. That class *mouths* its preference for a free, competitive society, while at the same time forcefully and even viciously denying to black people as a group the opportunity to compete.

We are not unmindful of other descriptions of the social utility of the middle class. Banfield and Wilson, in *City Politics*, concluded:

> The departure of the middle class from the central city is important in other ways. . . . The middle class supplies a social and political leavening in the life of a city. Middle-class people demand good schools and integrity in government. They support churches, lodges, parent–teacher associations, scout troops, better-housing committees, art galleries, and operas. It is the middle class, in short, that asserts a conception of the public interest. Now its activity is increasingly concentrated in the suburbs [p. 14].

But this same middle class manifests a sense of superior group position in regard to race. This class wants "good government" *for themselves*; it wants good schools *for its children*. At the same time, many of its members sneak into the black community by day, exploit it, and take the money home to their middle-class communities at night to support their operas and art galleries and comfortable homes. When not actually robbing, they will fight off the handful of more affluent black people who seek to move in; when they approve or even seek token integration, it applies only to black people like themselves—as "white" as possible. *This class is the backbone of institutional racism in this country.*

Thus we reject the goal of assimilation into middle-class America because the values of that class are in themselves anti-humanist and because that class as a social force perpetuates racism. We must face the fact that, in the past, what we have called the movement has not really questioned the middle-class values and institutions of this country. If anything, it has accepted those values and institutions without fully realizing their racist nature. Reorientation means an emphasis on the dignity of man, not on the sanctity of property. It means the creation of a society where human misery and poverty are repugnant to that society, not an indication of laziness or lack of initiative. The creation of new values means the establishment of a society based, as Killens expresses it in *Black Man's Burden*, on "free people," not "free enterprise" (p. 167). To do this means to modernize—*indeed, to civilize*—this country.

Supporting the old values are old political and economic structures; these must also be "modernized." We should at this point distinguish between "structures" and "system." By system, we have in mind the entire American complex of basic institutions, values, beliefs, etc. By structures, we mean the specific institutions (political parties, interest groups, bureaucratic administrations) which exist to conduct the business of the system. Obviously, the first is broader than the second. Also, the second assumes the legitimacy of the first. Our view is that, given the illegitimacy of the system, we cannot then proceed to transform that system with existing structures.

The two major political parties in this country have become non-viable entities for the legitimate representation of the real needs of masses—especially blacks—in this country. Walter Lippmann raised the same point in his syndicated column of December 8, 1966. He pointed out that the party system in the United States developed before our society became as technologically complex as it is now. He says that the ways in which men live and define themselves are changing radically. Old ideological issues, once the subject of passionate controversy, Lippmann argues, are of little interest today. He asks whether the great urban complexes—which are rapidly becoming the centers of black population in the U.S.—can be run with the same systems and ideas that derive from a time when America was a country of small villages and farms. While not addressing himself directly to the question of race, Lippmann raises a major question about our political institutions; and the crisis of race in America may be its major symptom.

Black people have seen the city planning commissions, the urban renewal commissions, the boards of education and the police departments fail to speak to their needs in a meaningful way. We must devise new structures, new institutions to replace those forms or to make them responsive. There is nothing sacred or inevitable about old institutions; the focus must be on people, not forms.

Existing structures and established ways of doing things have a way of perpetuating themselves and for this reason, the modernizing process will be difficult. Therefore, timidity in calling into question the boards of education or the police departments will not do. They must be challenged forcefully and clearly.

There is a growing recognition that the police are the most crucial institution maintaining the colonized status of Black Americans. And of all establishment institutions, police departments probably include the highest proportion of individual racists. This is no accident since central to the workings of racism (an essential component of colonization) are attacks on the humanity and dignity of the subject group. Through their normal routines the police constrict Afro-Americans to Black neighborhoods by harassing and questioning them when found outside the ghetto; they break up groups of youth congregating on corners or in cars without any provocation; and they continue to use offensive and racist language no matter how many inter-group understanding seminars have been built into the police academy. They also shoot to kill ghetto residents for alleged crimes such as car thefts and running from police officers.

Police are key agents in the power equation as well as the drama of dehumanization. In the final analysis they do the dirty work for the larger system by restricting the striking back of Black rebels to skirmishes inside the ghetto, thus deflecting energies and attacks from the communities and institutions of the larger power structure. In a historical review, Gary Marx notes that since the French revolution, police and other authorities have killed large numbers of demonstrators and rioters; the rebellious "rabble" rarely destroys human life. The same pattern has been repeated in America's recent revolts. Journalistic accounts appearing in the press recently suggest that police see themselves as defending the interests of white people against a tide of Black insurgence; furthermore the majority of whites appear to view "blue power" in this light. There is probably no other opinion on which the races are as far apart today as they are on the question of attitudes toward the police.

In many cases set off by a confrontation between a policeman and a Black citizen, the ghetto uprising has dramatized the role of law enforcement and the issue of police brutality. In their aftermath, movements have arisen to contain police activity. One of the first was the Community Alert Patrol in Los Angeles, a method of policing the police in order to keep them honest and constrain their violations of personal dignity. This was the first tactic of the Black Panther Party which originated in Oakland, perhaps the most significant group to challenge the police role in maintaining the ghetto as a colony. The Panthers' later policy of openly carrying guns (a legally protected right) and their intention of defending themselves against police aggression has brought on a series of confrontations with the Oakland police department. All indications are that the authorities intend to destroy the Panthers by shooting, framing up, or legally harassing their leadership—diverting the group's energies away from its primary purpose of self-defense and organization of the Black community to that of legal defense and gaining support in the white community.

Reprinted from "Internal Colonialism and Ghetto Revolt" by Robert Blauner in *Social Problems*, vol. 16, no. 4 (Spring 1969), pp. 404–405. With permission from The Society For the Study of Social Problems and the author.

If this means the creation of parallel community institutions, then that must be the solution. If this means that black parents must gain control over the operation of the schools in the black community, then that must be the solution. The search for new forms means the search for institutions that will, for once, make decisions in the interest of black people. It means, for example, a building inspection department that neither winks at violations of building codes by absentee slumlords nor imposes meaningless fines which permit them to continue their exploitation of the black community.

Essential to the modernization of structures is a broadened base of political participation. More and more people must become politically sensitive and active (we have already seen this happening in some areas of the South). People must no longer be tied, by small incentives or handouts, to a corrupting and corruptible white machine. Black people will choose their own leaders and hold those leaders responsible to *them.* A broadened base means an end to the condition described by James Wilson in *Negro Politics,* whereby "Negroes tended to be the objects rather than the subjects of civic action. Things are often done for, or about, or to, or because of Negroes, but they are less frequently done *by* Negroes" (p. 133). Broadening the base of political participation, then, has as much to do with the quality of black participation as with the quantity. We are fully aware that the black vote, especially in the North, has been pulled out of white pockets and "delivered" whenever it was in the interest of white politicians to do so. That vote must no longer be controllable by those who have neither the interests nor the demonstrated concern of black people in mind.

As the base broadens, as more and more black people become activated, they will perceive more clearly the special disadvantages heaped upon them as a group. They will perceive that the larger society is growing more affluent while the black society is retrogressing, as daily life and mounting statistics clearly show (see Chapters I and VIII). V. O. Key describes what often happens next, in *Politics, Parties and Pressure Groups:* "A factor of great significance in the setting off of political movements is an abrupt change for the worse in the status of one group relative to that of other groups in society. . . . A rapid change for the worse . . . in the relative status of any group . . . is likely to precipitate political action" (p. 24). Black people will become increasingly active as they notice that their retrogressive status exists in large measure because of values and institutions arraigned against them. They will begin to stress and strain and call the entire system into question. Political modernization will be in motion. We believe that it is now in motion. One form of that motion is Black Power.

The adoption of the concept of Black Power is one of the most legitimate and healthy developments in American politics and race relations in our time. The concept of Black Power speaks to all the needs mentioned in this chapter. It is a call for black people in this country to unite, to recognize their heritage, to build a sense of community. It is a call for black people to begin to define their own goals, to lead their own organizations and to support those organizations. It is a call to reject the racist institutions and values of this society.

The concept of Black Power rests on a fundamental premise: *Before a group can enter the open society, it must first close ranks.* By this we mean that group solidarity is necessary before a group can operate effectively from a bargaining position of strength in a pluralistic society. Traditionally, each new ethnic group in this society has found the route to social and political viability through the organization of its own institutions with which to represent its needs within the larger society. Studies in voting behavior specifically, and political behavior generally, have made it clear that politically the American pot has not melted. Italians vote for Rubino over O'Brien; Irish for Murphy over Goldberg, etc. This phenomenon may seem distasteful to some, but it has been and remains today a central fact of the American political system. There are other examples of ways in which groups in the society have remembered their roots and used this effectively in the political arena. Theodore Sorensen describes the politics of foreign aid during the Kennedy Administration in his book *Kennedy:*

> No powerful constituencies or interest groups backed foreign aid. The Marshall Plan at least had appealed to Americans who traced their roots to the Western European nations aided. But there were few voters who identified with India, Colombia or Tanganyika [p. 351].

The extent to which black Americans can and do "trace their roots" to Africa, to that extent will they be able to be more effective on the political scene.

A white reporter set forth this point in other terms when he made the following observation about white Mississippi's manipulation of the anti-poverty program:

> The war on poverty has been predicated on the notion that there is such a thing as a community which can be defined geographically and mobilized for a collective effort to help the poor. This theory has no relationship to reality in the deep South. In every Mississippi county there are two communities. Despite all the pious platitudes of the moderates on both sides, these two communities habitually see their interests in terms of conflict rather than cooperation. Only when the Negro community can muster enough political, economic and professional strength to compete on somewhat equal terms, will Negroes believe in the possibility of true cooperation and whites accept its necessity. En route to integration, the Negro community needs to develop a greater independence—a chance to run its own affairs and not cave in whenever "the man" barks—or so it seems to me, and to most of the knowledgeable people with whom I talked in Mississippi. To OEO, this judgment may sound like black nationalism. . . .[2]

The point is obvious: black people must lead and run their own organizations. Only black people can convey the revolutionary idea—and it is a revolutionary idea—that black people are able to do things themselves. Only they can help create in the community an aroused and continuing black consciousness that will provide the basis for political strength. In the past, white allies have often furthered white supremacy without the whites involved realizing it, or even wanting to do so. Black people must come together and do things for themselves. They must achieve self-identity and self-determination in order to have their daily needs met.

Black Power means, for example, that in Lowndes County, Alabama, a black sheriff can end police brutality. A black tax assessor and tax collector and county board of revenue can lay, collect, and channel tax monies for the building of better roads and schools serving black people. In such areas as Lowndes, where black people have a majority, they will attempt to use power to exercise control. This is what they seek: control. When black

[2] Christopher Jencks, "Accommodating Whites: A New Look at Mississippi," *The New Republic* (April 16, 1966).

people lack a majority, Black Power means proper representation and sharing of control. It means the creation of power bases, of strength, from which black people can press to change local or nation-wide patterns of oppression —instead of from weakness.

It does not mean *merely* putting black faces into office. Black visibility is not Black Power. Most of the black politicians around the country today are not examples of Black Power. The power must be that of a community, and emanate from there. The black politicians must start from there. The black politicians must stop being representatives of "downtown" machines, whatever the cost might be in terms of lost patronage and holiday handouts.

Black Power recognizes—it must recognize—the ethnic basis of American politics as well as the power-oriented nature of American politics. Black Power therefore calls for black people to consolidate behind their own, so that they can bargain from a position of strength. But while we endorse the *procedure* of group solidarity and identity for the purpose of attaining certain goals in the body politic, this does not mean that black people should strive for the same kind of rewards (i.e., end results) obtained by the white society. The ultimate values and goals are not domination or exploitation of other groups, but rather an effective share in the total power of the society.

Nevertheless, some observers have labeled those who advocate Black Power as racists; they have said that the call for self-identification and self-determination is "racism in reverse" or "black supremacy." This is a deliberate and absurd lie. There is no analogy—by any stretch of definition or imagination—between the advocates of Black Power and white racists. Racism is not merely exclusion on the basis of race but exclusion for the purpose of subjugating or maintaining subjugation. The goal of the racists is to keep black people on the bottom, arbitrarily and dictatorially, as they have done in this country for over three hundred years. The goal of black self-determination and black self-identity—Black Power—is full participation in the decision-making processes affecting the lives of black people, and recognition of the virtues in themselves as black people. The black people of this country have not lynched whites, bombed their churches, murdered their children and manipulated laws and institutions to maintain oppression. White racists have. Congressional laws, one after the other, have not been necessary to stop black people from oppressing others and denying others the full enjoyment of their rights. White racists have made such laws necessary. The goal of Black Power is positive and functional to a free and viable society. No white racist can make this claim.

A great deal of public attention and press space was devoted to the hysterical accusation of "black racism" when the call for Black Power was first sounded. A national committee of influential black churchmen affiliated with the National Council of Churches, despite their obvious respectability and responsibility, had to resort to a paid advertisement to articulate their position, while anyone yapping "black racism" made front-page news. In their statement, published in the *New York Times* of July 31, 1966, the churchmen said:

> We, an informal group of Negro churchmen in America, are deeply disturbed about the crisis brought upon our country by historic distortions of important human realities in the controversy about "black power." What we see shining through the variety of rhetoric is not anything new but the same old problem of power and race which has faced our beloved country since 1619.
>
> . . . The conscience of black men is corrupted because having no power to implement the demands of conscience, the concern for justice in the absence of justice becomes a chaotic self-surrender. Powerlessness breeds a race of beggars. We are faced with a situation where powerless conscience meets conscienceless power, threatening the very foundations of our Nation.
>
> We deplore the overt violence of riots, but we feel it is more important to focus on the real sources of these eruptions. These sources may be abetted inside the Ghetto, but their basic cause lies in the silent and covert violence which white middle class America inflicts upon the victims of the inner city.
>
> . . . In short, the failure of American leaders to use American power to create equal opportunity *in life* as well as *law*, this is the real problem and not the anguished cry for black power.
>
> . . . Without the capacity to participate with power, i.e., to have some organized political and economic strength to really influence people with whom one interacts, integration is not meaningful.
>
> . . . America has asked its Negro citizens to fight for opportunity as *individuals*, whereas at certain points in our history what we have needed most has been opportunity for the *whole group*, not just for selected and approved Negroes.
>
> . . . We must not apologize for the existence of this form of group power, for we have been oppressed as a group and not as individuals. We will not find our way out of that oppression until both we and America accept the need for Negro Americans, as well as for Jews, Italians, Poles, and white Anglo-Saxon Protestants, among others, to have and to wield group power.[3]

It is a commentary on the fundamentally racist nature of this society that the concept of group strength for black people must be articulated—not to mention defended. No other group would submit to being led by others. Italians do not run the Anti-Defamation League of B'nai B'rith. Irish do not chair Christopher Columbus Societies. Yet when black people call for black-run and all-black organizations, they are immediately classed in a category with the Ku Klux Klan. This is interesting and ironic, but by no means surprising: the society does not expect black people to be able to take care of their business, and there are many who prefer it precisely that way.

In the end, we cannot and shall not offer any guarantees that Black Power, if achieved, would be non-racist. No one can predict human behavior. Social change always has unanticipated consequences. If black racism is what the larger society fears, we cannot help them. We can only state what we hope will be the result, given the fact that the present situation is unacceptable and that we have no real alternative but to work for Black Power. The final truth is that the white society is not entitled to reassurances, even if it were possible to offer them.

We have outlined the meaning and goals of Black Power; we have also discussed one major thing which it is not. There are others of greater importance. The advocates of Black Power reject the old slogans and meaningless rhetoric of previous years in the civil rights struggle. The language of yesterday is indeed irrelevant: progress, non-violence, integration, fear of "white backlash," coalition. Let us look at the rhetoric and see why these terms must be set aside or redefined.

One of the tragedies of the struggle against racism is that up to this point there has been no national organization which could speak to the growing militancy of young black people in the urban ghettos and the black-belt South. There has been only a "civil rights" movement, whose tone of voice was adapted to an audience of middle-class whites. It served as a sort of buffer zone between that audience and angry young blacks. It claimed to speak for the needs of a community, but it did not speak in the tone of that community. None of its so-called leaders could go into a rioting community and be listened to. In a sense, the blame must be shared—along with the mass media—by those leaders for what happened in Watts, Harlem, Chicago, Cleveland and other places. Each time the black people in those cities saw Dr. Martin Luther King get slapped they became angry. When they saw little black girls bombed to death *in a church* and civil rights workers ambushed and murdered, they were angrier; and when nothing happened, they were steaming mad. We had nothing to offer that they could see, except to go out and be beaten again. We helped to build their frustration.

We had only the old language of love and suffering. And in most places—that is, from the liberals and middle class—we got back the old language of patience and progress. The civil rights leaders were saying to the country: "Look, you guys are supposed to be nice guys, and we are only going to do what we are supposed to do. Why do you beat us up? Why don't you give us what we ask? Why don't you straighten yourselves out?" For the masses of black people, this language resulted in virtually nothing. In fact, their objective day-to-day condition worsened. The unemployment rate among black people increased while that among whites declined. Housing conditions in the black communities deteriorated. Schools in the black ghettos continued to plod along on outmoded techniques, inadequate curricula, and with too many tired and indifferent teachers. Meanwhile, the President picked up the refrain of "We Shall Overcome" while the Congress passed civil rights law after civil rights law, only to have them effectively nullified by deliberately weak enforcement. "Progress is being made," we were told.

Such language, along with admonitions to remain non-violent and fear the white backlash, convinced some that that course was the *only* course to follow. It misled some into believing that a black minority could bow its head and get whipped into a meaningful position of power. The very notion is absurd. The white society devised the language, adopted the rules and had the black community narcotized into believing that that language and those rules were, in fact, relevant. The black community was told time and again how *other* immigrants finally won *acceptance:* that is, by following the Protestant Ethic of Work and Achievement. They worked hard; therefore, they achieved. We were not told that it was by building Irish Power, Italian Power, Polish Power or Jewish Power that these groups got themselves together and operated from positions of strength. We were not told that "the American dream" wasn't designed for black people. That while today, to whites, the dream may *seem* to include black people, it cannot do so by the very nature of this nation's political and economic system, which imposes institutional racism on the black masses if not upon every individual black. A notable comment on that "dream" was made by Dr. Percy Julian, the black scientist and director of the Julian Research Institute in Chicago, a man for whom the dream seems to have come true. While not subscribing to "black power" as he understood it, Dr. Julian clearly understood the basis for it: "The false concept of basic Negro inferiority is one of the curses that still lingers. It is a problem created by the white man. Our children just no longer are going to accept the patience we were taught by our generation. We were taught a pretty little lie—excel and the whole world lies open before you. *I obeyed the injunction and found it to be wishful thinking.*" (Authors' italics)[4]

A key phrase in our buffer-zone days was non-violence. For years it has been thought that black people would not literally fight for their lives. Why this has been so is not entirely clear; neither the larger society nor black people are noted for passivity. The notion apparently stems from the years of marches and demonstrations and sit-ins where black people did not strike back and the violence always came from white mobs. There are many who still sincerely believe in that approach. From our viewpoint, rampaging white mobs and white night-riders must be made to understand that their days of free head-whipping are over. Black people should and must fight back. Nothing more quickly repels someone bent on destroying you than the unequivocal message: "O.K., fool, make your move, and run the same risk I run—of dying."

When the concept of Black Power is set forth, many people immedi-

[4] *The New York Times* (April 30, 1967), p. 30.

ately conjure up notions of violence. The country's reaction to the Deacons for Defense and Justice, which originated in Louisiana, is instructive. Here is a group which realized that the "law" and law enforcement agencies would not protect people, so they had to do it themselves. If a nation fails to protect its citizens, then that nation cannot condemn those who take up the task themselves. The Deacons and all other blacks who resort to self-defense represent a simple answer to a simple question: what man would not defend his family and home from attack?

But this frightened some white people, because they knew that black people would now fight back. They knew that this was precisely what *they* would have long since done if *they* were subjected to the injustices and oppression heaped on blacks. Those of us who advocate Black Power are quite clear in our own minds that a "non-violent" approach to civil rights is an approach black people cannot afford and a luxury white people do not deserve. It is crystal clear to us—and it must become so with the white society—*that there can be no social order without social justice.* White people must be made to understand that they must stop messing with black people, or the blacks *will* fight back!

Next, we must deal with the term "integration." According to its advocates, social justice will be accomplished by "integrating the Negro into the mainstream institutions of the society from which he has been traditionally excluded." This concept is based on the assumption that there is nothing of value in the black community and that little of value could be created among black people. The thing to do is siphon off the "acceptable" black people into the surrounding middle-class white community.

The goals of integrationists are middle-class goals, articulated primarily by a small group of Negroes with middle-class aspirations or status. Their kind of integration has meant that a few blacks "make it," leaving the black community, sapping it of leadership potential and know-how. As we noted in Chapter I, those token Negroes—absorbed into a white mass—are of no value to the remaining black masses. They become meaningless show-pieces for a conscience-soothed white society. Such people will state that they would prefer to be treated "only as individuals, not as Negroes"; that they "are not and should not be preoccupied with race." This is a totally unrealistic position. In the first place, black people have not suffered as individuals but as members of a group; therefore, their liberation lies in group action. This is why SNCC—and the concept of Black Power—affirms that helping *individual* black people to solve their problems on an *individual* basis does little to alleviate the mass of black people. Secondly, while color blindness *may* be a sound goal ultimately, we must realize that race is an overwhelming fact of life in this historical period. There is no black man in this country who can live "simply as a man." His blackness is an ever-present fact of this racist society, whether he recognizes it or not. It is unlikely that this or the next generation will witness the time when race will no longer be relevant in the conduct of public affairs and in public policy decision-making. To realize this and to attempt to deal with it does not make one a racist or overly preoccupied with race; it puts one in the forefront of a significant *struggle.* If there is no intense struggle today, there will be no meaningful results tomorrow.

"Integration" as a goal today speaks to the problem of blackness not only in an unrealistic way but also in a despicable way. It is based on complete acceptance of the fact that in order to have a decent house or education, black people must move into a white neighborhood or send their children to a white school. This reinforces, among both black and white, the idea that "white" is automatically superior and "black" is by definition inferior. For this reason, "integration" is a subterfuge for the maintenance of white supremacy. It allows the nation to focus on a handful of Southern black children who get into white schools at a great price, and to ignore the ninety-four percent who are left in unimproved all-black schools. Such situations will not change until black people become equal in a way that means something, and integration ceases to be a one-way street. Then integration does not mean draining skills and energies from the black ghetto into white neighborhoods. To sprinkle black children among white pupils in outlying schools is at best a stop-gap measure. The goal is not to take black children out of the black community and expose them to white middle-class values; the goal is to build and strengthen the black community.

"Integration" also means that black people must give up their identity, deny their heritage. We recall the conclusion of Killian and Grigg: "At the present time, integration as a solution to the race problem demands that the Negro foreswear his identity as a Negro." The fact is that integration, as traditionally articulated, would abolish the black community. The fact is that what must be abolished is not the black community, but the dependent colonial status that has been inflicted upon it.

The racial and cultural personality of the black community must be preserved and that community must win its freedom while preserving its cultural integrity. Integrity includes a pride—in the sense of self-acceptance, not chauvinism—in being black, in the historical attainments and contributions of black people. No person can be healthy, complete and mature if he must deny a part of himself; this is what "integration" has required thus far. This is the essential difference between integration as it is currently practiced and the concept of Black Power.

The idea of cultural integrity is so obvious that it seems almost simple-minded to spell things out at this length. Yet millions of Americans resist such truths when they are applied to black people. Again, that resistance is a comment on the fundamental racism in the society. Irish Catholics took care of their own first without a lot of apology for doing so, without any dubious language from timid leadership about guarding against "backlash." Everyone understood it to be a perfectly legitimate procedure. Of course, there would be "backlash." Organization begets counterorganization, but this was no reason to defer.

The so-called white backlash against black people is something else: the embedded traditions of institutional racism being brought into the open and calling forth overt manifestations of individual racism. In the summer of 1966, when the protest marches into Cicero, Illinois, began, the black people knew they were not allowed to live in Cicero and the white people knew it. When blacks began to demand the right to live in homes in that town, the whites simply reminded them of the status quo. Some people called this "backlash." It was, in fact, racism defending itself. In the black community, this is called "White folks showing their color." It is ludicrous to blame black people for what is simply an overt manifestation of white racism. Dr. Martin Luther King stated clearly that the protest marches were not the cause of the racism but merely exposed a long-term cancerous condition in the society.

I BELIEVE I'M GOING TO DIE

Fred Hampton

These are excerpts from the transcript of "The Murder of Fred Hampton," a documentary film on the life and death of the chairman of the Black Panther party's Illinois chapter. Mr. Hampton and another Black Panther, Mark Clark, were killed in a police raid on Panther headquarters in Chicago, Dec. 4, 1969. The film has been shown in Chicago and Cannes.

I was born in a so-called bourgeois community and had some of the better things you could say of life. And I found that even some of the better things of life for black people wasn't too cool. And I found that there was more people starvin' than there was people eatin'. And I found there was more people didn't have clothes than did have clothes. And I found that I just happened to be one of the few. And I made a commitment to myself that I wouldn't stop doin' what I'm doin' until all those people were free.

We talkin' about we goin' ta make some changes in this system. We know they have our pictures. We know they lookin' for us. We know they want us. But we're still sayin' that even though we could be—in a sense—as far as this system goes—"on the mountaintop"—we in the Black Panther party—because of our dedication and understanding what's in the valley—knowing that the people are in the valley—knowing that we originally came from the valley—knowing that our plight is the same plight as the people in the valley—knowing that our enemy is on the mountaintop—our freedoms in the valley . . . we say even though it's nice to be on the mountaintop—we're goin' back to the valley!

I want you to know that I want you to think. If you ever think about me and if you think about me Niggers and if you ain't gonna do no revolutionary act, forget about me. I don't want myself on your mind if you're not going to work for the people. Like we always said, if you're asked to make a commitment at the age of 20 and you say, I don't want to make a commitment only because of the simple reason that I'm too young to die, I want to live a little bit longer. What you did is, you're dead already.

You have to understand that people have to pay the price for peace. If you dare to struggle, you dare to win. If you dare not struggle then damnit—you don't deserve to win. Let me say peace to you if you're willing to fight for it.

I've been gone for a little while. At least my body's been gone for a little while. But I'm back now and I believe that I'm back to stay. I believe that I'm going to do my job and I believe that I was born not to die in a car wreck; I don't believe that I'm going to die in a car wreck. I don't believe I'm going to die slipping on a piece of ice; I don't believe I'm going to die because I got a bad heart; I don't believe I'm going to die because of lung cancer. I believe that I'm going to be able to die doing the things I was born for. I believe that I'm going to be able to die high off the people. I believe that I will be able to die as a revolutionary in the international revolutionary proletarian struggle. And I hope that each one of you will be able to die in the international proletarian revolutionary struggle or you'll be able to live in it. And I think that struggle's going to come. Why don't you live for the people? Why don't you struggle for the people? Why don't you die for the people?

STRONG MEN

Sterling A. Brown

They broke you in like oxen,
They scourged you,
They branded you,
They made your women breeders,
They swelled your numbers with bastards. . . .
They taught you the religion they disgraced.

You sang:
Keep a-inchin' along
Lak a po' inch worm. . . .

You sang:
Bye and bye
I'm gonna lay down dis heaby load. . . .

You sang:
Walk togedder, chillen,
Dontcha git weary. . . .
The strong men keep a-comin' on
The strong men git stronger.

They point with pride to the roads you built for them,
They ride in comfort over the rails you laid for them.
They put hammers in your hands
And said—Drive so much before sundown.

You sang:
Ain't no hammah
In dis lan',
Strikes lak mine, bebby,
Strikes lak mine.

They cooped you in their kitchens,
They penned you in their factories,
They gave you the jobs that they were too good for,
They tried to guarantee happiness to themselves
By shunting dirt and misery to you.

THE FAILURE OF BLACK SEPARATISM

Bayard Rustin

We are living in an age of revolution—or so they tell us. The children of the affluent classes pay homage to their parents' values by rejecting them; this, they say, is a youth revolution. The discussion and display of sexuality increases—actors disrobe on stage, young women very nearly do on the street—and so we are in the midst of a sexual revolution. Tastes in music and clothing change, and each new fashion too is revolutionary. With every new social phenomenon now being dubbed a "revolution," the term has in fact become nothing more than a slogan which serves to take our minds off

From *Harper's Magazine*, vol. 240 (January 1970), pp. 25–29, 32–34 (excerpts). By permission from the author and publisher.

an unpleasant reality. For if we were not careful, we might easily forget that there is a conservative in the White House, that our country is racially polarized as never before, and that the forces of liberalism are in disarray. Whatever there is of revolution today, in any meaningful sense of the term, is coming from the Right.

But we are also told—and with far greater urgency and frequency—that there is a black revolution. If by revolution we mean a radical escalation of black aspirations and demands, this is surely the case. There is a new assertion of pride in the Negro race and its cultural heritage, and although the past summer was marked by the lack of any major disruptions, there is among blacks a tendency more pronounced than at any time in Negro history to engage in violence and the rhetoric of violence. Yet if we look closely at the situation of Negroes today, we find that there has been not the least revolutionary reallocation of political or economic power. . . .

Any appearance that we are in the grip of a black revolution . . . is deceptive. The problem is not whether black aspirations are outpacing America's ability to respond but whether they have outpaced her willingness to do so. Lately it has been taken almost as axiomatic that with every increase in Negro demands, there must be a corresponding intensification of white resistance. This proposition implies that only black complacency can prevent racial polarization, that any political action by Negroes must of necessity produce a reaction. But such a notion ignores entirely the question of what *kind* of political action, guided by what *kind* of political strategy. One can almost assert as a law of American politics that if Negroes engage in violence as a tactic they will be met with repression, that if they follow a strategy of racial separatism they will be isolated, and that if they engage in antidemocratic activity, out of the deluded wish to skirt the democratic process, they will provoke a reaction. To the misguided, violence, separatism, and minority ultimatums may seem revolutionary, but in reality they issue only from the desperate strivings of the impotent. Certainly such tactics are not designed to enhance the achievement of progressive social change. Recent American political history has proved this point time and again with brutal clarity.

The irony of the revolutionary rhetoric uttered in behalf of Negroes is that it has helped in fact to promote conservatism. On the other hand, of course, the reverse is also true: the failure of America to respond to the demands of Negoes has fostered in the minds of the latter a sense of futility and has thus seemed to legitimize a strategy of withdrawal and violence. Other things have been operating as well. The fifteen years since *Brown vs. Topeka* have been for Negroes a period of enormous dislocation. The modernization of farming in the South forced hundreds of thousands of Negroes to migrate to the North where they were confronted by a second technological affliction, automation. Without jobs, living in cities equipped to serve neither their material nor spiritual needs, these modern-day immigrants responded to their brutal new world with despair and hostility. The civil-rights movement created an even more fundamental social dislocation, for it destroyed not simply the legal structure of segregation but also the psychological assumptions of racism. Young Negroes who matured during this period witnessed a basic challenge to the system of values and social relations which had presumed the inferiority of the Negro. They have totally rejected this system, but in doing so have often substituted for it an exaggerated and distorted perception both of themselves and of the society. As if to obliterate the trace of racial shame that might be lurking in their souls they have embraced racial chauvinism. And as if in reply to past exclusions (and often in response to present insecurities), they have created their own patterns of exclusiveness.

The various frustrations and upheavals experienced recently by the Negro community account in large part for the present political orientation of some of its most vocal members: seeing their immediate self-interest more in the terms of emotional release than in those of economic and political advancement. One is supposed to think black, dress black, eat black, and buy black without reference to the question of what such a program actually contributes to advancing the cause of social justice. Since real victories are thought to be unattainable, issues become important in so far as they can provide symbolic victories. Dramatic confrontations are staged which serve as outlets for radical energy but which in no way further the achievement of radical social goals. So that, for instance, members of the black community are mobilized to pursue the "victory" of halting construction of a state office building in Harlem, even though it is hard to see what actual economic or social benefit will be conferred on the impoverished residents of that community by their success in doing so.

Such actions constitute a politics of escape rooted in hopelessness and further reinforced by government inaction. Deracinated liberals may romanticize this politics, nihilistic New Leftists may imitate it, but it is ordinary Negroes who will be the victims of its powerlessness to work any genuine change in their condition.

The call for Black Power is now over three years old, yet to this day no one knows what Black Power is supposed to mean and therefore how its proponents are to unite and rally behind it. If one is a member of CORE, Black Power posits the need for a separate black economy based upon traditional forms of capitalist relations. For SNCC the term refers to a politically united black community. US would emphasize the unity of black culture, while the Black Panthers wish to impose upon black nationalism the philosophies of Marx, Lenin, Stalin, and Chairman Mao. Nor do these exhaust all the possible shades and gradations of meaning. If there is one common theme uniting the various demands for Black Power, it is simply that blacks must be guided in their actions by a consciousness of themselves as a separate race.

Now, philosophies of racial solidarity have never been unduly concerned with the realities that operate outside the category of race. The adherents of these philosophies are generally romantics, steeped in the traditions of their own particular clans and preoccupied with the simple biological verities of blood and racial survival. Almost invariably their rally cry is racial self-determination, and they tend to ignore those aspects of the material world which point up divisions within the racially defined group. . . .

To Negroes for whom race is the major criterion, . . . divisions by wealth and status are irrelevant. Consider, for instance, the proposals for black economic advancement put forth by the various groups of black nationalists. These proposals are all remarkably similar. For regardless of one's particular persuasion—whether a revolutionary or a cultural nationalist or an unabashed black capitalist—once one confines one's analysis to the ghetto, no proposal can extend beyond a strategy for ghetto development and black enterprise. This explains in part the recent popularity of black capitalism and, to a lesser degree, black cooperatives: once both the economic strategy and goal are defined in terms of black self-determination, there is simply not much else available in the way of ideas. . . .

[A] separate black economy appears to offer hope for what Roy Innis has called "a new social contract." According to Innis's theory, the black community is essentially a colony ruled by outsiders; there can be no peace between the colony and the "mother country" until the former is ruled by some of its own. When the colony is finally "liberated" in this way, all conflicts can be resolved through negotiation between the black ruling class and the white ruling class. Any difficulties within the black community, that is, would become the responsibility of the black elite. But since self-determination in the ghetto, necessitating as it would the expansion of a propertied black middle class, offers the advantage of social stability, such difficulties would be minimal. How could many whites fail to grasp the obvious benefit to themselves in a program that promises social peace without the social inconvenience of integration and especially without the burden of a huge expenditure of money? Even if one were to accept the colonial analogy—and it is in many ways an uninformed and extremely foolish one—the strategy implied by it is fatuous and unworkable. Most of the experiments in black capitalism thus far have been total failures. As, given the odds, they should continue to be. For one thing, small businesses owned and run by blacks will, exactly like their white counterparts, suffer a high rate of failure. In fact, they will face even greater problems than white small businesses because they will be operating in predominantly low income areas where the clientele will be poor, the crime rate and taxes high, and the cost of land, labor, and insurance expensive. They will have to charge higher prices than the large chains, a circumstance against which "Buy Black" campaigns will in the long or even the short run have little force. On the other hand, to create large-scale black industry in the ghetto is unthinkable. The capital is not available, and even if it were, there is no vacant land. In Los Angeles, for example, the area in which four-fifths of the Negroes and Mexican-Americans live contains only 0.5 percent of all the vacant land in the city, and the problem is similar elsewhere. Overcrowding is severe enough in the ghetto without building up any industry there.

Another current axiom of black self-determination is the necessity for community control. Questions of ideology aside, black community control is as futile a program as black capitalism. Assuming that there were a cohesive, clearly identifiable black community (which, judging by the factionalism in neighborhoods like Harlem and Ocean Hill–Brownsville, is a far from safe assumption), and assuming that the community were empowered to control the ghetto, it would still find itself without the money needed in order to be socially creative. . . .

The truth of the matter is that community control as an idea is provincial and as a program is extremely conservative. It appears radical to some people because it has become the demand around which the frustrations of the Negro community have coalesced. In terms of its capacity to deal with the social and economic causes of black unrest, however, its potential is strikingly limited. The call for community control in fact represents an adjustment to inequality rather than a protest against it. Fundamentally, it is a demand for a change in the racial composition of the personnel who administer community institutions: that is, for schools, institutions of public and social service, and political organizations—as all of these are presently constituted—to be put into the keeping of a new class of black officials. Thus in a very real sense, the notion of community control bespeaks a fervent hope that the poverty-stricken ghetto, once thought to be a social problem crying for rectification, might now be deemed a social good worthy of acceptance. Hosea Williams of SCLC, speaking once of community control, unwittingly revealed the way in which passionate self-assertion can be a mask for accommodation: "I'm now at the position Booker T. Washington was about sixty or seventy years ago," Williams said. "I say to my brothers, 'Cast down your buckets where you are'—and that means there in the slums and ghettos."

There is indeed profound truth in the observation that people who seek social change will, in the absence of real substantive victories, often seize upon stylistic substitutes as an outlet for their frustrations. . . .

The response of guilt and pity to social problems is by no means new. It is in fact, as old as man's capacity to rationalize or his reluctance to make real sacrifices for his fellow man. Two hundred years ago, Samuel Johnson, in an exchange with Boswell, analyzed the phenomenon of sentimentality:

> Boswell: "I have often blamed myself, Sir, for not feeling for others, as sensibly as many say they do."
>
> Johnson: "Sir, don't be duped by them any more. You will find these very feeling people are not very ready to do you good. They *pay* you by *feeling*."

Today, payments from the rich to the poor take the form of "Giving a Damn" or some other kind of moral philanthropy. At the same time, of course, some of those who so passionately "Give a Damn" are likely to argue that full employment is inflationary.

We are living in a time of great social confusion—not only about the strategies we must adopt but about the very goals these strategies are to bring us to. Only recently whites and Negores of good will were pretty much in agreement that racial and economic justice required an end to segregation and the expansion of the role of the federal government. Now it is a mark of "advancement," not only among "progressive" whites but among the black militants as well, to believe that integration is passé. Unintentionally (or as the Marxists used to say, objectively), they are lending aid and comfort to traditional segregationists like Senators Eastland and Thurmond. Another "advanced" idea is the notion that government has gotten too big and that what is needed to make the society more humane and livable is an enormous new move toward local participation and decentralization. One cannot question the value or importance of democratic participation in the government, but just as misplaced sympathy for Negroes is being put to use by segregationists, the liberal preoccupation with localism is serving the cause of conservatism. Two years of liberal encomiums to decentralization have intellectually legitimized the concept, if not the name, of states' rights and have set the stage for the widespread acceptance of Nixon's "New Federalism."

The new anti-integrationism and localism may have been motivated by sincere moral conviction, but hardly by intelligent political thinking. It should be obvious that what is needed today more than ever is a political strategy that offers the real possibility of economically uplifting millions of impoverished individuals, black and white. Such a strategy must of necessity give low priority to the various forms of economic and psychological experimentation that I have discussed, which at best deal with issues peripheral to the central problem and at worst embody a frenetic escapism. These experiments are based on the assumption that the black community can be transformed from within when, in fact, any such transformation must depend on structural changes in the entire society. Negro poverty, for example, will not be eliminated in the absence of a total war on poverty. We need, therefore, a new national economic policy. We also need new policies in housing, education, and health care which can deal with these problems as they relate to Negroes within the context of a national solution. A successful strategy, therefore, must rest upon an identification of those central institutions which, if altered sufficiently, would transform the social and economic relations in our society; and it must provide a politically viable means of achieving such an alteration.

Surely the church is not a central institution in this sense. Nor is Roy Innis's notion of dealing with the banking establishment a useful one. For the banks will find no extra profit—quite the contrary—in the kind of fundamental structural change in society that is required. . . .

While the church, private enterprise, and other institutions can, if properly motivated, play an important role, finally it is the trade-union movement and the Democratic party which offer the greatest leverage to the black struggle. The serious objective of Negroes must be to strengthen and liberalize these. The trade-union movement is essential to the black struggle because it is the only institution in the society capable of organizing the working poor, so many of whom are Negroes. It is only through an organized movement that these workers, who are now condemned to the margin of the economy, can achieve a measure of dignity and economic security. I must confess I find it difficult to understand the prejudice against the labor movement currently fashionable among so many liberals. These people, somehow for reasons of their own, seem to believe that white workers are affluent members of the Establishment (a rather questionable belief, to put it mildly, especially when held by people earning over $25,000 a year) and are now trying to keep the Negroes down. The only grain of truth here is that there *is* competition between black and white workers which derives from a scarcity of jobs and resources. But rather than propose an expansion of those resources, our stylish liberals underwrite that competition by endorsing the myth that the unions are the worst enemy of the Negro.

In fact it is the program of the labor movement that represents a genuine means for reducing racial competition and hostility. Not out of a greater tenderness of feeling for black suffering—but that is just the point. Unions organize workers on the basis of common economic interests, not by virtue of racial affinity. Labor's legislative program for full employment, housing, urban reconstruction, tax reform, improved health care, and expanded educational opportunities is designed specifically to aid both whites and blacks in the lower and lower-middle classes where the potential for racial polarizations is most severe. And only a program of this kind can deal simultaneously and creatively with the interrelated problems of black rage and white fear. It does not placate black rage at the expense of whites, thereby increasing white fear and political reaction. Nor does it exploit white fear by repressing blacks. Either of these courses strengthens the demagogues among both races who prey upon frustration and racial antagonism. Both of them help to strengthen conservative forces—the forces that stand to benefit from the fact that hostility between black and white workers keeps them from uniting effectively around issues of common economic interest.

President Nixon is in the White House today largely because of this hostility; and the strategy advocated by many liberals to build a "new coalition" of the affluent, the young, and the dispossessed is designed to keep him there. The difficulty with this proposed new coalition is not only that its constituents comprise a distinct minority of the population, but that its affluent and youthful members—regardless of the momentary direction of their rhetoric—are hardly the undisputed friends of the poor. Recent Harris polls, in fact, have shown that Nixon is most popular among the college educated and the young. Perhaps they were attracted by his style or the minimal concessions he has made on Vietnam, but certainly their approval cannot be based upon his accomplishments in the areas of civil rights and economic justice.

If the Republican ascendancy is to be but a passing phenomenon, it must once more come to be clearly understood among those who favor social progress that the Democratic party is still the only mass-based political organization in the country with the potential to become a majority movement for social change. And anything calling itself by the name of political activity must be concerned with building precisely such a majority movement. In addition, Negroes must abandon once and for all the false assumption that as 10 percent of the population they can by themselves effect basic changes in the structure of American life. They must, in other words, accept the necessity of coalition politics. As a result of our fascination with novelty and with the "new" revolutionary forces that have emerged in recent years, it seems to some the height of conservatism to propose a strategy that was effective in the past. Yet the political reality is that without a coalition of Negroes and other minorities with the trade-union movement and with liberal groups, the shift of power to the Right will persist and the democratic Left in America will have to content itself with a well-nigh permanent minority status.

The bitterness of many young Negroes today has led them to be unsympathetic to a program based on the principles of trade unionism and electoral politics. Their protest represents a refusal to accept the condition of inequality, and in that sense, it is part of the long, and I think, magnificent black struggle for freedom. But with no comprehensive strategy to replace the one I have suggested, their protest, though militant in rhetoric and intention, may be reactionary in effect.

The strategy I have outlined must stand or fall by its capacity to achieve political and economic results. It is not intended to provide some new wave of intellectual excitement. It is not intended to suggest a new style of life or a means to personal salvation for disaffected members of the middle class. Nor is either of these the proper role of politics. My strategy is not meant to appeal to the fears of threatened whites, though it would calm those fears and increase the likelihood that some day we shall have a truly integrated society. It is not meant to serve as an outlet for the terrible frustrations of

Negroes, though it would reduce those frustrations and point a way to dignity for an oppressed people. It is simply a vehicle by which the wealth of this nation can be redistributed and some of its more grievous social problems solved. This in itself would be quite enough to be getting on with. In fact, if I may risk a slight exaggeration, by normal standards of human society I think it would constitute a revolution.

THE CRISIS IN LOCAL GOVERNMENT

Louis L. Knowles and Kenneth Prewitt

The immigrant minorities depended on the machine-boss style of politics to secure for themselves a niche in the power structure of the city. This system allowed every neighborhood and ethnic minority to have at least a single voice in the city council, and the local alderman was a familiar figure to much of the population of his ward. However, as the party organization became entrenched, it tended to lose much of its representative quality and to rely solely on the power of patronage jobs to sustain itself. In core-city areas that became populated by black people, the party machine would buy off the best of the leadership and entrench their control through the use of the patronage system. The black population, with its unique need for a political voice which could be used against the exploiters of its neighborhoods, was inadequately represented in machine politics. But at least there was some sense of identification with the political power structure of the city.

Reform politics has not been the boon to the black community that many would suppose. The new nonpartisan politics of the cities emphasizes efficiency and neutrality of officials. Local leaders should be technocrats rather than politicans, according to this theory. Consequently city government has become highly professionalized and unresponsive to the opinions of minorities of all types. Lane states:

> Municipal reforms of this nature: nonpartisanship, smaller city councils, the replacement of mayors by city-managers, may serve admirable technical purposes and in the long run be in the best interests of most groups in the community—but they weaken the political ties of the disorganized and depressed groups in the community. And, in doing this, they serve a strong, but usually repressed, interest of the community "power elite," whose focus is ostensibly upon the gains in efficiency and honesty brought about by the reforms, but who profit from the political apathy of the underdog.[1]

[1] Robert E. Lane, *Political Life* (New York: The Free Press of Glencoe, 1960), pp. 270–71.

In the old politics an ethnic or religious minority could control its own ward and be assured of at least one representative in the ruling body. In the new city, the trend is toward at-large elections, which benefit only the groups that hold a majority in the entire city.

> Other things being equal, Negro political strength in the city organizations tends to be directly proportional to the size and density of the Negro population and inversely proportional to the size of the basic political unit.[2]

A similar dilemma awaits our metropolitan centers in the near future as the pressure mounts for government structures that will include suburbs as well as the urban centers. The arguments for regional planning are strong. Taxable capital is moving out of the city and into the white suburbs, but the money is desperately needed to meet the social problems of the inner city. The funds will be welcomed by city governments that are increasingly feeling the pinch caused by the exodus of industry and the influx of the poor. But the money will inevitably create a demand among suburbanites that they have a say in its use. Just as black people are approaching the point where they could seize a large share of power in city government, they may find themselves faced with a regional government over which they have little or no control.

Liberal whites argue that events such as the elections of Stokes and Hatcher to the mayorships of Cleveland and Gary show that black people are gradually arriving at their rightful place in the political process. The Stokes and Hatcher elections were significant in that both men relied heavily on solid ghetto support for their victories. Big city elections will become easier for black candidates to win as the black population passes 50 percent. But black people can never hope to approach a voting majority in most electoral districts, although they will continue to constitute a significant minority. Most black candidates for office will still have to appeal to a large segment of the white community if they hope to be elected. Thus, although a small number of cases where black people have been elected to political positions do exist, a great majority of these black leaders fail to effect desperately needed social change. In terms of strict definition, the black man may be represented, but in terms of actual political power, he is still a second-class citizen.

In machine politics the black politician had to conform to the rules of the game as they were set by the white bosses. In the new, nonpartisan style of governing, the black leader must compromise the demands of his people to appeal to large blocs of white voters. In either case, the process of "co-optation" cripples black representation in government. For the purposes of this study, "co-optation" can be defined as the process whereby individuals

[2] James Q. Wilson, *Negro Politics* (New York: The Free Press of Glencoe, 1960), p. 27.

are assimilated and committed to the institutions and the values of the dominant group in the society. The dominant group in our society is, of course, white. This holds true whether one accepts the "pluralist" model of society, in which power resides in a number of focal points, or the "elite" model, which suggests a unified "power elite." As Carmichael and Hamilton point out,

> American pluralism quickly becomes a monolithic structure on issues of race. When faced with demands from black people, the multi-faction whites unite and present a common front.[3]

What does co-optation mean to the black who wants and needs his leaders to push for social reform? A specific example will illustrate that in order for blacks to attain positions of power, they must "sell-out"—accept and espouse the goals and ideals of the established power group. In 1939, William L. Dawson, a black member of the City Council in Chicago, a militant, and a Republican, switched parties with the full backing of the Democratic machine that controls Chicago politics. As James Q. Wilson points out in his book, *Negro Politics*:

> Dawson, before being co-opted into the Democratic Party, was an outspoken and vigorous champion of racial causes. Once inside an organization that was strong and which manifestly held the key to the future, race matters were subdued.[4]

Wilson further states:

> . . . the civic issues which the Negro protest and improvement associations define as important—open occupancy, fair employment practices, medical integration—are not common topics in the politicians' contacts with the voters.[5]

As young organizations value change, so mature organizations value order, and the leading Negro politicians have so completely moved from youthful change to present order that their aversion to issues, publicity, and protest action has smothered all sense of the urgent need to press the demands of the ghetto on the public. The co-optation of his leader into the dominant power group left the black man in Chicago with a figurehead leader and no one in power to push for needed legislation.

[3] Stokely Carmichael and Charles V. Hamilton, *Black Power: The Politics of Liberation in America* (New York: Vintage Books, 1967), p. 7.

[4] Wilson, p. 36.

[5] *Ibid.*, p. 54.

13 The old shell game

THE STRUCTURE OF POWER IN AMERICAN SOCIETY

C. Wright Mills

I

Power has to do with whatever decisions men make about the arrangements under which they live, and about the events which make up the history of their times. Events that are beyond human decision do happen; social arrangements do change without benefit of explicit decision. But in so far as such decisions are made, the problem of who is involved in making them is the basic problem of power. In so far as they could be made but are not, the problem becomes who fails to make them.

We cannot today merely assume that in the last resort men must always be governed by their own consent. For among the means of power which now prevail is the power to manage and to manipulate the consent of men. That we do not know the limits of such power, and that we hope it does have limits, does not remove the fact that much power today is successfully employed without the sanction of the reason or the conscience of the obedient.

Surely nowadays we need not argue that, in the last resort, coercion is the "final" form of power. But then, we are by no means constantly at the last resort. Authority (power that is justified by the beliefs of the voluntarily obedient) and manipulation (power that is wielded unbeknown to the powerless)—must also be considered, along with coercion. In fact, the three types must be sorted out whenever we think about power.

In the modern world, we must bear in mind, power is often not so authoritative as it seemed to be in the medieval epoch: ideas which justify rulers no longer seem so necessary to their exercise of power. At least for many of the great decisions of our time—especially those of an international sort—mass "persuasion" has not been "necessary"; the fact is simply accomplished. Furthermore, such ideas as are available to the powerful are often neither taken up nor used by them. Such ideologies usually arise as a response to an effective debunking of power; in the United States such opposition has not been effective enough recently to create the felt need for new ideologies of rule.

There has, in fact, come about a situation in which many who have lost faith in prevailing loyalties have not aquired new ones, and so pay no attention to politics of any kind. They are not radical, not liberal, not conservative, not reactionary. They are inactionary. They are out of it. If we accept the Greek's definition of the idiot as an altogether private man, then we must conclude that many American citizens are now idiots. And I should not be surprised, although I do not know, if there were not some such idiots even in Germany. This—and I use the word with care—this spiritual condition seems to me the key to many modern troubles of political intellectuals, as well as the key to much political bewilderment in modern society. Intellectual "conviction" and moral "belief" are not necessary, in either the rulers or the ruled, for a ruling power to persist and even to flourish. So far as the role of ideologies is concerned, their frequent absences and the prevalence of mass indifference are surely two of the major political facts about the western societies today.

How large a role any explicit decisions do play in the making of history is itself an historical problem. For how large that role may be depends very much upon the means of power that are available at any given time in any given society. In some societies, the innumerable actions of innumerable men modify their milieux, and so gradually modify the structure itself. These modifications—the course of history—go on behind the backs of men. History is drift, although in total "men make it." Thus, innumerable entrepreneurs and innumerable consumers by ten-thousand decisions per minute may shape and re-shape the free-market economy. Perhaps this was the chief kind of limitation Marx had in mind when he wrote, in *The 18th Brumaire*: that "Men make their own history, but they do not make it just as they please; they do not make it under circumstances chosen by themselves. . . ."

But in other societies—certainly in the United States and in the Soviet Union today—a few men may be so placed within the structure that by their decisions they modify the milieux of many other men, and in fact nowadays the structural conditions under which most men live. Such elites of power also make history under circumstances not chosen altogether by themselves, yet compared with other men, and compared with other periods of world history, these circumstances do indeed seem less limiting.

I should contend that "men are free to make history," but that some men are indeed much freer than others. For such freedom requires access to the means of decision and of power by which history can now be made. It has not always been so made; but in the later phases of the modern epoch it is. It is with reference to this epoch that I am contending that if men do not make history, they tend increasingly to become the utensils of history-makers. . .

The history of modern society may readily be understood as the story of the enlargement and the centralization of the means of power—in economic, in political, and in military institutions. The rise of industrial society has involved these developments in the means of economic production. The rise of the nation-state has involved similar developments in the means of violence and in those of political administration. . . .

Yet so great is the reach of the means of violence, and so great the economy required to produce and support them, that we have in the immediate past witnessed the consolidation of these two world centres, either of which dwarfs the power of Ancient Rome. As we pay attention to the awesome means of power now available to quite small groups of men we come to realize that Caesar could do less with Rome than Napoleon with France; Napoleon less with France then Lenin with Russia. But what was Caesar's power at its height compared with the power of the changing inner circles of Soviet Russia and the temporary administrations of the United States? We come to realize—indeed they continually remind us—how a few men have access to the means by which in a few days continents can be turned into thermonuclear wastelands. That the facilities of power are so enormously enlarged and so decisively centralized surely means that the powers of quite small groups of men, which we may call elites, are now of literally inhuman consequence.

My concern here is not with the international scene but with the United States in the middle of the twentieth century. I must emphasize "in the middle of the twentieth century" because in our attempt to understand any society we come upon images which have been drawn from its past and which often confuse our attempt to confront its present reality. That is one minor reason why history is the shank of any social science: we must study it if only to rid ourselves of it. In the United States, there are indeed many such images and usually they have to do with the first half of the nineteenth century. At that time the economic facilities of the United States were very widely dispersed and subject to little or to no central authority.

The state watched in the night but was without decisive voice in the day.

One man meant one rifle and the militia were without centralized orders. . . .

But then we must immediately add: all that is of the past and of little relevance to our understanding of the United States today. Within this society three broad levels of power may now be distinguished. I shall begin at the top and move downward.

II

The power to make decisions of national and international consequence is now so clearly seated in political, military, and economic institutions that other areas of society seem off to the side and, on occasion, readily subordinated to these. The scattered institutions of religion, education and family are increasingly shaped by the big three, in which history-making decisions now regularly occur. Behind this fact there is all the push and drive of a fabulous technology; for these three institutional orders have incorporated this technology and now guide it, even as it shapes and paces their development.

As each has assumed its modern shape, its effects upon the other two have become greater, and the traffic between the three has increased. There is no longer, on the one hand, an economy, and, on the other, a political order, containing a military establishment unimportant to politics and to money-making. There is a political economy numerously linked with military order and decision. This triangle of power is now a structural fact, and it is the key to any understanding of the higher circles in America today. For as each of these domains has coincided with the others, as decisions in each have become broader, the leading men of each—the high military, the corporation executives, the political directorate—have tended to come together to form the power elite of America.

The political order, once composed of several dozen states with a weak federal-centre, has become an executive apparatus which has taken up into itself many powers previously scattered, legislative as well as administrative, and which now reaches into all parts of the social structure. The long-time tendency of business and government to become more closely connected has since World War II reached a new point of explicitness. Neither can now be seen clearly as a distinct world. The growth of executive government does not mean merely the "enlargement of government" as some kind of autonomous bureaucracy: under American conditions, it has meant the ascendency of the corporation man into political eminence. Already during the New Deal, such men had joined the political directorate; as of World War II they came to dominate it. Long involved with government, now they have moved into quite full direction of the economy of the war effort and of the post-war era.

The economy, once a great scatter of small productive units in somewhat automatic balance, has become internally dominated by a few hundred corporations, administratively and politically inter-related, which together hold the keys to economic decision. This economy is at once a permanent-war economy and a private-corporation economy. The most important relations of the corporation to the state now rest on the coincidence between military and corporate interests, as defined by the military and the corporate rich, and accepted by politicians and public. Within the elite as a whole, this coincidence of military domain and corporate realm strengthens both of them and further subordinates the merely political man. Not the party politician, but the corporation executive, is now more likely to sit with the military to answer the question: what is to be done?

The military order, once a slim establishment in a context of civilian distrust, has become the largest and most expensive feature of government; behind smiling public relations, it has all the grim and clumsy efficiency of a great and sprawling bureaucracy. The high military have gained decisive political and economic relevance. The seemingly permanent military threat places a premium upon them and virtually all political and economic actions are now judged in terms of military definitions of reality: the higher military have ascended to a firm position within the power elite of our time.

In part at least this is a result of an historical fact, pivotal for the years since 1939: the attention of the elite has shifted from domestic problems—centered in the 'thirties around slump—to international problems—centered in the 'forties and 'fifties around war. By long historical usage, the government of the United States has been shaped by domestic clash and balance; it does not have suitable agencies and traditions for the democratic handling of international affairs. In considerable part, it is in this vacuum that the power elite has grown.

(i) To understand the unity of this power elite, we must pay attention to the psychology of its several members in their respective milieux. In so far as the power elite is composed of men of similar origin and education, of similar career and style of life, their unity may be said to rest upon the fact that they are of similar social type, and to lead to the fact of their easy intermingling. This kind of unity reaches its frothier apex in the sharing of that prestige which is to be had in the world of the celebrity. It achieves a more solid culmination in the fact of the interchangeability of positions between the three dominant institutional orders. It is revealed by considerable traffic of personnel within and between these three, as well as by the rise of specialized go-betweens as in the new style high-level lobbying.

(ii) Behind such psychological and social unity are the structure and the mechanics of those institutional hierarchies over which the political directorate, the corporate rich, and the high military now preside. How each of these hierarchies is shaped and what relations it has with the others determine in large part the relations of their rulers. Were these hierarchies scattered and disjointed, then their respective elites might tend to be scattered and disjointed; but if they have many interconnections and points of coinciding interest, then their elites tend to form a coherent kind of grouping. The unity of the elite is not a simple reflection of the unity of institutions, but men and institutions are always related; that is why we must understand the elite today in connection with such institutional trends as the development of a permanent-war establishment, alongside a privately incorporated economy, inside a virtual political vacuum. For the men at the top have been selected and formed by such institutional trends.

Washington, Aug. 12—Military and industrial leaders got together here today to honor Representative L. Mendel Rivers, the South Carolina Democrat who is chairman of the House Armed Services Committee and one of the defense establishment's foremost advocates.

Vice President Agnew praised Mr. Rivers for his "willingness to go to bat for the so-called and often discredited military–industrial complex" as 1,150 generals, Congressmen and defense contractors applauded in the ballroom of the Washington Hilton Hotel.

The three-hour gathering, with soldiers in Revolutionary War uniforms and lunch topped off by flags fluttering in mounds of baked alaska, was sponsored by the Washington Chapter of the Air Force Association.

The announced purpose of the occasion was the presentation to Mr. Rivers of the group's "Distinguished American Award" and a lapel pin bearing six stars; the gathering also appeared to represent a bipartisan show of strength by the military–industrial complex in a period of growing criticism of defense spending.

The Republican Vice-President said that the nation was fortunate to have men such as Mr. Rivers and another Democrat, Senator John C. Stennis of Mississippi, chairman of the Senate Armed Services Committee, to stand with the White House against "sizable and influential elements in both houses of Congress who feel we have not gone far enough in re-ordering priorities."

Unity across Lines

In turn, the Democratic master of ceremonies, John R. Blandford, chief counsel of Mr. Rivers's committee and a major general in the Marine Corps Reserve, said that when Mr. Agnew speaks, "people listen, and the great majority like what they hear."

One of the heartiest rounds of applause went to Senator Strom Thurmond, Republican of South Carolina, when he told the audience that a Senate majority had defeated one of several efforts to curb the Administration's antiballistic missile program shortly before the luncheon began.

The 15-page printed program, its cover red, white and blue, listed some 75 defense-oriented companies whose "cooperation" or "participation" had made the luncheon possible.

After a cocktail period that ended, with military precision, after the allotted 45 minutes, the diners paraded into the ballrooms to Sousa marches played by the Air Force ceremonial band. All wore name tags affixed to replicas of the United States flag as they took their places in front of red or blue napkins on white tablecloths.

The Airmen of Note, an Air Force dance band, played a pop concert during lunch and, later, the Army's Old Guard Fife and Drum Corps demonstrated how colonial military bands looked and sounded.

The martial air, commingled with frequent references to the patriotism of Mr. Rivers—"No man in America, including our Presidents, has done more for our national defense," said Senator Thurmond—also had undertones of humor.

Mr. Agnew said he wanted "to lay to rest the ugly, vicious, dastardly rumor" that Mr. Rivers, whose Charleston, S. C., district is chock full of military installations, "is trying to move the Pentagon piecemeal to South Carolina."

"Even when it appeared Charleston might sink into the sea from the burden," said the Vice President. Mr. Rivers's response was, "I regret that I have but one Congressional district to give my country to—I mean to give to my country."

The audience interrupted Mr. Agnew's remarks eight times with applause, 14 times with laughter.

James M. Naughton, "Rep. Rivers Is Honored as Top Defense Advocate," *The New York Times*, August 13, 1970.

About politics in industrial society, debate continues unchecked, particularly where the exercise of power is veiled, even denied by those who exert it; where the ephemera of politics and the surface play of the political elements concentrate attention upon themselves; where political decisions are influenced, nay determined, by events and alignments of forces in spheres ostensibly remote from the workings of the state; where, on the contrary, the state is so inextricably linked to other institutions that its distinctiveness is no longer obvious.

Norman Birnbaum, *The Crisis of Industrial Society* (New York: Oxford University Press, 1969), p. 41.

(iii) Their unity, however, does not rest solely upon psychological similarity and social intermingling, nor entirely upon the structural blending of commanding positions and common interests. At times it is the unity of a more explicit co-ordination.

To say that these higher circles are increasingly co-ordinated, that this is *one* basis of their unity, and that at times—as during open war—such co-ordination is quite wilful, is not to say that the co-ordination is total or continuous, or even that it is very surefooted. Much less is it to say that the power elite has emerged as the realization of a plot. Its rise cannot be adequately explained in any psychological terms.

Yet we must remember that institutional trends may be defined as opportunities by those who occupy the command posts. Once such opportunities are recognized, men may avail themselves of them. Certain types of men from each of these three areas, more far-sighted than others, have actively promoted the liaison even before it took its truly modern shape. Now more have come to see that their several interests can more easily be realized if they work together, in informal as well as in formal ways, and accordingly they have done so.

The idea of the power elite is of course an interpretation. It rests upon and it enables us to make sense of major institutional trends, the social similarities and psychological affinities of the men at the top. But the idea is also based upon what has been happening on the middle and lower levels of power, to which I now turn.

III

There are of course other interpretations of the American system of power. The most usual is that it is a moving balance of many competing interests. The image of balance, at least in America, is derived from the idea of the economic market: in the nineteenth century, the balance was thought to occur between a great scatter of individuals and enterprises; in the twentieth century, it is thought to occur between great interest blocs. In both views, the politician is the key man of power because he is the broker of many conflicting powers.

I believe that the balance and the compromise in American society—the "countervailing powers" and the "veto groups," of parties and associations, of strata and unions—must now be seen as having mainly to do with the middle levels of power. It is these middle levels that the political journalist and the scholar of politics are most likely to understand and to write about—if only because, being mainly middle class themselves, they are closer to them. Moreover these levels provide the noisy content of most "political" news and gossip; the images of these levels are more or less in accord with the folklore of how democracy works; and, if the master-image of balance is accepted, many intellectuals, especially in their current patrioteering, are readily able to satisfy such political optimism as they wish to feel. Accordingly, liberal interpretations of what is happening in the United States are now virtually the only interpretations that are widely distributed.

But to believe that the power system reflects a balancing society is, I think, to confuse the present era with earlier times, and to confuse its top and bottom with its middle levels.

By the top levels, as distinguished from the middle, I intend to refer, first of all, to the scope of the decisions that are made. At the top today, these decisions have to do with all the issues of war and peace. They have also to do with slump and poverty which are now so very much problems of international scope. I intend also to refer to whether or not the groups that struggle politically have a chance to gain the positions from which such top decisions are made, and indeed whether their members do usually hope for such top national command. Most of the competing interests which make up the clang and clash of American politics are strictly concerned with their slice of the existing pie. Labour unions, for example, certainly have no policies of an international sort other than those which given unions adopt for the strict economic protection of their members. Neither do farm organizations. The actions of such middle-level powers may indeed have consequence for top-level policy; certainly at times they hamper these policies. But they are not truly concerned with them, which means of course that their influence tends to be quite irresponsible.

The facts of the middle levels may in part be understood in terms of the rise of the power elite. The expanded and centralized and interlocked hierarchies over which the power elite preside have encroached upon the old balance and relegated it to the middle level. . . .

Fifty years ago many observers thought of the American state as a mask behind which an invisible government operated. But nowadays, much of what was called the old lobby, visible or invisible, is part of the quite visible government. The "governmentalization of the lobby" has proceeded in both the legislative and the executive domain, as well as between them. The executive bureaucracy becomes not only the centre of decision but also the arena within which major conflicts of power are resolved or denied resolution. "Administration" replaces electoral politics; the manoeuvring of cliques (which include leading Senators as well as civil servants) replaces the open clash of parties.

The shift of corporation men into the political directorate has accelerated the decline of the politicians in the Congress to the middle levels of power; the formation of the power elite rests in part upon this relegation. It rests also upon the semi-organized stalemate of the interests of sovereign localities, into which the legislative function has so largely fallen; upon the virtually complete absence of a civil service that is a politically neutral but politically relevant, depository of brain-power and executive skill; and it rests upon the increased official secrecy behind which great decisions are made without benefit of public or even of Congressional debate.

IV

There is one last belief upon which liberal observers everywhere base their interpretations and rest their hopes. That is the idea of the public and the associated idea of public opinion. Conservative thinkers, since the French Revolution, have of course Viewed With Alarm the rise of the public, which they have usually called the masses, or something to that effect. "The populace is sovereign," wrote Gustave Le Bon, "and the tide of barbarism mounts." But surely those who have supposed the masses to be well on their way to triumph are mistaken. In our time, the influence of publics or of masses within political life is in fact decreasing, and such influence as on occasion they do have tends, to an unknown but increasing degree, to be guided by the means of mass communication.

In a society of publics, discussion is the ascendant means of communication, and the mass media, if they exist, simply enlarge and animate this discussion, linking one face-to-face public with the discussions of another. In a mass society, the dominant type of communication is the formal media, and publics become mere markets for these media: the "public" of a radio programme consists of all those exposed to it. When we try to look upon the United States today as a society of publics, we realize that it has moved a considerable distance along the road to the mass society.

In official circles, the very term, "the public," has come to have a phantom meaning, which dramatically reveals its eclipse. The deciding elite can identify some of those who clamour publicly as "Labour," others as "Business," still others as "Farmer." But these are not the public. "The public" consists of the unidentified and the non-partisan in a world of defined and partisan interests. In this faint echo of the classic notion, the public is composed of these remnants of the old and new middle classes whose interests are not explicitly defined, organized, or clamorous. In a curious adaptation, "the public" often becomes, in administrative fact, "the disengaged expert," who, although ever so well informed, has never taken a clear-cut and public stand on controversial issues. He is the "public" member of the board, the commission, the committee. What "the public" stands for, accordingly, is often a vagueness of policy (called "open-mindedness"), a lack of involvement in public affairs (known as "reasonableness"), and a professional disinterest (known as "tolerance").

All this is indeed far removed from the eighteenth-century idea of the public of public opinion. That idea parallels the economic idea of the magical market. Here is the market composed of freely competing entrepreneurs; there is the public composed of circles of people in discussion. As price is the result of anonymous, equally weighted, bargaining individuals, so public opinion is the result of each man's having thought things out for himself and then contributing his voice to the great chorus. To be sure, some may have more influence on the state of opinion than others, but no one group monopolizes the discussion, or by itself determines the opinions that prevail.

In this classic image, the people are presented with problems. They discuss them. They formulate viewpoints. These viewpoints are organized, and they compete. One viewpoint "wins out." Then the people act on this view, or their representatives are instructed to act it out, and this they promptly do.

Such are the images of democracy which are still used as working justifications of power in America. We must now recognize this description as more a fairy tale than a useful approximation. The issues that now shape man's fate are neither raised nor decided by any public at large. The idea of a society that is at bottom composed of publics is not a matter of fact; it is the proclamation of an ideal, and as well the assertion of a legitimation masquerading as fact.

I cannot here describe the several great forces within American society as well as elsewhere which have been at work in the debilitation of the public. I want only to remind you that publics, like free associations, can be deliberately and suddenly smashed, or they can more slowly wither away. But whether smashed in a week or withered in a generation, the demise of the public must be seen in connection with the rise of centralized organizations, with all their new means of power, including those of the mass media of distraction. These, we now know, often seem to expropriate the rationality and the will of the terrorized or—as the case may be—the voluntarily indifferent society of masses. In the more democratic process of indifference the remnants of such publics as remain may only occasionally be intimidated by fanatics in search of "disloyalty." But regardless of that, they lose their will for decision because they do not possess the instruments for decision; they lose their sense of political belonging because they do not belong; they lose their political will because they see no way to realize it.

The political structure of a modern democratic state requires that such a public as is projected by democratic theorists not only exist but that it be the very forum within which a politics of real issues is enacted.

It requires a civil service that is firmly linked with the world of knowledge and sensibility, and which is composed of skilled men who, in their careers and in their aspirations, are truly independent of any private, which is to say, corporation, interests.

It requires nationally responsible parties which debate openly and clearly the issues which the nation, and indeed the world, now so rigidly confronts.

It requires an intelligentsia, inside as well as outside the universities, who carry on the big discourse of the western world, and whose work is relevant to and influential among parties and movements and publics.

And it certainly requires, as a fact of power, that there be free associations standing between families and smaller communities and publics, on the one hand, and the state, the military, the corporation, on the other. For unless these do exist, there are no vehicles for reasoned opinion, no instruments for the rational exertion of public will.

Such democratic formations are not now ascendant in the power structure of the United States, and accordingly the men of decision are not men selected and formed by careers within such associations and by their performance before such publics. The top of modern American society is increasingly unified, and often seems wilfully co-ordinated: at the top there has emerged an elite whose power probably exceeds that of any small group of men in world history. The middle levels are often a drifting set of stalemated forces: the middle does not link the bottom with the top. The bottom of this society is politically fragmented, and even as a passive fact, increasingly powerless: at the bottom there is emerging a mass society.

These developments, I believe, can be correctly understood neither in terms of the liberal nor the marxian interpretation of politics and history. Both these ways of thought arose as guidelines to reflection about a type of society which does not now exist in the United States. We confront there a new kind of social structure, which embodies elements and tendencies of all modern society, but in which they have assumed a more naked and flamboyant prominence.

That does not mean that we must give up the ideals of these classic political expectations. I believe that both have been concerned with the problem of rationality and of freedom: liberalism, with freedom and rationality as supreme facts about the individual; marxism, as supreme facts about man's role in the political making of history. What I have said here, I suppose, may be taken as an attempt to make evident why the ideas of freedom and of rationality now so often seem so ambiguous in the new society of the United States of America.

CLASS DISTINCTIONS: THE TRINITY

Saul D. Alinsky

The setting for the drama of change has never varied. Mankind has been and is divided into three parts: the Haves, the Have-Nots, and the Have-a-Little, Want Mores.

On top are the Haves with power, money, food, security, and luxury. They suffocate in their surpluses while the Have-Nots starve. Numerically the Haves have always been the fewest. The Haves want to keep things as they are and are opposed to change. Thermopolitically they are cold and determined to freeze the status quo.

On the bottom are the world's Have-Nots. On the world scene they are by far the greatest in numbers. They are chained together by the common misery of poverty, rotten housing, disease, ignorance, political impotence, and despair; when they are employed their jobs pay the least and they are deprived in all areas basic to human growth. Caged by color, physical or political, they are barred from an opportunity to represent themselves in the politics of life. The Haves want to keep; the Have-Nots want to get. Thermopolitically they are a mass of cold ashes of resignation and fatalism, but inside there are glowing embers of hope which can be fanned by the building of means of obtaining power. Once the fever begins the flame will follow. They have nowhere to go but up.

They hate the establishment of the Haves with its arrogant opulence, its police, its courts, and its churches. Justice, morality, law, and order, are mere words when used by the Haves, which justify and secure their status quo. The power of the Have-Nots rests only with their numbers. It has been said that the Haves, living under the nightmare of possible threats to their possessions, are always faced with the question of "when do we sleep?" while the perennial question of the Have-Nots is "when do we eat?" The cry of the Have-Nots has never been "give us your hearts" but always "get off our backs"; they ask not for love but for breathing space.

Between the Haves and Have-Nots are the Have-a-Little, Want Mores—the middle class. Torn between upholding the status quo to protect the little they have, yet wanting change so they can get more, they become split personalities. They could be described as social, economic, and political schizoids. Generally, they seek the safe way, where they can profit by change and yet not risk losing the little they have. They insist on a minimum of three aces before playing a hand in the poker game of revolution. Thermopolitically they are tepid and rooted in inertia. Today in Western society and particularly in the United States they comprise the majority of our population.

Yet in the conflicting interests and contradictions within the Have-a-Little, Want Mores is the genesis of creativity. Out of this class have come, with few exceptions, the great world leaders of change of the past centuries: Moses, Paul of Tarsus, Martin Luther, Robespierre, Georges Danton, Samuel Adams, Alexander Hamilton, Thomas Jefferson, Napoleon Bonaparte, Giuseppe Garibaldi, Nikolai Lenin, Mahatma Gandhi, Fidel Castro, Mao Tse-tung, and others.

Just as the clash of interests within the Have-a-Little, Want Mores has bred so many of the great leaders it has also spawned a particular breed stalemated by cross interests into inaction. These Do-Nothings profess a commitment to social change for ideals of justice, equality, and opportunity, and then abstain from and discourage all effective action for change. They are known by their brand, "I agree with your ends but not your means." They function as blankets whenever possible smothering sparks of dissension that promise to flare up into the fire of action. These Do-Nothings appear publicly as good men, humanitarian, concerned with justice and dignity. In practice they are invidious. They are the ones Edmund Burke referred to when he said, acidly: "The only thing necessary for the triumph of evil is for good men to do nothing."

THE POLITICAL IMPACT OF THE CONGLOMERATE GIANTS

Morton S. Baratz

It is one thing to assert and illustrate that the so-called industrial oligarchs "have" power, not in the possessory sense, but in the sense that they can and do get others to comply with their wishes. It is quite another to demonstrate that their behavior significantly affects, either for good or ill, the shape and scope of political outcomes. The first proposition is merely interesting, whereas the second gets to the core of the matter.

Without attempting to rank them according to importance in the overall scheme of things and thereby finessing what is in the ultimate an ethical, as opposed to a scientific, question, we may identify four broad political consequences of industrial oligarchy. First, the great corporations have an appreciable effect upon which goals the larger society sets for itself and the priority accorded to each. Second, the power, authority, and influence of the giants limit the freedom of other segments of the society, in that the latters' options are in one degree or another constrained. Third, the preeminence of the giants results in the perpetuation of an authoritative allocation of values that is highly inequitable. Fourth, the great enterprises are accountable to none but themselves and are irresponsible, in the sense that most of those affected by their behavior are barred from participation in deciding how they behave.

Social goals

Toward the end of the 1950s, a sizable number of Americans became convinced that the country had lost its way, that it had lost sight of its ultimate objectives. A national soul-searching exercise was set in motion, an exercise capped by the creation under Presidential auspices of a Commission on National Goals, charged with developing "a broad outline of coordinated national policies and programs" and setting up "a series of goals in various areas of national activity."

The report of the commission contained a curious mixture of fifteen general and specific objectives, ranging from enhancement of the dignity of the individual, through improvement of living conditions, to preservation and strengthening of the United Nations. With few exceptions, the goals and the terms in which they were stated were acceptable to the majority of Americans. None, it may be noted, was worded such that its attainment was contingent upon any drastic change in the form or conduct of any established institutions. Underlying each goal-statement, that is to say, was the (inarticulate) premise that the established order would remain as is.

It would be too much to say that *all* our national objectives are molded by the industrial oligarchy. Social goals and social values are the result of a variety of factors, some long predating the rise of great corporations. Yet there is a striking concurrence between the goal hierarchy of the business giants and that of society. In Professor Galbraith's words:

> The state is strongly concerned with the stability of the economy. And with its expansion or growth. And with education. And with the technical and scientific advance. And, most notably, with national defense. These are *the* national goals. . . . All have their counterpart in the needs and goals of the technostructure [of the giant corporations]. It requires stability in demand for its planning. Growth brings promotion and prestige. It requires trained manpower. It needs government underwriting of research and development. Military and other technical procurement support its most developed form of planning. At each point the government has goals with which the technostructure can identify itself. Or, plausibly, these goals reflect adaptation of public goals to the goals of the technostructure.

Constraint upon choices

No man has unlimited freedom of choice. Each of us is constrained in one way or another, whether by limited resources, commitments previously made to others, deeply rooted values and beliefs, or some other factors. It is appropriate to say, nonetheless, that the fewer the options open to an individual (or group or institution), the less free he is.

Within this frame of reference, it is clear that when exercised, the power, authority, and influence of the conglomerate giants tend to curtail the freedom of others. To the extent, for example, that the great corporations prevent other concerns from entering given lines of production, they restrict freedom of enterprise and of occupational choice. Similarly, when the giants undertake to "stabilize" prices and output in particular markets, they limit the freedom of smaller rivals to pursue different policies, policies that would afford the latter higher profits, sales revenue, or whatever it is they would prefer to maximize.

Even governments—federal, state, and local—are affected in this general respect. "The growth of the automobile industry is [a] classic example: in its requirements of roads, parking facilities, policemen, courts, traffic engineers, and so forth. . . . we were not aware of the costs, or that a choice existed. We were presented with a *fait accompli.*" Similarly, public policy-makers go to considerable lengths to avoid taking actions that could conceivably jeopardize the financial integrity of the great enterprises: most doubts in the divestment proceedings arising out of antitrust suits, on levies upon unreasonable accumulations of surplus, on the vigor with which certain regulatory statutes will be enforced—most doubts will be resolved in favor of the corporation in question.

Benefits and privileges

It was observed earlier that the prevailing mobilization of bias in America is highly favorable to and strongly reinforced by the great corporations. Another way to put this proposition is that the American enterprise system is firmly grounded upon two "core institutions of privilege . . .—the right to reap private benefit from the use of the means of production and the right to utilize the dynamic forces of the marketplace for private enrichment"—the workings of which result in an authoritative allocation of values (wealth, income, prestige, power and its correlates, and so on) that is highly favorable to those who control the conglomerate giants.

To point this out is not to deny that some degree of inequality of benefits is a necessary, although insufficient, condition for the attainment of certain high-priority social objectives. Thus, although the proposition is difficult to put to empirical test, it is surely plausible that unequal rewards are required for attainment of technically efficient utilization of resources and of steady growth in output and employment. Furthermore, a system under which equal rewards were given for unequal effort would violate the popular conception of justice.

There are those who will insist that the prevailing degree of inequality in the distribution of values is no greater than the minimum necessary for efficiency and justice. Whether they are right or wrong cannot be established beyond a doubt, mainly because we lack the data and analytical tools to test the assertion. What *does* seem clear, however, is that the giant corporations are the prime beneficiaries of the existing order and that they effectively utilize their privileges not only to protect their share of total benefits but to enlarge it. In fact, so pervasive are the values, benefits, and myths that underpin the prevailing mobilization of bias that the giants can proceed on the assumption that neither their privileges nor the fruits thereof will ever seriously be called into question.

Accountability and responsibility

It is of the essence of constitutional democracy that those who make policy choices are fully accountable to the persons and groups affected by the policies. In this way, there is some degree of assurance that the policy-makers, conscious of the anticipated reactions of those whom they affect, will not make choices hostile to the interests of the latter. Furthermore, democracy implies responsibility; in Professor Spiro's words:

> [T]he individual should, within the limits of the possible, seek to become responsible for his own fate. As a member of vast human organizations, he can assume this responsibility only by contributing to those central decisions whose consequences will in turn affect him. The norm of individual responsibility thus demands that citizens be given such opportunities for policy contributions, and, further, that these contributions be proportionate to the extent to which the contributors will be affected by or exposed to the consequences of the policies.

There is little ground for doubt that the giant corporations are "undemocratic" in both of the above respects. Where ownership and control are separated, the managers are accountable to the shareholders in only a formal sense. Moreover, as any number of commentators have pointed out, important economic decisions—the rate of investment, the location of plants, the level of output and employment—are made by a figurative handful of men, none of whom was chosen by the overwhelming number of persons affected by their decisions (and nondecisions) and over whom society has only the most tenuous controls. And, what may be most important of all, although corporate policy-makers are attuned to the phenomenon of anticipated reactions, in practically none of their decisions (and nondecisions) is there full participation by most of those who must live with the consequences of the decisions (and nondecisions).

. . . One cannot defend production as satisfying wants if that production creates the wants.

Were it so that a man on arising each morning was assailed by demons which instilled in him a passion sometimes for silk shirts, sometimes for kitchen-ware, sometimes for chamber pots, and sometimes for orange squash, there would be every reason to applaud the effort to find the goods, however odd, that quenched this flame. But should it be that his passion was the result of his first having cultivated the demons, and should it also be that his effort to allay it stirred the demons to ever greater and greater effort, there would be question as to how rational was his solution. Unless restrained by conventional attitudes, he might wonder if the solution lay with more goods or fewer demons.

So it is that if production creates the wants it seeks to satisfy, or if the wants emerge *pari passu* with the production, then the urgency of the wants can no longer be used to defend the urgency of the production. Production only fills a void that it has itself created.

John Kenneth Galbraith, *The Affluent Society* (Boston: Houghton Mifflin Company, 1960), p. 153.

CORPORATE AMERICA

Andrew Hacker

Since the end of World War II the corporate form has emerged as the characteristic institution of American society. Its rise has rendered irrelevant time-honored theories of politics and economics, and its explosive growth has created a new breed of man whose behavior can no longer be accounted for by conventional rules of conduct.

There is still time for reflection on these developments. America is not yet dominated by the corporate way of life; indeed, were this so we would all be painfully aware of the fact, and discussion of it would be superfluous. As matters now stand the corporation is central to the nation's economy. The 150 largest own two-thirds of the productive assets of the nation.

But there remains a substantial segment of the economy that cannot be called corporate in any meaningful sense. The small business community stands alongside corporate America, and it still embraces most of the working and entrepreneurial population. Indeed, the 100 largest manufacturing corporations employ less than six million persons out of the total labor force, and the 500 largest provide jobs for only about four million more. The preponderance of employed Americans, then, do not owe their livelihoods directly to corporate America, and it will be some time before even a simple majority of them do.

Yet all signs are that the future lies with the great corporate institution. It is growing in wealth, in size, in power. No one can seriously contend that there will be a rebirth of small business or a contraction of corporate growth. The corporation, to be sure, is not at this time the typical institution of our economy or our society. There are too many other social and economic forms, noncorporate in character, to permit the assertion that General Motors or United States Steel represents our institutional life today. Refuge must rather be taken in the suggestion that the corporation is "prototypical"—typical not of what exists now, but rather of that which will be at some future time. To study the corporate form, therefore, is to speculate on the America of a generation yet to come. From contemporary reality must be extrapolated the trends that will become increasingly accentuated.

Case of American Electric

The problem, which extends beyond the simple one of definition, may be illustrated by an imaginary conversation taking place not too many years from now. The setting and the topic of the discussion happen to be political, but the dialogue would take much the same form were it extended to other spheres where corporate power is exercised.

From *Corporation Takeover*, ed. by Andrew Hacker (New York: Harper & Row, Publishers, 1964). Reprinted by permission of the author and the Center for the Study of Democratic Institutions in Santa Barbara, Calif.

By 1972 American Electric had completed its last stages of automation: employees were no longer necessary. Raw materials left on the loading platform were automatically transferred from machine to machine, and the finished products were deposited at the other end of the factory ready for shipment. AE's purchasing, marketing and general management functions could be handled by 10 directors with the occasional help of outside consultants and contractors.

Beginning in 1962 AE's employee pension fund had started investing its capital in AE stock. Gradually it bought more and more of the company's shares on the open market, and by 1968 it was the sole owner of AE. As employees became eligible for retirement—some of them prematurely, due to the introduction of automation—the fund naturally liquidated its capital to provide pensions. But instead of reselling its AE shares on the open market, the fund sold the stock to AE itself, which provided the money for pensions out of current income. By 1981 the last AE employee had died and the pension fund was dissolved. At this time, too, AE became the sole owner of its shares. It had floated no new issues, preferring to engage in self-financing through earnings.

By 1982 the 10 directors decided that AE would be well served by the passage of legislation restricting the imports of certain electrical equipment. They therefore secured the services of a public relations firm specializing in political campaigns. The objective was to educate the public and sway grassroots sentiment so that Congress would respond by passing the required bill. The public relations firm was given a retainer of $1 million and authorized to spend up to $5 million more on advertising and related activities.

Within months the public began to hear about the dire consequences that would follow the importation of alien generators. National security, national prosperity and the nation's way of life were threatened by a flood of foreign goods. The public relations firm placed several hundred advertisements in newspapers and magazines, and almost a thousand on television. At least 50 citizens' committees "spontaneously" arose to favor the legislation, and over 200 existing groups passed resolutions in its support. Lectures were given to women's clubs and films were shown in high schools. By the end of the year—an election year—public sentiment had been aroused and hardly a Congressman was unaware of the popular ferment.

The bill was introduced in both chambers and a good majority of Senators and Representatives, abiding by the wishes of their constituents, voted for it. The President signed the bill and it became law. AE's profits were substantially higher the following year.

The Investigation

A group of Senators, however, were curious about what had been going on and they decided to investigate AE's foray into the political arena. One of the directors was happy to testify, for he knew that no law had been violated. No bribes had been offered, certainly, and no contributions to legislators' campaigns had been made. Toward the end of the inquiry, after all of the techniques employed by the company and the public relations firm had been brought out, the following colloquy took place:

Director: . . . And if we undertook these educational and political activities, it was our view that they were dictated by the company's best interests.

Senator: Now when you say that these campaigns were on behalf of the "company's" interests, I am not clear what you mean. Were you acting for your stockholders in this instance?

Director: I am afraid, Senator, that I cannot say that we were. You see, American Electric has no stockholders. The company owns all its stock itself. We bought up the last of it several years ago.

Senator: Well, if not stockholders, then were you acting as a spokesman for American Electric's employees—say, whose jobs might be endangered if foreign competition got too severe?

Director: No, sir, I cannot say that either. American Electric is a fully automated company and we have no employees.

Senator: Are you saying that this company of yours is really no more than a gigantic machine? A machine that needs no operators and appears to own itself?

Director: I suppose that is one way of putting it. I've never thought much about it.

Senator: Then, so far as I can see, all of this political pressure that you applied was really in the interests of yourself and your nine fellow directors. You spent almost $6 million of this company's money pursuing your personal political predilections.

Director: I am afraid, Senator, that now I must disagree with you. The 10 of us pay ourselves annual salaries of $100,000, year in and year out, and none of us receives any bonuses or raises if profits happen to be higher than usual in a given year. All earnings are ploughed back into the company. We feel very strongly about this. In fact, we look on ourselves as civil servants, in a way. Secondly, I could not say that the decision to get into politics was a personal wish on our part. At least eight of the 10 of us, as private citizens that is, did not favor the legislation we were supporting. As individuals most of us thought it was wrong, and not in the national interest. But we were acting in the company's interest, and in this case we knew that it was the right thing to do.

Senator: And by the "company" you don't mean stockholders or employees, because you don't have any. And you don't mean the 10 directors, because you just seem to be salaried managers which the machine hires to run its affairs. In fact, when this machine gets into politics—or indeed any kind of activity—it has interests of its own which can be quite different from the personal interests of its managers. I am afraid I find all this rather confusing.

Director: It may be confusing to you, Senator, but I may say that it has been quite straightforward to us at American Electric. We are just doing the job for which we were hired—to look out for the company's interests.

Power without People

Far-fetched, to be sure, but how much so? Already, A. A. Berle tells us, the pension fund of one large corporation is buying up the stock of its parent company and is close to having a controlling interest. This corporation, he writes, "has self-contained control, and management is thus responsible to itself." Needless to say, the productive enterprise that can function without employees is not yet a reality. But automation is abolishing jobs and there is no guarantee that new positions will be created in their stead.

The questions put to corporate spokesmen center on the problem of who is represented in the exercise of corporate power, whether that power is at work in the political arena or any other segment of society. There remains in many American minds the belief that power should be representative, that the ability to control resources should act in the name of human beings if it is to be legitimate. The corporation, however, is power—the power of productive assets—without a human constituency. It has interests to promote and defend, but they are the interests of a machine more than those of the people who guide, and profit from, its workings. The managers who sit astride the corporate complexes do indeed have power; but it is the power bestowed on them by the resources of the enterprises they tend. Executives come and go, and their terms of office in the top positions are surprisingly short. But the productive assets remain, continually developing new interests to be safeguarded and new demands to be fulfilled.

The increasing irrelevance of people may be illustrated by some references to the role of the stockholder. To begin with, approximately a third of all stock purchases are held for less than six months. Thus an appreciable fraction of those who are the legal owners of corporate America are not permanent constituents of the firms in which they happen to hold shares, but rather transient investors with no sustained interest in the fortunes of the companies bearing the names on their stock certificates.

Even more important, it is no longer true that the significant owners of corporation stock are human beings whose interests are represented in the exercise of corporate power. Stockholders are now more and more not people but institutions, many of them also corporate in structure. If it is proposed that a corporation "represents" the owners of its shares, it will soon emerge that many of these owners are insurance companies, universities, banks, foundations, pension funds and investment houses. These institutions do, of course, have interests. But, again, they are not the interests of people.

That power may be rendered legitimate by demonstrating its representative quality has always been one of the foundations of democratic theory. If power is exercised by—and within—government agencies and voluntary associations, it can usually be shown that officials are elected by constituents who have consented to the uses of authority and who cast equal votes in determining the personnel and often the policies that are to prevail.

Authority may be delegated rather than direct, and consent may be tacit rather than active, but the presumption remains that power in public and private life has a representative base.

Social Pluralism

Correlative to this is the familiar pluralist model: a society composed of a multiplicity of groups and a citizenry actively engaged in the associational life. Some measure of equilibrium among forces is assumed, and if there is conflict it results in compromises not overly oppressive to any of the participants. And the groups with which we are dealing are presumed to be voluntary associations consisting of individual citizens who join together to further their common interests. Well suited to this scheme are the myriad professional, occupational, religious and other groups which speak in their members' names. Were groups such as the American Medical Association, the United Automobile Workers, the National Association for the Advancement of Colored People and the American Legion the only participants in the struggle for political and economic preferment, then the sociology of democracy would continue as an effective theory. For in cases like these it may still be assumed, in spite of tendencies toward bureaucratization, that the power of these associations is simply an extension of the individual interest and wills of their constituent members.

But when General Electric, American Telephone and Telegraph, and Standard Oil of New Jersey enter the pluralist arena, we have elephants dancing among the chickens. For corporate institutions are not voluntary associations of individuals, but rather associations of assets, and no theory yet propounded has declared that machines are entitled to a voice in the democratic process.

The Investment Decision

The fulcrum of corporate power, in the final analysis, is the investment decision. And the uses of capital for investment purposes are decided by small handfuls of corporate managers. They decide how much is to be spent; what products are to be made; where they are to be manufactured; and who is to participate in the processes of production. A single corporatin can draw up an investment program calling for the expenditure of several billions of dollars on new plants and products. A decision such as this may well determine the quality of life for a substantial segment of society: men and materials will move across continents; old communities will decay and new ones will prosper; tastes and habits will alter; new skills will be demanded and the education of a nation will adjust itself accordingly; even government will fall into line, providing public services necessitated by corporate developments.

The American corporate system continues, in major outlines, to be capitalist in structure. Talk of a welfare state, of a mixed economy, even of a managerial revolution is of limited utility, for the fact remains that the major decisions in the economy are private. These decisions are made within closed circles, and public agencies may not intrude in any effective way.

Experience has thus far shown that public agencies set up to regulate private enterprise are soon brought to a close sympathy with the industries they were supposed to be regulating. This should occasion no great surprise. Corporations are powerful and they will use their resources to maintain a favorable climate for themselves. This is the politics of capitalism. It is not at all expressive of a conspiracy but rather a harmony of political forms and economic interests on a plane determined by the ongoing needs of corporate institutions.

No Middle Ground

Are there alternatives to corporate capitalism? Few voices are heard nowadays suggesting the public ownership of major industries, and it is just as well, for the odds are that nationalization would end in disillusionment. The problem is that there is no real middle ground. This was known to both Adam Smith and Karl Marx, but it is a fact hard to swallow in an age that seeks reason along the course of moderation.

Suppose that America followed the British pattern and nationalized a few industries such as railroads, electricity and coal mines. But instead of becoming agencies of the public interest, these industries would soon enter service as handmaidens of the private sector of the economy. For the preponderance of economic power would remain in corporate hands, and the effective efforts would be made to ensure that the industries in the public sector were suitably docile and did not serve as vehicles for serious planning that might jeopardize corporate interests.

On the other hand, there is the extreme proposal that the state nationalize all industry, thus once and for all destroying private economic power. This was and is the Marxian prescription, offered with the full understanding that the old order must be felled with one stroke if the new is to rise from its ashes. But the problems of irresponsibility in corporate America are minor compared with those of totalitarianism, and the Marxist alternative to capitalism is hardly one that those who have known a free society can be expected to embrace with enthusiasm.

Hence the frustrations that mark any search for a middle ground. We hear much of regulation, of intervention, of planning on the part of government. But, to take only the last, who are to be the planners? What is to be their source of power, as against their legal authority, and who will give force to their decisions? And is it possible to prevent corporate institutions from seducing, capturing and otherwise infiltrating those who are mandated to plan the economy in the public interest?

The Second America

The American people were not asked to consent to the rise of the corporation, yet they have had to adjust their lives to the imperatives of this pervasive institution. Not a few citizens have been recruited to corporate careers, and for them recent years have been a period of prosperity and progress. The new middle class has thus far found higher incomes and enhanced status, economic security and interesting work in the corporate world. To them society appears rational and they have few problems that can specifically be called "public" or "political." If this constituency of the corporation were able to embrace the whole of the working population, then despite the increased concentration of power it could at least be suggested that corporate America was bestowing its largesse upon all. But this is not the case.

There are losers as well as winners in the growth of corporate organization and technology. Not all who work for corporations have secure, let alone ascending, careers. The unskilled and the untrained continue to be hired at hourly wages, and then only for those hours when their services are required. Many of the unemployed are, indeed, corporate unemployed: they have been laid off from jobs they once had with corporations or have not been hired for jobs that corporate technology has been able to abolish.

By the same token trade unions are in decline, a development at least partly attributable to corporate technological innovations that have swelled the number of white-collar workers as a proportion of the employed population. Indirectly, and to some extent directly, corporate decisions have therefore both increased unemployment and diminished the role of unions. The latter consequence is a serious blow to the doctrine of social pluralism, for organized labor has been traditionally counted upon as a source of countervailing power against the strength of corporate management. Insofar as they are weakened, they deprive society of yet another check to the power of the corporation.

It may well be that two Americas are emerging, one a society protected by the corporate umbrella and the other a society whose members have failed to affiliate themselves with the dominant institutions.

What of this second America? In part it will consist of small businessmen and other independent spirits who manage to do well without corporate attachments. But, more importantly, it will be comprised of the unemployed, the ill-educated and the entire residue of human beings who are not needed by the corporate machine.

Little thought has been given to these people. How are they to earn their livings and support themselves? How will they maintain their self-esteem? If this pool grows to substantial proportions, if it finds political leadership, if it gives vent to its resentments and frustrations—then, and perhaps then only, will a force arise to challenge the great corporate institutions. For then power will meet power, the power of a mass movement confronting the power of the machine. The discard heap the machine itself created may arise to devour its progenitor.

This revolution—with or without violence, whether from the left or from the right—will only be averted if the corporation can make room in its evnirons for those who demand entry. Has it the jobs, the resources, the will and the imagination to achieve this? Thus far corporate America has escaped open attack because the new technology is not yet at the point where its victims outnumber its beneficiaries.

But technology advances according to rules of its own, and support for the machine will diminish as accelerated automation contracts the corporate constituency. In this event the second America, the society of losers, may grow in numbers and power with increasing rapidity. The outcome may not be a pleasant one.

BLUE-COLLAR DISCONTENT IN "LEISURE SOCIETY"

Nicholas Von Hoffman

WASHINGTON—The August issue of *Fortune* magazine reports that on a Friday last April, GM's Chevrolet assembly plant in Baltimore closed down in the middle of the 3:30-to-midnight shift. The reason was that more than 200 of 2,700 employes didn't show up for work. This wasn't a unique occurrence. In four years, absenteeism in the plant has gone from about 3 percent to 7.5 percent.

The *Fortune* article ("Blue Collar Blues on the Assembly Line" by Judson Gooding) depicts a condition of large and growing negligence among auto workers, particularly the young:

> The deep dislike of the job and the desire to escape become terribly clear twice each day when shifts end and the men stampede out of the plant gates to the parking lots, where they sometimes actually endanger lives in their desperate haste to be gone. . . . An average of 5 percent of GM's hourly workers are missing from work without explanation every day. . . . On some days, notably Mondays and Fridays, the figure goes as high as 10 percent. Tardiness has increased, making it even more difficult to start up the production line when a shift begins. . . .
>
> The quit rate at Ford last year was 25.2 percent. . . . Some assembly-line workers are so turned off, managers report with astonishment, they just walk away in mid-shift and don't even come back to get their pay for the time they have worked. . . . In some plants worker discontent has

> reached such a degree that there has been overt sabotage. Screws have been left in brake drums, tool handles welded into fender compartments to cause mysterious, unidentifiable and eternal rattles, paint scratched and upholstery cut.

A lot of quick, but not necessarily sound, conclusions can be jumped at here. It may be said that this is but another example of what the new Secretary of Labor, James D. Hodgson, calls a "crisis in craftsmanship," but people who believe that have never worked on an assembly line.

These are tough, monotonous jobs, that, even when done well, afford none of the satisfaction that arises from mastering a craft. Factory workers work for one thing—money; but, as *Fortune* remarks, these new, younger workers "have never experienced economic want or fear—or even insecurity. In the back of their minds is the knowledge that public policy will not allow them to starve, whatever may happen."

In their confidence they won't suffer economic privation, they resemble their collegiate counterparts. There are other similarities. If the contemporary college student arrives on campus with better training, the young factory worker starts his job with two more years of schooling than the older men.

"Along the main production line and in the subassembly areas," *Fortune* notes, along with others who have been looking into factories recently, "there are beards, and shades, long hair here, a peace medallion there, occasionally some beads—above all, young faces, curious eyes."

Working-class youth is moving in the direction of what was once the upper-middle-class-youth culture. This is true not only of dress and of pot smoking, which is endemic among young workers in some factories, but also in attitude toward the company.

Fortune's interviews with the young workers reveal them saying things about their employers that are remarkably similar to the complaints of college students: the job is boring, you are just a number, you feel tied down, you're in a jail cell—except they have more time off in prison. You can't do personal things, get a haircut, get your license plates or make a phone call.

Interestingly enough, the auto companies seem to be showing more sensitivity to the problems than many of the colleges and universities, which have simply concentrated on counterinsurgency techniques.

Ford shows a movie to new employes that honestly says that work is no fun: "It's a drag at first, but you realize you got to do it; so you do it." Some GM plants reward punctuality with initialed drinking glasses, but as one executive is quoted as saying, "If they won't come in for $32.40 a day, they won't come in for a monogrammed glass."

Another approach is to eliminate the dull jobs by automation, but there are limits to how far you can go with that; another tack is to eliminate all the intelligent workers, hiring only imbeciles who may not mind the repetitive boredom, but there still may be more jobs than there are morons to fill them.

The auto industry isn't the only one to experience a decrease in the reliability and quality of its labor force. Another notable example is the phone companies, but the complaint is really general, although the reasons for this I-don't-give-a-bleep attitude are easier to speculate on than prove.

Speculation suggests that many people aren't infinitely acquisitive, that they set a certain standard of comfort and enjoyment of material goods for themselves, and that, once they reach it, they stop working unless they're doing something they enjoy.

The people who complain most angrily about slipshod workmanship are often people who earn a living doing something they love. They don't have to put up with the boss, the foreman or the office manager—those names that stand for constraint, compulsion and social discipline in our society.

It's not just the hippie communards who have aspired to independence; it's every guy who has wanted to be his own boss. For a lot of people the difference between a good job and a rotten one that deprives a man of his pride is whether he has to punch a time card and take his coffee breaks at a prescribed time.

These feelings in relation to the boss and the company have always been with us. What's new is the heavily advertised idea of the "leisure society." Never has the distinction between work and play been clearer or more depressing. You can't turn on the television without getting your nose rubbed into it.

The *Fortune* article says that one of the biggest sources of discontent is enforced overtime. In the past workers wanted overtime. Now a growing number don't, either because their base pay is sufficient for the way they want to live or the extra money doesn't mean that much.

One of the reasons is high taxes. Why make the extra money if so much of it goes for people on welfare, especially when it is generally believed that the rich escape taxation just as they escape their military obligations?

THE POWER ELITE

C. Wright Mills

The structural trends of modern society and the manipulative character of its communication technique come to a point of coincidence in the mass society, which is largely a metropolitan society. The growth of the metropolis, segregating men and women into narrowed routines and environments, causes them to lose any firm sense of their integrity as a public. The members of publics in smaller communities know each other more or less fully, because they meet in the several aspects of the total life routine. The members of masses in a metropolitan society know one another only as fractions in specialized milieux: the man who fixes the car, the girl who serves your lunch, the saleslady, the women who take care of your child at school during the day. Prejudgment and stereotype flourish when people meet in such ways. The human reality of others does not, cannot, come through.

People, we know, tend to select those formal media which confirm what they already believe and enjoy. In a parallel way, they tend in the metropolitan segregation to come into live touch with those whose opinions are similar to theirs. Others they tend to treat unseriously. In the metropolitan society they develop, in their defense, a blasé manner that reaches deeper than a manner. They do not, accordingly, experience genuine clashes of viewpoint, genuine issues. And when they do, they tend to consider it mere rudeness.

Sunk in their routines, they do not transcend, even by discussion, much less by action, their more or less narrow lives. They do not gain a view of the structure of their society and of their role as a public within it. The city is a structure composed of such little environments, and the people in them tend to be detached from one another. The "stimulating variety" of the city does not stimulate the men and women of "the bedroom belt," the one-class suburbs, who can go through life knowing only their own kind. If they do reach for one another, they do so only through stereotypes and prejudiced images of the creatures of other milieux. Each is trapped by his confining circle; each is cut off from easily identifiable groups. It is for people in such narrow milieux that the mass media can create a pseudo-world beyond, and a pseudo-world within themselves as well.

Publics live in milieux but they can transcend them—individually by intellectual effort; socially by public action. By reflection and debate and by organized action, a community of publics comes to feel itself and comes in fact to be active at points of structural relevance.

But members of a mass exist in milieux and cannot get out of them, either by mind or by activity, except—in the extreme case—under "the organized spontaneity" of the bureaucrat on a motorcycle. We have not yet reached the extreme case, but observing metropolitan man in the American mass we can surely see the psychological preparations for it.

We may think of it in this way: When a handful of men do not have jobs, and do not seek work, we look for the causes in their immediate situation and character. But when twelve million men are unemployed, then we cannot believe that all of them suddenly "got lazy" and turned out to be "no good." Economists call this "structural unemployment"—meaning, for one thing, that the men involved cannot themselves control their job chances.

Structural unemployment does not originate in one factory or in one town, nor is it due to anything that one factory or one town does or fails to do. Moreover, there is little or nothing that one ordinary man in one factory in one town can do about it when it sweeps over his personal milieu.

Now, this distinction, between social structure and personal milieu, is one of the most important available in the sociological studies. It offers us a ready understanding of the position of "the public" in America today. In every major area of life, the loss of a sense of structure and the submergence into powerless milieux is the cardinal fact. In the military it is most obvious, for here the roles men play are strictly confining; only the command posts at the top afford a view of the structure of the whole, and moreover, this view is a closely guarded official secret. In the division of labor too, the jobs men enact in the economic hierarchies are also more or less narrow milieux and the positions from which a view of the production process as a whole can be had are centralized, as men are alienated not only from the product and the tools of their labor, but from any understanding of the structure and the processes of production. In the political order, in the fragmentation of the lower and in the distracting proliferation of the middle-level organization, men cannot see the whole, cannot see the top, and cannot state the issues that will in fact determine the whole structure in which they live and their place within it.

This loss of any structural view or position is the decisive meaning of the lament over the loss of community. In the great city, the division of milieux and of segregating routines reaches the point of closest contact with the individual and the family, for, although the city is not the unit of prime decision, even the city cannot be seen as a total structure by most of its citizens.

On the one hand, there is the increased scale and centralization of the structure of decision; and, on the other, the increasingly narrow sorting out of men into milieux. From both sides, there is the increased dependence upon the formal media of communication, including those of education itself. But the man in the mass does not gain a transcending view from these media; instead he gets his experience stereotyped, and then he gets sunk further by that experience. He cannot detach himself in order to observe, much less to evaluate, what he is experiencing, much less what he is not experiencing. Rather than that internal discussion we call reflection, he is accompanied through his life-experience with a sort of unconscious, echoing monologue. He has no projects of his own: he fulfills the routines that exist. He does not transcend whatever he is at any moment, because he does not, he cannot, transcend his daily milieux. He is not truly aware of his own daily experience and of its actual standards: he drifts, he fulfills habits, his behavior a result of a planless mixture of the confused standards and the uncriticized expectations that he has taken over from others whom he no longer really knows or trusts, if indeed he ever really did.

He takes things for granted, he makes the best of them, he tries to look ahead—a year or two perhaps, or even longer if he has children or a mortgage—but he does not seriously ask, What do I want? How can I get it? A vague optimism suffuses and sustains him, broken occasionally by little miseries and disappointments that are soon buried. He is smug, from the standpoint of those who think something might be the matter with the mass style of life in the metropolitan frenzy where self-making is an externally busy branch of industry. By what standards does he judge himself and his efforts? What is really important to him? Where are the models of excellence for this man?

He loses his independence, and more importantly, he loses the desire to be independent: in fact, he does not have hold of the idea of being an independent individual with his own mind and his own worked-out way of life. It is not that he likes or does not like this life; it is that the question does not come up sharp and clear so he is not bitter and he is not sweet about conditions and events. He thinks he wants merely to get his share of what is around with as little trouble as he can and with as much fun as possible.

Such order and movement as his life possesses is in conformity with external routines; otherwise his day-to-day experience is a vague chaos—although he often does not know it because, strictly speaking, he does not truly possess or observe his own experience. He does not formulate his desires; they are insinuated into him. And, in the mass, he loses the self-confidence of the human being—if indeed he has ever had it. For life in a society of masses implants insecurity and furthers impotence; it makes men uneasy and vaguely anxious; it isolates the individual from the solid group; it destroys firm group standards. Acting without goals, the man in the mass just feels pointless.

THE NEW FORMS OF CONTROL

Herbert Marcuse

A comfortable, smooth, reasonable, democratic unfreedom prevails in advanced industrial civilization, a token of technical progress. Indeed, what could be more rational than the suppression of individuality in the mechanization of socially necessary but painful performances; the concentration of individual enterprises in more effective, more productive corporations; the regulation of free competition among unequally equipped economic subjects; the curtailment of prerogatives and national sovereignties which impede the

From *One-Dimensional Man* by Herbert Marcuse, pp. 1–18 (excerpts). (Emphases are those of the editors.)

international organization of resources. That this technological order also involves a political and intellectual coordination may be a regrettable and yet promising development.

The rights and liberties which were such vital factors in the origins and earlier stages of industrial society yield to a higher stage of this society: they are losing their traditional rationale and content. Freedom of thought, speech, and conscience were—just as free enterprise, which they served to promote and protect—essentially *critical* ideas, designed to replace an obsolescent material and intellectual culture by a more productive and rational one. Once institutionalized, these rights and liberties shared the fate of the society of which they had become an integral part. The achievement cancels the premises.

To the degree to which freedom from want, the concrete substance of all freedom, is becoming a real possibility, the liberties which pertain to a state of lower productivity are losing their former content. Independence of thought, autonomy, and the right to political opposition are being deprived of their basic critical function in a society which seems increasingly capable of satisfying the needs of the individuals through the way in which it is organized. Such a society may justly demand acceptance of its principles and institutions, and reduce the opposition to the discussion and promotion of alternative policies *within* the status quo. In this respect, it seems to make little difference whether the increasing satisfaction of needs is accomplished by an authoritarian or a non-authoritarian system. Under the conditions of a rising standard of living, non-conformity with the system itself appears to be socially useless, and the more so when it entails tangible economic and political disadvantages and threatens the smooth operation of the whole. Indeed, at least in so far as the necessities of life are involved, there seems to be no reason why the production and distribution of goods and services should proceed through the competitive concurrence of individual liberties.

Freedom of enterprise was from the beginning not altogether a blessing. As the liberty to work or to starve, it spelled toil, insecurity, and fear for the vast majority of the population. If the individual were no longer compelled to prove himself on the market, as a free economic subject, the disappearance of this kind of freedom would be one of the greatest achievements of civilization. The technological processes of mechanization and standardization might release individual energy into a yet uncharted realm of freedom beyond necessity. The very structure of human existence would be altered; the individual would be liberated from the work world's imposing upon him alien needs and alien possibilities. The individual would be free to exert autonomy over a life that would be his own. If the productive apparatus could be organized and directed toward the satisfaction of the vital needs, its control might well be centralized; such control would not prevent individual autonomy, but render it possible.

This is a goal within the capabilities of advanced industrial civilization, the "end" of technological rationality. In actual fact, however, the contrary trend operates: the apparatus imposes its economic and political requirements for defense and expansion on labor time and free time, on the material and intellectual culture. By virtue of the way it has organized its technological base, **contemporary industrial society tends to be totalitarian.** For "totalitarian" is not only a terroristic political coordination of society, but also a non-terroristic economic-technical coordination which operates through the manipulation of needs by vested interests. It thus precludes the emergence of an effective opposition against the whole. Not only a specific form of government or party rule makes for totalitarianism, but also a specific system of production and distribution which may well be compatible with a "pluralism" of parties, newspapers, "countervailing powers," etc.

Today political power asserts itself through its power over the machine process and over the technical organization of the apparatus. The government of advanced and advancing industrial societies can maintain and secure itself only when it succeeds in mobilizing, organizing, and exploiting the technical, scientific, and mechanical productivity available to industrial civilization. And this productivity mobilizes society as a whole, above and beyond any particular individual or group interests. The brute fact that the machine's physical (only physical?) power surpasses that of the individual, and of any particular group of individuals, makes the machine the most effective political instrument in any society whose basic organization is that of the machine process. But the political trend may be reversed; essentially **the power of the machine is only the stored-up and projected power of man.** To the extent to which the work world is conceived of as a machine and mechanized accordingly, it becomes **the *potential* basis of a new freedom for man.**

Contemporary industrial civilization demonstrates that it has reached the stage at which "the free society" can no longer be adequately defined in the traditional terms of economic, political, and intellectual liberties, not because these liberties have become insignificant, but because they are too significant to be confined within the traditional forms. **New modes of realization** are needed, corresponding to the new capabilities of society.

Such new modes can be indicated only in negative terms because they would amount to the negation of the prevailing modes. Thus economic freedom would mean **freedom *from* the economy**—from being controlled by economic forces and relationships; freedom from the daily struggle for existence, from earning a living. Political freedom would mean **liberation of the individuals *from* politics over which they have no effective control.** Similarly, intellectual freedom would mean the restoration of individual thought now absorbed by mass communication and indoctrination, **abolition of "public opinion"** together with its makers. The unrealistic sound of these propositions is indicative, not of their utopian character, but of the strength of the forces which prevent their realization. The most effective and enduring form of warfare against liberation is the implanting of material and intellectual needs that perpetuate obsolete forms of the struggle for existence.

The intensity, the satisfaction and even the character of human needs, beyond the biological level, have always been preconditioned. Whether or not the possibility of doing or leaving, enjoying or destroying, possessing or rejecting something is seized as a *need* depends on whether or not it can be seen as desirable and necessary for the prevailing societal institutions and interests. In this sense, human needs are historical needs and, to the extent to which the society demands the repressive development of the individual, his needs themselves and their claim for satisfaction are subject to overriding critical standards.

We may distinguish both true and **false needs.** "False" are those which are superimposed upon the individual by particular social interests in his repression: the needs which perpetuate toil, aggressiveness, misery, and injustice. Their satisfaction might be most gratifying to the individual, but this happiness is not a condition which has to be maintained and protected if it serves to arrest the development of the ability (his own and others) to recognize the disease of the whole and grasp the chances of curing the disease. The result then is euphoria in unhappiness. Most of the prevailing needs to relax, to have fun, to behave and consume in accordance with the advertisements, to love and hate what others love and hate, belong to this category of false needs.

Such needs have a societal content and function which are determined by external powers over which the individual has no control; the development and satisfaction of these needs is heteronomous. No matter how much such needs may have become the individual's own, reproduced and fortified by the conditions of his existence; no matter how much he identifies himself with them and finds himself in their satisfaction, they continue to be what they were from the beginning—products of a society whose dominant interest demands repression.

The prevalence of **respressive needs** is an accomplished fact, accepted in ignorance and defeat, but a fact that must be undone in the interest of the happy individual as well as all those whose misery is the price of his satisfaction. The only needs that have an unqualified claim for satisfaction are the vital ones—nourishment, clothing, lodging at the attainable level of culture. The satisfaction of these needs is the prerequisite for the realization of *all* needs, of the unsublimated as well as the sublimated ones.

For any consciousness and conscience, for any experience which does not accept the prevailing societal interest as the supreme law of thought and behavior, the established universe of needs and satisfactions is **a fact to be questioned**—questioned in terms of truth and falsehood. These terms are historical throughout, and their objectivity is historical. The judgment of needs and their satisfaction, under the given conditions, involves standards of *priority*—standards which refer to the optimal development of the individual, of all individuals, under the optimal utilization of the material and intellectual resources available to man. The resources are calculable. "Truth" and "falsehood" of needs designate objective conditions to the extent to which the universal satisfaction of vital needs and, beyond it, the progressive alleviation of toil and poverty, are universally valid standards. But as historical standards, they do not only vary according to area and stage of development, they also can be defined only in (greater or lesser) *contradiction* to the prevailing ones. What tribunal can possibly claim the authority of decision?

In the last analysis, the question of what are true and false needs must be answered by the individuals themselves, but only in the last analysis; that is, if and when they are free to give their own answer. As long as they are kept incapable of being autonomous, as long as they are indoctrinated and manipulated (down to their very instincts), their answer to this question cannot be taken as their own. By the same token, however, no tribunal can justly arrogate to itself the right to decide which needs should be developed and satisfied. Any such tribunal is reprehensible, although our revulsion does not do away with the question: how can the people who have been the object of effective and productive domination by themselves create the conditions of freedom?

The more rational, productive, technical, and total the repressive administration of society becomes, the more unimaginable the means and ways by which the administered individuals might break their servitude and seize their own liberation. To be sure, to impose Reason upon an entire society is a paradoxical and scandalous idea—although one might dispute the righteousness of a society which ridicules this idea while making its own population into objects of total administration. **All liberation depends on the consciousness of servitude,** and the emergence of this consciousness is always hampered by the predominance of needs and satisfactions which, to a great extent, have become the individual's own. The process always replaces one system of preconditioning by another; the optimal goal is the replacement of false needs by true ones, **the abandonment of repressive satisfaction.**

The distinguishing feature of advanced industrial society is its effective suffocation of those needs which demand liberation—**liberation also from that which is tolerable and rewarding and comfortable**—while it sustains and absolves the destructive power and repressive function of the affluent society. Here, the social controls exact the overwhelming need for the production and consumption of waste; the need for stupefying work where it is no longer a real necessity; the need for modes of relaxation which soothe and prolong this stupefication; the need for maintaining such deceptive liberties as free competition at administered prices, a free press which censors itself, free choice between brands and gadgets.

Under the rule of a repressive whole, liberty can be made into a powerful instrument of domination. The range of choice open to the individual is not the decisive factor in determining the degree of human freedom, but *what* can be chosen and what *is* chosen by the individual. The criterion for free choice can never be an absolute one, but neither is it entirely relative. **Free election of masters does not abolish the masters or the slaves.** Free choice among a wide variety of goods and services does not signify freedom if these goods and services sustain social controls over a life of toil and fear—that is, if they sustain alienation. And the spontaneous reproduction of superimposed needs by the individual does not establish autonomy; it only testifies to the efficacy of the controls.

Our insistence on the depth and efficacy of these controls is open to the objection that we overrate greatly the indoctrinating power of the "media," and that by themselves the people would feel and satisfy the needs which are now imposed upon them. The objection misses the point. The preconditioning does not start with the mass production of radio and television and with the centralization of their control. The people enter this stage as preconditioned receptacles of long standing; the decisive difference is in the flattening out of the contrast (or conflict) between the given and the possible, between the satisfied and the unsatisfied needs. Here, the so-called equalization of class distinctions reveals its ideological function. If the worker and his boss enjoy the same television program and visit the same resort places, if the typist is as attractively made up as the daughter of her employer, if the Negro owns a Cadillac, if they all read the same newspaper, then this assimilation indicates not the disappearance of classes, but the extent to which the needs and satisfactions that serve the preservation of the Establishment are shared by the underlying population.

Indeed, in the most highly developed areas of contemporary society, the transplantation of social into individual needs is so effective that the difference between them seems to be purely theoretical. Can one really distinguish between the mass media as instruments of information and entertainment, and as agents of manipulation and indoctrination? Between the automobile as nuisance and as convenience? Between the horrors and the comforts of functional architecture? Between the work for national defense and the work for corporate gain? Between the private pleasure and the commercial and political utility involved in increasing the birth rate?

We are again confronted with one of the most vexing aspects of advanced industrial civilization: the rational character of its irrationality. Its productivity and efficiency, its capacity to increase and spread comforts, to turn waste into need, and destruction into construction, the extent to which this civilization transforms the object world into an extension of man's mind and body makes the very notion of alienation questionable. The people recognize themselves in their commodities; they find their soul in their automobile, hi-fi set, split-level home, kitchen equipment. The very mechanism which ties the individual to his society has changed, and social control is anchored in the new needs which it has produced.

The prevailing forms of social control are technological in a new sense. To be sure, the technical structure and efficacy of the productive and destructive apparatus has been a major instrumentality for subjecting the population to the established social division of labor throughout the modern period. Moreover, such integration has always been accompanied by more obvious forms of compulsion: loss of livelihood, the administration of justice, the police, the armed forces. It still is. But in the contemporary period, the technological controls appear to be the very embodiment of Reason for the benefit of all social groups and interests—to such an extent that all contradiction seems irrational and all counteraction impossible.

No wonder then that, in the most advanced areas of this civilization, the social controls have been introjected to the point where even individual protest is affected at its roots. The intellectual and emotional refusal "to go along" appears neurotic and impotent. This is the socio-psychological aspect of the political event that marks the contemporary period: the passing of the historical forces which, at the preceding stage of industrial society, seemed to represent the possibility of new forms of existence.

But the term "introjection" perhaps no longer describes the way in which the individual by himself reproduces and perpetuates the external controls exercised by his society. Introjection suggests a variety of relatively spontaneous processes by which a Self (Ego) transposes the "outer" into the "inner." Thus introjection implies the existence of an inner dimension distinguished from and even antagonistic to the external exigencies—an individual consciousness and an individual unconscious *apart from* public opinion and behavior.[1] The idea of "inner freedom" here has its reality: it designates the private space in which man may become and remain "himself."

Today this private space has been invaded and whittled down by technological reality. Mass production and mass distribution claim the *entire* individual, and industrial psychology has long since ceased to be confined to the factory. The manifold processes of introjection seem to be ossified in almost mechanical reactions. The result is, not adjustment but *mimesis:* an immediate identification of the individual with *his* society and, through it, with the society as a whole.

This immediate, automatic identification (which may have been characteristic of primitive forms of association) reappears in high industrial civilization; its new "immediacy," however, is the product of a sophisticated, scientific management and organization. In this process, the "inner" dimen-

[1] The change in the function of the family here plays a decisive role: its "socializing" functions are increasingly taken over by outside groups and media. See my *Eros and Civilization* (Boston: Beacon Press, 1955), p. 96 ff.

sion of the mind in which opposition to the status quo can take root is whittled down. The loss of this dimension, in which the power of negative thinking—the critical power of Reason—is at home, is the ideological counterpart to the very material process in which advanced industrial society silences and reconciles the opposition. The impact of progress turns Reason into submission to the facts of life, and to the dynamic capability of producing more and bigger facts of the same sort of life. The efficiency of the system blunts the individuals' recognition that it contains no facts which do not communicate the repressive power of the whole. If the individuals find themselves in the things which shape their life, they do so, not by giving, but by accepting the law of things—not the law of physics but the law of their society.

I have just suggested that the concept of alienation seems to become questionable when the individuals identify themselves with the existence which is imposed upon them and have in it their own development and satisfaction. This identification is not illusion but reality. However, the reality constitutes a more progressive stage of alienation. The latter has become entirely objective; the subject which is alienated is swallowed up by its alienated existence. There is only one dimension, and it is everywhere and in all forms. The achievements of progress defy ideological indictment as well as justification; before their tribunal, the "false consciousness" of their rationality becomes the true consciousness.

This absorption of ideology into reality does not, however, signify the "end of ideology." On the contrary, in a specific sense advanced industrial culture is *more* ideological than its predecessor, inasmuch as today the ideology is in the process of production itself.[2] In a provocative form, this proposition reveals the political aspects of the prevailing technological rationality. The productive apparatus and the goods and services which it produces "sell" or impose the social system as a whole. The means of mass transportation and communication, the commodities of lodging, food, and clothing, the irresistible output of the entertainment and information industry carry with them prescribed attitudes and habits, certain intellectual and emotional reactions which bind the consumers more or less pleasantly to the producers and, through the latter, to the whole. The products indoctrinate and manipulate; they promote a false consciousness which is immune against its falsehood. And as these beneficial products become available to more individuals in more social classes, the indoctrination they carry ceases to be publicity; it becomes a way of life. It is a good way of life—much better than before—and as a good way of life, it militates against qualitative change. Thus emerges a pattern of *one-dimensional thought and behavior* in which ideas, aspirations, and objectives that, by their content, transcend the established universe of discourse and action are either repelled or reduced to terms of this uni-

[2] Theodor W. Adorno, *Prismen. Kulturkritik und Gesellschaft.* (Frankfurt: Suhrkamp, 1955), p. 24 f.

verse. They are redefined by the rationality of the given system and of its quantitative extension. . . .

One-dimensional thought is systematically promoted by the makers of politics and their purveyors of mass information. Their universe of discourse is populated by self-validating hypotheses which, incessantly and monopolistically repeated, become hypnotic definitions or dictations. For example, "free" are the institutions which operate (and are operated on) in the countries of the Free World; other transcending modes of freedom are by definition either anarchism, communism, or propaganda. "Socialistic" are all encroachments on private enterprises not undertaken by private enterprise itself (or by government contracts), such as universal and comprehensive health insurance, or the protection of nature from all too sweeping commercialization, or the establishment of public services which may hurt private profit. This **totalitarian logic of accomplished facts** has its Eastern counterpart. There, freedom is the way of life instituted by a communist regime, and all other transcending modes of freedom are either capitalistic, or revisionist, or leftist sectarianism. In both camps, non-operational ideas are non-behavioral and subversive. The movement of thought is stopped at barriers which appear as the limits of Reason itself.

Such limitation of thought is certainly not new. Ascending modern rationalism, in its speculative as well as empirical form, shows a striking contrast between extreme critical radicalism in scientific and philosophic method on the one hand, and an uncritical quietism in the attitude toward established and functioning social institutions. Thus Descartes' *ego cogitans* was to leave the "great public bodies" untouched, and Hobbes held that "the present ought always to be preferred, maintained, and accounted best." Kant agreed with Locke in justifying revolution *if and when* it has succeeded in organizing the whole and in preventing subversion.

However, these accommodating concepts of Reason were always contradicted by the evident misery and injustice of the "great public bodies" and the effective, more or less conscious rebellion against them. Societal conditions existed which provoked and permitted real dissociation from the established state of affairs; a private as well as political dimension was present in which dissociation could develop into effective opposition, testing its strength and the validity of its objectives.

With the gradual closing of this dimension by the society, the self-limitation of thought assumes a larger significance. The interrelation between scientific-philosophical and societal processes, between theoretical and practical Reason, asserts itself "behind the back" of the scientists and philosophers. The society bars a whole type of oppositional operations and behavior; consequently, the concepts pertaining to them are rendered illusory or meaningless. Historical transcendence appears as metaphysical transcendence, not acceptable to science and scientific thought. The operational and behavioral point of view, practiced as a "habit of thought" at large, becomes the view of the established universe of discourse and action, needs and aspirations. The "cunning of Reason" works, as it so often did, in the interest of the powers that be. The insistence on operational and behavioral concepts turns against the efforts to free thought and behavior *from* the given reality and *for* the suppressed alternatives. Theoretical and practical Reason, academic and social behaviorism meet on common ground: that of **an advanced society which makes scientific and technical progress into an instrument of domination.**

"Progress" is not a neutral term; it moves toward specific ends, and these ends are defined by the possibilities of ameliorating the human condition. Advanced industrial society is approaching the stage where continued progress would demand the radical subversion of the prevailing direction and organization of progress. This stage would be reached when material production (including the necessary services) becomes automated to the extent that all vital needs can be satisfied while necessary labor time is reduced to marginal time. From this point on, technical progress would transcend the realm of necessity, where it served as the instrument of domination and exploitation which thereby limited its rationality; technology would become subject to **the free play of faculties** in the struggle for the pacification of nature and of society.

Such a state is envisioned in Marx's notion of **the "abolition of labor."** The term "pacification of existence" seems better suited to designate the historical alternative of a world which—through an international conflict which transforms and suspends the contradictions within the established societies—advances on the brink of a global war. "Pacification of existence" means the development of man's struggle with man and with nature, under conditions where the competing needs, desires, and aspirations are no longer organized by vested interests in domination and scarcity—an organization which perpetuates the destructive forms of this struggle.

Today's fight against this historical alternative finds a firm mass basis in the underlying population, and finds its ideology in the rigid orientation of thought and behavior to the given universe of facts. Validated by the accomplishments of science and technology, justified by its growing productivity, the status quo defies all transcendence. Faced with the possibility of pacification on the grounds of its technical and intellectual achievements, the mature industrial society closes itself against this alternative. Operationalism, in theory and practice, becomes the theory and practice of *containment.* Underneath its obvious dynamics, this society is a thoroughly static system of life: self-propelling in its **oppressive productivity** and in its beneficial coordination. Containing of technical progress goes hand in hand with its growth in the established direction. In spite of the political fetters imposed by the status quo, the more technology appears capable of creating the conditions for pacification, the more are the minds and bodies of man organized against this alternative.

The most advanced areas of industrial society exhibit throughout these two features: a trend toward consummation of technological rationality, and intensive efforts to contain this trend within the established institutions. Here is **the internal contradiction of this civilization:** the irrational element in its rationality. It is the token of its achievements. The industrial society which makes technology and science its own is organized for the ever-more-effective domination of man and nature, for the ever-more-effective utilization of its resources. It becomes irrational when the success of these efforts opens new dimensions of human realization. Organization for peace is different from organization for war; the institutions which served the struggle for existence cannot serve the pacification of existence. **Life as an end is qualitatively different from life as a means.**

Such **a qualitatively new mode of existence** can never be envisaged as the mere by-product of economic and political changes, as the more or less spontaneous effect of the new institutions which constitute the necessary prerequisite. Qualitative change also involves a change in the *technical* basis on which this society rests—one which sustains the economic and political institutions through which the "second nature" of man as an aggressive object of administration is stabilized. **The techniques of industrialization are political techniques;** as such, they prejudge the possibilities of Reason and Freedom.

To be sure, labor must precede the reduction of labor, and industrialization must precede the development of human needs and satisfactions. But as all freedom depends on the conquest of alien necessity, the realization of freedom depends on the *techniques* of this conquest. The highest productivity of labor can be used for the perpetuation of labor, and the most efficient industrialization can serve the restriction and manipulation of needs.

When this point is reached, domination—in the guise of affluence and liberty—extends to all spheres of private and public existence, integrates all authentic opposition, absorbs all alternatives. Technological rationality reveals its political character as it becomes the great vehicle of better domination, creating a truly totalitarian universe in which society and nature, mind and body are kept in a state of permanent mobilization for the defense of this universe.

14 Breaking the pattern of submission

UNITED STATES DECLARATION OF INDEPENDENCE

In Congress, July 4, 1776
The unanimous Declaration of the thirteen United States of America

When in the course of human events, it becomes necessary for one people to dissolve the political bands which have connected them with another, and to assume among the powers of the earth, the separate and equal station to which the Laws of Nature and of Nature's God entitle them, a decent respect to the opinions of mankind requires that they should declare the causes which impel them to the separation.

We hold these truths to be self-evident, that all men are created equal, that they are endowed by their Creator with certain unalienable rights, that among these are life, liberty and the pursuit of happiness. That to secure these rights, governments are instituted among men, deriving their just powers from the consent of the governed. That whenever any form of government becomes destructive of these ends, it is the right of the people to alter or to abolish it, and to institute new government, laying its foundation on such principles and organizing its powers in such form, as to them shall seem most likely to effect their safety and happiness. Prudence, indeed, will dictate that governments long established should not be changed for light and transient causes; and accordingly all experience hath shown, that mankind are more disposed to suffer, while evils are sufferable, than to right themselves by abolishing the forms to which they are accustomed. But when a long train of abuses and usurpations, pursuing invariably the same object evinces a design to reduce them under absolute despotism, it is their right, it is their duty, to throw off such government, and to provide new guards for their future security. Such has been the patient sufferance of these Colonies; and such is now the necessity which constrains them to alter their former systems of government. The history of the present King of Great Britain is a history of repeated injuries and usurpations, all having in direct object the establishment of an absolute tyranny over these States. To prove this, let facts be submitted to a candid world.

He has refused his assent to laws, the most wholesome and necessary for the public good.

He has forbidden his Governors to pass laws of immediate and pressing importance, unless suspended in their operation till his assent should be obtained; and when so suspended, he has utterly neglected to attend to them.

He has refused to pass other laws for the accommodation of large districts of people, unless those people would relinquish the right of representation in the Legislature, a right inestimable to them and formidable to tyrants only.

He has called together legislative bodies at places unusual, uncomfortable, and distant from the depository of their public records, for the sole purpose of fatiguing them into compliance with his measures.

He has dissolved representative houses repeatedly, for opposing with manly firmness his invasions on the rights of the people.

He has refused for a long time, after such dissolutions, to cause others to be elected; whereby the legislative powers, incapable of annihilation, have returned to the people at large for their exercise; the State remaining in the meantime exposed to all the dangers of invasion from without and convulsions within.

He has endeavoured to prevent the population of these states; for that purpose obstructing the laws of naturalization of foreigners; refusing to pass others to encourage their migration hither, and raising the conditions of new appropriations of lands.

He has obstructed the administration of justice, by refusing his assent to laws for establishing judiciary powers.

He has made judges dependent on his will alone, for the tenure of their offices, and the amount and payment of their salaries.

He has erected a multitude of new offices, and sent hither swarms of officers to harass our people, and eat out their substance.

He has kept among us, in times of peace, standing armies without the consent of our legislatures.

He has affected to render the military independent of and superior to the civil power.

He has combined with others to subject us to a jurisdiction foreign to our constitution, and unacknowledged by our laws; giving his assent to their acts of pretended legislation:

For quartering large bodies of armed troops among us:

For protecting them, by a mock trial, from punishment for any murders which they should commit on the inhabitants of these States:

For cutting off our trade with all parts of the world:

For imposing taxes on us without our consent:

For depriving us in many cases, of the benefits of trial by jury:

For transporting us beyond seas to be tried for pretended offences:

For abolishing the free system of English laws in a neighbouring Province, establishing therein an arbitrary government, and enlarging its boundaries so as to render it at once an example and fit instrument for introducing the same absolute rule into these Colonies:

For taking away our Charters, abolishing our most valuable laws, and altering fundamentally the forms of our governments:

For suspending our own Legislatures, and declaring themselves invested with power to legislate for us in all cases whatsoever.

He has abdicated government here, by declaring us out of his protection and waging war against us.

He has plundered our seas, ravaged our coasts, burnt our towns, and destroyed the lives of our people.

He is at this time transporting large armies of foreign mercenaries to complete the works of death, desolation and tyranny, already begun with circumstances of cruelty and perfidy scarcely paralleled in the most barbarous ages, and totally unworthy the head of a civilized nation.

He has constrained our fellow citizens taken captive on the high seas to bear arms against their country, to become the executioners of their friends and brethren, or to fall themselves by their hands.

He has excited domestic insurrections amongst us, and has endeavoured to bring on the inhabitants of our frontiers, the merciless Indian savages, whose known rule of warfare, is an undistinguished destruction of all ages, sexes, and conditions.

In every stage of these oppressions we have petitioned for redress in the most humble terms: our repeated petitions have been answered only by repeated injury. A prince whose character is thus marked by every act which may define a tyrant is unfit to be the ruler of a free people.

Nor have we been wanting in attention to our British brethren. We have warned them from time to time of attempts by their legislature to extend an unwarrantable jurisdiction over us. We have reminded them of the circumstances of our emigration and settlement here. We have appealed to their native justice and magnanimity, and we have conjured them by the ties of our common kindred to disavow these usurpations, which would inevitably interrupt our connections and correspondence. They too have been deaf to the voice of justice and of consanguinity. We must, therefore, acquiesce in the necessity, which denounces our separation, and hold them, as we hold the rest of mankind, enemies in war, in peace friends.

We, therefore, the Representatives of the United States of America, in General Congress assembled, appealing to the Supreme Judge of the world for the rectitude of our intentions, do, in the name, and by authority of the good people of these Colonies, solemnly publish and declare, That these United Colonies are, and of right ought to be Free and Independent States;

that they are absolved from all allegiance to the British Crown, and that all political connection between them and the State of Great Britain, is and ought to be totally dissolved; and that as Free and Independent States, they have full power to levy war, conclude peace, contract alliances, establish commerce, and to do all other acts and things which Independent States may of right do. And for the support of this declaration, with a firm reliance on the protection of Divine Providence, we mutually pledge to each other our lives, our fortunes, and our sacred honor.

I am charged with inciting black people to commit an offense by way of protest against the law, a law which neither I nor any of my people had any say in preparing. . . . I consider myself neither morally nor legally bound to obey laws made by a body in which I have no representation. That the will of the people is the basis of the authority of government is a principle universally acknowledged as sacred throughout the civilized world and constitutes the basic foundation of this country. It should be equally understandable that we, as black people, should adopt the attitude that we are neither morally nor legally bound to obey laws which were not made with our consent and which seek to oppress us.

H. Rapp Brown, speech delivered in Lincoln Park, Chicago, August 1968.

STRIDE TOWARD FREEDOM

Martin Luther King, Jr.

Since the philosophy of nonviolence played such a positive role in the Montgomery Movement, it may be wise to turn to a brief discussion of some basic aspects of this philosophy.

First, it must be emphasized that nonviolent resistance is not a method for cowards; it does resist. If one uses this method because he is afraid or merely because he lacks the instruments of violence, he is not truly nonviolent. This is why Gandhi often said that if cowardice is the only alternative to violence, it is better to fight. He made this statement conscious of the fact that there is always another alternative: no individual or group need submit to any wrong, nor need they use violence to right the wrong; there is the way of nonviolence resistance. This is ultimately the way of the strong man. It is not a method of stagnant passivity. The phrase "passive resistance" often gives the false impression that this is a sort of "do-nothing method" in which the resister quietly and passively accepts evil. But nothing is further from the truth. For while the nonviolent resister is passive in the sense that he is not physically aggressive toward his opponent, his mind and emotions are always active, constantly seeking to persuade his opponent that he is wrong. The method is passive physically, but strongly active spiritually. It is not passive nonresistance to evil, it is active nonviolent resistance to evil.

A second basic fact that characterizes nonviolence is that it does not seek to defeat or humiliate the opponent, but to win his friendship and understanding. The nonviolent resister must often express his protest through noncooperation or boycotts, but he realizes that these are not ends themselves; they are merely means to awaken a sense of moral shame in the opponent. The end is redemption and reconciliation. The aftermath of nonviolence is the creation of the beloved community, while the aftermath of violence is tragic bitterness.

A third characteristic of this method is that the attack is directed against forces of evil rather than against persons who happen to be doing the evil. It is evil that the nonviolent resister seeks to defeat, not the persons victimized by evil. If he is opposing racial injustice, the nonviolent resister has the vision to see that the basic tension is not between races. As I like to say to the people in Montgomery: "The tension in this city is not between white people and Negro people. The tension is, at bottom, between justice and injustice, between the forces of light and the forces of darkness. And if there is a victory, it will be a victory not merely for fifty thousand Negroes, but a victory for justice and the forces of light. We are out to defeat injustice and not white persons who may be unjust."

A fourth point that characterizes nonviolent resistance is a willingness to accept suffering without retaliation, to accept blows from the opponent without striking back. "Rivers of blood may have to flow before we gain our freedom, but it must be our blood," Gandhi said to his countrymen. The nonviolent resister is willing to accept violence if necessary, but never to inflict it. He does not seek to dodge jail. If going to jail is necessary, he enters it "as a bridegroom enters the bride's chamber."

One may well ask: "What is the nonviolent resister's justification for this ordeal to which he invites men, for this mass political application of the ancient doctrine of turning the other cheek?" The answer is found in the realization that unearned suffering is redemptive. Suffering, the nonviolent resister realizes, has tremendous educational and transforming possibilities. "Things of fundamental importance to people are not secured by reason alone, but have to be purchased with their suffering," said Gandhi. He continues: "Suffering is infinitely more powerful than the law of the jungle for converting the opponent and opening his ears which are otherwise shut to the voice of reason."

A fifth point concerning nonviolent resistance is that it avoids not only external physical violence but also internal violence of spirit. The nonviolent resister not only refuses to shoot his opponent but he also refuses to hate him. At the center of nonviolence stands the principle of love. The nonviolent resister would contend that in the struggle for human dignity, the oppressed people of the world must not succumb to the temptation of becoming bitter or indulging in hate campaigns. To retaliate in kind would do nothing but intensify the existence of hate in the universe. Along the way of life, someone must have sense enough and morality enough to cut off the chain of hate. This can only be done by projecting the ethic of love to the center of our lives. . . .

A sixth basic fact about nonviolent resistance is that it is based on the conviction that the universe is on the side of justice. Consequently, the believer in nonviolence has deep faith in the future. This faith is another reason why the nonviolent resister can accept suffering without retaliation. For he knows that in his struggle for justice he has cosmic companionship. It is true that there are devout believers in nonviolence who find it difficult to believe in a personal God. But even these persons believe in the existence of some creative force that works for universal wholeness. Whether we call it an unconscious process, an impersonal Brahman, or a Personal Being of matchless power and infinite love, there is a creative force in this universe that works to bring the disconnected aspects of reality into a harmonious whole. . . .

Where Do We Go from Here?

The bus struggle in Montgomery, Alabama, is now history. As the integrated buses roll daily through the city they carry, along with their passengers, a meaning-crowded symbolism. Accord among the great majority of passengers is evidence of the basic good will of man for man and a portent of peace in the desegregated society to come. Occasional instances of discord among passengers are a reminder that in other areas of Montgomery life segregation yet obtains with all of its potential for group strife and personal conflict. Indeed, segregation is still a reality throughout the South.

Where do we go from here? Since the problem in Montgomery is merely symptomatic of the larger national problem, where do we go not only in Montgomery but all over the South and the nation? Forces maturing for years have given rise to the present crisis in race relations. What are these forces that have brought the crisis about? What will be the conclusion? Are we caught in a social and political impasse, or do we have at our disposal the creative resources to achieve the ideals of brotherhood and harmonious living?

The last half century has seen crucial changes in the life of the American Negro. The social upheavals of the two world wars, the great depression, and the spread of the automobile have made it both possible and necessary for the Negro to move away from his former isolation on the rural plantation. The decline of agriculture and the parallel growth of industry have drawn large numbers of Negroes to urban centers and brought about a gradual improvement in their economic status. New contacts have led to a broadened outlook and new possibilities for educational advance. All of these factors have conjoined to cause the Negro to take a fresh look at himself. His expanding life experiences have created within him a consciousness that he is an equal element in a larger social compound and accordingly should be given rights and privileges commensurate with his new responsibilities. Once plagued with a tragic sense of inferiority resulting from the crippling effects of slavery and segregation, the Negro has now been driven to reëvaluate himself. He has come to feel that he is somebody. His religion reveals to him that God loves all His children and that the important thing about a man is not "his specificity but his fundamentum"—not the texture of his hair or the color of his skin but his eternal worth to God.

This growing self-respect has inspired the Negro with a new determination to struggle and sacrifice until first-class citizenship becomes a reality. This is the true meaning of the Montgomery Story. One can never understand the bus protest in Montgomery without understanding that there is a new Negro in the South, with a new sense of dignity and destiny. . . .

Finally, the Negro himself has a decisive role to play if integration is to become a reality. Indeed, if first-class citizenship is to become a reality for the Negro he must assume the primary responsibility for making it so. Integration is not some lavish dish that the federal government or the white liberal will pass out on a silver platter while the Negro merely furnishes the appetite. One of the most damaging effects of past segregation on the personality of the Negro may well be that he has been victimized with the delusion that others should be more concerned than himself about his citizenship rights.

In this period of social change, the Negro must come to see that there is much he himself can do about his plight. He may be uneducated or poverty-stricken, but these handicaps must not prevent him from seeing that he has within his being the power to alter his fate. The Negro can take direct action against injustice without waiting for the government to act or a majority to agree with him or a court to rule in his favor.

Oppressed people deal with their oppression in three characteristic ways. One way is acquiescence: the oppressed resign themselves to their doom. They tacitly adjust themselves to oppression, and thereby become conditioned to it. In every movement toward freedom some of the oppressed prefer to remain oppressed. Almost 2800 years ago Moses set out to lead the children of Israel from the slavery of Egypt to the freedom of the promised land. He soon discovered that slaves do not always welcome their deliverers.

They become accustomed to being slaves. They would rather bear those ills they have, as Shakespeare pointed out, than flee to others that they know not of. They prefer the "fleshpots of Egypt" to the ordeals of emancipation.

There is such a thing as the freedom of exhaustion. Some people are so worn down by the yoke of oppression that they give up. A few years ago in the slum areas of Atlanta, a Negro guitarist used to sing almost daily: "Ben down so long that down don't bother me." This is the type of negative freedom and resignation that often engulfs the life of the oppressed.

But this is not the way out. To accept passively an unjust system is to coöperate with that system; thereby the oppressed become as evil as the oppressor. Noncoöperation with evil is as much a moral obligation as is coöperation with good. The oppressed must never allow the conscience of the oppressor to slumber. Religion reminds every man that he is his brother's keeper. To accept injustice or segregation passively is to say to the oppressor that his actions are morally right. It is a way of allowing his conscience to fall asleep. At this moment the oppressed fails to be his brother's keeper. So acquiescence—while often the easier way—is not the moral way. It is the way of the coward. The Negro cannot win the respect of his oppressor by acquiescing; he merely increases the oppressor's arrogance and contempt. Acquiescence is interpreted as proof of the Negro's inferiority. The Negro cannot win the respect of the white people of the South or the peoples of the world if he is willing to sell the future of his children for his personal and immediate comfort and safety.

A second way that oppressed people sometimes deal with oppression is to resort to physical violence and corroding hatred. Violence often brings about momentary results. Nations have frequently won their independence in battle. But in spite of temporary victories, violence never brings permanent peace. It solves no social problem; it merely creates new and more complicated ones.

Violence as a way of achieving racial justice is both impractical and immoral. It is impractical because it is a descending spiral ending in destruction for all. The old law of an eye for an eye leaves everybody blind. It is immoral because it seeks to humiliate the opponent rather than win his understanding; it seeks to annihilate rather than to convert. Violence is immoral because it thrives on hatred rather than love. It destroys community and makes brotherhood impossible. It leaves society in monologue rather than dialogue. Violence ends by defeating itself. It creates bitterness in the survivors and brutality in the destroyers. A voice echoes through time saying to every potential Peter, "Put up your sword." History is cluttered with the wreckage of nations that failed to follow this command.

If the American Negro and other victims of oppression succumb to the temptation of using violence in the struggle for freedom, future generations will be the recipients of a desolate night of bitterness, and our chief legacy to them will be an endless reign of meaningless chaos. Violence is not the way.

The third way open to oppressed people in their quest for freedom is the way of nonviolent resistance. Like the synthesis in Hegelian philosophy, the principle of nonviolent resistance seeks to reconcile the truths of two opposites—acquiescence and violence—while avoiding the extremes and immoralities of both. The nonviolent resister agrees with the person who acquiesces that one should not be physically aggressive toward his opponent; but he balances the equation by agreeing with the person of violence that evil must be resisted. He avoids the nonresistance of the former and the violent resistance of the latter. With nonviolent resistance, no individual or group need submit to any wrong, nor need anyone resort to violence in order to right a wrong.

It seems to me that this is the method that must guide the actions of the Negro in the present crisis in race relations. Through nonviolent resistance the Negro will be able to rise to the noble height of opposing the unjust system while loving the perpetrators of the system. The Negro must work passionately and unrelentingly for full stature as a citizen, but he must not use inferior methods to gain it. He must never come to terms with falsehood, malice, hate, or destruction.

Nonviolent resistance makes it possible for the Negro to remain in the South and struggle for his rights. The Negro's problem will not be solved by running away. He cannot listen to the glib suggestion of those who would urge him to migrate en masse to other sections of the country. By grasping his great opportunity in the South he can make a lasting contribution to the moral strength of the nation and set a sublime example of courage for generations yet unborn.

By nonviolent resistance, the Negro can also enlist all men of good will in his struggle for equality. The problem is not a purely racial one, with Negroes set against whites. In the end, it is not a struggle between people at all, but a tension between justice and injustice. Nonviolent resistance is not aimed against oppressors but against oppression. Under its banner consciences, not racial groups, are enlisted.

If the Negro is to achieve the goal of integration, he must organize himself into a militant and nonviolent mass movement. All three elements are indispensable. The movement for equality and justice can only be a success if it has both a mass and militant character; the barriers to be overcome require both. Nonviolence is an imperative in order to bring about ultimate community. . . .

The Negro, once a helpless child, has now grown up politically, culturally, and economically. Many white men fear retaliation. The job of the Negro is to show them that they have nothing to fear, that the Negro understands and forgives and is ready to forget the past. He must convince the white man that all he seeks is justice, *for both himself and the white man.* A mass movement exercising nonviolence is an object lesson in power under discipline, a demonstration to the white community that if such a movement attained a degree of strength, it would use its power creatively and not vengefully.

Nonviolence can touch men where the law cannot reach them. When the law regulates behavior it plays an indirect part in molding public sentiment. The enforcement of the law is itself a form of peaceful persuasion. But the law needs help. The courts can order desegregation of the public schools. But what can be done to mitigate the fears, to disperse the hatred, violence, and irrationality gathered around school integration, to take the initiative out of the hands of racial demagogues, to release respect for the law? In the end, for laws to be obeyed, men must believe they are right.

Here nonviolence comes in as the ultimate form of persuasion. It is the method which seeks to implement the just law by appealing to the conscience of the great decent majority who through blindness, fear, pride, or irrationality have allowed their consciences to sleep.

The nonviolent resisters can summarize their message in the following simple terms: We will take direct action against injustice without waiting for other agencies to act. We will not obey unjust laws or submit to unjust practices. We will do this peacefully, openly, cheerfully because our aim is to persuade. We adopt the means of nonviolence because our end is a community at peace with itself. We will try to persuade with our words, but if our words fail, we will try to persuade with our acts. We will always be willing to talk and seek fair compromise, but we are ready to suffer when necessary and even risk our lives to become witnesses to the truth as we see it.

The way of nonviolence means a willingness to suffer and sacrifice. It may mean going to jail. If such is the case the resister must be willing to fill the jail houses of the South. It may even mean physical death. But if physical death is the price that a man must pay to free his children and his white brethren from a permanent death of the spirit, then nothing could be more redemptive.

What is the Negro's best defense against acts of violence inflicted upon him? As Dr. Kenneth Clark has said so eloquently, "His only defense is to meet every act of barbarity, illegality, cruelty and injustice toward an individual Negro with the fact that 100 more Negroes will present themselves in his place as potential victims." Every time one Negro school teacher is fired for believing in integration, a thousand others should be ready to take the same stand. If the oppressors bomb the home of one Negro for his protest, they must be made to realize that to press back the rising tide of the Negro's courage they will have to bomb hundreds more, and even then they will fail.

Faced with this dynamic unity, this amazing self-respect, this willingness to suffer, and this refusal to hit back, the oppressor will find, as oppressors have always found, that he is glutted with his own barbarity. Forced to stand before the world and his God splattered with the blood of his brother, he will call an end to his self-defeating massacre.

American Negroes must come to the point where they can say to their white brothers, paraphrasing the words of Gandhi: "We will match your capacity to inflict suffering with our capacity to endure suffering. We will meet your physical force with soul force. We will not hate you, but we cannot in all good conscience obey your unjust laws. Do to us what you will and we will still love you. Bomb our homes and threaten our children; send your hooded perpetrators of violence into our communities and drag us out on some wayside road, beating us and leaving us half dead, and we will still love you. But we will soon wear you down by our capacity to suffer. And in winning our freedom we will so appeal to your heart and conscience that we will win you in the process."

Realism impels me to admit that many Negroes will find it difficult to follow the path of nonviolence. Some will consider it senseless; some will argue that they have neither the strength nor the courage to join in such a mass demonstration of nonviolent action. As E. Franklin Frazier points out in *Black Bourgeoisie*, many Negroes are occupied in a middle-class struggle for status and prestige. They are more concerned about "conspicuous consumption" than about the cause of justice, and are probably not prepared for the ordeals and sacrifices involved in nonviolent action. . . .

The nonviolent approach does not immediately change the heart of the oppressor. It first does something to the hearts and souls of those committed to it. It gives them new self-respect; it calls up resources of strength and courage that they did not know they had. Finally it reaches the opponent and so stirs his conscience that reconciliation becomes a reality.

I suggest this approach because I think it is the only way to reëstablish the broken community. Court orders and federal enforcement agencies will be of inestimable value in achieving desegregation. But desegregation is only a partial, though necessary, step toward the ultimate goal which we seek to realize. Desegregation will break down the legal barriers, and bring men together physically. But something must happen so to touch the hearts and souls of men that they will come together, not because the law says it, but because it is natural and right. In other words, our ultimate goal is integration which is genuine intergroup and interpersonal living. Only through nonviolence can this goal be attained, for the aftermath of nonviolence is reconciliation and the creation of the beloved community.

It is becoming clear that the Negro is in for a season of suffering. As victories for civil rights mount in the federal courts, angry passions and deep prejudices are further aroused. The mountain of state and local segregation laws still stands. Negro leaders continue to be arrested and harassed under city ordinances, and their homes continue to be bombed. State laws continue to be enacted to circumvent integration. I pray that, recognizing the necessity of suffering, the Negro will make of it a virtue. To suffer in a righteous cause is to grow to our humanity's full stature. If only to save himself from bitterness, the Negro needs the vision to see the ordeals of this generation as the opportunity to transfigure himself and American society. If he has to go to jail for the cause of freedom, let him enter it in the fashion Gandhi urged his countrymen, "as the bridegroom enters the bride's chamber"—that is, with a little trepidation but with a great expectation.

Nonviolence is a way of humility and self-restraint. We Negroes talk a great deal about our rights, and rightly so. We proudly proclaim that three-fourths of the people of the world are colored. We have the privilege of watching in our generation the great drama of freedom and independence as it unfolds in Asia and Africa. All of these things are in line with the work of providence. We must be sure, however, that we accept them in the right spirit. In an effort to achieve freedom in America, Asia, and Africa we must not try to leap from a position of disadvantage to one of advantage, thus subverting justice. We must seek democracy and not the substitution of one tyranny for another. Our aim must never be to defeat or humiliate the white man. We must not become victimized with a philosophy of black supremacy. God is not interested merely in the freedom of black men, and brown men, and yellow men; God is interested in the freedom of the whole human race.

The nonviolent approach provides an answer to the long debated question of gradualism *versus* immediacy. On the one hand it prevents one from falling into the sort of patience which is an excuse for do-nothingism and escapism, ending up in standstillism. On the other hand it saves one from the irresponsible words which estrange without reconciling and the hasty judgment which is blind to the necessities of social process. It recognizes the need for moving toward the goal of justice with wise restraint and calm reasonableness. But it also recognizes the immorality of slowing up in the move toward justice and capitulating to the guardians of an unjust status quo. It recognizes that social change cannot come overnight. But it causes one to work as if it were a possibility the next morning.

Through nonviolence we avoid the temptation of taking on the psychology of victors. Thanks largely to the noble and invaluable work of the NAACP, we have won great victories in the federal courts. But we must not be self-satisfied. We must respond to every decision with an understanding of those who have opposed us, and with acceptance of the new adjustments that the court orders pose for them. We must act in such a way that our victories will be triumphs for good will in all men, white and Negro.

Nonviolence is essentially a positive concept. Its corollary must always be growth. On the one hand nonviolence requires noncoöperation with evil; on the other hand it requires coöperation with the constructive forces of good. Without this constructive aspect noncoöperation ends where it begins. Therefore, the Negro must get to work on a program with a broad range of positive goals. . . .

This then must be our present program: Nonviolent resistance to all forms of racial injustice, including state and local laws and practices, even when this means going to jail; and imaginative, bold, constructive action to end the demoralization caused by the legacy of slavery and segregation, inferior schools, slums, and second-class citizenship. The nonviolent struggle, if conducted with the dignity and courage already shown by the people of Montgomery and the children of Little Rock, will in itself help end the demoralization; but a new frontal assault on the poverty, disease, and ignorance of a people too long ignored by America's conscience will make victory more certain.

In short, we must work on two fronts. On the one hand, we must continue to resist the system of segregation which is the basic cause of our lagging standards; on the other hand we must work constructively to improve the standards themselves. There must be a rhythmic alternation between attacking the causes and healing the effects.

This is a great hour for the Negro. The challenge is here. To become the instruments of a great idea is a privilege that history gives only occasionally. Arnold Toynbee says in *A Study of History* that it may be the Negro who will give the new spiritual dynamic to Western civilization that it so desperately needs to survive. I hope this is possible. The spiritual power that the Negro can radiate to the world comes from love, understanding, good will, and nonviolence. It may even be possible for the Negro, through adherence to nonviolence, so to challenge the nations of the world that they will seriously seek an alternative to war and destruction. In a day when Sputniks and Explorers dash through outer space and guided ballistic missiles are carving highways of death through the stratosphere, nobody can win a war. Today the choice is no longer between violence and nonviolence. It is either nonviolence or nonexistence. The Negro may be God's appeal to this age—an age drifting rapidly to its doom. The eternal appeal takes the form of a warning: "All who take the sword will perish by the sword."

Ellsberg Says He'll Be Jailed

NEW ORLEANS—(AP)—Dr. Daniel Ellsberg, charged with unauthorized possession of secret government documents, says he expects to be jailed. He has admitted releasing the Pentagon papers to the press.

He made the prediction in an address at a rally of the Southern Christian Leadership Conference.

"If it weren't for the example set by the Rev. Martin Luther King, Jr., I wouldn't be where I am now, which is on my way to jail under indictment for having found a way to actively resist an evil war," Ellsberg said.

"I would have been an accomplice in the war.

"In the fall of 1968, I read a book entitled 'Strive for Freedom.' They (the government) should have burned that book if they wanted me to keep secrets. It was a book about duty and conscience. It was a book by Martin Luther King.

"You don't learn only from books—I learned from the young men and women who had to go to prison to keep from being accomplices in murder.

"If I didn't stand for what was right, how could I not go to prison for what I believe in. If I go, I'll be in good company. I'll be helping all of you to say 'No' to this war. The way Martin Luther King said 'No' to injustice."

The Denver Post, Aug. 15, 1971.

RULES FOR RADICALS*

Saul D. Alinsky

Change comes from power, and power comes from organization. In order to act, people must get together.

Power is the reason for being of organizations. When people agree on certain religious ideas and want the power to propagate their faith, they organize and call it a church. When people agree on certain political ideas and want the power to put them into practice, they organize and call it a political party. The same reason holds across the board. Power and organization are one and the same.

The organizer knows, for example, that his biggest job is to give the people the feeling that they can do something, that while they may accept the idea that organization means power, they have to experience this idea in action. The organizer's job is to begin to build confidence and hope in the idea of organization and thus in the people themselves: to win limited victories, each of which will build confidence and the feeling that "if we can do so much with what we have now just think what we will be able to do when we get big and strong." It is almost like taking a prize-fighter up the road to the championship—you have to very carefully and selectively pick his opponents, knowing full well that certain defeats would be demoralizing and end his career. Sometimes the organizer may find such despair among the people that he has to put on a cinch fight. . . .

* Show in class the 59 minute film "Saul Alinsky Went to War." Available from Contemporary Films, McGraw-Hill Films. Produced by National Film Board of Canada.

The organizer simultaneously carries on many functions as he analyzes, attacks, and disrupts the prevailing power pattern. The ghetto or slum in which he is organizing is *not* a disorganized community. There is no such animal as a disorganized community. It is a contradiction in terms to use the two words "disorganization" and "community" together: the word community itself means an organized, communal life; people living in an organized fashion. The people in the community may have experienced successive frustrations to the point that their will to participate has seemed to atrophy. They may be living in anonymity and may be starved for personal recognition. They may be suffering from various forms of deprivation and discrimination. They may have accepted anonymity and resigned in apathy. They may despair that their children will inherit a somewhat better world. From your point of view they may have a very negative form of existence, but the fact is that they are organized in that way of life. Call it organized apathy or organized nonparticipation, but that is their community pattern. They are living under a certain set of arrangements, standards, way of life. They may in short have surrendered—but life goes on in an organized form, with a definite power structure; even if it is, as Thoreau called most lives, "quiet desperation."

Therefore, if your function is to attack apathy and get people to participate it is necessary to attack the prevailing patterns of organized living in the community. *The first step in community organization is community disorganization.* The disruption of the present organization is the first step toward community organization. Present arrangements must be disorganized if they are to be displaced by new patterns that provide the opportunities and means for citizen participation. *All change means disorganization of the old and organization of the new.*

This is why the organizer is immediately confronted with conflict. The organizer dedicated to changing the life of a particular community must first rub raw the resentments of the people of the community; fan the latent hostilities of many of the people to the point of overt expression. He must search out controversy and issues, rather than avoid them, for unless there is controversy people are not concerned enough to act. The use of the adjective "controversial" to qualify the word "issue" is a meaningless redundancy. There can be no such thing as a "non-controversial" issue. When there is agreement there is no issue; issues only arise when there is disagreement or controversy. An organizer must stir up dissatisfaction and discontent; provide a channel into which the people can angrily pour their frustrations. He must create a mechanism that can drain off the underlying guilt for having accepted the previous situation for so long a time. Out of this mechanism, a new community organization arises. But more on this point later.

The job then is getting the people to move, to act, to participate; in short, to develop and harness the necessary power to effectively conflict with the prevailing patterns and change them. When those prominent in the status quo turn and label you an "agitator" they are completely correct, for that is, in one word, your function—to agitate to the point of conflict. . . .

Tactics means doing what you can with what you have. Tactics are those consciously deliberate acts by which human beings live with each other and deal with the world around them. In the world of give and take, tactics is the art of how to take and how to give. Here our concern is with the tactic of taking; how the Have-Nots can take power away from the Haves.

For an elementary illustration of tactics, take parts of your face as the point of reference; your eyes, your ears, and your nose. First the eyes; if you have organized a vast, mass-based people's organization, you can parade it visibly before the enemy and openly show your power. Second the ears; if your organization is small in numbers, then do what Gideon did: conceal the members in the dark but raise a din and clamor that will make the listener believe that your organization numbers many more than it does. Third, the nose; if your organization is too tiny even for noise, stink up the place.

Always remember the first rule of power tactics:

Power is not only what you have but what the enemy thinks you have.[1]

The second rule is: *Never go outside the experience of your people.* When an action or tactic is outside the experience of the people, the result is confusion, fear, and retreat. It also means a collapse of communication, as we have noted.

The third rule is: *Wherever possible go outside of the experience of the enemy.* Here you want to cause confusion, fear, and retreat.

General William T. Sherman, whose name still causes a frenzied reaction throughout the South, provided a classic example of going outside the enemy's experience. Until Sherman, military tactics and strategies were based on standard patterns. All armies had fronts, rears, flanks, lines of communication, and lines of supply. Military campaigns were aimed at such standard objectives as rolling up the flanks of the enemy army or cutting the lines of supply or lines of communication, or moving around to attack from the rear. When Sherman cut loose on his famous March to the Sea, he had no front or rear lines of supplies or any other lines. He was on the loose and living on the land. The South, confronted with this new form of military invasion, reacted with confusion, panic, terror, and collapse. Sherman swept on to inevitable victory. It was the same tactic that, years later in the early days of World War II, the Nazi Panzer tank divisions emulated in their

[1] Power has always derived from two main sources, money and people. Lacking money, the Have-Nots must build power from their own flesh and blood. A mass movement expresses itself with mass tactics. Against the finesse and sophistication of the status quo, the Have-Nots have always had to club their way. In early Renaissance Italy the playing cards showed swords for the nobility (the word *spade* is a corruption of the Italian word for sword), chalices (which became hearts) for the clergy, diamonds for the merchants, and clubs as the symbol of the peasants.

far-flung sweeps into enemy territory, as did our own General Patton with the American Third Armored Division.

The fourth rule is: *Make the enemy live up to their own book of rules.* You can kill them with this, for they can no more obey their own rules than the Christian church can live up to Christianity.

The fourth rule carries within it the fifth rule: *Ridicule is man's most potent weapon.* It is almost impossible to counterattack ridicule. Also it infuriates the opposition, who then react to your advantage.

The sixth rule is: *A good tactic is one that your people enjoy.*[2] If your people are not having a ball doing it, there is something very wrong with the tactic.

The seventh rule: *A tactic that drags on too long becomes a drag.* Man can sustain militant interest in any issue for only a limited time, after which it becomes a ritualistic commitment, like going to church on Sunday mornings. New issues and crises are always developing, and one's reaction becomes, "Well, my heart bleeds for those people and I'm all for the boycott, but after all there are other important things in life"—and there it goes.

The eighth rule: *Keep the pressure on,* with different tactics and actions, and utilize all events of the period for your purpose.

The ninth rule: *The threat is usually more terrifying than the thing itself.*

The tenth rule: *The major premise for tactics is the development of operations that will maintain a constant pressure upon the opposition.* It is this unceasing pressure that results in the reactions from the opposition that are essential for the success of the campaign. It should be remembered not only that the action is in the reaction but that action is itself the consequence of reaction and of reaction to the reaction, ad infinitum. The pressure produces the reaction, and constant pressure sustains action.

The eleventh rule is: *If you push a negative hard and deep enough it will break through into its counterside*; this is based on the principle that every positive has its negative. . . .

The twelfth rule: *The price of a successful attack is a constructive alternative.* You cannot risk being trapped by the enemy in his sudden agreement with your demand and saying "You're right—we don't know what to do about this issue. Now you tell us."

The thirteenth rule: *Pick the target, freeze it, personalize it, and polarize it.*

In conflict tactics there are certain rules that the organizer should always regard as universalities. One is that the opposition must be singled out as the target and "frozen." By this I mean that in a complex, interrelated, urban society, it becomes increasingly difficult to single out who is to blame for

[2] "Alinsky takes the iconoclast's pleasure in kicking the biggest behinds in town and the sport is not untempting . . ."—William F. Buckley, Jr., *Chicago Daily News,* October 19, 1966.

any particular evil. There is a constant, and somewhat legitimate, passing of the buck. In these times of urbanization, complex metropolitan governments, the complexities of major interlocked corporations, and the interlocking of political life between cities and countries and metropolitan authorities, the problem that threatens to loom more and more is that of identifying the enemy. Obviously there is no point to tactics unless one has a target upon which to center the attacks. One big problem is a constant shifting of responsibility from one jurisdiction to another—individuals and bureaus one after another disclaim responsibility for particular conditions, attributing the authority for any change to some other force. In a corporation one gets the situation where the president of the corporation says that he does not have the responsibility, it is up to the board of trustees or the board of directors, the board of directors can shift it over to the stockholders, etc., etc. And the same thing goes, for example, on the Board of Education appointments in the city of Chicago, where an extra-legal committee is empowered to make selections of nominees for the board and the mayor then uses his legal powers to select names from that list. When the mayor is attacked for not having any blacks on the list, he shifts the responsibility over to the committee, pointing out that he has to select those names from a list submitted by the committee, and if the list is all white, then he has no responsibility. The committee can shift the responsibility back by pointing out that it is the mayor who has the authority to select the names, and so it goes in a comic (if it were not so tragic) routine of "who's on first" or "under which shell is the pea hidden?" . . .

It should be borne in mind that the target is always trying to shift responsibility to get out of being the target. There is a constant squirming and moving and strategy—purposeful, and malicious at times, other times just for straight self-survival—on the part of the designated target. The forces for change must keep this in mind and pin that target down securely. If an organization permits responsibility to be diffused and distributed in a number of areas, attack becomes impossible.

I remember specifically that when the Woodlawn Organization started the campaign against public school segregation, both the superintendent of schools and the chairman of the Board of Education vehemently denied any racist segregationist practices in the Chicago Public School System. They took the position that they did not even have any racial-identification data in their files, so they did not know which of their students were black and which were white. As for the fact that we had all-white schools and all-black schools, well, that's just the way it was.

If we have been confronted with a politically sophisticated school superintendent he could have very well replied, "Look, when I came to Chicago the city school system was following, as it is now, a neighborhood school policy. Chicago's neighborhoods are segregated. There are white neighborhoods and black neighborhoods and therefore you have white schools and black schools. Why attack me? Why not attack the segregated neighborhoods and change them?" He would have had a valid point, of sorts; I still shiver when I think of this possibility; but the segregated neighborhoods would have passed the buck to someone else and so it would have gone into a dog-chasing-his-tail pattern—and it would have been a fifteen-year job to try to break down the segregated residential pattern of Chicago. We did not have the power to start that kind of a conflict. One of the criteria in picking your target is the target's vulnerability—where do you have the power to start? Furthermore, any target can always say, "Why do you center on me when there are others to blame as well?" When you "freeze the target," you disregard these arguments and, for the moment, all the others to blame.

Then, as you zero in and freeze your target and carry out your attack, all of the "others" come out of the woodwork very soon. They become visible by their support of the target.

The other important point in the choosing of a target is that it must be a personification, not something general and abstract such as a community's segregated practices or a major corporation or City Hall. It is not possible to develop the necessary hostility against, say City Hall, which after all is a concrete, physical, inanimate structure, or against a corporation, which has no soul or identity, or a public school administration, which again is an inanimate system.

John L. Lewis, the leader of the radical C.I.O. labor organization in the 1930s, was fully aware of this, and as a consequence the C.I.O. never attacked General Motors, they always attacked its president, Alfred "Ice-water-In-His-Veins" Sloan; they never attacked the Republic Steel Corporation but always its president, "Bloodied Hands" Tom Gridler, and so with us when we attacked the then-superintendent of the Chicago public school system, Benjamin Willis. Let nothing get you off your target.

With this focus comes a polarization. As we have indicated before, all issues must be polarized if action is to follow. The classic statement on polarization comes from Christ: "He that is not with me is against me" (Luke 11:23). He allowed no middle ground to the money-changers in the Temple. One acts decisively only in the conviction that all the angels are on one side and all the devils on the other. A leader may struggle toward a decision and weigh the merits and demerits of a situation which is 52 percent positive and 48 percent negative, but once the decision is reached he must assume that his cause is 100 percent positive and the opposition 100 percent negative. He can't toss forever in limbo, and avoid decision. He can't weigh arguments or reflect endlessly—he must decide and act. Otherwise there are Hamlet's words:

> And thus the native hue of resolution
> Is sicklied o'er with the pale cast of thought,
> And enterprises of great pith and moment
> With this regard their currents turn awry,
> And lose the name of action.

Many liberals, during our attack on the then-school superintendent, were pointing out that after all he wasn't a 100 percent devil, he was a regular churchgoer, he was a good family man, and he was generous in his contributions to charity. Can you imagine in the arena of conflict charging that so-and-so is a racist bastard and then diluting the impact of the attack with qualifying remarks such as "He is a good churchgoing man, generous to charity, and a good husband"? This becomes political idiocy. . . .

The real action is in the enemy's reaction.

The enemy properly goaded and guided in his reaction will be your major strength.

Tactics, like organization, like life, require that you move with the action.

The scene is Rochester, New York, the home of Eastman Kodak—or rather Eastman Kodak, the home of Rochester, New York. Rochester is literally dominated by this industrial giant. For anyone to fight or publicly challenge Kodak is in itself completely outside of Rochester's experience. Even to this day this company does not have a labor union. Its attitudes toward the general public make paternalistic feudalism look like participatory democracy.

Rochester prides itself on being one of America's cultural crown jewels; it has its libraries, school system, university, museums, and its well-known symphony. As previously mentioned we were coming in on the invitation of the black ghetto to organize them (they literally organized to invite us in). The city was in a state of hysteria and fear at the very mention of my name. Whatever I did was news. Even my old friend and tutor, John L. Lewis, called me and affectionately growled, "I resent the fact that you are more hated in Rochester than I was." This was the setting.

One of the first times I arrived at the airport I was surrounded by reporters from the media. The first question was what I thought about Rochester as a city and I replied, "It is a huge southern plantation transplanted north." To the question why was I "meddling" in the black ghetto after "everything" that Eastman Kodak had done for the blacks (there had been a bloody riot, National Guard, etc., the previous summer), I looked blank and replied, "Maybe I am innocent and uninformed of what has been happening here, but as far as I know the only thing Eastman Kodak has done on the race issue in America has been to introduce color film." The reaction was shock, anger, and resentment from Kodak. They were not being attacked or insulted—they were being laughed at, and this was insufferable. It was the first dart tossed at the big bull. Soon Eastman would become so angry that it would make the kind of charges that finally led to its own downfall.

The next question was about my response to a bitter personal denunciation of me from W. Allen Wallis, the president of the University of Rochester and a present director of Eastman Kodak. He had been the head of the Department of Business Administration, formerly, at the University of Chicago. He was at the university when it was locked in bitter warfare with the black organization in Woodlawn. "Wallis?" I replied. "Which one are you talking about—Wallace of Alabama, or Wallis of Rochester—but I guess there isn't any difference, so what was your question?" This reply (1) introduced an element of ridicule and (2) it ended any further attacks from the president of the University of Rochester, who began to suspect that he was going to be shafted with razors, and that an encounter with me or with my associates was not going to be an academic dialogue.

It should be remembered that you can threaten the enemy and get away with it. You can insult and annoy him, but the one thing that is unforgivable and that is certain to get him to react is to laugh at him. This causes an irrational anger. . . .

For example, I have emphasized and re-emphasized that tactics means you do what you can with what you've got, and that power in the main has always gravitated towards those who have money and those whom people follow. The resources of the Have-Nots are (1) no money and (2) lots of people. All right, let's start from there. People can show their power by voting. What else? Well, they have physical bodies. How can they use them? Now a melange of ideas begins to appear. Use the power of the law by making the establishment obey its own rules. Go outside the experience of the enemy, stay inside the experience of your people. Emphasize tactics that your people will enjoy. The threat is usually more terrifying than the tactic itself. Once all these rules and principles are festering in your imagination they grow into a synthesis.

I suggested that we might buy one hundred seats for one of Rochester's symphony concerts. We would select a concert in which the music was relatively quiet. The hundred blacks who would be given the tickets would first be treated to a three-hour pre-concert dinner in the community, in which they would be fed nothing but baked beans, and lots of them; then the people would go to the symphony hall—with obvious consequences. Imagine the scene when the action began! The concert would be over before the first movement! (If this be a Freudian slip—so be it!)

Let's examine this tactic in terms of the concepts mentioned above.

First, the disturbance would be utterly outside the experience of the establishment, which was expecting the usual stuff of mass meetings, street demonstrations, confrontations and parades. Not in their wildest fears would they expect an attack on their prize cultural jewel, their famed symphony orchestra. Second, all of the action would ridicule and make a farce of the law for there is no law, and there probably never will be, banning natural physical functions. Here you would have a combination not only of noise but also of odor, what you might call natural stink bombs. Regular stink bombs are illegal and cause for immediate arrest, but there would be absolutely nothing here that the Police Department or the ushers or any other servants of the establishment could do about it. The law would be completely paralyzed.

People would recount what had happened in the symphony hall and the reaction of the listener would be to crack up in laughter. It would make the Rochester Symphony and the establishment look utterly ridiculous. There would be no way for the authorities to cope with any future attacks of a similar character. What could they do? Demand that people not eat baked beans before coming to a concert? Ban anyone from succumbing to natural urges during the concert? Announce to the world that concerts must not be interrupted by farting? Such talk would destroy the future of the symphony season. Imagine the tension at the opening of any concert! Imagine the feeling of the conductor as he raised his baton!

With this would come certain fall-outs. On the following morning, the matrons, to whom the symphony season is one of the major social functions, would confront their husbands (both executives and junior executives) at the breakfast table and say, "John, we are not going to have our symphony season ruined by *those people!* I don't know what they want but whatever it is, something has got to be done and this kind of thing has to be stopped!"

Lastly, we have the universal rule that while one goes outside the experience of the enemy in order to induce confusion and fear, one must not do the same with one's own people, because you do not want them to be confused and fearful. Now, let us examine this rule with reference to the symphony tactic. To start with, the tactic is within the experience of the local people; it also satisfies another rule—that the people must enjoy the tactic. Here we have an ambivalent situation. The reaction of the blacks in the ghetto—their laughter when the tactic was proposed—made it clear that the tactic, at least in fantasy, was within their experience. It connected with their hatred of Whitey. The one thing that all oppressed people want to do to their oppressors is shit on them. Here was an approximate way to do this. However, we were also aware that when they found themselves actually in the symphony hall, probably for the first time in their lives, they would find themselves seated amid a mass of whites, many of them in formal dress. The situation would be so much *out of their experience* that they might congeal and revert back to their previous role. The very idea of doing what they had come to do would be so embarrassing, so mortifying, that they would do almost anything to avoid carrying through the plan. But we also knew that the baked beans would compel them physically to go through with the tactic regardless of how they felt.

I must emphasize that tactics like this are not just cute; any organizer knows, as a particular tactic grows out of the rules and principles of revolution, that he must always analyze the merit of the tactic and determine its strengths and weaknesses in terms of these same rules.

Imagine the scene in the U.S. Courtroom in Chicago's recent conspiracy trial of the seven if the defendants and counsel had anally trumpeted their contempt for Judge Hoffman and the system. What could Judge Hoffman, the bailiffs, or anyone else, do? Would the judge have found them in contempt for farting? Here was a tactic for which there was no legal precedent. The press reaction would have stunk up the judge for the rest of time.

Another tactic involving the bodily functions developed in Chicago during the days of the Johnson-Goldwater campaign. Commitments that were made by the authorities to the Woodlawn ghetto organization were not being met by the city. The political threat that had originally compelled these commitments was no longer operative. The community organization had no alternative but to support Johnson and therefore the Democratic administration felt the political threat had evaporated. It must be remembered here that not only is pressure essential to compel the establishment to make its initial concession, but the pressure must be maintained to make the establishment deliver. The second factor seemed to be lost to the Woodlawn Organization.

Since the organization was blocked in the political arena, new tactics and a new arena had to be devised.

O'Hare Airport became the target. To begin with, O'Hare is the world's busiest airport. Think for a moment of the common experience of jet travelers. Your stewardess brings you your lunch or dinner. After eating, most people want to go to the lavatory. However, this is often inconvenient because your tray and those of your seat partners are loaded down with dishes. So you wait until the stewardess has removed the trays. By that time those who are seated closest to the lavatory have got up and the "occupied" sign is on. So you wait. And in these days of jet travel the seat belt sign is soon flashed, as the airplane starts its landing approach. You decide to wait until after landing and use the facilities in the terminal. This is obvious to anyone who watches the unloading of passengers at various gates in any airport—many of the passengers are making a beeline for the men's or the ladies' room.

With this in mind, the tactic becomes obvious—we tie up the lavatories. In the restrooms you drop a dime, enter, push the lock on the door—and you can stay there all day. Therefore the occupation of the sit-down toilets presents no problem. It would take just a relatively few people to walk into these cubicles, armed with books and newspapers, lock the doors, and tie up all the facilities. What are the police going to do? Break in and demand evidence of legitimate occupancy? Therefore, the ladies' restrooms could be occupied completely; the only problem in the men's lavatories would be the stand-up urinals. This, too, could be taken care of, by having groups busy themselves around the airport and then move in on the stand-up urinals to line up four or five deep whenever a flight arrived. An intelligence study was launched to learn how may sit-down toilets for both men and women, as well as stand-up urinals, there were in the entire O'Hare Airport complex and how many men and women would be necessary for the nation's first "shit-in."

The consequences of this kind of action would be catastrophic in many ways. People would be desperate for a place to relieve themselves. One can see children yelling at their parents, "Mommy, I've got to go," and desperate mothers surrendering, "All right—well, do it. Do it right here." O'Hare would soon become a shambles. The whole scene would become unbelievable and the laughter and ridicule would be nationwide. It would probably get a front page story in the London *Times*. It would be a source of great mortification and embarrassment to the city administration. It might even create the kind of emergency in which planes would have to be held up while passengers got back aboard to use the plane's toilet facilities.

The threat of this tactic was leaked (again there may be a Freudian slip here, and again, so what?) back to the administration, and within forty-eight hours the Woodlawn Organization found itself in conference with the authorities who said that they were certainly going to live up to their commitments and they could never understand where anyone got the idea that a promise made by Chicago's City Hall would not be observed. At no point, then or since, has there ever been any open mention of the threat of the O'Hare tactic. Very few of the members of the Woodlawn Organization knew how close they were to writing history. . . .

. . . [O]ne of the major department stores in the nation was brought to heel by the following threatened tactic. Remember the rule—the threat is often more effective than the tactic itself, but *only* if you are so organized that the establishment knows not only that you have the power to execute the tactic but that you definitely will. You can't do much bluffing in this game; if you're ever caught bluffing, forget about ever using threats in the future. On that point you're dead.

There is a particular department store that happens to cater to the carriage trade. It attracts many customers on the basis of its labels as well as the quality of its merchandise. Because of this, economic boycotts had failed to deter even the black middle class from shopping there. At the time its employment policies were more restrictive than those of the other stores. Blacks were hired for only the most menial jobs.

We made up a tactic. A busy Saturday shopping date was selected. Approximately 3,000 blacks all dressed up in their good churchgoing suits or dresses would be bused downtown. When you put 3,000 blacks on the main floor of a store, even one that covers a square block, suddenly the entire color of the store changes. Any white coming through the revolving doors would take one pop-eyed look and assume that somehow he had stepped into Africa. He would keep right on going out of the store. This would end the white trade for the day.

For a low-income group, shopping is a time-consuming experience, for economy means everything. This would mean that every counter would be occupied by potential customers, carefully examining the quality of merchandise and asking, say, at the shirt counter, about the material, color, style, cuffs, collars, and price. As the group occupying the clerks' attention around the shirt counters moved to the underwear section, those at the underwear section would replace them at the shirt counter, and the personnel of the store would be constantly occupied.

Now pause to examine the tactic. It is legal. There is no sit-in or unlawful occupation of premises. Some thousands of people are in the store "shopping." The police are powerless and you are operating within the law.

This operation would go on until an hour before closing time, when the group would begin purchasing everything in sight to be delivered C.O.D.! This would tie up truck-delivery service for at least two days—with obvious further heavy financial costs, since all the merchandise would be refused at the time of delivery.

The threat was delivered to the authorities through a legitimate and "trustworthy" channel. Every organization must have two or three stool pigeons who are trusted by the establishment. These stool pigeons are invaluable as "trustworthy" lines of communication to the establishment. With all plans ready to go, we began formation of a series of committees: a transportation committee to get the buses, a mobilization committee to work with the ministers to get their people to their buses, and other committees with other specific functions. Two of the key committees deliberately included one of these stoolies each, so that there would be one to back up the other. We knew the plan would be quickly reported back to the department store. The next day we received a call from the department store for a meeting to discuss new personnel policies and an urgent request that the meeting take place within the next two or three days, certainly before Saturday!

The personnel policies of the store were drastically changed. Overnight, 186 new jobs were opened. For the first time, blacks were on the sales floor and in executive training.

This is the kind of tactic that can be used by the middle class too. Organized shopping, wholesale buying plus charging and returning everything on delivery, would add accounting costs to their attack on the retailer with the ominous threat of continued repetition. This is far more effective than canceling a charge account. Let's look at the score: (1) sales for one day are completely shot; (2) delivery service is tied up for two days or more; and (3) the accounting department is screwed up. The total cost is a nightmare for any retailer, and the sword remains hanging over his head. The middle class, too, must learn the nature of the enemy and be able to practice what I have described as mass jujitsu, utilizing the power of one part of the power structure against another part.

372-387

TO MISSISSIPPI YOUTH

Malcolm X

At the end of 1964, a delegation of thirty-seven teenagers from McComb, Mississippi, came to New York for their Christmas vacation. The eight-day trip was sponsored by the Student Nonviolent Coordinating Committee for young people who had been outstanding in the civil-rights struggle in their home town.

The McComb youth attended various meetings and discussions in Harlem. Toward the end of their stay, on December 31, 1964, they visited the Hotel Theresa to learn what Malcolm X stood for. The following is a small portion of what he told them.

One of the first things I think young people, especially nowadays, should learn is how to see for yourself and listen for yourself and think for yourself. Then you can come to an intelligent decision for yourself. If you form the habit of going by what you hear others say about someone, or going by what others think about someone, instead of searching that thing out for yourself and seeing for yourself, you will be walking west when you think you're going east, and you will be walking east when you think you're going west. This generation, especially of our people, has a burden, more so than any other time in history. The most important thing that we can learn to do today is think for ourselves.

It's good to keep wide-open ears and listen to what everybody else has to say, but when you come to make a decision, you have to weigh all of what you've heard on its own, and place it where it belongs, and come to a decision for yourself; you'll never regret it. But if you form the habit of taking what someone else says about a thing without checking it out for yourself, you'll find that other people will have you hating your friends and loving your enemies. This is one of the things that our people are beginning to learn today—that it is very important to think out a situation for yourself. If you don't do it, you'll always be maneuvered into a situation where you are never fighting your actual enemies, where you will find yourself fighting your own self.

I think our people in this country are the best examples of that. Many of us want to be nonviolent and we talk very loudly, you know, about being nonviolent. Here in Harlem, where there are probably more black people concentrated than any place in the world, some talk that nonviolent talk too.

From *Malcolm X Speaks*, ed. by George Breitman (New York: Grove Press, Inc., 1965), pp. 137–146.

But we find that they aren't nonviolent with each other. You can go out to Harlem Hospital, where there are more black patients than any hospital in the world, and see them going in there all cut up and shot up and busted up where they got violent with each other.

My experience has been that in many instances where you find Negroes talking about nonviolence, they are not nonviolent with each other, and they're not loving with each other, or forgiving with each other. Usually when they say they're nonviolent, they mean they're nonviolent with somebody else. I think you understand what I mean. They are nonviolent with the enemy. A person can come to your home, and if he's white and wants to heap some kind of brutality on you, you're nonviolent; or he can come to take your father and put a rope around his neck, and you're nonviolent. But if another Negro just stomps his foot, you'll rumble with him in a minute. Which shows you that there's an inconsistency there.

I myself would go for nonviolence if it was consistent, if everybody was going to be nonviolent all the time. I'd say, okay, let's get with it, we'll all be nonviolent. But I don't go along with any kind of nonviolence unless everybody's going to be nonviolent. If they make the Ku Klux Klan nonviolent, I'll be nonviolent. If they make the White Citizens Council nonviolent, I'll be nonviolent. But as long as you've got somebody else not being nonviolent, I don't want anybody coming to me talking any nonviolent talk. I don't think it is fair to tell our people to be nonviolent unless someone is out there making the Klan and the Citizens Council and these other groups also be nonviolent.

Now, I'm not criticizing those here who are nonviolent. I think everybody should do it the way they feel is best, and I congratulate anybody who can be nonviolent in the face of all that kind of action in that part of the world. I don't think that in 1965 you will find the upcoming generation of our people, especially those who have been doing some thinking, who will go along with any form of nonviolence unless nonviolence is going to be practiced all the way around.

If the leaders of the nonviolent movement can go into the white community and teach nonviolence, good. I'd go along with that. But as long as I see them teaching nonviolence only in the black community, we can't go along with that. We believe in equality, and equality means that you have to put the same thing over here that you put over there. And if black people alone are going to be the ones who are nonviolent, then it's not fair. We throw ourselves off guard. In fact, we disarm ourselves and make ourselves defenseless. . . .

The Organization of Afro-American Unity is a nonreligious group of black people who believe that the problems confronting our people in this country need to be re-analyzed and a new approach devised toward trying to get a solution. Studying the problem, we recall that prior to 1939 all of our people, in the North, South, East and West, no matter how much education we had, were segregated. We were segregated in the North just as much as we were segregated in the South. Even now there's as much segregation in the North as there is in the South. There's some worse segregation right here in New York City than there is in McComb, Mississippi; but up here they're subtle and tricky and deceitful, and they make you think you've got it made when you haven't even begun to make it yet.

Prior to 1939, our people were in a very menial position or condition. Most of us were waiters and porters and bellhops and janitors and waitresses and things of that sort. It was not until war was declared with Germany, and America became involved in a manpower shortage in regards to her factories plus her army, that the black man in this country was permitted to make a few strides forward. It was never out of some kind of moral enlightenment or moral awareness on the part of Uncle Sam. Uncle Sam only let the black man take a step forward when he himself has his back to the wall.

In Michigan, where I was brought up at that time, I recall that the best jobs in the city for blacks were waiters out at the country club. In those days if you had a job waiting table in the country club, you had it made. Or if you had a job at the State House. Having a job at the State House didn't mean that you were a clerk or something of that sort; you had a shoeshine stand at the State House. Just by being there you could be around all those big-shot politicians—that made you a big-shot Negro. You were shining shoes, but you were a big-shot Negro because you were around big-shot white people and you could bend their ear and get up next to them. And ofttimes you were chosen by them to be the voice of the Negro community.

Around that time, 1939 or '40 or '41, they weren't drafting Negroes in the army or the navy. A Negro couldn't join the navy in 1940 or '41. They wouldn't take a black man in the navy except to make him a cook. He couldn't just go and join the navy, and I don't think he could just go and join the army. They weren't drafting him when the war first started. This is what they thought of you and me in those days. For one thing, they didn't trust us; they feared that if they put us in the army and trained us in how to use rifles and other things, we might shoot at some targets that they hadn't picked out. And we would have. Any thinking man knows what target to shoot at. If a man has to have someone else to choose his target, then he isn't thinking for himself—they're doing the thinking for him.

The Negro leaders in those days were the same type we have today. When the Negro leaders saw all the white fellows being drafted and taken into the army and dying on the battlefield, and no Negroes were dying because they weren't being drafted, the Negro leaders came up and said, "We've got to die too. We want to be drafted too, and we demand that you take us in there and let us die for our country too." That was what the Negro leaders did back in 1940, I remember. A. Philip Randolph was one of the leading Negroes in those days who said it, and he's one of the Big Six right now; and this is why he's one of the Big Six.

So they started drafting Negro soldiers then, and started letting Negroes get into the navy. But not until Hitler and Tojo and the foreign powers were strong enough to put pressure on this country, so that it had its back to the wall and needed us, [did] they let us work in factories. Up until that time we couldn't work in the factories; I'm talking about the North as well as the South. And when they let us work in the factories, at first they let us in only as janitors. After a year or so passed by, they let us work on machines. We became machinists, got a little more skill. If we got a little more skill, we made a little more money, which enabled us to live in a little better neighborhood. When we lived in a little better neighborhood, we went to a little better school, got a little better education and could come out and get a little better job. So the cycle was broken somewhat.

But the cycle was not broken out of some kind of sense of moral responsibility on the part of the government. No, the only time that cycle was broken even to a degree was when world pressure was brought to bear on the United States government. They didn't look at us as human beings—they just put us into their system and let us advance a little bit farther because it served their interests. They never let us advance a little bit farther because they were interested in us as human beings. Any of you who have a knowledge of history, sociology, or political science, or the economic development of his country and its race relations—go back and do some research on it and you'll have to admit that this is true.

It was during the time that Hitler and Tojo made war with this country and put pressure on it [that] Negroes in this country advanced a little bit. At the end of the war with Germany and Japan, then Joe Stalin and Communist Russia were a threat. During that period we made a little more headway. Now the point that I'm making is this: Never at any time in the history of our people in this country have we made advances or progress in any way based upon the internal good will of this country. We have made advancement in this country only when this country was under pressure from forces above and beyond its control. The internal moral consciousness of this country is bankrupt. It hasn't existed since they first brought us over here and made slaves out of us. They make it appear they have our good interests at heart, but when you study it, every time, no matter how many steps they take us forward, it's like we're standing on a—what do you call that thing?—a treadmill. The treadmill is moving backwards faster than we're able to go forward in this direction. We're not even standing still—we're going backwards.

In studying the process of this so-called progress during the past twenty years, we of the Organization of Afro-American Unity realized that the only time the black man in this country is given any kind of recognition, or even listened to, is when America is afraid of outside pressure, or when she's afraid of her image abroad. So we saw that it was necessary to expand the problem and the struggle of the black man in this country until it went above and beyond the jurisdiction of the United States. . . .

I was fortunate enough to be able to take a tour of the African continent during the summer. I went to Egypt, then to Arabia, Kuwait, Lebanon, Sudan, Ethiopia, Kenya, Tanganyika, Zanzibar, Nigeria, Ghana, Guinea, Liberia and Algeria. I found, while I was traveling on the African continent, I had already detected it in May, that someone had very shrewdly planted the seed of division on this continent to make the Africans now show genuine concern with our problem, just as they plant seeds in your and my minds so that we won't show concern with the African problem. . . .

I also found that in many of these African countries the head of state is genuinely concerned with the problem of the black man in this country; but many of them thought if they opened their mouths and voiced their concern that they would be insulted by the American Negro leaders. Because one head of state in Asia voiced his support of the civil-rights struggle [in 1963] and a couple of the Big Six had the audacity to slap his face and say they weren't interested in that kind of help—which in my opinion is asinine. So the African leaders only had to be convinced that if they took an open stand at the governmental level and showed interest in the problem of black people in this country, they wouldn't be rebuffed.

And today you'll find in the United Nations, and it's not an accident, that every time the Congo question or anything on the African continent is being debated, they couple it with what is going on, or what is happening to you and me, in Mississippi and Alabama and these other places. In my opinion, the greatest accomplishment that was made in the struggle of the black man in America in 1964 toward some kind of real progress was the successful linking together of our problem with the African problem, or making our problem a world problem. Because now, whenever anything happens to you in Mississippi, it's not just a case of somebody in Alabama getting indignant, or somebody in New York getting indignant. The same repercussions that you see all over the world when an imperialist or foreign power interferes in some section of Africa—you see repercussions, you see the embassies being bombed and burned and overturned—nowadays, when something happens to black people in Mississippi, you'll see the same repercussions all over the world.

I wanted to point this out to you because it is important for you to know that when you're in Mississippi, you're not alone. As long as you think you're alone, then you take a stand as if you're a minority or as if you're outnumbered, and that kind of stand will never enable you to win a battle. You've got to know that you've got as much power on your side as that Ku Klux Klan has on its side. And when you know that you've got as much power on your side as the Klan has on its side, you'll talk the same kind of language with that Klan as the Klan is talking with you. . . .

I think in 1965, whether you like it, or I like it, or they like it, or not, you will see that there is a generation of black people becoming mature to the point where they feel that they have no more business being asked to take a peaceful approach than anybody else takes, unless everybody's going to take a peaceful approach.

So we here in the Organization of Afro-American Unity are with the struggle in Mississippi one thousand percent. We're with the efforts to register our people in Mississippi to vote one thousand percent. But we do not go along with anybody telling us to help nonviolently. We think that if the government says that Negroes have a right to vote, and then some Negroes come out to vote, and some kind of Ku Klux Klan is going to put them in the river, and the government doesn't do anything about it, it's time for us to organize and band together and equip ourselves and qualify ourselves to protect ourselves. And once you can protect yourself, you don't have to worry about being hurt. . . .

If you don't have enough people down there to do it, we'll come down there and help you do it. Because we're tired of this old runaround that our people have been given in this country. For a long time they accused me of not getting involved in politics. They should've been glad I didn't get involved in politics, because anything I get in, I'm in it all the way. If they say we don't take part in the Mississippi struggle, we will organize brothers here in New York who know how to handle these kind of affairs, and they'll slip into Mississippi like Jesus slipped into Jerusalem.

That doesn't mean we're against white people, but we sure are against the Ku Klux Klan and the White Citizens Councils; and anything that looks like it's against us, we're against it. Excuse me for raising my voice, but this thing, you know, gets me upset. Imagine that—a country that's supposed to be for freedom and all of that kind of stuff when they want to draft you and put you in the army and send you to Saigon to fight for them—and then you've got to turn around and all night long discuss how you're going to just get a right to register and vote without being murdered. Why, that's the most hypocritical government since the world began! . . .

I hope you don't think I'm trying to incite you. Just look here: Look at yourselves. Some of you are teen-agers, students. How do you think I feel—and I belong to a generation ahead of you—how do you think I feel to have to tell you, "We, my generation, sat around like a knot on a wall while the whole world was fighting for its human rights—and you've got to be born into a society where you still have that same fight." What did we do, who preceded you? I'll tell you what we did: Nothing. And don't you make the same mistake we made. . . .

You get freedom by letting your enemy know that you'll do anything to get your freedom; then you'll get it. It's the only way you'll get it. When you get that kind of attitude, they'll label you as a "crazy Negro," or they'll call you a "crazy nigger"—they don't say Negro. Or they'll call you an extremist or a subversive, or seditious, or a red or a radical. But when you stay radical long enough, and get enough people to be like you, you'll get your freedom. . . .

So don't you run around here trying to make friends with somebody who's depriving you of your rights. They're not your friends, no, they're your enemies. Treat them like that and fight them, and you'll get your freedom; and after you get your freedom, your enemy will respect you. And we'll respect you. And I say that with no hate. I don't have hate in me. I have no hate at all. I don't have any hate. I've got some sense. I'm not going to let somebody who hates me tell me to love him. I'm not that wayout. And you, young as you are, and because you start thinking, you're not going to do it either. The only time you're going to get in that bag is if somebody puts you there. Somebody else, who doesn't have your welfare at heart. . . .

I want to thank all of you for taking the time to come to Harlem and especially here. I hope that you've gotten a better understanding about me. I put it to you just as plain as I know how to put it; there's no interpretation necessary. And I want you to know that we're not trying to advocate any kind of indiscriminate, unintelligent action. Any kind of action that you are ever involved in that's designed to protect the lives and property of our mistreated people in this country, we're with you one thousand percent. And if you don't feel you're qualified to do it, we have some brothers who will slip in, as I said earlier, and help train you and show you how to equip yourself and let you know how to deal with the man who deals with you. . . .

THE NEW AMERICAN REVOLUTION

Tom Hayden

> We for ten years incessantly and ineffectually besieged the throne as supplicants; we reasoned, we remonstrated with Parliament in the most mild and decent language . . .
>
> *from* THE DECLARATION OF THE CAUSES AND THE NECESSITY OF TAKING UP ARMS
> *The Continental Congress, July 1775*

> I feel that I am a citizen of the American dream, and that the revolutionary struggle of which I am a part is a struggle against the American nightmare. . . .
>
> *Eldridge Cleaver*

If we look at any revolutionary movement, we see that it evolves through three overlapping stages. The first is *protest*, in which people petition their rulers for specific policy changes. When the level of protest becomes massive, the rulers begin to apply pressures to suppress it. This in turn drives the people towards the second stage, *resistance*, in which they begin to contest the legitimacy of the rulers. As this conflict sharpens, resistance leads to a *liberation* phase in which the ruling structure disintegrates and "new guards" are established by the people. America in the Sixties experienced primarily the protest phase, but resistance has already become commonplace among the blacks and the young. Temporary periods of liberation have even been achieved—as when students occupied Columbia University for one week and learned they could create new relationships and govern themselves. Of course, these experiences only provide a glimpse of liberation as long as the government has sufficient police power to restore university officials to office.

In the resistance phase it becomes necessary to lay plans for defeating the police and building a new society. It is a time of showdown in which the government will either crush the resistance and restore its own power, or undergo constant failure, eroding its own base to a very dangerous point. Because it challenges the legitimacy of the way things are ordered, resistance acquires the responsibility of proposing and creating new arrangements.

So your brother's bound and gagged
And they chained him to a chair,
Won't you please come to Chicago
Just to sing?
In a land that's known as freedom
How can such a thing be fair,
Won't you please come to Chicago
For the help that we can bring?
We can change the world,
Re-arrange the world.
It's dying to get better.
Politicians, sit yourself down,
There's nothing for you here,
Won't you please come to Chicago
For a ride?
Don't ask Jack to help you
'Cause he'll turn the other ear,
Won't you please come to Chicago
Or else join the other side?
We can change the world,
Re-arrange the world.
It's dying (if you believe in justice)
It's dying (if you believe in freedom)
It's dying (then everything's all right)
It's dying (rules and regulations, who needs 'em?)
Open up the door!

Somehow people must be free
I hope the day comes soon,
Won't you please come to Chicago,
Show your face?
From the bottom of the ocean
To the mountains of the moon,
Won't you please come to Chicago,
No one else can take your place?
We can change the world,
Re-arrange the world.
It's dying (if you believe in justice)
It's dying (if you believe in freedom)
It's dying (then everything's all right)
It's dying (rules and regulations, who needs 'em?)
Open up the door!

The general outlines of what we want are by now as clear as possible without developing a rigid blueprint. We have to abolish a private property system which turns over the benefits of our wealth and technology to a few, and which in its drive for new markets collides with the aspirations of people all over the world. We need to turn this situation around so that our technology can be used by the world's people for the development of their economies and cultures. In this socialist transformation, decision-making power must be in the hands of the people most affected.

What is less clear is the kind of structural rearrangement which will be required to achieve these goals. A radical movement always begins to create within itself the structures which will eventually form the basis of the new society. So it is necessary to look at the structure of motion-now-in-progress to understand what must be destroyed and what must be built. We need a new Continental Congress to explore where our institutions have failed and to declare new principles for organizing our society.

The first principle of any new arrangement is *self-determination for our internal colonies*. In the Seventies the Third World revolutions will sharpen not only on other continents but here inside the U.S. The black ghettos are a chain of islands forming a single domestic colony. The same is true of the Puerto Rican people struggling for independence in San Juan, New York and Chicago; the Chicano people of the Southwest; and the Asians and Indians struggling in their small urban and rural communities. The concept of "integration" which so dominated consciousness in the Sixties is now blinding most people to the new reality of self-determination. Underlying the desire for integration is the even deeper belief that America is "one nation, indivisible." It seems unthinkable that this country might literally be broken up into self-determining parts (nations on the same land), yet that is more or less what is evolving. The failure of the U.S. to make progress in the areas of education, jobs, housing and land reform here at home, the constant recourse to repressive violence at a time when the "revolution of rising expectations" is nowhere stronger than in America, can only make Third World people turn towards independence.

The second principle of rearrangement should be the creation of *Free Territories in the Mother Country*. Already we are seen as alien and outside White Civilization by those in power. It is necessary for us to create amidst the falling ruins of this Empire a new, alternative way of life more in harmony with the interests of the world's people.

Abbie is a pioneer in this struggle, but so far "Woodstock Nation" is purely cultural, a state of mind shared by thousands of young people. The next stage is to make this "Woodstock Nation" an organized reality with its own revolutionary institutions and, starting immediately, with roots in its own territory. At the same time, the need to overcome our inbred, egoistic, male, middle-class character, and especially to create solidarity with Third World struggles, has to become a foremost part of our consciousness.

The new people in white America are clustering in ghetto communities of their own: Berkeley, Haight-Ashbury, Isla Vista, Madison, Ann Arbor, the East Village, the Upper West Side. These communities, often created on the edge of universities, are not the bohemian enclaves of ten years ago. Those places, like Greenwich Village and North Beach, developed when the alienated were still a marginal group. Now millions of young people have nowhere else to go. They live cheaply in their own communities; go to school or to various free universities; study crafts and new skills; learn self-defense; read the underground press; go to demonstrations. The hard core of these new territories is the lumpen-bourgeoisie, drop-outs from the American way of life. But in any such community there is a cross-section of people whose needs overlap. In Berkeley, for example, there are students, street people, left-liberals and blacks, together constituting a radical political majority of the city. Communities like this are nearly as alien to police and "solid citizens" as are the black ghettos.

The importance of these communities is that they add a dimension of territory, of real physical space, to the consciousness of those within. The final break with mainstream America comes, after all, when you literally *cannot* live there, when it becomes imperative to live more closely with "your own kind."

Until recently people dropped out in their minds, or into tiny bohemian enclaves. Now they drop out collectively, into territory. In this situation feelings of individual isolation are replaced by a common consciousness of large numbers sharing the same needs. It is possible to go anywhere in America and find the section of town inhabited by the drop-outs, the freaks and the radicals. It is a nationwide network of people with the same oppression, the same language, the same music, the same styles, the same needs and grievances: the very essence of a new society taking root and growing up in the framework of the old.

The ruling class views this pattern with growing alarm. They analyze places like Berkeley as "red zones" like the ones they attempt to destroy in Vietnam. Universities and urban renewal agencies everywhere are busy moving into and destroying our communities, breaking them up physically, escalating the rents, tearing down cheap housing and replacing it with hotels, convention centers and university buildings. Politicians declare a "crime wave" (dope) and double the police patrols. Tens of thousands of kids are harassed, busted, moved on.

In every great revolution there have been such "liberated zones" where radicalism was most deeply rooted, where people tried to meet their own needs while fighting off the official governing power. If there is revolutionary change inside the Mother Country, it will originate in the Berkeleys and Madisons, where people are similarly rooted and where we are defending ourselves against constantly growing aggression.

The concept of Free Territories does *not* mean local struggles for "community control" in the traditional sense—battles which are usually limited to electoral politics and maneuvering for control of funds from the state or federal government. Our struggles will largely ignore or resist outside administration and instead build and defend our own institutions.

Nor does the concept mean withdrawal into comfortable radical enclaves remote from the rest of America. The Territories should be centers from which a challenge to the whole Establishment is mounted.

Such Free Territories would have four common points of identity:

First, *they will be utopian centers of new cultural experiment.* "All Power to the Imagination" has real meaning for people experiencing the breakdown of our decadent culture. In the Territories all traditional social relations—starting with the oppression of women—would be overturned, or at least re-examined. The nuclear family would be replaced by a mixture of communes, extended families, children's centers and new schools. Women would have their own communes and organizations. Work would be redefined as a task done for the community, or as play. Drugs would be commonly used as a means of deepening self-awareness. Urban structures would be destroyed, to be replaced with parks, closed streets, expanded backyards inside blocks, and a village atmosphere in general would be encouraged. Education would be reorganized along revolutionary lines, with children really participating. Music and art would be freed from commercial control and widely performed in the community. At all levels the goal would be to eliminate egoism, competition and aggression from our personalities.

Second, *the Territories will be internationalist. Cultural experiment without internationalism is privilege; internationalism without cultural rev-*

olution is false consciousness. People in our Territories would act as citizens of an international community, an obstructive force inside imperialism. Solidarity committees to aid all Third World struggles would be in constant motion. Each Territory would see itself as an "international city." The flags, music and culture of other countries and other liberation movements would permeate the Territory. Travel and "foreign relations" with other nations would be commonplace. All imperialist institutions (universities, draft boards, corporations) in or near the Territory would be under constant siege. An underground railroad would exist to support revolutionary fugitives.

Third, *the Territories will be centers of constant confrontation, battlefronts inside the Mother Country.* Major institutions such as universities and corporations would be under constant pressure either to shut down or to serve the community. The occupying police would be systematically opposed. Stores would be pressured to transform themselves into community-serving institutions. Tenant unions would seek to break the control of absentee landlords and to transform local housing into communal shelter. There would be continual defiance of tax, draft and drug laws. Protest campaigns of national importance, such as the anti-war movement, would be initiated from within the Territories. The constant process of confrontation would not only weaken the control of the power structure, but would serve also to create a greater sense of our own identity, our own possiblities.

Fourth, *they will be centers of survival and self-defense.* The Territories would include free medical and legal services, child-care centers, drug clinics, crash pads, instant communication networks, job referral and welfare centers—all the basic services to meet people's needs as they struggle and change. Training in physical self-defense and the use of weapons would become commonplace as fascism and vigilantism increase.

Insurgent, even revolutionary, activity will occur outside as well as inside the Territories. Much of it will be within institutions (workplaces, army bases, schools, even "behind enemy lines" in the government). But the Territories will be like models or beacons to those who struggle within these institutions, and the basic tension will tend always to occur between the authorities and the Territories pulling people out of the mainstream.

The Territories will establish once and for all the polarized nature of the Mother Country. No longer will Americans be able to think comfortably of themselves as a homogeneous society with a few extremists at the fringes. No longer will politicians and administrators be able to feel confident in their power to govern the entire U.S. Beneath the surface of official power, the Territories will be giving birth to new centers of power.

In the foreseeable future, Free Territories will have to operate with a strategy of "dual power"—that is, people would stay within the legal structure of the U.S., involuntarily if for no other reason, while building new forms with which to replace that structure. The thrust of these new forms will be resistance against illegitimate outside authority, and constant attempts at self-government.

Mother Country radicalism will have its unique organization forms. Revolutionary movements have turned towards the concept of a centralized, disciplined, nationally-based "vanguard" party which leads a variety of mass organizations representing specific interests (women, labor, students, etc.). This organizational form is logical where people are already disciplined by their situation (as in a large factory) or where the goal is "state power." But it is not so clear that such an organizational form is necessary—at least now—for Mother Country radicalism. Certainly the excessive individualism and egoism which dominate the culture of young people must be overcome if we are going to survive, much less make a revolution. But the organizational form must be consistent with the kind of revolution we are trying to make. For that reason *the collective* in some form should be the basis of revolutionary organization.

A revolutionary collective would not be like the organizations to which we give part-time attachment today, the kind where we attend meetings, "participate" by speaking and voting, and perhaps learn how to use a mimeograph machine. The collectives would be much more about our *total* lives. Instead of developing our talents within schools and other Establishment institutions, we would develop them primarily within our own collectives. In these groups we would learn politics, self-defense, languages, ecology, medical skills, industrial techniques—everything that helps people grow towards independence. Thus the collectives would not be just organizational weapons to use against the Establishment, but organs fostering the development of revolutionary people.

The emphasis in this kind of organization is on power from below. It begins with a distrust of highly centralized or elite-controlled organizations. But we should also recognize that decentralization can degenerate into anarchy and tribalism. Collectives must stress the need for unity and cooperation, especially on projects which require large numbers or when common interests are threatened. We should seek the advantages of coordinated power while avoiding the problem of an established hierarchy. A network of collectives can act as the "revolutionary council" of a given Territory and a network of such councils can unite the Territories across the United States. In addition to such political coordination, the Territories can be united through the underground press and culture, through conferences and constant travel.

Finally and above all, the concept of Free Territories does not imply that the youth movement is already "revolutionary," except in its potential. Free Territories are only a form in which the struggle goes on. Both the "student movement" and the "youth culture" still must deal with the permeation of *white, male, middle-class attitudes*. Neither students on strike nor stoned freaks in the street constitute a real revolutionary force. There must be still more transformation of our character on all levels. Male chauvinism must be overthrown in the political movement and the rock culture; individualism and egoism must be replaced by a collective spirit; narrow, middle-class demands for privilege must be replaced by demands in the interest of the tax-paying masses. The most critical immediate problem we have to clear up is our relationship to the Third World liberation movement.

The creation of Free Territories in the Mother Country is not separate from the national liberation battles of Third World people. The Territories are a way to prepare for the vast international uprising which will be the next American Revolution.

We must not follow the chauvinist path taken by the Left in other colonial periods. Our support for black liberation must be unconditional. We must begin by making it clear that there will be no racism and no racist escapism in the peace movement or in Woodstock Nation. If we are serious about becoming new men and women, free of the bloody legacy of white American civilization, then we have the responsibility of becoming the first white people in history to live beyond racial definitions of interest. There is something racist about Woodstock Nation—not the familiar racism of George Wallace, but an attitude of distance that comes from living in the most comfortable oppression the world has ever known. We are constantly in danger of escaping into a cultural revolution of our own, a tiny island of post-scarcity hedonism, pacifism and fantasy far from the blood and fire of the Third World.

White radicals can follow the path of their own legitimate revolution, however, without abandoning the Vietnamese and the blacks. In fact we cannot realize our own needs without the destruction of the same colonial system that brutalizes the Third World. We are at one end of a line of resistance whose other end is rooted in black America and the Third World. Young white people today, whether working-class or middle-class, are the first privileged generation with no real interest in inheriting the capitalist system. We have experienced its affluence and know that life involves far more than suburban comfort. We know further that this system contains its own self-destruct: racism, exploitation and militarism lead nowhere in the contemporary world but to war and waste. As we look out over the top of imperialism we should be able to see that our true allies are those who live below and beyond its privilege, the wretched of the earth.

Certainly there is a gap between the children of affluence and the children of squalor. Our need for a new life style, for women's liberation, for the transformation of work, for a new environment and educational system, cannot be described in the rhetoric of Third World revolution where poverty, exploitation and fascist violence are the immediate crisis. We cannot be black; nor can our needs be entrusted to a Third World vanguard of any kind.

But our destiny and possible liberation cannot be separated from the

Third World vanguards. The change toward which we are inevitably moving is one in which the white world yields power and resources to an insistent mankind. There is no escape—either into rural communes or existential mysticism—from this dynamic of world confrontation. By our deeds each day we are determining what role, if any, we will have in the world's future. What we have and have not done, for Bobby and for Cuba and for Vietnam, measures exactly our stature in the new world being created.

Some will cry that this cosmic formulation denies the issue of priorities. How shall it be settled whether to work first against racism, or the war, or male supremacy, or the production speed-up? Historically the White Left has argued that colonial liberation should wait for socialist revolution or be submerged in a black-white working-class coalition. In the same vein, some Panthers today argue that the women's movement should wait until blacks are liberated. Special interests seem constantly in danger of being betrayed, and so we fragment into groups with particular, immediate priorities.

At first this fragmentation appears hopeless. But the fact that so many different people are moving at once for their own liberation suggests an inspiring possibility. *We are living in a time of universal desire for a new social order, a time when total revolution is on the agenda:* not a limited and particular "revolution" for national identity here, for the working class there, for women here—but *for all of mankind* to build a new, freer way of life by sharing the world's vast resources equally and fraternally. The world's people are so interdependent that a strike for freedom anywhere creates vibrations everywhere. The American Empire itself is so worldwide in scope that mankind has for the first time not only a common spirit but a common enemy. Through their particular struggles, more and more revolutionaries see the possibilities of the "new man" envisioned by Che Guevara. Formed in an international upheaval, such a human being would be universal in character for the first time in history. To become such a whole person in the present means fighting not only around immediate self-interest but against all levels of oppression at once.

It is in this context that priorities, especially the priority of Bobby Seale's trial, should be understood. Vanguards will be discovered in action, and priorities will be created where total showdowns between the status quo and revolution appear. Bobby's case, and the repression of the Panthers generally, embodies just such a showdown. Bobby and the Panthers were the first to raise the battle cry of liberation inside America, the first black revolutionary party with an internationalist perspective, the first to threaten imperialism totally from within. The U.S. government certainly sees the Panthers this way; that is why it is attempting, through Bobby's trial, to demonstrate that genocide awaits all who rebel. All those who value their own liberation must go with the Panthers and Bobby as they become symbols of humanity making a time-honored stand: Freedom or Death.

VOLUNTEERS

Marty Balin and Paul Kantner

Look whats happening out in the streets
    Got a revolution   Got to revolution
Hey Im dancing down the streets
    Got a revolution   Got to revolution
Aint it amazing all the people I meet
    Got a revolution   Got to revolution

One generation got old
One generation got soul
This generation got no destination to hold
    Pick up the cry

Hey now its time for you and me
    Got a revolution   Got to revolution
Come on now were marching to the sea
    Got a revolution   Got to revolution
Who will take it from you
We will and who are we
    We are volunteers
        volunteers
        volunteers

PART FOUR
FEAR

All liberation depends on the consciousness of servitude.
Herbert Marcuse

Who do we fear?
We fear "the enemy."
Who is the enemy?
The enemy is They; the enemy is the Other.
Other than Us: a threat to the body politic.
A foreign object that must be excised.
G. M. Swatez

We have come, finally, to the problem of fear, another part of the complex American social reality. It is our fears as well as our aspirations that shape the quality of life in America. We are afraid of many things, from being mugged on the streets to the threat of nuclear holocaust, of not having enough of the material things of life, of not being successful, and of being vulnerable to others. We project these fears outward to mold a fearful social environment beset with problems of pollution, poverty, and powerlessness. With fear so finely interwoven into the fabric of American society, one might conclude that the quality of life would be improved if only we were less afraid. But fear is not always socially destructive, for the fear of starvation, of death from preventable disease, and of natural catastrophe has been a powerful force for constructive social innovation. The selections that follow can support a much different conclusion: that to cope successfully with the problem of fear we must become fully afraid. In any case, we must begin by confronting the fears that we have and by understanding the conditions that produced them.

Part Four surveys some of the fears that haunt Americans and some of the social purposes that they serve. It examines the gut reactions of middle America to unsafe streets, lenient courts, and permissive schools and parents, as in the following:

> The judges and courts are not harsh enough. These people who commit crimes don't get enough time in prison and they don't get it soon enough. . . . An important factor in the crime crisis, experts agree, is the permissive attitude of parents, educators, courts—the public generally. . . . The war on crime has to start with attitudes. It must start in the grade school—maybe even in kindergarten. . . . Crime that goes unpunished breeds crime. . . . All of this has been brought about by the breakdown of proper instruction and discipline in the home, in the schools and in the churches. . . . (See "Why the Street Are Not Safe")

Social changes that have threatened the position of the blue-collar classes have in the recent past produced a politics of fear. Or has fear always been an indispensible tool of American politicians? Other readings examine the fears of minority groups. Schools in the South were desegregated in the 1960s, but Negro parents were often afraid to take advantage of the new order of things:

> Out of a population of some fifty thousand Negroes, there had only been forty-five applications [to a white high school in the South after integration decree]. People had said that they would send their children, had talked about it, had made plans; but, as the time drew near, when the application blanks were actually in their hands, they said, "I don't believe I'll sign this right now. I'll sign later." Or, "I've been thinking about this. I don't believe I'll send him right now." "Why?" I asked. But to this she couldn't or wouldn't give me any answer. (See Baldwin's *A Fly in Buttermilk*)

And radicalism from the left increasingly plays on fear to accomplish its version of "constructive action":

> After careful consideration we have come to the conclusion that no constructive action will be taken until you are convinced that repressive tactics cannot keep the fruits of repression from your own homes and families. (See Handbill given to whites in Chicago suburbs)

Such fears, as the selections in Chapter 15 suggest, play an obvious role in maintaining the existing social order. The society, in turn, perpetuates fear.

Fear is developed and perpetuated through a variety of complex social mechanisms. It is in part the result of such barriers as race, class, sex, and religion, that separate us from each other, that define the groups of people whom we distrust, hate, and fear. We fear the "others" who are not like us, and this becomes a reinforcing and self-sustaining social process—Laing has captured the essence of it in one of his knots: "Jack is frightened because Jill is dangerous; Jill appears dangerous because Jack is frightened." Our perception of the groups to which we belong and the behavior expected of us by these groups is, in turn, the product of socialization. All societies socialize the young both to restrict and to encourage certain behavior. The ways in which social sanctions and roles are learned in American society are examined in Chapter 16. These selections suggest that fear is not inherent in human nature, but is learned—the product of socialization. Certainly the way that we are socialized makes significant behavioral change a fearful experience. We learn at an early age to be conformists—to adhere to the mores and norms of our group or to face the consequences. When desirable change is both known and possible, excessive maintenance of group norms can become paralyzing, a kind of social illness; this explains Baldwin's observation that ". . . the future is like heaven—everyone exalts it, but no one wants to go there now."

Chapter 17 extends this individual learning to examine the social, economic, political, and spatial structures that institutionalize fear in potentially dangerous ways. The major pattern is the reinforcing system of isolation or "separateness" that then perpetuates both hate and fear. These three conditions thus maintain each other. The reader should note the similarities in this process of isolation, hate, and fear with reference, for example, to the

American Indians, Blacks in the ghetto, and the Ku Klux Klan. In each, the groups involved come to hold the view that one's own group is the center of everything, and all others are scaled and rated with reference to that view (See Williams).

Chapter 18 reflects on the dangers that emerge from the society dominated by extreme ethnocentrism and automatic obedience to established authority. In such circumstances unbelievable atrocities can be imposed on one's fellow man as in Elliot's fantasy where "the individual, even the leader, has no significant choice to make in the current of events. The current is part of a natural law, it is immoral, cruel, wasteful, useless and mysterious." Milgram's scientific experiments on human obedience provide us with an empirical base that lends plausibility to Elliot's chilling fantasy.

In conclusion, Chapter 19 presents what the editors of this volume believe to be the only direction in which the solution to pollution, poverty, powerlessness, and fear in American society can be found. Stated simply: The individual must come to define his "in group" to include all of humanity. Structuring society such that this is possible is very complicated and all of the requirements, at this point in time, may be largely unknown, although we believe a number of them may be found in the materials of this volume. It is for this reason we have ended with a chapter entitled, "Be Fully Afraid and Yet Not Stop." In other words, you are encouraged to rethink what you believe to be necessary to achieve for all Americans a high quality of life, to confront both personally and analytically the fears that necessary changes evoke, and then to act.

15 What? Me worry?

Only a few months ago, I sat talking with a Negro friend, who seemed very depressed.

"What's bugging you?" I asked.

"I had a nightmare last night," he said. "You know, the last time in Watts, I was out on the streets trying to cool it. Well, in my nightmare it happened again, but this time I wasn't cooling it, this time I was up on a roof with a rifle, sniping. And down below on the street, there was a white guy and I shot him, I killed him. And you know who he was? He was you. I killed you."

Paul Jacobs, *Prelude to Riot* (New York: Random House, 1966).

The more Jack is afraid of Jill
the more frightened is Jack that
Jill will think
that Jack is afraid

the more Jill is afraid of Jack
the more frightened is Jill that
Jack will think
that Jill is afraid

the more afraid Jack is of Jill
the more frightened Jack is
not to be frightened of Jill
because it is very dangerous not to be afraid when
faced with one so dangerous

Jack is frightened because Jill is dangerous
Jill appears dangerous because Jack is frightened

WHY STREETS ARE NOT SAFE: SPECIAL REPORT ON CRIME*

Fear has become a part of life for millions of Americans. Crime, spreading, is increasingly vicious. A survey of authorities spotlights the causes, suggests some remedies.

One of the great puzzles of urban America is this: Why is there so much crime?

Year after year, the problem keeps spiraling. Violence is spreading. Terror strikes in the suburbs as well as the slums. People are being slain, robbed, beaten, slashed, vandalized by youths and adults, white and black. Many offenses are marked by a sinister senselessness.

Latest figures of the Federal Bureau of Investigation showed major crime increasing at a rate of 11 percent last year compared with 1968. The over-all rate of rise for violent crimes—murder, rape, robbery, aggravated assault—was 12 percent. Street robbery was up 18 percent; residential robbery, 22 percent.

Capital's Plight. Alarm is nationwide. A symbol of the crime crisis is Washington, D. C., of which the Senate Majority Leader, Mike Mansfield, of Montana, said recently:

> It is a capital blanketed in fear. Fear stalks the streets. It seeps into office and home. It afflicts rich and poor. . . . It spreads and will continue to spread into what were supposed to be the "safe" suburbs. . . . People flee the streets at dark and, more and more, even in daylight.

The situation in many other cities, the FBI's uniform crime reports indicate, is as menacing as it is in the nation's capital—or worse. People are asking:

Why? What is behind the grim upsurge? Who are the criminals? What motivates them? Narcotics? Poverty? Racial malice? Class hatred? Envy? Frustration?

Who is to blame? Courts? Police? Parents? Schools?

To get answers, staff members of "U. S. News & World Report" talked with prosecutors, police chiefs, jurists, members of Congress and other officials across the country.

* Show in class 31 minute color film "Night and Fog" available from Contemporary Films, McGraw-Hill Films. After brief discussion show film "Obedience" (44 minutes). Available from Audio-Visual Services, Pennsylvania State University, University Park, Pa., 16802.

Reprinted from "U. S. News & World Report," vol. 68, no. 11 (March 16, 1970), pp. 15–19.

On these pages are the views of experts on causes of the frightening growth of crime in America, where it is heading, what can be done to halt it.

Narcotics

"The 'junkie' would kill his mother . . ."

Many authorities relate the intensifying problem of drug addiction to the flooding tide of crime.

In New York City, U. S. District Attorney Whitney North Seymour, Jr., calls narcotics the principal cause of street crime. Mr. Seymour comments: "The addict needs a steady flow of dollars to finance his habit. To get the money, he preys on the community."

Says New York City Council President Sanford D. Garelik, former chief inspector of the world's largest police department:

> The most important new element in crime is the increase in use of narcotics. Extent of that increase is illustrated by the fact that there are 10 times as many deaths from overdoses of heroin in New York City now as there were 10 years ago.

The New York State Narcotics Addiction Control Commission estimates that the average heroin addict—"fencing" stolen goods at a fraction of their value—must steal $150 worth every day to support a $30.50-a-day habit.

Robbery: a Way of Life. From Daniel Gutman, dean of the New York Academy of the Judiciary: "In my opinion, 75 percent of the crime on the streets is committed by drug addicts."

George Schuyler, Negro author and columnist, has this to say about his New York neighborhood:

> I was mugged in this area. My wife was mugged a block away. I know scores who have been mugged and robbed. The drug traffic has developed an element which lives solely by robbery. This element has expanded and extended all over the city and gone into the suburbs.

Across the continent, in Pasadena, Calif., an affluent suburb of Los Angeles, a police official says the armed-robbery rate rose about 25 percent last year. The reason: "Narcotics. The user has to have his 'fix.' He must get the money somehow. So he robs."

From testimony before a congressional committee by Police Chief Jerry Wilson of Washington, D. C.:

> . . . The narcotics problem is adding considerably to the problem of crime. We find this problem even among juvenile holdup men. . . . It is not at all unusual to arrest a 16 or 17-year-old in a holdup and find that they are narcotics users. If we could really cure our narcotics problems we could do a great deal toward curing our over-all crime problem.

Death from Drugs. Drug addiction of juveniles is causing concern everywhere. In New York City, 36 teen-agers died of drug abuse in the first two months of this year.

A crash program to cope with the narcotics problem is urged by Mr. Garelik and others. The ex-police inspector contends:

> It's just a delusion to think that law enforcement can do the job alone. Dealing with this problem requires an across-the-board effort to change the attitudes of young people who think that experimentation with narcotics is the "in thing."

Says Joseph Barriteau, a Negro who is an official of the New York City Youth Services Agency:

> Wipe out the drug traffic or we'll never solve the problem of crime in the streets . . . The "junkie" is not only sick, he is dangerous. He would kill his mother if he had to do it to get the money he must have for drugs.

Social Ills

"Poverty in the midst of plenty"

Police Chief Joseph P. Kimble of Beverly Hills, Calif., believes that too many refuse to recognize that there is a direct link between crime in the streets and social conditions.

"For millions," says Mr. Kimble, "there is poverty in the midst of plenty, substandard housing, inferior education and a lack of promising jobs."

The California lawman calls poverty a "sewer" out of which the only ladder available is money. More often than not, Mr. Kimble says, there is a temptation to turn to crime to get the money.

A similar viewpoint is expressed by Senator Joseph D. Tydings (Dem.), of Maryland, whose work on anticrime measures has won him an award from the American Society of Criminologists.

"*Cancer of Inner City.*" Speaking of what he terms the "basic, underlying problem," Senator Tydings says:

> The decay of the central city is much more serious than most people realize. The average person does not comprehend the extent of family breakdowns, how impoverished the schools are, how bad the welfare system is in holding the family together, how bad transportation is. The cancer of the inner city is much worse than generally realized.

In the same vein, Virgil W. Peterson, who recently retired after 28 years as director of the Chicago Crime Commission, observes that most major crimes occur in areas characterized by "overcrowding, poor housing, poor schools, few recreational facilities, newly arrived families."

Some sociologists argue that as poor people swarm into cities from rural areas where they have lived in comparative isolation, and see the glitter and affluence of the urban scene, many turn to crime out of frustration or envy.

Gordon Hawkins, of the University of Chicago's Center for Studies in Criminal Justice, notes evidence that criminal activity increases along with social, industrial and commercial progress, as the division between rich and poor becomes sharper and more obvious.

Edward D. Brady, director of personnel security for the Chicago board of education, blames "increasing polarization of the races" for most of the violence in the city's schools.

Poverty Equals Crime. This conviction is voiced by Daniel P. Moynihan, urban-affairs expert and counselor to President Nixon: "If you want to get rid of crime, get rid of poverty and racial isolation—and don't kid yourself, the correlation is absolute."

A somewhat different attitude is taken by Irving Reichert, executive director of the San Francisco commission on crime, who says:

> For years, people have been saying that lack of education, poverty and racial discrimination bring about crime. I'm not sure that we know that. If we did eliminate poverty and improve education, maybe then we could raise people from street criminals to business criminals. People are more concerned about street crime than business crime, but the money loss from street crimes and burglaries is almost insignificant when compared to fraud against consumers and corporate violations of law. . . . Street theft is the poor man's way of getting ahead.

But Mr. Reichert concedes that he has "never found a psychologist who can explain the senseless beatings" that accompany many street crimes.

Criminal Justice

"Our system is a failure"

From an address by Washington Police Chief Jerry Wilson before the International Association of Chiefs of Police:

> Our criminal-justice system is a failure. We are not preventing crime; we are not apprehending and convicting enough offenders; we are not rehabilitating enough convicts.
>
> As Chief Justice Warren Burger has said: "Many people . . . will be deterred from serious crimes if they believe that justice is swift and sure. Today no one thinks that."

Mr. Wilson's complaints include:

A bail system under which "a defendant, no matter how heinous the crime charged or how strong the evidence against him, can go free if he can pay the premium."

Personal-recognizance release which produces "an atmosphere in which criminals feel that nothing will happen to them, regardless of how often they commit crimes, regardless of how often they are arrested."

"Seemingly interminable delays" in court action.

Safe To Break Law? Nationwide, a large proportion of armed crime is committed by juveniles. In Washington, for example, teen-agers commit 45 percent of the armed robberies. In this situation, courts become targets for mounting criticism.

An advisory panel headed by Judge Alfred Burka, of the District of Columbia Court of General Sessions, says this in a report to Congress on armed violence:

> The way the criminal justice system operates at present is an abomination of justice and, undoubtedly, a significant contributor to armed crimes. The juvenile court proceeds so slowly in adjudicating its cases that juveniles often feel that it is "safe" to commit a crime . . .

Urging pretrial detention and speedy prosecution of accused persons, juvenile and adult, the panel notes that in the District of Columbia "one out of every three armed-robbery suspects released on bail is arrested for another offense before he comes to trial."

Criticism of court decisions which are asserted to show more concern for the rights of accused offenders than for the safety of society is widespread. Senator Tydings argues, however: "Blaming unpopular decisions is a way to blame the courts for all the problems."

What is needed in the judicial area, Senator Tydings says, is "elimination of the tremendous delay in bringing cases to trial." He adds: "The courts ought to modernize their administration. Judges ought to work hard."

Judges Too Lenient? There is a swelling cry for swifter justice, stiffer sentences, sterner treatment of "repeaters."

In Houston, Tex., 10,000 bankers and other executives petitioned for denial of bail bonds to suspects convicted of previous crimes. The petition says that "our laws and our courts have been promiscuous in freeing convicted criminals on bond after their arrest for repeated offenses."

A frequently made comment is echoed by George Schuyler, the New York Negro columnist: "The judges and courts are not harsh enough. These people who commit crimes don't get enough time in prison and they don't get it soon enough."

Widely cited as a cause of crime is the prison system.* Senator Tydings says that many prisons are "stockades run by criminals—crime schools." He contends that there is "no rehabilitation," that "prisons are turning out people far more dangerous than when they went in."

Police Problems

Forces "spread too thin"

A grumble often heard among crime fighters is that police manpower is being used improperly.

The police, says Richard E. Friedman, executive director of the Better Government Association of Chicago, are "spread too thin over too many areas."

Mr. Friedman continues:

> The basic function of laws governing crime is to protect persons and property. Criminal law has been extended beyond its primary purpose into purely personal or social spheres. The result is that the efforts of police, prosecutors and the judiciary have been diluted and priorities have been confused.
>
> For example, the police must abandon much of their efforts to curb crimes of violence—such as muggings and rapes—to concentrate on social and personal matters such as political protest and drunkenness. The police are given the dirty work of resolving the whole spectrum of unresolved social, moral and political problems that politicians and the public have failed to solve.

In their recently published book, "The Honest Politician's Guide to Crime Control," Norval Morris and Gordon Hawkins of the University of Chicago urge a complete overhaul of the criminal-law system to combat rising crime rates.

Half of the nontraffic arrests made each year, the Chicago criminologists say, are for offenses which do not involve violence or loss of property. The authors maintain that statutes forcing police to devote so much time to relatively minor offenses should be revoked or changed.

"What's important to people is walking safely on the streets," Messrs. Morris and Hawkins emphasize. "The police should be free to protect people and property."

* See John C. Esposito and Larry J. Silverman, *Vanishing Air*, p. 79, Part One.

VIOLENT CRIME: **UP 131%**

CRIMES OF VIOLENCE IN U.S.: RISING 10 TIMES AS FAST AS POPULATION

In 9 years, from 1960 to 1969—

POPULATION **UP 13%**

Source: Federal Bureau of Investigation

MURDERS
1960 9,000
1969* 14,900
Change in past 9 years **UP 66%**

FORCIBLE RAPES
1960 16,860
1969* 36,300
Change in past 9 years **UP 115%**

ROBBERIES
1960 107,390
1969* 301,000
Change in past 9 years **UP 180%**

AGGRAVATED ASSAULTS
1960 152,000
1969* 307,800
Change in past 9 years **UP 103%**

ALL CRIMES OF VIOLENCE
1960 285,200
1969* 660,000

*1969 crime figures are estimates based on official figures for first 9 months of year

Reprinted from "U. S. News & World Report," March 16, 1970.

Mr. Morris insists, in separate comment, that "we need a massive overhaul of our use of men, money and resources." He adds: "Out of an average $932 each person pays in taxes, $400 goes to national defense . . . less than $4 goes to criminal-law enforcement."

Need for "Better" Police. The idea that major crimes can be cut just by putting more policemen on police forces is not supported by statistics, says Craig Broadus of the San Francisco Committee on Crime. The answer, in Mr. Broadus's opinion, is not just more manpower, but better manpower. He explains:

> Those men you put out must be carefully selected, adequately trained, and you have to know where to put them at what time. This is where the computer helps. You have to have ample staff services, high-speed access to records. A cop is only as good as his records.

Moral Issue

"It's a permissive society"

An important factor in the crime crisis, experts agree, is the permissive attitude of parents, educators, courts—the public generally. "It's a permissive society," is a statement made in one form or another by many policemen, prosecutors and other specialists in the causes of crime.

For example, District Attorney Lewis Slaton of Fulton County, Georgia, explains why he believes poverty is not the real trigger for most violent crimes:

> They're not committing these offenses because they're hungry.
>
> The motivation seems to be that society has such a permissive attitude that even if the criminal gets caught, some lawyer will get him off or the judge will tap his wrists with probation.

In Phoenix, Ariz., Police Capt. Doeg Nelson expresses a conviction that a breakdown in basic family discipline ranks high as a reason for the increase in crime.

Carol S. Vance, district attorney in Houston, Tex., sets forth a similar view that "we are in for trouble" because too many parents and adults generally have "let this become a kid's world, without exercising the concern and discipline needed today."

Mr. Vance believes that the crime explosion results from "a new type of amorality—people with a complete indifference to life and with no social, religious or cultural values."

Contempt for Law. Col. Wilson Speir, head of the Texas department of public safety and the Texas Rangers, says crime will keep increasing "as long as we have a growing disrespect for law and authority and some people think it fashionable to select the laws they will obey and those they will disobey."

Police Chief James D. Wright of Sausalito, Calif., says that many times he has heard young burglars say: "Why should I work? I can make more with burglaries."

Hans W. Matick, codirector of the Center for Studies in Criminal Justice at the University of Chicago, points out that many elements of the crime problem were analyzed by presidential commissions in recent years. But, Mr. Matick says: "There's nobody out there listening." He adds:

> If we really wanted to reduce crime we could. Just compare the amount of money spent on it with that spent for such things as farm subsidies, the space program, the oil depletion allowance.

"Tolerance" for Crime? Chief Kimble of Beverly Hills fears that the American public has developed "a tolerance for crime and violence" just as an addict develops tolerance for certain drugs.

"We have come to accept crime and violence as natural by-products of living in a 'stress society,' " Chief Kimble comments ruefully.

The Californian warns that, if this attitude continues, "the streets of every city will become more dangerous than the jungles of Vietnam."

The fact that there is a ready market for stolen goods is cited by Craig Broadus of the San Francisco Committee on Crime as an indication of changing standards. Thieves, Mr. Broadus observes, "couldn't fence the stuff if there hadn't been a general breakdown in morality and honesty."

Spurring Crime

A "climate of violence"

Factors contributing to the rising crime rate, some authorities assert, are lurid movies, scenes of violence on television, and obscene or inflammatory printed matter.

"The militance of youthful rebels, black and white, often seems to be glorified by the news cameras," a police official remarks.

> Anarchy is made to seem commonplace. Depravity is big at the movie box offices now that censorship of almost any kind has been rejected by the courts.
>
> All of this contributes to a weakening of public morality, to the increasing disregard of the old standards of right and wrong.

Capt. Patrick V. Needham, executive assistant to Chicago's police superintendent, says that "a climate of violence" has been fostered, with undoubted effect on the growth of serious lawbreaking.

This comment from Judge Sam Phillips McKenzie of the Fulton County, Georgia, superior court is typical of many: "It may be that violence pervades the times in which we live—it's portrayed so often and so routinely on television."

Capt. Doeg Nelson of the Phoenix police department notes that from the time they are children, Americans see "excitement and affluence" pictured on television.

"It's hard to see these things and not want to be a part of them," the Arizona officer observes.

In Long Beach, Calif., Police Sgt. James D. Reed says that young thugs who "stalk older people, like animals stalking their prey," robbing and brutally beating their victims, want "excitement and money in their pockets."

Sergeant Reed calls such attacks a "symbol of our times."

Experts analyzing the causes of the steadily climbing rate of serious crime see no prospect of early solution.

Some call for a massive attack on social problems as the answer. Others, such as Clarence D. Rogers, Jr., a prosecutor in Cleveland, urge drastic reform of the penal system. Still others demand swifter, harsher justice.

Another view comes from District Judge Arthur E. Higgs of Bay County, Michigan, who says: "The war on crime has to start with attitudes. It must start in the grade schools—maybe even in kindergarten."*

* See Harry L. Gracey, *Learning the Student Role: Kindergarten as Academic Boot Camp*, pp. 261–274, Part Three.

Crime and Its Causes—the View from Congress

Senator John L. McClellan (Dem.), of Arkansas, is known as an investigator of crime, riots and civil disorders. He is chairman of the Senate Permanent Subcommittee on Investigations. Representative Emanuel Celler (Dem.), of New York, is chairman of the House Judiciary Committee. Following are their views, as expressed to members of the staff of "U. S. News & World Report," on why crime keeps rising in this country.

Senator McClellan: *"The chance of being punished for a serious crime is less than 1 out of 20."*

"We do not have adequate law enforcement," said Senator McClellan. "I think crime is somewhat contagious. Crime that goes unpunished breeds crime. When the impression is created that crime does pay, those who are not inclined to be industrious and who would rather drift, live by their wits and avoid work are attracted to crime. That's one source of the rising crime rate.

"Another is that a good many people find crime necessary to support the drug habit.

"Another is the general climate in this nation—of civil disobedience, of nonconformity and of disrespect for authority—this so-called philosophy of each 'doing his own thing' irrespective of its relation to or impact upon others. A great deal of it is in the nature of rebellion against constituted authority.

"All of this has been brought about by the breakdown of proper instruction and discipline in the home, in the schools and in the churches. That's fundamental.

"I don't think there's any question about laxity in law enforcement. The fact is that the chance of being apprehended, convicted and punished for a serious crime is less than 1 out of 20. More than half the crimes committed are not even detected by the police. Of those detected, many go unsolved. Of those suspects indicted, increasingly many are acquitted. Then, of those convicted or who plead guilty, many are granted probation and are really never punished.

"So people take chances. The odds of being punished have shifted strongly and favorably to the criminal.

"Our police forces are understaffed, inadequately trained, and poorly equipped. They are not modernized to compete mechanically and technologically with the techniques available to the criminal, although we are trying now to give them more modern and effective tools.

"Much of the responsibility for lack of law enforcement lies with the Supreme Court. The tone is set at the top. The Court has by recent decisions established so many legal technicalities that serve to shield and protect one accused of crime that the weapons and methods that once were legally available to law-enforcement officials have lost much of their strength and effectiveness. The police are handicapped by the courts.

"Racial tensions also contribute to an atmosphere that is conducive to crime. Anything that creates tensions between peoples arouses emotions of distrust, anger and prejudice which act to incite violence.

"The very fact that there is repeated and continuous talk about people having been mistreated or oppressed arouses and perpetuates resentment that engenders hate and a desire for retaliation and revenge."

Representative Celler: *"We have more guns per capita than any other nation in the world."*

"We are a pluralistic society, and we have a tremendous burst of population—particularly in the cities, where a malefactor can easily lose himself and avoid detection," said Representative Celler.

"We have the very rich and the very poor, which creates feelings of unrest among those who are impoverished, and the temptation to equalize their conditions with the more fortunate by theft is prevalent.

We have the clash between white and black, which exacerbates the situation.

"We have the slums and other ills of overpopulated cities, with their rat-infested tenements which create . . . discord and discontent which easily become the basis of crime.

"Then you must remember also that we are a nation, more or less, of violence. Our birth came out of violence—the Revolution. All throughout our history we have been fighting the perils and the difficulties of the frontier.

"We probably have more guns and pistols per capita than any other nation in the world, and there isn't any real control over them—all of which adds to the violence and adds naturally to crime in the streets with the use of these lethal implements. Our police protection is woefully inadequate. More federal money is needed to help the cities uproot crime and prevent the causes of crime.

"Drug addiction is deeply involved in the crime problem. I think our treatment of drug addiction is wrong. I think a drug addict is like an alcoholic—he is a sick person, diseased. And a drug addict—but not the seller of drugs—should be treated like a diseased person, not like a convict. He should get treatment."

THE USES OF SIDEWALKS: SAFETY

Jane Jacobs

Streets in cities serve many purposes besides carrying vehicles, and city sidewalks—the pedestrian parts of the streets—serve many purposes besides carrying pedestrians. These uses are bound up with circulation but are not identical with it and in their own right they are at least as basic as circulation to the proper workings of cities.

A city sidewalk by itself is nothing. It is an abstraction. It means something only in conjunction with the buildings and other uses that border it, or border other sidewalks very near it. The same might be said of streets, in the sense that they serve other purposes besides carrying wheeled traffic in their middles. Streets and their sidewalks, the main public places of a city, are its most vital organs. Think of a city and what comes to mind? Its streets. If a city's streets look interesting, the city looks interesting; if they look dull, the city looks dull.

More than that, and here we get down to the first problem, if a city's streets are safe from barbarism and fear, the city is thereby tolerably safe from barbarism and fear. When people say that a city, or a part of it, is

From *The Death and Life of Great American Cities*, by Jane Jacobs, pp. 29–32.

dangerous or is a jungle what they mean primarily is that they do not feel safe on the sidewalks.

But sidewalks and those who use them are not passive beneficiaries of safety or helpless victims of danger. Sidewalks, their bordering uses, and their users, are active participants in the drama of civilization versus barbarism in cities. To keep the city safe is a fundamental task of a city's streets and its sidewalks.

This task is totally unlike any service that sidewalks and streets in little towns or true suburbs are called upon to do. Great cities are not like towns, only larger. They are not like suburbs, only denser. They differ from towns and suburbs in basic ways, and one of these is that cities are, by definition, full of strangers. To any one person, strangers are far more common in big cities than acquaintances. More common not just in places of public assembly, but more common at a man's own doorstep. Even residents who live near each other are strangers, and must be, because of the sheer number of people in small geographical compass.

The bedrock attribute of a successful city district is that a person must feel personally safe and secure on the street among all these strangers. He must not feel automatically menaced by them. A city district that fails in this respect also does badly in other ways and lays up for itself, and for its city at large, mountain on mountain of trouble.

Today barbarism has taken over many city streets, or people fear it has, which comes to much the same thing in the end. "I live in a lovely, quiet residential area," says a friend of mine who is hunting another place to live. "The only disturbing sound at night is the occasional scream of someone being mugged." It does not take many incidents of violence on a city street, or in a city district, to make people fear the streets. And as they fear them, they use them less, which makes the streets still more unsafe.

To be sure, there are people with hobgoblins in their heads, and such people will never feel safe no matter what the objective circumstances are. But this is a different matter from the fear that besets normally prudent, tolerant and cheerful people who show nothing more than common sense in refusing to venture after dark—or in a few places, by day—into streets where they may well be assaulted, unseen or unrescued until too late.

The barbarism and the real, not imagined, insecurity that gives rise to such fears cannot be tagged a problem of the slums. The problem is most serious, in fact, in genteel-looking "quiet residential areas" like that my friend was leaving.

It cannot be tagged as a problem of older parts of cities. The problem reaches its most baffling dimensions in some examples of rebuilt parts of cities, including supposedly the best examples of rebuilding, such as middle-income projects. The police precinct captain of a nationally admired project of this kind (admired by planners and leaders) has recently admonished residents not only about hanging around outdoors after dark but has urged them never to answer their doors without knowing the caller. Life here has much in common with life for the three little pigs or the seven little kids of the nursery thrillers. The problem of sidewalk and doorstep insecurity is as serious in cities which have made conscientious efforts at rebuilding as it is in those cities that have lagged. Nor is it illuminating to tag minority groups, or the poor, or the outcast with responsibility for city danger. There are immense variations in the degree of civilization and safety found among such groups and among the city areas where they live. Some of the safest sidewalks in New York City, for example, at any time of day or night, are those along which poor people or minority groups live. And some of the most dangerous are in streets occupied by the same kinds of people. All this can also be said of other cities.

Deep and complicated social ills must lie behind delinquency and crime, in suburbs and towns as well as in great cities. This book will not go into speculation on the deeper reasons. It is sufficient, at this point, to say that if we are to maintain a city society that can diagnose and keep abreast of deeper social problems, the starting point must be, in any case, to strengthen whatever workable forces for maintaining safety and civilization do exist—in the cities we do have. To build city districts that are custom made for easy crime is idiotic. Yet that is what we do.

The first thing to understand is that the public peace—the sidewalk and street peace—of cities is not kept primarily by the police, necessary as police are. It is kept primarily by an intricate, almost unconscious, network of voluntary controls and standards among the people themselves, and enforced by the people themselves. In some city areas—older public housing projects and streets with very high population turnover are often conspicuous examples—the keeping of public sidewalk law and order is left almost entirely to the police and special guards. Such places are jungles. No amount of police can enforce civilization where the normal, casual enforcement of it has broken down.

The second thing to understand is that the problem of insecurity cannot be solved by spreading people out more thinly, trading the characteristics of cities for the characteristics of suburbs. If this could solve danger on the city streets, then Los Angeles should be a safe city because superficially Los Angeles is almost all suburban. It has virtually no districts compact enough to qualify as dense city areas. Yet Los Angeles cannot, any more than any other great city, evade the truth that, being a city, it *is* composed of strangers not all of whom are nice. Los Angeles' crime figures are flabbergasting. Among the seventeen standard metropolitan areas with populations over a million, Los Angeles stands so pre-eminent in crime that it is in a category by itself. And this is markedly true of crimes associated with personal attack, the crimes that make people fear the streets.

Handbill Passed out on Sheridan Road, Chicago's North Side, in the Days Just Following the Assassination of Martin Luther King, Jr.

This is a warning. . . . Not that we think it will do any good, but we feel obliged to give it before we engage in our next activity. You who drive Sheridan Road to work, you who live on the North Shore—you are no longer safe.

Til now you have been assured of your safety—you are white, you are relatively wealthy, you are fifteen miles from the nearest riot area, and most of all, you are protected by your military agents of the police force and the National Guard. Because of your safety you have not felt obliged to deal with the deterioration of American society and the repression of certain of its citizens.

You have it in your power to change things. The people who drive Sheridan Road to and from work control over half the jobs in the Chicago area, you control their content and you control who will fill them. You reap most of the benefits from a system which is built on the back of Blacks and poor Whites. And you give sanction to this system by doing nothing to change it.

After careful consideration we have come to the conclusion that no constructive action will be taken until you are convinced that repressive tactics cannot keep the fruits of repression from your own homes and families. So long as you believe that the problem is a Black one you will feel that you can use force to keep it locked in the ghetto. This message is to warn you that those days are over, that the Black man is no longer isolated in his fight for freedom, that his fight is also ours.

We have considered all alternatives and found them wanting. We feel that nothing less than positive, constructive force in your own communities will make you see that repression cannot be effective, and we are all personally committed to coming back again and again whatever the consequences. We are not poor ourselves but we are dedicated to destroying the oppression of those who are.

And we are white, all white. We can walk down your streets unimpeded and frequently unnoticed. We can go anywhere. Many of us are undistinguishable from your neighbors. And wherever we go from now on, we will bring to you and your families the costs which you have escaped, the fruits of your economic policies and position, the response of repressed and frustrated people.

The Black man in America is no longer an isolated phenomenon. He can no longer be avoided, because we will make you pay the price which he is too visible and too distant to bring to your homes. We cannot force you to alter the existing economic system which you control, but we can see that you pay for your profits.

TABLE 55 Assaults on Police Officers, 1970, Percent Distribution of Weapons Used
[5,091 agencies; 1970 population 123,525,000]

Population Group	*Total Assaults*	*Firearms*	*Knife or Cutting Instrument*	*Other Dangerous Weapon*	*Hands, Fists, Feet, etc.*
TOTAL ALL	38,467	2,240	1,094	3,962	31,171
AGENCIES	100.0	5.8	2.8	10.3	81.0
Group I (over 250,000)	17,252	7.2	2.9	12.1	77.7
(over 1,000,000)	10,640	6.2	3.1	11.1	79.7
(500,000 to 1,000,000)	3,357	12.2	3.4	18.3	66.1
(250,000 to 500,000)	3,255	5.6	1.9	9.2	83.3
Group II (100,000 to 250,000)	4,126	4.7	2.3	11.3	81.7
Group III (50,000 to 100,000)	4,047	4.0	2.6	9.7	83.6
Group IV (25,000 to 50,000)	3,715	3.3	2.2	6.3	88.2
Group V (10,000 to 25,000)	3,805	4.3	2.9	5.9	86.9
Group VI (under 10,000)	2,978	4.5	3.1	10.4	82.0
Suburban agencies[1]	7,648	5.0	3.1	8.9	83.0
Sheriffs	2,544	8.3	4.2	9.5	78.0

Geographic Division	*Total Assaults*	*Firearms*	*Knife or Cutting Instrument*	*Other Dangerous Weapon*	*Hands, Fists, Feet, etc.*
Total	38,467	2,240	1,094	3,962	31,171
	100.0	5.8	2.8	10.3	81.0
New England	2,306	3.6	2.1	12.3	82.0
Middle Atlantic	7,034	4.0	3.3	3.6	89.1
East North Central	11,179	6.3	2.6	13.3	77.9
West North Central	2,237	10.5	2.7	12.0	74.8
South Atlantic	5,730	5.8	2.8	9.9	81.6
East South Central	1,155	2.9	2.5	2.6	92.0
West South Central	3,044	6.7	3.1	10.1	80.1
Mountain	1,520	8.6	3.0	9.6	78.8
Pacific	4,262	5.7	3.2	14.6	76.5

[1] Includes suburban city and county police agencies within metropolitan areas. Excludes core cities. Suburban cities are also included in other city groups. Due to rounding percentage may not add to 100.0.

U.S. Government Printing Office, Washington, D.C., p. 165.

[Eds. note: "Hands, Fists, Feet, etc."?!]

It was somewhat arresting to discover that back in the approximately 26,000 acres of suburban Maryland parkland nearby are lurking two machine guns, shotguns, a .30-caliber carbine and a 30-06 rifle equipped with a telescopic sight, all owned by the Maryland-National Capital Park and Planning Commission police. That's a lot of hardware. But even more intriguing was a remark by Capt. Donald Leslie of the Prince George's County division that he thinks of this as "classified information . . . because if you give out all this information, then everybody would know our armaments and in the time of a riot situation that's something we would not prefer."

If Staff Writer Stephen Neary's report constituted a security leak of "classified information," we shudder to think what "secret" or "top secret" or "tippy-top-secret, eyes-only" sorts of armaments are stashed in the woods. Should duffers on the six M-NCPPC golf courses tote mine detectors? Are we likely to stumble on an ABM site or a polaris sub at the bottom of one of the skating rinks?

Fortunately, Capt. Leslie assured our reporter that the machine guns are only for use "in extreme emergency-type situations" that apparently have yet to happen, such as "when your own men are pinned down by sniper fire." At that point, the besieged park policemen still would need to get permission from the parks department director, who in turn would consult the commission's executive director. For now, the arsenal is under lock and key, we're informed. While we wouldn't want to endanger any of our park troops, it does seem like a good time to reassess the M-NCPPC defense budget and see if we can't afford some disarmament in the parks.—*Washington Post*

"Arsenal-in-the-Parks," *Christian Science Monitor* (July 29, 1970).

A massive underground shelter to shield business executives and their records from nuclear bomb attacks or civil insurrections is being planned in central California.

Bekins Moving & Storage Company, architect of the plan, said it has bought land for a shelter capable of housing 1,000 executives and office personnel 40 feet underground for up to 30 days.

A brochure the firm is using to promote the bunker among large United States corporations calls it a corporate survival center.

Ranchland Site

Its main purpose will be to protect such firms in the event of nuclear war, but Bekins officials here said it would help offset increasing fears within the business world over rioting, bombing attacks, and destruction of files.

The shelter, which will be topped by a jet landing strip for quick access, will house a computer center, a communications center, a large records storage unit, offices, living quarters, a morgue, and a cafeteria able to serve 1,000 persons in 90 minutes.

The space put aside for offices can serve as alternative headquarters for a limited number of business firms during any emergency, the brochure said.

Bekins officials said construction of the bunker was tentatively scheduled to begin next year on a 200-acre ranchland site in the Diablo Mountains near Coalinga, midway between San Francisco and Los Angeles.

Some firms, the officials said, were thinking of moving into the underground complex as soon as it was ready and setting up alternative headquarters there.

Banks, oil companies, construction and manufacturing firms are among those said to be interested.

Space inside the shelter would be leased to them at $100,000 a year each on a 10-year lease.

Reuters, "Huge California Underground Shelter to Shield Executives and Records," *Christian Science Monitor* (July 1970). Reprinted by permission of **Reuters.**

FEAR

Patricia C. Sexton

Many slum dwellers live in a generalized state of fear—of being robbed, knifed, attacked, bullied, or having their children injured. The fear colors their whole lives: their ability to learn, to work, to stay sane and healthy, to venture out of their apartments or block, to live openly and freely, to be friends with their neighbors, to trust the world, outsiders, themselves. Fear is a crippler in the slum.

In East Harlem, with its vast youth population, only 10 percent of the nonstreet acreage is park. So children play in the streets. In Morningside Manhattan, a neighboring area with more money and fewer children, 37 percent of the acreage is park. In East Harlem, the streets take up almost half of all acreage; it is here that children play and the business of life is carried on. Cars have more room than children.

In New York most people who get enough money to do it move out. They move to the edge of town or to the suburbs or farther. Many of

From *Spanish Harlem* by Patricia Cayo Sexton, pp. 116–119. Copyright © 1965 by Patricia Cayo Sexton. Reprinted by permission of Harper & Row, Publishers, Inc.

them prefer the excitement of the city and hate long-distance commuting, but they do it "for the sake of the children"—good schools, open space, safety from crime, housing space for big families. Most of the people in East Harlem who live in bad housing are either too poor to move out or don't know where to go. They remain with their children.

East Harlem's children seem afraid. Almost all of them have witnessed crime or violence in the neighborhood or at school, and they are afraid. The children complain about the older boys from higher grades and from the junior high schools who hang around the school and bully them:

> Some boys come from junior highs to the halls, and they carry knives, and they say to the little boys, "Give me your money or we'll cut you up and all that."
>
> Five years ago when this school was uncivilized, you know, it was real bad, and this kid he came to school, and he was crazy, he was drunk, you know, and he was big and he had a knife, and he said he was going to cut Mr. A_____'s hair. So I ran. I was scared, and I went to tell, but where were all the teachers at? And I hear the teachers screaming out loud, and they were all locked up in there.

Many children complained about the bad men and bad children and about the things they "learn" in the streets. One child said:

> There's too much bad men. I say everywhere is a bad neighborhood. Not like around here but everywhere you go you could see a bad one. On the west side on a hundred fifth, in Brooklyn, where my grandmother lives, it's real quiet. You walk in there, and you could hear a pin drop. At 7 o'clock everybody's in their house, and nobody's in the street. That's better than around here, 'cause nobody disturbs you. This neighborhood is worse than other places. Too much big people teach the little kids too much bad things. The boys take the pocketbooks and pass it to each other. Too much people got too much bad ideas. The little kids learned it from the big ones. The little kids can be worse as the big kids. As they grow up they get worse.

Though the youth "gangs" are mainly gone from East Harlem, the "clubs" remain and sometimes their activities are indistinguishable from those of the fighting gangs.[1]

And they report much worse things than gambling, things they have witnessed themselves or that happened to relatives or neighbors:

[1] Despite recent substitution of narcotics for knives among fighting gangs, delinquency is more than twice the city rate. Among the remaining youth clubs are: Red Wings, Viceroys, Dragons, Enchanters, Enforcers, Elegants, Untouchables.

> The neighborhood is lousy. Like if the people, say, rap on your door, and they bust in the door, they steal from you. And yesterday right in front of everybody, a man shot a man in the back with a 35. Shot him in the back.

> There was this little biddy, she went down to 100th and First Avenue, and came back and met these boys at 111th Street and they took her up to apartment, and they beat her up bad and her face was swollen, and they gave her an injection, an overdose of narcotics. They all took narcotics. And then she dies. And they find her in bed dead in the apartment.

> Every Sunday my mother goes to see my brother at the state hospital, and she takes his things, and I help her because, you know, her hands they hurt, and this finger she had a big bumps on it. So every Sunday I take her things to the bus, and when coming back, there was this man, he was standing next to the stoop, and these other two men came out and shot at him. He put that thing on so you couldn't hear the shot, and he killed the man, and then they went away, and I was there when everything happen. Some people are killing other people for nothing, they're taking away their lives.

Parents are often so afraid of the street and the strange things that happen there that many of them keep small children at home, summer and winter. Discussions with children show that knowledge and fear of crime, fights, abuse from other children, are at the top of their minds. Children talk about it so much and so freely that it seems almost a preoccupation. Fear can be so damaging to the human personality and to learning potential that those who inquire into the causes of limited growth among slum children had better look at the streets as well as the home and the school.

Few people outside the law enforcement agencies deal with crime directly, and no one has tried to test the dimensions of fear in the slum.

Preston Wilcox, a Negro social worker, said, "One reason crime is rampant in East Harlem is that Negroes won't turn other Negroes in to a white policeman. Whites just don't know the type of treatment Negroes get from the police." The same is said to apply to Puerto Ricans. If this is the case, some means should be devised of allowing local citizens to help enforce the law. Wilcox also suggested that "instead of adding more police—nobody thinks that will do any good—they should sit around with people and ask what they can do to make their houses safer. That's the only way to do anything about it. One person suggested sealing off the roofs; that's where the thugs and addicts hang out, and there's no reason to leave them open anyhow. People have a lot of good ideas."

Again, the familiar theme: The people of East Harlem need to take power and exert controls over their own destiny.

A FLY IN BUTTERMILK

James Baldwin

"You can take the child out of the country," my elders were fond of saying, "but you can't take the country out of the child." They were speaking of their own antecedents, I supposed; it didn't, anyway, seem possible that they could be warning me; I took myself out of the country and went to Paris. It was there I discovered that the old folks knew what they had been talking about: I found myself willy-nilly, alchemized into an American the moment I touched French soil.

Now, back again after nearly nine years, it was ironical to reflect that if I had not lived in France for so long I would never have found it necessary —or possible—to visit the American South. The South had always frightened me. How deeply it had frightened me—though I had never seen it—and how soon, was one of the things my dreams revealed to me while I was there. And this made me think of the privacy and mystery of childhood all over again, in a new way. I wondered where children got their strength—the strength, in this case, to walk through mobs to get to school.

"You've got to remember," said an older Negro friend to me, in Washington, "that no matter what you see or how it makes you feel, it can't be compared to twenty-five, thirty years ago—you remember those photographs of Negroes hanging from trees?" I looked at him differently. *I* had seen the photographs—but *he* might have been one of them. "I remember," he said, "when conductors on streetcars wore pistols and had police powers." And he remembered a great deal more. He remembered, for example, hearing Booker T. Washington speak, and the day-to-day progress of the Scottsboro case, and the rise and bloody fall of Bessie Smith. These had been books and headlines and music for me but it now developed that they were also a part of my identity.

"You're just one generation away from the South, you know. You'll find," he added, kindly, "that people will be willing to talk to you . . . if they don't feel that you look down on them just because you're from the North."

The first Negro I encountered, an educator, didn't give me any opportunity to look down. He forced me to admit, at once, that I had never been to college; that Northern Negroes lived herded together, like pigs in a pen; that the campus on which we met was a tribute to the industry and determination of Southern Negroes. "Negroes in the South form a *community.*"

My humiliation was complete with his discovery that I couldn't even drive a car. I couldn't ask him anything. He made me feel so hopeless an example of the general Northern spinelessness that it would have seemed a spiteful counterattack to have asked him to discuss the integration problem which had placed his city in the headlines.

At the same time, I felt that there was nothing which bothered him more; but perhaps he did not really know what he thought about it; or thought too many things at once. His campus risked being very different twenty years from now. Its special function would be gone—and so would his position, arrived at with such pain. The new day a-coming was not for him. I don't think this fact made him bitter but I think it frightened him and made him sad; for the future is like heaven—everyone exalts it but no one wants to go there now. And I imagine that he shared the attitude, which I was to encounter so often later, toward the children who were helping to bring this future about: admiration before the general spectacle and skepticism before the individual case.

That evening I went to visit G., one of the "integrated" children, a boy of about fifteen. I had already heard something of his first day in school, the peculiar problems his presence caused, and his own extraordinary bearing.

He seemed extraordinary at first mainly by his silence. He was tall for his age and, typically, seemed to be constructed mainly of sharp angles, such as elbows and knees. Dark gingerbread sort of coloring, with ordinary hair, and a face disquietingly impassive, save for his very dark, very large eyes. I got the impression, each time that he raised them, not so much that they spoke but that they registered volumes; each time he dropped them it was as though he had retired into the library.

We sat in the living room, his mother, younger brother and sister, and I, while G. sat on the sofa, doing his homework. The father was at work and the older sister had not yet come home. The boy had looked up once, as I came in, to say, "Good evening, sir," and then left all the rest to his mother.

Mrs. R. was a very strong-willed woman, handsome, quiet-looking, dressed in black. Nothing, she told me, beyond name-calling, had marked G.'s first day at school; but on the second day she received the last of several threatening phone calls. She was told that if she didn't want her son "cut to ribbons" she had better keep him at home. She heeded this warning to the extent of calling the chief of police.

"He told me to go on and send him. He said he'd be there when the cutting started. So I sent him." Even more remarkably perhaps, G. went.

No one cut him, in fact no one touched him. The students formed a wall between G. and the entrances, saying only enough, apparently, to make their intention clearly understood, watching him, and keeping him outside. (I asked him, "What did you feel when they blocked your way?" G. looked up at me, very briefly, with no expression on his face, and told me, "Nothing, sir.") At last the principal appeared and took him by the hand and they entered the school, while the children shouted behind them, "Nigger-lover!"

G. was alone all day at school.

"But I thought you already knew some of the kids there," I said. I had been told that he had friends among the white students because of their previous competition in a Soapbox Derby.

"Well, none of them are in his classes," his mother told me—a shade too quickly, as though she did not want to dwell on the idea of G.'s daily isolation.

"We don't have the same schedule," G. said. It was as though he were coming to his mother's rescue. Then, unwillingly, with a kind of interior shrug, "Some of the guys had lunch with me but then the other kids called them names." He went back to his homework.

I began to realize that there were not only a great many things G. would not tell me, there was much that he would never tell his mother.

"But nobody bothers you, anyway?"

"No," he said. "They just—call names. I don't let it bother me."

Nevertheless, the principal frequently escorts him through the halls. One day, when G. was alone, a boy tripped him and knocked him down and G. reported this to the principal. The white boy denied it but a few days later, while G. and the principal were together, he came over and said, "I'm sorry I tripped you; I won't do it again," and they shook hands. But it doesn't seem that this boy has as yet developed into a friend. And it is clear that G. will not allow himself to expect this.

I asked Mrs. R. what had prompted her to have her son reassigned to a previously all-white high school. She sighed, paused; then, sharply, "Well, it's not because I'm so anxious to have him around white people." Then she laughed. "I really don't know how I'd feel if I was to carry a white baby around who was calling me Grandma." G. laughed, too, for the first time. "White people say," the mother went on, "that that's all a Negro wants. I don't think they believe that themselves."

Then we switched from the mysterious question of what white folks believe to the relatively solid ground of what she, herself, knows and fears.

"You see that boy? Well, he's always been a straight-A student. He didn't hardly have to work at it. You see the way he's so quiet now on the sofa, with his books? Well, when he was going to ——— High School, he didn't have no homework or if he did, he could get it done in five minutes. Then, there he was, out in the streets, getting into mischief, and all he did all day in school was just keep clowning to make the other boys laugh. He wasn't learning nothing and didn't nobody care if he *never* learned nothing and I could just see what was going to happen to him if he kept on like that."

The boy was very quiet.

"What were you learning in ——— High?" I asked him.

"Nothing!" he exploded, with a very un-boyish laugh. I asked him to tell me about it.

"Well, the teacher comes in," he said, "and she gives you something to read and she goes out. She leaves some other student in charge . . ." ("You can just imagine how much reading gets done," Mrs. R. interposed.) "At the end of the period," G. continued, "she comes back and tells you something to read for the next day."

So, having nothing else to do, G. began amusing his classmates and his mother began to be afraid. G. is just about at the age when boys begin dropping out of school. Perhaps they get a girl into trouble; she also drops out; the boy gets work for a time or gets into trouble for a long time. I was told that forty-five girls had left school for the maternity ward the year before. A week or ten days before I arrived in the city eighteen boys from G.'s former high school had been sentenced to the chain gang.

"My boy's a good boy," said Mrs. R., "and I wanted to see him have a chance."

"Don't the teachers care about the students?" I asked. This brought forth more laughter. How could they care? How much could they do if they *did* care? There were too many children, from shaky homes and worn-out parents, in aging, inadequate plants. They could be considered, most of them, as already doomed. Besides, the teachers' jobs were safe. They were responsible only to the principal, an appointed official, whose judgment, apparently, was never questioned by his (white) superiors or confreres.

The principal of G.'s former high school was about seventy-five when he was finally retired and his idea of discipline was to have two boys beat each other—"under his supervision"—with leather belts. This once happened with G., with no other results than that his parents gave the principal a tongue-lashing. It happened with two boys of G.'s acquaintance with the result that, after school, one boy beat the other so badly that he had to be sent to the hospital. The teachers have themselves arrived at a dead end, for in a segregated school system they cannot rise any higher, and the students are aware of this. Both students and teachers soon cease to struggle.

"If a boy can wash a blackboard," a teacher was heard to say, "I'll promote him."

I asked Mrs. R. how other Negroes felt about her having had G. reassigned.

"Well, a lot of them don't like it," she said—though I gathered that they did not say so to her. As school time approached, more and more people asked her, "Are you going to send him?" "Well," she told them, "the man says the door is open and I feel like, yes, I'm going to go on and send him."

Out of a population of some fifty thousand Negroes, there had been only forty-five applications. People had said that they would send their children, had talked about it, had made plans; but, as the time drew near, when the application blanks were actually in their hands, they said, "I don't believe I'll sign this right now. I'll sign it later." Or, "I been thinking about this. I don't believe I'll send him right now."

"Why?" I asked. But to this she couldn't, or wouldn't, give me any answer.

I asked if there had been any reprisals taken against herself or her husband, if she was worried while G. was at school all day. She said that, no, there had been no reprisals, though some white people, under the pretext of giving her good advice, had expressed disapproval of her action. But she herself doesn't have a job and so doesn't risk losing one. Nor, she told me, had anyone said anything to her husband, who, however, by her own proud suggestion, is extremely closemouthed. And it developed later that he was not working at his regular trade but at something else.

As to whether she was worried, "No," she told me; in much the same way that G., when asked about the blockade, had said, "Nothing, sir." In her case it was easier to see what she meant: she hoped for the best and would not allow herself, in the meantime, to lose her head. "I don't feel like nothing's going to happen," she said, soberly. "I *hope* not. But I know if anybody tries to harm me or any one of my children, I'm going to strike back with all my strength. I'm going to strike them in God's name."

G., in the meantime, on the sofa with his books, was preparing himself for the next school day. His face was as impassive as ever and I found myself wondering—again—how he managed to face what must surely have been the worst moment of his day—the morning, when he opened his eyes and realized that it was all to be gone through again. Insults, and incipient violence, teachers, and—exams.

"One among so many," his mother said, "that's kind of rough."

"Do you think you'll make it?" I asked him. "Would you rather go back to ——— High?"

"No," he said, "I'll make it. I ain't going back."

"He ain't thinking about going back," said his mother—proudly and sadly. I began to suspect that the boy managed to support the extreme tension of his situation by means of a nearly fanatical concentration on his schoolwork; by holding in the center of his mind the issue on which, when the deal went down, others would be *forced* to judge him. Pride and silence were his weapons. Pride comes naturally, and soon, to a Negro, but even his mother, I felt, was worried about G.'s silence, though she was too wise to break it. For what was all this doing to him really?

"It's hard enough," the boy said later, still in control but with flashing eyes, "to keep quiet and keep walking when they call you nigger. But if anybody ever spits on me, I *know* I'll have to fight."

His mother laughs, laughs to ease them both, then looks at me and says, "I wonder sometimes what makes white folks so mean."

This is a recurring question among Negroes, even among the most "liberated"—which epithet is meant, of course, to describe the writer. The next day, with this question (more elegantly phrased) still beating in my mind, I visited the principal of G.'s new high school. But he didn't look "mean" and he wasn't "mean": he was a thin, young man of about my age, bewildered and in trouble. I asked him how things were working out, what he thought about it, what he thought would happen—in the long run, or the short.

"Well, I've got a job to do," he told me, "and I'm going to do it." He said that there hadn't been any trouble and that he didn't expect any. "Many students, after all, never see G. at all." None of the children have harmed him and the teachers are, apparently, carrying out their rather tall orders, which are to be kind to G. and, at the same time, to treat him like any other student.

I asked him to describe to me the incident, on the second day of school, when G.'s entrance had been blocked by the students. He told me that it was nothing at all—"It was a gesture more than anything else." He had simply walked out and spoken to the students and brought G. inside. "I've seen them do the same thing to other kids when they were kidding," he said. I imagine that he would like to be able to place this incident in the same cheerful if rowdy category, despite the shouts (which he does not mention) of "nigger-lover!"

Which epithet does not, in any case, describe him at all.

"Why," I asked, "is G. the only Negro student here?" According to this city's pupil-assignment plan, a plan designed to allow the least possible integration over the longest possible period of time, G. was the only Negro student who qualified.

"And, anyway," he said, "I don't think it's right for colored children to come to white schools just *because* they're white."

"Well," I began, "even if you don't like it . . ."

"Oh," he said quickly, raising his head and looking at me sideways, "I never said I didn't like it."

And then he explained to me, with difficulty, that it was simply contrary to everything he'd ever seen or believed. He'd never dreamed of a mingling of the races; had never lived that way himself and didn't suppose that he ever would; in the same way, he added, perhaps a trifle defensively, that he only associated with a certain stratum of white people. But, "I've never seen a colored person toward whom I had any hatred or ill-will."

His eyes searched mine as he said this and I knew that he was wondering if I believed him.

I certainly did believe him; he impressed me as being a very gentle and honorable man. But I could not avoid wondering if he had ever really *looked* at a Negro and wondered about the life, the aspirations, the universal humanity hidden behind the dark skin. As I wondered, when he told me that race relations in his city were "excellent" and had not been strained by recent developments, how on earth he managed to hold on to this delusion.

I later got back to my interrupted question, which I phrased more tactfully.

"Even though it's very difficult for all concerned—this situation—doesn't it occur to you that the reason colored children wish to come to white schools isn't because they want to be with white people but simply because they want a better education?"

"Oh, I don't know," he replied, "it seems to me that colored schools are just as good as white schools." I wanted to ask him on what evidence he had arrived at this conclusion and also how they could possibly be "as good" in view of the kind of life they came out of, and perpetuated, and the dim prospects faced by all but the most exceptional or ruthless Negro students. But I only suggested that G. and his family, who certainly should have known, so thoroughly disagreed with him that they had been willing to risk G.'s present well-being and his future psychological and mental health in order to bring about a change in his environment. Nor did I mention the lack of enthusiasm envinced by G.'s mother when musing on the prospect of a fair grandchild. There seemed no point in making this man any more a victim of his heritage than he so gallantly was already.

"Still," I said at last, after a rather painful pause, "I should think that the trouble in this situation is that it's very hard for *you* to face a child and treat him unjustly because of something for which he is no more responsible than—than *you* are."

The eyes came to life then, or a veil fell, and I found myself staring at a man in anguish. The eyes were full of pain and bewilderment and he nodded his head. This was the impossibility which he faced every day. And I imagined that his tribe would increase, in sudden leaps and bounds was already increasing.

For segregation has worked brilliantly in the South, and, in fact, in the nation, to this extent: it has allowed white people, with scarcely any pangs of conscience whatever, to *create*, in every generation, only the Negro they wished to see. As the walls come down they will be forced to take another, harder look at the shiftless and the menial and will be forced into a wonder concerning them which cannot fail to be agonizing. It is not an easy thing to be forced to re-examine a way of life and to speculate, in a personal way, on the general injustice.

"What do you think," I asked him, "will happen? What do you think the future holds?"

He gave a strained laugh and said he didn't know. "I don't want to think about it." Then, "I'm a religious man," he said, "and I believe the Creator will always help us find a way to solve our problems. If a man loses that, he's lost everything he had." I agreed, struck by the look in his eyes.

"You're from the North?" he asked me, abruptly.

"Yes," I said.

"Well," he said, "you've got your troubles too."

"Ah, yes, we certainly do," I admitted, and shook hands and left him. I did not say what I was thinking, that our troubles were the same trouble and that, unless we were very swift and honest, what is happening in the South today will be happening in the North tomorrow.

A TISSUE OF FEARS

Newsday

The Black Panthers are a small (1,000 strong) but sinewy organization of militant ghettoites with a professed commitment to the overthrow of hated white institutions and a penchant for fierce rhetoric: among lesser contributions to the language of violence, they are said to have coined the soubriquet "pigs" as more or less the compensatory equivalent of "niggers." The Panthers also do more than talk. They believe in guns for self-defense, and they are not at all squeamish about using them, defensively or otherwise: in their three-year history they have killed at least a few policemen. They are a bellicose and threatening group, barely accepted even in their own ghettos. They don't hate all white men, but hate enough of them to warrant uneasiness, and they make no secret of their special hatred for white men wearing blue uniforms.

For their part, the police have been anything but indifferent to the threat. In recent weeks, two Illinois leaders of the organization were killed and four members wounded in a raid by Chicago police, under circumstances that cast serious doubts on the credibility of the law officers involved. Four days later, Los Angeles police staged a massive pre-dawn raid in which three Panthers (as well as three policemen) were wounded, 21 were arrested and a store of guns was seized. In all, according to the Panthers, 23 members of the organization have been killed and over 90 arrested since January, 1968, and while these figures are undocumented, there is evidence enough that the Panther leadership has been virtually decimated during that period. The Panthers are now convinced that they are the objects of a nationwide conspiracy by law enforcement agencies aimed at destroying their organization.

The existence of high-level conspiracies is always hard for Americans to believe. Certainly, as one police officer acknowledged, there is sufficient anti-

From *Newsday* (December 19, 1969), pp. 17–18. Reprinted from Newsday, Long Island.

Panther animus among local lawmen to account for the rash of shootings and arrests without any need to attribute them to a nationwide plot.

Nevertheless, a group of 25 distinguished citizens were alarmed enough about the escalating warfare to convene an independent commission of inquiry this week. Led by such normally judicious men as Ramsey Clark, Roy Wilkins, Whitney Young and Arthur Goldberg, the conmission intends to conduct an "orderly and dispassionate" investigation and make its findings known to the public. "However one views the Panthers," said the group's first announcement, the police actions against them raise "grave questions over the whole range of civil rights and civil liberties as applied to the Panthers," and over "the process of justice" employed.

In its larger implications, we can think of few questions more important for Americans to confront in the '70s. We are concerned about "the process of justice" not solely as it is applied by agents of the law but as it has lately come to be applied by each of us to those we regard as dangerously hostile. The police–Panther vendetta is only the leading edge of all the bitter clashes of interest that have divided us in the past few years. Looked at closely, the polarization of sympathies in this country is a tissue of fears. Not what we believe in, but what we are afraid of, has begun to determine where we stand, whether the issue is crime in the streets or war in Vietnam, white middle class protest or black militancy. Thus there are those who are frightened enough by the bristling, revolutionary aspect of the Panthers to approve almost any measures taken to subdue them, and those who are even more frightened by a climate of fear in which such approval can be taken for granted. Many are frightened, also, by a climate of opinion in which those who oppose the war are seen as traitors, and those who support it are seen, in turn, as war-lovers; those who criticize law and order campaigns are aberrantly enamored of criminals, and those who favor tough police measures are inevitably fascistic. The desperate embracing of such simple-mindedness is the most frightening thing of all that has happened in the latter part of the sixties.

We began this overlong discourse with a recitation of the Panthers' sins. Having said it, we apologize for finding it necessary to say at all. What is so disturbing about the present trend of virtue is that in order to raise a question of justice, one first, as a dubious token of impartiality, states the case for injustice. But it is our point, finally, that there has never been an adequate case for injustice. On any level—in the courts, on the streets, or in the public forum—justice is a far more complex matter than the forces of good overriding the forces of villainy. If Americans learn nothing else in the '70s, they must learn to deal with that complexity. It is by the way we administer, in the broad sense, the intricate "process of justice" that we will either ameliorate our corrosive domestic conflicts in the next decade or plunge into even greater turmoil than we have known.

CHICAGO, April 5—I want to protest the proposed postage increase. One cent is enough; the remainder will only pad the pockets of the bigwigs.

I also want to protest our high taxes on everything. They are only used to pad the pockets of officials.

And I protest the truckers' strike. It is only going to raise the cost of food and other things. Milk will go up, then bread, then everything else. I am having a hard time with a budget of $40 a week for food for three adults. I even quit smoking because it got too expensive to blow smoke out of my nose.

The strike will close factories and keep supplies from coming in, and workers who live from week to week will have to be laid off. I want to protest against everyone who is responsible for this rotten mess we are in.

Mrs. C.

"Protest," *Chicago Tribune* (April 5, 1970).

MURDER IN PARKWOLD [and] FEAR

Maxwell Anderson and Kurt Weill

Servant: What do you want?
Johannes: We want money and clothes.
Servant: It's Johannes! I know you!
You cannot do such a thing.
Johannes: Do you want to die?
(shot)
Mathew: Quick! Get out!
Woman's voice: He was shot at night.
Negro Chorus: Murder in Parkwold!
Woman's voice: Nobody knows why or by whom.
White Chorus: Murder in Parkwold!
Man's voice: There was one shot only!
Negro Chorus: Murder in Parkwold!
Man's voice: The servant had called out.
White Chorus: Murder in Parkwold!
Negro Chorus: Murder in Parkwold!

All: In Parkwold among the great houses,
among the lighted streets
And the wide gardens.
White Woman's voice: There are not enough police!
Solo tenor: Murder in Parkwold!
Murder in Parkwold!

Murder in Parkwold.
Murder in Parkwold.
Woman's voice: These streets are full of evil. I'm afraid.
Man: It's alright. Take my arm
This is a shabby neighborhood
Woman: Hush!
Negro singers: It is fear!
It is fear!
Who can enjoy the lovely land,
the seventy years,
the sun that pours down on the earth
when there is fear in the heart?
White singers: Who can walk quietly in the dusk
where behind the dusk there are whispers and reckless hands?
Yes, we fear them.
For they are many and we are few.
Negro singers: Who can be content when he dares not raise his voice
(It is fear)
For fear of the whip, the guard,
the loss of his house
(It is fear)
For fear of the mines and the prisons,
And the cell from which there is no return!
Yes, we fear them,
Though we are many and they are few.
White singers: Who can lie peacefully abed
When in the dark without window
is troubled by those who hate you
for what you are and what you do?
Negro singers: You think you know what it is to fear?
Or to hate?
What is there you have not taken from us
except hate and fear?
Yes, we fear them,
Though we are many and they are few.
White singers: Men are not safe in the streets,
Not safe in their houses

(It is fear)
There are brutal murders,
(It is fear)
robberies
(It is fear)
Tonight again a man lies dead.
Yes, it is fear!
Yes, it is fear!
Fear of the few for the many,
Fear of the many for the few.
It is fear!

THE TEETH MOTHER NAKED AT LAST

Robert Bly

I

Massive engines lift beautifully from the deck.
Wings appear over the trees, wings with eight hundred
    rivets.

Engines burning a thousand gallons of gasoline a minute
    sweep over the huts with dirt floors.

The chickens feel the new fear deep in the pits of their
    beaks.
Buddha with Padma Sambhava.
Slate ships float on the China Sea,
gray bodies born in Roanoke,
the ocean to both sides expanding, "buoyed on the dense
    marine."

Helicopters flutter overhead. The death-
bee is coming. Supersabres
like knots of neurotic energy sweep
around and return.
This is Hamilton's triumph.
This is the advantage of a centralized bank.
B-52's come from Guam. All the teachers
die in flames. The hopes of Tolstoy fall asleep in the
    ant-heap.
Do not ask for mercy.

Now the time comes to look into the past-tunnels,
the hours given and taken in school,
the scuffles in coatrooms,
foam leaps from his nostrils,
now we come to the scum you take from the mouths
of the dead,

now we sit beside the dying, and hold their hands, there
is hardly time for goodbye,
the staff sergeant from North Carolina is dying—you
hold his hand,
he knows the mansions of the dead are empty, he has
an empty place
inside him, created one night when his parents came
home drunk,
he uses half his skin to cover it,
as you try to protect a balloon from sharp objects. . . .

Artillery shells explode. Napalm canisters roll end over
end.
800 steel pellets fly through the vegetable walls.
The six-hour infant puts his fists instinctively to his
eyes to keep out the light.
But the room explodes,
the children explode.
Blood leaps on the vegetable walls.

Yes, I know, blood leaps on the walls—
No need to cry at that—
Do you cry at the wind pouring out of Canada?
Do you cry at the reeds shaken at the edges of the sloughs?
The Marine battalion enters.
This happens when the seasons change,
This happens when the leaves begin to drop from the
trees too early
"Kill them: I don't want to see anything moving."
That happens when the ice begins to show its teeth
in the ponds
that happens when the heavy layers of lake water press
down on the fish's head, and sends him deeper,
where his tail swirls slowly, and his brain passes
him pictures of heavy reeds, of vegetation fallen on
vegetation. . . .

Hamilton saw all this in detail:
*"Every banana tree slashed, every cooking utensil
smashed, every mattress cut."*

Now the Marine knives sweep around like sharp-edged
jets; how easily they slash open the rice bags,
the mattresses. . . .
ducks are killed with $150 shotguns.

Old women watch the soldiers.

II

Excellent Roman knives slip along the ribs.

A stronger man starts to jerk up the strips of flesh.

*Let's hear it again, you believe in the Father, the Son,
and the Holy Ghost?*

A long scream unrolls.

More.

*From the political point of view, democratic institutions
are being built in Vietnam, wouldn't you agree?*

A green parrot shudders under the fingernails.
Blood jumps in the pocket.
The scream lashes like a tail.

"Let us not be deterred from our task by the voices
of dissent. . . ."

The whines of jets
pierce like a long needle.

As soon as the President finishes his press conference,
black wings carry off the words,
bits of flesh still clinging to them.

* * *

The ministers lie, the professors lie, the television lies,
the priests lie. . . .
These lies mean that the country wants to die.
Lie after lie starts out into the prairie grass,
like enormous trains of Conestoga wagons. . . .

And a long desire for death flows out, guiding
the enormous caravans from beneath,
stringing together the vague and foolish words.

It is a desire to eat death,
to gobble it down,
to rush on it like a cobra with mouth open,

It's a desire to take death inside,
to feel it burning inside, pushing out velvety hairs,
like a clothes brush in the intestines

This is the thrill that leads the President on to lie

* * *

The Chief Executive enters; the Press Conference
begins:
First the President lies about the date the Appalachian
Mountains rose

Then he lies about the population of Chicago, then
about the weight of the adult eagle, next about the
acreage of the Everglades

He lies about the number of fish taken every year in the
Arctic, he has private information about which
city *is* the capital of Wyoming, he lies about the
birthplace of Attila the Hun

He lies about the composition of the amniotic fluid, he
insists that Luther was never a German, and insists
that only the Protestants sold indulgences,

That Pope Leo X *wanted* to reform the church, but the
"liberal elements" prevented him,

That the Peasants' War was fomented by Italians from
the North.
And the Attorney General lies about the time the sun
sets.

* * *

This is only the deep longing for death.
It is the longing for someone to come and take us by
the hand to where they all are sleeping:
where the Egyptian Pharoahs are asleep, and your own
mother,
and all those disappeared children, who used to go
around with you in a swing at grade school. . . .

Do not be angry at the President—he is longing to take
in his hand
the locks of death hair—
to meet his own children sleeping, or unborn. . . .

He is drifting sideways toward the dusty places

That's what it's like for a rich country to make war,
That's what it's like to bomb huts (afterwards described
as "structures")
That's what it's like to kill marginal farmers (afterwards
described as "Communists")

This is what it's like to watch the altimeter needle
going mad

Baron 25, this is 81. Are there any friendlies in the area?
81 from 25, negative on the friendlies. I'd like you to
take out as many structures as possible located in those
trees within 200 meters east and west of my smoke mark.

diving, the green earth swinging, cheeks hanging back,
red pins blossoming ahead of us, 20 millimeter
cannon fire, leveling off, rice fields shooting by
like telephone poles, smoke rising, hut roofs loom
up huge as landing fields, slugs going in, half the
huts on fire, figures running, palm trees burning,
shooting past, up again; blue sky, cloud mountains

That is what it's like to have a gross national product

It's because a hospital room in the average American
city now costs $60 a day that we bombed hospitals
in the North

It's because the aluminum window-shade business is
doing so well in the United States that we roll fire
over entire villages

It's because the milk trains coming into New Jersey hit
the right switches every day that the best Vietnamese
men are cut in two by American bullets that follow
each other like freight cars

This is what it's like to send firebombs down in 110°
heat from air-conditioned cockpits,

This is what it's like to be told to fire into a reed hut
with an automatic weapon,

It's because we have new packaging for smoked oysters
that bomb holes appear in the rice paddies

It is because we have so few women sobbing in back
rooms,
because we have so few children's heads torn apart by
high-velocity bullets,

because we have so few tears falling on our own hands
that the Super Sabre turns and screams down toward
the earth

It's because tax-payers move to the suburbs that we
transfer populations.
The Marines use cigarette lighters to light the thatched
roofs of huts
because so many Americans own their own homes.

16 *Carefully taught*

TEACHING REBELLION AT UNION SPRINGS

Patricia Michaels

In 1967 I got a job teaching high school in a small industrial community in upstate New York. I didn't think the job would have political significance for me. I had been involved in civil rights demonstrations and anti-Vietnam marches and in general I identified with the movement. I had also taught in an urban ghetto school. No liberal or left activity existed in Union Springs, so I saw my job there as a retreat from politics and as an opportunity to teach without the pressures of the ghetto. But in fact teaching in Union Springs turned out to be a profoundly political experience. I learned there that decent human relations, meaningful work and education are impossible in this country even in those little red schoolhouses that seemed impervious to the crisis affecting the rest of society.

One of my first discoveries was that most of my students, who looked like Wonder Bread children, were non-college bound and hostile to school. I asked them why they hadn't quit when they were sixteen. Most replied, like a chorus, "Because to get a good job you have to go to school." They understood that the boredom and discipline were preparation for the future. One boy parroted an administrator on the subject of keeping his shirt tails in: "When you work in a factory you're going to have to follow rules you don't like, so you'd better get used to them now."

After a few weeks of teaching, I began to discover that the school was designed to teach the majority of students to adjust to the lives already laid out for them after high school. It reinforced what they had learned at home and in grade school: to blunt feelings; distrust feelings you do have; accept boredom and meaningless discipline as the very nature of things. The faculty and the administration saw themselves as specializers in this process. This point was brought home to me at one faculty meeting following an assembly. In an effort to bring culture to Union Springs, the school sponsored a cello concert, one of several longhair events. The students tired of having their "horizons broadened," hooted and howled throughout the con-

From *No More Teacher's Dirty Looks* (San Francisco: Bay Area Radical Teachers' Organizing Committee and Socialist Revolution), pp. 34–39. By permission of Patricia Michaels.

cert. The cellist was almost as indignant as the teachers and administration. The teachers expressed the sentiment that somehow they had failed to do their job: to train kids to accept things they did not like. Teacher after teacher admitted that while the assembly may have been boring, so were many things in life. *They* had made it, so could the kids. "Culture isn't supposed to be fun," said the principal, "But if you get something out of it, that's all that counts. For most of our kids this is the only time they'll ever get to hear a cellist and their lives will be richer for it."

The school was also designed to promote a definition of work that excluded emotional satisfaction. To the degree that the kids accepted this definition, they distrusted the very classes they enjoyed. Students would often tell me, "This isn't English, it's too much fun," or "School is where you learn—not have a good time." Enjoyment was drinking, speeding cars, minor lawbreaking activities that involved little creativity or effort. Having defined school (i.e., work) as joyless, joy, they thought, must be effortless.

They didn't connect their feelings of depression and anger with the socialization they were undergoing. While putting themselves down as failures, they would tell me everything that was wrong with the school. The petty vandalism, the screaming in the halls, the "cutting up" in class were their means of psychological survival. They didn't see this behavior as an attack on the school system. They were certain too, that if they didn't shape up, they would pay a terrible price.

Their response to the first novel we read in class, Warren Miller's "The Cool World," reflected their sense of futility. They admired Duke, the gang leader hero, and thought he was "cool" because he said what he felt and did what he wanted. At the same time, he was "stupid" because his actions could only lead to poverty, violence and death. They were infuriated at the ending of the novel when Duke "gets rehabilitated." In the endings that they wrote as an exercise, they had Duke killed or imprisoned. As one boy wrote, "This was the only honest ending because the price you pay for doing what you want is defeat in one form or another."

Resigned to the "realities" of life, they had difficulty accepting praise. They had been taught they were unworthy and to distrust anyone who thought they were not. Praise challenged their self-image. John B., for example, was a senior who planned to pump gas after he got out of the army. He also wrote poetry. He alternated between being proud of his work and telling me that it was "bullshit." He was threatened by his creativity. The school had "tracked" him into a "low achiever" class since grade one and after eighteen years he wasn't about to challenge that authoritative definition. The only other job he considered was as a state policeman. "At least you'd have some power," he told me.

The student body was split between the working class "greasers" and the middle class "scholars" or honors students. The students from working class homes saw the honors kids as sellouts, phonies and undeservedly privileged. The honors kids, for example, had a lounge. The rest of the student body congregated in the bath rooms.

The honors students were more ambivalent in their attitudes towards the greasers. Their own school experience was a grind, and they both resented and envied the relative casualness of the other students.

A few college-bound kids protested against my leniency in grades and the lack of discipline in my classes. They demanded that I lower the grades of the "less gifted" and enforce school rules. Some honors students admitted that behind their demands was a conception of learning as drudgery. Success, in turn, meant the failure of others. But this, they added, was the way things are. Society, they were convinced, owed them nothing. Reality was the status quo and people should be judged by how well they coped with that reality.

The "scholars'" game in school consisted of conning the teachers. Establish your reputation and slide through. At times, they acknowledged the hypocrisy of the game, but rarely acted on it. While the "scholars" had nothing but contempt for the administration and most of the faculty, they couldn't get close to the other kids because of their unwillingness to give up the privileges that came with being honors students.

The student body was also divided along sexual lines. Men at Union Springs were more individually rebellious: they expressed their hatred of the school in ways that were considered "manly": haphazard disobedience, drinking before coming to school, vandalism. The women, however, were passive about school on a daily basis, since their major concern was the prestige that came from having a boyfriend, and their status among the men.

One day I assigned my senior class an article about a girl who had been thrown out of college for living with her boyfriend. The boys in the class acknowledged that while they wouldn't marry a girl who did "that," they didn't think it was the school's right to punish her. The girls said nothing. In their compositions they expressed anger at the injustice of punishing the girl and not the boy. One girl wrote: "It's always the girl who suffers in this situation, nothing ever happens to the boy."

The following day I spoke with the girls (the boys were out of the room) and asked why they hadn't said in class what they had written on their papers. They said that they were afraid. One girl told me that the only time she would talk freely in a class was if no boys whom she liked romantically were present.

On another occasion a boy criticized my assigning a novel that contained obscene language, because, he said, it embarrassed him to read those words in front of girls. At the end of the class, a few girls told me that while people should be free to read and write what they wanted, they were glad at least one boy respected them enough to watch his language.

In spite of these divisions among the students, the oppressiveness of the school sometimes brought them together in action. Smoking in the bathrooms was the most controversial issue in the school. Breaking the smoking rules enraged the teachers. Several of them spent their free time catching the smokers, bringing them into the office and getting them suspended for three days. The administration, in an act of desperation (20 cigarette butts had been found on the floor in one day), removed the entrance doors to the bathrooms. After unsuccessfully petitioning the principal, twenty-five students lined up in front of the men's room and refused to proceed to their first period class. The principal threatened to call the police if they wouldn't obey his order to move.

Inside the faculty room, some teachers said they wanted to bust heads and hoped that the administration would allow it. Others joked about how our students were trying to imitate the college kids.

In an assembly later that afternoon, the principal announced that he was replacing the bathroom doors, but only because of the responsible behavior of the majority of students. "All over the country," he said, "bearded rebels are tearing up the schools and causing trouble and now we have their younger versions at Union Springs. "We know," he added, "that while the troublemakers demonstrate, the cream of the crop is dying in Vietnam. These are the true heroes. The boys who stood in front of the men's room this morning are the riff-raff."

The students had not thought of the demonstrators as riff-raff. They were among the most popular kids in school. But neither had they seen them as part of a national movement. By making that association, the principal had helped to break down some of the students' antagonisms towards the left. Later, when SDS people tried to link up with students at Union Springs, some of the ground work had already been laid by the principal.

By my second year at Union Springs, I was intensely sensitive to the repressiveness of the school system and my own role in it. My way of dealing with that was to make my classes more relevant to students' lives. I told them to write about what they felt in the language with which they were most comfortable. The first papers I received were filled with obscenity, and I criticized them on stylistic rather than moral grounds. In the second papers, the students' efforts to shock me changed into honest attempts at good writing. I told one class of seniors who were working on short stories that I would mimeograph and distribute some of their work. The most popular story was a satire concerning soldiers in Vietnam; it was sprinkled with obscenity. I said that I would reprint the story as promised, but I wanted the class to be aware of the risk. They all agreed that the author had written what he felt and that there was nothing objectionable about the piece.

A few weeks later the principal told me that I would have to "cease and desist" from accepting students' work that made use of "poor" language. The principal also criticized me for playing rock music in my classes. "You're allowing too much freedom in your classes." He told me that while these methods were all right for "Negro kids," since "that's the kind of life they're used to" or for very responsible college-bound students, they were not all right for youngsters whose future success in the Army or on their jobs depended on their following rules.

As a result of my classes, he said, students were becoming defiant and teachers and parents were complaining. He said that I was doing a disservice to students in allowing them a freedom that they were not going to have later on.

Up to that point I had not thought of my work as political. In fact, I had berated myself because I hadn't spent more time talking about the war, Blacks, tracking, and so on. Movement friends I had spoken with warned me that far from "radicalizing" my students, I was providing them with a "groovy classroom," making school more palatable, and adjustment to a corrupt system easier for them. After speaking with the principal, however, I concluded that my classroom methods were political. In order for the students to fit into the society, they had to believe certain things about themselves, about their teachers, and about their work. By permitting my students to use their own language in the classroom and to wander the halls without passes, by helping them to discover that school work could be creative, I was challenging the values of the school and, therefore, those of society. That was the beginning for the students of understanding the relation between their lives and the movement.

I told the principal that I could not comply with his order but would discuss the issue with my class. He warned me that I was close to losing my job and that he couldn't figure out why I wanted to be a martyr for the students.

The next day I told my class what had happened. They agreed that we should continue to do what we were doing, though a few students argued that I was teaching revolution and disrespect for authority. One boy told me that his father said that if I were teaching in Russia I would have been jailed long ago. Other students defended our classroom activities, saying that this was the first time they'd been able to express themselves in school. "Everybody in town is calling Mrs. Michaels a Communist," one girl said. "Everything they don't like around here, they call Communist. We've done nothing wrong and neither has she. Those who don't like it here should transfer to another class and not ruin it for the rest of us."

Although the students expressed concern about my losing my job, they knew that the issue was them, as well as myself. It wasn't my class that was on the line, but our class. Crucial to their understanding of the issue as it deepened was my continuing to inform them of developments. By breaking down the traditional teacher–student relationship, I could speak with them not only about their own oppression but mine as well. In that process, the students had begun to listen to me when I raised questions about the war, the draft and the tracking system, though they weren't ready yet to ask those questions for themselves.

In January of my second year, a local SDS chapter sponsored a festival and several workshops for high school students. I announced the events to my students and urged them to go. In spite of warnings from administrators, teachers and parents, a number of students attended. Several teachers showed up to "learn about SDS," but the students knew that they were spies.

The SDS organizer asked the students if they wanted the teachers to stay. "They are part of thc reason we're here," one boy said. "We can never talk honestly in their presence and we can't now. They have to leave." When the teachers refused to go, the students walked out of the room and set up another workshop: a liberating experience; defiance without punishment; a taste of collective power.

The festival changed the students' attitude towards the left. Their disdain for the "peace freaks" was based on a stereotype of the cowardly college student. Their brothers were fighting in Vietnam and if the leftists took their beliefs seriously, they "would be fighting too." One boy told me that the only time he took college demonstrators seriously was when he saw them on TV at the Chicago convention. The students at Union Springs disliked the college protesters because they saw them as a privileged group and they couldn't figure out why they were rebelling.

Students at Union Springs felt ambivalent about leftist culture. Although they talked about "filthy hippies," they listened to the Doors and the Rolling Stones. Rock music was vital to their lives. To hate hippies was difficult for them because Mick Jagger was one too. The longhaired radicals who spoke to them at the SDS festival acted tough, brave, and "tuned" into the kids' experiences. That the principal and teachers defined these people as outlaws only made them more attractive.

The Festival and the presence of high school students at an SDS function frightened the community. The newspapers were filled with letters for the next few weeks condemning SDS and the students who attended. Kids brought the newspapers into school and we discussed reasons for the community's and administration's terror at SDS' presence. Gradually the kids began to connect the local issue with the anti-Communist, pro-war rhetoric they had heard all their lives. They had begun to identify their own rebellion with the rebellion of the people they had earlier called "rioters" "peace creeps," and "commies."

Earlier that year I had talked with some students about Cuba. They had insisted that Castro was a dictator who filled the prisons with anyone who disagreed with him, and that the United States ought to invade the island. When I questioned the reliability of media reporting, they didn't respond.

Only after they read the distortions about themselves in the local newspaper stories, did my argument have some meaning for them. When they were not involved in their own struggle, they accepted what the TV and the newspapers told them. They had even resented my raising questions about Cuba, Vietnam, or Blacks. As one student told me after I talked with him about the war, "Our government couldn't be doing all of those terrible things." What made those "terrible things" believable to him was his new found consciousness of what the school had been doing to him everyday and how the principal and teachers responded when he began to act.

In the months that followed the SDS conference, I talked with students in class, during free periods, and in my home, where many of them became frequent visitors, about everything from Vietnam to dating problems. In April of that year, some of them joined an SDS demonstration against Westmoreland.

As the opportunity to rebel began to develop at Union Springs High, many of the women held back. They didn't see the relevance of the rebellion to their own lives and some even discouraged the boys from participating since it disrupted the normal social life of the school. The girls who did participate, however, were the most militant and committed of the rebels. Some were girls whose dating unpopularity had made high school hell for them and who identified with me because in my classroom they could assert themselves in ways that won them respect. Others were girls who were more assured of their popularity and because they were not hung up in the individualism of the boys, could act together more easily.

The male students, on the other hand, were beginning to challenge the traditional values of individualism and competitiveness that had made it difficult for them to rebel together. Previously much of their prestige had depended upon *individual* defiance. As one boy told me earlier that year: "I talk back to teachers, but when everybody starts doing it, it doesn't mean anything anymore."

About two weeks after the Westmoreland demonstration, seven students decided that they were going to boycott an honors assembly and asked if they could use my room. The assembly was an annual ritual to humiliate the majority of students and to honor the "handful" who had "achieved." The students felt that their refusal to participate was justified, but were uncomfortable about the action. One boy said: "Listen, I don't like this. 'Cutting up' in class is fun, but this is different. It's too serious. I'm not scared or anything, but everybody's acting like it's such a big deal." The boy may have expected punishment for his action but he felt threatened because he had involved himself with six others in a collective decision to defy the school system. If they escaped without punishment, he would be only one among seven heroes. If they got into trouble, his act couldn't be dismissed as a prank. Another boy replied, "This is different from setting a cherry bomb off in the halls and running away. We're identifying ourselves and we're trying to figure out why we're doing it. If you don't see that, you'd better leave."

In early May, I was fired. Many students prepared to sit in. They made signs, held meetings and argued with their parents, who urged them not to get involved. The administration responded with threats of police, suspensions, and warnings to seniors who "might not graduate" if they participated. Administrators phoned the parents of the student leaders and urged them to keep their kids at home. Police watched the entrance of my house. On the morning of the sit-in, teachers in the halls urged the students to hurry to class. Many students did stay home. Others were confused and stood around the halls. About 50 sat in. Six students were suspended for five days and one boy was beaten by the vice-principal when he refused to move on to class.

The next morning the principal met with the students and tried to calm them. There wasn't anything they or he could do to get me back in school, he said. But he would listen to their grievances about the school. After a few days of restlessness and more meetings with students, Union Springs High had ostensibly returned to normal.

But many students had changed during my two years there. When I first met them, they had been resigned to the limited world that the school had defined for them. They didn't believe that they were capable of creating anything larger. Experiences in my classes and their struggle opened the possibility of new definitions of work, of teachers and themselves. When they had to defend those discoveries to parents, contemporaries and school personnel the students learned how to work together.

I did not come to Union Springs to be a political organizer. I came to teach. But I refused to be the teacher that both the administration and students expected me to be. I had rejected the role of cop and socializer not out of any revolutionary commitment, but out of my need to relate to my students. This same need made me reject the labels "lower track," "non–college-bound," "slow learner," that were placed on my students. My refusal to play the traditional teacher role was linked to my refusal to accept them as inferior because they had been treated as such. By breaking down their stereotypes of themselves and of me, I also helped them break down their self-confining images of the world around them.

One letter I received from a female student indicated the achievement as well as the limitations of my work at Union Springs:

> Up until you came to us, I'm sure no student knew where he or she stood in school. They didn't know the powers they had. Now we know them and are trying to use them as best we can. It's going to take time to get organized, but the way things are going now, I'm sure the time will come. I remember the time I was accused of smoking. The principal told me that I had no alternative but to admit I was smoking. I told him that I wasn't and that he could get the Supreme Court on it if he wanted to, but he couldn't prove it.

> That was the first time I really used the power I had and I won. It doesn't seem like much power when it was all over, but I can still remember looking at his face and noticing that his smirk was gone and that he really looked afraid of me. I don't know if you realize it or not, but that small power has affected almost every kid in school and I think that's why you were fired.

Energy had been released at Union Springs, but where will students go with this energy, what will they do with it in that same school this year, in the army, in the factories, and in their marriages? The students were ready to join a movement. Right now there is no movement for them to join. Those who are still in school write me that Union Springs is quiet again. Those who are out say pretty much the same thing. The movement that speaks to the needs they experienced and acted on at Union Springs is yet to be created.

"Got him!"

Reprinted with permission of Oliphant and The Denver Post.

"PDA" Outlawed in High School

HIGHLAND PARK, ILL.—(AP)—School authorities have notified high school students that public display of affection (PDA) is in poor taste and consequently not acceptable in school.

Mark Panther, assistant principal, defined the administration policy on PDA.

"Holding hands isn't bad," he said, "but when a guy has [a] girl up against a locker and starts rubbing her, this is in poor judgment."

He said PDA is "degrading to the individuals involved and embarrassing to those in the vicinity who have to observe this."

Commenting on school policy, Panther said:

"This rule is in simple good taste and this is an educational institution, not a love-in. This is one place that sets the pattern for society. There'd be no holds barred if this rule goes."

"'PDA' Outlawed In High School," *Denver Post* (August 10, 1970).

THE FEAR OF EQUALITY

Robert E. Lane

. . . Since 1848, it has been assumed that the drive for a more equalitarian society, its effective social force, would come from the stratum of society with the most to gain, the working classes. This was thought to be the revolutionary force in the world—the demand of workers for a classless society sparked by their hostility to the owning classes. It was to be the elite among the workers, not the *lumpenproletariat*, not the "scum," who were to advance this movement. Just as "liberty" was the central slogan of the bourgeois revolution, so "equality" was the central concept in the working class movement. Hence it was natural to assume that whatever gains have been made in equalizing the income and status of men in our society came about largely from working class pressure.

But on closer investigation the demands for greater liberty or "freedom" turn out to have been of an ambiguous nature. The middle classes sought freedom of speech and action in large part for the economic gains that this would give them, and moralized their action with the theology of freedom. But the freedom that they gained was frightening, for it deprived them of the solidary social relationships and the ideological certainty which often gave order and meaning to their lives. On occasion, then, they sought to "escape from freedom." The older unfree order had a value which the earlier social commentators did not appreciate.

There is a parallel here with the movement toward a more equalitarian society. The upper working class, and the lower middle class, support specific measures embraced in the formula "welfare state," which have equalitarian consequences. But, so I shall argue, many members of the working classes do not want equality. They are afraid of it. In some ways they already seek to escape from it. Equality for the working classes, like free-

From *The American Political Science Review*, vol. 53 (March 1959), pp. 35–51. Reprinted with permission of the author and the publisher.

dom of the middle classes, is a worrisome, partially rejected, by-product of the demand for more specific measures. Inequality has values to them which have been overlooked. It is these attitudes on status and equality that I shall explore here.

I. Extended Interviews with Fifteen Men

This discussion is based upon extended interviews of from ten to fifteen hours each (in from four to seven sessions) with a sample of American urban male voters. The sample is a random selection from the white members on a list of 220 registered voters in a moderate income (not low income) housing development where income is permitted to range between $4,000 and $6,500, according to the number of dependents in the family. Out of fifteen asked to participate, fifteen agreed, for a modest cash consideration. The characteristics of the sample, then, are as follows:

> They are all men, white, married, fathers, urban, Eastern seaboard.
>
> Their incomes range from $2,400 to $6,300 (except for one who had just moved from the project. His income was $10,000 in 1957).
>
> Ten had working class (blue collar) occupations such as painter, plumber, oiler, railroad fireman, policeman, machine operator.
>
> Five had white collar occupations such as salesman, bookkeeper, supply clerk.
>
> Their ages ranged from 25 to 54; most are in their thirties.
>
> Twelve are Catholic, two Protestants, one is Jewish.
>
> All are native born; their nationality backgrounds are: six Italian, five Irish, one Polish, one Swedish, one Russian, one Yankee. Most are second or third generation Americans.
>
> All were employed at the time of the interviews.
>
> Their educational distribution was: three had only grammar school education; eight had some high school; two finished high school; one had some college; one completed graduate training.

The interviews with these men were taped, with the permission of the interviewees, and transcribed. They were conducted by means of a schedule of questions and topics followed by conversational improvised probes to discover the underlying meanings of the answers given. The kinds of questions employed to uncover the material to be reported are illustrated by the following: "What do you think the phrase 'All men are created equal' means?" "How would you feel if everyone received the same income no matter what his job?" "Sometimes one hears the term 'social class'—as in working class or middle class. What do you think this term 'social class' means?" "What class do you belong to?" "How do you feel about it?" There were also a number of questions dealing with status, private utopias, feelings of privilege or lack of privilege, and other topics, throughout the interview schedule which sometimes elicited responses bearing on the question of social and economic equality.

II. How to Account for One's Own Status?

It is my thesis that attitudes toward equality rest in the first instance upon one's attitude towards one's own status. Like a large number of social beliefs, attitudes towards equality take their direction from beliefs about the self, the status of the self, one's self-esteem or lack thereof. It is necessary, therefore, first to explore how people see themselves in American hierarchical society.

The American culture and the democratic dogma have given to the American public the notion that "all men are created equal." Even more insistently, the American culture tells its members: "achieve," "compete," "be better, smarter, quicker, richer than your fellow men"; in short, "be unequal." The men I interviewed had received these inequalitarian messages, some eagerly, some with foreboding. Having heard them, they must account for their status, higher than some, lower than others. They must ask themselves, for example, "Why didn't I rise out of the working class, or out of the 'housing project class,' or out of the underpaid office help class?" And, on the other hand, "Why am I better off than my parents? or than the fellows down the road in the low rental project? or the fellows on relief?" Men confronted with these questions adopt a variety of interesting answers.

Is it up to me? The problem of accounting for status is personally important for these men only if they think that their decisions, effort, and energy make a difference in their position in life. Most of my subjects accepted the view that America opens up opportunity to all people; if not in equal proportions, then at least enough so that a person must assume responsibility for his own status. . . .

III. Reducing the Importance of the Struggle

When something is painful to examine, people look away, or, if they look at it, they see only the parts they want to see. They deny that it is an important something. So is it often with a person's class status when the reference is upward, when people must account not for the strength of their position, but for its weakness. How do they do this?

In the first place they may *insulate themselves*, limit their outlook and range of comparisons. . . . A second device for reducing the importance of class position is to *deny its importance*. This is not to deny the importance of getting ahead, but to limit this to the problem of job classification, or occupational choice—nothing so damaging to the self-esteem as an ordering of persons on a class scale. . . .

A third device for reducing the significance of the struggle for status and "success" is *resignation*, a reluctant acceptance of one's fate. When some men assume this posture of resignation one senses a pose; their secret hopes and ambitions will not down. For others it rings true. . . .

IV. People Deserve Their Status

If one accepts the view that this is a land of opportunity in which merit will find a way, one is encouraged to accept the status differences of society. But it is more than logic which impels our men to accept these differences. There are satisfactions of identification with the going social order; it is easier to accept differences which one calls "just" than those that appear "unjust"; there are the very substantial self-congratulatory satisfactions of comparison with those lower on the scale. Thus this theme of "just desserts" applies to one's own group, those higher, and those lower.

So Kuchinsky says: "If you're a professor, I think you're entitled to get what you deserve. I'm a painter and I shouldn't be getting what you're getting." Furthermore, confidence in the general equity of the social order suggests that the rewards of one's own life are proportionate to ability, effort, and the wisdom of previous decisions. On ability, Costa, a machine operator, says:

> I believe anybody that has the potential to become a scientific man, or a professor, or a lawyer, or a doctor, should have the opportunity to pursue it, but there's a lot of us that are just made to run a machine in a factory. No matter what opportunities some of us might have had, we would never have reached the point where we could become people of that kind. I mean everybody isn't Joe DiMaggio. . . .

But the most usual mistake or deficiency accounting for the relatively humble position is failure to continue one's education due to lack of family pressure ("they should have made me"), or youthful indiscretion, or the demands of the family for money, or the depression of the thirties.

The Upper Classes Deserve To Be Upper. Just as they regard their own status as deserved, so also do they regard the status of the more eminently successful as appropriate to their talents. Rapuano, an auto parts supply man, reports:

> Your income—if you're smart, and your ability calls for a certain income, that's what you should earn. If your ability is so low, why hell, then you should earn the low income. ["Do you think income is proportionate to ability now?"] I would say so. Yes.

But there is a suggestion in many of the interviews that even if the income is divorced from talent and effort, in some sense it is appropriate. Consider Sokolsky again, a machine operator and part-time janitor, discussing the tax situation:

> Personally, I think taxes are too hard. I mean a man makes, let's say $150,000. Well, my God, he has to give up half of that to the government—which I don't think is right. For instance if a man is fortunate enough to

> win the Irish Sweepstakes, he gets 150—I think he has about $45,000 left. I don't think that's right.

Even if life is a lottery, the winner should keep his winnings. . . .

The concept of "education" is the key to much of the thinking on social class and personal status. In a sense, it is a "natural" because it fits so neatly into the American myth of opportunity and equality, and provides a rationale for success and failure which does minimum damage to the souls of those who did not go to college. Thus in justifying their own positions, sometimes with reference to the interview situation, my clients imply, "If I had gone to college (like you) I would be higher up in this world." Costa, a machine operator, speaks this theme:

> Now what would be the advantage of you going 20 years to school so you wind up making $10,000 a year, and me going 8 years to school, making $10,000. You would be teaching the young men of tomorrow, the leaders of tomorrow, and I would be running a machine. You have a lot more responsibility to the country as a whole than I would have. Why shouldn't you be rewarded in proportion. . . .

What is it about education that justifies differences in income? In the above interviews it is clear that education is thought to increase skills which should be suitably rewarded. Furthermore, it appears that the time necessary for educational preparation deserves some reward—a recurrent theme. With education goes responsibility—and responsibility should be rewarded. But there is also some suggestion in the interview material that the pain and hard (unpleasant) work associated with going to school deserves compensation. People who did not like school themselves may be paying homage to those who could stick it out. It is a question whether O'Hara, a maintenance oiler, implies this when he says:

> I think a person that is educated deserves more than somebody that isn't. Somebody who really works for his money really deserves it more than somebody that's lazy and just wants to hang around.

In this and other ways, education serves as a peg on which to hang status; and, like "blood," whether a person got the education or not is not his "fault," or at least it is only the fault of an irresponsible youth, not a grown man.

The Lower Classes Deserve No Better than They Get. By and large those in the lower orders are those who are paid daily (not weekly) or are on relief; they live in slums or in public housing projects (but not middle income projects); they do not live respectable lives; they have only grammar school education; they may have no regular jobs. Closer to home, these slightly lower in status are people like "The lady next door who has a little less than I have," the man who can't afford to take care of his kids properly in the project, people who spend their money on liquor, the person with less skill in the same line of work.

The rationale for their lower status turns chiefly on two things: their lack of education and therefore failure to know what they want or failure to understand lifesmanship, and their general indifference. It is particularly this "not caring" which seems so salient in the upper working class mind. This is consonant with the general view that success is a triumph of the will and a reflection of ability. Poverty is for lazy people, just as middle status is for struggling people. . . .

In general, there is little sympathy given to those lower in the scale, little reference to the overpowering forces of circumstance, only rare mention of sickness, death of a breadwinner, senility, factories moving out of town, and so forth. The only major cause of poverty to which no moral blame attaches is depression or "unemployment"—but this is not considered a strikingly important cause in the minds of my clients. They are Christian in the sense that they believe "The poor ye have with you always," but there is no trace of a belief that the poor are in any way "blessed."

V. What if There Were Greater Equality of Opportunity and Income?

We have examined here the working (and lower middle) class defenses of the present order. They are well organized and solidly built. By and large these people believe that the field is open, merit will tell. They may then deprecate the importance of class, limit their perspectives, accept their situation reluctantly or with satisfaction. They may see the benefits of society flowing to their own class, however they define it. They tend to believe that each person's status is in some way deserved.

How would these lower middle and working class men feel about a change in the social order such that they and their friends might suddenly be equal to others now higher or lower in the social order? Most of them wouldn't like it. They would fear and resent this kind of equality.

Abandonment of a Rationale. Changing ideas is a strain not to be lightly incurred, particularly when these ideas are intimately related to one's self-esteem. The less education one has, the harder it is to change such ideas. Painfully these men have elaborated an explanation for their situation in life; it helps explain things to their wives who take their status from them; it permits their growing children to account for relative social status in school; it offers to each man the satisfactions of social identity and a measure of social worth. Their rationales are endowed with moral qualities; the distribution of values in the society is seen as just and natural. While it gives satisfactions of an obvious kind to those who contemplate those beneath them, it also gives order and a kind of reassurance, oddly enough, to those who glance upwards towards "society" or "the four hundred." This reassurance is not unlike the reassurance provided by the belief in a Just God while injustices rain upon one's head. The feudal serf, the Polish peasant, the Mexican peon believed that theirs was a moral and a "natural order"—so also the American working man.

The Problem of Social Adjustment. Equality would pose problems of social adjustments, of manners, of how to behave. Here is Sokolsky, unprepossessing, uneducated, and nervous, with a more prosperous brother in the same town. "I'm not going to go over there," he says, "because every time I go there I feel uncomfortable." On the question of rising from one social class to another, his views reflect this personal situation:

> I think it's hard. Let's say—let's take me, for instance. Suppose I came into a lot of money, and I moved into a nice neighborhood—class—maybe I wouldn't know how to act then. I think it's very hard, because people know that you just—word gets around that you . . . never had it before you got it now. Well, maybe they wouldn't like you . . . maybe you don't know how to act.

The kind of equality with others which would mean a rapid rise in his own status is a matter of concern, mixed, of course, with pleasant anticipation at the thought of "telling off" his brother.

Consider the possibility of social equality including genuine fraternization, without economic equality. Sullivan, a railroad fireman, deals with this in graphic terms:

> What is the basis of social class? Well, things that people have in common . . . Money is one, for instance, like I wouldn't feel very comfortable going around with a millionaire, we'll say . . . He could do a lot and say a lot—mention places he'd been and so on—I mean I wouldn't be able to keep up with him . . . and he wouldn't have to watch his money, and I'd have to be pinching mine to see if I had enough for another beer, or something.

And, along the lines of Sokolsky's comments, Sullivan believes that moving upwards in the social scale is easier if one moves to a new place where one has not been known in the old connection. Flynn holds that having the right interests and conversational topics for the new and higher social group will make it possible— but otherwise it could be painful. Kuchinsky, the house painter, says "I suppose it would feel funny to get into a higher class, but I don't believe I would change. I wouldn't just disregard my friends if I came into any money." Clinging to old friends would give some security in that dazzling new world.

De Angelo, a factory operative, also considers the question of whether the higher status people will accept the *arriviste*, but for himself, he dismisses it:

> I wouldn't worry much about whether they would accept or they wouldn't accept. I would move into another class. I mean—I mean—I don't worry much about that stuff. If people don't want to bother with me, I don't bother with them, that's all.

These fears, while plausible and all too human on the face of it, emerged unexpectedly from the interview material designed to capture ideas and emotions on other aspects of class status. They highlight a resistance to equalitarian movements that might bring the working class and this rejecting superior class—whether it is imaginary or not—in close association. If these were revolutionaries, one might phrase their anxieties: "Will my victims accept me?" But they are not revolutionaries.

These are problems of rising in status to meet the upper classes face to face. But there is another risk in opening the gates so that those of moderate circumstances can rise to higher status. Equality of opportunity, it appears, is inherently dangerous in this respect: there is the risk that friends, neighbors, or subordinates will surpass one in status. O'Hara has this on his mind. Some of the people who rise in status are nice, but:

> You get other ones, the minute they get a little, they get big-headed and they think they're better than the other ones—where they're still—to me they're worse than the middle class. I mean, they should get down, because they're just showing their illiteracy—that's all they're doing.

Sokolsky worries about this possibility, too, having been exposed to the slights of his brother's family. But the worry over being passed by is not important, not salient. It is only rarely mentioned.

Deprivation of a Meritorious Elite. It is comforting to have the "natural leaders" of a society well entrenched in their proper place. If there were equality there would no longer be such an elite to supervise and take care of people—especially "me." Thus Woodside, our policeman, reports:

> I think anybody that has money—I think their interest is much wider than the regular working man. . . . And therefore I think that the man with the money is a little bit more educated, for the simple reason he has the money, and he has a much wider view of life—because he's in the knowledge of it all the time.

Here and elsewhere in the interview, one senses that Woodside is glad to have such educated, broad-gauged men in eminent positions. He certainly opposes the notion of equality of income. Something similar creeps into Johnson's discussion of social classes. He feels that the upper classes, who "seem to be very nice people," are "willing to lend a helping hand—to listen to you. I would say they'd help you out more than the middle class [man] would help you out even if he was in a position to help you out." Equality, then, would deprive society, and oneself, of a group of friendly, wise, and helpful people who occupy the social eminences.

The Loss of the Goals of Life. But most important of all, equality, at least equality of income, would deprive people of the goals of life. Every one of the fifteen clients with whom I spent my evenings for seven months believed that equality of income would deprive men of their incentive to work, achieve, and develop their skills. These answers ranged, in their sophistication and approach, across a broad field. The most highly educated man in the sample, Farrel, answers the question "How would you feel if everyone received the same income in our society?" by saying:

> I think it would be kind of silly. . . . Society, by using income as a reward technique, can often insure that the individuals will put forth their best efforts.

He does not believe, for himself, that status or income are central to motivation—but for others, they are. Woodside, our policeman, whose main concern is not the vistas of wealth and opportunity of the American dream, but rather whether he can get a good pension if he should have to retire early, comes forward as follows:

> I'd say that [equal income]—that is something that's pretty—I think it would be a dull thing, because life would be accepted—or it would—rather we'd go stale. There would be no initiative to be a little different, or go ahead.

Like Woodside, Flynn, a white collar worker, responds with a feeling of personal loss—the idea of such an equality of income would make him feel "very mad." Costa, whose ambitions in life are most modest, holds that equality of income "would eliminate the basic thing about the wonderful opportunity you have in this country." Then, for a moment the notion of his income equalling that of the professional man passes pleasantly through his mind: "Don't misunderstand me—I like the idea"; then again, "I think it eliminates the main reason why people become engineers and professors and doctors."

Rapuano, whose worries have given him ulcers, projects himself into a situation where everyone receives the same income, in this case a high one:

> If everyone had the same income of a man that's earning $50,000 a year, and he went to, let's say 10 years of college to do that, why hell, I'd just as soon sit on my ass as go to college and wait till I could earn $50,000 a year, too. Of course, what the hell am I going to do to earn $50,000 a year—now that's another question.

But however the question is answered, he is clear that guaranteed equal incomes would encourage people to sit around on their anatomy and wait for their pay checks. But he would like to see some levelling, particularly if doctors, whom he hates, were to have their fees and incomes substantially reduced.

That These Sacrifices Shall Not Have Been in Vain. The men I talked to were not at the bottom of the scale; not at all. They were stable breadwinners, churchgoers, voters, family men. They achieved this position in life through hard work and sometimes bitter sacrifices. They are distinguished from the lower classes through their initiative, zeal and responsibility, their willingness and ability to postpone pleasures or to forego them entirely. In their control of impulse and desire they have absorbed the Protestant ethic. At least six of them have two jobs and almost no leisure. In answering questions on "the last time you remember having a specially good time" some of them must go back ten to fifteen years. Nor are their good times remarkable for their spontaneous fun and enjoyment of life. Many of them do not like their jobs, but stick to them because of their family responsibilities—and they do not know what else they would rather do. In short, they have sacrificed their hedonistic inclinations, given up good times, expended their energy and resources in order to achieve and maintain their present tenuous hold on respectability and middle status.

Now in such a situaton to suggest that men be equalized and the lower orders raised and one's own hard-earned status given to them as a right and not a reward for effort, seems to them desperately wrong. In the words of my research assistant, David Sears, "Suppose the Marshall Plan had provided a block and tackle for Sisyphus after all these years. How do you think he would have felt?" Sokolsky, Woodside, and Dempsey have rolled the stone to the top of the hill so long, they despise the suggestion that it might have been in vain. Or even worse, that their neighbors at the foot of the hill might have the use of a block and tackle.

The World Would Collapse. As a corollary to the view that life would lose its vigor and its savor with equality of income, there is the image of an equalitarian society as a world running down, a chaotic and disorganized place to live. The professions would be decimated: "People pursue the higher educational levels for a reason—there's a lot of rewards, either financial or social," says Costa. Sullivan says, "Why should people take the headaches of responsible jobs if the pay didn't meet the responsibilities?" For the general society, Flynn, a white collar man, believes that "if there were no monetary incentive involved, I think there'd be a complete loss. It would stop all development—there's no doubt about it." McNamara, a bookkeeper, sees people then reduced to a dead level of worth: with equal income "the efforts would be equal and pretty soon we would be worth the same thing." In two contrasting views, both suggesting economic disorganization, Woodside believes "I think you'd find too many men digging ditches, and no doctors," while Rapuano believes men would fail to dig ditches or sewers "and where the hell would we be when we wanted to go to the toilet?"

Only a few took up the possible inference that this was an attractive, but impractical ideal—and almost none followed up the suggestion that some equalization of income, if not complete equality, would be desirable. The fact of the matter is that these men, by and large, prefer an inequalitarian society, and even prefer a society graced by some men of great wealth. As they look out upon the social scene, they feel that an equalitarian society would present them with too many problems of moral adjustment, interpersonal social adjustment, and motivational adjustment which they fear and dislike. But perhaps, most important, their life goals are structured around achievement and success in monetary terms. If these were taken away, life would be a desert. These men view the possibility of an equalitarian world as a paraphrased version of Swinburne's lines on Jesus Christ, "Thou hast conquered, oh pale equalitarian, and the world has grown gray with thy breath."

VI. Some Theoretical Implications

Like any findings on the nature of men's social attitudes and beliefs, even in such a culture-bound inquiry as this one, the new information implies certain theoretical propositions which may be incorporated into the main body of political theory. Let us consider seven such propositions growing more or less directly out of our findings on the fear of equality:

(1) The greater the emphasis in a society upon the availability of "equal opportunity for all," the greater the need for members of that society to develop an acceptable rationalization for their own social status.

(2) The greater the strain on a person's self-esteem implied by a relatively low status in an open society, the greater the necessity to explain this status as "natural" and "proper" in the social order. Lower status people generally find it less punishing to think of themselves as correctly placed by a just society than to think of themselves as exploited, or victimized by an unjust society.

(3) The greater the emphasis in a society upon equality of opportunity, the greater the tendency for those of marginal status to denigrate those lower than themselves. This view seems to such people to have the factual or even moral justification that if the lower classes "cared" enough they could be better off. It has a psychological "justification" in that it draws attention to one's own relatively better status and one's own relatively greater initiative and virtue.

(4) People tend to care less about *equality* of opportunity than about the availability of *some* opportunity. Men do not need the same life chances as everybody else, indeed they usually care very little about that. They need only chances (preferably with unknown odds) for a slightly better life than they now have. Thus: Popular satisfaction with one's own status is related less to equality of opportunity than to the breadth of distribution of some

opportunity for all, however unequal this distribution may be. A man who can improve his position one rung does not resent the man who starts on a different ladder half way up.

These propositions are conservative in their implications. The psychological roots of this conservatism must be explored elsewhere, as must the many exceptions which may be observed when the fabric of a social order is so torn that the leaders, the rich and powerful, are seen as illegitimate—and hence "appropriately" interpreted as exploiters of the poor. I maintain, however, that these propositions hold generally for the American culture over most of its history—and also, that the propositions hold for most of the world most of the time. This is so even though they fly in the face of much social theory—theory often generalized from more specialized studies of radicalism and revolution. Incidentally, one must observe that it is as important to explain why revolutions and radical social movements do *not* happen as it is to explain why they do.

The more I observed the psychological and physical drain placed upon my sample by the pressures to consume—and therefore to scratch in the corners of the economy for extra income—the more it appeared that competitive consumption was not a stimulus to class conflict, as might have been expected, but was a substitute for or a sublimation of it. Thus we would say:

(5) The more emphasis a society places upon consumption—through advertising, development of new products, and easy installment buying—the more will social dissatisfaction be channeled into intra-class consumption rivalry instead of inter-class resentment and conflict. The Great American Medicine Show creates consumer unrest, working wives, and dual-jobholding, not antagonism toward the "owning classes."

As a corollary of this view: (6) The more emphasis a society places upon consumption, the more will labor unions focus upon the "bread and butter" aspects of unionism, as contrasted to its ideological elements.

We come, finally, to a hypothesis which arises from this inquiry into the fear of equality but goes much beyond the focus of the present study. I mention it here in a speculative frame of mind, undogmatically, and even regretfully:

(7) The ideals of the French Revolution, liberty and equality, have been advanced because of the accidental correspondence between these ideals and needs of the bourgeoisie for freedom of economic action and the demands of the working class, very simply, for "more." Ideas have an autonomy of their own, however, in the sense that once moralized they persist even if the social forces which brought them to the fore decline in strength. They become "myths"—but myths erode without support from some major social stratum. Neither the commercial classes nor the working classes, the historical beneficiaries of these two moralized ideas (ideals or myths), have much affection for the ideals in their universal forms. On the other hand, the professional classes, particularly the lawyers, ministers, and

teachers of a society, very often do have such an affection. It is they, in the democratic West, who serve as the "hard core" of democratic defenders, in so far as there is one. It is they, more frequently than others, who are supportive of the generalized application of the ideals of freedom and equality to all men. This is not virtue, but rather a different organization of interests and a different training. Whatever the reason, however, it is not to "The People," not to the business class, not to the working class, that we must look for the consistent and relatively unqualified defense of freedom and equality. The professional class, at least in the American culture, serves as the staunchest defender of democracy's two greatest ideals.

Declaration—That "Commie Junk"

MIAMI (AP)—Only one person out of 50 approached on Miami streets by a reporter agreed to sign a typed copy of the Declaration of Independence.

Two called it "commie junk," one threatened to call the police and another warned Miami Herald reporter Colin Dangaard: "Be careful who you show that kind of antigovernment stuff to, buddy."

A questionnaire, circulated among 300 young adults attending a Youth for Christ gathering, showed that 28 percent thought an excerpt from the Declaration was written by Lenin.

The youths, mostly high school seniors, were then asked to describe briefly what sort of person they thought would make such a statement.

Among other things, the author of the Declaration was called:

"A person of communism, someone against our country."

"A person who does not have any sense of responsibility."

"A hippie."

"A red-neck revolutionist."

"Someone trying to make a change in government—probably for his own selfish reasons."

Next Dangaard typed up the Declaration in petition form, stood all day on a sidewalk and asked middle-aged passersby to read it and sign it.

Only one man agreed—and he said it would cost the pollster a quarter for his signature.

Comments from those who took the trouble to read the first three paragraphs:

"This is the work of a raver."

"Somebody ought to tell the FBI about this sort of rubbish."

"Meaningless."

"I don't go for religion, Mac."

"The boss'll have to read this before I can let you put it in the shop window. But politically I can tell you he don't lean that way."

Chicago Daily News (July 12, 1970).

Insufficient social cohesion (atomization, personal isolation) is experienced by the individual as alienation, as separation—separation from work, separation from neighbors, separation from friends and relatives, from government, from self. The phenomenal correspondent of alienation is a generalized low-level anxiety that tends to be focused, when it becomes intolerable, on features of the environment that are experienced as most isolated from the social group to which one experiences most attachment. This is the social-psychological process of scapegoating.

Whom do we fear? We fear the enemy. Who is the enemy? The enemy is They; the enemy is the Other. Other than Us: a threat to the body politic. A foreign object that must be excised. The social processes of denial, displacement, and projection.

Gerald M. Swatez

THE POLITICS OF EXPERIENCE

R. D. Laing

Normal alienation from experience

The relevance of Freud to our time is largely his insight and, to a very considerable extent, his *demonstration* that the *ordinary* person is a shriveled, desiccated fragment of what a person can be.

As adults, we have forgotten most of our childhood, not only its contents but its flavor; as men of the world, we hardly know of the existence of the inner world: we barely remember our dreams, and make little sense of them when we do; as for our bodies, we retain just sufficient proprioceptive sensations to coordinate our movements and to ensure the minimal requirements for biosocial survival—to register fatigue, signals for food, sex, defecation, sleep; beyond that, little or nothing. Our capacity to think, except in the service of what we are dangerously deluded in supposing is our self-interest and in conformity with common sense, is pitifully limited: our capacity even to see, hear, touch, taste and smell is so shrouded in veils of mystification that an intensive discipline of unlearning is necessary for *anyone* before one can begin to experience the world afresh, with innocence, truth and love. . . .

Many of us do not know, or even believe, that every night we enter zones of reality in which we forget our waking life as regularly as we forget our dreams when we awake. Not all psychologists know of fantasy as a modality of experience,[1] and the, as it were, contrapuntal interweaving of different experiential modes. Many who are aware of fantasy believe that fantasy is the farthest that experience goes under "normal" circumstances. Beyond that are simply "pathological" zones of hallucinations, phantasmagoric mirages, delusions.

This state of affairs represents an almost unbelievable devastation of our experience. Then there is empty chatter about maturity, love, joy, peace.

This is itself a consequence of and further occasion for the divorce of our experience, such as is left of it, from our behavior.

What we call "normal" is a product of repression, denial, splitting, projection, introjection and other forms of destructive action on experience (see below). It is radically estranged from the structure of being.

The more one sees this, the more senseless it is to continue with generalized descriptions of supposedly specifically schizoid, schizophrenic, hysterical "mechanisms."

There are forms of alienation that are relatively strange to statistically "normal" forms of alienation. The "normally" alienated person, by reason of the fact that he acts more or less like everyone else, is taken to be sane. Other forms of alienation that are out of step with the prevailing state of alienation are those that are labeled by the "normal" majority as bad or mad.

The condition of alienation, of being asleep, of being unconscious, of being out of one's mind, is the condition of the normal man.

Society highly values its normal man. It educates children to lose themselves and to become absurd, and thus to be normal.

Normal men have killed perhaps 100,000,000 of their fellow normal men in the last fifty years.

Our behavior is a function of our experience. We act according to the way we see things.

If our experience is destroyed, our behavior will be destructive.

If our experience is destroyed, we have lost our own selves.

How much human *behavior*, whether the interactions between persons themselves or between groups and groups, is intelligible in terms of human *experience?* Either our inter-human behavior is unintelligible, in that we are simply the passive vehicles of inhuman processes whose ends are as obscure as they are at present outside our control, or our own behavior towards each other is a function of our own experience and our own intentions, however alienated we are from them. In the latter case, we must take final responsibility for what we make of what we are made of.

We will find no intelligibility in behavior if we see it as an inessential

[1] See R. D. Laing, *The Self and Others* (London: Tavistock Publications, 1961; Chicago: Quadrangle Press, 1962), especially Part I.

phase in an essentially inhuman process. We have had accounts of men as animals, men as machines, men as biochemical complexes with certain ways of their own, but there remains the greatest difficulty in achieving a human understanding of man in human terms. . . .

Men have always been weighed down not only by their sense of subordination to fate and chance, to ordained external necessities or contingencies, but by a sense that their very own thoughts and feelings, in their most intimate interstices, are the outcome, the resultant, of processes which they undergo.

A man can estrange himself from himself by mystifying himself and others. He can also have what he does stolen from him by the agency of others.

If we are stripped of experience, we are stripped of our deeds; and if our deeds are, so to speak, taken out of our hands like toys from the hands of children, we are bereft of our humanity. We cannot be deceived. Men can and do destroy the humanity of other men, and the condition of this possibility is that we are interdependent. We are not self-contained monads producing no effects on each other except our reflections. We are both acted upon, changed for good or ill, by other men; and we are agents who act upon others to affect them in different ways. Each of us is the other to the others. Man is a patient-agent, agent-patient, interexperiencing and interacting with his fellows.

It is quite certain that unless we can regulate our behavior much more satisfactorily than at present, then we are going to exterminate ourselves. But as we experience the world, so we act, and this principle holds even when action conceals rather than discloses our experience.

We are not able even to *think* adequately about the behavior that is at the annihilating edge. But what we think is less than what we know; what we know is less than what we love; what we love is so much less than what there is. And to that precise extent we are so much less than what we are.

Yet if nothing else, each time a new baby is born there is a possibility of reprieve. Each child is a new being, a potential prophet, a new spiritual prince, a new spark of light precipitated into the outer darkness. Who are we to decide that it is hopeless?

The Mystification of Experience

It is not enough to destroy one's own and other people's experience. One must overlay this devastation by a false consciousness inured, as Marcuse puts it, to its own falsity.

Exploitation must not be seen as such. It must be seen as benevolence. Persecution preferably should not need to be invalidated as the figment of a paranoid imagination; it should be experienced as kindness. Marx described mystification and showed its function in his day. Orwell's time is already with us. The colonists not only mystify the natives, in the ways that Fanon so clearly shows,[2] they have to mystify themselves. We in Europe and North America are the colonists, and in order to sustain our amazing images of ourselves as God's gift to the vast majority of the starving human species, we have to interiorize our violence upon ourselves and our children and to employ the rhetoric of morality to describe this process.

In order to rationalize our industrial-military complex, we have to destroy our capacity to see clearly any more what is in front of, and to imagine what is beyond, our noses. Long before a thermonuclear war can come about, we have had to lay waste our own sanity. We begin with the children. It is imperative to catch them in time. Without the most thorough and rapid brainwashing their dirty minds would see through our dirty tricks. Children are not yet fools, but we shall turn them into imbeciles like ourselves, with high I.Q.'s if possible.

From the moment of birth, when the Stone Age baby confronts the twentieth-century mother, the baby is subjected to these forces of violence, called love, as its mother and father, and their parents and their parents before them, have been. These forces are mainly concerned with destroying most of its potentialities, and on the whole this enterprise is successful. By the time the new human being is fifteen or so, we are left with a being like ourselves, a half-crazed creature more or less adjusted to a mad world. This is normality in our present age.

Love and violence, properly speaking, are polar opposites. Love lets the other be, but with affection and concern. Violence attempts to constrain the other's freedom, to force him to act in the way we desire, but with ultimate lack of concern, with indifference to the other's own existence or destiny.

We are effectively destroying ourselves by violence masquerading as love.

I am a specialist, God help me, in events in inner space and time, in experiences called thoughts, images, reveries, dreams, visions, hallucinations, dreams of memories, memories of dreams, memories of visions, dreams of hallucinations, refractions of refractions of refractions of that original Alpha and Omega of experience and reality, that Reality on whose repression, denial, splitting, projection, falsification, and general desecration and profanation our civilization as much as on anything is based.

We live equally out of our bodies and out of our minds.

Concerned as I am with this inner world, observing day in and day out its devastation, I ask why this has happened?

One component of an answer, suggested in Chapter I, is that we can *act* on our *experience* of ourselves, others and the world, as well as take action on the world through behavior itself. Specifically this devastation is largely the work of *violence* that has been perpetrated on each of us, and

[2] Frantz Fanon, *The Wretched of the Earth* (London: MacGibbon and Kee, 1965); also Frantz Fanon, *Studies in a Dying Colonialism* (New York: Monthly Review Press, 1965).

by each of us on ourselves. The usual name that much of this violence goes under is *love.*

We act on our experience at the behest of the others, just as we learn how to behave in compliance with them. We are taught what to experience and what not to experience, as we are taught what movements to make and what sounds to emit. A child of two is already a moral mover and moral talker and moral experiencer. He already moves the "right" way, makes the "right" noises, and knows what he should feel and what he should not feel. His movements have become stereometric types, enabling the specialist anthropologist to identify, through his rhythm and style, his national, even his regional, characteristics. As he is taught to move in specific ways out of the whole range of possible movements, so he is taught to experience out of the whole range of possible experience.

Much current social science deepens the mystification. Violence cannot be seen through the sights of positivism.

A woman grinds stuff down a goose's neck through a funnel. Is this a description of cruelty to an animal? She disclaims any motivation or intention of cruelty. If we were to describe this scene "objectively," we would only be denuding it of what is "objectively," or better, ontologically present in the situation. Every description presupposes our ontological premises as to the nature (being) of man, of animals, and of the relationship between them.

If an animal is debased to a manufactured piece of produce, a sort of biochemical complex—so that its flesh and organs are simply material with a certain texture in the mouth (soft, tender, tough), a taste, perhaps a smell—then to describe the animal *positively* in those terms is to debase oneself by debasing being itself. A *positive* description is not "neutral" or "objective." In the case of geese-as-raw-material-for-pâté, one can only give a negative description if the description is to remain underpinned by a valid ontology. That is to say, the description moves in the light of what this activity is a brutalization of, a debasement of, a desecration of: namely, the true nature of human beings and of animals.

The description must be *in light of* the fact that the human beings have so brutalized themselves, have become so banal and stultified, that they are unaware of their own debasement. This is not to superimpose onto the "neutral" description certain value judgements that have lost all criteria of "objective" validity, that is to say, any validity that anyone feels needs to be taken really seriously. On "subjective" matters, anything goes. Political ideologies, on the other hand, are riddled with value judgements, unrecognized as such, that have no ontological validity. Pedants teach youth that such questions of value are unanswerable, or untestable, or unverifiable, or not really questions at all, or that what we require are metaquestions. Meanwhile Vietnam goes on.

Under the sign of alienation every single aspect of the human reality is subject to falsification, and a positive description can only perpetuate the alienation which it cannot itself describe, and succeeds only in further deepening it because it disguises and masks it the more.

We must then repudiate a positivism that achieves its "reliability" by successfully masking what is and what is not, by serializing the world of the observer, by turning the truly given into *capta* which are *taken as given,* by denuding the world of being and relegating the ghost of being to a shadow land of subjective "values."

The theoretical and descriptive idiom of much research in social science adopts a stance of apparent "objective" neutrality. But we have seen how deceptive this can be. The choice of syntax and vocabulary is a political act that defines and circumscribes the manner in which "facts" are to be experienced. Indeed, in a sense it goes further and even creates the facts that are studied.

The "data" (given) of research are not so much given as *taken* out of a constantly elusive matrix of happenings. We should speak of *capta* rather than data. The quantitatively interchangeable grist that goes into the mills of reliability studies and rating scales is the expression of a processing that we do *on* reality, not the expression of the processes *of* reality.

Natural scientific investigations are conducted on objects, or things, or the patterns of relations between things, or on systems of "events." Persons are distinguished from things in that persons experience the world, whereas things behave in the world. Thing-events do not experience. Personal events are experiential. Natural scientism is the error of turning persons into things by a process of reification that is not itself part of true natural scientific method. Results derived in this way have to be dequantified and dereified before they can be reassimilated into the realm of human discourse.

Fundamentally, the error is the failure to realize that there is an ontological discontinuity between human beings and it-beings.

Human beings relate to each other not simply externally, like two billiard balls, but by the relations of the two worlds of experience that come into play when two people meet.

If human beings are not studied as human beings, then this once more is violence and mystification.

In much contemporary writing on the individual and the family there is assumed some not-too-unhappy confluence, not to say pre-established harmony, between nature and nurture. Some adjustments may have to be made on both sides, but all things work together for good to those who want only security and identity.

Gone is any sense of possible tragedy, of passion. Gone is any language of joy, delight, passion, sex, violence. The language is that of a boardroom. No more primal scenes, but parental coalitions; no more repression of sexual ties to parents, but the child "rescinds" its Oedipal wishes. For instance:

> The mother can properly invest her energies in the care of the young child when economic support, status, and protection of the family are provided by the father. She can also better limit her cathexis of the child to maternal feelings when her wifely needs are satisfied by her husband.[3]

Here is no nasty talk of sexual intercourse or even "primal scene." The economic metaphor is aptly employed. The mother "invests" in her child. What is most revealing is the husband's function. The provision of economic support, status and protection, in that order.

There is frequent reference to security, the esteem of others. What one is supposed to want, to live for, is "gaining pleasure from the esteem and affection of others."[4] If not, one is a psychopath.

Such statements are in a sense true. They describe the frightened, cowed, abject creature that we are admonished to be, if we are to be normal—offering each other mutual protection from our own violence. The family as a "protection racket."

Behind this language lurks the terror that is behind all this mutual back-scratching, this esteem-, status-, support-, protection-, security-giving and getting. Through its bland urbanity the cracks still show.

In our world we are "victims burning at the stake, signaling through the flames," but for some, things go blandly on. "Contemporary life requires adaptability." We require also to "utilize intellect," and we require "an emotional equilibrium that permits a person to be malleable, to adjust himself to others without fear of loss of identity with change. It requires a basic trust in others, and a confidence in the integrity of the self."[5]

Sometimes there is a glimpse of more honesty. For instance, when we "consider society rather than the individual, each society has a vital interest in the *indoctrination* of the infants who form its new *recruits.*"[6]

What these authors say may be written ironically, but there is no evidence that it is.

Adaptation to what? To society? To a world gone mad?

The family's function is to repress Eros; to induce a false consciousness of security; to deny death by avoiding life; to cut off transcendence; to believe in God, not to experience the Void; to create, in short, one-dimensional man; to promote respect, conformity, obedience; to con children out of play; to induce a fear of failure; to promote a respect for work; to promote a respect for "respectability."

Let me present here two alternative views of the family and human adaptation:

[3] T. Lidz, *The Family and Human Adaptation* (London: Hogarth Press, 1964), p. 54.

[4] Ibid., page 34.

[5] Ibid., pages 28–29.

[6] Ibid., page 19.

> Men do not become what by nature they are meant to be, but what society makes them. . . . generous feelings . . . are, as it were, shrunk up, seared, violently wrenched, and amputated to fit us for our intercourse with the world, something in the manner that beggars maim and mutilate their children to make them fit for their future situation in life.[7]

and:

> In fact, the world still seems to be inhabited by savages stupid enough to see reincarnated ancestors in their newborn children. Weapons and jewelry belonging to the dead men are waved under the infant's nose if he makes a movement, there is a great shout—Grandfather has come back to life. This "old man" will suckle, dirty his straw and bear the ancestral name; survivors of his ancient generation will enjoy seeing their comrade of hunts and battles wave his tiny limbs and bawl; as soon as he can speak they will inculcate recollections of the deceased. A severe training will "restore" his former character, they will remind him that "he" was wrathful, cruel or magnanimous, and he will be convinced of it despite all experience to the contrary. What barbarism! Take a living child, sew him up in a dead man's skin, and he will stifle in such senile childhood with no occupation save to reproduce the avuncular gestures, with no hope save to poison future childhoods after his own death. No wonder, after that, if he speaks of himself with the greatest precautions, half under his breath, often in the third person; this miserable creature is well aware that he is his own grandfather.
>
> These backward aborigines can be found in the Fiji Islands, in Tahiti, in New Guinea, in Vienna, in Paris, in Rome, in New York—wherever there are men. They are called parents. Long before our birth, even before we are conceived, our parents have decided who we will be.[8]

In some quarters there is a point of view that science is neutral, and that all this is a matter of value judgements.

Lidz calls schizophrenia a failure of human adaptation. In that case, this too is a value judgement. Or is anyone going to say that it is an objective fact? Very well, let us call schizophrenia a successful attempt not to adapt to pseudo-social realities. Is this also an objective fact? Schizophrenia is a failure of ego functioning. Is this a neutralist definition? But what is, or who is, the "ego"? In order to get back to what the ego is and what actual reality it most nearly relates to, we have to desegregate it, de-depersonalize it, de-extrapolate, de-abstract, de-objectify, de-reify, and we get back to you and me, to our particular idioms or styles of relating to each other in social context. The ego is by definition an instrument of adaptation, so we are back

[7] E. Colby (ed.), *The Life of Thomas Holcroft, continued by William Hazlitt* (London: Constable & Co., 1925), Volume II, page 82.

[8] J. P. Sartre, Foreword to *The Traitor* by André Gorz (London: Calder, 1960), pages 14–15.

to all the questions this apparent neutralism is begging. Schizophrenia is a successful avoidance of ego-type adaptation? Schizophrenia is a label affixed by some people to others in situations where an interpersonal disjunction of a particular kind is occurring. This is the nearest one can get at the moment to something like an "objective" statement, so called.

The family is, in the first place, the usual instrument for what is called socialization, that is, getting each new recruit to the human race to behave and experience in substantially the same way as those who have already got here. We are all fallen Sons of Prophecy, who have learned to die in the Spirit and be reborn in the flesh.

This is also known as selling one's birthright for a mess of pottage.

Here are some examples from Jules Henry, an American professor of anthropology and sociology, in his study of the American school system:

> The observer is just entering her fifth-grade classroom for the observation period. The teacher says, "Which one of you nice, polite boys would like to take (the observer's) coat and hang it up?" From the waving hands, it would seem that all would like to claim the honor. The teacher chooses one child, who takes the observer's coat. . . . The teacher conducted the arithmetic lessons mostly by asking, "Who would like to tell the answer to the next problem?" This question was followed by the usual large and agitated forest of hands, with apparently much competition to answer.
>
> What strikes us here are the precision with which the teacher was able to mobilize the potentialities of the boys for the proper social behavior, and the speed with which they responded. The large number of waving hands proves that most of the boys have already become absurd; but they have no choice. Suppose they sat there frozen?
>
> A skilled teacher sets up many situations in such a way that a *negative attitude can be construed only as treason*. The function of questions like, "Which one of you nice, polite boys would like to take (the observer's) coat and hang it up? is to blind the children into absurdity—to compel them to acknowledge that it is better to exist absurd than not to exist at all. The reader will have observed that the question is not put, "Who *has* the answer to the next problem?" but "Who *would like to tell* it?" What at one time in our culture was phrased as a challenge in skill in arithmetic, becomes an invitation to group participation. The essential is *that nothing is but what it is made to be by the alchemy of the system.*
>
> In a society where competition for the basic cultural goods is a pivot of action, people cannot be taught to love one another. It thus becomes necessary for the school to teach children how to hate, and without appearing to do so, for our culture cannot tolerate the idea that babes should hate each other. How does the school accomplish this ambiguity?[9]

[9] Excerpts from *Culture Against Man*, by Jules Henry. Copyright © 1963 by Random House, Inc. Reprinted by permission of the publisher.

Here is another example given by Henry:

> Boris had trouble reducing 12/16 to the lowest terms, and could only get as far as 6/8. The teacher asked him quietly if that was as far as he could reduce it. She suggested he "think." Much heaving up and down and waving of hands by the other children, all frantic to correct him. Boris pretty unhappy, probably mentally paralyzed. The teacher quiet, patient, ignores the others and concentrates with look and voice on Boris. After a minute or two she turns to the class and says, "Well, who can tell Boris what the number is?" A forest of hands appears, and the teacher calls Peggy. Peggy says that four may be divided into the numerator and the denominator.[10]

Henry comments:

> Boris's failure made it possible for Peggy to succeed; his misery is the occasion for her rejoicing. This is a standard condition of the contemporary American elementary school. To a Zuni, Hopi or Dakota Indian, Peggy's performance would seem cruel beyond belief, for competition, the wringing of success from somebody's failure, is a form of torture foreign to those noncompetitive cultures.
>
> Looked at from Boris's point of view, the nightmare at the blackboard was, perhaps, a lesson in controlling himself so that he would not fly shrieking from the room under enormous public pressure. Such experiences force every man reared in our culture, over and over again, night in, night out, even at the pinnacle of success, to dream not of success, but of failure. In school the external nightmare is internalized for life. Boris was not learning arithmetic only; he was learning the *essential nightmare also. To be successful in our culture one must learn to dream of failure.*[11]

It is Henry's contention that in practice education has never been an instrument to free the mind and the spirit of man, but to bind them. We think we want creative children, but what do we want them to create?

> If all through school the young were provoked to question the Ten Commandments, the sanctity of revealed religion, the foundations of patriotism, the profit motive, the two-party system, monogamy, the laws of incest, and so on . . .[12]

. . . there would be such creativity that society would not know where to turn.

Children do not give up their innate imagination, curiosity, dreaminess easily. You have to love them to get them to do that. Love is the path through permissiveness to discipline; and through discipline, only too often, to betrayal of self.

[10] Ibid., page 27.
[11] Ibid., pages 295–296.
[12] Ibid., page 288.

What school must do is to induce children to want to think the way school wants them to think. "What we see," in the American kindergarten and early schooling process, says Henry, "is the pathetic surrender of babies." You will, later or sooner, in the school or in the home.

It is the most difficult thing in the world to recognize this in our own culture.

In a London class, average age ten, the girls were given a competition. They had to bake cakes and the boys were to judge them. One girl won. Then her "friend" let out that she had bought her cake instead of baking it herself. She was disgraced in front of the whole class.

Comments:

(1) The school is here inducting children into sex-linked roles of a very specific kind.

(2) Personally, I find it obscene that girls should be taught that their status depends on the taste they can produce in boys' mouths.

(3) Ethical values are brought into play in a situation that is at best a bad joke. If coerced into such game-playing by adults, the best a child can do is to play the system without getting caught. I most admire the girl who won and hope she will choose her "friends" more carefully in future.

What Henry describes in American schools is a strategy that I have observed frequently in British families studied by my colleagues and myself.

The double action of destroying ourselves with one hand, and calling this love with the other, is a sleight of hand one can marvel at. Human beings seem to have an almost unlimited capacity to deceive themselves, and to deceive themselves into taking their own lies for truth. By such mystification, we achieve and sustain our adjustment, adaptation, socialization. But the result of such adjustment to our society is that, having been tricked and having tricked ourselves out of our minds, that is to say, out of our own personal worlds of experience, out of that unique meaning with which potentially we may endow the external world, simultaneously we have been conned into the illusion that we are separate "skin-encapsuled egos." Having at one and the same time lost our *selves* and developed the illusion that we are autonomous *egos*, we are expected to comply by inner consent with external constraints, to an almost unbelievable extent.

We do not live in a world of unambiguous identities and definitions, needs and fears, hopes, disillusions. The tremendous social realities of our time are ghosts, specters of murdered gods and our own humanity returned to haunt and destroy us. The Negroes, the Jews, the Reds. *Them.* Only you and I dressed differently. The texture of the fabric of these socially shared hallucinations is what we call reality, and our collusive madness is what we call sanity.

Let no one suppose that this madness exists only somewhere in the night or day sky where our birds of death hover in the stratosphere. It exists in the interstices of our most intimate and personal moments.

We have all been processed on Procrustean beds. At least some of us have managed to hate what they have made of us. Inevitably we see the other as the reflection of the occasion of our own self-division.

The others have become installed in our hearts, and we call them ourselves. Each person, not being himself either to himself or the other, just as the other is not himself to himself or to us, in being another for another neither recognizes himself in the other, nor the other in himself. Hence being at least a double absence, haunted by the ghost of his own murdered self, no wonder modern man is addicted to other persons, and the more addicted, the less satisfied, the more lonely.

Once more there is a turn of the spiral, another round of the vicious circle, another twist of the tourniquet. For now love becomes a further alienation, a further act of violence. My need is a need to be needed, my longing a longing to be longed for. I act now to install what I take to be myself in what I take to be the other person's heart. Marcel Proust wrote:

> How have we the courage to wish to live, how can we make a movement to preserve ourselves from death, in a world where love is provoked by a lie and consists solely in the need of having our sufferings appeased by whatever being has made us suffer?

But no one makes us suffer. The violence we perpetrate and have done to us, the recriminations, reconciliations, the ecstasies and the agonies of a love affair, are based on the socially conditioned illusion that two actual persons are in relationship. Under the circumstances, this is a dangerous state of hallucination and delusion, a mishmash of fantasy, exploding and imploding, of broken hearts, reparation and revenge.

Yet within all this, I do not preclude the occasions when, most lost, lovers may discover each other, moments when recognition does occur, when hell can turn to heaven and come down to earth, when this crazy distraction can become joy and celebration.

And, at the very least, it befits Babes in the Wood to be kinder to each other, to show some sympathy and compassion, if there is any pathos and passion left to spend.

But when violence masquerades as love, once the fissure into self and ego, inner and outer, good and bad occurs, all else is an infernal dance of false dualities. It has always been recognized that if you split Being down the middle, if you insist on grabbing *this* without *that*, if you cling to the good without the bad, denying the one for the other, what happens is that the dissociated evil impulse, now evil in a double sense, returns to permeate and possess the good and turn it into itself.

When the great Tao is lost, spring forth benevolence and righteousness.

When wisdom and sagacity arise, there are great hypocrites.

When family relations are no longer harmonious, we have filial children and devoted parents.

When a nation is in confusion and disorder, patriots are recognized.

We must be very careful of our selective blindness. The Germans reared children to regard it as their duty to exterminate the Jews, adore their leader, kill and die for the Fatherland. The majority of my own generation did not regard it as stark raving mad to feel it better to be dead than Red. None of us, I take it, has lost too many hours' sleep over the threat of imminent annihilation of the human race and our own responsibility for this state of affairs.

In the last fifty years, we human beings have slaughtered by our own hands coming on for one hundred million of our species. We all live under constant threat of our total annihilation. We seem to seek death and destruction as much as life and happiness. We are as driven to kill and be killed as we are to let live and live. Only by the most outrageous violation of ourselves have we achieved our capacity to live in relative adjustment to a civilization apparently driven to its own destruction. Perhaps to a limited extent we can undo what has been done to us and what we have done to ourselves. Perhaps men and women were born to love one another, simply and genuinely, rather than to this travesty that we call love. If we can stop destroying ourselves we may stop destroying others. We have to begin by admitting and even accepting our violence, rather than blindly destroying ourselves with it, and therewith we have to realize that we are as deeply afraid to live and to love as we are to die.

TOO OLD TO GO 'WAY, LITTLE GIRL

Janis Ian

Don't go out in the street, Little Girl,
And don't go out into town.
You don't know who you'll meet, Little Girl.
There are bad men around.

Uh ho your mother she's in love with you,
She tells you you oughtn't go with guys.
So go to bed at ten, let your mother tuck you in,
And turn on your Mickey Mouse nite lite.
Then you make it with your mind.

Don't go out into town, Little Girl,
Stay safe in your house, Girl.
Your mother's wails, the enquirer's tales
Keep you mmm hiding, denying.

Don't go into the park, Little Girl,
You know those men they're all the same.
Stay inside alone after dark, Little Girl.
A boy wants just one thing.

Mmm don't talk about sex, you might get hexed.
God'll punish you for your dirty mind.
Now there's no escaping, you'd enjoy a raping
Just to find out the facts of life.
Mama says maintain your pride.

Don't go out into town, Little Girl,
Stay safe in your house, Girl.
Your mother's wails, the enquirer's tales
Keep you mmm hiding, denying.

Don't go into your mind, Little Girl,
The windows they're only made of glass.
Don't let me catch you trying to pry, Little Girl,
Mirrors of illusion tumble fast.
Uh ho you're too far gone for anyone.
I'd like to help but I can only sigh.
You'd best maintain your mother's pride,
You lost yours the time you obeyed
When she said don't fraternize.
Got no place to hide.

Don't go out into town, Little Girl,
Stay safe in the house, Little Girl.
When your mother's gone you'll continue to run.
Keep on mmm hiding, denying.

17 Isolation / Hate ↔ Fear

FORCED ASSIMILATION

Edward H. Spicer

The view that forcible assimilation of the Indians was fully justified received expression in statements of many government officials and others from the 1870s into the 1900s. Some of the major emphases are set forth in the following excerpts from various documents.[1]

In our intercourse with the Indians it must always be borne in mind that we are the most powerful party . . . We . . . claim the right to control the soil which they occupy, and we assume that it is our duty to coerce them, if necessary, into the adoption and practice of our habits and customs. (Columbus Delano, *Report of the Secretary of the Interior, 1872.* pp. 3–4.)

The education of small numbers is overborne and lost in the mass of corrupting and demoralizing surroundings. Children at [the nonreservation boarding] school are hostages for good behavior of parents. (R. H. Pratt in *U.S. Bureau of Indian Affairs Annual Report*, 1878, pp. 173–75.)

Agents are expected to keep the [boarding] schools filled with Indian pupils, first by persuasion; if this fails, then by withholding rations or annuities or by such other means as may reach the desired end. (U.S. Bureau of Indian Affairs, *Regulations*, 1884, p. 94.)

[1] The first four are quoted in J. S. Slotkin, *The Peyote Religion*, Glencoe, Ill., 1956, p. 85; the last three in Loring B. Priest, *Uncle Sam's Stepchildren*, New Brunswick, N.J., 1942, pp. 242–43.

The multiplicity of tribes represented, enabled a mixing of tribes in dormitory rooms. The rooms held three to four each and it was arranged that no two of the same tribe were placed in the same room. This not only helped in the acquirement of English but broke up tribal and race clannishness, a most important victory in getting the Indian toward real citizenship. (R. H. Pratt, *The Indian Industrial School: Carlisle, Penna.* Carlisle, Penna., 1908, p. 21.)

We have a full right, by our own best wisdom, and then even by compulsion, to dictate terms and conditions to them; to use constraint and force; to say what we intend to do, and what they must and shall do. . . . This rightful power of ours will relieve us from conforming to, or even consulting to any troublesome extent, the views and inclinations of the Indians whom we are to manage. A vast deal of folly and mischief has come of our attempts to accommodate ourselves to them, to humor their whims and caprices, to indulge them in their barbarous ways and their inveterate obstinacy. Henceforward they must conform to our best views of what is for their good. The Indian must be made to feel he is in the grasp of a superior. (George E. Ellis, *The Red Man and the White Man in North America,* Boston, 1882, p. 572.)

I believe the Government should adopt a more vigorous policy with the Indian people. I can see no reason why a stronge Government like ours should not govern and control them and compel each one to settle down and stay in one place, his own homestead, wear the white man's clothing, labor for his own support, and send his children to school. I can see no reason why . . . good and true men and women should come to an Indian agency and labor honestly and earnestly for three or four or a dozen years trying to coax or persuade the Indians to forsake their heathenish life and adopt the white man's manner of living, and then go away feeling they have thrown away, almost, the best years of their lives. The truth is the Indians hate the white man's life in their hearts, and will not adopt it until driven by necessity. (United States Indian Office, *Annual Report of the Commissioner of Indian Affairs*, 1884 [Statement by Agent Armstrong of the Crows], p. 111.)

Some races are plastic and can be molded: some races are elastic and can be bent; but the Indian is neither; he is formed out of rock, and when you change his form you annihilate his substance. . . . Civilization destroys the Indian . . . and the sooner the country understands that all these efforts are valueless unless they are based upon force supplemented by force and continued by force, the less money we shall waste and the less difficulty we shall have. (United States Congress, *Congressional Record,* IV, p. 393 [Senator Ingalls of Kansas].)

* Show in class 6 minute film "Buffy."

MY COUNTRY 'TIS OF THY PEOPLE YOU'RE DYING

Buffy Sainte-Marie

Now that your big eyes are finally opened,
Now that you're wond'ring "how must they feel?,"
Meaning them that you've chased 'cross America's movie screens.
Now that you're wond'ring "how can it be real,"
That the ones you've called colorful, noble and proud
In your school propaganda, they starve in their splendor!
You've asked for my comment, I simply will render:
My country 'tis of thy people you're dying.

Now that the long houses "breed superstition"
You force us to send our toddlers away to your schools
Where they're taught to despise their traditions;
Forbid them their languages, then further say that
American history really began when Columbus set out of Europe!
And stress that the nation of leeches that's conquered
This land are the biggest and bravest and boldest and best!
And yet where in your history books is the tale
Of the genocide basic to this country's birth?
Of the preachers who lied? How the Bill of Rights failed?
How a nation of patriots returned to their earth?
And where will it tell of the liberty bell as it rang
With a thud over Kinzua mud? And of brave Uncle Sam
In Alaska this year?
My country 'tis of thy people you're dying.

Here how the bargain was made for the West,
With her shivering children in zero degrees,
"Blankets for your land", so the treaties attest.
Oh, well, blankets for land is a bargain indeed—
But the blankets were those Uncle Sam had collected,
From smallpox diseased dying soldiers that day,
And the tribes were wiped out and the history books censored!
A hundred years of your statesmen have felt it's better this way,
Yet a few of the conquered have somehow survived—
Their blood runs the redder though genes have been paled,
From the Grand Canyon's caverns to Craven's sad hills,

The wounded, the losers, the robbed sing their tale,
From Los Angeles County to upstate New York,
The white nation fattens while others grow lean.
Oh the tricked and evicted, they know what I mean;
My country 'tis of thy people you're dying!

The past it just crumbled: the future just threatens;
Our life blood's shut up in your chemical tanks.
And now here you come, bill of sale in your hand,
And surprise in your eyes that we're lacking in thanks,
For the blessings of civilization you've brought us,
The lessons you've taught us, the ruin you've wrought us!
Oh see what our trust in America's bought us!
My country 'tis of thy people you're dying!

Now that the pride of the sires receive charity,
Now that we're harmless and safe behind laws,
Now that my life's to be known as your heritage,
Now that even the graves have been robbed,
Now that our own chosen way is your novelty,
Hands on our hearts, we salute you your victory,
Choke on your blue, white and scarlet hypocrisy,
Pitying the blindness that you've never seen,
That the eagles of war whose wings lent you glory,
They were never no more than carrion crows;
Pushed the wrens from their nest, stole their eggs, changed their story,
The mockingbird sings it—it's all that she knows,
"Ah what can I do?" say a powerless few,
With a lump in your throat and a tear in your eye,
Can't you see that their poverty's profiting you?
My country 'tis of thy people you're dying!

STRANGERS NEXT DOOR: ETHNIC RELATIONS IN AMERICAN COMMUNITIES

Robin M. Williams, Jr.

Ethnocentrism

Ethnocentrism, says William Graham Sumner, is that ". . . view of things in which one's own group is the center of everything, and all others are scaled and rated with reference to it." It is a fact that men classify

From Robin M. Williams, Jr., *Strangers Next Door: Ethnic Relations in American Communities*, pp. 17–27, 28–49, 64–71 (excerpts). © 1964. Reprinted by permission of Prentice-Hall, Inc., Englewood Cliffs, New Jersey.

their fellows in a variety of ways and react to others as members of social categories. What is the nature of these groups that men form? How do they form them, and why? What is the nature of ethnocentric feelings, and how strong are they? The answers to these questions will constitute the main part of this chapter. We will also consider, in the final pages of this chapter, whether ethnocentrism necessarily results in prejudice. . . .

WHY WE ARE ETHNOCENTRIC

All individuals need group belongingness and group anchorage. Without stable relationships to other persons, without some group ties, the individual becomes insecure, anxious, and uncertain of his identity. In order to receive the emotional support of the group (that is, the family group, the neighborhood or school peer group) the individual must heed the opinions of other group members. In the homogeneous family group he learns definite codes for behavior within the group and for behavior towards other groups. The child discovers very early that agreement with group opinions and codes is rewarding. He learns that the teachings of one's parents and close associates are helpful in getting what he wants and avoiding what he does not want. To the extent to which the child finds the instruction of elders and peers reliable for achieving rewarding results, he learns to give credence to their opinions. The child's need is great for relationships of trust that mediate reality to him. And through group attachments and loyalties he learns also of group antipathies and conflicts. He perceives groups, then, as social units in which he can expect security and love or danger and negative emotional experience.

Secure identity as a member of an ingroup is not a free good, contrary to some first appearances, but is only to be had at a price. Often one must have already established credentials of other group memberships and of personal qualities and achievements. Furthermore, maintenance of a clear, full, and secure identity within the ingroup requires conformity to group norms. More exactly, the price of one's group identity is responsible reciprocity with other members, a reciprocity defined by mutually accepted norms.

THE OVERLAPPING OF GROUPS

Particularly in our complex society, most individuals are members of more than one group. The child, aware at first only of his membership in a kinship group, slowly becomes conscious of other memberships. Piaget reports that only at the age of ten to eleven were the children he studied capable of understanding that they could be members of both a locality and a nation, and of understanding what a nation is. By adulthood then, the individual is aware of a plurality of group memberships that help him identify himself. The person is rare in urban America today who feels a clear and strong sense of identification with one and only one grouping or segment of the community and nation. The typical individual is a member of many ingroups (groups of intimate belonging; "we-groups") and may relate himself to many other reference groups (those that matter to him, and upon whose opinions he relies).

It is difficult to realize fully the enormous significance of alternative group memberships. If the individual can belong to only one group, that group inevitably becomes all-important to him. In it all his satisfactions are found and are controlled and limited. It encompasses and constricts all his experience. However, totalistic character of group membership diminishes in complex and fluid societies. The growth of alternative possibilities of group membership and group reference depends upon the number and variety of distinctive groupings, but the sheer multiplication of groupings is far from the whole story. Changes in the criteria of membership are accentuated by changes in the functions of groups and by shifts in the alignments among and between groups. The characteristics that actually are statistically typical of a grouping or category at one time cease to be typical later. . . .

Ethnocentric feelings

POSITIVE ETHNOCENTRISM

What are the components of the sentiments of ethnocentrism? George Peter Murdock says, "Always the 'we-group' and its codes are exalted, while 'other groups' and their ways are viewed with suspicion, hostility and contempt." It is true that satisfaction with one's own group (Oog) sometimes is accompanied by negative feelings toward other groups, but for the moment let us examine the attitude that ethnocentric groups have toward themselves. The most important are:

(1) A belief in the unique value of Oog.

(2) Satisfaction with membership in Oog.

(3) Solidarity, loyalty, or cooperation with regard to Oog.

(4) Preference for association with members of Oog.

(5) Belief in the rightness of Oog's relationships with other groups.

The attitudes toward other groups that often accompany the five sentiments just mentioned are:

(1) Judging other groups by Oog's standards.

(2) Belief that Oog is superior to other groups, in all ways or in some ways.

(3) Ignorance of other groups.

(4) Lack of interest in other groups.

(5) Hostility towards other groups.

NEGATIVE ETHNOCENTRISM

It is not true, as is often assumed, that every group, people, or society considers itself superior in some generalized sense to all others or even to most others. There are many well-documented instances in which positive loyalty to the ingroup goes along with some appreciation of outgroup values and practices. One's own group does provide the norms for judging other groups, and in various particular ways an outgroup may be seen as superior. For instance, a tribe that prides itself upon its skill in the building of boats can recognize that the products of another tribe represent superior craftsmanship. This admission need not result in a general devaluation of Oog; it is negative ethnocentrism only in its admission of specific points of inferiority. One still retains one's ingroup standards and a basic adherence to its values.

Yet, the phenomena of self-hatred and self-deprecation of one's own membership group are common and must be taken into account. History is replete with voluntary exiles, expatriates, outgroup emulators, social climbers, renegades, and traitors. Also, the dominant attitude in a whole people can be one of accepting at least some of the low evaluations of outsiders. Peter A. Munch has given a fascinating account of such attitudes among the inhabitants of the remote island of Tristan da Cahuna. Among the villagers in southern Italy whose amoral familism has been described by Edward C. Banfield, the desire to emigrate, the awareness of poverty, and the deprecation of the local society are evident. Other examples can be found, as in numerous instances of tribal peoples overwhelmed by conquest and subordinated to technologically advanced rulers. But the most important manifestations of negative sentiments toward the individual's own membership group occur in subordinated minority groups that are objects of prejudice and discrimination. . . .

Does positive ethnocentrism necessarily result in prejudice?

Whether strong negative feelings toward an outgroup always develop along with positive feelings of ethnocentrism is a question that has been explored in numerous studies. On the one hand we have Mary Ellen Goodman's study of Negro and white children, which showed that racial preferences were associated with hostility in only a minority of cases. On the other hand, William Graham Sumner is usually singled out among American sociologists as favoring the idea that ingroup solidarity is related to outgroup hostility. What he says, however, is somewhat ambiguous: "The relationship of comradeship and peace in the we-group and that of hostility and war toward others-groups are correlative to each other." Sumner was thinking primarily of preliterate groups with relatively clear boundaries in situations in which threat and counterthreat affected the group as a whole. Even so, his statement bears the marks of caution: he says "are correlative" rather than "necessarily occur together." The consensus of studies, however, seems to be that continued interaction between culturally distinctive peoples need not result in conflict. One group may be assimilated by another, or there are even rare examples of sustained contacts between two endogamous and ethnocentric peoples with little conflict and little or no assimilation of one culture to the other. Such accommodative relations seem to rest upon an economic interdependence that is mutually advantageous and essentially noncompetitive. Much more common, unfortunately, are asymmetrical relations in which cultural differences become signals for discriminating behavior by members of a more powerful collectivity.

Whether or not prejudice results is dependent on such complicated factors as (1) the nature of the social system of which the groups are a part, (2) the extent to which one group is a threat (economically or otherwise) to the other, and (3) the degree of understanding or misunderstanding of one group towards another. Other significant factors that will be discussed in subsequent chapters are the personality structures and dynamics of individuals within the groups.

THE NATURE OF THE SOCIAL SYSTEM

When ethnic distinctions have been built into the cultural definitions and the norms of routine behavior in a social system, prejudiced attitudes and discriminatory behavior will be characteristic of normal personalities in that system. The manifestation of prejudice is not necessarily a symptom of unusual psychological needs or of neurotic or psychotic tendencies. When prejudice is normal in a society its manifestations are found among the respectable members of the population who are most firmly embedded in and committed to the legitimate organizations and conventional behavior characteristic of that social system. (Conversely, as shown by the findings in Southport, low prejudice is found most often among persons who are most likely to be free from the most constrained adherence to the general conventions of the community.) That is, when ethnic differences are the result of deeply rooted historical cleavages, it is usual for prejudice to accompany ethnocentrism.

THREAT

If for any reason two clearly distinguished social categories or collectivities are so situated in a society that their members frequently come into competition, the likelihood is high that negative stereotyping (a common variety of prejudice) will reinforce a sense of difference and that hostile attitudes will tend to restrict interaction and/or cause conflict. Whether the competition is economic, political, sexual, or for prestige, if one group perceives another as a threat, prejudice results. A central implication of Rokeach's extensive résumé of research on dogmatism is that a closed belief system is a consequence of threat. It is implied by this formulation that the greater the threat: (1) the more rigid the belief system that develops in response, (2) the more intense the affects supporting the beliefs, and (3) the more punitive the sanctions against disbelief.

Certain individuals and segments of the population will be so located in the social structure as to be especially likely to attach the meaning of threat, injury, deprivation, or punishment to the presence and behavior of one or more ethnic groups. Concretely, this most often means economic competition. For example, a white union member on strike sees "his" job taken by a Negro; a Protestant businessman believes his profits are reduced by the competition offered by a Jewish merchant. Or the so-called realistic threat may be noneconomic, such as when legislation thought to have been passed at the public behest of Catholic spokesmen confronts the Protestant with legal restrictions on dissemination of birth-control information or materials. Another example might be the Mexican-American father who is deeply concerned with the preservation of customary roles of women and fears the example set for his daughters by Anglo-American schoolmates.

When two ethnocentric groups come into a mutually threatening relationship, the stage for group conflict is fully set. Short of the cycle of threat-hostility-threat that is the classical prelude to group conflict—from gang fights, to riots, to global wars—we can observe a quieter prejudice, stabilized in systems of preferential ranking and preferential social access and personal association.

UNDERSTANDING AND MISUNDERSTANDING

The notion that understanding will always lead to the reduction of prejudice and/or the diminution of conflict has limitations that are often overlooked, ignored, or underestimated. Deadly enemies often understand one another all too well. Conversely, some groups manage to live together in a state of uneasy but tolerable accommodation when an accurate and detailed knowledge of each other's real sentiments and intentions would precipitate severe conflict. Understanding will reduce antipathy and the likelihood of conflict only if the groups like or respect what they discover by understanding each other or if one group finds that the threat posed by the other, though real, is not so severe, unalterable, or immediate as previously believed.

When persons feel themselves to be members of a group and identify themselves with that group's corporate views or policies in competition with another group, they necessarily find it difficult to comprehend the other group's position. An ingenious experiment by Blake and Manton suggests that under these conditions a loss in competition leads to hostility both toward impartial judges and toward the winning group, ". . . with feelings expressed that the decision was completely unjustified in the light of the 'evidence.'" Even though the members of the competing groups reported that they understood the competitor's views as well as they understood those of their own group, they, in fact, did not. In all groups, the members knew their own group's position best and were inclined toward distortion in their comprehension of the other group's position.

Misunderstanding Another Group's Beliefs and Values Many observers, noting the relative unimportance of skin color biologically—and the failure of scientific studies to produce significant evidence of genetically determined racial differences in intelligence—have been puzzled to observe that many individuals persist in exhibiting prejudice towards those with physical racial characteristics. In studies done by Rokeach it has been revealed that prejudice may not be a result of the fact that the other person is of a different racial category, national origin, or religious group affiliation but a result of the prejudiced person's assuming that the other individual's beliefs and values are incongruent with his own. He found that white students both in the North and in the South prefer a Negro with similar beliefs to a white person with different beliefs. But in most situations many white persons would take it for granted that the Negro person did differ from them in basic ways. Thus misunderstanding or lack of knowledge of the outgroup frequently results in prejudice.

Possibly one can now see why a wide range of concepts and types of data must be dealt with in order to begin to understand the causes and the nature of prejudice. Intergroup behavior involves three great systems of human social action: the culture, the social system, and the personality system. Accordingly, we need to study cultural content—"stereotypes," beliefs, and evaluations; and we need to study personality as related to cultural content and to social interaction. We must analyze interaction both in terms of general patterns of intergroup contact and in terms of specific situations. And even while we deal with each of these sets of factors, we must remember that they all are simultaneously engaged in those person-to-person communications that are conceived by the participants to have an intergroup character.

We shall begin with a general discussion of the kinds of prejudice that exist. We shall then examine the manifestations of prejudice—social-distance feelings and stereotypes. In this discussion of manifestations we will begin to see how a cultural heritage defines the social objects for prejudices. When we have described basic patterns of prejudice, we shall look at who the prejudiced are.

When Ethnocentrism Becomes Prejudice

The many faces of prejudice

Prejudice is a broad concept having no clear meanings until we give meanings to it. As a general rule the term should always be understood in the specific context in which it is used. There are positive and negative prejudices (though in literature dealing with intergroup relations negative prejudice, or prejudice *against* some group, is nearly always implied). And although a prejudice is always a prejudgment, prejudgments may be based on direct experience or on second-hand experience. Prejudices may be very important to the persons who hold them, or they may be peripheral to the main concerns of the prejudiced. . . .

Also, prejudices may be highly specific toward a particular outgroup or generalized toward all outgroups. Prejudices may be primarily cognitive (stereotyping), affective (attraction or aversion), or evaluative (for example, attitudes toward questions of public policy concerning racial minorities). Mention of all these varieties will be made elsewhere in this book. We begin, however, with a look at two aspects of prejudice, social-distance feelings and stereotypes—two results of ethnocentrism that are inert but potentially active.

Manifestations of prejudice

SOCIAL-DISTANCE FEELINGS

Social-distance feelings are feelings of unwillingness among members of a group to accept or approve a given degree of intimacy in interaction with a member of an outgroup. Specific aspects of social-distance feelings are: (1) feelings of group difference, (2) dislike of the outgroup, (3) feelings of inappropriateness, (4) fear of anticipated reactions of the ingroup, (5) aversion to and fear of anticipated responses of the outgroup, (6) generalized feelings of shyness or discomfort regarding unfamiliar social situations.

Source of Social-Distance Feelings It has already been mentioned that the individual learns norms of appropriate behavior toward his own group and toward outgroups from the primary groups in which he has membership. Social-distance feelings, then, may reflect the individual's conformity to the expectations and demands of his ingroup rather than his attitudes toward members of the outgroup. All other things being the same, both his acceptance of the norms and his actual conformity with them will be the more likely, the more he has a positive desire to associate with and be approved by the members of his group. His conformity, by the same token, will be a way of avoiding negative sanctions, including disapproval. . . .

Variations in the Findings We found marked differences in what was thought to be appropriate behavior from one city to another, from one school to another within the same city, and from the more insulated to the less insulated students within the same school. In the case of dancing with Negroes, 45 percent of the white students found it unpleasant in one school in Hometown, 89 percent in another school in Steelville. Similarly in the case of going to a party and finding that most of the people are Jewish, the variation in finding this experience unpleasant was 35 percent to 55 percent. There was even variation from one grade in the same high school to another, depending upon the setting. At the time when the questionnaires were filled in by the students, the eleventh grade in Hometown Southside High School had several outstanding Negro students, one of whom held a high leadership position in the school. Among those white students in this grade having a Negro friend, there was a strikingly small number who found it unpleasant to dance with a Negro.

What "Others" Will Think The connection between the social-distance feelings of any particular individual and the social atmosphere of his group setting is reflected in the high correlation between an individual's personal feelings about dancing with a Negro and how he thinks his family and friends feel about it. Undoubtedly the individual to some degree simply attributes his own attitudes to others, but he also often correctly reports the real feelings of others in his own social circles. The field interviews emphasized how very much individuals tend to see their own behavior through the eyes of the significant other persons with whom they associate. How comfortable or uncomfortable a person feels when dancing with a Negro depends heavily on how he thinks it appears to his friends. In a prejudiced environment, the stares and gossiping that may accompany such a situation when most of the onlookers disapprove are almost certain to stir up feelings of discomfort in the participant.

Furthermore, social-distance feelings appear to reflect the reactions of parents and friends just as much as or more than they reflect the experience of fairly close social contacts with Negroes. Even if one has invited a Negro fellow student to one's home, or has engaged with him in some social activity, one is still likely to find it unpleasant to dance with a Negro if one thinks his family or friends would disapprove. . . .

STEREOTYPES

What They Are and How They Emerge Along with social-distance feelings, stereotypes are one of the most common manifestations of prejudice. Stereotypes are labels or identities we assign to people that show what we believe these persons are like and how we think they will behave. Human beings, particularly when they feel little interest in individuals within a class of objects or people, tend to ignore the perceptible differences among these objects or people and tend to view all members of the class as being the same. Gouldner says of group members' forming stereotypes:

> . . . (1) They observe or impute to a person certain characteristics. . . . (2) These observed or imputed characteristics are then related to and interpreted in terms of a set of culturally prescribed *categories* which have been learned during the course of socialization. Conversely, the culturally learned categories focus attention upon certain aspects of the individual's behavior and appearance. (3) In this manner the individual is "pigeonholed"; that is, he is held to be a certain "type" of person, a teacher,

> Negro, boy, man, or woman. The process . . . can be called the assignment of a "social identity." The types or categories to which he has been assigned *are* his social identities.[1]

Thus stereotypes need not be based on direct sensory experience with the stereotyped object. An individual may describe the alleged characteristics of a group without ever having observed the members of that category.

Their Function with Regard to Culture, Personality, and Society Stereotypes constitute a part of culture, a part of an organized aggregate of shared symbols, beliefs, and values. Considered as part of a system or prejudice, stereotypes are operative in defining both the objects of action and the evaluative standards applied to social objects. Indeed, the maintenance of established stereotypes over long periods of time is possible partly because there are systems of action primarily devoted to their maintenance. These systems range from processes of inculcation within the family to the incorporation of stereotypes in song and story and to societywide dissemination through media of mass communication. Stereotypes are also components of social and personality systems: as summaries of and rationalizations for past experiences, they have sociological implications; as predictions of the behavior of others they give direction to psychological energies. The function of stereotypes as far as social systems are concerned is that the sharing of stereotypes reassures the holders and helps maintain systems of group privileges and power. In situations of competition and conflict, stereotypes simplify the alignments, sharpen group boundaries, and facilitate ingroup consensus. . . .

On What Are Stereotypes Based? Stereotyping, like rumor, is especially likely to thrive on the combination of interest and ignorance. Thus stereotypes emerge as distillations of the political, economic, and cultural alignments of nations as interpreted by leaders and intellectuals, especially through mass media and in reference to dramatic public events. What one person or one group believes about another is usually expressed without any immediate confrontation of evidence. Stereotypes may contain a core of truth, but the amount of truth may be very little indeed. Consider the personality stereotypes attached to personal names such as Percival or Ebenezer. How accurate are they? Is it true that red hair indicates a quick temper? If so, how much of the redhead's behavior is due to a self-fulfilling prophecy?

Does Hostility Cause Stereotyping? Although it has sometimes been thought that stereotypes were causes rather than effects of hostility, experiments have demonstrated that if two groups having no preconceived stereotypes develop hostility towards one another in a situation of rivalry and conflict, each will also spontaneously develop definite negative stereotypes

[1] Alvin W. Gouldner, "Cosmopolitans and Locals: Toward an Analysis of Latent Social Roles—I," *Administrative Science Quarterly*, II, No. 3 (December, 1957), 283.

concerning the other. Sherif showed that individuals who were initially inclined to be friendly toward one another became hostile when placed in opposing groups. Experimental situations that engaged two rival groups in competing and mutually frustrating activities led to the development of hostile attitudes and highly unfavorable stereotypes in each group toward the other group and its members. The positive or negative characteristics attributed by each group to the other tended to reflect the actual functional relationships between the two.

Sherif gives partial support to the view that stereotypes are symptomatic of hostility rather than causes of it when he says, "A number of field studies and experiments indicate that if the functional relations between groups are positive, favorable attitudes are formed towards the outgroup. If the functional relationships between groups are negative, they give rise to hostile and unfavorable stereotypes in relation to the outgroup."

How Stereotypes Perpetuate Hostility Of course, whenever real cultural differences exist between two populations living in proximity, the differences will have consequences for the interaction which develops. This is quite evident, for example, in those interactions that are rendered very difficult by mutual lack of knowledge of the other's language. Other cultural differences may have important effects, even if not always so immediately obvious. Where actual differences in culture become closely associated with definite statuses and roles, many stereotypes may come to have considerable descriptive value. A system of group dominance and subordination can create conditions that reinforce stereotypes. For example, to the degree that members of a dominant group feel that the system of group relations is unjust, or to the extent that they project their own reactions to deprivation upon the subordinate group, so will they expect hostility from the subordinates.

The expected hostility, since it may at any time be expressed in aggressive behavior, is perceived as a standing threat. A typical group response to this sense of threat is to insist upon rigid patterns of segregation, deference, and discrimination. These patterns, of course, perpetuate the closed cycle just described.

Stability of Stereotypes. Stereotypes are petrified expectations that are relatively unyielding to social change. They are usually more or less impervious to new evidence that is incongruent with their content. Experimental evidence, indeed, indicates that persons most readily learn materials that are in agreement with or supportive of their own attitudes concerning intergroup issues. When people were given the task of learning statements, those who favored racial segregation learned plausible prosegregation statements and implausible antisegregation statements much more rapidly than they did plausible antisegregation and implausible prosegregation statements. Persons opposed to segregation showed the corresponding reverse tendencies.

Resistance to alteration through new information or evaluation is characteristic of stereotypes.

However, under the impact of unusual and momentous events, stereotypes can be shattered and reformed. Stereotypes sometimes are altered radically and dramatically within a relatively short period of time. The American stereotype of Japan and the Japanese people changed from that of the Madame Butterfly era to World War II's image of a cruel and treacherous people, then back again to a benign image of industry, cleanliness, modernism, and friendliness as actual relations between the nations changed. Between 1942 and 1948, the stereotypes of Americans held in several European countries changed drastically to an emphasis on unfavorable characteristics. Such rapid and massive changes run far beyond any corresponding change in knowledge of the typical, actual personal characteristics of individuals when functioning "at home" within national groups.

Stereotypes in a Larger Setting Stereotypes are usually embedded in a larger set of ideas and beliefs about the nature of man and society and, indeed, of the universe. Arising in some collective historical experience, initial generalizations about the characteristics and behavior of outgroups are sometimes reshaped and reworked in relation to these comprehensive beliefs. An illustration of this point is the ante-bellum development of justifications for slavery in the United States. The theory of Aryan superiority promulgated during the past hundred years and culminating in the "blood and soil" doctrine of Nazi Germany is an even more remarkable case in point.

Specific Stereotypes Stereotypes that refer to social categories, statuses, groups, or collectivities are usually stated in terms of qualities (traits, properties, characteristics) conceived as if somehow inherent in the objects: Americans are materialistic; Italians are excitable; Orientals are inscrutable; professors are absent-minded; women are flighty; white people are cruel. Such imputations of qualities very easily become expectations of behavior; and these stereotypes have the same overgeneralized and rigid character as those of physical appearance or psychological states.

Negative stereotypes used by majority-group members in the United States to stigmatize outgroups usually are the reversed images of dominant positive traits. The epithet of laziness reflects the value of industriousness. Ignorance contrasts with the virtues of competence, education, self-improvement. Dishonesty is the opposite of upright, moral, fair dealings. "Sexually loose" is the antithesis of Puritan reserve. "Loud and noisy" is the converse of the ideals of public decorum, the strict control of impulse, the taboos against giving in to emotion. Even the stereotype of the "power of the Catholic Church" acquires much of its negative resonance from some Protestant views of the church as a man-made vehicle of religious expression. . . .

The language of prejudice

Stereotypes are part of a whole way of talking about outgroups. This special universe of discourse has its own distinctive vocabulary, its own idiom, its own peculiar style. The derogatory epithets (and other terms expressing disparagement or awareness of group difference) which arise in most sizable ingroups that exist for any considerable period of time constitute the "language of prejudice." We may define the language of prejudice as an aggregate of words and phrases applied (accidentally or intentionally, directly or indirectly) to express contempt, derision, stereotypic assumptions, or, at least, a belief that there are generalized group differences, to another social category or to an individual because of his membership in that category.

In all the communities studied evidence was found that the language of prejudice—for Negroes and whites, Jews and gentiles, Mexicans and Anglo-Americans, and so on—acted as a cue for intergroup tension and as a barrier to effective communication between ethnic groupings. These reactions are more noticeable in smaller than in larger communities, partly because opportunity for casual intergroup contact is greater in the smaller communities where less residential segregation exists, and partly because the small proportion of ethnics and the low number of intergroup contacts on the part of white majority-group persons result in a lack of experience in intergroup communication and a correlative lack of sophistication and insight. In the one most intensively studied instance, the most noticeable elements of the language of prejudice experienced and discussed by Hometown's Negro community might be subdivided into those that are accidental and those that are intentional on the part of whites, and into those that are indirect references and those that are direct racial references.

ACCIDENTAL-INDIRECT

Phrases Pertaining to Color These phrases follow an historical tradition of equating whiteness with purity or desirability and blackness with evil. Examples are: "That's darn white of you," "free, white, and twenty-one," "He treated me white," or "Your face may be black, but your heart's as white as mine."

Disparagement of Other Minorities This behavior may take the form of whites telling Negroes jokes about Jews, Italians, Catholics, etc. or confidential statements such as "you Negroes are all right with me, but it's those Jews I don't like." In some instances, the Negro's negative reaction is based on the recognition of necessity for interminority solidarity; in more instances, it is based on the Negro's recognition of the phenomenon of group prejudice and categorical thinking, even though it refers to another minority group.

ACCIDENTAL-DIRECT

Racial Testimonials In many cases, Hometown Negroes reported that whites seek to establish rapport by making favorable categorical statements of their preference for Negroes or by making assertions that Negroes are not inferior to whites; for example, "I like Negro people," "What the hell—you're as good as I am," or the statement sometimes referred to by Negroes as the "black mammy speech": "I've loved the colored ever since I was rocked to sleep in the arms of my black mammy." Though some Negroes are aware that the testimonial is sometimes the product of a white person's guilt feelings, others feel that the ingratiating statements are employed in order to disarm and exploit the Negro, or that they are overprotesting their affection for Negroes. One Negro explained testily that "I don't like too much butter on my bread."

The Racial Slip To the Negroes of Hometown, the most noticeable and disturbing of all the elements of the language of prejudice, despite its accidental nature, is the racial slip. This involves unintentional phrases in the speech of whites that carry epithets or other expressions that are disparaging of minorities, for example, "I worked like a nigger," "I jewed him down," "There's a nigger in the woodpile," or words that Negro public school youths complain are frequently employed by teachers—reference to Brazil nuts as "nigger-toes," or reference to a type of garden weed as "nigger-heads." Slips cause particular apprehension among Negroes because (1) the epithet that is used is disturbing, despite its accidental nature, (2) the Negro person is often aware of the white person's acute embarrassment when he becomes aware of the disturbing nature of what he has said, and (3) the Negro is often aware that he is expected to make a protest to the slip that he would often prefer to avoid.

INTENTIONAL-INDIRECT

Stereotyped Preconceptions of Negroes Many Negroes know the stereotypes about them held by whites, and they express disapproval of white people who expect all Negroes to be able to dance and sing, or who assume that each Negro knows thoroughly all aspects of Negro life in the South and in Africa, or who think that each Negro knows all other Negroes, or who believe that Negroes are lazy, ignorant, and happy-go-lucky, or who believe that all Negroes are sexually immoral. This disapproval is particularly great among higher-status Negroes whose way of life is similar to that of middle-class whites, but who may partially share the white person's stereotypic view of lower-status Negroes, and resent being placed in a similar category.

Caricatures of the Negro Negroes also express disapproval at the way Negro life is parodied in the media of communication; they often cite the examples of the former radio shows of "Amos 'n Andy" and "Beulah," the "Little Black Sambo" children's fable, and certain cinema characters. The annoyance is more extreme when in interracial contacts, they are addressed by whites in imitations of Negro dialect, parodied by white's imitations of stereotypic Negro characters, or called names drawn from derogatory stories, like "Sambo," "Nicodemus," or "Rastus." Occasionally, the attempts by proprietors of business establishments to show Negroes that their patronage is not wanted may take the form of indirect caricatures, parodies of Southern Negro speech, or addressing the Negro by stereotypic names.

INTENTIONAL-DIRECT

Jokes, Songs, and Stories Disparaging Negroes Embedded in American culture are a number of so-called darky jokes, comic stories in pseudo-Negro dialect, stories ridiculing the stereotyped traits of the Negro, or songs that contain racial epithets. These are intentional to the extent that the white person is usually aware that they have racial implications; the fact that they offend some Negroes is often accidental, since the lack of interracial understanding may make the white person unaware that Negroes could take offense at what is often considered mere good fun. A few whites hold the mistaken assumption that telling a darky joke is an act of friendly recognition of the Negro, and are seriously surprised and disturbed if Negroes express objection.

Intentional Use of Racial Epithets Situations of interracial tension often involve purposive words of contempt on the part of whites, like "smoke," "jig," "coon," or "shine." Some Negroes have been able to recall as many as twenty of these epithets. However, as far as Negro reactions are concerned, the one most negatively evaluated term is the word "nigger"—a word so intensely disliked that the Negro press generally prints it as "n——r," regardless of the context. Its connotations, drawn largely from Southern experiences, produce in most Negroes a bitterness, anger, and occasional fury that is usually far greater in its intensity than most white persons realize. Hence, many of the actual incidents of tension and violence in interracial situations are produced through the utterance of this epithet by whites. This reaction also causes Negroes to resent less intentionally disparaging terms like "Negress," the Southern white pronunciation of Negro as "Nigra," and even the nonracial word "niggardly."

In a general sense, the language of prejudice exists because of several anti-Negro aspects of American culture that are unreflectively absorbed by many, perhaps most, American white people in the process of growing-up. A white person whose interracial contacts are rare may, then, on encountering a Negro, search through his limited store of knowledge about Negroes and make inappropriate comments; a white person may attempt to establish a joking relationship with a Negro, which is acceptable in his own informal social groups but inconsistent with the Negro's past interracial experience (for example, joking about women and sex; calling friends "boy"—an expression of friendship to many whites, but regarded by Southern-born

Negroes as an expression of white contempt); a white person in attempting to indicate his lack of prejudice may accidentally employ inappropriate techniques or make slips; finally, the white person in anger or contempt may employ power words, epithets that he knows will disturb the minority-group member. . . .

Our summary may be stated in this way: Prejudice on the part of majority group members results in a tendency to use certain terms and expressions that disparage minority-group members. Minority-group members in varying degrees are aware of these symbols and tend to react negatively to them, and particularly to affectively-laden outgroup epithets.

The prejudiced

> Every group has their own way. I'm afraid of the colored. I don't like them. They have razors and kill each other and things. Where we lived when we were first married, out of spite a woman sold her house to colored. They brought a lot of colored to Elmira. People sold their homes. They were always fighting with razors. They're ugly people. You dasn't say "colored" to them or they'll fight. I've seen people say "nigger" to them and they beat 'em up. I had no trouble with 'em. I didn't say anything to them. I feel sorry for 'em. Domineering niggers marry whites, and whites marry niggers. Their children, some are white and some are black. In Omaha they push the whites off the streets. They hold hands in a line and push you off. They call you "white trash." In Omaha, Nebraska, they have bold niggers. Course, they're not all that way. What I've seen have been.
>
> *Prejudiced respondent*

Who are the prejudiced? The next section will be devoted to a discussion of the social correlates of prejudice. In a complex society we may suspect variations in degree of prejudice among people who live in different geographic areas, among the various socioeconomic classes and those with varying amounts of education, among people with different religious affiliations, among those who belong to different political parties and other organizations, and among those who differ with regard to age, sex, and marital status. . . .

Summary The main generalizations concerning social correlates of prejudice emerging from the data are:

(1) The Southern sample exhibits the greatest frequency of social-distance prejudice. The Far Western city has the largest proportion of relatively tolerant or accepting individuals. The Northeastern and Midwestern samples fall in between.

(2) Educational level is significantly associated with degree of prejudice: the higher the educational level, the less frequent are high degrees of prejudice toward Negroes, Jews, and Mexican-Americans.

(3) Individuals who identify themselves with the upper class tend to be slightly more prejudiced than other white gentiles toward Jews. While the relationships between social-distance feelings toward Negroes and self-chosen class identity are not clear cut, there is some tendency for persons who say that they belong to the working class to be more likely than those who consider themselves to be upper class to maintain attitudes of aversion concerning close social contacts. In both instances, those who identify with the middle class fall in between these two categories in prejudice toward Jews and Negroes.

(4) Persons who work in relatively high-status occupations tend to be more prejudiced toward Jews, whereas those in lower status occupations are the more likely to have feelings of social distance toward Negroes and Mexican-Americans.

(5) There are no large or consistent differences among the various Protestant denominations nor between Protestants and Catholics in the extent of prejudice toward Jews, Negroes, or Mexican-Americans.

(6) Individuals who report that they *seldom* attend religious services tend to be more prejudiced than those who report that they *often* attend *or* those who say they *never* attend. The regular churchgoers are the group showing least frequency of social-distance reactions, followed by the non-attenders, whereas it is the infrequent attenders—perhaps the "imperfectly churched" or "conventionally religious"—who are most likely to show exclusionistic prejudice. It appears, however, that the observed differences are partly due to correlated differences in education.

(7) Political party affiliation or preference is not strongly related to differences in prejudice, although in the cities studied, there is a slight tendency for the greatest frequency of intolerance to appear among Democrats. Independent voters are most likely to be free of feelings of social distance toward racial and ethnic minorities.

(8) Individuals who report membership in clubs and organizations tend to be consistently more tolerant of Negroes and Mexican-Americans than those who do not belong to such groups. (Organizational membership is not predictive of attitudes toward association with Jewish persons.) The apparent effects of organizational membership are confounded with, and may be largely reducible to, effects related to educational level and social class.

(9) On the whole, there is a slight tendency among adults for the prevalence of prejudices against close social contacts with Negroes, Jews and Mexican-Americans to be greater among older persons.

(10) Females are slightly more likely than males to be prejudiced against the three minorities named.

(11) Individuals who are either divorced, separated, or widowed tend to be slightly more often prejudiced than those who are married or single. No clear conclusions can be drawn from comparisons of single with married people.

In general, individuals who are closely bound to the dominant mores of the particular subgroup tend more often to be prejudiced toward minorities. Examples from our data who fit into this category are residents of the South, females, older people, and nonindependent voters. There are exceptions to this general rule. For example, it might be expected that church members who often attend religious services would be more intolerant than others, when, in fact the tendency is for them to be more tolerant. On the whole, however, it seems fair to say that individuals who are less closely bound with traditional subgroup ties appear to be more tolerant.

TENDENCIES OF THE PREJUDICED

Prejudiced people share certain tendencies with regard to the inconsistency and confusion of their responses, their ignorance of the true feelings of outgroup members, the degree of their guilt feelings about the treatment of minorities, and the degree to which they generalize prejudices.

Inconsistency and Confusion Christie has said that logically incompatible stereotypes may be held together because they express a common attitude or feeling. Indeed, many individuals place different evaluations upon the very desirability of logical consistency in giving responses. Such differences in evaluation may be systematically associated with various social strata, educational levels, and ethnic categories. For example, there are scattered but consistent evidences that relatively uneducated Negro respondents are especially likely to agree to interview or questionnaire items, to give more inconsistent answers as between original and reversed forms of items, and to give more "don't know" or "can't answer" responses.

Our firsthand interviews gave many vivid impressions of the tendency, especially in authoritarian and generally hostile individuals, for various stereotypes to blur and interlock. Some respondents spoke of all racial, ethnic, and religious groupings other than their own as nationalities (as, "There are a lot of different nationalities in this town, like Negroes, those Catholics, and some Greeks"). Some respondents spoke of Jews as a nationality; others talked of the Jewish race, even while referring to Negroes as a class of people. . . .

Ignorance of True Feelings of Outgroup Members of dominant social groupings who insist upon deferential behavior from the lower orders are strongly disposed to regard the respectful behavior they require as evidence that their subordinates fully accept the system. In modern America very rarely is this self-assuring assumption correct. Probably most of the white respondents in Southport are unaware that 40 percent of the local Negroes feel that they have more in common to discuss with a Negro in New York than with a white resident of Southport. Certainly some would show surprise if they knew that anger or annoyance at hearing the word "nigger" is reported by no less than 92 percent of the Negroes in the city. The assumption that minority-group members are well satisfied with their lot is often voiced, whether defensively or naïvely, by many members of dominant social groups who feel well satisfied with their own way of life. . . .

Guilt Feelings Examining America's treatment of minorities, Gunnar Myrdal called the problem of the Negro in the United States the "American Dilemma."[2] How much this dilemma is experienced by different types of Americans as personal reaction is difficult to determine. But in answer to a direct question: *Do you ever feel guilty about the way Negroes are treated —would you say never, sometimes, or fairly often?,* 33 percent of a cross section of white adults in Southport said "sometimes" and 8 percent said "often."

The people in our sample gave an overwhelming demonstration of the proverbial public expression of confidence of the white Southerner in his superior understanding of Negroes. At the level of lip-service, this confidence, even if it be defensive and mistaken, is still widespread. We asked, *Do you think that Southerners understand Negroes better than Northerners or not so well as Northerners do?* The replies:

"Better"	70 percent
"About the same"	12 percent
"Not so well"	9 percent
"Do not know" or no answer	9 percent

At the same time, our Southport respondents were willing to testify in the ratio of 2:1 that Negroes are better off in the South than in the North.

Of course, all this testimony may be defensive or overcompensatory. Short of depth interviews, which we were not in a position to conduct, we could not deal directly with this problem. Nevertheless, the survey responses give some indirect clues as to possible underlying attitudes that may be at variance to an important extent with the explicit picture of positive appraisal, optimism, and lack of guilt. Having asked about whether white people in the South feel guilty, we went on to inquire, *How about you, personally, do you ever feel guilty about the way Negroes are treated—would you say never, sometimes, or fairly often?* When responding in these specifically personal terms, 8 percent said they feel guilty "fairly often" and

[2] *An American Dilemma* (New York: Harper & Row, Publishers, 1944).

another 33 percent admitted to guilt feelings "sometimes." Can we take these responses as really indicative of guilt? It seems likely that in a Deep South city in the early 1950s there would not be many people who, in a confidential interview, would testify to guilt unless they did feel it. How many others of the 57 percent who said they never feel guilty may have unconscious guilt we have no way of guessing.

These Southern adults are much more likely to deny feelings of guilt than are high-school youths in the far more liberal atmosphere of a Western city. In a survey of high-school students in Phoenix just two years after desegregation, the youths in the Phoenix Union High School were asked, *How often do you feel guilty about the way Negroes in the United States are treated—would you say never, sometimes, or fairly often?* The replies:

Never	16 percent
Sometimes	64 percent
Fairly often	20 percent

Putting side by side the answers to the two questions about guilt asked in Southport raises the possibility that we may be dealing with pluralistic ignorance. Although the two questions are not strictly comparable, it is clear that more people admit to guilt feelings in themselves than believe that other whites feel guilty. Both estimates cannot be right, and it seems likely that the social control of opinions concerning Negro–white relations leads to underestimation by local people of the extent of doubt and uneasiness generated by the system. Such mutual ignorance of others' private feelings undoubtedly is one of the mechanisms by which imperfectly integrated social arrangements are maintained in opposition to pressures toward change.

Other kinds of defensive beliefs and systematic ignorance may work in a similar way to support the *status quo.*

The expansion of Negro ghettoes in northern United States cities increases mobility more dramatically. Typically, the highly segregated and rapidly growing Negro area can only expand into nearby white neighborhoods. If the whites panic, the turnover takes place very rapidly, affecting up to 75 percent of the dwellings within two or three years. The mobility rate increases as the normal rate of white outmigration (about 50 percent in five years) is accelerated by racial and economic fears; but, as in any neighborhood, the most mobile elements, the young and the renters, leave first. The crucial stage in the changeover is not the acceleration of white outmigration, but the almost total cessation of white inmigration.

Brian J. L. Berry and Frank E. Horton (ed.), *Geographic Perspectives on Urban Systems* (Englewood Cliffs, New Jersey: Prentice-Hall, Inc., 1970), p. 401.

492–509

THE TROUBLE AT ROUND ROCK

The Nephew of Former Big Man[1]

The Bureau of Indian Affairs in the 1940s assigned a trained linguist to the job of helping Navajos develop a literature in their own language. A transcription was devised and publication of a monthly newspaper and a series of historical narratives begun. The following was recorded in Navajo, translated into English, and published in both languages in 1952 along with other accounts by eye-witnesses of the same events.

In the Fort Sumner Treaty we were told to place our children in school. So when we got back policemen were sent from Fort Defiance down toward Round Rock to carry out this provision. To get all of the children they went from hogan to hogan.

The leader of one of the parties was a man named Charlie. Others in this party were one called Bobbed Hair, one by the name of Bead Clan Gambler, another called Slender Silver Maker, and the one who was known as The Interpreter (Chee Dodge), as well as several others.

For a long time the men and womenfolk had held back their children. So on the dates set for bringing the children to Round Rock, very few were brought in. When the children were taken there a man by the name of Black Horse said, "No," and stood against the children being taken away to school. There was one man by the name of Limper, who may still be hunched with old age (still alive). There was one called Slow One, and there were Canyon De Chelly Man, Tall Bitter Water Clansman, Ugly Knife, Sucker, Weela, and Gray Haired Man. All of these said, "No," and stood against the proposal. And then many young men joined with them. All of these men are now perhaps dead.

Here at this meeting to get children together for school the man known as Black Horse stubbornly balked on it. "What the devil, you can jerk our children away from us if you want to. If you want trouble over this matter go to it," he shouted. Several others who were of like mind were behind him. In fact, they had probably conspired with him.

The one called Little Chief (Shipley) came also. He was the Agent. But when a hot argument got under way in the meeting, the Navajos threw the Agent out. Then things really happened. The man called Bead Clan Gambler

[1] Left-Handed Mexican Clansman *et al.*, *The Trouble at Round Rock.* Navajo Historical Series: 2, United States Indian Service, Phoenix, Arizona, 1952, pp. 34–35.

got the Agent back from those who had laid hands on him. This Bead Clan Gambler was a husky man. As the mob made away with the Agent he dashed in among them and grabbed the Agent up under one arm (like a football). When the mobsters would have jumped him he straight-armed them and bowled them over backward, and running hard he beat them to a flour storage room. When he had gotten the Agent in there he piled things against the door from within, and the mob was frustrated. The Interpreter (Chee Dodge) also took refuge in the flour storage room. It was said that they stayed inside for several days without going outside. And while they were in there they dirtied the flour.

The news of this trouble spread all about, even up into the Monument Valley. Everyone said, "They're not going to take our children away, that's all there is to it." People were ready to fight. Some said that no soldiers had come to the scene of the trouble. Some said that bear hunters had been brought to the rescue, but the truth is that it wasn't these. That was just a tale. Soldiers came from Fort Defiance. They were sent for from there, and those who came moved up on top of Row of Willows (near Wheatfields). At that time there was a beautiful meadow there. There was not a single wash at that time. There they were encamped. When they moved again they went to the burned trading post at Black Rock Spring (near Tsailee). After camping there for two days they moved on. They moved down to Blue Clay Point (near Round Rock).

This was not the only time a school party went out. They went out many times. Summer and winter they would go about telling the people to place their children in school.

When the soldiers who were sent for arrived to fight, my older sister, who was the wife of Weela, acted as a peacemaker. Here she acted as go-between to restore the peace. One man took credit for restoring peace. He was a man called White Man. I heard him saying that he was the one who restored the peace. I told him, "You are a liar. You just made that story up. It was my sister who restored the peace. I know it. I am sure of it." So that is how Black Horse made trouble by holding back the children.

Now school is a wonderful thing. They had no reason for keeping us out of school, I'm convinced of that. School is not a thing of no value. It is something to be longed for and sought after. Had I gone to school I wonder how I would be today. By school we mean an endless learning. It's a means for accomplishment without end.

People who have children, and who put them in school, are right in so doing. I think they are indeed lucky children. I was one of those who spoke in favor of schools in days gone by. Not long ago a paper was brought up before us in a meeting. They said, "Here's a list of the men who asked for education, and here's one of the men. These men knew the advantages of schooling." They said this, mentioning my part in it. When they mentioned me in this connection I almost wept. I was right when I took that stand.

Had I gone to school I often wonder how good a leader I might have become.

Long ago our forbears went after one another with weapons over this question of schooling. On account of differences over education they threw out an Agent. It nearly brought tragedy. When people were about to come to blows my sister restored the peace. These things happened just about the time when my mind had become mature enough to reason and remember, so I know whereof I speak. And to many things which occurred I was a witness, while in others I took an active part. So the people nearly came to blows over schools. But now education is, without doubt, the right thing. So go on children. Go to school. Study hard. In the future you will profit by it. . . .

A BOARDING SCHOOL EXPERIENCE

Francis La Flesche[1]

Francis La Flesche, Omaha, attended a mission boarding school in the 1860s. The following is from the preface to a book which he wrote about his schoolboy years.

. . . Among my earliest recollections are the instructions wherein we were taught respect and courtesy toward our elders; to say "thank you" when receiving a gift, or when returning a borrowed article; to use the proper and conventional term of relationship when speaking to another; and never to address any one by his personal name; we were also forbidden to pass in front of persons sitting in the tent without first asking permission; and we were strictly enjoined never to stare at visitors, particularly at strangers. To us there seemed to be no end to the things we were obliged to do, and to the things we were to refrain from doing.

From the earliest years the Omaha child was trained in the grammatical use of his native tongue. No slip was allowed to pass uncorrected, and as a result there was no child-talk such as obtains among English-speaking children—the only difference between the speech of old and young was in the pronunciation of words which the infant often failed to utter correctly, but this difficulty was soon overcome, and a boy of ten or twelve was apt to speak as good Omaha as a man of mature years.

[1] From Francis La Flesche, *The Middle Five* (Madison: The University of Wisconsin Press; © 1963 by the Regents of the University of Wisconsin), pp. xvi–xx.

Like the grown folk, we youngsters were fond of companionship and of talking. In making our gamesticks and in our play, we chattered incessantly of the things that occupied our minds, and we thought it a hardship when we were obliged to speak in low tones while older people were engaged in conversation. When we entered the Mission School, we experienced a greater hardship, for there we encountered a rule that prohibited the use of our own language, which rule was rigidly enforced with a hickory rod, so that the new-comer, however socially inclined, was obliged to go about like a little dummy until he had learned to express himself in English.

All the boys in our school were given English names, because their Indian names were difficult for the teachers to pronounce. Besides, the aboriginal names were considered by the missionaries as heathenish, and therefore should be obliterated. No less heathenish in their origin were the English substitutes, but the loss of their original meaning and significance through long usage had rendered them fit to continue as appellations for civilized folk. And so, in the place of Tae-noo'-ga-wa-zhe, came Philip Sheridan; in that of Wa-pah'-dae, Uysses S. Grant; that of Koo'-we-he-ge-ra, Alexander, and so on. Our sponsors went even further back in history, and thus we had our David and Jonathan, Gideon and Isaac, and, with the flood of these new names, came Noah. It made little difference to us that we had to learn the significance of one more word as applied to ourselves, when the task before us was to make our way through an entire strange language. So we learned to call each other by our English names, and continued to do so even after we left school and had grown to manhood.

The names thus acquired by the boys are used in these sketches in preference to their own, for the reason that Indian words are not only difficult to pronounce, but are apt to sound all alike to one not familiar with the language, and the boys who figure in these pages might lose their identity and fail to stand out clearly in the mind of the reader were he obliged to continually struggle with their Omaha names.

In the talk of the boys I have striven to give a reproduction of the peculiar English spoken by them, with was composite, gathered from the imperfect comprehension of their books, the provincialisms of the teachers, and the slang and bad grammar picked up from uneducated white persons employed at the school or at the Government Agency. Oddities of speech, profanity, localisms, and slang were unknown in the Omaha language, so when such expressions fell upon the ears of these lads they innocently learned and used them without the slightest suspicion that there could be bad as well as good English.

The misconception of Indian life and character so common among the white people has been largely due to an ignorance of the Indian's language, of his mode of thought, his beliefs, his ideals, and his native institutions. Every aspect of the Indian and his manner of life has always been strange to the white man, and this strangeness has been magnified by the mists of prejudice and the conflict of interests between the two races. While these in time may disappear, no native American can ever cease to regret that the utterances of his father have been constantly belittled when put into English, that their thoughts have frequently been travestied and their native dignity obscured. The average interpreter has generally picked up his knowledge of English in a random fashion, for very few have ever had the advantage of a thorough education, and all have had to deal with the difficulties that attend the translator. The beauty and picturesqueness, and euphonious playfulness, or the gravity of diction which I have heard among my own people, and other tribes as well, are all but impossible to be given literally in English.

The talk of the older people, when they speak in this book, is, as well as I can translate it, that of every day use.

Most of the country now known as the State of Nebraska (the Omaha name of the river Platt, descriptive of its shallowness, width, and low banks) had for many generations been held and claimed by our people as their own, but when they ceded the greater part of this territory to the United States government, they reserved only a certain tract for their own use and home. It is upon the eastern part of this reservation that the scene of these sketches is laid, and at the time when the Omahas were living near the Missouri River in three villages, some four or five miles apart. The one farthest south was known as Ton'-won-ga-hae's village; the people were called "wood eaters," because they cut and sold wood to the settlers who lived near them. The middle one was Ish'-ka-da-be's village, and the people designated as "those who dwell in earth lodges," they having adhered to the aboriginal form of dwelling when they built their village. The one to the north and nearest the Mission was E-sta'-ma-za's village, and the people were known as the "make-believe white-men," because they built their houses after the fashion of the white settlers. Furniture, such as beds, chairs, tables, bureaus, etc., were not used in any of these villages, except in a few instances, while in all of them the Indian costume, language, and social customs remained as yet unmodified.

In those days the Missouri was the only highway of commerce. Toiling slowly against the swift current, laden with supplies for the trading posts and for our Mission, came the puffing little steamboats from the "town of the Red-hair," as St. Louis was called by the Indians, in memory of the auburn locks of Governor Clark,—of Lewis and Clark fame. We children used to watch these noisy boats as they forced their way through the turbid water and made a landing by running the bow into the soft bank.

The white people speak of the country at this period as "a wilderness," as though it was an empty tract without human interest or history. To us Indians it was as clearly defined then as it is today; we knew the boundaries of tribal lands, those of our friends and those of our foes; we were familiar with every stream, the contour of every hill, and each peculiar feature of the landscape had its tradition. It was our home, the scene of our history, and we loved it as our country.

A STUDY IN NATIVISM: THE AMERICAN RED SCARE OF 1919–1920

Stanley Coben

At a victory loan pageant in the District of Columbia on May 6, 1919, a man refused to rise for the playing of "The Star-Spangled Banner." As soon as the national anthem was completed an enraged sailor fired three shots into the unpatriotic spectator's back. When the man fell, the *Washington Post* reported, "the crowd burst into cheering and handclapping." In February of the same year, a jury in Hammond, Indiana, took two minutes to acquit the assassin of an alien who yelled, "To Hell with the United States." Early in 1920, a clothing store salesman in Waterbury, Connecticut, was sentenced to six months in jail for having remarked to a customer that Lenin was "the brainiest," or "one of the brainiest" of the world's political leaders. Dramatic episodes like these, or the better known Centralia Massacre, Palmer Raids, or May Day riots, were not everyday occurrences, even at the height of the Red Scare. But the fanatical one hundred percent Americanism reflected by the Washington crowd, the Hammond jury, and the Waterbury judge pervaded a large part of our society between early 1919 and mid-1920.

Recently, social scientists have produced illuminating evidence about the causes of eruptions like that of 1919–1920. They have attempted to identify experimentally the individuals most responsive to nativistic appeals, to explain their susceptibility, and to propose general theories of nativistic and related movements. These studies suggest a fuller, more coherent picture of nativisitic upheavals and their causes than we now possess, and they provide the framework for this attempt to reinterpret the Red Scare.

Psychological experiments indicate that a great many Americans—at least several million—are always ready to participate in a "red scare." These people permanently hold attitudes which characterized the nativists of 1919–1920: hostility toward certain minority groups, especially radicals and recent immigrants, fanatical patriotism, and a belief that internal enemies seriously threaten national security.

In one of the most comprehensive of these experiments, psychologists Nancy C. Morse and Floyd H. Allport tested seven hypotheses about the

Abridged from the *Political Science Quarterly*, 79 (March 1964), 52–75.

causes of prejudice and found that one, national involvement or patriotism, proved to be "by far the most important factor" associated with prejudice. Other widely held theories about prejudice—status rivalry, frustration, aggression, and scapegoat hypotheses, for example—were found to be of only secondary importance. Summarizing the results of this and a number of other psychological experiments, Gordon W. Allport, a pioneer in the scientific study of prejudice, concluded that in a large proportion of cases the prejudiced person is attempting to defend himself against severe inner turmoil by enforcing order in his external life. Any disturbance in the social *status quo* threatens the precarious psychic equilibrium of this type of individual, who, according to Allport, seeks "an island of institutional safety and security. The nation is the island he selects. . . . It has the definiteness he needs."

Allport pointed out that many apprehensive and frustrated people are not especially prejudiced. What is important, he found,

> is the way fear and frustration are handled. The institutionalistic way—especially the nationalistic—seems to be the nub of the matter. What happens is that the prejudiced person defines "nation" to fit his needs. The nation is first of all a protection (the chief protection) of him as an individual. It is his in-group. He sees no contradiction in ruling out of its beneficent orbit those whom he regards as threatening intruders and enemies (namely, American minorities). What is more, the nation stands for the status quo. It is a conservative agent; within it are all the devices for safe living that he approves. His nationalism is a form of conservatism.

Substantial evidence, then, suggests that millions of Americans are both extraordinarily fearful of social change and prejudiced against those minority groups which they perceive as "threatening intruders." Societal disruption, especially if it can easily be connected with the "intruders," not only will intensify the hostility of highly prejudiced individuals, but also will provoke many others, whose antagonism in more stable times had been mild or incipient, into the extreme group.

A number of anthropologists have come to conclusions about the roots of nativism which complement these psychological studies. Since the late nineteenth century, anthropologists have been studying the religious and nativistic cults of American Indian tribes and of Melanesian and Papuan groups in the South Pacific. Recently, several anthropologists have attempted to synthesize their findings and have shown striking parallels in the cultural conditions out of which these movements arose. In every case, severe societal disruption preceded the outbreak of widespread nativistic cult behavior. According to Anthony F. C. Wallace, who has gone farthest toward constructing a general theory of cult formation, when the disruption has proceeded so far that many members of a society find it difficult or impossible to fulfill their physical and psychological needs, or to relieve severe anxiety through the ordinary culturally approved methods, the society will be susceptible to what Wallace has termed a "revitalization movement." This is a convulsive attempt to change or revivify important cultural beliefs and values, and frequently to eliminate alien influences. Such movements promise and often provide participants with better means of dealing with their changed circumstances, thus reducing their very high level of internal stress.

American Indian tribes, for example, experienced a series of such convulsions as the tide of white settlers rolled west. The Indians were pushed onto reservations and provided with Indian agents, missionaries, and physicians, who took over many of the functions hitherto assumed by chiefs and medicine men. Indian craftsmen (and craftswomen) were replaced by dealers in the white man's implements. Most hunters and warriors also lost their vocations and consequently their self-respect. What an anthropologist wrote of one tribe was true of many others: "From cultural maturity as Pawnees they were reduced to cultural infancy as civilized men."

One of the last major religious upheavals among the Indians was the Ghost Dance cult which spread from Nevada through Oregon and northern California in the eighteen-seventies, and a similar movement among the Rocky Mountain and western plains Indians about 1890. Although cult beliefs varied somewhat from tribe to tribe, converts generally were persuaded that if they followed certain prescribed rituals, including the dance, they would soon return to their old ways of living. Even their dead relatives would be restored to life. Most Indians were too conscious of their military weakness to challenge their white masters directly. Ghost Dancers among the Dakota Sioux, however, influenced by the militant proselyter Sitting Bull, became convinced that true believers could not be harmed by the white man's bullets and that Sioux warriors would drive the intruders from Indian lands. Their dreams were rudely smashed at the massacre of Wounded Knee Creek in December 1890.

The Boxer movement in China, 1898 to 1900, resembled in many respects the Indian Ghost Dance cults; however, the Boxers, more numerous and perhaps less demoralized than the Indians, aimed more directly at removing foreign influences from their land. The movement erupted first in Shantung province where foreigners, especially Japanese, British, and Germans, were most aggressive. A flood of the Yellow River had recently deprived about a million people in the province of food and shelter. Banditry was rampant, organized government ineffective. The Boxer movement, based on the belief that these tragic conditions were due almost entirely to the "foreign devils" and their agents, determined to drive the enemy out of China. Boxers went into action carrying charms and chanting incantations supposed to make them invulnerable to the foreigners' bullets. The first object of the Boxers' nativistic fury were Chinese who had converted to Christianity, the intruders' religion. The patriots then attacked railroad and telegraph lines, leading symbols of foreign influence. Finally, the Boxers turned against the foreigners themselves, slaughtering many. Not until after the Boxers carried on a two-month siege of the foreign community in Peking did American, European, and Japanese armies crush the movement. . . .

Dominant as well as conquered peoples, Ralph Linton has pointed out, undergo nativistic movements. Dominant groups, he observed, are sometimes threatened "not only by foreign invasion or domestic revolt but also by the invidious process of assimilation which might, in the long run, destroy their distinctive powers and privileges." Under such circumstances, Linton concluded, "the frustrations which motivate nativistic movements in inferior or dominated groups" are "replaced by anxieties which produce very much the same [nativistic] result" in dominant groups. . . .

The ferocious outbreak of nativism in the United States after World War I was not consciously planned or provoked by any individual or group, although some Americans took advantage of the movement once it started. Rather, the Red Scare, like the Gaiwiio and Boxer movements described above, was brought on largely by a number of severe social and economic dislocations which threatened the national equilibrium. The full extent and the shocking effects of these disturbances of 1919 have not yet been adequately described. Runaway prices, a brief but sharp stock market crash and business depression, revolutions throughout Europe, widespread fear of domestic revolt, bomb explosions, and an outpouring of radical literature were distressing enough. These sudden difficulties, moreover, served to exaggerate the disruptive effects already produced by the social and intellectual ravages of the World War and the preceding reform era, and by the arrival, before the war, of millions of new immigrants. This added stress intensified the hostility of Americans strongly antagonistic to minority groups, and brought new converts to blatant nativism from among those who ordinarily were not overtly hostile toward radicals or recent immigrants.

Citizens who joined the crusade for one hundred percent Americanism sought, primarily, a unifying force which would halt the apparent disintegration of their culture. The movement, they felt, would eliminate those foreign influences which the one hundred percenters believed were the major cause of their anxiety.

Many of the postwar sources of stress were also present during World War I, and the Red Scare, as John Higham has observed, was partly an exaggeration of wartime passions. In 1917–1918 German-Americans served as the object of almost all our nativistic fervor; they were the threatening intruders who refused to become good citizens. "They used America," a patriotic author declared in 1918 of two million German-Americans, "they never loved her. They clung to their old language, their old customs, and cared nothing for ours. . . . As a class they were clannish beyond all other races coming here." Fear of subversion by German agents was almost as extravagant in 1917–1918 as anxiety about "reds" in the postwar period. Attorney General Thomas Watt Gregory reported to a friend in May 1918 that "we not infrequently receive as many as fifteen hundred letters in a single day suggesting disloyalty and the making of investigations."

Opposition to the war by radical groups helped smooth the transition among American nativists from hatred of everything German to fear of radical revolution. The two groups of enemies were associated also for other reasons. High government officials declared after the war that German leaders planned and subsidized the Bolshevik Revolution. When bombs blasted homes and public buildings in nine cities in June 1919, the director of the Justice Department's Bureau of Investigation asserted that the bombers were "connected with Russian bolshevism, aided by Hun money." In November 1919, a year after the armistice, a popular magazine warned of "the Russo-German movement that is now trying to dominate America. . . ."

Even the wartime hostility toward German-Americans, however, is more understandable when seen in the light of recent anthropological and psychological studies. World War I disturbed Americans not only because of the real threat posed by enemy armies and a foreign ideology. For many citizens it had the further effect of shattering an already weakened intellectual tradition. When the European governments decided to fight, they provided shocking evidence that man was not, as most educated members of Western society had believed, a rational creature progressing steadily, if slowly, toward control of his environment. When the great powers declared war in 1914, many Americans as well as many Europeans were stunned. The *New York Times* proclaimed a common theme—European civilization had collapsed: The supposedly advanced nations, declared the *Times*, "have reverted to the condition of savage tribes roaming the forests and falling upon each other in a fury of blood and carnage to achieve the ambitious designs of chieftains clad in skins and drunk with mead." Franz Alexander, director for twenty-five years of the Chicago Institute of Psychoanalysis, recently recalled his response to the outbreak of the World War:

> The first impact of this news is [*sic*] unforgettable. It was the sudden intuitive realization that a chapter of history had ended. . . . Since then, I have discussed this matter with some of my contemporaries and heard about it a great deal in my early postwar psychoanalytic treatments of patients. To my amazement, the others who went through the same events had quite a similar reaction. . . . It was an immediate vivid and prophetic realization that something irrevocable of immense importance had happened in history.

Americans were jolted by new blows to their equilibrium after entering the war. Four million men were drafted away from familiar surroundings and some of them experienced the terrible carnage of trench warfare. Great numbers of women left home to work in war industries or to replace men in other jobs. Negroes flocked to Northern industrial areas by the hundreds of thousands, and their first mass migration from the South created violent racial antagonism in Northern cities.

During the war, also, Americans sanctioned a degree of government control over the economy which deviated sharply from traditional economic individualism. Again, fears aroused before the war were aggravated, for the reform legislation of the Progressive era had tended to increase government intervention, and many citizens were further perturbed by demands that the federal government enforce even higher standards of economic and social morality. By 1919, therefore, some prewar progressives as well as conservatives feared the gradual disappearance of highly valued individual opportunity and responsibility. Their fears were fed by strong postwar calls for continued large-scale government controls—extension of federal operation of railroads and of the Food Administration, for example.

The prime threat to these long-held individualistic values, however, and the most powerful immediate stimulus to the revitalistic response, came from Russia. There the Bolshevik conquerors proclaimed their intention of exporting Marxist ideology. If millions of Americans were disturbed in 1919 by the specter of communism, the underlying reason was not fear of foreign invasion—Russia, after all, was still a backward nation recently badly defeated by German armies. The real threat was the potential spread of communist ideas. These, the one hundred percenters realized with horror, possessed a genuine appeal for reformers and for the economically underprivileged, and if accepted they would complete the transformation of America.

A clear picture of the Bolshevik tyranny was not yet available; therefore, as after the French Revolution, those who feared the newly successful ideology turned to fight the revolutionary ideals. So the *Saturday Evening Post* declared editorially in November 1919 that "History will see our present state of mind as one with that preceding the burning of witches, the children's crusade, the great tulip craze and other examples of softening of the world brain." The *Post* referred not to the Red Scare or the impending Palmer Raids, but to the spread of communist ideology. Its editorial concluded: "The need of the country is not more idealism, but more pragmatism; not communism, but common sense." One of the most powerful patriotic groups, the National Security League, called upon members early in 1919 to "teach 'Americanism.' This means the fighting of Bolshevism . . . by the creation of well defined National Ideals." Members "must preach Americanism and instil the idealism of America's Wars, and that American spirit of service which believes in giving as well as getting." New York attorney, author, and educator Henry Waters Taft warned a Carnegie Hall audience late in 1919 that Americans must battle "a propaganda which is tending to undermine our most cherished social and political institutions and is having the effect of producing widespread unrest among the poor and the ignorant, especially those of foreign birth."

When the war ended Americans also confronted the disturbing possibility, pointed up in 1919 by the struggle over the League of Nations, that Europe's struggles would continue to be their own. These factors combined to make the First World War a traumatic experience for millions of citizens. As Senator James Reed of Missouri observed in August 1919, "This country is still suffering from shell shock. Hardly anyone is in a normal state of mind. . . . A great storm has swept over the intellectual world and its ravages and disturbances still exist."

The wartime "shell shock" left many Americans extraordinarily susceptible to psychological stress caused by postwar social and economic turbulence. Most important for the course of the Red Scare, many of these disturbances had their greatest effect on individuals already antagonistic toward minorities. First of all, there was some real evidence of danger to the nation in 1919, and the nation provided the chief emotional support for many Americans who responded easily to charges of an alien radical menace. Violence flared throughout Europe after the war and revolt lifted radicals to power in several Eastern and Central European nations. Combined with the earlier Bolshevik triumph in Russia these revolutions made Americans look more anxiously at radicals here. Domestic radicals encouraged these fears; they became unduly optimistic about their own chances of success and boasted openly of their coming triumph. Scores of new foreign language anarchist and communist journals, most of them written by and for Southern and Eastern European immigrants, commenced publication, and the established radical press became more exuberant. These periodicals never tired of assuring readers in 1919 that "the United States seems to be on the verge of a revolutionary crisis." American newspapers and magazines reprinted selections from radical speeches, pamphlets, and periodicals so their readers could see what dangerous ideas were abroad in the land. Several mysterious bomb explosions and bombing attempts, reported in bold front page headlines in newspapers across the country, frightened the public in 1919. To many citizens these seemed part of an organized campaign of terror carried on by alien radicals intending to bring down the federal government. The great strikes of 1919 and early 1920 aroused similar fears.

Actually American radical organizations in 1919 were disorganized and poverty-stricken. The Communists were inept, almost without contact with American workers and not yet dominated or subsidized by Moscow. The IWW [International Workers of the World] was shorn of its effective leaders, distrusted by labor, and generally declining in influence and power. Violent anarchists were isolated in a handful of tiny, unconnected local organizations. One or two of these anarchist groups probably carried out the "bomb conspiracy" of 1919; but the extent of the "conspiracy" can be judged from the fact that the bombs killed a total of two men during the year, a night watchman and one of the bomb throwers, and seriously wounded one person, a maid in the home of a Georgia senator.

Nevertheless, prophecies of national disaster abounded in 1919, even among high government officials. Secretary of State Robert Lansing confided to his diary that we were in real peril of social revolution. Attorney General

A. Mitchell Palmer advised the House Appropriations Committee that "on a certain day, which we have been advised of," radicals would attempt "to rise up and destroy the Government at one fell swoop." Senator Charles Thomas of Colorado warned that "the country is on the verge of a volcanic upheaval." And Senator Miles Poindexter of Washington declared, "There is real danger that the government will fall." A West Virginia wholesaler, with offices throughout the state, informed the Justice Department in October 1919 that "there is hardly a respectable citizen of my acquaintance who does not believe that we are on the verge of armed conflict in this country." William G. McAdoo was told by a trusted friend that "Chicago, which has always been a very liberal minded place, seems to me to have gone mad on the question of the 'Reds.' " Delegates to the Farmers National Congress in November 1919 pledged that farmers would assist the government in meeting the threat of revolution.

The slight evidence of danger from radical organizations aroused such wild fear only because Americans had already encountered other threats to cultural stability. However, the dislocations caused by the war and the menace of communism alone would not have produced such a vehement nativistic response. Other postwar challenges to the social and economic order made the crucial difference.

Of considerable importance was the skyrocketing cost of living. Retail prices more than doubled between 1915 and 1920, and the price rise began gathering momentum in the spring of 1919. During the summer of 1919 the dominant political issue in America was not the League of Nations; not even the "red menace" or the threat of a series of major strikes disturbed the public as much as did the climbing cost of living. The *Washington Post* early in August 1919 called rising prices, "the burning domestic issue. . . ." Democratic National Chairman Homer Cummings, after a trip around the country, told President Woodrow Wilson that more Americans were worried about prices than about any other public issue and that they demanded government action. When Wilson decided to address Congress on the question the Philadelphia *Public Ledger* observed that the administration had "come rather tardily to a realization of what is uppermost in the minds of the American people."

Then the wave of postwar strikes—there were 3,600 of them in 1919 involving over 4,000,000 workers—reached a climax in the fall of 1919. A national steel strike began in September and nationwide coal and rail walkouts were scheduled for November 1. Unions gained in membership and power during the war, and in 1919 labor leaders were under strong pressure to help workers catch up to or go ahead of mounting living costs. Nevertheless, influential government officials attributed the walkouts to radical activities. Early in 1919, Secretary of Labor William B. Wilson declared in a public speech that recent major strikes in Seattle, Butte, Montana, and Lawrence, Massachusetts, had been instituted by the Bolsheviks and the I.W.W. for the sole purpose of bringing about a nationwide revolution in the United States. During the steel strike of early fall, 1919, a Senate investigating committee reported that "behind this strike there is massed a considerable element of I.W.W.'s, anarchists, revolutionists, and Russian soviets. . . ." In April 1920 the head of the Justice Department's General Intelligence Division, J. Edgar Hoover, declared in a public hearing that at least fifty percent of the influence behind the recent series of strikes was traceable directly to communist agents.

Furthermore, the nation suffered a sharp economic depression in late 1918 and early 1919, caused largely by sudden cancellations of war orders. Returning servicemen found it difficult to obtain jobs during this period, which coincided with the beginning of the Red Scare. The former soldiers had been uprooted from their homes and told that they were engaged in a patriotic crusade. Now they came back to find "reds" criticizing their country and threatening the government with violence, Negroes holding good jobs in the big cities, prices terribly high, and workers who had not served in the armed forces striking for higher wages. A delegate won prolonged applause from the 1919 American Legion Convention when he denounced radical aliens, exclaiming, "Now that the war is over and they are in lucrative positions while our boys haven't a job, we've got to send those scamps to hell." The major part of the mobs which invaded meeting halls of immigrant organizations and broke up radical parades, especially during the first half of 1919, was comprised of men in uniform.

A variety of other circumstances combined to add even more force to the postwar nativistic movement. Long before the new immigrants were seen as potential revolutionists they became the objects of widespread hostility. The peak of immigration from Southern and Eastern Europe occurred in the fifteen years before the war; during that period almost ten million immigrants from those areas entered the country. Before the anxious eyes of members of all classes of Americans, the newcomers crowded the cities and began to disturb the economic and social order. Even without other postwar disturbances a nativistic movement of some strength could have been predicted when the wartime solidarity against the German enemy began to wear off in 1919.

In addition, not only were the European revolutions most successful in Eastern and to a lesser extent in Southern Europe, but aliens from these areas predominated in American radical organizations. At least ninety percent of the members of the two American Communist parties formed in 1919 were born in Eastern Europe. The anarchist groups whose literature and bombs captured the imagination of the American public in 1919 were composed almost entirely of Italian, Spanish, and Slavic aliens. Justice Department announcements and statements by politicians and the press stressed the predominance of recent immigrants in radical organizations. Smoldering prejudice against new immigrants and identification of these immigrants with European as well as American radical movements, combined with other sources of postwar stress to create one of the most frenzied and one of the most widespread nativistic movements in the nation's history.

The result, akin to the movements incited by the Chinese Boxers or the Indian Ghost Dancers, was called Americanism or one hundred percent Americanism. Its objective was to end the apparent erosion of American values and the disintegration of American culture. By reaffirming those beliefs, customs, symbols, and traditions felt to be the foundation of our way of life, by enforcing conformity among the population, and by purging the nation of dangerous foreigners, the one hundred percenters expected to heal societal divisions and to tighten defenses against cultural change.

Panegyrics celebrating our history and institutions were delivered regularly in almost every American school, church, and public hall in 1919 and 1920. Many of these fervent addresses went far beyond the usual patriotic declarations. Audiences were usually urged to join a crusade to protect our hallowed institutions. Typical of the more moderate statements was Columbia University President Nicholas Murray Butler's insistence in April 1919 that "America will be saved, not by those who have only contempt and despite for her founders and her history, but by those who look with respect and reverence upon the great series of happenings extending from the voyage of the Mayflower. . . ."

The American flag became a sacred symbol. Legionaries demanded that citizens "Run the Reds out from the land whose flag they sully." Men suspected of radical leanings were forced to kiss the stars and stripes. A Brooklyn truck driver decided in June 1919 that it was unpatriotic to obey a New York City law obliging him to fly a red cloth on lumber which projected from his vehicle. Instead he used as a danger signal a small American flag. A policeman, infuriated at the sight of the stars and stripes flying from a lumber pile, arrested the driver on a charge of disorderly conduct. Despite the Brooklyn patriot's insistence that he meant no offense to the flag, he was reprimanded and fined by the court.

Recent immigrants, especially, were called to show evidence of real conversion. Great pressure was brought to bear upon the foreign-born to learn English and to forget their native tongues. As Senator William S. Kenyon of Iowa declared in October 1919, "The time has come to make this a one-language nation." An editorial in the *American Legion Weekly* took a further step and insisted that the one language must be called "American. Why even in Mexico they do not stand for calling the language the Spanish language."

Immigrants were also expected to adopt our customs and to snuff out remnants of Old World cultures. Genteel prewar and wartime movements to speed up assimilation took on a "frightened and feverish aspect." Welcoming members of an Americanization conference called by his department, Secretary of the Interior Franklin K. Lane exclaimed in May 1919, "You have been gathered together as crusaders in a great cause. . . . There is no other question of such importance before the American people as the solidifying and strengthening of true American sentiment." A Harvard University official told the conference that "The Americanization movement . . . gives men a new and holy religion. . . . It challenges each one of us to a renewed consecration and devotion to the welfare of the nation." The National Security League boasted, in 1919, of establishing one thousand study groups to teach teachers how to inculcate "Americanism" in their foreign-born students. A critic of the prevailing mood protested against "one of our best advertised American mottoes, 'One country, one language, one flag,' " which, he complained, had become the basis for a fervent nationwide program.

As the postwar movement for one hundred percent Americanism gathered momentum, the deportation of alien nonconformists became increasingly its most compelling objective. Asked to suggest a remedy for the nationwide upsurge in radical activity, the Mayor of Gary, Indiana, replied, "Deportation is the answer, deportation of these leaders who talk treason in America and deportation of those who agree with them and work with them." "We must remake America," a popular author averred, "We must purify the source of America's population and keep it pure. . . . We must insist that there shall be an American loyalty, brooking no amendment or qualification." As Higham noted, "In 1919, the clamor of 100 percenters for applying deportation as a purgative arose to an hysterical howl. . . . Through repression and deportation on the one hand and speedy total assimilation on the other, 100 percenters hoped to eradicate discontent and purify the nation."

Politicians quickly sensed the possibilities of the popular frenzy for Americanism. Mayor Ole Hanson of Seattle, Governor Calvin Coolidge of Massachusetts, and General Leonard Wood became the early heroes of the movement. The man in the best political position to take advantage of the popular feeling, however, was Attorney General A. Mitchell Palmer. In 1919, especially after the President's physical collapse, only Palmer had the authority, staff, and money necessary to arrest and deport huge numbers of radical aliens. The most virulent phase of the movement for one hundred percent Americanism came early in 1920, when Palmer's agents rounded up for deportation over six thousand aliens and prepared to arrest thousands more suspected of membership in radical organizations. Most of these aliens were taken without warrants, many were detained for unjustifiably long periods of time, and some suffered incredible hardships. Almost all, however, were eventually released.

After Palmer decided that he could ride the postwar fears into the presidency, he set out calculatingly to become the symbol of one hundred percent Americanism. The Palmer raids, his anti-labor activities, and his frequent pious professions of patriotism during the campaign were all part of this effort. Palmer was introduced by a political associate to the Democratic party's annual Jackson Day dinner in January 1920 as "an American whose

Americanism cannot be misunderstood." In a speech delivered in Georgia shortly before the primary election (in which Palmer won control of the state's delegation to the Democratic National Convention), the Attorney General asserted: "I am myself an American and I love to preach my doctrine before undiluted one hundred percent Americans, because my platform is, in a word, undiluted Americanism and undying loyalty to the republic." The same theme dominated the address made by Palmer's old friend, John H. Bigelow of Hazleton, Pennsylvania, when he placed Palmer's name in nomination at the 1920 National Convention. Proclaimed Bigelow: "No party could survive today that did not write into its platform the magic word 'Americanism.' . . . The Attorney-General of the United States has not merely professed, but he has proved his true Americanism. . . . Behind him I see a solid phalanx of true Americanism that knows no divided allegiance."

Unfortunately for political candidates like Palmer and Wood, most of the social and economic disturbances which had activated the movement they sought to lead gradually disappeared during the first half of 1920. The European revolutions were put down; by 1920 communism seemed to have been isolated in Russia. Bombings ceased abruptly after June 1919, and fear of new outrages gradually abated. Prices of food and clothing began to recede during the spring. Labor strife almost vanished from our major industries after a brief railroad walkout in April. Prosperity returned after mid-1919 and by early 1920 business activity and employment levels exceeded their wartime peaks. At the same time, it became clear that the Senate would not pass Wilson's peace treaty and that America was free to turn its back on the responsibilities of world leadership. The problems associated with the new immigrants remained; so did the disillusionment with Europe and with many old intellectual ideals. Nativism did not disappear from the American scene; but the frenzied attempt to revitalize the culture did peter out in 1920. The handful of unintimidated men, especially Assistant Secretary of Labor Louis F. Post, who had used the safeguards provided by American law to protect many victims of the Red Scare, found increasing public support. On the other hand, politicians like Palmer, Wood, and Hanson were left high and dry, proclaiming the need for one hundred percent Americanism to an audience which no longer urgently cared.

It is ironic that in 1920 the Russian leaders of the Comintern finally took charge of the American Communist movement, provided funds and leadership, and ordered the Communist factions to unite and participate actively in labor organizations and strikes. These facts were reported in the American press. Thus a potentially serious foreign threat to national security appeared just as the Red Scare evaporated, providing a final illustration of the fact that the frenzied one hundred percenters of 1919–1920 were affected less by the "red menace" than by a series of social and economic dislocations.

Although the Red Scare died out in 1920, its effects lingered. Hostility toward immigrants, mobilized in 1919–1920, remained strong enough to force congressional passage of restrictive immigration laws. Some of the die-hard one hundred percenters found a temporary home in the Ku Klux Klan until that organization withered away during the mid-twenties. As its most lasting accomplishments, the movement for one hundred percent Americanism fostered a spirit of conformity in the country, a satisfaction with the *status quo*, and the equation of reform ideologies with foreign enemies. Revitalization movements have helped may societies adapt successfully to new conditions. The movement associated with the American Red Scare, however, had no such effect. True, it unified the culture against the threats faced in 1919–1920; but the basic problems—a damaged value system, an unrestrained business cycle, a hostile Russia, and communism—were left for future generations of Americans to deal with in their own fashion.

5-10-36

18 Here?

THE NRACP

George P. Elliott

THE NATIONAL RELOCATION AUTHORITY: COLORED PERSONS

Office of Public Relations *Colored Persons Reserve Nevada*

Dear Herb,

Pardon the letterhead. I seem to have brought no stationery of my own, it's a dull walk to the commissary, and I found this paper already in the desk drawer.

Your first letter meant more to me than I can say, and the one I received yesterday has at last aroused me from my depression. I will try to answer both of them at once. You sensed my state of mind, I could tell it from little phrases in your letter—"open your heart, though it be only to a sunset;" "try reading *Finnegans Wake*; if you ever get *into* it you won't be able to fight your way out again for months." I cherish your drolleries. They are little oases of high-light and quiet in this rasping, blinding landscape.

How I hate it! Nothing but the salary keeps me here—nothing. I have been driven into myself in a very unhealthy way. Long hours, communal eating, the choice between a badly lighted reading room full of people and my own cell with one cot and two chairs and a table, a swim in a chlorinated pool, walks in this violent, seasonless, arid land—what is there? There seem to be only two varieties of people here: those who "have culture," talk about the latest *New Yorker* cartoons, listen to imitation folk songs and subscribe to one of the less popular book clubs; and those who play poker, talk sports and sex, and drink too much. I prefer the latter type as people, but unfortunately I do not enjoy any of their activities except drinking. Since I know the language and mores of the former type, and have more inclination toward them, I am thrown with people whom I dislike intensely. In this muddle I find myself wishing, selfishly, that you were here; your companionship would mean so much to me now. But you knew better than I what the Colored Persons Reserve would mean—you were most wise to stay in Washington, most wise. You will be missing something by staying there, but I assure you it is something well worth missing.

I must mention the two universal topics of conversation. From the filing clerks to my division chief I know of no one, including myself, who does not talk absorbedly about mystery stories. A few watered-down eclectics say they haven't much preference in mysteries, but the folk songers to a man prefer the tony, phony Dorothy Sayers–S.S. Van Dine type of pseudo-literary snobbish product, and the horsy folk prefer the Dashiell Hammett romantic cum violent realism. There is one fellow—a big domed Irishman named O'Doone who wears those heavy rimmed, owlish glasses that came into style a couple of years ago just after the war—who does nothing but read and reread Sherlock Holmes, and he has won everyone's respect in some strange fashion by this quaint loyalty. He's quite shy, in a talkative, brittle way, but I think I could grow fond of him.

Everyone finds a strong need to read the damnable things, so strong that we prefer the absolute nausea of reading three in one day—I did it once myself for three days on end—to not reading any. What is it actually that we prefer not to do? I can only think of Auden's lines, "The situation of our time Surrounds us like a baffling crime." Of our time and of this job.

What are we doing here? That is the other subject none of us can let alone. We are paid fantastic salaries (the secretary whom I share with another writer gets four hundred dollars a month, tell Mary *that* one), and for one whole month we have done nothing while on the job except to read all the provisions and addenda to the Relocation Act as interpreted by the Authority or to browse at will in the large library of literature by and about Negroes, from sociological studies to newspaper poetry in dialect. You know the Act generally of course, but I hope you are never for any reason subjected to this Ph.D.-candidate torture of reading to exhaustion about a subject in which you have only a general interest. But the *why* of this strange and expensive indoctrination is totally beyond me. I thought that I was going to do much the same sort of public relations work here on the spot as we had been doing in the State Department; I thought the salary differential was just a compensation for living in this hellhole. That's what everyone here had thought too. It appears, however, that there is something more important brewing. In the whole month I have been here I have turned out only a couple of articles describing the physical charms of this desiccated cesspool; they appeared in Negro publications which I hope you have not even heard of. Beyond that I have done nothing but bore myself to death by reading Negro novels and poetry.

They are a different tribe altogether; I would be the last to deny that their primeval culture is wonderful enough to merit study—but not by me. I have enough trouble trying to understand the rudiments of my own culture without having this one pushed off onto me.

I have been stifled and confused for so long that all my pent-up emotions have found their worthiest outlet in this letter to you, my dear friend. I have been vowing (as we used to vow to quit smoking, remember?) to stop reading mysteries, but my vows seldom survive the day. Now I do solemnly swear and proclaim that each time I have the urge to read a mystery I will instead write a letter to you. If these epistles become dull and repetitious just throw them away without reading them. I'll put a mark—say an M—on the envelope of these counter-mystery letters, so you needn't even open them if you wish. I'm sure there will be a lot of them.

Does this sound silly? I suppose it does. But I am in a strange state of mind. There's too much sunlight and the countryside frightens me and I don't understand anything.

Bless you,
Andy

March 14

Dear Herb,

It wasn't as bad as I had feared, being without mysteries. We get up at seven and go to work at eight. Between five and six in the afternoon there's time for a couple of highballs. From seven or so, when dinner is over, till ten or eleven—that's the time to watch out for. After you have seen the movie of the week and read *Time* and *The New Yorker* you discover yourself, with that autonomic gesture with which one reaches for a cigarette, wandering toward the mystery shelf and trying to choose between Carter Dickson and John Dickson Carr (two names for the same writer, as I hope you don't know). On Sundays there's tennis in the early morning and bowling in the afternoon. But those gaping rents in each tightly woven, just tolerable day remain, no matter what you do. At first I thought I should have to tell myself bedtime stories. One evening I got half-drunk in the club rooms and absolutely potted alone in my own room afterward. First time in my life. Another time O'Doone and I sat up till midnight composing an "Epitaph for a Mongoose." I can't tell you how dreary some of our endeavors were; O'Doone still quotes one of mine occasionally. He's a strange fellow. I can't exactly figure him out but I like him in an oblique sort of way. Neither of us fits into any of three or four possible schemes of things here, and we share a good deal in general outlook. But he can amuse himself with a cerebral horseplay which only makes me uneasy. O'Doone has a French book—God knows where he got it—on Senegalese dialects; he goes around slapping stuffy people on the back and mumbling, "Your grandmother on your father's side was a pig-faced gorilla" or else a phrase which in Senegalese has something to do with transplanting date trees but which in English sounds obscene, and then he laughs uproariously. In any event, he's better off than I, who am amused by almost nothing.

Now that you have been spared the threatened dejection of my counter-mystery letters I must confess to the secret vice which I have taken up in the past week. It grows upon me too; it promises to become a habit which only age and infirmity will break. I had thought it a vice of middle age (and perhaps it is—are we not thirty-eight, Herb? When does middle age commence?). I *take walks*. I talk long walks alone. If I cannot say that I enjoy them I do look forward to them with the eagerness with which an adolescent will sometimes go to bed in order to continue the dream which waking has interrupted.

Not that my walks are in any way dreamlike. They are perfectly real. But they take place in a context so different from any of the social or intellectual contexts of the CPR day and they afford such a strong emotional relief to it that I think they may be justly compared to a continued dream. My walks, however, have a worth of their own such as dreams can never have. Instead of taking me from an ugly world to a realm of unexplained symbols they have driven me toward two realities, about which I must confess I have had a certain ignorance: myself and the natural world. And standing, as I feel I do, at the starting point of high adventure I feel the explorer's excitement and awe, and no self-pity at all.

I have recaptured—and I am not embarrassed to say it—the childhood delight in stars. That's a great thing to happen to a man, Herb: to be able to leave the smoke-and-spite-laden atmosphere of bureaucracy, walk a few miles out into the huge, silent desert, and look at the stars with a delight whose purity needs no apology and whose expansiveness need find no words for description. I am astonished by the sight of a Joshua tree against the light blue twilight sky, I am entranced by the vicious innocence of one of the kinds of cactus that abound hereabouts. I enjoy these garish sunsets with a fervor that I once considered indecent. I cannot say that I like this desert—certainly not enough to live in it permanently—but it has affected me very deeply. I think that much of my trouble during my first month here was resisting the force of the desert. Now I no longer resist it, yet I have not submitted to it; rather I have developed a largeness of spirit, a feeling of calm and magnificence. Which I am sure is in part lightheadedness at having such a weight of nasty care removed all at once, but which is wonderful while it lasts.

But it's not *just* lightheadedness. Some obstruction of spirit, an obstruction of whose existence I was not even aware, has been removed within me, so that now I can and dare observe the complexities of that catalogued, indifferent, unaccountable natural world which I had always shrugged at. One saw it from train windows, one dealt with it on picnics, one admired the nasturtiums and peonies of one's more domesticated friends, one approved of lawns and shade trees. What then? What did one know of the rigidity of nature's order or of the prodigality with which she wastes and destroys and errs? I came here furnished only with the ordinary generic names of things—snake, lizard, toad, rabbit, bug, cactus, sagebrush, flower, weed—but already I have watched a road runner kill a rattlesnake and I am proud that I know how rabbits drink. Do you know how rabbits drink? If you ask what difference it makes to know this I can happily reply, "None at all, but it gives me pleasure." A pleasure which does not attempt to deny mortality, but accepts it and doesn't care—a true pleasure and one worth cherishing.

11 P.M.

I owe it to you, I know, to give a somewhat less personal, less inward account of this place. But a calculated, itemized description of anything, much less of so monstrous a thing as a desert, is beyond me. Instead I'll try to give you an idea of what effect such physical bigness can have upon the people in it.

Our buildings are situated at the head of a very long valley—the Tehuala River Valley—which is partially arable and which is good for grazing purposes in both the upper and lower regions. The highway into the valley (that is, the highway that leads to the east, as well as the railroad) runs not far from our settlement. Being public relations, we are located just within the fence, a huge, barbarous fence with guards. We have had a rather surprising number of visitors already, and hundreds more are expected during the summer. Our eight buildings are flat-roofed, gray, of a horizontal design, and air-conditioned. But our view of the valley is cut off by a sharp bend about four or five miles below us. The tourists, in other words, can see almost nothing of the valley or of the Reserve stretching for eight hundred miles to the southwest, for this is the only public entrance to the Reserve and no airplanes are permitted over any part of it. Around the turn in the upper valley is yet another even more barbarous, even better guarded fence, past which no one goes except certain Congressmen, the top officials (four, I believe) in the NRACP, and SSE (Special Service Employees, who, once they have gone past that gate, do not return and do not communicate with the outside world even by letter). All this secrecy—you can fill in details to suit yourself—is probably unnecessary, but it does succeed in arousing an acute sense of mystery and speculation about the Reserve.

Well, being no more than human I walked the five miles to the bend the other day, climbed a considerable hill nearby, and looked out over the main sweep of the valley for the first time. I was hot and tired when I reached the foot of the hill so I sat down—it was around 5:30—and ate the snack I had brought. When I reached the top of the hill the sun was about to set; the long shadows of the western hills lay over the floor of the valley and in some places extended halfway up the hills to the east. Far, far to the west, just to the north of the setting sun, was a snow-capped mountain, and immediately in front of me, a mile and a half or so away, stretched the longest building I have ever seen in my life. It had a shed roof rising away from me and there were no windows on my side of the building. Nothing whatsoever broke the line of its continuous gray back. It was at least a mile long, probably longer. Beyond it lay dozens of buildings exactly like this one except for their length; some of them ran, as the long one did, east and west, some ran north and south, some aslant. I could not estimate to my satisfaction how large most of them were; they seemed to be roughly the size of small factories. The effect which their planner had deliberately calculated and achieved was that of a rigidly patterned, unsymmetrical (useless?) articulation of a restricted flat area. Nothing broke the effect, and for a reason which I cannot define these buildings in the foreground gave such a focus and order to the widening scene that lay before me that I stood for the better part of an hour experiencing a pure joy—a joy only heightened by my grateful knowledge that these Intake buildings were designed to introduce an entire people to the new and better world beyond. The fine farms and ranches and industries and communities which would arise from these undeveloped regions took shape in the twilight scene before me, shimmering in the heat waves rising from the earth.

But presently it was quite dark—the twilights are very brief here—and I was awakened from my reverie by the lights going on in one of the buildings before me. I returned to the PR settlement and to my solitary room in a state of exaltation which has not yet deserted me.

For an hour, the Universe and History co-extended before me and they did not exclude me. For while I am but a grain on the shore of event only within my consciousness did this co-extending take place and have any meaning. For that long moment mine was the power.

I will write again soon.

Andy

March 20

Dear Herb,

You complain that I didn't say anything directly about my voyage of discovery into myself as I had promised in my last letter. And that the internal high pressures of urban life are blowing me up like a balloon in this rarefied atmosphere.

Maybe so. I'll try to explain what has been going on. But I forgot to take a cartographer on my voyage, so that my account may resemble, in crudeness, that of an Elizabethan freebooter in Caribbean waters. (If I had the energy I'd try to synthesize these balloon voyage metaphors, but I haven't.)

It all began when I asked myself on one of my walks why I was here, why I had taken this job. $8,000 a year—yes. The social importance of the project—maybe (but not my personal importance to the project). Excitement at being in on the beginning of a great experiment in planning—yes. The hope of escaping from the pressures of Washington life—yes. These are valid reasons all of them, but on the other side—why I should want *not* to come here—are better reasons altogether. An utter absence of urban life. No friends. No chance of seeing Betty. The loss of permanent position (this one you pointed out most forcefully) in State for a better paid but temporary job here. Too inadequate a knowledge of my duties, or of the whole NRACP for the matter, to permit me to have made a decision wisely. And an overpowering hatred of restrictions. Never once, Herb, for three years to be allowed to leave this Reserve! I've been sweating here for seven weeks, but 156 weeks! Christ!) Now I had known, more or less, all these factors before I came here, all these nice rational, statistical factors. But when I asked myself the other night in the false clarity of the desert moonlight why I had chosen to come, why really, I still could not answer myself satisfactorily. For I was still certain of one thing: that none of the logical reasons, none of my recognized impulses would have brought me here singly or combined.

Being in the mood I also asked myself why I had continued to live with Clarice for five years after I had known quite consciously that I did not love her but felt a positive contempt for her. Betty accounted for part of it, and the usual fear of casting out again on one's own. But I would not have been on my own in any obvious sense; I am sure you know of my love affairs during those five years; I could have married any of three or four worthy women. I asked myself why it was that from the moment Clarice decided once and for all to divorce me (she did the deciding, not me; I don't think you knew that) I lost my taste for my current inamorata and have not had a real affair since.

These questions I was unable to answer, but at least I was seriously asking them of myself. I was willing and able to face the answers. The key to the answer came from my long-limbed, mildly pretty, efficient, but (I had originally thought) frivolous and banal secretary, Ruth. She is one of those women who because they do not have an "intellectual" idea in their noodles are too frequently dismissed as conveniently decorative but not very valuable. Perhaps Ruth really is that, but she has made two or three remarks recently which seem to me to display an intuitive intelligence of a considerable order. Yet they may be merely aptly chosen, conventional observations; it is hard to tell. She interests me. She has a maxim which I resent but cannot refute: "There are those who get it and those who dish it out; I intend to be on the side of the dishers." (Is this the post-Christian golden rule? It has its own power, you know.) In any case, the other day I was sitting in my cubicle of an office, in front of which Ruth's desk is placed—she services two of us. I had my feet up on the desk in a rather indecorous fashion, and I had laid the book I was reading on my lap while I smoked a cigarette. I suppose I was daydreaming a little. Suddenly Ruth opened the door and entered. I started, picked up the book, and took my feet off the table top.

Ruth cocked an eye at me and said, "You like to feel guilty, don't you? All I wanted to know was whether you could spare time for a cup of coffee."

So we went to the café and had coffee and didn't even mention her statement or its cause.

But it set me thinking; the longer I thought about it the better I liked it. I had always discounted wild, Dostoevskian notions like that as being too perverse to be true, but now I am not at all sure that frivolous, red-nailed Ruth wasn't right. So long as Clarice had been there to reprove me for my infidelities I had indulged in them. When her censorship was removed, the infidelities or any love affairs at all lost their spice, the spice being the guilt that she made me feel about them. Then, having divorced Clarice, I took this job. The job is a sop to my sense of guilt at being white and middle-class (that is to say, one of Ruth's "dishers"), a sop because I am participating in an enterprise whose purpose is social justice. At the same time it is a punishment because of the deprivations I am undergoing; yet the actual luxury of my life and my actual status in the bureaucracy, high but not orthodox, privileged yet not normally restricted, nourishes the guilt which supports it. I suppose Freud could tell me what it is that causes the sense of guilt in the first place, but I am not going to bother to find out. There are certain indecencies about which one ought not to inquire unless one has to. Social guilt—that is to say a sense of responsibility toward society—is a good thing to have, and I intend to exploit it in myself. I intend to satisfy it by doing as fine a job as I possibly can; furthermore I intend to find a worthy European family, Italian perhaps, who are impoverished and to support them out of my salary. I must confess that the CARE packages we sent to Europe immeddiately after the war made me feel better than all the fine sentiments I ever gave words to.

I am grateful that I came here. I have been thrown back upon myself in a way that has only benefited me.

We begin work soon. The first trainload of Negroes arrived today, five hundred of them. They are going through Intake (the buildings I described in my last letter) and our work, we are told, will commence within a few days. Exactly what we are to do we will be briefed on tomorrow. I look forward to it eagerly.

Andy

I read this letter over before putting it in the envelope. That was a mistake. All the excitement about myself which I had felt so keenly sounds rather flat as I have put it. There must be a great deal for me yet to discover. As you know, I have never spent much of my energy in intimacies, either with myself or with other people. One gets a facsimile of it when talking about the universal stereotypes of love with a woman. But this desert has thrown me back upon myself, and from your letter I take it you find my explorations of interest. However, you must not expect many more letters in so tiresome a vein. I will seal and mail this one tonight lest I repent in the morning.

April 10

Dear Herb,

I have not known how to write this letter, though I've tried two or three times in the past week to do it. I'm going to put it in the form of a homily with illustrations. The text: "There are those who get it and those who dish it out; I intend to be on the side of the dishers."

First, in what context did it occur? It is the motto of a charming young woman (any doubts I may have expressed about her are withdrawn as of now; she is all one could ask for) who is not malicious and who does not in the least want to impose her beliefs or herself upon other people. She sends one hundred dollars a month to her mother, who is dying of cancer in a county hospital in Pennsylvania. When she told me she was sending the money I asked her why.

"Why?" said Ruth. "I'm disappointed in you to ask me such a thing."

"All right be disappointed, but tell me why."

She shrugged in a humorous way. "She's my mother. And anyway," she added, "we're all dying, aren't we?"

The important thing to note about Ruth is that she means it but she doesn't care. Just as she doesn't really care whether you like her clothes or her lovely hair; she does and you should—the loss is yours if you don't. She was reared in a perfectly usual American city, and she has chosen from its unconscious culture the best in custom and attitude.

But she said it here in the public relations division of the Colored Persons Reserve, here where there is as much getting and dishing out as anywhere in the world, where the most important Negro in the Reserve, its president, may be in a very real sense considered inferior to a white window washer. The first time O'Doone heard her say it (he had dropped by to talk awhile and Ruth had joined us) he made the sign of the cross in the air between himself and Ruth and backed clear out of the room. He didn't return either. I'm sure he's not religious. I don't know why he did that.

What does the statement imply? Primarily it makes no judgment and does not urge to action. It is unmoral. "There is a condition such that some people must inflict pain and others must receive it; since it is impossible to be neutral in this regard and since I like neither to give nor to take injury I shall choose the path of least resistance. I shall ally myself with the inflictors not because I like their side and certainly not because I dislike the other side but only because in that way I myself am least interfered with." No regret, no self-deception (*it is impossible to be neutral*), only true resignation. This circumstance is as it is, and it will not and should not be otherwise. There is a certain intensity of joy possible after resignation of this order greater than we frustrated hopers know. (Where do I fit into this scheme? I think I have discovered one thing about myself from contemplating Ruth's maxim: I want profoundly to be a disher, but my training has been such, or perhaps I am only so weak, that I am incapable of being one with a clear conscience. Consequently I find myself in a halfway position: dishing it out, yes, but at the behest of people I have never seen, and to people I will never know.) Ruth took a job with the NRACP for the only right reason: not for any of my complicated ones nor for the general greed but because she saw quite clearly that here was one of the very pure instances of getting it and of dishing it out. She left a job as secretary to an executive in General Electric for this. I think she gets a certain pleasure from seeing her philosophy so exquisitely borne out by event. Ruth is twenty-seven. I think I am in love with her. I am sure she is not in love with me.

Tell me, Herb, does not this maxim ring a bell in you? This girl has had the courage to put into deliberate words her sense of the inevitable. Do you not admire her for it? And is she not right? She is right enough. If you doubt it let me tell you what our job here is.

The authorities consider the situation potentially explosive enough to warrant the most elaborate system of censorship I have ever heard of. To begin with there is a rule that during his first week in the Reserve every Negro may write three letters to persons on the outside. After that period is over only one letter a month is permitted. Now all letters leaving here during the first week are sent to PR where they are censored and typed in the correct form (on NRACP letterhead); the typed copies are sent on and the originals are filed. The reason for this elaborate system is interesting enough and probably sound; every endeavor is to be made to discourage any leaking out of adverse reports on conditions in the CPR. There are some fourteen million Negroes in the nation not all of whom are entirely pleased with the prospect of being relocated, and there are an indeterminate number of Caucasian sympathizers—civil liberties fanatics for the most part—who could cause trouble if any confirmation of their suspicions about the CPR should leak out. We have put out a staggering amount of data on the climatic, agricultural, power production, and mining conditions of the region, and we have propagandized with every device in the book. Yet we know well enough how long it takes for propaganda to counteract prejudice, and sometimes how deceptive an apparent propaganda success can be. We are more than grateful that almost the entire news outlet system of the nation is on our side.

Well, after the letters of the first week have been typed and sent the writer's job begins. Every effort is made to discourage the interned Negroes from writing to the outside. For one thing we keep in our files all personal letters incoming during the first month. Anyone who continues to write to an internee after this month needs to be answered. The filing clerks keep track of the dates, and forward all personal letters to us. (The clerks think we send the letters on to the internees.) We then write appropriate responses to the letters in the style of the internee as we estimate it from his three letters. We try to be as impersonal as possible, conveying the idea that everything is fine. Why do we not forward the letters to the internees to answer? First of all we do, if the internees request it. They are told that they will receive letters only from those persons whose letters they request to see, and such a request involves yards of red tape. Very few are expected to use the cumbersome mechanism at all. Secondly we write the letters for them simply to save ourselves time and trouble. We would have a lot of rewriting to do anyway; this method assures us of complete control and an efficient modus operandi. Any Negro outside who writes too many insistent letters will be, at our request, relocated within a month; we do not want any unnecessary unhappiness to result from the necessarily painful program. Friends and relatives are to be reunited as fast as possible. Whole communities are to be relocated together to avoid whatever wrenches in personal relationships we can avoid.

Is not this getting it and dishing it out on a fine scale? All for very good reasons I know, but then is it not conceivable that there are always good reasons for the old crapperoo? Sometimes I feel absolutistic enough to say, *if it's this bad for any ultimate reason whatsoever then to hell with it.* After which sentiment comes the gun at the head. But then reason reinstates my sense of the relativity of values, and on I go writing a letter to Hector Jackson of South Carolina explaining that I've been so busy putting up a chicken house and plowing that I haven't had a chance to write but I hope to see you soon. (I doubt if I will.)

Andy

I forgot to mention—I have a special job, which is to censor the letters of all the clerical personnel in PR. One of my duties is to censor any reference to the censorship! A strange state of affairs. None of them know that this job is mine; most think the censor must be some Mail Department employee. I must say one looks at some people with new eyes after reading their correspondence.

I need hardly say—but in case there is any doubt I will say—that this letter is absolutely confidential. How much of our system will become publicly known I cannot guess but naturally I don't want to jump the official gun in this regard.

April 12

Dear Herb,

Let me tell you about the strange adventure I had last evening. I am still not quite sure what to make of it.

Immediately after work I picked up a few sandwiches and a pint of whiskey and walked out into the desert on one of my hikes. One more meal with the jabber of the café and one more of those good but always good in the same way dinners and I felt I should come apart at the seams. (Another thing I have learned about myself: I am ill-adapted to prison life.) I had no goal in view; I intended to stroll.

But I found myself heading generally in the direction of the hill from which I had looked over the Tehuala Valley and the city of CPR Intake buildings. I came across nothing particularly interesting in a natural history way so that by early dusk I was near to the hill. I decided to climb it again and see what I could see.

The first thing I saw, in the difficult light of dusk, was a soldier with a gun standing at the foot of the hill. I came around a large clump of cactus and there he was, leaning on his rifle. He immediately pointed it at me and told me to go back where I belonged. I objected that I had climbed this hill before and that I could see no reason why I shouldn't do it again. He replied that he didn't see any reason either, but I couldn't just the same; they were going to put up another fence to keep people like me away. I cursed at the whole situation; if I had dared I would have cursed him too, for he had been rude as only a guard with a gun can be. But before I left I pulled out my pint and took a slug of it. The guard was a changed man.

"Christ," he said, "give me a pull."

"I should give you a pull."

"Come on," he said, "I ain't had a drop since I came to this hole. They won't even give us beer."

"All right, if you'll tell me what the hell's going on around here."

He made me crouch behind a Joshua tree, and he himself would not look at me while he talked. I asked him the reason for all the precautions.

"They got a searchlight up top the hill with machine guns. They sweep the whole hill all the time. They can see plain as day in the dark. They keep an eye on us fellows down here. I know. I used to run the light."

"I haven't seen any light," I said.

He glanced at me with scorn.

"It's black," he said. "They cut down all the bushes all around the top part of that hill. Anybody comes up in the bare place—pttt! *Any*body. Even a guard."

"I still don't see any light."

"Man, it's black light. You wear glasses and shine this thing and you can see better than you can with a regular light searchlight. It's the stuff. We used to shoot rabbits with it. The little bastards never knew what hit them!"

I didn't want to appear simple so I didn't ask any more questions about the black light. He was an irascible fellow, with a gun and a knife, and he had drunk most of the bottle already.

"Why do you let me stay at all?" I asked.

"Can't see good in the dusk. Not even them can't."

I couldn't think of anything more to say.

"I used to be guard on the railroad they got inside. Say, have they got a system! Trains from the outside go through an automatic gate. All the trainmen get on the engine and drive out. Then we come up through another automatic gate and hook on and drag it in. Always in the daytime. Anybody tried to hop train, inside or out—pttt! Air-conditioned box cars made out of steel. Two deep they come. Never come in at night."

"Are you married?"

"Ain't nobody married up front, huh?"

I didn't answer.

"Well, is there?"

"No, but there could be if anybody felt like it."

"Well, there ain't even a woman inside. Not a damn one. They let us have all the nigger women we want. Some ain't so bad. Most of them fight a lot."

He smashed the pint bottle on a rock nearby. "Why didn't you bring some real liquor, God damn you?" he said in a low voice full of violence. "Get the hell back home where you belong. Get out of here. It's getting dark. I'll shoot the guts out of you too. Bring me something I can use next time, huh? Get going.

"Stay under cover," he shouted after me. "They're likely to get you if they spot you. They can't miss if it's dark enough."

The last I heard of him he was coughing and spitting and swearing. I was as disgusted as scared, and I must confess I was scared stiff.

I walked homeward, slowly recovering my emotional balance, trying to understand what had happened to me with that guard, the meaning of what he had told me. For some absurd reason the tune *In the Gloaming* kept running through my head in the idiotic way tunes will; I was unable to concentrate intelligently upon the situation.

I heard a sound at some distance to my left. I stopped, suddenly and inexplicably alarmed to the point of throbbing temples and clenched fists. A slim figure in brown came through the cactus; as it approached I could see that it was a young woman. She did not see me, but her path brought her directly to where I was standing. I did not know whether to accost her at a distance or to let her come upon me where I stood. By the time I had decided not to accost her I could see that it was Ruth.

"Why Ruth!" I cried with all the emotion of relief and gratified surprise in my voice and perhaps something more. "What are you doing here?"

She started badly, then seeing who it was she hurried up to me and to my surprise took my arms and put them around her body. "Andy, I am so glad to see you. Some good angel must have put you here for me."

I squeezed her, we kissed, a friendly kiss, then she drew away and shook herself. She had almost always called me Mr. Dixon before; there was a real affection in her "Andy."

"What's the matter?" I asked her. "Where have you been?"

"I didn't know you took walks too."

"Oh yes. It's one way to keep from going nuts."

She laughed a little and squeezed my arm. I could not refrain from kissing her again, and this time it was not just a friendly kiss.

"Where did you go?" I asked again.

"To that hill. I went up there a couple of times before. There was a guard there who wanted to lay me."

We didn't speak for a few moments.

"I think he almost shot me for giving him the brushoff. I didn't look back when I left, but I heard him click his gun. You don't know how glad I was to see you."

So we kissed again and this time it was serious.

"Wait a minute," she said, "wait a minute."

She unlocked her arm from mine, and we continued on our way not touching.

"I had some trouble with a guard too," I said. "I wonder why they're so damned careful to keep us away."

"Mine told me they didn't want us to get any funny ideas. He said things aren't what they seem to be in there."

"Didn't you ask him what he meant?"

"Sure. That's when he said I'd better shut up and let him lay me or else he'd shoot me. So I walked off. I'm not going to call on *him* again."

I put my arm around her. I can't tell you how fond I was of her at that moment, of her trim, poised body, her courage, her good humor, her delightful rich voice and laughter. But she only kissed me gently and withdrew.

"I want to keep my head for a while, darling," she said.

I knew what she meant. We walked on in silence, hand in hand. It was moonlight. If I was lightheaded now I knew why.

When we were about half a mile from our buildings we came across O'Doone also returning from a walk.

"Well," he said brightly, "it *is* a nice moon, isn't it?"

It wouldn't do to say that we had met by accident; I was embarrassed, but Ruth's fine laugh cleared the air for me.

"Nicest I ever saw," she said.

"Did you ever walk up that hill," I asked him, "where you can see out over the valley?"

"Once," he said in a surprisingly harsh voice. "I'd rather play chess."

We went into one of the recreation rooms and O'Doone beat me at three games of chess. Ruth sat by, knitting—a sweater for a cousin's baby. We talked little, but comfortably. It would have been a domestic scene if it had not been for the fifty or sixty other people in the room.

Herb, what does it all mean?

Andy

April 20

Dear Herb,

[If all goes well you will receive the following letter from Ruth's cousin, who will be informed by O'Doone's sister to forward it to you. O'Doone's sister will also send you instructions on how to make the invisible ink visible. I first wrote the letter in visible ink, intending to mail it in the usual way, I was prepared to take all the certainly drastic consequences that would come from its being read by someone of authority. But O'Doone's invisible ink (what a strange fellow to have brought a quart of it here! He said he had brought it only to play mysterious letter games with his nephew. I wonder.) and Ruth's baby sweater, upon the wrapping of which I write this, combined to save me. If the authorities catch *this* I don't care what happens. It takes so long to write lightly enough in invisible ink for no pen mark to show on the paper that I doubt if I will have the patience to use it often. Most of my letters will be innocuous in regular ink. I may add an invisible note or two, between the lines, in the margin, or at the end. O'Doone says it's not any of the ordinary kinds and if we're careful the authorities are not likely to catch us. O'Doone is strange. He refused to take this whole ink matter for anything more than a big joke, as though we were digging a tunnel under a house, O'Doone pretending we are just tunneling in a strawstack to hide our marbles, myself trying to protest (but being laughed at for my lapse in taste) that we are really undermining a house in order to blow it up. Which perhaps we are. In any event I don't have the energy left to rewrite this letter, I'll merely copy it off invisibly.]

I cannot tell you how shocked I was to discover the familiar, black censor's ink over five lines in your last letter. The censor censored! I had not thought of that. In my innocence I had thought that we writers in the higher brackets could be trusted to be discreet. One would think I was still a loyal subscriber to the *Nation* I was so naïve. But no—I am trusted to censor the letters of inferiors (I suspect my censorship is sample-checked by someone), but my own letters are themselves inspected and their dangerous sentiments excised. And, irony of ironies, your own references to the fact that my letters were censored were themselves blacked out.

Who is it that does this? The head of PR here? That's a strange way to make him waste his time. One of his assistants? Then the head must censor the assistant's letters. And the chief board of the NRACP censors the head's letters? And the President theirs? And God his? And . . . ?

Which is the more imprisoned: the jailer who thinks he is free and is not, or the prisoner who knows the precise boundaries of his liberty and accepting them explores and uses all the world he has?

I am a jailer who knows he is not free. I am a prisoner who does not know the limits of his freedom. All this I voluntarily submitted to in the name of a higher freedom. Ever since my adolescence, when the New Deal was a faith, liberty has been one of the always repeated, never examined articles of my creed. Well, I have been examining liberty recently, and she's a pure fraud.

One thing I have learned: you don't just quietly put yourself on the side of Ruth's dishers, you become one of them yourself. A disher *has* to dish it out, he cannot help it at all, and he pays for it. Or maybe I am only paying for my guilt-making desire to be a more important disher that I am.

Ruth was surprised at my distress upon receiving your censored letter. She only shrugged. What had I expected, after all? It was inevitable, it was a necessity. That's the key word, Herb, *necessity*. Not liberty, *necessity*. True liberty is what the prisoner has, because he accepts *necessity*. That's the great thing, to recognize and accept *necessity*.

I've been working slowly toward a realization of this. I think my decision to work in the NRACP came from recognizing the social necessity of it. The Negro problem in America was acute and it was insoluble by any liberal formula. This solution gives dignity and independence to the Negroes. It staves off the depression by the huge demand for manufactured products, for transportation, for the operations of the NRACP itself; but perhaps most important of all, it establishes irrevocably in the American people's mind the wisdom and rightness of the government, for if capitalism must go (as it must) it should be replaced peaceably by a strong and wise planned state. Such a state we are proving ourselves to be. Very well. I accepted this. But what I forgot was that I, I the individual, I Andrew Dixon, must personally submit to the stringencies of necessity. The relics of the New Deal faith remained to clutter up my new attitude. This experience, coming when and as it did, particularly coming when Ruth's courageous wisdom was nearby to support me, has liberated me (I hope) into the greater freedom of the prisoner of necessity.

At least such are my pious prayers. I cannot say I am sure I fully understand all the strictures of necessity. I *can* say I do not enjoy those I understand. But pious I will remain.

Remember the days when we thought we could *change* necessity? Democracy and all that? How much older I feel!

Andy

May 1

Mary my dear,

Please let me apologize—sincerely too, Mary—for having neglected you so cruelly for the past months. Herb tells me you are quite put out, and well you might be. I can find no excuses for it, but I will stoutly maintain that it was not a question of hostility or indifference to you, my dear. Actually I have been going through something of a crisis, as Herb may have been telling you. It has something to do with the desert, and something to do with the NRACP, and a lot to do with the charming young woman whose picture I enclose. She is Ruth Cone. We are getting married in a couple of Sundays—Mother's Day. Why Mother's Day I really don't know, but she wants it so there's no help. The details of our plighting troth might amuse you.

A couple of evenings ago I was playing chess in the recreation room with a man named O'Doone, my only friend here. Ruth was sitting beside us knitting some rompers for a cousin's baby. From time to time we would chat a little; it was all very comfortable and unromantic. O'Doone, between games, went to the toilet. When he had left Ruth said to me with a twinkle in her eye, "Andy darling, don't you see what I am doing?" I replied, "Why yes, my sweet, knitting tiny garments. Is it . . .?" And we both laughed heartily. It was a joke, you see, a mild comfortable little joke, and no one would have thought of it a second time except that when we had finished laughing it was no longer a joke. Her face became very sober and I am sure mine did too. I said, "Do you want children, Ruth?" "Yes," she replied. "Do you want to have my children?" "Yes," she said again, without looking at me. Then with the most charming conquest of modesty that you can imagine she turned her serious little face to me, and we very lightly kissed. O'Doone had returned by then. "Well," he said in a bright way, "do I interrupt?" "Not at all," I answered, "we have just decided to get married." He burbled a little, in caricature of the overwhelmed, congratulating friend, pumped our hands, and asked us when we were marrying. "I don't know," I said. "Why not tomorrow?" "Oh no," said Ruth severely, "how can I assemble my trousseau?" At which O'Doone went off into a braying laugh and we set up the chess pieces. "Bet you five to one," he said, "I win this game in less than sixty moves." I wouldn't take his bet. It took him about forty moves to beat me. Thus did Dixon and Cone solemnly vow to share their fortunes.

It's the first marriage in PR. Everybody will attend. The chief promised me Monday off and temporary quarters in one of the guest suites. We are to get a two-room apartment in the new dormitory that is nearly completed. Such privacy and spaciousness will make us the envy of the whole community. I'm sure there will be a spate of marriages as soon as the dormitory is completed. We will not be married by a holy man, partly because neither of us believes in it and partly because there isn't one of any kind on the premises. (I wonder why there were those detailed questions about religious beliefs on our application forms.) There was a little trouble at first about who was authorized to marry people here. The PR chief, as the only person permitted to leave the place, went out and got himself authorized to do it legally. I think he rather fancies himself in the capacity of marrier. He runs to paternalism.

Ruth urges me—she assumes quite rightly that I have not done it already—to tell you some of the homely details of life here. Of our sleeping rooms the less said the better. The beds are comfortable, period. We live quite communally, but very well. There's a fine gymnasium with swimming pool and play fields attached—tennis, baseball, squash, fencing, everything but golf. There's the best library (surely the best!) in the world on American Negro affairs, and a reasonably good one of modern literature. We have comfortable working quarters and a long working day. There is a fine desert for us to walk around in, and I have come to need an occasional stroll in the desert for spiritual refreshment. And we eat handsomely, except for vegetables. In fact, the only complaint that I have of the cooking is the monotony of its excellence: roast, steak, chop, stew. Almost never liver and kidneys and omelettes and casseroles, and always frozen vegetables. Well, probably the Negroes will be producing plenty of vegetables within a few weeks. There's lots of liquor of every kind. There is a sort of department store where one can buy everything one needs and most of the luxuries one could want in this restricted life. There's a movie a week—a double-feature with news and cartoon—and bridge or poker every day. A microcosmic plenitude.

As for the rest of our routine life here I can think of nothing interesting enough to mention. We work and avoid work, backbite, confide, suspect. It's a bureaucratic existence, no doubt of that.

Will this epistle persuade you to forgive me?

Now you must write to me—soon.

Devotedly yours,
Andy

(*In invisible ink, between the lines of the preceding letter*)

O'Doone, who sometimes gives his opinions very obliquely, came to me today with some disturbing figures. He wasn't in the least jaunty about them and I must confess that I am not either.

According to *Time*, which seems to know more about the CPR than we do, there have been about 50,000 Negroes interned already, and these 50,000 comprise nearly all the wealthy and politically powerful Negroes in the nation (including an objectionable white-supremacy Senator one of whose great-great-grandmothers turns out to have been black). The leaders were interned first, reasonably enough, to provide the skeleton of government and system in the new state which they are to erect. *But*, O'Doone points out, we have yet to receive from them a request for letters from an outsider, and if any Negroes at all are going to make such requests it must surely be these, the most important, the least afraid of red tape. (He also pointed out that not one of the entertainers or athletes of prominence has been interned. That, I'm afraid, is all too easily explained.) You see, says O'Doone, you see? But he didn't say, Why? to me, and I'm glad he didn't, for I can't even guess why.

Another statistic he had, concerned the CPR itself. We all know that the figures on natural resources in the CPR are exaggerated. Grossly. Fourteen million people cannot possibly live well in this area, and O'Doone demonstrated that fact to me most convincingly. Economically, the Negro problem in the U.S. has been that they provided a larger cheap-labor market than consumer market. Now the false stimulus of capitalizing their beginnings here will keep American industry on an even keel for years and years, but after that what? O'Doone bowed out at that point, but I think I can press the point a little further. They will provide a market for surplus commodities great enough to keep the pressures of capitalism from blowing us sky high, meanwhile permitting the transition to a planned state to take place. Very astute, I think, very astute indeed.

June 12

Dear Herb,

Why I have not written, you ought to be able to guess. I will not pretend to any false ardors about Ruth. She is wise and winning as a woman, and everything one could ask for as a wife. I love her dearly. She has not read very widely or profoundly, but I think she is going to do something about that soon. We are happy together and I think we shall continue to be happy during the difficult years to come. What more can I say?

Why are happiness and contentment and the sense of fulfillment so hard to write about? I can think of nothing to say, and besides Ruth is just coming in from tennis (it's 9:30 Sunday morning).

10 P.M.

Ruth has gone to bed so I will continue in another vein.

I have been discovering that the wells of pity, which have lain so long locked and frozen in my eyes, are thawed in me now. I am enclosing a letter which came in from a Negress in Chicago to her lover in the CPR, and his response. It is the first letter from inside except for the usual three during the first week that I have read. Apparently a few have been coming out now and then, but this is my first one. I cannot tell you how I pitied both these unhappy people. When Ruth read them she said, "My, what a mean man! I hope he has to collect garbage all his life." I cannot agree with her. I think his little note betrays an unhappiness as great as the woman's, and even more pitiable for being unrecognized, unappreciated. Judge for yourself. I can think of nothing to add.

Andy

> Honey, dear child, why don't you write to me? Don't you even remember all those things you told me you'd do no matter what? And you're not even in jail, you just in that place where we all going to go to sooner or later. O I sure hope they take me there with you. I can't live without you. But I don't even know who to ask to go there with you. I went to the policeman and they said they didn't know nothing about it. I don't know what to do. You don't know how I ache for you honey, It's just like I got a tooth pulled out but it ain't no tooth it's worse, and there is no dentist for it neither. There's a fellow at the store keeps bothering me now and again, but I assure him I don't want him, I got a man. I thought I had a man, you, but I don't hear nothing from you. Maybe you got something there, I don't see how you could do it not after those things you said, but if you have tell me so I can go off in some hole and die. I don't want this Lee Lawson, he's no good, it's you I want, sweetheart, you tell me it's all right. I *got* to hear from you or I'll just die.

> Dear ———,
>
> I've been so busy baby, you wouldn't believe how busy I've been. You'll be coming here pretty soon and then you'll feel better too. It's nice here. We'll get along fine then. You tell that guy to leave you be. You're my gal. Tell him I said so.
>
> Yours truly.
>
> ———

(*In invisible ink*)

I didn't include these letters because I thought they were in the Héloïse–Abélard class, but because I wanted to say something about them and also because they gave me more invisible space.

The man's response came to us already typed. That very much astonished me, and O'Doone, when I told him, let fly a nasty one. "I suppose," he said, "they have a couple of writers in there writing a few letters in place of the Negroes, which we then relay. Complicated isn't it?" Not complicated, upsetting. Devastating. What if it were true? (And I must say this letter has an air more like the PR rewrite formula than like a real letter. Then *none* of the Negroes would have even filtered connection with the outside world.) Why? Why fool even us? Is there no end to the deception and doubt of this place?

O'Doone posed another of his puzzles yesterday. He read in the current PR weekly bulletin that the CPR has been shipping whole trainloads of leather goods and canned meats to China and Europe for relief purposes, under the government's supervision, of course. O'Doone came into my office at once, waving the bulletin and chortling. "How do you like it?" he cried. "Before we get a carrot out of them the Chinese get tons of meat." Then a sudden light seemed to dawn on his face. "Where did all the cattle come from?"

A strange thing happened: O'Doone's intelligent, sensitive face collapsed. The great domed forehead remained almost unwrinkled, but his features looked somehow like one of those children's rubber faces which collapse when you squeeze them. No anguish, no anxiety, only collapse. He left without a word. I wish he had never come here with that news.

Last night I lay awake till three or four o'clock. I could hear trucks and trains rumbling occasionally throughout the night, entering and leaving the Reserve. But that guard I met at the foot of the hill told me that they only bring internees in the daytime. Are those shipments? How can it be? Sometimes I am sick at heart with doubt and uncertainty.

I dreamt last night that I was a Gulliver, lying unbound and unresisting on the ground while a thousand Lilliputians, all of them black, ate at me. I would not write the details of that dream even in invisible ink. Not even in plain water.

July 4

Dear Herb,

Hail Independence Day! Some of the overgrown kids around here are shooting off firecrackers. No one is working. It is all very pleasant. I suppose March 20th will be the Independence Day of the new Negro nation—the day when the first trainload arrived. How long ago that seems already. I do not think I have ever been through so much in so short a time.

Now for the real news. Ruth is pregnant! Amazing woman, she remains outwardly as humorous and self-contained as ever. No one else knows her condition because she wants to avoid as much as possible of the female chatter that goes with pregnancy. She insists upon playing tennis still. Yet she is not all calmness and coolness; when we are lying in bed together before going to sleep she croons little nonsense hymns to pregnancy in my ear, and yesterday afternoon at the office she walked into my cubicle and placed my hand over her womb. Then she kissed me with an unviolent passion that I have never known before in my life. I tell you, she's a wonderful woman.

How miraculous is conception and growth! I no more understand such things than I really understand about the stars and their rushings. One event follows another, but I'm sure I don't know why. If you permit yourself to, you get back to an archaic awe realizing that you have started off a chain of miracles. I never had a sense of littleness when observing the naked heavens, of man's puniness, of my own nothingness. Perhaps it was a fear of that feeling which for so long prevented me from looking upward at all. I mentioned my reaction to O'Doone on one of the first occasions of our meeting. He nodded and said, "But is not a man more complex than a star, and in every way but one that we know of more valuable?" What he said remains with me yet, and when I am presented with the vastness of the stars and the forces which operate within them I am impressed and excited but not depressed by the imagined spectacle. Their bigness does not make me little. My own complexity does not make them simple. Perhaps man is no longer the center of the universe, but neither is anything else. That I have learned.

But when I am presented with the proof of the powers that men (and myself) possess, I still feel a little off balance. When Clarice was pregnant with Betty I had no such feeling. I felt annoyed chiefly. But now, in this desert, in the CPR, I have been sent back at last to fundamentals, to the sources of things; I realize fully how unaccountable is birth of life. Ruth, who never departed far from the sources, is less embarrassed in admitting her sense of mystery.

One thing I am going to teach this child if it can be taught anything: that the humane tradition has been tried and found wanting. It's over, finished, kaput. A new era of civilization commences. Once kindness and freedom were good for something, but no more. *Put yourself in his place*—never. Rather, fight to stay where you are. I think we are entering upon an age of reason and mystery. Reason which accepts and understands the uttermost heights and depths of human power, man's depravity, and his nobility—and, understanding these, dares use them toward a great and future goal, the goal of that stern order which is indispensable to the fullest development of man. Mystery toward all that is not explainable, which is a very great deal. Rationalism failed, for it asserted that everything was ultimately explainable. We know better. We know that to destroy a man's sense of mystery is to cut him off from one of the sources of life. Awe, acceptance, and faith are wonderful sources of power and fulfillment. I have discovered them. My child shall never forget them.

Andy

(*In invisible ink*)

I have put the gun to my temple, Herb, I have pointed the knife at my heart. But my nerve failed me. There were a few days when I was nearly distracted. My division chief told me to stay home till I looked better, but I dared not. I think it was only Ruth's pregnancy that saved me. My newly awakened sense of mystery plus my powers of reason have saved me. This is the third letter I have written you in a week, but I threw the others away. I knew they were wild and broken, and I was not sure at all that I was physically able to write in such a manner as to avoid detection.

It came to a head two weeks ago. O'Doone entered my office, his face looking bright and blasted. He dropped a booklet on my desk and left after a few comments of no importance. The booklet was an anthropologist's preliminary report on certain taboos among American Negroes; the fellow had been interviewing them in Intake. There was nothing of special interest about it that I could see except that it was written in the past tense.

I expected O'Doone to reclaim the booklet any day. For some reason he had always done the visiting to me, not I to him. He was very restless and I am slothful. But a week passed and no O'Doone. I did not meet him in the café nor in the recreation room. I went to his own room, but he did not answer. The next day I went to his office and his secretary told me he had not shown up for two days. I returned to his room. It was locked. The janitor unlocked it for me. When I entered I saw him lying dead on his bed. "Well, old boy," I said to drive the janitor away, I don't know why, "feeling poorly?" He had drunk something. There was a glass on the table by his bed. There was no note. His face was repulsive. (That is a mystery I have learned to respect, how hideous death is.) He was cold and somehow a little sticky to the touch. I covered his face with a towel and sat down. I knew I should call someone, but I did not want to. I knew the janitor would remember letting me in and my staying too long. Yet I felt that was something I must do. What it was I could not remember, something important. It took me an eternity to remember: the invisible ink. I knew where he had kept it; it was not there. I looked throughout his room and it was simply gone. I left.

I still did not notify anyone of his suicide. I was not asking myself why he had done it. Or perhaps I was only shouting, Where's the ink? in a loud voice to cover up the little question, Why? I went to our rooms and straight to the liquor shelf, took down the Scotch, poured myself a stiff one, and drank. It was horrible; I spat it out, cursing. Then I recognized the odor; O'Doone had come over, poured out the Scotch (I hope he enjoyed it himself), and filled the bottle with the invisible ink. At that I broke down in the most womanish way and cried on the bed (never ask, Why? Why? Why?).

Ruth found me there some time later. I told her everything that had happened, and she immediately pulled me together. She had the sense to know I had been acting more oddly than was wise. She notified the right people and O'Doone was disposed of. No one asked me any embarrassing questions, and no official mention of O'Doone's end was made anywhere.

I must continue this on a birthday card.

(*In invisible ink on a large, plain Happy Birthday card to Mary*)

I had still not allowed myself to ask why he had done it, but Ruth put the thing in a short sentence. "He was too soft-hearted to stand it here." She was right; he was a Christian relic. He knew more than he could bear. I resolved to go that very evening again to the hill where the black searchlight threatened the night.

Some sandwiches. Four half-pints of whiskey. A hunting knife (a foolish gesture, I know). Plain drab clothes. The long walk in the still hot, late-afternoon sun. Sunset. The huge, sudden twilight. Then I was within sight of a guard (not the same one I had seen before) standing by the new fence at the foot of the hill.

I crept up toward him under cover of brush and cactus till I was close enough to toss a half-pint of whiskey in his direction. His bored, stupid face immediately became animated by the most savage emotions. He leveled his gun and pointed it in my general direction. He could not see me, however, and rather than look for me he crouched, eyes still searching the underbrush, to reach for the bottle. He drained it in five minutes.

"Throw me some more," he whispered loudly.

"Put the gun down."

I aimed my voice away from him, hoping that he would not spot me. I was lying flat beneath a large clump of sagebrush. There was a Joshua tree nearby and several cactus plants. He pointed the gun at one of the stalks of cactus and crept up toward it. Then he suddenly stopped, I don't know why, and walked back to his post.

"What yer want?" he asked.

I tossed out another bottle. He jumped again, then got it and drank it.

"What's going on in there?"

"They're fixing up the niggers," he said. "You know as much about it as I do."

He began to sing *Oh! Susannah* in a sentimental voice. It was beginning to get too dark for my safety. I was desperate.

I tossed out another bottle, only not so far this time. When he leaned for it I said very clearly, "You look like a butcher."

He deliberately opened the bottle and drank off half of it. "Butcher, huh? Butcher?" He laid down his gun and took his villainous knife out. "I'm no butcher. I won't have nothing to do with the whole slimy mess. I won't eat them, no sir, you can do that for me. But I can do a little carving, I think. No butcher, you son of a bitch. You dirty, prying, nigger-eating son of a bitch. I'll learn you to call me a butcher."

He was stalking the cactus again. He lunged forward at it and with much monotonous cursing and grunting dealt with it murderously. Meanwhile I crawled out on the other side of the sagebrush and ran for it. He never shot at me. Nothing happened except that I too ran full tilt into a cactus and had to walk hours in agony of flesh as well as of spirit. I vomited and retched till I thought I would be unable to walk further.

I must continue this letter some other way.

Andy

(*In invisible ink on the papers wrapping another sweater for Ruth's cousin's baby*)

I told Ruth nothing of what I had learned; not even *her* great sense of the inevitable could survive such a shock, I think. Yet sometimes it seems to me that she must surely know it all. I do not want to know whether she knows. Could I support it if she did?

It was more painful pulling the cactus needles out than it had been acquiring them. But she removed them all, bathed the little wounds with alcohol, and put me to bed. The next morning I awoke at seven and insisted upon going to work. I sat all day in my office, eating crackers and drinking milk. I didn't accomplish a thing. It was then that my chief told me to take it easy for a while. I was in a sort of stupor for a couple of days; yet to everyone's consternation I insisted on going to work. I accomplished nothing and I intended to accomplish nothing, it was just that I could not tolerate being alone. In fact today was the first day I have been alone for more than five minutes since I returned from the walk. But today I have regained a kind of composure, or a semblance of composure, which for a time I despaired of ever possessing again. And I know that by the time I have given shape enough to my thoughts to put them on this paper for you to read I shall have gained again a peace of mind. To have you to write to, Herb, that is the great thing at this point. Without you I do not know what I would have done.

So much for my emotions. My thinking, my personal philosophy, has gone through at least as profound an upheaval as they. In the chaos of my mind, in which huge invisible chunks of horror hit me unexpectedly from unexpected angles again and again, my first coherent and sensible idea came in the form of a question. "Why did they make it possible for me to find out what has been going on?" (For I finally realized that it was no fluke that I had discovered it, or O'Doone either, or anyone with the suspicions and the courage for it. When the atom bombs were being produced, the whole vast undertaking was carried off without a single leak to the outside. So if I had been able in so simple a way to find out what had been going on in the CPR it was only because they didn't care. They could have stopped me.)

Then I thought, invisible ink is scarcely new in the history of things. Perhaps they have been reading my correspondence with you all along and will smile at this letter as they have smiled at others. Or perhaps they haven't taken the trouble to read it because they simply don't care.

Perhaps the authorities not only did not care if we gradually found out, but wanted us to. Why should they want us to? Why, if that were true, should they have put up so formidable a system—double fences, censorship, lies, etc., etc.—of apparent preventatives?

The only answer that makes sense is that they want the news to sift out gradually and surreptitiously to the general population—illegally, in the form of hideous rumors to which people can begin to accustom themselves. After all, many knew generally that something like the atom bomb was being manufactured. Hiroshima was not the profound and absolute shock in 1945 that it would have been in 1935, and a good deal of the preparation for its general acceptance was rumor. It is in the people's interest that the CPR function as it does function, and especially so that they can pretend that they have nothing to do with it. The experience of the Germans in the Jew-extermination camps demonstrated that clearly enough. It would do no good for me to go around crying out the truth about NRACP, because few would believe me in the first place and my suppression would only give strength to the rumors—which are required and planned for anyhow.

But I still had to set myself the task of answering, Why? What drove them (whoever *they* are) to the decision to embark upon a course which was not only revolutionary but dangerous? I accepted the NRACP as inevitable, as *necessity*; there remained only the task of trying to understand wherein lay the mystery of the *necessity* and of adjusting myself to the situation. The individual, even the leader, has no significant choice to make in the current of events. That current is part of natural law; it is unmoral, cruel, wasteful, useless, and mysterious. The leader is he who sees and points out the course of history so that we may pursue that course with least pain. It is odd that we Americans have no such leader; what we have is committees and boards and bureau heads who collectively possess leadership and who direct our way almost impersonally. There is nothing whatsoever that I myself would like so much as to be one of those wise, courageous, anonymous planners. I think I possess the wisdom. But in place of courage I have a set of moral scruples dating from an era when man was supposed to have a soul and when disease took care of overpopulation. The old vestigial values of Christianity must be excised in the people as they are being excised in me. The good and the lucky are assisting at the birth of a new age; the weak and unfit are perishing in the death of an old. Which shall it be for us?

For my own part I think I am in a state of transition from being one of the unfit to being one of the fit. I feel it. I will it. There are certain external evidences of it. For example, I was face to face with the truth at the end of April, but instead of acknowledging what I saw I turned to my love for Ruth. Yet that refusal to recognize the truth did not long survive the urgings of my sense of necessity. And I remember when being confronted with piecemeal evidences of truth that I was unable to explain a number of them.

You know, Herb, how accomplished a rationalizer I can be, yet this time I did not even *try* to rationalize many of the facts.

It is dawn outside. I cannot read this letter over, so I am not entirely sure how incoherent it is. I feel that I have said most of what I wanted to say. I am not very happy. I think I shall sleep the better for having written this. I eat nothing but bread and fruit and milk. A bird is singing outside; he is making the only sound in the world. I can see the hill which separates us from the Intake buildings. It's a pleasant hill, rather like an arm extending out from the valley sides, and I am glad it is there. I am cold now, but in three hours it will be warm and in five hours hot. I am rambling I know. But suddenly all my energy has leaked out. I walk to the door to see Ruth so happily sleeping, mysteriously replenishing life from this nightly portion of death, and I think of that baby that she is bearing and will give birth to. If it were not for her and the baby I am sure I should have gone mad. Is not that a mystery, Herb? Our child shall be fortunate; it is the first conscious generation of each new order in whom the greatest energy is released. There are splendid things ahead for our child.

It is not my fault. I did not know what I was doing. How could I have known? What can I do now?

I stare at the lightening sky. Exhausted, I do not know why I do not say farewell and go to bed. Perhaps it is because I do not want to hear that little lullaby that sings in my ears whenever I stop: I have eaten human flesh, my wife is going to have a baby; I have eaten human flesh, my wife is going to have a baby.

Remember back in the simple days of the Spanish Civil War when Guernica was bombed how we speculated all one evening what the worst thing in the world could be? This is the worst thing in the world, Herb. I tell you, the worst. After this, nothing.

Perhaps if I lay my head against Ruth's breast and put her hands over my ears I can go to sleep. Last night I recited Housman's "Loveliest of trees, the cherry now" over and over till I went to sleep, not because I like it particularly but because I could think of nothing else to recite.

My wife is going to have a baby, my wife is going to have a baby, my wife is going to have a baby.

Bless you,
Andy

SOME CONDITIONS OF OBEDIENCE AND DISOBEDIENCE TO AUTHORITY

Stanley Milgram

Postscript

Almost a thousand adults were individually studied in the obedience research, and there were many specific conclusions regarding the variables that control obedience and disobedience to authority. Some of these have been discussed briefly in the preceding sections, and more detailed reports will be released subsequently.

There are now some other generalizations I should like to make, which do not derive in any strictly logical fashion from the experiments as carried out, but which, I feel, ought to be made. They are formulations of an intuitive sort that have been forced on me by observation of many subjects responding to the pressures of authority. The assertions represent a painful alteration in my own thinking; and since they were acquired only under the repeated impact of direct observation, I have no illusion that they will be generally accepted by persons who have not had the same experience.

With numbing regularity good people were seen to knuckle under the demands of authority and perform actions that were callous and severe. Men who are in everyday life responsible and decent were seduced by the trappings of authority, by the control of their perceptions, and by the uncritical acceptance of the experimenter's definition of the situation, into performing harsh acts.

What is the limit of such obedience? At many points we attempted to establish a boundary. Cries from the victim were inserted; not good enough. The victim claimed heart trouble; subjects still shocked him on command. The victim pleaded that he be let free, and his answers no longer registered on the signal box; subjects continued to shock him. At the outset we had not conceived that such drastic procedures would be needed to generate disobedience, and each step was added only as the ineffectiveness of the earlier techniques became clear. The final effort to establish a limit was the Touch-Proximity condition. But the very first subject in this condition subdued the victim on command, and proceeded to the highest shock level. A quarter of the subjects in this condition performed similarly.

The results, as seen and felt in the laboratory, are to this author disturbing. They raise the possibility that human nature, or—more specifically—the kind of character produced in American democratic society, cannot be counted on to insulate its citizens from brutality and inhumane treatment at the direction of malevolent authority. A substantial proportion of people do what they are told to do, irrespective of the content of the act and with-

From *Human Relations*, vol. 18 (February, 1965), pp. 74–75 (excerpt). Reprinted by permission of the publisher.

out limitations of conscience, so long as they perceive that the command comes from a legitimate authority. If in this study an anonymous experimenter could successfully command adults to subdue a fifty-year-old man, and force on him painful electric shocks against his protests, one can only wonder what government, with its vastly greater authority and prestige, can command of its subjects. There is, of course, the extremely important question of whether malevolent political institutions could or would arise in American society. The present research contributes nothing to this issue.

In an article titled "The Dangers of Obedience," Harold J. Laski wrote:

> . . . civilization means, above all, an unwillingness to inflict unnecessary pain. Within the ambit of that definition, those of us who heedlessly accept the commands of authority cannot yet claim to be civilized men.
>
> . . . Our business, if we desire to live a life, not utterly devoid of meaning and significance, is to accept nothing which contradicts our basic experience merely because it comes to us from tradition or convention or authority. It may well be that we shall be wrong; but our self-expression is thwarted at the root unless the certainties we are asked to accept coincide with the certainties we experience. That is why the condition of freedom in any state is always a widespread and consistent skepticism of the canons upon which power insists.

Vietnam Prices: One Man Worth $4.25; Buffalo, $100

A disgruntled Denver GI's letter to his folks indicates the price of water buffalo is up and the cost of man is down in Vietnam.

Spec. 4 Dennis Adamek, 19, sent a letter to his father, Dale Adamek, 2442 W. 38th Ave., which arrived Saturday. The soldier, in part, wrote:

"First off, we killed a Vietnamese civilian yesterday (likely the letter was written about a week ago). He was 78 years old. He was tending his water buffalo in an area where he wasn't supposed to be.

"One of our tanks took some weapons outside the perimeter to test fire them. He (the victim) was 1,400 meters away, almost a mile.

"The men in the tank didn't even see the water buffalo, much less the old man. They killed three buffalo and wounded two. We have to pay $100 each for the buffalo and $4.25 plus a casket for the man. I ain't lying."

The elder Adamek said he doesn't know which outfit his son is in or where it is located. He said Dennis does not like to be involved in war and that he "doesn't see why we have to be over there."

The soldier is a radio technician and has been in the Army since October 1969 and in Vietnam since about June 1.

Dennis has approximately three years of service remaining, said Adamek, a Denver Water Board employee.

"Vietnam Prices: One Man Worth $4.25; Buffalo, $100," *Rocky Mountain News* (August 10, 1970).

"I'm glad I have the company's assurances of safety—I glow in the dark!"

Reprinted with permission of Oliphant and The Denver Post.

FEAR

Ron Jendryaszek

Fear:
To feel
Caught in yourself,
Knowing that you are
Crowded within a world, alone,
And that you're dying,
Without having lived,
Free from
Fear

By permission of Ron Jendryaszek (student in tryout class with this book).

19 "Be fully afraid and yet not stop."

FEAR

Gerald M. Swatez

Destruction. Exploitation. Domination. And finally, Alienation. We traverse here four stations of the death instinct, and their common meaning is separation, unwholeness. The radical separation of man from man has become the poisonous essence of our society; with it is the separation of man from society that is the consequence, unintended but necessary, of rooting our social bond (the law, in this rational–legal order) in man's separateness from man. We have come to the experience of the phenomenon of a social order crumbling. Our experience is of the social world. If the social world is disintegrating, if the rules of social behavior require us to make ourselves more and more separate from each other, then our experience is of alienation from other, alienation from self. Our experience is of anxiety—the separation of the now from the morrow. We fear the fear we *will* feel, and can not even allow ourselves to fully experience the fear we *do* feel.

The fear is primordial, not realistic. It is the fixated, freaked-out memory of the birth trauma, of the frustrating breast, of the intruding father. Our culture does not draw integrating energy from our common experiences of loss and separation; rather, it uses these feelings to drive the acquisitive impulse—to objectify our desire for connection, to represent connection through possession, by energizing material symbols of wholeness that prohibit wholeness in reality.

The fear we feel, and the malaise, is the experience of our real selves, our union with others and with the All, falling away, ever falling, ever breaking.

We have placed our faith in partial "objective" (reified, materialized) idols of ourselves, in the machine and the bureaucracy. We have sacrificed our freedom to idols; we are a nation of idolators. And the fear we feel in the all-pervasive presence of our innumerable golden calves is the fear of the wrath of God.

We are all afraid.
WE HAVE NOTHING TO FEAR BUT FEAR ITSELF!
Of course we're afraid. We're afraid of germs. We're
afraid of dirt. We're afraid of the dark. We're afraid
of the Bomb. We're afraid of the Red Menace. We're
afraid of the Black Panthers, and of drugs, and of pain.
We're afraid to be bad.
We're afraid of sex. We're afraid to be alone. We're
afraid of other people. Other people. Other.
We are the other people.

The core, the source, of social problems today—whether pollution, poverty, crime, war, drug addiction, social chaos, or governmental tyranny—is the unwillingness of each of us to face himself, the unwillingness of each of us to face each other with honesty, with candor. The evasions we use to hide from ourselves and from each other are the psychoneurotic processes of denial, displacement, projection, and their structural concomitants. These are most obvious in the social process of scapegoating, blaming others (Them. The Enemy.) for what we do and feel. Our very culture encourages, and our social structure manifests, the pretense that what we have learned to condemn in ourselves is not part of ourselves, but is someone else, someone who deserves to be punished, or destroyed, or cured; and the pretense that what we have learned to praise in ourselves is not really part of ourselves, but is located in the things around us (My flag deserves more respect than I, personally, do.). Our social structure is evasive, alienative, destructive.

"Be fully afraid and yet not stop" advises admitting to fear, but acting rightly, nonetheless, and allowing fantasy to guide our action in opening up ourselves, our culture, and our society.

HIJACK THE STARSHIP!

. . . history is
transforming the question
of reorganizing human society
and human nature
in the spirit of play
from a speculative possibility
to a realistic necessity.

Norman O. Brown, *Life Against Death* (New York: Vintage Books, 1959), p. 34.

POPULATION, RESOURCES, ENVIRONMENT: ISSUES IN HUMAN ECOLOGY

Paul R. Ehrlich and Anne H. Ehrlich

In the United States, the leadership consists mainly of those people who are most likely to have the ethnocentrism of their society embedded in their characters. Our images of leadership and our political and elective processes seem to require this. Our leaders are unlikely to be familiar with the values and attitudes of other cultures. They are equally unlikely to know anything about the psychology of aggression. They are most likely to have deep emotional investments in patriotic ideals and the glorification of the American way of life, and to have contempt for other cultures. Few have any insight into the psychological tricks which we have built into our world view in order to conceal reality. They do not understand why we talk of military "hardware" instead of weapons, why we say we can "take out" an enemy city instead of "destroy it, killing every man, woman, and child," why we talk of "casualties" in Vietnam instead of "dead and maimed." They do not understand how our preconceptions about the Russians, the Chinese, the Cubans, and other unfamiliar peoples badly distort our perceptions of their behavior. *Moreover, American leaders do not understand that the leaders of the other countries have equally distorted perceptions of our actions and motives.* They have no way of understanding. If the men now leading most nations really had been sensitive to such things as cultural relativity, it is unlikely that they ever would have become political leaders. . . .

The basic need is evident: Once again, it is a change in human attitudes so that the "in group" against which aggression is forbidden expands to include *all* of humanity.

The study of attitudes tends to emphasize the role of fantasy in transforming nature—or in leaving nature severely alone as, in some sense, sacred. To borrow a distinction adumbrated by theologians, it depicts man's *world* rather than man's environment. Man's world is a fabric of ideas and dreams, some of which he manages to give visible form. For the privilege of having fantasies, of possessing a world rather than simply an environment, man pays with the risk of disaster and the certainty of ultimate impermanence in all his efforts. . . . [The] works of man may be seen as reified fantasies; fantasies that have acquired varying degrees of transient substance through the ingenuity and stubbornness of our more practical dreamers.

Yi-Fu Tuan, "Attitudes toward Environment: Themes and Approaches," *Environmental Perception and Behavior*, ed. David Lowenthal, Department of Geography Research Paper No. 109, University of Chicago (1967), pp. 16–17.

THE TEACHINGS OF DON JUAN

Carlos Castaneda

"When a man starts to learn, he is never clear about his objectives. His purpose is faulty; his intent is vague. He hopes for rewards that will never materialize, for he knows nothing of the hardships of learning.

"He slowly begins to learn—bit by bit at first, then in big chunks. And his thoughts soon clash. What he learns is never what he pictured, or imagined, and so he begins to be afraid. Learning is never what one expects. Every step of learning is a new task, and the fear the man is experiencing begins to mount mercilessly, unyielding. His purpose becomes a battlefield.

"And thus he has stumbled upon the first of his natural enemies: Fear! A terrible enemy—treacherous, and difficult to overcome. It remains concealed at every turn of the way, prowling, waiting. And if the man, terrified in its presence, runs away, his enemy will have put an end to his quest."

"What will happen to the man if he runs away in fear?"

"Nothing happens to him except that he will never learn. He will never become a man of knowledge. He will perhaps be a bully, or a harmless, scared man; at any rate, he will be a defeated man. His first enemy will have put an end to his cravings."

"And what can he do to overcome fear?"

"The answer is very simple. He must not run away. He must defy his fear, and in spite of it he must take the next step in learning, and the next, and the next. He must be fully afraid, and yet he must not stop. That is the rule! And a moment will come when his first enemy retreats. The man begins to feel sure of himself. His intent becomes stronger. Learning is no longer a terrifying task.

"When this joyful moment comes, the man can say without hesitation that he has defeated his first natural enemy."

"Does it happen at once, don Juan, or little by little?"

"It happens little by little, and yet the fear is vanquished suddenly and fast."

"But won't the man be afraid again if something new happens to him?"

Originally published by the University of California Press, 1968, pp. 57–60. Reprinted by permission of The Regents of the University of California.

"No. Once a man has vanquished fear, he is free from it for the rest of his life because, instead of fear, he has acquired clarity—a clarity of mind which erases fear. By then a man knows his desires; he knows how to satisfy those desires. He can anticipate the new steps of learning, and a sharp clarity surrounds everything. The man feels that nothing is concealed.

"And thus he has encountered his second enemy: Clarity! That clarity of mind, which is so hard to obtain, dispels fear, but also blinds.

"It forces the man never to doubt himself. It gives him the assurance he can do anything he pleases, for he sees clearly into everything. And he is courageous because he is clear, and he stops at nothing because he is clear. But all that is a mistake; it is like something incomplete. If the man yields to this make-believe power, he has succumbed to his second enemy and will fumble with learning. He will rush when he should be patient, or he will be patient when he should rush. And he will fumble with learning until he winds up incapable of learning anything more."

"What becomes of a man who is defeated in that way, don Juan? Does he die as a result?"

"No, he doesn't die. His second enemy has just stopped him cold from trying to become a man of knowledge; instead, the man may turn into a buoyant warrior, or a clown. Yet the clarity for which he has paid so dearly will never change to darkness and fear again. He will be clear as long as he lives, but he will no longer learn, or yearn for, anything."

"But what does he have to do to avoid being defeated?"

"He must do what he did with fear: he must defy his clarity and use it only to see, and wait patiently and measure carefully before taking new steps; he must think, above all, that his clarity is almost a mistake. And a moment will come when he will understand that his clarity was only a point before his eyes. And thus he will have overcome his second enemy, and will arrive at a position where nothing can harm him anymore. This will not be a mistake. It will not be only a point before his eyes. It will be true power.

"He will know at this point that the power he has been pursuing for so long is finally his. He can do with it whatever he pleases. His ally is at his command. His wish is the rule. He sees all that is around him. But he has also come across his third enemy: Power!

"Power is the strongest of all enemies. And naturally the easiest thing to do is to give in; after all, the man is truly invincible. He commands; he begins by taking calculated risks, and ends in making rules, because he is a master.

"A man at this stage hardly notices his third enemy closing in on him. And suddenly, without knowing, he will certainly have lost the battle. His enemy will have turned him into a cruel, capricious man."

"Will he lose his power?"

"No, he will never lose his clarity or his power."

"What then will distinguish him from a man of knowledge?"

"A man who is defeated by power dies without really knowing how to handle it. Power is only a burden upon his fate. Such a man has no command over himself, and cannot tell when or how to use his power."

"Is the defeat by any of these enemies a final defeat?"

"Of course it is final. Once one of these enemies overpowers a man there is nothing he can do."

"Is it possible, for instance, that the man who is defeated by power may see his error and mend his ways?"

"No. Once a man gives in he is through."

"But what if he is temporarily blinded by power, and then refuses it?"

"That means his battle is still on. That means he is still trying to become a man of knowledge. A man is defeated only when he no longer tries, and abandons himself."

"But then, don Juan, it is possible that a man may abandon himself to fear for years, but finally conquer it."

"No, that is not true. If he gives in to fear he will never conquer it, because he will shy away from learning and never try again. But if he tries to learn for years in the midst of his fear, he will eventually conquer it because he will never have really abandoned himself to it."

"How can he defeat his third enemy, don Juan?"

"He has to defy it, deliberately. He has to come to realize the power he has seemingly conquered is in reality never his. He must keep himself in line at all times, handling carefully and faithfully all that he has learned. If he can see that clarity and power, without his control over himself, are worse than mistakes, he will reach a point where everything is held in check. He will know then when and how to use his power. And thus he will have defeated his third enemy.

"The man will be, by then, at the end of his journey of learning, and almost without warning he will come upon the last of his enemies: Old age! This enemy is the cruelest of all, the one he won't be able to defeat completely, but only fight away.

"This is the time when a man has no more fears, no more impatient clarity of mind—a time when all his power is in check, but also the time when he has an unyielding desire to rest. If he gives in totally to his desire to lie down and forget, if he soothes himself in tiredness, he will have lost his last round, and his enemy will cut him down into a feeble old creature. His desire to retreat will overrule all his clarity, his power, and his knowledge.

"But if the man sloughs off his tiredness, and lives his fate through, he can then be called a man of knowledge, if only for the brief moment when he succeeds in fighting off his last, invincible enemy. That moment of clarity, power, and knowledge is enough."

A considerable new message . . . . The current fantasy . . . . Fantasy is a word [Ken] Kesey has taken to using more and more, for all sorts of plans, ventures, world views, ambitions. It is a good word. It is ironic and it isn't. It refers to everything from getting hold of a pickup truck—"that's our fantasy for this weekend"—to some scary stuff out on the raggedy raggedy edge. . . .

Tom Wolfe, *The Electric Kool-Aid Acid Test* (New York: Farrar, Strauss and Giroux, 1968), p. 29.

THE PURSUIT OF LONELINESS

Philip E. Slater

The goal of many early Americans was to find or to create or to participate in a utopian community, but they became distracted by the dream of personal aggrandizement and found themselves farther and farther from this goal. When we think today of the kind of social compliance that exists in such communities (as well as in the primitive communities we romanticize so much) we shrink in horror. We tell each other chilling stories of individuals in imagined societies of the future being forced to give up their dreams for the good of the group, of not being allowed to stand out. But this, in some degree, is just the price we must pay for a tolerable life in a tolerable community. We need to understand this price, to consider it, to reflect on its consequences and the consequences of not paying it. . . .

Past efforts to build utopian communities failed because they were founded on scarcity assumptions. But scarcity is now shown to be an unnecessary condition, and the distractions that it generated can now be avoided. . . . Hence the only obstacle to utopia is the persistence of the competitive motivational patterns that past scarcity assumptions have spawned. Nothing stands in our way except our invidious dreams of personal glory. Our horror of group coercion reflects our reluctance to relinquish these dreams, although they have brought us nothing but misery, discontent, hatred, and chaos. If we can overcome this horror, however, and mute this vanity, we may again be able to take up our original utopian task.

Philip E. Slater, *The Pursuit of Loneliness: American Culture at the Breaking Point*, pp. 149–150.

WITHIN YOU, WITHOUT YOU

George Harrison

We were talking—about the space
between us all
And the people—who hide themselves
behind a wall of illusion
Never glimpse the truth—then it's far
too late—when they pass away.
We were talking—about the love we all
could share—when we find it
To try our best to hold it there—with
our love
With our love—we could save the world
—if only they knew.
Try to realize it's all within yourself
no one else can make you change
And to see you're really only very small,
and life flows on within you and without
you.
We were talking—about the love that's
gone so cold and the people,
Who gain the world and lose their soul—
they don't know—they can't see—are
you one of them?
When you've seen beyond yourself—
then you may find, peace of mind, is
waiting there—
And the time will come when you see
we're all one, and life flows on within
you and without you.

The doctrines of the quiet past are inadequate to the stormy present. As we must see anew and feel anew, so must we think anew and act anew, and then we will save our country.

Abraham Lincoln

WE CAN BE TOGETHER

Paul Kantner

We can be together
Ah you and me
We should be together

We are all outlaws in the eyes of America
In order to survive we steal cheat lie
    forge fred hide and deal
We are obscene lawless hideous dangerous
    dirty violent and young

But we should be together
Come on all you people standing around
Our life's too fine to let it die and
We can be together

All your private property is
Target for your enemy
And your enemy is
We

We are forces of chaos and anarchy
Everything they say we are we are
And we are very
Proud of ourselves

Up against the wall
Up against the wall fred
Tear down the walls
Tear down the walls

Come on now together
Get it on together
Everybody together

We should be together
We should be together my friends
We can be together
We will be

We must begin here and now
A new continent of earth and fire
Tear down the walls
Come on now gettin higher and higher
Tear down the walls
Tear down the walls
Tear down the walls
Won't you try

Symptoms of growth may look like breakdown or derangement; the more we are allowed by the love of others and by self-understanding to live through our derangement into the new arrangement, the luckier we are. It is unfortunate when our anxiety over what looks like personal confusion or dereliction blinds us to the forces of liberation at work.

M. C. Richards, *Centering: In Pottery, Poetry, & the Person* (Middletown, Conn.: Wesleyan Univ. Press, 1964), pp. 132–133.

Be Patient
Trust Yourself
Help Each Other